Social Studies for the Elementary and Middle Grades

SECOND EDITION

Social Studies for the Elementary and Middle Grades

A CONSTRUCTIVIST APPROACH

Cynthia Szymanski Sunal
The University of Alabama–Tuscaloosa

Mary Elizabeth Haas
West Virginia University

Boston ■ New York ■ San Francisco
Mexico City ■ Montreal ■ Toronto ■ London ■ Madrid ■ Munich ■ Paris
Hong Kong ■ Singapore ■ Tokyo ■ Cape Town ■ Sydney

Series Editor: Traci Mueller
Series Editorial Assistant: Janice Hackenberg
Senior Marketing Manager: Elizabeth Fogarty
Editorial-Production Service: Omegatype Typography, Inc.
Composition Buyer: Linda Cox
Manufacturing Buyer: Andrew Turso
Cover Administrator: Joel Gendron
Electronic Composition: Omegatype Typography, Inc.

For related titles and support materials, visit our online catalog at www.ablongman.com.

Between the time Website information is gathered and then published, it is not unusual for some sites to have closed. Also, the transcription of URLs can result in typographical errors. The publisher would appreciate notification where these errors occur so that they may be corrected in subsequent editions.

Library of Congress Cataloging-in-Publication Data

Sunal, Cynthia S.
    Social studies for the elementary and middle grades : a constructivist approach / Cynthia Szymanski Sunal, Mary Elizabeth Haas.—2nd ed.
        p.   cm.
    Includes bibliographical references and index.
    ISBN 0-205-41258-0
    1. Social sciences—Study and teaching (Elementary)—United States.   2. Social sciences—Study and teaching (Middle school)—United States.   3. Constructivism (Education)—United States.   I. Haas, Mary E.   II. Title.
LB1584.S88 2005
372.83'044—dc22

                                                                                        2004047843

Printed in the United States of America

10   9   8   7   6   5   4   3   2   1   09   08   07   06   05   04

Contents

v

chapter 3

Helping Students Develop Social Studies Inquiry Skills 48

chapter 4

Helping Students Construct Concepts 85

chapter 5

Helping Students Use Inquiry to Build Generalizations 117

chapter 6

Using Instructional Strategies That Help Students Learn   134

chapter 7

Helping Students Relate to Individuals and Communities   173

chapter 8

Helping Students Become Citizens in a Democratic Society in an Ever More Interdependent World   210

chapter 9

Helping All Students Experience Meaningful Social Studies   251

chapter 10

Helping Students Interpret History   276

chapter 11

Helping Students Interpret the Earth and Its People
through Geography   314

chapter 12

Helping Students Make Economic Decisions 353

chapter 13

Helping Students Understand Local and Global Societies 389

chapter 14

Helping Students Learn through Multiple Assessments and Evaluation   416

chapter 15

Planning Units of Various Lengths and Formats   447

Preface

Social Studies for the Elementary and Middle Grades: A Constructivist Approach, second edition, views social studies as a powerful part of the kindergarten through middle school program. Its power comes from meaningful learning of social studies content, skills, and values to promote democratic behavior in and among citizens.

This edition continues to strongly focus on *meaningful learning of powerful social studies.* Such learning is built on recognizing that students must construct knowledge in their own minds for it to be meaningful to them. To help teachers create powerful social studies, we discuss: (1) the strategies for teaching powerful social studies, (2) the structure of the knowledge to be learned, and (3) the theory and research explaining meaningful learning in social studies. Our discussion is embedded in over 25 years of teaching experience in public schools and an equal number of years in higher education teaching, supervising, and carrying out reaserch.

The research literature in social studies and on constructivism contributed heavily to the approach we take in this book. As we work with the research literature, conduct our own research, and develop and teach social studies lessons, we use the theories and strategies we discuss in this book. We find the learning cycle approach to structuring lessons and units provides flexibility, ensuring the inclusion of the best aspects of major thoeries describing how students learn. We have applied the learning cycle in teaching social studies concepts, generalizations, skills, and values.

Social studies incorporates rich opportunities to involve students in active investigation of the issues, problems, consequences, and successes people encounter in the social world. This book serves as an example of such social studies as it involves the reader in considering many examples and illustrations of how to teach social studies. This second edition includes new discussion of global education both within a new chapter and infused throughout the book. This edition also infuses technology throughout the chapters, makes frequent literature connections, and addresses issues of diversity within the chapters. Additonal interviews with exemplary teachers and classroom scenarios have been added to further bring the reader into classrooms. A learning cycle unit has been added. Lesson plans for the range of grade levels, from kindergarten through middle school, are provided. These lesson plans move the reader from the interviews and classroom scenes to planning procedures that produce powerful social studies curriculum and teaching. The learning cycle lesson plans illustrate various ways of combining individual instructional strategies with important content from multiple social science disciplines, history, and other contributing disciplines to create meaningful learning.

COMPANION
WEBSITE

Two icons appear in the margins of this book to make it more convenient for you to use. The NCSS (National Council for the Social Studies) icon identifies references to NCSS documents and social studies standards of importance to teachers. The CW icon refers you to the companion website (www.ablongman.com/sunal2e), where you will find supporting materials and many links to useful websites.

Opportunities for application and reflection of the ideas in this book are emphasized in the Time for Reflection: What Do You Think? activities. Readers benefit most from these sections when they are used as they are encountered in the book and when they share their answers with others. Readers are invited to use these activities to enter into dialogue with the authors, course instructors, and peers. Instructors may want to use these activities as starters for class discussions as they build a community of teachers and learners who create powerful social studies education. Readers should use them to help construct their own knowledge of social studies education.

Major curriculum movements, such as science-related social issues, civic action, and full involvement of diverse learners in the classroom are discussed throughout the book as their impact on many social studies topics is considered. The National Council for the Social Studies Standards and the various content standards for history, economics, geography, and civics are all emphasized in the text and learning cycles. Because of the important roles of history, geography, economics, values, political science, and global education in the social studies curriculum, chapters are devoted to each. These chapters identify content and appropriate strategies that can be utilized in teaching information from each of these disciplines. Assessment is integrated throughout the chapters and is also discussed in depth in a separate chapter. Internet resources supporting and extending the discussion of powerful social studies instruction and curriculum are found at the end of each chapter and on an accompanying companion website. Each chapter ends with a suggested activity designed to expand your understanding through personally applying ideas developed in the chapter. Additional expansion activities for each chapter are also at the companion website.

This textbook guides the user in planning and teaching powerful social studies lessons and units. It elaborates on the steps for using a wide range of specific instructional strategies and guides the selection of appropriate content. Therefore, it is a comprehensive reference for those who are teaching and developing the social studies curriculum. The authors welcome your questions and comments through the companion website.

ACKNOWLEDGMENTS

We would like to thank the reviewers of this edition for their helpful comments: Cathy Kim, Muhlenberg College, and Mary Ann Maslak, St. John's University. We also thank our social studies colleagues who have examined and taught with the first edition and offered encouragement and suggestions. We are also grateful for the questions and suggestions from our students that have helped us to reflect on how they are constructing their ideas and skills for teaching meaningful social studies.

Social Studies for the Elementary and Middle Grades

CHAPTER 1

Meaningful Social Studies and the Student

INTRODUCTION

Think back to your elementary and middle school years. What memories surface when you think of social studies? Record your memories on the following lines.

_____

_____

Some teacher candidates and inservice teachers have said these things:

- *Units on a Country.* Every month, we studied a different country, arranging our desks in the shape of that country and being responsible for learning all about the part of the country where our desk was located, its culture, occupations, natural resources, and so on. At the end of the month, we shared what we had found out. During the month, we sampled food from our country, sang songs, and listened to stories. I loved it and was always excited about which country would be next.

- *Memorizing States and Their Capitals.* I don't remember ever looking at a map to try to find a state capital, although I probably did. I found this easy because I'm good at memorization, but for many, memorizing those state capitals was a chore because we kept taking quizzes until we got 100 percent.

- *Field Trips.* I can remember two really great field trips. One was to a local doughnut store. The kitchen smelled wonderful. We were impressed at how mechanized doughnut making was. At the end of the field trip, we each got to pick out six doughnuts and take them with us. The other field trip was to a state park with mounds built by Native Americans long ago. They were huge. I wanted ➤

1

➤ so much to know what had happened to the people who built these mounds. Why were there no villages around these mounds now? After the trip, I read everything I could find about these people.

- *Writing Reports.* We had to write a report on somebody or something related to each unit we studied. At first, I enjoyed it, but after a while, I got so tired of them. It was really boring listening to each student read his or her report.

- *Worksheets and Questions.* There were always so many questions to answer at the end of the chapters. We would also be given worksheets to fill in. The teacher called them "fun sheets," but we knew they were no fun.

- *Discussions.* One year my teacher really encouraged us to say what we thought about things. We brought up a lot of issues that were important to us, such as why we were the last stop on the school bus route and got home later than anyone at the other schools. We had not considered the fact that we also started school later. After some discussion, we decided that this fact did not make up for our long afternoons and petitioned the school board for a change.

- *Role Playing.* I was shy but I did enjoy role playing. Because I could think of it as a school assignment, I put aside my shyness and really got involved. It seemed to make me understand situations much better. My teacher did some economics-related role playing that I enjoyed most of all.

Some of these memories are positive, and some are negative. What term best describes your social studies memories: mostly positive, mostly negative, or a mixture of both?

_____

Social studies is capable of engaging students so deeply that in 10, 20, or 30 years, they will reminisce fondly about social studies activities. Notice that the most positive memories occurred when students' minds were actively involved in constructing new knowledge or revising knowledge they already had.

CHAPTER OVERVIEW

Your past experience with social studies is used throughout the chapter to help you consider several questions: What is social studies? What are the sources of social studies content? What are the characteristics of social studies teaching? How do the answers to these questions relate to what you and society believe about children and how learning is accomplished? Over the years, social studies educators have offered multiple answers. As you work through this chapter and the book, you are presented with different perspectives on social studies. Reflect on these perspectives and discuss them with your peers. Do they view children and learning in similar or different ways than you do?

CHAPTER OBJECTIVES

1. Reflect on your own experience in social studies.
2. Describe participatory citizenship.

3. Define social studies.
4. Explain why social studies is multidisciplinary.
5. Reflect on the characteristics of powerful social studies.
6. Describe a format for social studies instruction.
7. Evaluate a social studies lesson plan.

SOCIAL STUDIES IN THE ELEMENTARY AND MIDDLE SCHOOL

Personal reflection helps to develop a deeper understanding of key ideas underlying the teaching of social studies. Reflective activities help you compare your own knowledge with new ideas. Such comparisons help you to understand effective social studies teaching.

Most of our lives and social worlds involve everyday experiences. Reflecting on our experiences and observing and talking with children help us to understand the nature of the social world and how we come to make meaning of all we observe and hear. Imagine children at a shopping mall. They observe, play, model people, and explore—all without being "taught." They might ask questions such as "Can you look at the mall map and find a short way to the toy store?" or "Where did Grandma and Grandpa go to buy their new shoes when they were little?" or "How does the baker know how many cookies to make for the cookie store in the food court?" or "How come all the teenagers hang out around the food court?"

These questions spring from a natural exploration of our social world that begins at birth and continues as the tools of language, reading, and mathematics are mastered and used to investigate the social world. Social studies happens every time a child figures out a shortcut to take home or asks a question about whether the classroom rules should be changed because "we keep fighting about whose turn it is." This book begins with a discussion of social studies in elementary and middle schools that examines the origin of children's knowledge and presents a glimpse of two classroom scenes that illustrate the teaching of social studies.

A Third-Grade Classroom Scene

Ms. Cannon, a third-grade teacher for the past 3 years, begins her study of a textbook chapter "What Is a Law?" by dividing her 24 students into cooperative groups of four and asking each group to select a representative to serve in a classroom legislature.

The representatives hold their first meeting a couple of days later. Other students are able to observe the meeting or can participate in activities available at the classroom centers. The legislators talk about problems in the classroom and decide to meet with their groups to identify three problems of greatest interest to their group members.

At their next meeting, the legislature discusses the problems each group identified and agrees they will work on one of the problems. They choose confusion at the end of the day when everyone is getting ready to go home. They decide to make a law. The law reads, "When the classroom clock says 2:50, everyone will start to pick up litter off the floor. When you have 10 pieces of litter, throw them in the wastebasket and go to your cubby. When you have your stuff out of the cubby, get in the bus line or the walker line to go home." The legislature writes out the law and posts it on a bulletin board. Each representative talks about the law with his or her group.

At their next meeting, Ms. Cannon suggests that the legislature talk to group members in a few days to decide whether their law is working. They agree to do so. After some discussion, the legislature decides that, after the law has been in effect for a few days, they will ask their group members to write down their evaluation of how the new law is working.

At a meeting a week later, the legislature discusses the written and oral comments they received about the new law. They list these comments on a chart in one of two columns labeled *good* or *bad*. Only a few comments are bad. They all deal with an individual student's inability to find 10 pieces of litter to pick up because other students were faster at picking up the litter. The legislature decides that this could be a problem with the law. They decide to reevaluate how it is working in 2 weeks. Meanwhile, they think about the other two problems they identified and about which one they should discuss at their next meeting.

The next day Ms. Cannon asks the class to list the steps that were followed by the legislature in enacting the new law. The class then develops a definition for the term *legislature* and records it on a chart. ■

A Seventh-Grade Classroom Scene

Mr. Powell, a seventh-grade teacher, wants his students to think about the role of geographical characteristics in building a house at a particular site. He begins by giving students information about two 40-acre pieces of property for sale at similar prices. The information for each property contains an aerial photograph of the piece of land and some notes from a realtor about the characteristics of the property. One piece of property is high on a mountain ridge and is hilly with a thick forest. It has a stony stream that cuts a path back and forth through it. The other piece of property is located in a valley. It is mostly flat and swampy with very few trees.

Mr. Powell presents two questions, writing them on the board: (1) Which piece of property would be the easier and cheaper on which to build a house and road? (2) Would your ideas be the same or different if you were building a house and road on the property in 1870? He divides the class into small groups, assigns roles, and says, "Discuss these questions in groups for 15 minutes and be ready to explain to the class the reasoning for your answer to each question."

Most groups decide that the hilly property is a more difficult site on which to build a house and road. They do not consider the problems resulting from swampy ground. The groups think that the difference is minimal between building on either piece of property in 1870 or today. One group says, "It would just be slower to build them in 1870 because you would use horses instead of trucks and bulldozers."

The lesson continues with Mr. Powell noting, "Some of you have said you could use more information to make your conclusions. Let's see whether we can find more evidence you can use." He provides the students with access to the Internet, a newspaper listing excavating companies and construction firms that they can call, and a map of the local area from the U.S. Geological Survey.

In their groups, students discuss the information they gather, make charts grouping the information, and decide whether this new information supports their earlier conclusions. Later in the lesson, the students are given more information on the properties, including a report indicating whether the soil is appropriate for a septic tank and how deep a well needs to be to get water. Mr. Powell asks them to think about the two original questions and decide whether they want to revise their ideas about the answers or whether they think the extra evidence supports the previous answers. ■

TIME FOR REFLECTION: WHAT DO YOU THINK?

What are some words you expect the students in Ms. Cannon's class to use to describe social studies?_____

_____

What do you think Ms. Cannon's definition of social studies is? _____

_____

_____

What are some words you expect the students in Mr. Powell's class to use to describe social studies?_____

_____

What do you think Mr. Powell's definition of social studies is? _____

_____

_____

Powerful social studies is meaningful, integrative, value based, challenging, and active (National Council for the Social Studies, 1994b). The National Council for the Social Studies (NCSS) described its vision of powerful teaching and learning in a 1992 position statement summarized in Figure 1.1. Social studies learning is the student's personal construction of meaning from information collected through the senses and from social interaction with others that is interpreted in terms of the student's prior knowledge of the social world (Scheurman & Newman, 1998; Sunal, Sunal, & Haas, 1996).

➤ BUILDING ON DIVERSITY

Meaningful Social Studies

Every student brings to the classroom unique personal experiences, different perspectives on the world, and different ideas about how to act in social situations. Each student has inclinations toward certain ways of learning. Some students are excellent auditory learners, whereas others are excellent visual learners. Some students have traveled widely, whereas others have never left their community. Students come from two-parent families, single-parent families, extended families, blended families, or another type of family. The diversity found in every classroom is huge, even when that classroom is in a tiny rural community or takes in a close-knit ethnic community in a large city. Such diversity serves as a deep and broad resource for meaningful social studies experiences. When teachers build on the diversity found among their students, social studies is personal, relevant, and important. Students find there is much to be appreciated in diversity while recognizing that, despite our diversity, we all share many experiences, wishes, and goals.

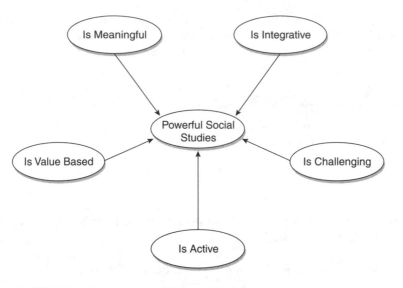

FIGURE 1.1 Powerful Social Studies

Source: Expectations of Excellence: Curriculum Standards for Social Studies, by the National Council for the Social Studies, 1994, Washington, DC: National Council for the Social Studies.

The view that students construct their own knowledge has great implications for social studies education. Students must have information to act on—evidence developed through their own experience that can be related to the ideas and skills being taught. Students collect this evidence by making observations of, and interacting with, people, educational materials, and objects. Students think about information, relating it to their prior experiences and knowledge. They consider the information they acquire using familiar ways of thinking. They make predictions and encounter challenges. It is through such challenges to our present way of thinking that we come to understand new ideas (Sunal, Sunal, & Haas, 1996).

Students need to classify and describe the materials, experiences, and information they observe. Performing such tasks comes naturally, but often students are uncertain about doing these tasks or are not particularly good at doing them. It is only after encountering activities that challenge them and make them think that students discover regular patterns in the world and make conclusions about them. A pattern is a regular activity that has occurred in the past and is expected to occur again in the future. The world is full of patterns, as the following examples demonstrate:

- People wear fewer and lighter clothes in summer.
- Groups have social relationships that tell members who should lead and who should follow.
- Past events influence current events.

Students' inferences and conclusions about their observations of the world are drawn from and interpreted in terms of the values they, their families, and their communities have. These values are often challenged, reconsidered, and clarified during social studies activities. Throughout social studies instruction, students integrate information from a variety of sources that represent differing perspectives. They make decisions and solve problems about what they need and what is important to them. Thus, social studies is a powerful construction process that goes on in students' minds. The NCSS describes its vision of powerful social studies teaching and learning in the 1992 position statement summarized in Figure 1.1. Figure 1.2 illustrates how the processes of powerful learning and teaching both start and end with students' interaction with the world.

Unfortunately, lessons taking place in some classrooms do not use the ideas, materials, and instructional strategies long advocated by social studies educators and found to be effective by researchers. In some classrooms, the dominant instructional strategy is teaching directly from the textbook with little or no additional activities other than fact-oriented worksheets. Priority is given to covering most of the textbook in the time available for social studies rather than to thinking and understanding. The full responsibility for learning the content is placed on the students. The

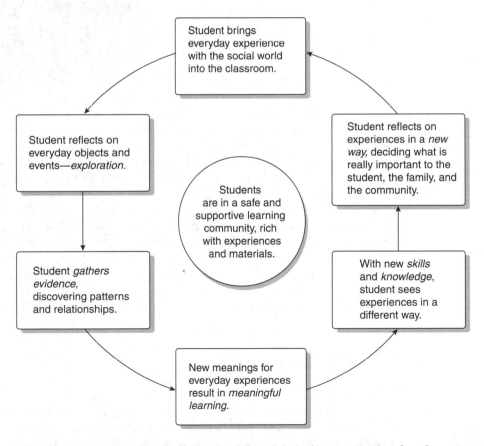

FIGURE 1.2 Model of Meaningful Social Studies Instruction for Elementary and Middle School

Social studies field trips are a way to make the great connection integrating social studies with the other content areas.

content to be learned typically consists of memorizing terms and their spellings. This type of instruction does not really teach social studies (Shaver, Davis, & Helburn, 1979; Superka, Hawke, & Morrissett, 1980).

Fortunately, many teachers perceive social studies teaching in ways that support the NCSS description of powerful social studies. When elementary teachers who are members of the National Council for the Social Studies were surveyed about their teaching of social studies, they indicated that their greatest satisfaction in teaching social studies is knowing they are teaching important content and skills. Although 90 percent of these teachers use a textbook in social studies instruction, many (45 percent) use it no more than once a week, and 8 percent use no textbook at all. These teachers described their teaching units as focusing on social science and social studies content that often was integrated with other school subjects and that used multiple and combined teaching strategies (Haas & Laughlin, 1999a).

➤ **USING TECHNOLOGY**

Deciding Whether and When

Technology resources such as the Internet and CD-ROMs offer many opportunities for teachers to move away from using only textbooks as teaching resources. Teachers can use a website such as CNN Interactive at http://www.cnn.com to involve   ➤

CW
COMPANION
WEBSITE

students in current issues or for relating historical events to today's issues. Or teachers can use a CD-ROM such as Lewis and Clark Rediscovery developed by Infi-Media, Inc. (www.infimedia-inc.com) to enable students to use excerpts from the journals of members of the Lewis and Clark expedition to examine significant events in the journey and important decision points faced by the expedition.

Technology "is as old as the first crude tool invented by prehistoric people" (National Council for the Social Studies, 1994b, p. 28). Deciding when and how to use technology in social studies instruction is an example of real social studies problem solving. Technology has altered, and continues to alter, the course of education. It brings teachers surprises, and it challenges their beliefs and values. Teachers must be ready for these changes and give careful consideration to the possible outcomes of technology use and their consequences for learning knowledge and democratic social relationships among people and things.

Like all instructional resources, technology used to support the teaching of social studies must reflect social studies goals and learning outcomes. Today, computer technology serves as (1) an information resource, (2) a learning tool, (3) a storage device, (4) a facilitator of communication, and (5) an integrator of information (Perkins, 1992). Teachers need to consider the following questions when deciding whether and when to use a technology:

1. How and when can technology facilitate the basic elements of instruction?
2. For which social studies activities are the costs in time and money of obtaining and using technology appropriate investments?
3. What learning experiences might be improved for my students if technology is used?

EDUCATION FOR ACTIVE CITIZENSHIP

A general goal for school curriculum should be facilitating students' development of an awareness, appreciation, and understanding of key social studies concepts and processes required for personal decision making, participation in civic and cultural affairs, and economic productivity (National Council for the Social Studies, 1994b; National Research Council, 1996). *Citizenship* means active participation in community and national decision making (Barr, Barth, & Shermis, 1977; Goodman & Adler, 1985).

Being an active, participatory citizen means that students ask questions, determine answers to questions based on related information, and act to bring about changes in their everyday social world. This process of awareness, appreciation, and understanding of the social world is learned fully only through social studies. As our technological society continues to change, it creates many concerns that require decision making from citizens. Making thoughtful decisions requires citizens to have content knowledge in many areas and to know how to use and evaluate the evidence their knowledge gives them. Yet many students seem turned off by social studies when they enter middle school. This is a serious problem for a complex democratic society in which citizens are expected to make informed decisions.

While agreeing with the general goal of citizenship education in social studies, some educators place a greater emphasis on any one of the following six viewpoints:

1. Teaching history and geography
2. Understanding social science
3. Facilitating cultural transmission
4. Supporting personal development
5. Developing reflective thinking skills
6. Encouraging rational problem solving, decision making, and social action

Each of these supports citizenship education as a general goal in social studies.

The No Child Left Behind Act of 2001 identified three core subjects to be taught in K–12 that contribute to developing an understanding of citizenship in all students. These subjects are civics and government, history, and geography. The National Assessment of Educational Progress (NAEP) will be used nationwide to test students' knowledge of these three core subjects. States will also test students' achievement in these areas with tests they select to track students' progress toward understanding citizenship knowledge and skills.

Social studies has been called "the great connection" by Goodman and Adler (1985). It is seen as the core to which all parts of the elementary and middle school curriculum can be tied. Social studies can integrate mathematics, science, art, music, physical education, health, reading, language arts, and all the other content areas. Such integration is important. The school curriculum often splits knowledge into many separate areas of study, but the real world in which citizens live and work is not so compartmentalized. Social studies is an interdisciplinary approach relying heavily on the content of social science and history to achieve its goal of preparing people to be active citizens of a democracy.

SOCIAL STUDIES IS ESSENTIAL

Social studies plays a critical role in our lives. When social studies consists of memorizing facts, reading textbooks, watching videos, answering questions, and illustrating knowledge already learned, its impact on students is minimal. These activities provide little help for students when they try to understand how and why people act as they do and whether particular behaviors are good or worthy of adopting. But when social studies is perceived as an integral part of the intellectual development of students, and as a set of relevant experiences, it becomes an essential part of the curriculum.

When social studies focuses student attention by confronting interesting problems related to their social world, students will naturally want to observe, ask questions, research information, express observations and ideas in drawings, argue for their viewpoints, and act to change things. When students "do" social studies, they draw on thinking skills and knowledge from the entire school curriculum as they construct an understanding of their social world and seek to solve the problems it presents. Rather than being relegated to something to do when there is time, social studies must be a fundamental part of the overall school curriculum.

DEFINITION OF SOCIAL STUDIES

Throughout the past century, the definition of social studies tended to change as knowledge of subject matter increased and developed and as more was learned about how children and youth construct meaningful knowledge. Social studies educators always maintained the importance of teaching democratic traditions to the next generation and advocated that social studies instruction should be an active process through which students come to understand the social world and participate as a citizen of that world. Originally, they focused on doing this through studying the history of western civilization and geography. Today's formal definition, adopted by the NCSS and highlighted in *Expectations for Excellence: Curriculum Standards for Social Studies,* lists the many disciplines that contribute knowledge needed by citizens in a democracy with multicultural demographic characteristics (1994b, p. vii).

> Social studies is the integrated study of the social sciences and humanities to promote civic competence. Within the school program, social studies provides coordinated, systematic study drawing upon such disciplines as anthropology, archaeology, economics, geography, history, law, philosophy, religion, and sociology, as well as appropriate content from the humanities, mathematics, and natural sciences. The primary purpose of social studies is to help young people develop the ability to make informed and reasoned decisions for the public good as citizens of a culturally diverse, democratic society in an interdependent world.

The NCSS curriculum standards document describes an important aspect of social studies as "promoting knowledge of and involvement in civic affairs" (p. vii). Civic issues, whether pertaining to health care, crime, or foreign policy, are complex and draw on several disciplines. Health care issues, for example, require some understanding of law, biology, psychology, history, and sociology. The defining characteristic of social studies is that it is multidisciplinary in nature, encompassing and integrating knowledge and processes from many disciplines. The formal definition of social studies given above emphasizes the multidisciplinary aspect of social studies and the many perspectives it seeks to integrate.

The multidisciplinary nature of social studies in the schools has been described as being like an orchestra (NCSS, 1994b, p. ix). Just as an orchestra plays specific pieces of music, schools implement the study of specific topics at certain grade levels. Sometimes, in an orchestra, one instrument leads while others play supporting notes. In a social studies unit about changes in the community, history might take the lead while geography and economics support the unit. In a unit titled "New Jobs and Careers in the United States: What Is My Future?" the study of economics might lead with the support of geography, psychology, and history.

SOCIAL STUDIES CURRICULUM

During the 1990s, national standards were developed for social studies along with other areas of education. These standards describe

- What students from kindergarten through grade 12 should be taught
- How students should be taught
- How students' achievement should be evaluated (NCSS, 1994b, p. viii)

The 10 themes of the social studies standards are listed and defined in Figure 1.3. Each theme incorporates one or more of the disciplines contributing to social studies content. Each theme also incorporates one to three major concepts associated with the disciplines. The first theme, Culture, incorporates ideas from anthropology, sociology, geography, and history. The second theme, Time, Continuity, and Change, emphasizes history along with other disciplines. The third theme, People, Places, and Environment, is strongly represented by geography and to a lesser extent, economics, culture, and civic ideals. A major message is that social studies is multidisciplinary and not rooted in any single discipline. The themes of Science, Technology, and Society and Global Connections clearly demonstrate a multidisciplinary focus.

Expectations for Excellence: Curriculum Standards for Social Studies is a document created by a national task force of social studies teachers and teacher educators. This document was reviewed and revised by many more social studies professionals before it received final approval of its content by the NCSS Board of Directors in 1994. It was designed for use by state governments and departments of education, school districts, schools, individual teachers, book publishers, parents, and community members. The complete document, published by NCSS as *Bulletin #89,* describes learning experiences in primary, intermediate, middle/junior high, and high school for each of the themes. It also specifies student performance expectations for each theme within each grade level.

COMPANION
WEBSITE

More information about the national social studies standards can be found on the Internet at the website of the National Council for the Social Studies. The Educational Standards and Curriculum Frameworks for Social Studies website maintains an annotated list of Internet sites with K–12 educational standards and curriculum frameworks documents. The listings are by social studies organization and by state. Both sites can be found on the website for this text.

TIME FOR REFLECTION: WHAT DO YOU THINK?

Return to the scenarios of lessons taught by Ms. Cannon and Mr. Powell.

1. Which of the 10 themes is the primary theme in Ms. Cannon's scenario? Why do you think so? _____

_____

Theme	Description
• *Culture*	Human beings create, learn, and adapt culture. Cultures are dynamic systems of beliefs, values, and traditions that exhibit both commonalities and differences. Understanding culture helps us understand ourselves and others.
• *Time, Continuity, and Change*	Human beings seek to understand their historic roots and to locate themselves in time. Knowing what things were like in the past and how things change and develop helps us answer important questions about our current condition.
• *People, Places, and Environment*	Today's students are aware of the world beyond their personal locations. As students study this content, they create their spatial views and geographic perspectives. Social, cultural, economic, and civic demands require such knowledge to make informed and critical decisions about relationships between people and their environment.
• *Individual Development and Identity*	Personal identity is shaped by one's culture, by groups, and by institutional influences. Examination of various forms of human behavior enhances understanding of the relationship between social norms and emerging personal identities, the relationships between social processes that influence identity formation, and the ethical principles underlying individual action.
• *Individuals, Groups, and Institutions*	Institutions exert enormous influence over us. Institutions are organizations that embody and promote the core social values of their members. It is important for students to know how institutions are formed, what controls and influences them, how they control and influence individuals and culture, and how institutions can be maintained or changed.
• *Power, Authority, and Governance*	Understanding the development of structures of power, authority, and governance and their evolving functions is essential for the emergence of civic competence.
• *Production, Distribution, and Consumption*	Decisions about exchange, trade, and economic policy and well-being are global in scope. The role of government in policy making varies over time and from place to place. Systematic study of an interdependent world economy and the role of technology in economic decision making is essential.
• *Science, Technology, and Society*	Technology is as old as the first crude tool invented by prehistoric humans. Our modern life would be impossible without technology and the science that supports it. Today's technology forms the basis for many difficult social choices.
• *Global Connections*	The realities of global interdependence require understanding of the increasingly important and diverse global connections among societies. Persisting and emerging global issues require solutions.
• *Civic Ideals and Practices*	All people have a stake in examining civic ideals and practices across time and in diverse societies, as well as in determining how to close the gap between present practices and the ideals on which our democratic republic is based. An understanding of civic ideals and the practice of citizenship is critical to full participation in society.

F I G U R E   1 . 3 **The 10 Themes of the Social Studies Standards**

Source: Expectations of Excellence: Curriculum Standards for Social Studies, by the National Council for the Social Studies, 1994, Washington, DC: National Council for the Social Studies.

➤ 2. Which of the 10 themes is the primary theme in Mr. Powell's scenario? Why do you think so?_____

_____

3. Are there other themes you find in Ms. Cannon's scenario? If so, which ones?

_____

_____

4. Are there other themes you find in Mr. Powell's scenario? If so, which ones?

_____

_____

COMPANION
WEBSITE

COMPANION
WEBSITE

COMPANION
WEBSITE

Standards have also been developed for major disciplines contributing to social studies that describe what to teach in the discipline and how to teach it. Three standards books have been developed for history: *National Standards for United States History: Exploring the American Experience (Grades 5–12), National Standards for World History: Exploring Paths to the Present (Grades 5–12)*, and *National Standards for History: Expanding Children's World in Time and Space (Grades K–4)* (National Center for History in the Schools, 1994). These describe what students should know about history and what thinking skills will help them investigate history. The document *Geography for Life: National Geography Standards 1994* (National Council for Geographic Education, 1994) describes a set of 18 national standards identifying what students should know and what thinking skills will help them learn geographic content from kindergarten through grade 12. The *Voluntary National Content Standards in Economics* (National Council on Economic Education, 1997) serves as a guide to helping K–12 students develop economic understanding. The Center for Civic Education (1994) produced the *National Standards for Civics and Government* to help teachers develop curricula to guide students' construction of key concepts of government essential for participation as a citizen of a democratic society. Each of the national standards documents focuses on three aspects of social studies that are essential in our lives: (1) supporting the community and the common good of its people, (2) identifying both common and multiple perspectives—unity and diversity in human society, and (3) applying social studies knowledge, skills, and democratic values to civic action

Many states and local school districts have shown leadership in identifying key standards for their social studies curriculum. The national social studies standards found in *Expectations for Excellence: Curriculum Standards for Social Studies* (National Council for the Social Studies, 1994b), as well as the discipline-specific standards in subjects such as geography, have been used in guiding the development of many state and local courses of study. Some states and school districts have added to or otherwise revised their courses of study so that they align with national standards to some extent. Other states and school districts have highly independent courses of study. So, whereas social studies represents a mixed picture in terms of its curriculum, guidelines are available from many sources to help teachers develop an appropriate and meaningful curriculum for their students. National, state, and local standards all indicate that the teacher's task is to support learning that really does increase a student's competence and confidence in using important social studies knowledge and skills to have a better life and to contribute more as a citizen.

CURRICULUM PATTERNS IN SOCIAL STUDIES

Perhaps the curriculum pattern most frequently used in social studies during the last half of the twentieth century was the expanding environments approach (Superka, Hawke, & Morrissett, 1980). In this approach, kindergarten students focus on themselves and their families. As they progress through the grades, they "expand out" from their personal world to explore a wide range of cultures and governments. In grade 8, students study U.S. history in greater depth. The expanding environments approach generally includes the topics shown in Table 1.1. The expanding environments

T A B L E 1 . 1

Topics in the Expanding Environments Approach to Social Studies

- Kindergarten
    Self
    School
    Community
    Home
- First grade
    Families
- Second grade
    Neighborhoods
- Third grade
    Communities
- Fourth grade
    State history
    Geographic regions
- Fifth grade
    U.S. history
- Sixth grade
    World cultures
    Western hemisphere studies
- Seventh grade
    World geography or history
- Eighth grade
    U.S. history

Source: "The Current and Future Status of the Social Studies," by D. Superka, S. Hawke, & I. Morrissett, 1980, *Social Education, 44*(5), 362–369.

approach has been typical of many kindergarten through grade 6 programs since 1955. But, seventh- and eighth-graders have studied virtually the same topics since 1916 (Morrissett, 1981; Superka, Hawke, & Morrissett, 1980).

This pattern has been questioned. Some critics question the underlying assumption that children are most familiar with their immediate environments and that their frames of reference are confined to it (Naylor & Diem, 1987). The media and the Internet have changed the abilities of younger children to encounter people and problems at ever greater distances, literally bringing the world into their homes. Others point out that the expanding environments approach does not make provision for teaching issues of immediate concern to children (Joyce & Alleman-Brooks, 1982).

Questioning and criticism have led to attempts to rethink the social studies curriculum. Some individuals agreed on and advocated a curriculum based on essential concepts drawn from history and the social sciences (Taba, Durkin, Fraenkel, & McNaughton, 1971). These concepts are given in Table 1.2. Centering the curriculum on social problems was supported by Dunfee (1977) and Engle and Ochoa (1988) as the basis for a curriculum.

Numerous curriculum projects during the 1960s and 1970s stressed the use of critical thinking, primary documents, and multimedia data sources that had been little used in the elementary schools. Among these were the Minnesota Social Studies Project (Capron, 1972) and the Social Roles Model (Superka & Hawke, 1982). The Minnesota project used the following sequence: kindergarten—the earth as the home of people; grades 1 and 2—families around the world; grades 3 and 4—communities around the world; grade 5—regional studies; grade 6—our economic system; grade 7—man and society; and grade 8—our political system. The Social Roles Model stressed social participation by students. Seven social roles were stressed: citizen, worker, consumer, family member, friend, member of various social groups, and self. Research studies with the Minnesota project in grades 1–5 led to the conclusion that the program achieved better results than other social studies programs that were not as well-defined or structured (Mitsakos, 1978). Little research has been done with the Social Roles Model so it is not possible to make conclusions about its effects.

In 1990, the California State Department of Education published a state framework for social studies, the *History–Social Science Framework for California Public Schools, Kindergarten Through Grade 12* (1988). The emphasis in this state framework for social studies is on history (see Table 1.3). Because California is a heavily populated and influential state, its framework has had effects on social studies curricula elsewhere.

The desire for improvement and better performance by U.S. students on standardized tests nationally and internationally resulted in the development of the national standards movement. The standards developed by NCSS, as well as the standards developed and based in a specific discipline such as geography or economics, grow in complexity and abstractness over the span of grades K–12. They do not make the assumptions about students found in the expanding environments approach. Instead, they view students as being able to participate in a wide range of experiences, ideas, and issues. In this book, the chapters on planning and instruction in the various content themes provide additional details on the various standards and how you can use them in planning lessons and assessments.

TABLE 1.2

Essential Concepts for Social Studies Curriculum

Causality: Events have antecedents

Conflict: Interaction involves struggle

Cooperation: Joint effort

Cultural change: Cultures never remain static

Differences: Both the natural and social worlds vary

Interdependence: People and groups are mutually dependent

Modification: As people and environments interact, both change

Power: Influence on decision making

Societal control: Liberty is constrained in all societies

Tradition: Values and ways of living are retained, to some extent

Values: Objects, behaviors, ideas, and institutions deemed important

Source: A Teacher's Handbook to Elementary Social Studies, by H. Taba, M. D. Durkin, J. E. Fraenkel, & A. H. McNaughton, 1971, Reading, MA: Addison-Wesley.

TABLE 1.3

California's History–Social Science Framework: Scope and Sequence

Kindergarten	Learning and working, now and long ago
First grade	A child's place in time and space
Second grade	People who make a difference
Third grade	Understanding continuity and change
Fourth grade	California: A changing state
Fifth grade	U.S. history and geography: Making a new nation, to 1850
Sixth grade	World history and geography: Ancient civilizations
Seventh grade	World history and geography: Medieval and early modern times
Eighth grade	U.S. history and geography: Growth and conflict
Ninth grade	One semester course electives in History–Social Science: our state, physical geography, cultural geography, humanities, anthropology, psychology, sociology, women's history, ethnic studies, area studies–culture, law-related education
Tenth grade	World history and geography: The modern world, 1789–present
Eleventh grade	U.S. history and geography: Continuity and change in the twentieth century
Twelfth grade	Principles of American democracy/economics (two 1-semester courses)

Source: History–Social Science Framework, 1988, Sacramento, CA: California State Department of Education.

PLANNING POWERFUL SOCIAL STUDIES LESSONS

Researchers have identified instructional strategies that students want to see used in social studies. Students want less reading and more group projects, field trips, independent work, discussions, clear examples, student planning, challenging learning experiences, class activities, role playing, and simulations (Schug, Todd, & Beery, 1984). In 1997, elementary teachers who were members of NCSS reported that they regularly used multiple resources in the classroom to address individual learning differences, along with cooperative learning, group learning, and individual choice in project selection (Haas & Laughlin, 1999a). However, the professional literature suggests that there doesn't seem to be a match between what most teachers have done in social studies and what students want to do.

Using the types of activities that children prefer does not by itself provide for powerful social studies learning. Teachers must carefully plan and assess lessons in order to provide the experiences that result in meaningful learning. Powerful social studies helps students construct meaningful learning by helping students relate facts and concepts to explain the world. Content is challenging, integrative, and value-based. Lessons involve students in active learning and processing of information described as "minds-on" learning. Although students may move about and physically handle learning materials, the physical activity is not incorporated for the sake of using muscles, taking a break, making a project to take home, or for fun. Additionally, teachers and students work together to keep a cooperative and supportive classroom climate that encourages students by providing opportunities to learn and grow rather than creating a restrictive atmosphere based on a fear of failure. Table 1.4 (p. 20) is a lesson plan employing powerful social studies ideas in a way that facilitates meaningful learning and construction of knowledge by students. The lesson, Making Good Rules, is designed for the primary grades. When teaching, the teacher is both a motivator and a guide as well as a provider of information. The teacher's role in helping students restructure their ideas is particularly important. Read this plan now, making note of the planned interactions between students and their teacher.

TIME FOR REFLECTION: WHAT DO YOU THINK?

Write down your initial reaction to the lesson Making Good Rules. _____
_____
_____

Reflect more on the lesson plan in Table 1.4 using the following questions for assistance. Discuss your responses to the questions below with a peer, if possible.

1. What are two different assumptions the teacher made about the prior experiences of the students for whom this lesson was planned? _____
_____
_____

➤ 2. What is the response the teacher expects from students when the teacher re-peatedly interrupts the game? _____

_____

3. In the lesson's development, the teacher wants the students to reach accurate con-clusions about rules that will give new meaning to their ideas about rules. The teacher also wants the students to generalize their new ideas to the law. What are two important conclusions students can reach from making a list of criteria for rules?
   Conclusion 1:_____
   Conclusion 2:_____

4. For what additional school activities are there rules that students might examine?

_____

_____

5. Why should teachers take the time to have students help write class rules rather than just listing the classroom rules?z_____

_____

6. Why would a class revise rules after they are made? _____

_____

_____

7. Why does a teacher post the rules in a prominent place in the classroom? _____

_____

_____

_____

8. How are the activities in this lesson related to the daily lives of students beyond the classroom? _____

_____

_____

9. What important ideas about writing and obeying the laws taught in this lesson are similar to those used in our democracy? _____

_____

_____

MAKING A LITERATURE CONNECTION ➤

Considering Quality for Social Studies Instruction

Literature can be used to extend and expand on the main idea of many social studies lessons. For primary-grade students, there are few high-quality literature selections dealing with the main idea of "making good rules." One possibility for grade 3, at the upper end of the pri-mary grades, is *Judge Judy Sheindlin's You Can't Judge a Book by Its Cover: Cool Rules for School,* by Judy Sheindlin and illustrated by Bob Tore. This book deals with the moral choices children encounter daily at school and assists them by examining the deeper meanings behind popular sayings such as "curiosity killed the cat." Judge Sheindlin presents a situation such as being given a note in a sealed envelope to give to your parents and some alternatives, including "don't open it because you will get in trouble" and "give the envelope to your parents and hope they are in a good mood." On the other hand, if middle school students have been discussing the need for making good rules and identifying positive values, more abundant useful literature is available. Two examples are *What Do You Stand For?: A Kid's*

TABLE 1.4

Learning Cycle	Making Good Rules

Grade Level: Primary
NCSS Standards: Power, Authority, and Governance

NCSS

Exploratory Introduction

Materials: Eraser

Objectives	Procedures	Assessments
Students discuss the need for rules in a game.	Arrange students in relay teams of eight to ten for an eraser relay. Teacher starts game but does not give any rules. Stop students for not playing correctly and give one or two directions and restart game only to stop it again. Repeat three to six times. Game rules include:	Record students' participation in discussion on a checklist.
	1. Pass the eraser down the row and then back up. Winning team is first to complete this. 2. Players must hold eraser with both hands. 3. First player bends down and passes eraser to the next player by reaching through his or her legs. 4. Next player passes the eraser over his or her head, and so on. 5. Players turn around after passing eraser. 6. When the eraser gets back to the first player everyone on the team sits down on the floor.	
	After the game is played correctly, repeat it several times. Teacher asks: "How did you like playing this relay? How important was it that everyone knew all of the rules? How do rules help us? Does everyone have to obey rules? What would happen if there were no rules?	

Lesson Development

Materials: Two statements on cards (see Procedures)

Objectives	Procedures	Assessments
	Display two statements and read them to the students: "When the stoplight is red, stop and wait until it is green	

Guide to Building Character by Barbara A. Lewis and edited by Pamela Espeland and *Jackie's Nine: Jackie Robinson's Values to Live* By by Sharon Robinson.

Teachers focus first on the quality of available literature. Quality considerations in social studies include the content and purpose of the selection. High-quality literature connections for social studies are accurate and appropriate and recognize different perspectives on an issue.

TABLE 1.4

Continued

	before going on. When the stoplight is red, stop and wait until it is green before going on—except if you are wearing red shoes."	
Students analyze a good and a poor rule and develop a list of characteristics of a good rule.	Teacher asks: "Could both of these statements be rules?" "How are they different?" "Is one a better rule than the other?" "Why?" Have students work with a partner to develop a list of characteristics that make a rule a good rule. Share ideas. List their ideas. Ask: "What are the characteristics that make a rule a good rule?" Develop a statement together that answers this question. Expect some of the following:	Criteria listed by pairs of students.
	It is needed for a good reason. It is clearly worded. It applies fairly and equally to all. It is easy to use or follow. It is agreed to by all.	
	"Besides when playing games, when do you have to obey rules?" "Who makes rules?" "What are some of the rules (laws) that people have to obey?" Check answers against criteria and summarize statement.	

Expansion

Materials: Rules for fire drills or the bus

Objectives	Procedures	Assessments
Students write rules using characteristics of a good rule, then apply them and evaluate them.	Students examine the rules for a fire drill or the bus rules. They practice them and compare them with their criteria. Students practice writing rules by making one or more for a specific classroom activity such as free reading time, science lab, or art class. Use the rules during the day. Discuss how well they worked. Rewrite, if needed. Post rules for later use. As the year progresses and new activities, such as field trips and parties, occur, have the students write, practice, and use appropriate rules for the class.	Record of student participation in developing, applying, and rewriting

SUMMARY

Participatory citizenship is an important goal in the development of every student. A participatory citizen has an awareness, appreciation, and basic understanding of key social studies concepts and processes required for personal decision making, participation in civic and cultural affairs, and economic productivity. Powerful social studies facilitates the construction of knowledge about the social world and our role as a participating citizen in it. Planning and teaching effective social studies lessons in the elementary and middle school classrooms constitute an exciting and complex task. Powerful social studies teaching involves students in activities, confronting them with situations they cannot adequately understand using only their prior knowledge. Teachers encourage observation, gathering and communicating evidence, and forming conclusions through a variety of procedures. Teachers foster interaction between students and with materials that result in "minds-on" social studies. This book will describe ways of creating and using powerful social studies to help you plan lessons that support students as they construct their understandings and become an active participant in a democracy.

Expanding ON THIS CHAPTER

Activity

COMPANION
WEBSITE

Draw a web illustrating your ideas about elementary and middle school social studies teaching. Include social studies knowledge, meaningful learning, exploration, social studies and students, gathering evidence, and everyday experience. Group and order your ideas, indicating relationships with arrows. Share your web with another member of the class, and discuss the similarities and differences between your webs. Why might there be differences in the webs that teachers draw? Do you think differences in the grade level you are teaching, or anticipate teaching, might be a contributor to the differences?

Recommended Websites to Visit

COMPANION
WEBSITE

National Council for the Social Studies
    www.ncss.org

No Child Left Behind Act of 2001, Pub. L. No. 107-110
    www.loc.gov/

National Center for History in the Schools: National Standards in History
    www.sscnet.ucla.edu/nchs/standards/

National Geography Standards
    www.nationalgeographic.com/education/xpeditions/standards/matrix.html

Voluntary National Content Standards in Economics
    http://store.ncee.net/volnatconsta.html

National Standards for Civics and Government
    www.civiced.org/stds_toc_preface.html

Teaching for Meaningful Learning in Social Studies

INTRODUCTION

During your schooling, you participated in many lesson experiences. You may have examined lesson plans in textbooks, the ERIC (Educational Resources Information Center) file, and Internet sources. Perhaps you have written lesson plans. Because of your experiences, you are well aware of the types of activities that teachers and students do during a lesson. List at least 10 tasks or activities that are included in a lesson plan.

_____   _____
_____   _____
_____   _____
_____   _____

Categorize the activities you listed into (1) those done by the teacher, (2) those done by the student, and (3) those done by both the teacher and student. During a lesson, what are some differences in the behaviors of teachers from those of students? What accounts for these differences?

_____
_____

CHAPTER OVERVIEW

Teachers strive to increase meaningful learning in social studies and to help students correct their alternative conceptions about the social world. This chapter focuses on how teachers plan lessons facilitating students' meaningful learning of social studies, developing an awareness, appreciation for, and ability to make decisions and participate successfully in everyday life (National Council for the Social Studies, 1994b).

Because of past experiences in school and life, students may resist or have trouble understanding new ideas. Teaching social studies effectively requires teachers to do more than tell students what they want them to know. They must help students know, for themselves, how to obtain information and use it to make decisions supporting a democratic society. How do students begin to learn about their social world in a meaningful way? How can teachers help students learn powerful social studies content so that it will be meaningful to them? How can teachers structure social studies lessons to apply what is known about how students learn? These questions form the focus of this chapter.

As you read and respond to this chapter, you may use much of what you learned in educational psychology classes and be challenged to understand how that knowledge is combined with social knowledge to plan better lessons for children and youth. You will be provided with a flexible structure for developing lessons. The same lesson structure can be applied to learning all levels and types of social studies information and inquiry skills and to developing attitudes, values, and morals.

CHAPTER OBJECTIVES

1. Explain the importance of understanding students' prior knowledge about the social studies content and skills to be taught.
2. Describe the effect of prior knowledge on learning new social studies knowledge.
3. Explain how rote memory learning of social studies differs from meaningful social studies learning.
4. Describe how students begin to understand social studies content, skills, and attitudes.
5. Describe a planning strategy that can be used to facilitate meaningful social studies learning.
6. Select activities for the various phases of a powerful social studies lesson.
7. Describe the essential parts of each phase of the learning cycle.
8. Explain why each phase of the learning cycle lesson must be included for successful student learning.
9. Construct appropriate activities for each phase of the learning cycle lesson.

HOW IS SOCIAL STUDIES BEST TAUGHT IN TODAY'S CLASSROOMS?

Social studies educators have long advocated that students must form meaning in their own minds by their own active efforts (Fraenkel, 1977; Saunders, 1992; Taba, 1967). Meaning cannot be pushed or poured into the mind by someone else. The meaning of cooperation with others, the process of identifying types of governments, the understanding of why citizens should vote, are examples of the range of social studies knowledge for which students must develop their own conception. To do so, students must work with social studies ideas until these ideas mean something to them. Teachers facilitate meaningful learning by planning and using social studies experiences that engage students in working through social studies ideas in their own minds.

APPLYING WHAT WE KNOW ABOUT MEANINGFUL LEARNING TO SOCIAL STUDIES CURRICULUM

Using Constructivist Theory in Social Studies Instruction

Meaningful social studies learning is an active construction process. It creates a network of experiences, ideas, and relationships educators call *knowledge*. Figure 2.1 illustrates the experiences students have as they construct their knowledge, skills, and attitudes in social studies. Starting with the earliest experiences in life, we begin building ever more complex networks of social studies knowledge. Meaningful social studies learning is a process of integrating and building various social studies ideas by adding, modifying, and connecting relationships between ideas. Making relationships also includes the abilities to explain, predict, and apply social studies information to many events (National Council for the Social Studies, 1994a). Learning social studies meaningfully involves and depends on the *prior knowledge* the learner brings to a situation, whether the learner's *attention is focused* on the ideas being presented, and the *mental and physical actions* of learners as they interact with events, people, and objects during instruction.

Learning through active mental and physical involvement is appropriate for higher-level goals of social studies, such as the following:

1. Understanding concepts (e.g., change and continuity)
2. Understanding generalizations (e.g., predicting relationships between the amount of diversity in a society and the degree of potential conflicts that might be found among its people)
3. Developing higher-level thinking skills (e.g., social studies processing skills, such as classifying different political positions, and higher skills, such as critical thinking, decision making, and problem solving)
4. Developing attitudes and dispositions about the social world (e.g., willingness to suspend judgment until a sufficient amount of evidence is available to form a reasonable conclusion)

NCSS

FIGURE 2.1 Knowledge Network of Experiences and Ideas Leading to a Person's Current Social Studies Idea

Using Behavioral Learning Theory in Social Studies Instruction

Teaching for active learning differs from traditional and behavioral orientations to social studies teaching. Traditional teaching is supported by a view that knowledge is transmitted by the teacher or textbook. When the teacher asks questions or gives an assignment, it is primarily to find out whether students have received the message. Such traditional social studies teaching is viewed as transmission and begins with the teacher or textbook presenting summarized information the student is expected to "recite" at a later time. Sometimes, this telling is followed by a highly teacher-guided activity designed to show the "truth" of the information. Telling students that cities are often located on rivers or asking them to repeat the definition of a city are examples of the traditional transmission view of instruction.

The transmission view of the social studies curriculum entails a list of items to be transmitted, a catalog of facts. Traditional teaching employs strategies that enhance memorization and recall. Students often enjoy memorizing facts they view as useful. The issue is whether the goal of the social studies curriculum is committing to memory a list of facts *or* whether it is meaningful learning that enables individuals to personally explain relationships and decide how to encounter social events in ways that are consistent with their values and those of their culture. A traditional program centered on memorizing facts does not encourage students to find meaning in what they are learning, nor does it help them make and test decisions.

Memorization is useful for recalling facts such as that 50 states make up the United States or that the name of one type of government is *monarchy.* But if students do not understand the meaning of those facts, they cannot connect them to form a bigger idea. Teaching social studies in this way fails to make connections with what a student already knows about the world. Direct teaching narrows learning objectives and limits social studies learning to the particular solution explained. It fails to encourage students to search their long-term memory and modify or replace inadequate ideas. When direct instruction dominates lessons, teachers often find it necessary to devote much attention to motivating and disciplining students. The passive and unrelated abstract approach of traditional teaching encourages students to become bored and distracted rather than engaged in social studies learning.

Teaching for meaningful learning does not replace all traditional strategies. Traditional social studies methods and behavioral teaching methods are appropriate for encouraging the recall and comprehension of information and the initial teaching of skills, that is, spelling social studies words, identifying names of presidents, citing an example of a propaganda technique in a commercial, learning to measure distance on a map, or recording data from a survey on a chart or graph. Although traditional teaching is appropriate in some instances, it deserves a small portion of students' and teachers' time and efforts in an elementary or middle school social studies curriculum.

AN EFFECTIVE STRATEGY TO ASSIST STUDENTS IN CONCEPTUAL CHANGE

Social studies knowledge begins when the learner actively works with events found in everyday life, both in and out of a classroom. It is saved in the learner's mind as a *new construction* made from sensory information obtained in the world and *reconstructions* of prior knowledge. For meaningful learning to occur in school, classroom experiences must first be perceived by students. Then, students mentally reconstruct the perception in their minds. This representation is transformed by each student to fit his or her own prior knowledge. Figure 2.2 illustrates the mental processes involved in meaningful learning.

Conceptual change occurs when students change their concepts. This is not easy to do. Students form their existing ideas from the experiences they have had. These ideas make sense to them. They do not give up their ideas without being convinced that the

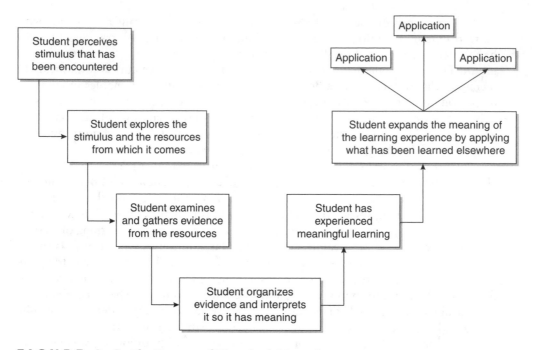

F I G U R E 2 . 2 The Process of Meaningful Learning during a Social Studies Lesson

new idea is better and more useful in their lives. So teachers involve students in meaningful social studies activities that foster conceptual change. They plan lessons that

- Motivate students to recall related prior knowledge
- Connect the new social studies idea to students' prior knowledge
- Allow students to compare and confront their prior knowledge with the new social studies idea
- Encourage students to use metacognition, to think about their own thinking (Costa, 2002; Pintrich, Marx, & Boyle, 1993)

Recently, three elementary and middle school teachers trying to foster conceptual change in their students expressed their views. Their comments provide insights into teaching for meaningful learning.

I see students in a completely different way. For the first time, I am really challenging them, not just spoon feeding them.

The idea of prior knowledge has transformed my view of social studies teaching.

It is enlightening to see what ideas the students have and how they can think through ideas if given the opportunity.

The lesson plan, "National Memorials and the Display of Power," in Table 2.1 is an example of a lesson plan that promotes meaningful learning by students by

TABLE 2.1

Learning Cycle	National Memorials and the Display of Power

Grade Level: Middle School and Intermediate
Theme or Standard: Power, Authority, and Governance

NCSS

Exploratory Introduction

Materials: Figures 2.3 and 2.4 for each student

Objectives	Procedures	Assessments
Students make inferences about an unfamiliar artifact.	Give each student copies of Figures 2.3 and 2.4. Tell students these are pictures of different views of the same memorial. Divide class into groups of three to five students. Have each group discuss the pictures by considering the following questions: 1. Which details in the pictures are familiar to you? 2. Which are unfamiliar or unusual? 3. Who do you think this person is? 4. From what culture do you think this person comes? Write the questions on a transparency for all to see. Following the discussion ask students to respond to the four questions in the guide by writing a short paragraph that describes what they see in each picture.	Completeness of paragraph: Has the student responded to all four questions?

Lesson Development

Materials: Figure 2.5 for each student, overhead transparencies of two to three political cartoons, pennies

Objectives	Procedures	Assessments
Students share ideas about what the artifact represents.	Have a reporter from each group read the paragraph to the class. Discuss or speculate on the following questions and record student responses: 1. What were the first things noticed? 2. What specifics stand out? 3. What are some possible reasons for making the memorial? 4. The face on the memorial is probably the face of _____.	Appropriate ideas are noted on a checklist of student names.
Students identify characteristics of the artifact and of coins that suggest a person's political power.	Read the following statement written by a fifth-grader: It seems like it's carved. It's a strong face, quiet and powerful. When people have a powerful ruler, they honor the ruler by making a statue like this.	Students identifying appropriate artifact/ coin characteristics noted on a checklist of student names.

continued

T A B L E   2 . 1

Continued

Have students discuss the following questions:

1. Does this student agree with your conclusions?
2. What evidence did the student use in making these conclusions?

Read further writing by the student:

> I looked at the memorial some more to check if my ideas about it were right. It looks like it's wearing a lot of crowns. The face looks calm. It's smiling a little. You see the same thing on all sides.

Discuss students' responses to the following questions:

1. Did you notice the same details?
2. What role do you think this person had in the society?
3. What do you think the people thought about or felt when they looked at the statue?
4. Has anyone personally seen a big memorial like this one?
5. Have you seen any pictures from another culture similar to this memorial?

Read more of what the fifth-grader wrote:

> This memorial reminds me of pictures I've seen of kings. Lots of times they are wearing a crown and have a calm face. This memorial has the face looking in all directions; this shows the ruler rules over all places that the ruler can see. I think that when a ruler is powerful, people honor that by making statues that show the ruler's power.

Discuss students' responses to the following questions:

1. Do you think this student's ideas are logical? Why?
2. How do people in the United States show that a president was important and had a lot of power?
3. In what different ways do we honor an important president or leader?

Examine a picture of Mount Rushmore or the Lincoln Memorial or the presidential faces on coins or paper money. Ask students whether these faces show any of the characteristics you have discussed.

TABLE 2.1

Continued

	Give students an explanation about the memorial in Figures 2.3 and 2.4. The memorial is in Kampuchea (Cambodia), in the old city of Angkor. Locate these on a world map. The memorial is of Jayavaraman VII, ruler of the Khmers, who lived in this area from 1181–1220 A.D. It is 50 feet tall and is made of stone. It tops the towers in the buildings of what was the capital city near the temple complex of Angkor Wat. Jayavaraman VII was a powerful king whose people also thought he was a god. He was a general, a conqueror of new lands, and a masterful builder of cities. Give students copies of Figure 2.5, another view of Jayavaraman VII's head topping a tower. Discuss Figure 2.5.	
Students summarize three characteristics used in depicting political power: size, frequency, and calmness of attitude.	To bring closure to the lesson, show the students a couple of political cartoons. Use a cartoon that clearly shows an emotion on the face of the leader. The more quickly the cartoon elicits a response, such as a laugh, from the students, the better. Ask students to explain whether these cartoons give them the same impression of the political leaders that the memorial gave them. Have students discuss for a few minutes with a partner their ideas about how a person's political power is demonstrated to the public. Then ask students to list their conclusions on the board.	The three characteristics are listed.
Students form a hypothesis that suggests where they find likenesses that convey political power.	Explain that authorities have identified three ways to convey political power: (1) bigger-than-life images with strong and powerful features, (2) a wide distribution of the person's image, and (3) a calm face that shows the leaders are secure in their power and goals. Ask students to examine the class list to see whether their ideas reflect what the experts say. Ask them to talk about these findings with their partner: Do they think the experts' three categories are correct? Ask each pair to develop a summary statement that incorporates all three of these ideas, beginning with the phrase: "In any culture you can identify which of its leaders were the most powerful because...." These should be shared in class.	Check off pairs forming appropriate hypothesis.

continued

TABLE 2.1

Continued

Expansion

Materials: Chart paper or transparencies

Objectives	Procedures	Assessments
Students identify, based on the evidence collected, the level of support each hypothesis has.	Have students discuss where they are likely to find likenesses of famous political leaders. (Answers include statues, money, stamps, paintings, TV public service announcements.) Record answers on a chart or transparency. Divide students into small groups of three to four students. Have each group select one location from the list and develop an investigation plan to test the statement they wrote at the end of the lesson development phase. If possible, students should find data on several different nations. (Note: TV public service announcements will be difficult for students to document. You may want to have a discussion instead of a group report about an announcement students have seen.) Have students carry out their investigations.	Use evidence to identify the level of support for each hypothesis.
Students summarize their conclusions regarding where likenesses conveying political power may be found.	Have each group make a presentation to the class that includes (1) an explanation of where they looked for information and how successful they were in finding the information and (2) several examples of representative evidence to support or disprove the hypothesis. Return to the list of locations and place one star next to the categories that provide some support for the hypothesis, two stars next to those that supply much support, and cross out any that do not support the hypothesis. Conclude by having students write a paragraph summarizing the findings of their individual groups. If possible the students should use a word processing program to type their reports and a drawing program to illustrate them. Reports and illustrations can be printed and displayed on a bulletin board titled "Ways Political Heroes Are Honored."	Students' summaries appropriately conclude where likenesses conveying political power may be found.

incorporating strategies for conceptual change. Figures 2.3, 2.4, and 2.5 are used as learning resources for the lesson. Examine these pictures and read through the lesson plan.

F I G U R E   2 . 3 **Front and Left Side View**   **F I G U R E   2 . 4** **Back and Right Side View**

F I G U R E   2 . 5 **A View of the Original Artifact**

TIME FOR REFLECTION: WHAT DO YOU THINK?

1. Give two reasons for using the pictures in Figures 2.3 and 2.4. _____
   _____
   _____

2. Why do you think the teacher recommends that the students discuss the pictures
   in small groups?_____
   _____

3. What three actions are the students expected to perform in completing the Exploratory Introduction? _____
   _____
   _____

4. How do you know that the teacher does not expect the students to be able to
   identify correctly the object in the picture or the culture that produced the objects?
   _____
   _____

5. The first set of questions in the Lesson Development is designed to get the class
   to share the ideas of each group and to make predictions or hypothesize. Why
   do you think the teacher records the statements?_____
   _____
   _____

6. What do you think a U.S. middle school (grades 5–8) student will predict that the
   object is? _____
   _____
   _____

7. Why do you think the teacher provides the students with a fictitious statement
   attributed to a fifth-grader? _____
   _____
   _____

8. Why does the teacher read the fifth-grader's response little by little rather than
   completely through all at once?_____
   _____
   _____

9. What is the purpose of looking at the penny or a picture of Mount Rushmore before providing the explanation for the object? _____
   _____
   _____

10. What is the purpose of using the cartoons? _____
   _____
   _____

11. What teaching strategy does the Expansion use to support the conclusion of the
   Lesson Development and encourage the students to further their understanding?
   _____
   _____

MAKING A LITERATURE CONNECTION ➤

Portraying Power

COMPANION WEBSITE

Teachers wishing to expand on the lesson about national memorials and the display of power through literature might find *B. Franklin, Printer* by David A. Adler an interesting resource on a famous individual who was politically powerful in his time. Students consider what national memorials exist to display the power he had, if any. *Franklin D. Roosevelt* (United States Presidents series) by Karen Bornemann Spies presents a powerful U.S. president. Students should examine the monument to this president in Washington, D.C., and consider what inferences can be drawn from that monument about his life and leadership. A resource for the Franklin D. Roosevelt (FDR) monument is http:www.nps.gov/fdrm/fdr/struggle.htm.

➤ USING TECHNOLOGY

Taking an Electronic Field Trip

COMPANION WEBSITE

The Internet offers many possibilities for visiting a distant or costly site via an electronic field trip. Electronic field trips fit well in the expansion phase of the learning cycle. Students can visit the home or library of one of the U.S. presidents as an expansion to the lesson on national memorials and political power. Visit presidential homes at the site of Teaching with Historic Places: www.cr.nps.gov/nr/twhp/. Planning and debriefing a field trip are vital to meaningful learning (see Chapter 6 for more information on social studies field trips). An Internet field trip can provide students with a firsthand learning experience that might not otherwise be possible (Wilson, Bagley, & Rice, 2000, p. 152). Teachers provide questions that lead students to explore a site thoroughly, analyze the information critically, and present their findings in their own words (Cotton, 1999).

When preparing for a virtual field trip, the teacher avoids confusion and problems in typing addresses by entering the home page address (URL) of the website as a bookmark. Additional problems are eliminated by providing written directions and help for students:

1. State limitations for printing and saving graphics and pictures.
2. Help students use the site efficiently and navigate through any problems identified in previewing the site.
3. Direct students' attention to important information needed to complete the assignment successfully.

An example of such directions and questions for a virtual field trip to Mount Vernon follows:

COMPANION WEBSITE

> Go to the Mount Vernon site: www.mountvernon.org. Click on Educational Resources, and complete the online Mansion Tour. Return to Educational Resources, and click on Biographical Information. As you read the brief biography, consider the pictures used. Do the pictures convey a sense of Washington's power? Why or why not?

PHASES OF A LEARNING CYCLE LESSON

A generic approach to planning social studies lessons encourages conceptual change regardless of the age of the student or the content of the social studies to be learned. The sequence of activities in a lesson designed to help students make conceptual change begins with students exploring new social studies information, a skill, or an attitude. This exploration leads to a more guided examination of the idea, skill, or attitude. It culminates in expanding the idea, skill, or attitude through additional practice and application in new settings. Because of the characteristics of each phase of the lesson, these three phases are called *exploratory introduction, development,* and *expansion.* Each phase has a specific purpose to accomplish. Teachers plan activities that flow from one to another. Teachers make many decisions in this process. While teaching the cycle, sometimes the teacher decides to return to an earlier part of it to provide additional instruction. This happens as assessment reveals the need for additional efforts in that phase.

The learning cycle approach is best used as part of an instructional program that also stresses creativity, the development of self-worth, self-reliance, and respect for the opinions of others. This teaching approach is compatible with knowledge gained from developmental studies involving students, from information processing studies examining the function of the brain, and from constructivist approaches to learning (Clark, 1990; Lawson, Abraham, & Renner, 1989). It also fosters the social studies standard *Individual Development and Identity* (National Council for the Social Studies, 1994b). This standard is fostered as children learn that they are able to understand the world around them and can make decisions and take actions that impact people and the world in a variety of ways.

When a teacher begins to plan a social studies lesson, several decisions are made. First, the teacher selects or develops one or more social studies objectives relevant to the curriculum and to the students' past experiences in the area. The local or state social studies curriculum guide or national social studies standards are resources to consult when making this decision. Once objectives have been selected, the teacher plans and sequences instructional activities that foster meaningful learning.

Exploratory Introduction

The *exploratory introduction* involves students with some (occasionally all) of the new social studies content, skills, or attitudes emphasized in the lesson. This makes students recall their existing personal knowledge and reveal it to others. While students are engaged in a specific activity relating their old learning to the new topic, the teacher diagnoses their existing ideas. Planning for effective exploration activities requires careful consideration.

Teachers need to be certain the activity encourages learning through students' own inquiry and focuses their interests on aspects of important social studies content, skill usage, or attitudes. To accomplish this, teachers provide only minimal guidance and allow adequate time for students to explore and investigate. An open or divergent key question is asked. This is a question for which many answers apply. Activities provide structure for student interaction with ideas and/or materials and usually require students to work with a partner or small group. Such an arrangement promotes students sharing prior ideas, predicting, hypothesizing, and testing their first thoughts. This often results in students raising important questions that promote inquiry.

The activities help students become aware of the purpose and importance of social studies content in the lesson. In an exploratory introduction, students are not expected to provide "correct" answers but to reveal what they now know and need to learn in the next phases of the lesson. Questions teachers might ask themselves as they plan the exploratory introduction include:

- What type of activities will confront students' existing knowledge of the new social studies content to be learned?
- What activities will help me diagnose students' prior knowledge of the new social studies content in the lesson?
- What activities will encourage students to recall and relate prior knowledge to the new social studies content or skill usage?
- What initial activities will encourage students in nonthreatening ways to reveal what they now know?

Ideally, the teacher creates an activity that presents students with a confusing situation in which they confront something with which they are only partially familiar. This results in their willingness to change their ideas and become confident again in their ability to process information correctly.

Students will be ready for the development activities because they provide them with opportunities to accommodate the new content or skill (Ginsburg & Opper, 1988). Successful exploratory introductions may result in some students modifying the structure of their social studies knowledge, but, more likely, they will uncover the need for additional activities on the topic or new skills to help them understand what puzzled them.

Development

Development builds on the results of the exploratory introduction. It requires more teacher direction as students are guided toward experiencing and developing new content or skills. The purpose of this part of the lesson is to explain and provide examples of key new social studies content or skills. These examples encourage students to construct relationships mentally using skills in data processing and reasoning. This phase of the lesson is more teacher guided than other parts of the lesson. A wide range of teaching strategies associated with both inquiry and direct teaching are used to promote and accomplish learning. The teacher brings this phase of the lesson to a closure when she is certain that the content or skill is clearly defined and described.

Teachers plan activities for the development phase that communicate information. Most important, the information communicated helps students resolve the questions and establish the relationships among facts explored earlier in the lesson. As students resolve questions and develop relationships, they define concepts and form conclusions. Throughout this process, they learn to select and use appropriate inquiry skills.

Students' experiences are shaped in many ways, through demonstrations, analogies, audiovisual materials, artifacts, textbooks, trade books, and other media. A variety of teacher and student interactions and the use of multimedia sources of information build explanations. Activities are designed to encourage students to develop as much of the new knowledge as possible by providing clear examples, modeling behaviors, and checking for understanding. Students have enough time to question, try out, and practice the new social studies ideas and skills. In doing this, teachers help students *accommodate* their thinking to the new ideas, skills, or attitudes.

Because students' short-term memory has limited capacity, teachers use resources that are more concrete in nature such as artifacts, pictures, graphs, guest speakers, and demonstrations accompanied by verbal explanations. Such resources enable students to hold on to the ideas under study as they refer to them during the lesson activities. Teachers provide clear examples of the new content to be learned. When appropriate, teachers provide guided practice through step-by-step procedures while at other times they explain ideas through the use of analogies or reenactments. Encountering the content or skill in several ways helps students construct meaning (Clark, 1990; Potari & Spiliotopoulou, 1996; Wade, 1994b).

At the end of the development, the students and teacher identify the major idea, skill, or attitude of the lesson. As the development phase is completed, most students have an understanding of the lesson objectives, but some still may not be clear about all ideas at this point. It is important to make certain that all students have a clear description during the lesson closure of the content or skill toward which they have been working so that they will be able to apply it in the next phase of the lesson. Students are encouraged to talk and write about the ideas.

One effective way to do this is to ask a general question, such as, What have you learned from our social studies experiences about _____ so far? Class members describe and help each other by adding to the description and clarifying their points. The teacher provides positive feedback, assessing students' progress through their comments and writing assignments. Should she decide that additional practice is needed for all or some students, she creates opportunities for this to happen. Finally, it is time to affirm that the learners revised their earlier ideas about the topic and identify some of the important new things learned through doing the activities.

When planning the development phase of a social studies lesson, teachers make decisions about the following questions:

> *How can the exploration experiences be further developed to focus on the basic social studies idea, skill, or attitude to be taught?*
> *How can the key social studies idea, skill, or attitude best be explained?*
> *How should the social studies idea, skill, or attitude be practiced, modeled, or demonstrated?*
> *What strategies or techniques can be used to assess the level of all students' understanding of the social studies idea, skill, or attitude?*
> *What activities can be provided to help special learners or to provide additional practice for those who may need it?*

Expansion

After the development phase is concluded, the lesson is not completed. It is essential to help students apply and transfer the new idea, skill, or attitude to different situations. This is what occurs during the *expansion* phase. Additional practice and application help students retrieve the social studies information or skills from their memories when needed. The teacher plans how to provide the experiences necessary for accomplishing transfer into long-term memory.

For an idea or skill to be used automatically from long-term memory, sufficient practice is needed. It should be spaced out over time and the idea or skill should be used in different contexts. After students receive initial instruction and perform activities to develop their understanding, they are ready to transfer it to situations that differ from their previous experience. Often, teachers omit this step to save time. Such a choice is a poor and costly one. Students need experience using the social studies idea in a new context over a period of time before it can be stabilized in long-term memory (National Council for the Social Studies, 1994b; Perkins & Salomon, 1991). Failure to include a related expansion activity immediately may result in the student forgetting what has been learned in the previous phases of the learning cycle.

The expansion phase begins with a short review of some of the ideas students have been studying. The students then engage in a task in which they make major decisions about how they use and present their knowledge related to the task or the skills they are learning. Expansion tasks include working with artifacts and primary source material, field trips, problem solving, decision making, interviewing or surveying, illustrating ideas through art, drama, or simulations, discussing in small groups, and writing reports or essays. The expansion phase of a lesson may be short, or it may take several days and involve out-of-school activities or homework. Length does not matter, but the inclusion of an expansion task is essential. Teachers will want to consider the amount of time they have available when deciding the length of time to devote to the expansion. If the task performed can integrate assessment of long-term instructional goals as well as social studies content, skills, and attitudes, then devoting several days to the expansion may be desirable.

Following the expansion activities, a brief chronological summary is completed of this cycle of events and important learning. This final closure is important in helping students put the lesson experiences together into a whole set of related events. It is best done by asking students to summarize, identifying what they learned and how they feel about their accomplishments. Students often like to display their work on a lesson in the classroom for several days after completing the study so they can enjoy and refer to it. The final removal of projects and displays for a lesson can provide an opportunity for a quick review and remembrance of the study and serve as a prompt to anticipate beginning a new and different social studies learning cycle lesson.

When planning the expansion phase of a social studies lesson, teachers make decisions about the following questions:

> *How much time can I devote to the Expansion at this time?*
> *What type of activities will students be able to organize and conclude in the time allowed for the Expansion?*
> *How can I structure the review portion of the Expansion so that it can be completed quickly and thoroughly?*
> *What other social studies concepts or generalizations are related to our topic of study?*
> *What other social studies learning situations provide an opportunity to use the content or skill we are learning?*

Highlights for each of the phases of the learning cycle lesson are shown in Table 2.2.

T A B L E   2 . 2

Learning Cycle	Sequencing Social Studies Instruction

Exploratory Introduction Phase Summary

The *exploratory introduction* allows students to confront and make evident their own thinking about, and knowledge of, the social studies idea or skill to be learned.

Purposes   To provide common background social studies experience that enables students' learning through their own actions and reactions to help them try out and confront their prior knowledge in a new setting

To introduce the new social studies idea or skill and relate prior knowledge to the new social studies idea or skill

To diagnose students' prior knowledge of the new social studies idea or skill

To bring out and make public students' prior knowledge on the new social studies idea or skill

Characteristics
1. Encourages learning through students' own inquiry and focuses interest
2. Involves minimal guidance or expectation on the teacher's part
3. Often provides an experience that confronts students' old way of thinking
4. Begins with a preplanned, open or divergent question from the teacher
5. Involves students in cooperative learning groups
6. Encourages observations of the world and raises questions for the students
7. Provides students with interaction with ideas and materials as well as collecting and organizing data
8. Encourages students' reflection in selecting resources, discussion, and debate
9. Encourages trying out prior ideas, suspending judgment, predicting, hypothesizing, and testing
10. Provides students with adequate time to relate prior knowledge to the new idea or skill
11. Allows students to know the purpose and objective of the social studies lesson
12. Allows teacher to know students' present understanding of the idea or skill

Development Phase Summary

Development builds on the exploratory introduction by using a more direct teaching format to help students experience and develop the idea or skill more fully, systematically, or to a higher order.

Purpose   To introduce a new social studies idea or skill leading students to apply new patterns of reasoning to their experiences, encouraging accommodation

Characteristics
1. Follows adequate exploration of the social studies idea or skill in which some development may have occurred
2. Encourages discussion of past experiences with the social studies idea or skill in the exploratory introduction phase and elsewhere

TABLE 2.2

Continued

    3. Allows learning from "explanation" through an interesting variety of teaching methods and student hands-on, minds-on learning activities

    4. Introduces an idea or skill in a structured manner through additional experience using a variety of mediums including the students' own senses, teacher explanation, technology interfaces, film, textbook readings, field trips, cooperative group discussion, Internet searches, guests to be interviewed, primary source materials, and others

    5. Encourages students to develop as much of the new idea or skill as possible through providing one or more complete cycles of explanation, giving clear examples and modeling, and checking for understanding

    6. Provides closure to the new idea or skill

Expansion Phase Summary

Expansion activities allow students to apply the idea or skill just taught in the development phase. They often include experiences during application that cause students to extend the range and context of the idea or skill.

Purpose   To apply the new idea or skill to additional examples to help stabilize it in the student's mind, fostering real understanding and long-term memory

Characteristics   1. Provides additional time and experiences for the social studies idea or skill to become part of the student's thought processes (conceptual change)

    2. Provides application activities in new, relevant contexts at the same time helping students recall their original alternative explanations

    3. Encourages retrieval from long-term memory by helping students form an abstraction from concrete examples

    4. Extends the range of applicability of the new social studies idea or skill outside the learning setting by transfer to other relevant contexts and times

    5. Provides a summary of the important events in the social studies lesson

TIME FOR REFLECTION: WHAT DO YOU THINK?

Teaching for meaningful learning in social studies requires thought and careful planning. The following list of statements represents a set of actions taken by a teacher when planning a social studies lesson. Sequence these actions in an order that would help students construct meaning regarding a social studies idea by placing the numerals 1, 2, or 3 in front of each statement. Identify initial actions that should take place in a lesson with the numeral 1. Identify actions that should be performed in the middle of a lesson with the numeral 2. Identify concluding actions in a social studies lesson with the numeral 3.

_____ 1. Provide clear examples of the new social studies idea or model the new skill.

➤

➤

_____ 2. Provide students practice in using the new social studies idea just explained.

_____ 3. Ask probing questions to diagnose students' prior knowledge on social studies ideas.

_____ 4. Provide a clear explanation of the new social studies idea.

_____ 5. Provide activities to help students transfer the new social studies knowledge to increasingly real-world situations.

_____ 6. Focus students' attention on social studies experiences.

_____ 7. Provide additional practice to help students use terms, definitions, and explanations learned previously in the lesson.

_____ 8. Ask students to clarify the new idea and justify statements with evidence.

_____ 9. Provide application activities in new, relevant contexts while helping students recall their original alternative explanations.

_____ 10. Encourage students working cooperatively in groups to recall and relate prior knowledge to the new social studies idea.

_____ 11. Elicit and discuss students' prior knowledge.

_____ 12. Help students try out and confront their prior knowledge.

_____ 13. Ask students to reflect on and explain related experiences, concepts, and terminology in their own words.

_____ 14. Provide a summary of the important events in the social studies lesson.

_____ 15. Provide a concise, brief closure of the main social studies lesson idea.

Consult the Characteristics sections of Table 2.2 to check the accuracy of your sequencing in the Time for Reflection activity. The actions you numbered 1 should be those found in the exploratory introduction phase of the lesson. The actions you numbered 2, those performed in the middle of the lesson, should be found in the development phase. The final actions, those you numbered 3, should be found in the expansion phase of the lesson. These expansion phase actions should bring the lesson to a conclusion through final review and application or practice in a new setting.

These phases of actions form a cycle. One set of actions leads to another. The last set of actions, belonging to the expansion phase of a lesson, can sometimes be the lead-in for another lesson. When this happens, students are involved in exploring the next new idea they will investigate even as they work to expand the idea they have just learned.

➤ **BUILDING ON DIVERSITY**

Opportunities to Include Multiple Perspectives

The learning cycle format offers many opportunities to build on the cultural diversity represented by students. Since the Exploration phase is open ended, it is expected that students' prior knowledge is diverse. As each student's prior knowledge

➤

➤ is brought out, other students often discover varying perspectives among their class-mates, setting up a confrontation to what the student currently thinks. During the Development phase, the focus is on reconstructing prior knowledge into a new idea or skill level or attitude. So all students have equal opportunities to reconstruct their prior knowledge. The different perspectives and skill levels among the students are used to both broaden and deepen the reconstruction. During Expansion, students use their newly reconstructed idea, skill level, or attitude in a new application that is different from the context in which they learned it. The more diverse the students, the wider is the possible set of applications.

CHOOSING ACTIVITIES APPROPRIATE TO EACH PHASE OF THE LEARNING CYCLE LESSON

Now try recognizing which actions belong to which phase in a lesson designed to teach the map skill of using the grid system and gaining information through observation. Two sets of activities describing ways to teach grid systems usage are listed below. The first set is for elementary students, and the second set is for middle childhood students. From each set, select one activity to use for the exploratory introduction phase, one to use during the development phase, and a third to use in the expansion phase. Record the numeral of each choice on the line provided at the end of the list of activities. When you have made your choices for each lesson, reflect on your reasons for the selections or discuss your selections with a classmate.

Elementary Lesson Activity Choices

1. The teacher says: "Think about where you are sitting. For example, I am sitting in front of Ellen and next to the sink. I will ask some students to tell the class where they are sitting in the room." Have each student pick another student's name from a jar and describe where that student is sitting. The teacher asks: "Did anyone have any problems in trying to describe the locations or in deciding who the person was whose location was being described?" Discuss student responses.

2. Create a grid on all or much of the classroom floor. Move students' desks so that each is in a square of the grid. Tape cards to the floor that identify rows with numbers and columns with letters. Ask students to identify their "address" by using a number and a letter. Have them put their address on any drawings or other papers they turn in. At the end of each day, select one or two students to act as mail carriers for the day, using the addresses to deliver finished papers and drawings for students to take home.

3. Using masking tape, make two columns on the floor. Divide them both by another tape strip to create four squares. Identify each row with a picture of a bird (e.g., robin and cardinal) and each column with a picture of a piece of clothing (e.g., pants and sweatshirt). Ask one student to stand in a square. Ask the other students to tell you which square the student is standing in. Repeat with students standing in different squares. Students should soon discover that each square has two names (it can

be robin–pants, robin–sweatshirt, cardinal–pants, or cardinal–sweatshirt). Encourage them to use both names. Repeat on another day with six squares, and later with eight squares. Eventually, introduce letters and numerals so the squares can be identified as A1, A2, B1, and so on.

4. Introduce students to the game bingo. Use cards that have letters and numerals identifying rows and columns. Play the game several times over a few weeks.

Write the number of the activity you choose from those above on the line beside the phase in which you would use that activity.

Exploratory Introduction ⎯⎯⎯⎯
Development ⎯⎯⎯⎯
Expansion ⎯⎯⎯⎯

Appropriate responses for the elementary practice lesson follow.

The first activity in the list is the approach that best represents an exploratory introduction activity. The development phase of a lesson formally introduces the new idea or skill, guiding students to construct new knowledge from their experiences. Therefore, a combination of discussion and a floor grid, found in elementary lesson activity 3, forms an effective development activity for defining a grid system, a concept essential to eventually understanding latitude and longitude. The expansion phase is the final part of any effective lesson designed for meaningful learning. Students apply the new idea in additional situations. Activity 2, in which students act as mail carriers, is an effective expansion activity with which to conclude the lesson. A follow-up to activity 2 for the expansion phase could be activity 4. Because it is more abstract than is activity 2, it is not preferred as a first expansion activity.

Middle Childhood Lesson Activity Choices

1. Provide students with travel magazines and other magazines with pictures of interesting places to visit. Have them select one they would most like to visit, but keep it a secret. Help them find it on a world map. Ask them to plan a 1- or 2-minute presentation for the class describing the place they would most like to visit, their "mystery place," without naming it. Next, tell them to give the other students clues by describing where it is located using two neighboring places. Have the other students try to guess what the mystery place is. Discuss problems that arose as they tried to guess each mystery place.

2. Ask groups of three students to plan a treasure hunt through five cities. Each city can be identified only by its location using latitude and longitude. Students should do some library research to identify an item that is made in each city. They should draw the item or find a picture of it, then place it in an envelope identified with the name of the city.

Each team goes on a treasure hunt designed by another team. Using a world map, they find each city by using its latitude and longitude coordinates. When all five cities have been located, each team makes a list of the names of the cities found at particular pairs of coordinates. Then they claim the envelopes printed with the names of these cities. They glue the items found in the envelopes onto a map, identify the city that belongs with each item, and display the map on a Treasure Hunt bulletin board.

3. Tape yarn onto a world map, forming a grid with 10 rows and 10 columns. Ask students to suggest a way of labeling the grid. (They might suggest, for example, letters and numerals.) Label the ends of each row and column with the system suggested. Then, have pairs of students pull a card out of a box and try to find the city named on the card. After finding it, ask the students to identify its location as closely as possible using the grid. Talk about problems they encounter, such as not being able to pinpoint a location well if it is in the center of a square or not directly on a grid line.

Ask whether anyone can tell the class what the equator is and where it is on the grid. Identify the equator for the students, if necessary, and label it. Ask them to identify whether their city is above (north) or below (south) of the equator on this map. Repeat this procedure with the prime meridian. Discuss whether these designations help students identify the location of their city or make it more confusing. Ask whether anybody can share something about latitude and longitude. Discuss comments. Then describe how the grid system currently on the map relates to latitude and longitude. Introduce finding locations with latitude and longitude. Introduce a globe and find latitude and longitude lines on it. Are these lines easier to understand with the globe? Practice finding their cities on the globe.

4. Ask students to find a city of their choice on the globe and then write down only its latitude and longitude on a strip of paper and place that in a jar. Ask each student to select a strip out of the jar, use the coordinates given to find a city, and write the name of the city on the strip of paper. Offer to assist any student who is having difficulty. Then have the class generate a list of cities they have heard of in the news. Ask students to choose five cities, find their coordinates, and write them on a sheet of paper. Check papers for accuracy.

Appropriate responses for the middle childhood practice lesson follow.

The first activity in the list is the approach that best represents an exploratory introduction activity. For the development phase of the lesson, activity 3 is a good choice. It starts with a map and a simple grid system and uses it as a beginning point for helping students invent for themselves an appropriate understanding of latitude and longitude. For the expansion phase, asking students to construct their own situation, as in the treasure hunt in activity 2, is an effective expansion activity with which to conclude the lesson. Activity 4 would also serve as a useful expansion activity because it engages students in demonstrating and practicing their own construction of the idea just explained in the development phase of the lesson.

WRITING YOUR OWN LEARNING CYCLE LESSON

Thus far, you have practiced identifying the characteristics of the phases of the learning cycle. Now it is time for you to try to write a learning cycle lesson of your own. Plan a brief lesson to teach the concept of family groups. For the purpose of this exercise, assume that the students come from homes with two parents, homes with a single parent, and homes with an extended family, and present information on only these three forms of families. Discuss your results of this activity with a peer.

1. Design an Exploratory Introduction activity suitable for introducing the topic of family groups and exploring students' prior knowledge of it in a social studies lesson. _____
   _____
   _____

2. Design a Development activity to follow the exploration above. _____
   _____
   _____
   _____

3. Describe an Expansion activity to follow the activity you gave for developing the idea of family groups. _____
   _____
   _____
   _____

PRINCIPLES OF TEACHING AND LEARNING THAT SUPPORT THE CURRICULUM STANDARDS FOR SOCIAL STUDIES

In the *Curriculum Standards for the Social Studies,* the National Council for the Social Studies (1994b) has outlined its principles for teaching and learning. Five main principles tell us that social studies teaching and learning are powerful when they are meaningful, integrative, value based, challenging, and active. This chapter has applied these principles. It has introduced an overview of social studies teaching and learning supported by the five main principles. Other chapters focus on selecting and writing appropriate objectives and assessing student learning.

SUMMARY

Social studies teaching must be appropriate to students' own prior knowledge if it is to be effective in helping them construct meaningful social studies learning. Before any formal social studies lesson, students are likely to have their own ideas about the concept, skill, or attitude that, until now, enabled them to explain and predict events to their satisfaction. Instead of teaching students entirely new content in social studies, teachers find it necessary to spend much of the instructional time helping students restructure their social studies knowledge, fostering conceptual change.

When students are presented with ideas in their social studies lessons, they have to modify and reconstruct their prior knowledge to understand the new ideas. This requires a willingness and an effort on the part of the learner to construct her knowledge schema through additional interactive experiences with the social world. It involves reorganizing prior knowledge along with newly acquired knowledge. A student's learning is not passive. Students control their own learning by their willingness to mentally engage in lessons. Teachers help each student construct ideas by using the ideas students bring with them to the classroom.

The purpose of this chapter is to introduce the teaching of social studies for meaningful learning. The following points summarize teaching as it is used to facilitate students' meaningful learning of social studies. The most worthwhile objectives of social studies units are learning major concepts, generalizations, inquiry skills, values, and attitudes. This requires a strategy of instruction different from traditional teaching used to recall facts. For these important social studies ideas and skills, teachers plan activities that encourage meaningful understanding.

Teachers identify important key social studies ideas and skills in advance, using a strategy that promotes conceptual change and meaningful learning. Lessons consist of a three-phase sequence of purposeful, interactive activities: exploratory introduction, development, and expansion. These phases help students explore their prior knowledge, integrate new ideas into their thought patterns, and apply new ideas and skills in diverse settings. Teachers continually assess progress toward attaining lesson objectives and may return to an earlier phase if further explanation or application of an idea, skill, or attitude is needed. Teachers ask students questions such as: What do you know about . . .? Why do you think . . .? How do you explain . . .? What evidence do you have? Teachers affirm student learning and encourage students to reflect on their social knowledge, attitudes, and actions.

Expanding ON THIS CHAPTER

Activity

COMPANION
WEBSITE

Design activities for a lesson teaching the concept of an *assembly line*. Children should conclude that the benefits of using an assembly line include "speed" and "efficiency" through the "division of labor."

a. Describe an Exploratory Introduction activity.
b. Describe a lesson Development activity that logically follows your Exploratory Introduction activity.
c. Describe an Expansion activity for this lesson on the concept of an *assembly line*.
d. Use Table 2.2 to evaluate the accuracy of your activities. Will each activity enable you to carry out the purpose of the phase of the lesson in which it is used? (If not, try to restructure it so that it will enable you to accomplish this purpose.)

Recommended Websites to Visit

COMPANION
WEBSITE

Teaching with Historic Places
    www.cr.nps.gov/nr/twhp/
The Awesome Library (of social studies lessons)
    www.awesomelibrary.org/Classroom/Social_Studies/Social_Studies.html
Library of Congress/National Digital Library
    www.loc.gov/
Marco Polo: Internet Content for Your Classroom
    www.marcopolo-education.org/index.aspx
PBS Teacher Source
    www.pbs.org/teachersource/
GEM: The Gateway to Educational Materials
    www.thegateway.org/

Helping Students Develop Social Studies Inquiry Skills

INTRODUCTION

Read the following sample fourth-grade social studies textbook passage. Identify, by their corresponding numbers, the statements in the passage that encourage growth in inquiry skills.

(1) All through our lives we work with other people. (2) We depend on other people and they depend on us. (3) We are **interdependent.** (4) We need to help each other and expect that everyone will do their share to make our lives happy. (5) We should do all we can to help other people. (6) We depend on our teachers to help us learn. (7) We depend on our families to feed, clothe, love, and protect us. (8) We depend on our neighbors to be our friends and help make our community a good place to live. (9) Our community depends on other communities. (10) We build roads to connect our communities. (11) We visit each other's stores. (12) We work together to make life better for everyone.

Discuss the passage and your responses with a peer in light of the following questions:

1. What social studies inquiry skills might be fostered by reading the passage?
2. Which statement(s) should be selected as a goal for a social studies lesson that helps students develop inquiry skills?
3. What activities should be used to encourage students to learn social studies inquiry skill(s)?

We return to this passage at the end of the chapter for additional reflection.

CHAPTER OVERVIEW

Inquiry in social studies involves the diverse ways in which we study our social world and propose explanations based on evidence for various events. Inquiry also refers to the activities students engage in as they investigate the social world and develop their knowledge of ideas in social studies. Students ask, find, and determine answers to questions growing out of everyday experiences. Learning involves developing thinking, or inquiry, skills (National Council for Social Studies, 1994b). Table 3.1 lists the general abilities students need to carry out social studies inquiries. Most elementary and middle school students are ready for experiences that give them concrete foundations for understanding abstract social studies ideas (Anderson, 1997; National Council for the Social Studies, 1994b). These foundations constitute the *inquiry skills:* (1) early inquiry skills, (2) social studies inquiry skills, (3) inquiry attitudes and dispositions, and (4) integrative thinking skills.

NCSS

TABLE 3.1
Abilities Needed to Do Inquiry

Grades K–4	Grades 5–8
Ask a question about phenomena/events in the social world	Identify questions that can be investigated
Plan and perform simple investigations	Plan and conduct investigations
Use simple equipment and tools to gather data	Use tools and technology to gather, analyze, and interpret data
Use data to develop descriptions and explanations	Use a range of inquiry skills to develop generalizations and models using data
Communicate descriptions of investigations and explanations	Communicate procedures for investigations and explanations

Inquiry skills help us develop an "explanation" for what we observe or investigate. The explanation students develop is the social studies "idea" or "knowledge" to be learned in the lesson. Students at various age levels and with various types of experiences develop different explanations from their personal experiences depending on the inquiry skills used or available to them. The challenge for the teacher is to make common experiences meaningful to students through the use of inquiry skills. Skill development requires classroom instruction during which students interact with each other. Assessment of inquiry skills is essential. Such assessment is communicated to students to help them understand that a high value is placed on learning inquiry skills.

CHAPTER OBJECTIVES

1. Explain the importance of planning for the development of social studies inquiry skills.

2. Describe types of skills needed by students to develop meaningful social studies learning.

3. Describe the difference in emphasis when planning social studies inquiry skills for the early childhood and middle childhood levels.

4. Describe the process of teaching social studies inquiry skills.

5. Identify conditions necessary for effectively teaching social studies inquiry skills.

6. Describe methods for assessing social studies inquiry skills during a lesson or unit.

USING INQUIRY SKILLS TO DEVELOP STUDENTS' SOCIAL STUDIES IDEAS

Knowledge develops through our experiences with the world and other individuals. Students use their prior knowledge and information from their experiences to construct new social studies knowledge. The success of this learning process depends on the level and kind of inquiry skills available to students. Teachers help students develop meaning from their experiences by encouraging the development of their inquiry skills. Throughout the year, inquiry skills are developed, practiced, and used in every social studies unit. If the use of inquiry skills is left out of a unit or is poorly developed, the ideas learned by students are less meaningful and rote memorization is likely to result (Sternberg, 1994).

The transfer of an inquiry skill from one context or topic area to another is an important goal. It cannot be assumed that transfer occurs automatically (Anderson, 1997). Transfer of an inquiry skill is likely to occur automatically only after a student has had many opportunities to practice the skill. For example, in a unit on landforms, students should identify and classify landforms to learn to distinguish hills from mountains. A few weeks later, the class begins working with a unit on economics in the community. The classification skill students developed in the earlier unit on landforms does not automatically transfer when they try to classify types of community businesses, such as manufacturing and service companies. The following discussion describes and examines inquiry skills in an effective K–8 social studies program.

EARLY INQUIRY SKILLS

COMPANION
WEBSITE

People use their five senses to investigate the environment: sight, hearing, taste, touch, and smell. Preschool children apply their senses to develop numerous early inquiry skills as they play. Early inquiry skills include pushing, pulling, sliding, and rolling. Children run their fingers through people's hair, touch clothes of different textures, feel the warmth generated by sitting in a comfortable adult lap, taste everything they can get into their mouths, and listen to the cadences of a caretaker's speech in varying social situations. These skills facilitate the investigation of the very young child's world. Later, other inquiry skills such as observation develop through continued experiences.

These early skills are learned before children experience any social studies content. For example, very young children feel the textures of a variety of clothing items before they understand how money is exchanged for clothing or how the seasons determine which clothing items are worn at various times. These early skills are basic prerequisites for understanding social studies concepts such as wants and needs, money, and production and distribution of goods. They are also prerequisites for later social studies inquiry skills.

COMPANION
WEBSITE

Early social studies experiences are important and focus on building these early inquiry skills. A table found on the website for this book describes some activities that develop early inquiry skills. It shows relationships between early inquiry skills and those learned later. Rich and diverse experiences at home and school provide learning opportunities and create students' prior knowledge. The social environment in which such experiences occur is important in the development of a child's attitudes toward learning.

> **BUILDING ON DIVERSITY**

Early Inquiry Skills

Kindergarteners begin school with numerous early inquiry skills developed through interactions with those around them and with their physical environments. Very young students are usually skilled at filling and emptying containers, smelling objects and people, spreading sand and mud, throwing objects, running, whining, whispering, and so forth. Such early inquiry skills enable young children to investigate social situations, often testing others' reactions—for example, how significant adults around them react to a thrown object, to whining, or to a whispered confidence.

Every student has a different set of early experiences. The culture of the home and its occupants dramatically affects the student. The neighborhood also exerts an influence, as do the media and the larger regional and national cultures. These influences are diverse, so children start school with different levels of skill development. Some students have advanced classification skills, while others' skills are limited. Some students have had lots of opportunities to talk with adults, while others have had few opportunities. Children use their inquiry skills to examine their social worlds. Teachers expect wide ranges of skills among their students and engage them in physical activities that foster early inquiry skills among those who lag in development and build on existing inquiry skills among others, creating a foundation for social studies inquiry skills.

SOCIAL STUDIES INQUIRY SKILLS

The early inquiry skills developed by very young children are incorporated into school social studies activities to develop social studies inquiry skills. These skills include both basic and higher-level integrative thought processes. They are important in social studies because they are necessary for exploration and investigation of the social world. Most children, and many adults, however, are not very good at using them (Glatthorn & Baron, 1991; Turner, 1994). Examples of social studies inquiry skills include observing, classifying, estimating, using maps, inferring, predicting, isolating and using variables, and interpreting data. The basic social studies inquiry skills are prerequisites for more complex inquiry skills. Table 3.2 provides examples of student behaviors related to each skill.

Each inquiry skill is built on a number of subskills, which need to be addressed. Table 3.2 describes behaviors that are necessary for elementary and middle school students to use each inquiry skill effectively. For instance, as younger students learn the skill of observing, teachers address the need for them to make many observations using all their senses. Teachers also encourage students to examine both qualitative and quantitative characteristics. If an event involves change, students are encouraged to make observations of the event during the change process as well as before and after it.

TIME FOR REFLECTION: WHAT DO YOU THINK?

Look closely at the photograph in Figure 3.1. Then answer the following questions without looking back:

- What is your first impression of where this picture was taken?
- What do you think the people in this picture are doing?

Look at Figure 3.1 again and respond to the following questions:

- What details do you notice on a second look that you did not notice when you first looked?
- Do these details support your first impression of where this picture was taken? If not, where do you now think it was taken?
- Do the details you noticed on a second look support your first impression of what these people are doing? If not, what do you now think they are doing?
- What can you remember seeing, experiencing, or reading that supports your idea of what these people are doing?

This activity asked you to look at a picture without telling you anything about it. Then you were asked to make some inferences regarding where it was taken and what is happening in it. After having a second opportunity to make observations about the picture, you were asked to recall anything you might have seen that would support your ideas. These questions incorporated the three characteristics that should exist in an exploration activity beginning a skills lesson: (1) diagnosing what students now know, (2) focusing students' attention, and (3) relating students' prior knowledge to the new learning.

By asking what your first impression was and what you could remember that might be related to the picture, the activity was diagnosing your prior knowledge and relating prior knowledge to new learning. The activity focused your attention by asking you to look at the picture and make some inferences about it. By reflecting on your responses to the questions above, you should be able to evaluate how appropriate your inferences were about the picture.

T A B L E   3 . 2

Social Studies Inquiry Skills K–8

Basic Skills

	Associated Behaviors
Observing	1. *Identify* and *name* characteristics of an object or event by using at least four senses. (Use of the sense of taste is restricted to specific teacher-designed situations.) 2. *Be aware of the need* to make numerous observations of objects and events. 3. *Pose questions* focusing on observations of objects, people, and events. 4. *Construct* descriptive and quantitative statements of observations. 5. *Construct* statements of observations describing observable changes in characteristics of an object or during an event. 6. *Distinguish* among statements based on observations and those based on inference.
Communicating	1. *Describe* the characteristics of an object or event in sufficient detail so that another person can identify it. 2. *Describe* changes in the characteristics of an object or during an event. 3. *Use* pictures, maps, tables, and graphs to communicate results obtained from observations. 4. *Describe* relationships and trends orally, in writing, in drawings, and using graphics.
Classifying	1. *Identify* and *name* observable characteristics of objects or events that could be used to group them. 2. *Order* a group of objects or events based on a single characteristic. 3. *Construct* a one-, two-, or multistage classification of a set of objects or events and name the observable characteristics on which the classification is based. 4. *Construct* two or more different classification schemes for the same set of objects or events with each scheme serving a different purpose. 5. *Construct* an operational definition of a single object or event based on a classification scheme.
Inferring	1. *Construct* one or more statements or explanations from a set of observations. 2. *Identify* observations supporting a given inference. 3. *Describe* alternative inferences for the same set of observations. 4. *Identify* inferences that should be accepted, modified, or rejected on the basis of additional observations.
Predicting	1. *Construct* a forecast of future events based on observed events. 2. *Order* a set of forecasts or predictions in terms of your confidence in them. 3. *Identify* predictions as (a) interpolations between observed events or (b) extrapolations beyond the range of observed events.

continued

TABLE 3.2

Continued

| Measuring and Estimating | 1. *Demonstrate* the use of simple tools to describe length, distance, and time.
2. *Describe* objects and events using measurements consistently during investigations.
3. *Construct* estimates of simple measurements of quantities such as length and area.
4. *Apply* rules for calculating derived quantities from two or more measurements.
5. *Distinguish* between accuracy and precision. |

Integrative Skills

	Associated Behaviors
Organizing, Interpreting, and Drawing Conclusions from Data	1. *Describe* the overall appearance of a graph or map and the relationships between individuals and groups of data. 2. *Construct* maps, tables, and graphs using information from observations. 3. *Construct* one or more statements of inferences or hypotheses from the information given in a table of data, graph, map, or picture. 4. *Use and construct* maps and graphs of various types to interpret data. 5. *Describe* data using the mean, median, and range where applicable. 6. *Use* technology hardware and software to gather, analyze, and interpret data. 7. *Distinguish* between linear and nonlinear relationships in data.
Isolating and Using Variables	1. *Identify* factors that may influence the behavior or characteristics of an event or set of events. 2. *Distinguish* among variables that are manipulated, responding, or held constant in an investigation or description of an investigation. 3. *Construct* a test to determine the effects of one variable (manipulated variable) on a second variable (the responding variable). 4. *Distinguish* among conditions that hold a given variable constant and conditions that do not hold a variable constant.
Formulating Hypotheses	1. *Distinguish* among statements of inference and hypothesis. 2. *Construct* a hypothesis relating potentially interacting variables. 3. *Construct* a test of a hypothesis. 4. *Distinguish* between observations that support a hypothesis and those that do not. 5. *Reconstruct* a hypothesis to increase its power to explain.
Solving Problems, Making Decisions, Investigating, Thinking Critically, and Thinking Creatively	1. *Acquire* background information. 2. *Establish* initial conditions for the investigation. 3. *Write* focus questions to guide inquiry. 4. *Collect and analyze* data while attempting to develop explanations. 5. *Reexamine and rewrite* explanations/plans if necessary.

FIGURE 3.1 **What Are These People Doing?**

Social studies inquiry skills can be grouped into four areas by their functions: data gathering, data organizing, data processing, and communicating (see Table 3.3). This sequence is used when planning an inquiry lesson or unit. Early in the lesson, several data-gathering skills are used. Later, data-organizing and data-processing social studies skills are encouraged. Student activities involving communication occur throughout the lesson. A stronger focus on communication occurs near the end of the lesson when final conclusions are made, shared, and evaluated. A well-planned social studies lesson or unit involves skills from each area.

Data-Gathering Skills

Data gathering is where learning begins. A number of skills are used to gather data in social studies: observing; measuring and estimating; researching and referencing; questioning; interviewing and surveying; interpreting books, charts, graphs, and maps; hypothesizing; and using technology to gather data. Students need many opportunities to practice using these skills and lots of constructive feedback when problems develop as they use them.

Data-Organizing Skills

Data gathering is the beginning point. The information gathered has little meaning to students unless they are helped to organize it so that it is usable. Skills that are

T A B L E   3 . 3

Functions of Social Studies Inquiry Skills

Data Gathering	Data Organizing	Data Processing	Communicating
Observing	Classifying	Constructing tables, maps, charts, and graphs	Reporting
Measuring and estimating skills	Ordering or sequencing	Finding patterns	Writing
Researching and referencing skills	Isolating and using variables	Predicting	Using graphing, mapmaking, and drawing
Questioning	Using technology to organize data	Interpreting observations	Formal discussing
Interviewing and surveying		Finding relationships	Informal discussing
Interpreting books, charts, graphs, and maps		Discussing to clarify ideas	Discussing to persuade
Hypothesizing		Inferring	Using technology to communicate data
Using technology to gather data		Evaluating hypotheses	
		Using technology to process data	

important in organizing data are classifying, ordering or sequencing, isolating and using variables, and using technology to organize data. These skills enable us to take individual pieces of information and make some sense of them. We do this by putting together pieces that show similar characteristics.

Data-Processing Skills

Once data is organized, it can be processed into concepts and generalizations using one or more of these skills: constructing tables, maps, charts, and graphs; finding patterns; predicting; interpreting observations; finding relationships; inferring; evaluating hypotheses; and using technology to process data.

Communicating Skills

Communicating is part of what defines us as social beings. It is essential to the thinking process enabling us to share the questions we raise, the hypotheses we develop, and the answers we find. Language in written, spoken, or signed form involves us in communication. Communication is a large part of our lives and takes place both formally and informally. Communication skills include reporting; writing; graphing, map-making, and drawing; formal discussing; informal discussing; and using technology to communicate data and conclusions.

OBSERVATIONS, INFERENCES, AND HYPOTHESES

Everyone has been involved with social studies inquiry skills in school. Yet many people have difficulty distinguishing among them or describing them. This is especially so with the skills of observing, inferring, and hypothesizing.

TIME FOR REFLECTION: WHAT DO YOU THINK?

This activity asks you to use your present knowledge to determine the skill used to form each of the statements below. Read the statements and determine which statements are observation, inference, or hypothesis.

CLASSROOM EVENT

A game was placed in a learning center. Students were told they could play the game throughout the school week in groups of two to four when they had finished their work and had some free time. The students found that the board game had colored squares on it in a pattern that covered the board. They also found nine small objects in a small box on top of the board. They did not find the rules to the game, nor would their teacher tell them how to play it. Students were asked to write about the game and their experiences with it in their social studies journals whenever they wanted to do so. Listed below are some of the statements students made during the week. Read their statements and identify which statements are observation, inference, or hypothesis by writing the letter O, I, or H, respectively, on the line corresponding to the statement.

_____ 1. "The game has squares on it." (Day 1)
_____ 2. "The pieces go with the game." (Day 1)
_____ 3. "All games have rules." (Day 1)
_____ 4. "The game has a box on top of it with nine pieces in it." (Day 3)
_____ 5. "We counted the squares in the game and there were fourteen red ones, six blue ones, twelve yellow ones, and nine purple ones." (Day 3)
_____ 6. "The game is like Monopoly." (Day 4)
_____ 7. The following statement was made by a small group of students who brought in several board games to compare to the one in the learning center: "All board games have the same kinds of parts." (Day 5)
_____ 8. "Rules are what make a game work." (Day 5)
_____ 9. "We tried to play the game nineteen times." (Day 5)
_____ 10. "When there are no rules for a game, people will start arguing because they can't agree on what to do." (Day 4)
_____ 11. "Someone must have lost the rules." (Day 1)
_____ 12. The following statement was given by a small group of students as a starting point for a project: "The more parts to a game—like the more squares of different colors it has and the more pieces—the harder it is to play."

➤

➤ How did you do? Check your responses with the following answers:

Statements 1, 4, 5, and 9 are observations.
Statements 2, 3, 6, 7, 8, and 11 are inferences.
Statements 7, 10, and 12 are hypotheses.

Read the following section to expand your idea of these skills.

Observations

Observations state characteristics of objects or events observed through the use of the senses. You should be able to identify the sense that is used to make an observation. For example, consider the following observation: The arrowhead felt smooth except for three sharp points along each side and a sharp point on top. This observation clearly involves the sense of touch. The arrowhead *feels* smooth. Sharp points can be *felt* on the top and sides, and the number of points can be *counted* on each side. Indirect observations are those made by another person: "Miranda told me that the beef jerky Tomas brought to class tasted salty." Observations represent a single case or event. They may be valid but cannot be used to make predictions. Observations lead to statements of fact.

Inferences

Inferences are based on observations or fact statements, but extend beyond what has been observed with the senses. Inferences are best-guess statements such as "It looks like it's raining outside." They are only partially supported, or even unsupported, descriptions or explanations of what has been observed. Inferences usually summarize and go beyond a set of observations that have common characteristics.

Classifying, predicting, and *generalizing* often result in inferences. *Classification inferences* define an object or event, and usually apply to all observed and unobserved cases. Statement 8 (above) is a classification inference. *Prediction inferences* attempt to determine the state of an object or event for which insufficient data is available to make an observation. In making a prediction, one must go beyond the data gathered and make judgments about an event based on information about closely similar events. Statements 2, 6, and 11 (above) are prediction inferences. *Generalization inferences* summarize and make conclusions about information gathered and may go beyond previous information about an object or event. A generalization is an example of this type of inference. Statement 3 (above) is a generalization inference. Inference statements can lead to the creation of concepts.

TIME FOR REFLECTION: WHAT DO YOU THINK?

If you were to design a lesson plan and use the exploratory introduction activity based on Figure 3.1 discussed previously in this chapter, what might be an objective for the activity? Can you identify specific content that was being taught in the exploratory activity?

➤

> A possible objective for the exploratory introduction activity follows: Students will infer where an event pictured is occurring and what is happening. You may note that this objective focuses on inferring, a social studies inquiry skill. The exploratory introduction activity using Figure 3.1 asked you to make inferences from the limited data contained in the picture. Afterward, you were asked to recall any information you might have had that would help you refine your initial inferences.
>
> No specific content was being taught in the exploration activity. However, it was not content free. As you may have inferred, this picture was taken in Africa. Specifically, it was taken in the town of Daura in northern Nigeria, during a Muslim festival celebrating the end of Ramadan, the annual fasting period. These people are passing through a gate leading to the palace of the Emir of Daura, a cultural and religious leader. In examining the picture, you have an opportunity to add to your information regarding another culture. You may have noted the clothing people are wearing, architectural details, or any number of other items. The questions above and the discussion here should help you review your original observations, think about your inferences, and enter any content you noted into your long-term memory.

Any activity focused on developing a skill uses some content. In the lesson using Figure 3.1, additional objectives may focus on content. However, to teach a skill well, the lesson should be integrated with content, but priority is given to the skill (Eggen, Kauchak, & Harder, 1979; Sunal & Haas, 1993).

Hypotheses

COMPANION
WEBSITE

A *hypothesis* describes the relationship of two or more variables constructed for investigation and testing. Simple hypotheses usually contain only two variables: the cause and the result. For example, consider the following hypothesis statement: The most popular lunch served in the school cafeteria is one that you can pick up in your hands and eat. Additional variables may be added as controls. Two controls might be added to this hypothesis for a class investigation: (1) All the lunches have been served on different days of the week. (2) All the lunches have a dessert. Based on personal observations and inferences, a person may make a generalized hypothesis for unobserved situations by saying that when variable *A* increases, variable *B* decreases. For example, when the number of kinds of vegetables served at lunch goes up, the popularity of the lunch goes down. Another hypothesis may claim that whenever the same variables are combined, the same event results. For example, any lunch that has a main part you can pick up and eat, such as pizza or hot dogs, is popular with students at this school.

Hypotheses typically condense large amounts of data and are general statements that cover all cases, not only those that are actually observed. Once a hypothesis has been stated, it is investigated and tested. A special word of caution is needed at this point: Hypotheses can be *proved* only if all possible cases are investigated and tested. Testing all cases is an impossible task, so hypotheses can only be *well supported* so one feels quite confident about the relationship. The first set of data found that contradicts the hypothesis results in the hypothesis no longer being supported. An unsupported hypothesis must be either dropped or revised to account for the new information.

People of all backgrounds carry out investigations, devising and using tests. Trying out different kinds of hand lotion on severely chapped hands and deciding which brand of garbage bag best holds one's garbage without breaking when carried out to the garbage can are examples of investigations that involve a test. Rarely do these investigations accurately test hypotheses, however, because the variables being tested are restricted by conditions, and testers may have little control over the conditions affecting the situation. For example, the person testing two types of hand lotion on chapped hands might not take into account how frequently the lotions are applied, how much is applied, and whether the furnace is on, drying the air and making it easier for the hands to remain chapped when one of the lotions is tested.

Effective problem solvers design tests that require more observations of the proposed related variables covered by the hypothesis than do the ones just described. For example, an individual may investigate the effectiveness of different types of hand lotion on severely chapped hands by requiring a variety of hand-wetting tasks when testing different brands of lotion. The individual wants to make sure extra tasks, such as washing the floor, are not performed while a brand of lotion is being tested. Such extra tasks may wet the hands more and cause the test of lotions to be unfair.

In summary, a statement that attempts to describe the relationship between variables and is general in the sense that it covers all cases, both observed and unobserved, is called a *hypothesis*. A hypothesis is a statement that can be investigated. A useful hypothesis statement clearly relates two variables in a general way. A hypothesis may be disproved when one set of observations does not agree with what the hypothesis predicts. An acceptable hypothesis is one with a lot of support. A hypothesis cannot be proved until all possible cases have been tested. Students must practice rewriting a hypothesis that needs to be modified or that was rejected when it was investigated. It is not an easy task.

Helping Students Develop Hypotheses.   Younger students can ask questions and carry out investigations when they are working with familiar items or situations. Hypothesis formation can be taught (Sunal & Sunal, 1999). The hypothesis is developed as a response to a specific inquiry. This process occurs in the lesson development phase of the learning cycle. Students are asked questions to get them thinking about what is needed to decide whether their original inquiry can be addressed:

> What do you need to know to answer your question?
> What do you now know about this?
> What do you need to try out?
> How could this material or event help us come up with answers to our question?
> What should be changed?
> What will happen as a result of the change?

Cooperative learning groups offer an opportunity for the give and take of ideas and are effective when trying to develop hypotheses.

Evaluating Hypotheses. After data is gathered and presented, students decide whether their hypotheses are supported. Four results are possible:

1. If the data is inadequate for making a decision, students decide they need additional data.
2. If the hypothesis is supported, students invent a generalization.
3. If the hypothesis is not supported by the data, students reconstruct their hypothesis.
4. If the hypothesis is not supported by the data, students may reject the hypothesis and construct a new tentative hypothesis based on the additional information.

TIME FOR REFLECTION: WHAT DO YOU THINK?

Elementary and middle school students constructed the following hypotheses to test during a week of school. Read the pairs of hypotheses below. Put an X on the line before the statement that identifies the better hypothesis in each pair.

_____ 1.a. The later the hour in the day, the more likely it will rain.

_____ 1.b. It rains more often on September 20 than on October 20.

_____ 2.a. A candidate who has the most debates with opponents will win an election.

_____ 2.b. The more debates there are, the more people notice a candidate.

_____ 3.a. The greater the perceived threat from another as determined by the number of attacks on communities by an opponent's soldiers, the more frequently protective walls are built around both large and small communities.

_____ 3.b. People build big structures such as castles or the Great Wall of China to protect themselves.

_____ 4.a. The longer a country has had a flag, the more likely it is to be a representative democracy.

_____ 4.b. Placing the flags of countries on a timeline will give us an answer.

_____ 5.a. Students who are taller than 5 feet are older than students who are 5 feet or less in height.

_____ 5.b. The taller the student, the older in months he or she will be.

_____ 6.a. Lots of towns are located along rivers.

_____ 6.b. The longer a river is, the greater the number of towns located along it is.

_____ 7.a. As inflation increases, the amount of money required to buy a house will increase, keeping up with the rate of inflation.

_____ 7.b. The more unstable the economy is, the greater the rate of inflation is.

_____ 8.a. People keep others farther away from them in the afternoon than in the morning.

_____ 8.b. The later in the day it is, the farther away people like to be from those standing near them.

_____ 9.a. The more hours of sunlight there are, the more tasks people report accomplishing.

_____ 9.b. The more sunlight there is, the more we do.

➤

> Answers and rationale follow.

In statements 1a, 2b, and 8b, the hypotheses are generalized statements.

In statements 3a and 9a, the hypotheses show clear relationships of two or more variables and are more readily disproved.

In statement 4a, the hypothesis attempts to describe a relationship between variables.

In statements 5b and 7a, the hypotheses are testable.

In statement 6b, the hypothesis is a generalized statement that shows a relationship between two or more variables.

DEVELOPING AND USING GUIDING HYPOTHESES

In social studies, students often develop *guiding hypotheses,* which have characteristics different in some ways from the hypotheses just described. Guiding hypotheses are tools that help an investigator raise questions and search for patterns. These hypotheses are not as precise as those just discussed. The investigator starts with an inquiry and then develops some guiding hypotheses to investigate it further. As interesting patterns are found in the search, a guiding hypothesis may be discarded and another one developed.

Teachers help students develop guiding hypotheses for different kinds of investigations. Students might do an *exploratory* investigation of an inquiry, a process that investigates something they do not understand very well. In this case it is not possible to develop a hypothesis that clearly links variables and describes a test that can be carried out. Instead, students are trying to discover or identify the important variables. Examples of questions that can be used in an exploratory investigation follow:

What is happening in this event? (For example, consider the enforcement of class rules.)

What are the important patterns we are seeing? (For example, everyone seems to ignore the rule about not borrowing pencils and other supplies from one another.)

How are these patterns linked to one another? (For example, students don't enforce the rule about borrowing materials because everyone gets short of materials once in a while and knows he or she will have to borrow from someone else.) (Marshall & Rossman, 1995)

To gather data related to their questions, students can conduct interviews.

Students might also develop guiding hypotheses as part of an *explanatory* investigation of an inquiry. In this case they try to explain the factors that are causing an event or action. They may also want to identify plausible networks of causes that shape the event. Questions they may ask follow:

What events, beliefs, attitudes, and policies are shaping this event? (For example, a new bridge across a nearby river has been proposed, and students note that three different locations are being considered, each having its vocal supporters or detractors.)

How do these factors interact to result in the event? (For example, the location for a new bridge across a nearby river has been chosen even though it means that a toxic dump at the foot of the bridge location will have to be cleaned up at great expense and a rare species of wildlife is endangered at the site of the other end of the bridge. What factors caused this bridge location to be chosen over the other two proposed locations?)

To collect data related to their inquiry, students might conduct interviews, carry out surveys, or read documents about the event.

Another type of investigation using guiding hypotheses is the *descriptive* study. Here students try to document the event of interest to them. To do so, they ask a question, such as "What are the important behaviors, events, beliefs, attitudes, and processes occurring in this event?" (For example, our school seems very crowded, and people are beginning to talk about adding on to the building. What is happening to make people think it is crowded?) To collect data related to their inquiry, they may observe the event closely, conduct interviews, carry out surveys, or read documents.

A last type of investigation using guiding hypotheses is the *predictive* study. Students try to predict the outcomes of an event. They might also try to forecast other events or people's behaviors as a result of this event. They may ask the following questions:

What will happen as a result of this event? (For example, what will happen to class sizes if an addition is built on to the school?)

Who will be affected by this event? (For example, will any of the students now in the school still be here when the addition is finished? Will new teachers have to be hired for the additional classrooms?)

In what ways will students be affected? (For example, will students be feeling less stressed because they have more personal space? Will students argue less over where to put stuff in the classrooms?)

To carry out such an investigation, students might use a survey questionnaire with a large group of people. This type of investigation is often closest to the studies carried out to test hypotheses that were discussed previously (Marshall & Rossman, 1995).

ATTITUDES AND DISPOSITIONS PROMOTING POWERFUL SOCIAL STUDIES

Attitudes and dispositions are affective responses that reflect our feelings and personal likes and dislikes. The development of attitudes promoting powerful learning is a fundamental goal of the social studies curriculum. We can plan for, model, and encourage the following attitudes in a social studies lesson: curiosity, respect for evidence, flexibility, responsibility to others and the environment, and appreciation of the social and natural worlds. These attitudes are not only important for learning social studies, but also essential to being an active and responsible citizen.

Curiosity

Curious students want to know about, to experience, to explore, and to investigate the things around them. This is an attitude that promotes all kinds of learning. Curiosity is often shown through questioning. Teachers foster curiosity by welcoming students' questions about people, objects, and events. Inviting students to pose questions is one way of valuing curiosity. Questioning brings satisfaction if it helps students share their pleasure and excitement with others. Satisfaction resulting from the expression of curiosity helps students sustain interest for longer periods and ask more thoughtful questions.

Curiosity is *wanting to know,* rather than a mere flow of questions. Wanting to know stimulates efforts to find out. A teacher encourages curiosity by asking students to explain a puzzling event related to a key idea. One goal of the exploratory introduction phase of a lesson is to create curiosity.

Respect for Evidence

To examine the social world and construct meaning about it, students gather evidence and use it to develop and test ideas. An explanation or theory is not useful to a student unless it fits the evidence or makes sense of what the student already knows.

Open-Mindedness. Students show they know that an unsupported statement is not necessarily true when they ask, "How do you know that's true?" or say, "Prove it." Adults often expect students to accept a statement based on the authority who made it. This can reduce students' desire to ask for evidence. If a teacher appears to accept statements from students without evidence or offers no evidence for a statement he or she makes to students, the attitude transmitted is that evidence is *not* necessary. Asking for evidence conveys the true nature of social studies as a process focused on solving specific types of problems.

Perseverance. Obtaining convincing evidence takes perseverance. Sometimes, gathering evidence to support explanations seems impossible to students. Perseverance involves waiting for new evidence to be reported, being willing to try again, learning from earlier difficulties, and changing one's ideas as a result of what is learned. Teachers model perseverance and provide students with some assignments that require seeking out information rather than just accepting the most easily available evidence.

Consideration of Conflicting Evidence. It is not easy to accept evidence that conflicts with what you think you already know. Cultivating a respect for evidence involves an awareness and a willingness to do so. Students are more likely to consider conflicting evidence if their teacher models this behavior, accepts mistakes, and rewards their efforts.

Reserving Judgment

Respect for evidence requires reserving judgment. An individual does not make a judgment until an effort is made to find out whether the information is conflicting.

Such information is willingly considered and used in making a decision. Students find this a difficult process that does not result in immediate satisfaction. Instead, a period of uncertainty and mental challenge exists before a judgment occurs.

Flexibility

The concepts and generalizations formed when trying to understand the social world change as evidence that contradicts them is developed. Unless flexibility exists, each experience that conflicts with existing ideas causes resistance. It becomes a rival idea instead of a part of the process of modifying and developing an existing one. The ability to be flexible and the recognition that conclusions are tentative are important qualities. Elementary and middle school students might not be able to fully understand the tentativeness of ideas, but teachers need to promote attitudes that enable them eventually to develop this understanding. One way of doing this in the classroom is to preface conclusions with a statement such as "As far as we can tell. . . ." It helps occasionally to talk with students about how their ideas have changed and how they used to think. Asking students to write and read about what they have learned in a small group helps them develop flexibility. Having students construct portfolios of their social studies experiences and receive feedback also promotes flexibility.

Responsibility to Others and to the Environment

Students are encouraged to investigate and explore relationships with others and their environment to understand them and to develop skills for further understanding. Growth of inquiry skills should be accompanied by the development of sensitivity and responsibility. This is expressed as an attitude of respect for, and willingness to care about, others and the environment.

A sense of responsibility toward someone or something is more likely to occur when a student has had experience with that person and thing or knows something about them. For example, students who have picked up litter in their classroom or from the school grounds understand the effort that goes into this task. These students are more likely to take care of their school or community than is someone who has not been so involved. Knowledge and experience help, although they are not enough to create an attitude of responsibility. Many of the concepts relating to responsibility for, and sensitivity to, people and the environment are complex. The interdependence of plants and animals in an ecosystem, for example, is not routinely considered when citizens make decisions in local communities. Concepts are often controversial, such as in the production of energy using nuclear fission.

Teachers can help students develop respectful attitudes toward others and the environment through examples and rules of conduct. Rules that teachers and students form together help when students begin to act responsibly. These rules can be expressed by expecting students to pick up pencils or crayons off the floor rather than step on and mash them, to water classroom plants on a regular basis, to wipe up a spill so that someone else won't slip on it, to wash their hands after covering a sneeze to reduce the spread of bacteria, and to provide enough space when sitting in a circle on the rug so that their neighbors have enough room to sit comfortably. The way to accomplish this is gradually to transfer responsibility to students for making decisions about how they should behave in their social and physical world.

Values, Morals, and Aesthetics

Although people use cognitive skills to gain knowledge, they are greatly affected by the affective domain. Often, it is an emotional aspect or implication that prompts people to examine a problem and take action. The skills used in the affective domain to make value and moral choices are the same as those used to examine cognitive issues. The difference is the content of the problem under consideration. Affective questions focus on making choices about preference, importance, correctness, and truth.

Values are decisions about the worth or importance of something based on a standard we have set. When we value something, we believe it is important or that it has worth. Value decisions are *morals* when the judgments involve rightness or wrongness. Chapter 7 discusses social studies education concerning values and morals in depth.

Aesthetics is the recognition of beauty and the assignment of value to it. People value that which they consider beautiful. Through painting, sculpture, ceramics, and weaving, artists express the beauty they see in nature and in social events. Musicians and writers also express the beauty they find in nature and in social events. Aesthetics encompasses all forms of expression, including music, literature, dance, and art. Thus, activities providing students with opportunities to search for beauty and examine values that people over the ages have assigned to the many designs and relationships found in nature and in the social world are incorporated into social studies.

Each generation must be educated to recognize and preserve relationships between people, places, and environment as production, distribution, and consumption take place among a larger and larger population. We need to examine and institute ways that allow nature and people to coexist. Developing an appreciation for natural beauty is a starting point for students to learn to value the natural environment in which they live. By incorporating cognitive, affective, and aesthetic perspectives in lessons, students have opportunities to examine important aspects of a problem before making a decision. In so doing, students use many skills and apply them to information from both the cognitive and affective domains.

MAKING A LITERATURE CONNECTION

Demonstrating Powerful Attitudes and Dispositions

Attitudes and dispositions strongly affect our education. When teachers model curiosity, respect for evidence, flexibility, and other powerful attitudes and dispositions, students typically respond positively. Modeling involves demonstrating the trait in action and encouraging students to display it.

Literature selections that demonstrate attitudes and dispositions promoting powerful social studies are available. *Curious George* by H. A. Rey is beloved by very young children, who watch the monkey's curiosity get him into all sorts of trouble and find that he always has challenging experiences but comes out fine. In *Straight to the Hoop* by John Coy, James, an inner-city 10-year-old, perseveres to prove himself on the basketball court. Responsibility toward others and perseverance are described in *Freedom School, Yes!* by Amy Littlesugar, as Jolie, her family, and friends, despite threats, persevere in aiding a young woman who has come to teach in a Mississippi Freedom School in the 1960s. *The Chimpanzees I Love: Saving Their World and Ours* by Jane Goodall clearly presents Dr. Goodall's respect for our environment as she enthusiastically works very hard to learn about and protect an endangered species.

TEACHING LESSONS IN WHICH STUDENTS USE INTEGRATIVE THINKING SKILLS

In everyday life, people make decisions, evaluate, and form judgments about their world. In responding to life's problems and issues, people need to be able to make careful and appropriate choices. To make such choices, people engage in critical thinking, problem solving and decision making, investigating, and creative thinking (see Table 3.4). Integrative thinking skills have a purpose. Determining the best color of clothing to wear in the winter, the best route to take to a relative's new home, or the size and type of air conditioner to buy for one's house when living in the Sonoran desert of Arizona all call for critical thought and skills associated with careful examination. These skills are important to use in powerful social studies lessons. They involve students in using many cognitive and affective skills as they reach a conclusion to a problem or issue in the lesson.

Critical Thinking

Critical thinking involves having good reasons for what you believe. *Critical thinking* includes careful, precise, persistent, and objective analysis of any knowledge claim or belief to judge its validity and worth (Ennis, 1991). Both before and after arriving at a conclusion, students need to be aware of, and willing to consider, the thought process they followed to reach the conclusion. Were their methods logical? Were they making unwarranted assumptions? Were they skipping a necessary step? Did the evidence support the conclusion? A willingness to consider the methods used helps students evaluate the process they used, discover problem areas, and reflect on how they might do things differently. Wanting to improve on their ideas and on the processes they use to come to conclusions is an important goal. It is a creative process that helps students identify problems and seek alternatives.

Critical thinking involves a complex set of dispositions and abilities (see Table 3.4). These dispositions include seeking reasons, trying to be well informed, taking into account the total situation, and looking for alternatives (National Council for the Social Studies, 1994b). In addition, critical thinking involves abilities such as focusing on a question, judging the credibility of a source, making and evaluating value judgments, defining terms, and deciding on an action (Ennis, 1991; National Council for the Social Studies, 1994b). Students can begin to develop, with appropriate assistance during the elementary grades, dispositions and abilities that make up critical thinking.

T A B L E   3 . 4

Sample Student Behaviors Involved When Using Integrative Skills

Critical Thinking—Understanding New Knowledge

Being open minded
Asking questions
Focusing on a question
Distinguishing relevant and irrelevant knowledge statements, value statements, and reasoning
Willing to analyze arguments and knowledge statements in terms of how well they explain
Desiring to use credible sources
Judging credibility of an argument or source
Tolerating ambiguity
Respecting evidence
Waiting for considerable evidence before judging
Being willing to search for more evidence
Being willing to revise in light of new evidence

Problem Solving—Resolving a Difficulty

Sensing a problem
Identifying important components of the problem
Putting elements of the problem into one's own words
Constructing or identifying a problem statement
Identifying alternative solution plans
Selecting a plan appropriate to the type of problem identified
Anticipating and planning for obstacles
Trying out the planned solution
Monitoring the process of working toward the solution
Adapting procedures as obstacles are encountered
Describing the solution resulting from the procedure
Validating the findings in terms of procedure and goal
Determining the efficiency and effectiveness of the overall process

Investigating—Testing an Idea or Explanation

Writing operational definitions as needed
Constructing a question to be answered
Writing a hypothesis that answers the question
Collecting and interpreting data related to the hypothesis
Writing a report of the investigation, including a statement about whether the data support the
    hypothesis

Creative Thinking—Creating Novel Ideas or Products

Demonstrating an interest in exploring the novel and the unexpected
Willing to try to create innovative or original thoughts, patterns, products, and solutions
Willing to take risks in creating and exploring new ideas and different viewpoints

T A B L E   3 . 4

Continued

Being aware of the potential of generating alternatives

Being aware of the potential of applying ideas, analogies, and models in new contexts

Being ready to change ideas or approaches as the situation evolves

Being willing to work at the edge of one's competence and to accept confusion and uncertainty

Learning to view failure as normal, interesting, and challenging

Being willing to set products or ideas aside and come back later to evaluate them from a distance

Feeling comfortable with and being motivated by intrinsic rather than extrinsic rewards

Problem Solving and Decision Making

Problem solving is a thinking strategy that attempts to resolve a difficulty. A good problem solver is familiar with, and capable of, using a variety of problem-solving strategies. Problem solving begins with problem finding and moves on to identifying, selecting, carrying out, and validating problem solutions (see Table 3.4). Becoming a better problem solver requires students to be able to reflect on their thought process to decide what a "good problem-solver" does (Barell, 1991). In an example suggested by Barell, a teacher, Ms. Mulcahy, talks with her first- and second-graders about how she thinks through life's dilemmas. The students then pose and resolve problems related to real situations they encounter, such as graffiti on school walls. Eventually, her students reflect on their thinking processes to decide what a good problem solver does:

- Takes irrelevant information or events out of the problem
- Looks at the problem from different angles and develops and tries out sample solutions, weighing them against each other
- Makes an informed decision by choosing the best alternative based on information obtained from the samples
- Considers and supports ideas provided by others, adds on to someone else's thinking
- Represents the ideas concretely, perhaps by writing or drawing them on a piece of paper or with a computer application (Barell, 1991)

Investigating

When teaching the skill of *investigating*, the teacher assists students in designing investigations that help them pose a wide variety of what-if questions to see what follows (Evans, Newmann, & Saxe, 1996; Schon, 1987). Most people are not very good at investigation in daily life. Three problems often arise when a person is not very good at investigation.

1. Collecting too few pieces of data can lead to an erroneous conclusion.

2. Collecting more data provides more information, but that data must be shown in an organized form; otherwise, relationships among the pieces of data may not be obvious.

3. Even when organizing the information, too small or too large a sequence may result in data that isn't very helpful.

Teachers help students refine their investigating skills by encouraging them to share their information with the class. Data collected by one group of students may lend or reduce support for one or more of several competing hypotheses. Sharing information is likely to broaden students' understanding of a problem because they come into contact with a wider range of data organized in varying formats by different groups.

During a learning cycle lesson involving investigating, students are encouraged to take different paths in their investigations depending on whether the data they collected are inadequate, support the hypothesis, or do not support it. Figure 3.2 on this book's website describes the paths of developing and reconstructing hypotheses.

COMPANION WEBSITE

If the data collected are inadequate and no decision can be made regarding whether a hypothesis is supported, students need to decide whether to try to collect more data and/or more appropriate data. If this can be done, they plan how to do it and then collect the additional data. Students sometimes find that it is not possible to obtain adequate data. The information might not exist in a form available to them. For example, students interested in the lives of a local group of Native Americans living in Nebraska during the late 1700s, before this region became a part of the United States, may find little or no information available. Students may, however, be able to make inferences based on information available on the Internet, in resource books, or via guest speakers from the local community college history department or the local historical society.

Under such circumstances, students can be asked to explain how valid or reliable they believe their hypothesis is. Or they might decide to pursue a different but related problem for which more information is available. If their hypothesis is not supported, the students repeat the processes of gathering, organizing, and presenting data and deciding whether the hypothesis is supported by this new set of data. If it is, they have developed a generalization as a result of their second attempt to solve the problem. If their data does not support the reconstructed hypothesis, they need to modify or construct a completely new hypothesis and repeat the process.

Creative Thinking

Creative thinking uses the basic thought processes to develop constructive, novel, or aesthetic ideas or products. Emphasis is on the use of prior knowledge to generate other possibilities in the same context or similar possibilities in other contexts, or to extend ideas in new directions. Creative ability builds on and extends awareness, interest, and willingness to explore, create change, and generate novel thoughts, products, and solutions. One part of Table 3.4 lists attitudes and dispositions that foster creative thinking.

Lesson activities allow students to generate, or select among, different purposes for exploring and understanding basic concepts. Students explore the range of meaning ideas have. Lessons on local government, for example, include such divergent purposes as helping students construct an idea of the role local government has in necessary but ordinary aspects of our lives, such as trash collection, the removal of snow on school bus routes, thus reducing the number of "snow days" for which schools are closed, and paving dirt roads in the 1950s as more people began to own cars. Students select and revise a problem related to a key idea, choose the methods to study the problem, and defend ideas derived from their study. Such assignments challenge students to use what they already know, applying it to what they see as new and challenging problems. They use their skills in the more difficult tasks of combining information, generating ideas, and communicating their ideas.

➤ **USING TECHNOLOGY**

COMPANION
WEBSITE

COMPANION
WEBSITE

Fostering Inquiry Skills

Technology can be used to expand students' control over their own learning by increasing the quality and extent of their experiences with information. In such classrooms, students are active seekers and constructors of knowledge with support from their teachers. Students' inquiries are facilitated by many public agencies. The federal government, for example, is making much of its current information and many of its archives and library resources available to the public. The Library of Congress, www.loc.gov/, is just one public agency with an ambitious program for placing its documents and pictures online. This website's pictures, sound recordings, maps, and documents interest students and prompt them to think about and ask questions.

Many newspapers and magazines have websites, and many allow free access to their articles. News organizations have tapped their video archives, developing special programs that are often sold on video with teacher guides. C-Span, www.c-span.org, is a joint venture involving many local and national news agencies that cooperate to provide free downloads of programs and lesson plans to teachers each week. The rights to use these materials vary among the programs. The table in the next Using Technology box provides an overview of the copyright laws for use in education.

Teachers use technology as a tool to facilitate social studies inquiry in five basic instructional elements: (1) providing authentic learning activities, (2) working in collaborative groups on projects, (3) providing information-rich classrooms, (4) connecting previously isolated teachers, and (5) promoting authentic evaluation tasks.

Technology assists students in gaining firsthand experience through their own inquiries by involving them in situations far beyond the time and space limitations of the classroom. This happens through several activities:

1. *Discussing* questions and *posing* problems to social scientists, historians, and others who use social studies understandings on their jobs
2. *Accessing* current news reports and documents
3. *Obtaining* photographs and short movies
4. *Making* virtual trips

CREATING AN ENVIRONMENT PROMOTING STUDENT THINKING IN SOCIAL STUDIES

Teaching for thinking requires deliberate planning and classroom conditions facilitating student interaction. Three strategies help create a proactive approach to teaching thinking in social studies: questioning, structuring, and modeling (Allen, 1996; Costa, 1991). Carefully planned questioning helps students connect prior knowledge, gather and process information into meaningful relationships, apply those relationships in new situations, and be aware of their own thinking during these processes.

Teaching for thinking starts with students' prior knowledge of an idea and leads to current experiences with the idea. Several questions may follow up students' initial responses:

What can you tell me about your past experience with events such as this?
What is your evidence for that statement?
What can you do now to become more sure about or comfortable with your answer?

Effective social studies teaching involves helping students ask more questions and providing them with fewer answers. To accomplish more effective questioning, teachers must be aware of and plan for higher-level thought questions, questions that ask for evidence to support responses, and questions that require students to become aware of their own thinking.

Lessons should provide opportunities and activities for students to engage in asking questions. Planning for questioning requires the use of wait time. *Wait time* involves waiting three to five seconds before asking a student to respond to your question and before responding to a student's answer. It is a research-supported technique that has been correlated with increased student thinking about ideas, with longer responses from students, and with more effective use of evidence in constructing responses (Rowe, 1987).

Structuring involves planning interactions between students and the learning environment. It is important that teachers maintain and extend student thinking about social studies ideas for greater periods of time than is now common in many classrooms. The classroom and outside school environment can be arranged so students can interact with real people, real objects, and real social experiences. Students need regular and frequent opportunities to talk about their thinking and to be involved in at least some risk taking in the learning process. A safe learning environment with a positive and creative atmosphere encourages students to listen to others' ideas and to work with each other. Such an environment helps students look at problems from many perspectives.

Modeling involves posing a problem and thinking out loud while demonstrating a solution. Using materials to provide observable cues is effective. For example, a teacher demonstrates how to use a map scale properly to measure distance on a map by acting out a complete procedure, explaining each step. Putting into action questioning, structuring, and modeling encourages students to integrate higher-order thought processes with social studies content.

Lesson Characteristics

An inquiry skill lesson has four major characteristics:

- A primary focus on a skill used in inquiry
- Concrete and/or manipulative experiences
- Use of content in an organized fashion
- Extensive practice of the skill (Sunal & Haas, 1993)

Concrete experiences use materials students can experience with their own senses. Such experiences might involve students in activities that feature a guest speaker dressed in Vietnam War military clothing, a 1910 glass bottle, a copy of the Declaration of Independence, or a videotape of a recent debate among presidential candidates. Students might try on a Vietnam War helmet, pick up a 1910 glass bottle and note its weight, handle the copy of the Declaration of Independence and try to trace an original signature with their finger, or count the number of times a presidential candidate looked over at an opponent during the five-minute period allotted for initial comments. Students need time to explore the materials or information available to make observations for use in later parts of the lesson.

Processing unfamiliar information is a difficult task that is made easier when concrete materials are available (Ginsburg & Opper, 1988). Evidence shows that children have limited space in their sensory memories (Glatthorn & Baron, 1991). They can address only a few items coming in through their senses at a time. When all the sensory memory space is being used, items simply are not addressed; no attention is paid to them. Having concrete examples in front of them allows students to work with greater amounts of new information. They do not have to hold it all in their sensory memory at once. Having an item enables a student to refer to it and makes it possible for the student to work with a greater variety of information at the same time. When concrete materials are not available, the teacher should decide whether to defer the topic until students can more adequately deal with it in the absence of examples or whether photographs, slides, video, computer software, Internet sites, or other less concrete materials can be used.

In the lesson, many different activities encourage and emphasize the development of inquiry skills. The teacher does not explicitly focus on concepts and generalizations but on the processes and steps that direct thinking in identifying or applying the concept or generalization. However, as opportunities to teach content occur during the activity, the teacher takes advantage of them.

Planning Activities to Teach Skills

Planning includes everything a teacher considers and prepares for classroom activities. Planning for skills activities includes

- Identifying the skill(s) to be developed
- Writing objectives
- Deciding which activities to use and sequencing them
- Obtaining the materials that will be used during the activity
- Setting up the grouping arrangement for the activity (Sunal & Haas, 1993)

Goals and Objectives. A skills lesson has two goals for students: developing skills and gathering an unspecified body of information (Sunal & Haas, 1993). Objectives for a skills lesson are developed from its goals. They identify the specific skill(s) students are to be constructing.

TIME FOR REFLECTION: WHAT DO YOU THINK?

Consider the objectives below. Which ones focus on teaching skills?

1. Sort old Valentine's Day cards into groups.
2. State the differences between a political and a topographic map.
3. Observe apple butter being made and list all the items used in the process.
4. Display a timeline by dressing in costumes from different time periods and standing in a line chronologically.
5. Watch adults as they attempt to find solutions to pushing heavily loaded grocery carts through supermarket doors that are sticking and difficult to push open.

Objective 1 focuses on teaching skills because its emphasis is on the processes of observing and classifying. Objective 2 is oriented toward the acquisition of the concepts of a political map and a topographic map rather than toward teaching skills. Students would need to have constructed the skill of observation to accomplish this objective. The construction of skill in observation is not the primary focus of this objective. A skill is being used to construct a concept. Objective 3 is oriented toward helping students construct the skill of observation. Objective 4 is focused on constructing the concept of a timeline. To achieve this objective, however, students have to be able to put costumes in chronological order, so they would be using a skill. Objective 5 is a skills activity objective in which students are observing and inferring.

Teaching Materials. To develop skills, students need information to process. The teacher provides students with materials that give them access to the information needed. If possible, each student or pair of students should be provided with a set of materials with which to work. When it is not possible to provide enough materials, the following alternatives can be considered:

- Ask the students to bring in materials.
- Set up a learning station if just a few materials are available.
- When just one object is available, organize opportunities for each student to explore the object with the teacher and/or person providing the object.
- When no materials are available, use media or electronic technology.

Grouping. Skills activities should use grouping arrangements that give students maximum opportunity to work with materials. Large groups, small groups, learning stations, or one-on-one interaction can be used equally well with careful planning.

➤ **USING TECHNOLOGY**

Broadcast Media and Computer Copyright Law:
What You Can and Cannot Do

Broadcast Media

What You Can Do
1. You can make a videotape or audiotape copy of a broadcast for educational uses.
2. The taped copy can be kept for 45 calendar days, and must be erased at the end of this period.
3. You can ask your media center or school-system media coordinator to record a program for you.
4. The taped program can be used once in your classroom during the first 10 school days of the 45-calendar-day period. It can be shown in its entirety or in part according to instructional objectives.
5. The taped program can be used for student review as a second use during the 45-calendar-day period.
6. School staff may view or listen to the program several times during the 45-calendar-day period.
7. Several additional copies can be made of the program for educational purposes. These copies must be erased when the original taped copy is erased.
8. If you want to keep the copy longer than the 45-day period, permission must be obtained from the copyright holder.

What You Cannot Do
1. You cannot change the original content of the program.
2. When program is used, you cannot skip the copyright notice in the program.
3. You cannot videotape premium videotape channels without prior permission.

Computers

What You Can Do
1. You can make one backup copy of a computer program.
2. You can adapt a computer program to another language if such an adaptation does not already exist.
3. You can add changes to the program so that it better fits your instructional needs.

What You Cannot Do
1. You cannot make additional copies other than the single backup copy of the computer program.

IMPLEMENTING ACTIVITIES THAT TEACH INQUIRY SKILLS

Skills activities are implemented after the objectives of the activity have been selected, the materials gathered, and the grouping arrangement decided. Implementation involves three steps: an exploratory introduction of the skill, guided development of the skill, and expansion of the skill as it is used in different situations.

Exploratory Introduction of a Skill

Skills activities typically begin with observation. For example, census rolls are visually observed, music from another culture is auditorily observed, an indigo blue-dyed hand-woven cloth from Niger is tactually observed by rubbing it between our fingers and visually observed by noticing that some of the blue dye has come off on our fingers. The exploratory introduction also challenges students' existing ability and creates a need for development of the skill that is the goal of the lesson. Once students have become aware of a need to reconstruct the skill, the teacher can move to the more guided development of the skill.

The activity using Figure 3.1 previously in this chapter was focused on inferring. After examining the picture, students may find that they are able to make inferences about it but feel unsure about those inferences. They are beginning to realize that inferences can be made with little information but that they may be inaccurate or inappropriate. They should be receptive to a teacher's introduction of additional pictures or other materials that provide them with information they can use to be more sure of the inferences they make.

Lesson Development

During the second phase of the lesson, the teacher guides students more directly in the construction of the skill. The teacher may ask leading questions, give explanations, and provide examples of the use of the skill. The teacher often guides students to recognize that they may have used the skill in a limited fashion, for example, making just a few observations of something that has the potential for many observations. Or, as with Figure 3.1, they may have made inferences based on very little information.

Although the teacher might not be focusing on the acquisition of specific facts, concepts, or generalizations, he or she takes advantage of opportunities to foster their acquisition. For example, following the exploratory introduction activity using Figure 3.1, the teacher may help students find Nigeria on a world map. Students might examine pictures of adobe buildings typically built in this area and compare them to adobe buildings in the southwestern United States. Students might note that most of the people are wearing light-colored clothing, then look at a graph of average monthly temperatures in this part of Nigeria and make inferences about how the preferred color of clothing might be related to temperature.

This phase of the lesson ends with a closure activity. This enables the teacher to assess how well students have developed the skill. If the skill being constructed is observation, for example, the teacher might set an item down in a central location in the room, ask each student to make observations of it, and then compile a class list of observations of the item encouraging students to contribute something not previously mentioned. Such a closure activity enables teachers to determine whether the students are ready to move on to the expansion phase of the skill or whether they need more guided development activities. Teachers ask guiding questions that stimulate the use of the skill and its prerequisite skills, if any. Teachers also model steps in using the skill. Students are asked to explain or describe how they developed their answers. Then teachers provide opportunities for students to use the skill.

Expansion

After students have initially acquired a skill, they need to practice and use it in situations that differ from the one in which they acquired it. At first, students practice the skill with teacher guidance. The teacher asks them to explain why they have decided something is or is not an observation, for example. As the teacher guides the practice, students take some responsibility for their own learning. By asking students to explain their response, the teacher is enabling them to discover for themselves whether they are correctly using the skill.

As an example, in a lesson focusing on the skill of inferring, the teacher might follow up some of the lesson activities related to Figure 3.1 by providing students with pictures of crowds of people in the United States. These might include a New Year's Eve crowd at Times Square in New York City or a beach in the summer. Students are asked questions that require them to make inferences about the pictures, for example, "What is your first impression of where this picture was taken?" and "What do you think the people in this picture are doing?"

Eventually, the students develop the inquiry skill being taught and can use it in different situations. The teacher then involves students in a quick practice activity to demonstrate their achievement of the skill. For example, the teacher might give each student a list of five observations about an item, such as the classroom whiteboard, and ask students to circle those observations that can be directly verified. Or the teacher might give students a new picture, provide them with a list of inferences about it, and ask them to identify the inference they are most unsure of based on the information they have in the picture. These types of activities serve as an opportunity to determine which students can move on to independent activity using the skill and which students need more guided practice or even reteaching.

The last part of expansion involves intensive independent activity. An example of independent activity with the skill of observation is giving students a simple map and asking them to list observations they can make about it. Independent activity with the skill of making inferences might involve students in examining a map of Nigeria that shows its river systems and making inferences regarding where agriculture might be expected because of the location of rivers and where large cities might have begun as a market for farm products from the local area. Students could check their inferences by using library or Internet resources.

For a skill to be used automatically from long-term memory, students need to practice the skill over a long period of time. Opportunities to use a skill should be a part of later lessons that do not have to focus primarily on the skill but may use it to teach a concept or as part of activities leading to the construction of a different skill.

TIME FOR REFLECTION: WHAT DO YOU THINK?

Read the following activities from a lesson for primary grades students. Then answer the questions that follow.

- **Exploratory Introduction.** Arrange students in a circle around a set of foods including sweet potatoes, peanuts, tomatoes, squash, pumpkins, field corn, yellow corn, and sunflower seeds. Encourage them to examine the items and describe their observations. Then ask them to put the items into two groups: those they think people eat and those that are not eaten. Tell them these were all plants that European immigrants acquired from Native Americans.
- **Lesson Development.** Discuss students' observations and classification of the items. Are they familiar with each item? Examine the two groups that were sorted. Ask students why they put each item in the group. Then ask small groups of three students to sort samples of the foods in any way they want. Talk about how they are sorting them by asking questions such as "Why did you put these together?" and "What is the same about the foods in this pile?" Have each student choose three items that go together and tell why. Ask the students, "What do people do when they put things into groups?" or "How do people decide that some things go together in one pile and other things belong together in another pile?"
- **Expansion.** Encourage students to taste small samples, both raw and cooked, of each food. Then have them use taste to sort the items into groups. Ask students to decide which is their favorite among the foods. Ask them to think of another food that tastes somewhat like their favorite. If they have difficulty, ask them to think of another food, not currently in the selection before them, that is similar in some way to their favorite food (i.e., color, texture). Then ask them to describe how it is similar. Finally, ask students to use magazines to find pictures of foods they like that are the same in some way, cut them out, paste them on a piece of paper shaped like a dinner plate, and write a description of how these foods are similar.

1. Which skill is being taught in this lesson?
2. Is the *primary focus* of this lesson on having students further develop their skill of classification?
3. What unit might this lesson be a part of?
4. What lesson might follow next in this unit?

This is a lesson in which the primary focus is on the skill of classification using Native American foods acquired by European immigrants as the content classified. The lesson could be part of several different units, including a unit on Native Americans or a unit on European settlement of North America. The next lesson in either of these units could focus on recognizing how most of these foods became part of the modern North American diet.

What other materials might the teacher have used as part of a unit on Native Americans to teach the skill of classification? What are three characteristics that might be used to classify these materials? Use the materials you have just suggested in a lesson teaching classification. Briefly describe an exploratory activity, lesson development, and an expansion activity.

ASSESSING THE USE OF INQUIRY SKILLS

It is often difficult to determine whether all students in a group have mastered a particular skill. Students' level of performance using inquiry skills is poorly assessed by standardized and most paper-and-pencil tests because such tests often measure only lower-level social studies content objectives. Assessing skills indicates they have value.

Regular daily record keeping makes the assessment of skills doable within the demands of a busy teaching day. Assessment of student thinking skills uses different types of records for different purposes. The type of record keeping depends on whether the record is intended for the parent, teacher, student, or for another purpose such as assessment by special education personnel.

A *task completion* record indicates a student has finished a task. It can indicate how well or to what level a task has been finished. A *task performance* record uses events occurring within a social studies unit. For example, a student task record in an early grades unit investigating geographic features of the neighborhood involves the completion of specific tasks such as the following:

- Making drawings of two personally identified geographic features using a variety of materials
- Listing observable characteristics of different geographic features such as a small hill on the playground
- Constructing a model of the hill

Table 3.5 illustrates a record form assessing tasks.

The type of information recorded for assessment ranges from a simple checkmark to a numerical rating scale, rubric, or a narrative comment. A checkmark indicates the student demonstrated or completed the task. Checkmarks are useful as a way to identify that progress has occurred, but they usually are not sufficient for evaluating student progress. The use of numerical, rubric, and narrative assessments helps diagnose students' strengths and weaknesses. Rubrics use criteria to assess and evaluate learning performance. See Table 3.6 for a sample rubric assessment. Rubric

TABLE 3.5

Record of Student Social Studies Activities

Topic	Student			
	Tanya	Travis	Natalie	Umberto
Drawing two geographic features using a variety of materials	X	X	X	X
Listing observable characteristics of geographic features	X	X	X	X
Constructing a model of one geographic feature	X	X		X

TABLE 3.6

Record of Student Skill Development

Topic	Student			
	Tanya	Travis	Natalie	Umberto
Observing				
Use of more than one sense while investigating the observable characteristics of a geographic feature	X	X	X	X
Classifying				
Classification of a variety of geographic features by their shape		X	X	X
Identifying Variables				
Identification of the height of the land as a variable related to the observable characteristics of some of the neighborhood's geographic features			X	X

and narrative assessment ratings are useful in deciding on future social studies instruction. Table 3.7 identifies levels for curiosity. Records may be kept on individual or classroom charts. Comparing student progress to the overall development of the skill or to other students allows a teacher to provide a more supportive and powerful social studies program.

Evaluation is a critically important task. It is necessary for planning effective social studies lessons, for providing feedback to students to enhance their learning, and for interacting meaningfully with students during classroom teaching. Chapter 14 provides an in-depth discussion of the use and techniques of social studies assessment.

HIERARCHY OF INQUIRY SKILLS

The categories of inquiry skills provide a way to scaffold the introduction of these skills in social studies lessons. During the early elementary grades, social studies lessons focus on basic skills such as observation, classification, communication, and measurement. At the middle school level, social studies lessons focus on students' independent use of basic skills and facilitate their learning of integrative inquiry skills. Table 3.8 illustrates the ever-increasing complexity of the skills addressed during the K–8 years. Inquiry skill learning requires relating the new skill to prerequisite skills, modeling the new skill, becoming aware of its components, and practicing and trans-

T A B L E   3 . 7

Sample Development Assessment for Curiosity

Curiosity Assessment

Lesson or Activity _____

Rating Level	Student			
	Tanya	*Travis*	*Natalie*	*Umberto*
Level 1				
Unaware of new things and shows little sign of interest even when these things are pointed out				
Level 2				
Often seems unaware of new things and shows little sign of interest even when these things are pointed out				
Level 3				
Is attracted by new things but looks at them only superficially or for a short time. Asks questions mostly about what things are and where they come from, rather than about how or why they work or relate to other things				
Level 4				
Usually shows interest in new or unusual things and notices details				
Level 5				
Shows interest in new or unusual things and notices details; seeks, by questioning or action, to find out about and to explain causes and relationships				

ferring it sufficiently so that it is performed automatically. The learning cycle lesson accomplishes these necessary steps while building students' interest and proficiency (Table 3.9).

T A B L E   3 . 8

Developmental Use of Thinking Skills in Social Studies Lessons

Thinking Skill	Components of Skills Used at Particular Grade Levels		
	Kindergarten	*Elementary School*	*Middle School*
Observation	Descriptive; uses all senses; needs to use real experiences	Quantitative; observes change; uses familiar situations	Relates theory and observations; can use imagined situations
Classification	Uses one attribute to classify	Can use multiple attributes to classify; can use a hierarchical system	Can create a hierarchical system
Communication	Can describe information coming directly from the senses, can begin recording data	Can make inferences from experiences; can begin graphical representation	Can describe using maps, charts, graphs qualitatively
Measuring and Estimating	Can make comparisons	Measures with some accuracy; begins estimating	Can use abstract measures and relations
Inferring	Uses inference but unaware of using it	Distinguishes among observations	Uses inference in developing theory
Predicting	Uses prediction but unaware of using it	Makes descriptive, concrete predictions	Makes quantitative, thorough predictions; uses qualitative description; uses abstract variables
Using Variables	Uses a single variable	Identifies, selects, uses multiple variables	Controls multiple variables
Hypothesizing	Begins using fair tests	Makes simple, concrete hypotheses; identifies hypotheses; judges; uses inductive thinking	Identifies and constructs tests; judges; uses inductive and deductive thinking
Investigating	Begins developing concept of fairness	Uses hypothesis testing	Uses and generates hypotheses

TABLE 3.9

Teaching Inquiry Skills Using the Learning Cycle

Exploratory Introduction

Help students try out and confront their prior knowledge of the inquiry skill.

Provide an opportunity for students to display the skill focused on in the lesson. Start students thinking with a "key" question involving them in an activity using the skill.

Relate previous experience to the lesson skill.

Lesson Development

Discuss the results of the exploratory activity, providing connections to the focus skill.

Provide an explanation of the new skill, describing how to use it, when it is used, for what purpose it is used, and how to know when to use it appropriately.

Provide clear examples or model the new skill.

Provide closure for the new skill, describing the steps necessary to use it.

Expansion

Provide practice activities for the new skill. Use interesting examples, not repetitive practice.

Provide activities where the skill is applied in new, relevant contexts.

Provide activities helping students transfer the new social studies inquiry skill to more and more real-world events.

Provide a summary of the skill, when it is used, and how to use it correctly.

SUMMARY

Ideas are made up of information and the related inquiry skills necessary for using and interpreting information meaningfully. Students perceive and interpret information from their experiences and use their prior knowledge to construct new knowledge. Construction of new knowledge is dependent on the level and kind of inquiry skills available to students. Beginning social studies lessons focus on helping students derive meaning from their everyday experiences by encouraging the development of their inquiry skills. After students have specific social studies experiences in an area and have developed basic inquiry skills, the focus of social studies teaching moves from a skills emphasis to a skills-and-content emphasis. Inquiry skill development requires purposeful unit and lesson planning and the use of methods that facilitate student interaction. Assessment and evaluation of a wide range of inquiry skills place a higher value on them and focus instruction on meaningful learning in students.

COMPANION
WEBSITE

Expanding ON THIS CHAPTER

Activity

Information, or data, is gathered, organized, processed, and finally communicated to others. Teachers sometimes rely on written papers as the way in which students are encouraged to communicate information. Consider a set of activities in which middle school students have been investigating the ethnic background of cowboys in the American West following the Civil War. They have found out that many cowboys were African American. What are appropriate means of communicating their information other than through a written paper?

Recommended Websites to Visit

COMPANION
WEBSITE

Decision Making, a lesson plan for grades 4, 5, and 6
   http://askeric.org/cgi-bin/printlessons.cgi/Virtual/Lessons/Social_Studies/ Psychology/PSY0004.html

Critical Thinking Strategies, a lesson plan for all grade levels
   http://askeric.org/cgi-bin/printlessons.cgi/Virtual/Lessons/Interdisciplinary/ INT0013.html

The Process of Sequencing: A Picture Card Game
   http://askeric.org/cgi-bin/printlessons.cgi/Virtual/Lessons/ Interdisciplinary/INT0059.html

Data Gathering: Vietnam, a middle school lesson
   http://askeric.org/cgi-bin/printlessons.cgi/Virtual/Lessons/Social_Studies/ World_History/Vietnam/VET0200.html

Environmental Explorer: A lesson using observation skills to analyze changes that people have made to the natural environment.
   www.nationalgeographic.com/resources/ngo/education/ideas58/58environ.html

Famous People: Selected Portraits from the Collections of the Library of Congress
   http://lcweb.loc.gov/rr/print/235_intr.html

The Library of Congress: The online catalog contains over 12 million bibliographic records representing books, serials, computer files, manuscripts, cartographic materials, music, sound recordings, and visual materials from the Library's collections.
   www.loc.gov/catalog/

Smithsonian Institution
   www.si.edu/

Al Bawaba, Middle East Gateway: Topics and materials include news, business, travel, entertainment, games, kids, shop, e-cards, downloads, editorial, report, and "in the Spotlight."
   www.albawaba.com

iTECH Inc: School Acceptable Use Policy Links
   www.aupaction.com/aupsonweb.html

ERIC Clearinghouse for Social Studies/Social Science Education (ERIC/Chess)
   www.indiana.edu/~ssdc/eric_chess.htm

Helping Students Construct Concepts

INTRODUCTION

An example of a fourth-grade social studies textbook passage appears below. Each sentence has been numbered for easy reference. Read the passage, then answer the questions that follow it.

(1) The place where a river begins is called its **source.** (2) Many rivers begin high in the mountains. (3) Water from rain, melted snow, and underground springs collects. (4) The water begins to run downhill as a **stream.** (5) The picture on this page shows a stream carrying water downhill. (6) It moves fast. (7) It carries pieces of sand, soil, and rock. (8) These pieces grind a deep, wide path into the earth. (9) The bottom of the path is the **riverbed.** (10) The sides of the stream are its **banks.**

(11) The stream cuts into the land and becomes lower than the earth around it. (12) It becomes larger as rain and melting snow add to it.

(13) Other, smaller streams join it. (14) Soon the stream is large enough to be called a **river.**

(15) Smaller rivers and streams, called **branches,** join the river.

(16) Branches are also known as **tributaries** (TRIB-yuh-tair-eez). (17) Look at the picture of tributaries flowing into a large river on the next page.

(18) A river **drains,** or carries away, water from the land around it. (19) The land drained by a river and its branches is called a **river basin.**

(20) Soil washed into the river is called **silt.** (21) The river collects lots of silt, small stones, and sand. (22) When the river reaches flat land, it slows down. (23) It no longer can carry a lot of silt, stones, and sand. (24) As the stream runs downhill, other streams join it. (25) Most of the silt, stones, and sand settle to the bottom and the river becomes shallower.

➤

(26) In some places the sand piles up. (27) Large piles become islands. (28) Small piles look like a low mound and are called **sandbars.** (29) Look at the picture of the sandbar on the next page. (30) Sometimes a sandbar is a mound under the water and boats can get grounded, or stuck, on it.

(31) Most rivers reach the ocean. (32) The place where the river empties into the ocean is called its **mouth.** (33) This is where the river drops the rest of its silt and the fresh water it brings mixes with the salt water of the ocean. (34) Look at the picture of a river's mouth on the next page.

If possible, discuss the passage and your responses with a peer.

1. What are four adjectives that describe your impressions of the passage and the social studies content it presents? _____

    _____

2. How do you think a fourth-grader will respond to the passage? _____

    _____

3. What can a teacher do to help the average fourth-grader better understand the passage? _____

    _____

4. What social studies concept(s) should be selected as objectives for a lesson?

    _____

5. What activities should be used to encourage meaningful learning of the social studies concept(s)? _____

    _____

    _____

We return to this passage at the end of the chapter for additional reflection.

CHAPTER OVERVIEW

Social studies involves mastery of key concepts and processes required for personal decision making, active participation in civic and cultural affairs, and economic productivity (National Council for Social Studies, 1994b).

Factual information, or facts, is based on observations and inferences about objects and events. Examples of two facts follow: (1) the Bill of Rights is part of the Constitution of the United States of America and (2) this author's family has two children, one girl and one boy. Concepts summarize a set of factual statements that have a common characteristic and distinguish any and all examples of the concept from nonexamples. The first fact, about the Bill of Rights, may be part of a set of facts used to construct the concept of governing documents. The second fact, about this author's family, may be part of a set of facts used to construct the concept of family.

The focus of this chapter is on facilitating students' learning of social studies concepts. Because students usually come to class with preconceived ideas and some misconceptions about the world, teachers plan and implement activities that encourage conceptual change toward greater accuracy.

CHAPTER OBJECTIVES

1. Identify and classify different types of concepts.
2. Identify and classify different levels of abstraction between concepts.
3. Describe the rationale for assessing and planning for working with students' alternative social studies conceptions.
4. Describe important elements of a teaching strategy that encourages and facilitates concept relearning or replacement.

CONCEPT TEACHING STARTS WITH REFLECTION AND PRACTICE

In lessons that focus on helping students construct a new concept or reconstruct an existing one, the teacher's role involves two tasks: (1) providing students with information to work with and (2) asking questions to focus their attention on important aspects of the information. Although the teacher serves as a guide during lesson development, activities are centered on interactions between students and their social environment. Activities enable students to work with examples of the concept. Eventually, students reconstruct their ideas or invent a definition of the concept using the information they have worked with during the lesson development.

A Fourth-Grade Classroom Scene

As an exploratory activity for her students, Ms. Carlson asked them the following questions. How do you think her fourth-grade students responded?

"Think about who sits next to you in one of your classes."
"If someone sits on your left, is it a boy or girl? What is this person's name?"
"If someone sits directly in front of you, is it a boy or girl? What is this person's name?"

Then, Ms. Carlson instructed her students to draw a simple map showing themselves and the students sitting near them. Later, Ms. Carlson asked, "Do you know the people who sit near you better than those who sit farther away from you?" Finally, she asked the students to think about what characteristic, or attribute, they used to select the people to include on their map. She asked her students, "What attribute did they all have in common?"

The attribute that was the focus of this exploratory activity was *location*. Students were asked to think about who was sitting in a classroom location near to them. They were not asked about others located farther away. To build on the exploratory activity, the following lesson development occurred. ■

A Fourth-Grade Classroom Scene: Lesson Development

Ms. Carlson asked the students to imagine the following scenario.

Imagine that the classroom walls have moved farther out so that the classroom is twice its size. When this happened, your chairs ended up being farther away from each other. Now the distance between your chairs is twice what it was before. The person who was on your left is still on your left. The person who was directly in front of you is still in front of you. The only thing that has changed is how far apart your chairs are. Even though the people around you are farther away from you, they are still on your left, or in front of you.

Ms. Carlson: What might we call someone who sits next to us in class or who lives next door to us at home? [The students quickly decide that such a person is called a *neighbor.*]

Ms. Carlson: Using the characteristic of location, how would you define *neighbor*?

Brian: A neighbor is "someone who is in a place close to you."

Ms. Carlson: Do you think Brian's definition of *neighbor* is a useful one for you? [The students tell her they think it is a useful definition. Ms. Carlson writes it on the board as their working definition.]

Ms. Carlson: Using Brian's definition of neighbor, if the person sitting on your left switched seats with someone on the other side of the room, would that person still be your neighbor? [After some discussion, students agree that the student who switched seats would no longer be a neighbor. They decide that an important attribute of neighbor is location and, specifically, closeness in location.] ■

FACTS AS SOCIAL STUDIES CONTENT

Facts about the world are first acquired through the five senses in the form of observations. Social studies facts are statements of observations of people, objects, and events. They come out of our direct, sensory experiences or indirectly through the experiences of others; we can hear or read about factual information others have acquired. For example, we might observe the construction of new houses in nearby fields. We count 12 new houses being built. Then, as we drive along, we notice another new set of houses and count 40 houses being built on that site. We are acquiring these facts *directly* through our observations. Or we may read in a newspaper about how many new houses are being built on the two sites. Now, we are *indirectly* acquiring these facts, which others have identified.

Today technology assists us in collecting data, making it available to all students. In the past, such information was available only to those who lived near government offices, museums, and large libraries. For example, information on the number of permits for new house construction and the locations of houses being built are kept in databases in city and county records departments. Another example of information that students and social scientists can both access through technology is the U.S. Central Intelligence Agency "CIA World Fact Book," www.odci.gov/cia/publications/factbook/. This site contains facts about other nations.

**COMPANION
WEBSITE**

Facts are single occurrences, taking place in the past or present. They result from observations. Facts do not allow us to predict an event or action (Eggen & Kauchak, 2001). Using the facts about the number of houses built in new developments, we cannot predict the number of houses that will be built in the next development begun in the city. Effective strategies for learning factual information differ greatly from those used in learning other social studies content.

Meaningful social studies content is not acquired by using or recalling facts when constructing or interpreting concepts. When recall is needed, a rote memory learning strategy can facilitate the learning of social studies facts. Rote memory learning requires repetition, immediate feedback, breaking down the content into small pieces, associating new material to be memorized to information previously learned, mnemonics, and attention to the motivational needs of the student (Joyce & Weil, 1992). Games, rewards, mnemonics, and quick pacing of instructional events are all effective techniques for facilitating the memorization of facts. Such rote instructional techniques should make up only a small part of social studies, probably no more than 10 percent of instructional time. Terminology, symbols, and spelling are factual information that might be included in a social studies curriculum. Useful facts a teacher might have students learn are the names of continents; the major steps for making a law; procedures for constructing a timeline; and names of coins used as money in our society.

Teachers plan in advance for the memorization of facts and relate these facts to other important social studies objectives. In a fourth-grade unit on landforms, for example, the names of specific mountains and volcanoes such as Mt. McKinley, Mt. Everest, and Mt. Kilimanjaro are facts that might be learned as a minor objective and activity in the unit. The background experiences involving factual information that students have are an important part of classroom social studies learning. In the absence of direct personal experience on the part of the students, a teacher may focus on teaching some facts so that students are better able to develop and understand more important concepts and generalizations. When the teacher shows students a video on mountains and volcanoes, such as one on Mt. McKinley, the video is the only source of common experiences the teacher knows the students can share. Direct experiences and the use of references for information provide important classroom sources of facts to be used in developing concepts.

In the past, traditional social studies lessons focused on fact-learning strategies. These often resulted in elementary and middle school students having weak understandings of more interesting and advanced concepts needed to form conclusions and make value decisions (National Council for the Social Studies, 1994a). Today's teachers are coming to the realization that only rarely should facts be the focus of what is taught.

There is too much factual information for anyone to learn. The number of social studies facts doubles every few years. Yet facts have little power to create useful or meaningful knowledge by themselves. A heavy use of fact-learning teaching strategies neglects important social studies concepts. Students do not learn important objectives. For example, emphasis on facts reduces learning the structure of U.S. government to memorizing the names of the branches of government and a statement explaining their powers. Yet the powerful social studies objective is developing a comprehensive, personal understanding of the judiciary, legislative, and executive branches of U.S. government. Each branch of government is a concept and should be taught using concept learning strategies.

Without an adequate background of facts, a student's understanding of concepts, such as individual, group, or consumer, remains vague. Facts are a necessary part of instruction but should not be the final outcome of lessons and units. Facts can only provide examples or partial meaning for the concepts basic to understanding social studies content, skills, attitudes, and values.

TIME FOR REFLECTION: WHAT DO YOU THINK?

Indicate which of the following are facts by placing an X on the line before the number.

_____ 1. The sand is white.

_____ 2. The line that forms a border around an area delimiting that area is its boundary.

_____ 3. People's lives are changed by revolutions in technology as new jobs are created and existing jobs disappear.

_____ 4. Juan Ponce de Leone explored Florida in 1513.

_____ 5. The quickest way for women to gain the right to vote was to amend the U.S. Constitution.

Of the five items above, items 1 and 4 are facts. Item 1 describes a specific observation. Item 4 identifies a specific event. Another example of a fact is, Martin Luther King, Jr., was a minister. This factual statement describes a specific person. An additional example is, freedom of the press is guaranteed by the Bill of Rights. This fact identifies a specific piece of content in the Bill of Rights.

Item 2 is a concept statement defining a boundary. A similar example is, all governors are the chief executives of their states. This is a concept statement describing a group of people: governors. An additional example is, volcanoes can be divided into two groups: explosive and free flowing. This concept statement describes and categorizes volcanoes.

Item 3 is a generalization because it describes a pattern relating three concepts: people's lives, their jobs, and technology. (Chapter 5 discusses generalizations in depth.) Both items 2 and 3 describe and summarize a set of similarities found between the facts from which they were formed. Item 5 is an inference, a statement that goes beyond the observations made.

Do not be concerned if you are finding it difficult to identify facts. It takes some practice before you can quickly and easily do this. The discussion of concepts that follows should help you better distinguish facts from concepts.

FORMING CONCEPTS

Concepts are formed by finding similarities between many facts and temporarily emphasizing those similarities. For example, lake is a concept formed by focusing on shape, contents, and sources of various bodies of water. We focus on *consistent similarities* that create the concept lake and ignore small differences between lakes, such as size and where they are found.

Providing Examples and Nonexamples

As concepts are formed, a number of examples and nonexamples of the concept must be examined (Baker & Piburn, 1997). Concepts are best introduced through one or more experiences with the concept during the exploratory introduction phase of the learning cycle. The exploration of a concept is followed by providing examples and nonexamples of the concept during the development phase of the learning cycle.

Examples are any and all individual items or events that have the characteristics of a given concept (Seiger-Ehrenberg, 2002, p. 291). When students are working with the concept of natural resources, for instance, a teacher might provide factual information through the use of highly concrete examples, such as a lump of coal, a piece of iron, and a glass of water. Students can also look for natural resources found within a 6-foot-square area marked off on the school grounds or in pictures. They can use their senses of sight and touch, a box of rock samples, and maps. They can look for natural resources in pictures and multimedia taken from spacecraft. As another example, when teaching the concept of lake, a teacher might use Internet pictures of Lake Erie, the Great Salt Lake, Lake Baikal, and a local lake and have students locate these lakes on a map.

Nonexamples are any and all individual items that may have some but not all the characteristics or critical attributes that exemplify a given concept (Seiger-Ehrenberg, 2002). As part of the process of constructing the concept of natural resources, for example, students might examine nonexamples such as pieces of plastic and nylon. Whereas these materials have some characteristics similar to those of a natural resource, they are not similar enough to be considered a natural resource. A lump of plastic may seem like a rock, but it is not made by natural processes but instead was manufactured by people. As a further example, a teacher may decide that students first need to learn that the following attribute is a beginning point for understanding the concept of natural resources: objects found on earth that people can use immediately. Then the teacher decides to use the following examples and nonexamples to help students construct an understanding of this attribute.

Example: Sort objects commonly found in the classroom into two groups representing their natural origins: metal objects and wooden objects.

Nonexample: Have students examine a piece of crumbly wood and a dry plant stem that, because they most likely have little immediate or short-term use, demonstrate that they cannot act as resources for people's use.

Identifying All Important Characteristics of a Concept

For effective instruction, it is important to identify all attributes or characteristics *essential* to a social studies concept. When concepts are complex, a child begins with a simple definition. As the child's experiences increase his or her abilities to understand an idea, the concept is refined and new attributes are added to its definition. Many social studies concepts such as democracy and justice have meanings that evolve over time as individuals mature and cultures change.

For example, in learning the concept friendship, young children may consider a friend's similarity to themselves an essential characteristic (Singleton & Asher, 1979). With help, students experience and consider several characteristics of friendship: (1) perceived similarity in age, race, sex, interest, degree of sociability, and values; (2) existence of mutual acceptance, admiration, and loyalty; (3) willingness to help each other and to be satisfied by the help received; (4) caring about what happens to a friend; and (5) mutual understanding and closeness with an expectation that friends be useful to each other (Kostelnik, Stein, Whiren, & Soderman, 1998). The fourth and fifth characteristics are usually understood by students in middle school but not by younger students. However, all elementary and middle school students can learn that some characteristics, such as the size or hair color of a friend, are not essential. It is important to help students distinguish nonessential characteristics from those that are essential.

Teachers play an important role in helping students identify the essential attributes of social studies concepts. A teacher uses a learning cycle that includes each of the first three essential characteristics of the concept of friendship to produce conceptual change in younger students. Older students can be asked to consider the fourth and fifth characteristics of friendship. For older students, a learning cycle could involve asking students, during the exploratory introduction phase, to make and discuss predictions and carry out tests using written scenarios in learning stations for several essential characteristics.

During the lesson development phase, students could discuss the results of the tests of their predictions. As the discussion progresses, they are provided with clear explanations of examples and nonexamples. The examples are carefully selected to make obvious the essential and nonessential characteristics of the concept.

The expansion phase involves asking students to make further applications and transfer the concept to situations outside the classroom context. This could involve an everyday situation, such as how to help a friend who has left his lunch at home and doesn't have any money to buy lunch, or a not-so-common situation, such as how to help a friend get elected as class representative to the school legislature even though you were thinking about trying to get elected yourself.

Differentiating Concepts from Facts

Concepts differ from facts in two major ways. First, factual statements are isolated bits of information acquired directly through the senses: seeing, hearing, tasting, feeling, or smelling. Concepts involve more than simple observation. Second, concepts summarize and classify observations into categories. Similarities are identified and generalized and expand the meaning of the facts being categorized. For example, consider the meaning derived from the facts in the following statement: A voter can be male or female, of any race or any religion, but has to be at least 18 years old.

The *summarizing* capability of a concept is very important. For example, people ride in many kinds of vehicles: big and small, with room for two or six, with or without air conditioning. To remember each of these with a name would take up a lot of mental capacity; so we form concepts that group together similar vehicles by shared characteristics, such as pick-up truck, sport utility vehicle, van, and limousine.

Concepts are defined by humans and reflect their cultures. Without concepts, all the facts we learn would be difficult to remember or use. For example, if students are involved with a unit on the concept of aggression and conflict management, a teacher might use examples of accidental aggression, such as tagging a friend too hard in a game of hide and seek, telling a joke that unexpectedly hurts someone's feelings, or crushing a butterfly in your hand in an effort to keep it from flying away. Another set of examples might deal with a child enjoying an aggressive action that inadvertently hurts someone: Roger feels satisfaction in a well-placed karate chop that knocks down Sammy's building, or Elizabeth laughingly bites Tulana because it feels good. Yet another example illustrates hostile aggression: Claudia pushes Jenny away from the water fountain because Jenny was first in line last time. Claudia sees this as "getting even," so it is premeditated and deliberate. Each of these instances of inadvertent or planned aggression is a fact. When they are examined in light of their shared characteristics, they make up the concept of aggression.

TIME FOR REFLECTION: WHAT DO YOU THINK?

Below is a sample elementary social studies textbook passage describing a portion of U.S. history. As you read the passage, pay close attention to how the concept is defined with specific criteria. Characterize the category with examples and nonexamples to provide the reader with greater meaning.

1. Identify and name the two important social studies concept(s) being defined in the sample passage. _____

2. Describe the criteria, or characteristics, provided for the concepts in the passage. _____

3. For each concept listed, determine whether examples and nonexamples are provided in the passage. If provided, describe them; if not, indicate they are not present. _____

Women's **suffrage,** or the right to vote, was important to many people. But, for a long time, women could not vote. After the Civil War, the Fifteenth Amendment gave African American men the right to vote. But women did not get the right to vote.

Between 1890 and 1919 the women's right to vote movement grew. Women gained the right to vote in many states, such as Montana. In 1916 Jeanette Rankin was elected to Congress by the people of Montana. She was the first woman to serve in the House of Representatives. Jeanette Rankin, Harriet Stanton Blatch, and Carrie Chapman Catt were some of the women who worked for suffrage for everyone.

Women were given the vote by one state, then another. But this was slow. The quickest way for all women to get the right to vote was by amending the Constitution.

➤

➤
> Some men believed women should not take part in government. They also thought that women could not do certain kinds of work or understand certain ideas. The work that women did during World War I helped change people's ideas. They saw that women could contribute much in government and work.
>
> In 1919, Congress passed an amendment to the Constitution. It said women could not be kept from voting. The amendment went to the states for **ratification,** or approval. Enough states gave their approval by August 26, 1920.

The major concept introduced in the sample textbook passage is the women's suffrage movement. Ratification is another social studies concept essential to the process of women gaining suffrage in the United States. Characteristics of the women's suffrage movement provided in the passage are (1) the right to vote for all women; (2) some states gave women the right to vote; (3) some men were against women's suffrage; and (4) an amendment would be the quickest way for all women to obtain voting rights. Among the examples provided is that Montana and some other states granted women suffrage. A nonexample is the Fifteenth Amendment giving African American men the right to vote.

Other examples and nonexamples of women gaining the right to vote are possible. Ratification appears once in the passage and is defined as "approval." The word *approval,* but not *ratification,* appears in the concluding sentence. The passage fails to mention any time limit or the number of states required for ratification. It does not mention that the amendment had to be approved by state legislatures at special state conventions called for the purpose of approving the amendment. No examples of states that ratified the amendment or of states that voted against it or failed to consider it are given. The names of three women who worked for suffrage are given. But no specific information about how they approached and accomplished their task is provided. The passage indicates that the approval of the amendment ended the women's suffrage movement on August 20, 1920.

Attention to the complete meaning of the concepts and the use of multiple examples and nonexamples would strengthen this textbook passage presentation of the concepts of the women's suffrage movement and ratification of amendments to the U.S. Constitution. Doing so would make the passage more realistic. It probably would help students understand that the rights of democracy must be claimed and used by its citizens if democracy is to continue to exist.

TYPES OF CONCEPTS

Concepts can be communicated in three ways:

1. *Formal definition:* A carefully worded sentence often using abstract terms, for example, that given in a dictionary
2. *Concept name:* A name indicated by a label or term
3. *Operational description:* A definition that describes the concept in practical, everyday language often accompanied by an example

To understand the *formal definition,* which entails abstract terms and relationships among concepts, is a difficult task for students. Read the following example of a formal concept definition for *bar scale*: "A bar scale is a series of marks made along a line at regular intervals to measure distance on a map." This type of definition is commonly found in elementary and middle school textbooks. Understanding this definition of *bar scale* requires knowledge of what is meant by a "series of marks," an "interval," a "regular interval," "measurement," "distance," and "map." Only when the student understands each of these concepts can they be put together to form a relationship that has meaning and can be applied to the bar scale found on a map.

Concept names are the labels or terms used to communicate the concept. *Map* is a concept name used to describe a class of objects. *Suffrage* is a concept name given to a class of actions and events. Some of the many concept names that are important in social studies are *culture, time, environment, individual, production, global connections, civic ideals,* and *governor.* Concept names communicate different meanings to individuals. Young students may be able to focus only on one aspect of *governor:* "can get things for me that I need." Older students may visualize a person who manages the work of many others and is responsible for putting into practice laws others make. Giving an event or object a concept name is a common textbook approach to social studies instruction. But just labeling something does not give it meaning. It is important to provide students with experiences, discussion, and time to reflect so they can give meaning to the concept name.

Operational definitions describe a concept by providing a test for deciding whether an object, action, or event is an example of the concept. The test is described in terms and experiences that are familiar to the student. The definition excludes all reasonable statements that do not represent the concept for students. If the object or event does not meet the test, it does not represent an example of the concept. An example of an operational definition is "Acting on impulse means that a person acts without thinking ahead: an idea or desire pops into their heads, and they are in motion; they see something they want and grab for it; they think something and blurt it out" (Calkins, 1995, p. 59). Frequently, operational definitions have two parts. The first part describes the conditions. The conditions include what is done in an event or to an object being defined, such as, "an idea or desire pops into their heads, and they are in motion." The second part describes the effect of what is observed or what happens as a result of what is done, for example, "they see something they want and grab it." Powerful social studies instruction focuses on the use of operational definitions to communicate the meaning of concepts.

TIME FOR REFLECTION: WHAT DO YOU THINK?

The following activity works with identifying and developing the skill of defining a concept by using operational definitions. For students, this skill is closely related to the skill of communicating. Making clear statements to others about the world is important. Also important is the idea that more than one satisfactory statement can be used to define a concept. Operational definitions define concepts so that they can be used in and outside classrooms in everyday situations.

➤

PART I

Indicate the type of concept description each of the following statements represents. Write O, F, or N on the line provided for **operational description, formal definition,** or **name,** respectively.

_____ 1. A branch is a stream or river that flows into a larger one.

_____ 2. Children are self-disciplined when they can judge for themselves what is right and wrong and then behave appropriately even when nobody else is available to tell them how to behave or to make sure that they do it.

_____ 3. Culture.

_____ 4. A schedule is an organized pattern of blocks of time that is arranged in a certain order and that allows individuals following it to predict future activities.

_____ 5. A continent is one of the Earth's main areas of land.

Items 1 and 5 are examples of formal definitions. These definitions involve language and terms that require additional definition. Items 2 and 4 represent operational definitions. These definitions adequately describe a procedure, concept, event, object, or property of an object in the situation in which it is used. Item 3 is a concept name.

PART II

Two definitions are provided for each of the following concepts. Choose the more appropriate operational definition for a sixth-grade student.

_____ 1.a. *Humor* is something that is perceived as funny because it is not compatible with the normal or expected pattern of events.

_____ 1.b. *Humor* is when something silly happens.

_____ 2.a. A *game* involves other players, has rules, and is highly social.

_____ 2.b. A *game* is not work.

_____ 3.a. A child taking on a *character role* is involved in pretend play.

_____ 3.b. A child taking on a *character role* engages in many behaviors appropriate for the part and demonstrates that the role is temporary and is defined by the actor in the present situation.

Humor and *game* in items 1 and 2, respectively, are more appropriately defined operationally using the first definitions (1a and 2a). The second choice (3b) is the more appropriate operational definition for *character role.* More appropriate definitions allow the student to follow a procedure or carry out an activity whose result defines the concept. The less operational statements refer to abstract procedures or terms or may involve experiences that students are not likely to have had.

In the Time for Reflection examples, it is not difficult to identify the more appropriate definition—one that students should be working with and learning. Other operational definitions may be more difficult to use or construct. For example, for a definition of *hyperactivity,* one might say that it is "inappropriate activity at a high energy level." However, one may find that all children are involved in inappropriate activity at times. Also, children usually show a high energy level at certain times during the day. So this operational definition may be more appropriate in some situations than in others. Additional description may be added to the definition if it is not useful. The operational definition of hyperactivity may be made more appropriate for teachers by expanding it as follows: "a persistent pattern of inattention and/or impulsivity that is more frequent and severe than is typically observed in individuals at a comparable level of development, often leading to inappropriate activity at a high energy level."

TIME FOR REFLECTION: WHAT DO YOU THINK?

Below are several beginnings of social studies definitions. Add to or change the definitions to make them more appropriate for a child in the upper grades of elementary school or in middle school.

1. *Citizen*: An official resident of a country who votes.
2. *Longitude*: A line that runs from the North Pole to the South Pole.
3. *Discrimination:* Unfair treatment.

➤ BUILDING ON DIVERSITY

Defining Concepts

Teachers ask students to define concepts on the basis of their own observations, thoughts, and experiences. Such definitions are operational definitions. Operational definitions are useful to students when they are built on their own experiences and observations rather than the teacher's experiences. To require students to use a definition that is not based on their own experience defeats the important process of helping students construct their own meaning. An operational definition is a tentative or working definition that can be modified and changed with new experiences. Teachers help students come to understand that definitions are constructed, then reconstructed, as we have new experiences with a concept. For meaningful learning, it is important to have the disposition to be willing to consider new evidence that will lead us to the reconstruction of the definition of a concept.

INTERRELATIONSHIPS AMONG CONCEPTS

Concepts are interrelated. Two concepts often share some of the same facts, and most concepts include other concepts as subconcepts. A garage, for example, can house a car, but it can also be a workshop or a storage area. People are flexible in the concepts they form, allowing them to account for the diversity in the social world.

A key concept in elementary and middle school social studies is government. Government includes the subconcept of branches of government. Branches of government, in turn, involves the subconcepts of judiciary, legislature, and executive, as well as other subconcepts. Executive, in turn, includes president, governor, and mayor, in addition to other subconcepts. These related concepts form a hierarchy. In a hierarchy, a key concept can incorporate many subconcepts. In turn, a concept can be a subconcept to another more inclusive concept. So judge can be a subconcept to judiciary, and judiciary can be a subconcept to branches of government. Providing concept maps and having students make their own concept maps can be an important tool to help students assess their own learning. Concept maps also help teachers diagnose learning problems.

Concept maps and *concept webs* are terms that are often used interchangeably. A concept map helps students develop interrelated knowledge and understandings. The concept map has been defined as a process that identifies concepts in a set of materials being studied, and that organizes those concepts into a hierarchical arrangement from the most general, most inclusive concept, to the least general, most specific concept (Farris & Cooper, 1994).

Consider a very simple concept map:

People—*eat*—apples.

Such a concept map shows how two concepts are related but does not describe a hierarchy. As an instructional or assessment device, a teacher might draw a concept

Students found the relationship between the stone quarry and the big building in their community and explained it in their book.

Things About Grafton That You Never Knew

by Grafton Elementary School Second Graders
who studied their community in-depth from December 1, 1998 to March 11, 1999

Grafton Elementary School
by Jonathon White

map for students and leave some blank spaces in it. In the example above, the teacher might leave a blank space where *apples* is found. Students might use the map in one or more of a number of ways: to discuss and decide what concepts should be written in the blanks or to carry out investigations and other activities to decide how to fill in the blanks. Depending on the objective, students may have many options for filling in the blank or only one acceptable option. Consider the following example:

The nation with highest income per person is _____.

In this case, only one option may be acceptable.

Teachers may use a concept map throughout a unit, beginning with students' prior knowledge and adding to it and revising it as the unit progresses. A concept web is very similar to the concept map. In a concept web, the most general and inclusive idea is placed in the center. Subconcepts are arranged around it and connected to it with a line. Then another layer of sub-subconcepts of each subconcept is arranged around the outside of each subconcept and connected to it with a line. Software is available to make concept webs easy to draw. One example of such software is Inspiration (Inspiration Software).

Most major concepts, such as government and map, include several subconcepts. To accurately construct the concept being taught, students need to understand its subconcepts. The facts summarized to form a key concept must be meaningful to the students. For example, when constructing the concept of map perspective, students must experience how all the sights they see differ depending on how far away they are or the direction from which they are seen. Students should experience seeing a tree on the playground from 1 foot away, 10 feet away, and 100 feet away. They should look at it from different directions and even over their shoulder. These experiences enable students to acquire important facts that are necessary to understanding the subconcept of perspective.

It is important to incorporate many opportunities for students to experience and interact with all important subconcepts. Teachers provide opportunities for students to compare and contrast the sets of characteristics that describe these concepts and the relationships among them. Teachers must understand the hierarchy among concepts if they are to teach concepts successfully and diagnose difficulties students are having in constructing these concepts.

TIME FOR REFLECTION: WHAT DO YOU THINK?

1. Identify a concept that includes *supply* and *demand* as subconcepts. _____

_____

_____

2. Identify a concept that includes *socialism* as a subconcept. _____

_____

_____

3. Identify one or more subconcepts of *supply*. _____

_____

_____

➤   4. Identify one or more subconcepts of *socialism.* _____

_____

_____

A concept that includes supply and demand as subconcepts is price. Possible subconcepts of supply include manufactured goods and producer. A sample concept map for a sixth-grade unit on supply and demand is shown in Figure 4.1. Possible concepts that include socialism as a subconcept are political system and economic theory. Each of these includes socialism as one system or theory along with others. Possible subconcepts of socialism include governmental ownership and state control of production.

FIGURE 4.1 Simple Concept Web

Teachers perform a *concept analysis* to assist them in considering how concepts are related to each other. In a concept analysis the following are identified:

- The concept name
- The concept definition
- Critical attributes or defining characteristics
- Several examples of the concept
- Critical superordinate concepts

- Critical subconcepts
- Critical coordinate concepts

A *superordinate concept* is a "bigger" or more inclusive concept into which a concept fits. State is a superordinate concept for county. A *coordinate concept* is one that is equivalent in some way to the concept under consideration. The two concepts may be related in terms of just one characteristic. Stream and brook are coordinate concepts. Mother and stepmother are coordinate concepts. Capitalism and communism are coordinate concepts for socialism. Coordinate concepts are related to each other but are not subconcepts nor superordinate concepts for each other. Table 4.1 illustrates a concept analysis of county.

Concepts are a major portion of the social studies content that students need to construct. To do this, students take a large number of facts and process them into manageable pieces. Individuals must learn each concept and process the information it represents on their own. As a result, each of us and every student within a class has a somewhat different understanding of a concept. The strength of well-defined concepts is such that even though we each form our own mental construction of a concept, its essential attributes are recognized by all of us.

T A B L E   4 . 1

A Concept Analysis

Step 1: Gather Information (Eggen & Kauchak, 2001)

1. Concept
2. Definition
3. Attributes or characteristics
4. Examples
5. Superordinate concepts
6. Subconcepts
7. Coordinate concepts

Step 2: Perform a Concept Analysis

1. Concept: county
2. Definition: the largest territorial division for local government within a state of the United States
3. Attributes or characteristics: an identifiable region within a state, a governmental unit, a provider of local services such as law enforcement and education
4. Examples: Wayne County, Michigan (large city), Fayette County, West Virginia (rural and small town), and Tuscaloosa County, Alabama (small city and rural area)
5. Superordinate concept: state
6. Subconcepts: large city, mid-sized city, small city, rural area
7. Coordinate concept: parish (found only in the state of Louisiana)

DIFFERENCES IN COMPLEXITY AND ABSTRACTNESS OF CONCEPTS

Concepts differ widely in their *complexity* and level of *abstractness* (Klausmeier, Ghatala, & Frayer, 1974; Martorella, 1994). Because of this difference, the level of abstractness of concepts must match students' developmental level of thinking. Consider the following concepts: wants, puddle, map, money, decade, highway, election, individual, and interdependence. Of the concepts listed, wants and puddle can be understood by very young children. Both are closely tied to everyday experiences in a child's world. A label and an operational definition can easily be associated with wants. A puddle is a concrete object a child can play in. Whereas both wants and puddle can be complex concepts, each is also tied to a number of concrete experiences the child can have. As a result, children having these experiences typically form an appropriate partial concept before or during the early grades. Experiences later in life contribute to a more complete understanding of each concept.

The concepts of map, money, decade, highway, election, and individual are appropriately introduced to, and understood at least partially by, elementary students. The more directly observable aspect or subconcepts of each key concept are the starting points. First- and second-grade students can experience properties of map subconcepts through

- Playing in a sandbox where they try to reproduce the schoolyard
- Playing with trucks and cars on the floor
- Drawing an object, such as a drinking cup, from different perspectives—from above, below, the side
- Sitting in different parts of schoolyard playground equipment, examining the same view from different locations
- Arranging models of furniture in a doll house or on a tabletop

Fourth- and fifth-grade students should investigate subconcepts such as scale, symbols, and grid systems. Investigating grid systems begins with arranging items in straight rows and columns, and playing bingo. These and later experiences build an increasingly deeper understanding of the key concept of grid systems. These understandings, in turn, become part of the more inclusive concept of map.

Among the most complex and abstract of the concepts listed previously is interdependence, which refers to a relationship in which two or more people, objects, or events depend in some ways on each other. It is a relationship that can be personally experienced in complex as well as simple ways. You can be interdependent with your dog, for example. You feed the dog and it gives you affection in exchange. Both of you benefit from the relationship. Our states and nation are interdependent with many other states and nations because each trades its natural resources and manufactured products for those others produce. Interdependence has some concrete, or directly observable, characteristics that can be appropriately experienced by elementary and middle school students. But often it is not directly observable or is on such a large scale, as in the case of interdependence among nations, that it is difficult for students to have relevant experiences.

The ease with which a concept can be learned depends on several factors:

- The number of critical attributes or characteristics it has
- How concrete these attributes are
- The reasoning skill level required to provide meaningful learning of all aspects of the concept (Tennyson & Cocchiarella, 1986)

A teaching technique that focuses on beginning with the simplest concepts or versions of a concept and moving gradually to more complex concepts was described by Robert Gagne (1965). He stressed the need to examine the entire learning sequence, then work in small steps from the simple to the complex.

Jean Piaget defined and categorized levels of mental development based on thought processes typically available to students (Piaget, 1963, 1970). The developmental levels of concern here are preoperational, concrete operational, and formal operational. Piaget found that most students enter school capable of performing preoperational thinking, develop concrete operational thinking during the early elementary grades, and begin to use formal thought processes in middle school. A description of the thought processes typically associated with preoperational, concrete operational, and formal operational developmental levels can be found on the website for this book.

COMPANION WEBSITE

Three types of concepts were described by Bruner, Goodnow, and Austin (1962): conjunctive, disjunctive, and relational. A *conjunctive* concept has a single, fixed set of characteristics that define the concept. An example of a conjunctive concept in social studies is a globe. It is a spherical object with a map of the earth drawn on it. This is the least complex type of concept to learn.

A *disjunctive* concept has two or more sets of alternative critical attributes that define it. A parent, for example, can be the father or mother of a child, by genetics or by adoption.

A *relational* concept is the most complex type of concept. It lacks clearly defined characteristics. Instead, its characteristics are defined by comparisons and relationships with other objects or events. An example of this concept is rich or wealthy. A million dollars may make you rich in a town where the average household income is $40,000 per year. But if you live in a town where several people have incomes of millions of dollars every year, you are not considered rich. Other social studies concepts that are relational are far away, justice, fairness, busy, democratic, and hardworking.

Much social studies content requires the use of diverse and higher-order reasoning. Yet most students' ability to do abstract thinking is limited. It is important to plan the learning of social studies concepts according to the reasoning patterns needed to understand the content communicated in the lesson. Although not limited to these specific stages, concepts *may* be called *sensory* or *preoperational, concrete,* or *formal,* depending on the type of thought processes required to begin constructing meaning about the concept. These labels indicate differences in the thinking required to understand a concept even at a basic level.

Effective teachers begin with sensory or concrete concepts and gradually progress to higher-level concepts. The differences between these categories of concepts can be summarized: *Sensory concepts* develop from students' use of early inquiry skills in activities. *Concrete concepts* develop as students begin to use a full range of inquiry skills, especially when introduced through real people, objects, and experiences. A concept usually can be considered concrete if one can grasp its meaning through direct experience. If a concept derives its meaning from the proficient use of inquiry skills and involves the position of the concept within a theoretical system, it is classified as *formal*. Using these classifications, wants and puddle are classified as preoperational. Map, money, decade, highway, election, and individual are classified as concrete concepts. Democratic process, governmental structures, and interdependence are classified as formal concepts.

Sensory Concepts

COMPANION
WEBSITE

Meaningful concepts can be developed before a concept name is given to the experiences. In learning the concept boundary, very young children use all their senses with each boundary encountered. They see, touch, smell, and perhaps lick or bite each item, forming a physical boundary. They also lie down on it, kick it, and, if it is small enough, throw it, put it under and in other things, and so on. These investigations are repeated with each boundary they encounter until they are able to group all these characteristics into the concept boundary. Then, when a boundary is encountered, not only do young students label it as a boundary, but also they understand it as a meaningful concept. The same events occur with many concepts, such as money, shelter, or hill.

Concrete Concepts

Concrete concepts are concepts whose meanings can be derived from firsthand experiences with people, objects, or events. Firsthand experiences must occur, or the experiences must be common to the students involved. Some concrete concepts, such as prejudice and map, are examples of concrete concepts for which higher-level inquiry skills are needed.

Drawings, maps, globes, and models establish many concepts as concrete. However, learners must be able to develop meaning from direct experience with a concept for it to become concrete. If the concrete materials themselves represent abstract models divorced from the experience of the students, the materials cannot fit the definition of a concrete concept. If a concept, when presented, can only be memorized and not meaningfully understood, students may form a misconception.

MAKING A LITERATURE CONNECTION

Recognizing Its Limitations

The discussion in this chapter describes some concepts as sensory, some as concrete, and some as formal. All concepts require real social and physical experiences the student uses to investigate the concept. Sometimes, literature selections seem to be able to replace real experiences. A few teachers, for example, will read a book during the exploration phase of a lesson in order to give all the students the same experience. Yet students' prior knowledge and experiences result in different understandings and interpretations of the book, and students do not have the same experiences nor the same information after the book is read. So replacing a concrete and sensory experience with reading a book is not acceptable if a social or physical experience is available. As an example, reading about a baseball game is not the same as attending a game or as playing in one. A book might well describe a student's pleasure at being selected to represent the class at a special event in the school system; however, that description is not equal to feeling the pleasure and pride that come when you find your classmates have voted for you to be their representative.

In a concept lesson, a literature selection may serve as a good choice to use late in the lesson when students have a clear personal understanding of the concept being constructed. Reading a book to review a concept or to expand its application during the expansion phase of a lesson is a much better practice than trying to initially confront an idea through the abstract words of a story.

Formal Concepts

Formal concepts derive their meaning from an established relationship with an assumption, model, or some other theoretical system. Meaning is not given to these concepts by information from the senses, but through imagination or through developing logical relationships within the system. The meaning of the concept is developed from the attributes or relations given to it by the set of assumptions within which it is a member. Examples of formal concepts are ethnic group, third-world nation, and revolution.

School is a concrete concept. What attributes of this photograph of a Paraguayan school fit with the attributes you use to identify a school?

The student who primarily uses concrete reasoning patterns does not reason beyond concrete objects, events, or experiences; has little power of reflection; and does not construct theoretical systems. Hearing a lecture or reading about revolution, third-world nations, ethnic groups, community, or other formal concepts does not provide such a student with the necessary experiential background to understand these concepts. Instead, instruction should begin with exploratory experiences and concrete concepts.

The fact that social studies concepts can be interpreted either as sensory, concrete, or formal, helps in planning a learning activity that leads students to construct their own meaning. Learning that begins with a concrete version of a concept is likely to make a more secure connection with the students' previous understanding. The learning cycle is a way to help students achieve meaningful understanding of a concept. Most students are likely to have an understanding of concrete concepts such as transportation, rules, buying and selling, and sharing. Through exploratory activities, they can apply their understanding and discover the limitations of their concrete concepts. For instance, they can discover the difficulty of estimating an appropriate selling price for popcorn based only on the cost of the ingredients without considering the cost of popping equipment, such as a microwave oven, or how much profit is appropriate. For this reason, teachers make allowances in the amount of time available for investigation by different students.

Powerful Concept Instruction

COMPANION
WEBSITE

Students of all ages describe social studies concepts differently from those accepted as accurate in the professional literature. In the past, these alternative conceptions have been considered misconceptions and critical barriers to learning. Students may have formed their alternative concept on the basis of the limited facts and experiences they have available. The concepts may be technically inaccurate or incomplete, but they represent an effort by the student to abstract similarities.

A young child may, for example, decide that a voter cannot be a police officer because she has never seen anyone in a uniform at the voting booths when she accompanies family members. The child has formed this concept on the basis of the limited facts available to her. Or the individual may not have abstracted essential attributes. For example, the child may have noted that everyone waiting in line to vote was talking about how angry he or she was with a recent raise state legislators had voted for themselves. The child may decide that you cannot vote unless you are angry about an issue. Although the concept is inaccurate, it does represent an effort by the child to abstract similarities.

As more facts are acquired through active experiences that challenge the student, or as the student reviews the inventory of facts, the concept may change and become more accurate. Teachers provide opportunities for students to have experiences that add to their inventory of facts. Teachers also provide opportunities for students to discuss the facts they have acquired and relate these facts to the concepts formed. To learn a new concept, students must be mentally involved in *conceptual change*—reshaping and restructuring their prior knowledge. The starting point in the process of conceptual change is students' prior knowledge. Their prior knowledge has proved successful for them in the past but differs from the intended knowledge to be gained from the lesson (Sanger & Greenbowe, 1997).

During the early part of a social studies lesson, the exploratory introduction, each student identifies his or her existing concept. A problematic social studies experience and discussion related to the concept encourages students to think about their views. Thinking about their views leads to a confrontation between their alternative conception and the conception intended by the social studies lesson. Dissatisfaction with the existing conceptions is critical to the process of conceptual change. Only at this time do students realize that they must reorganize or replace their prior knowledge because their existing concepts are inadequate to understand the new experiences. To be useful, retained, and transferred to a new setting, the new conception must be clear, understandable, plausible, and successful for the student (Berliner & Casanova, 1987). This process of *awareness, reconstruction,* and *application* makes up the sequence of events in the learning cycle. It is teaching for understanding.

Teachers may influence students' thinking and conceptions in ways that are intended, in ways that are unanticipated, or perhaps not at all (Duit, 1987). When might teaching have little effect on students' concepts? Four types of instances may result in little or no effects. First, students have already formed concepts on their own, sometimes by giving an idea a lot of thought (Rye & Rubba, 1998). Many concepts develop as students try to make sense of their social and physical environments. In school, students are sometimes involved in situations using concepts that the teacher defines differently than do the students. One or two instructional experiences in school might not be enough to convince students to reconstruct their own concept.

Second, teachers are often unaware of students' inaccurate or incomplete concepts. Through setting up an open-ended exploratory introduction activity, teachers observe, listen, and work with students, noting their current understanding of a concept.

Third, teachers often make unfounded assumptions about the teaching and learning process. Sometimes teachers assume that students have no prior concepts. At other times, teachers assume that if students have prior concepts, these are easily replaced by new concepts they are taught. Both assumptions are often false. Much of the time, students have prior concepts that they do not easily reconstruct because conceptual change is a difficult and demanding process.

Fourth, teachers and students often fail to communicate with each other. Teachers try to convey meaning using words, diagrams, or symbols. The student has to find the meaning in them. The constructed meaning may not be the meaning intended by the teacher. This is particularly likely if the vocabulary used by the teacher, textbook, or worksheet is not familiar to the student. In this case, the following may result:

The student may ignore what the teacher is saying.

The teacher may ignore what the student is saying.

The teacher may insist that students use the "correct" words; students may sound like they understand the concept but, actually, they don't.

The teacher rephrases student responses, making them accurate without addressing students' misunderstandings.

> **BUILDING ON DIVERSITY**

Cultural Factors and Concepts

Lynch (1998, p. 24) described culture as a "second skin" that becomes visible only when we brush up against one that's different. Sometimes well-prepared lessons fail to help students define a concept. When this happens, a teacher might well remember Lynch's simile. Students' culture might be involved. Because our culture is a framework for our lives, it includes our food, clothing, furniture, art, games, and habits, as well as our deep beliefs and values. The way we look at the world, the way we relate to one another, and the way we bring up our children are culturally defined (Ayers, 1993). It is important for teachers also to recognize that there are many variations within each culture, including educational level, socioeconomic status, occupation, temperament, and personal experience, all of which are factors that influence our values and beliefs. Finally, children might not reconstruct the concepts we are trying to help them build because of other factors in their lives stemming from the culture they bring to school, including race, language, ethnicity, religion, gender, family, age, lifestyle, and political orientation. In such a case, students do not all achieve the lesson's objectives. What does the teacher do? Reteaching the lesson using different strategies might help. Some students, for example those from Middle Eastern cultures, consider their role in a group to be important. These students might benefit from a cooperative group approach to activities through which the concept is constructed. To teach concepts well, teachers need to know some basic information about the cultures and languages of their students. A good resource describing the learning styles and appropriate teaching styles found among students from various cultures is *Understanding Your International Students: A Cultural, Educational, and Linguistic Guide,* edited by Jeffra Flaitz (Ann Arbor, MI: University of Michigan Press, 2003). Another resource is *Passport to Learning: Teaching Social Studies to ESL Students,* Bulletin 101, by Barbara Cruz, Joyce Nutta, Jason O'Brien, Carine Feyten, and Jane Govoni (Silver Spring, MD: National Council for the Social Studies, 2003).

How can teachers influence students' social studies concepts? Five important actions must take place. These actions are summarized in the learning cycle sequence in Table 4.2.

- First, teachers need to provide students with an opportunity to become familiar with the context in which the concept to be discussed belongs. Students try out their ideas by explaining an event or object for themselves during the exploratory introduction.
- Second, to influence students' concepts successfully, teachers help students become aware of ideas they bring to the lesson. Bringing out prior knowledge begins during the exploratory phase of the lesson and continues throughout the lesson with revisions, changes, and additions being noted. Students describe, write, draw, and act out their understanding or meaning of the data related to the main concept of the lesson. Students use their own words in these activities, identifying the evidence supporting their ideas. Instructional activ-

TABLE 4 . 2

Teaching a Concept Using the Learning Cycle

Phase	Planning Required
Exploratory Introduction	Help students try out and confront their prior knowledge of the social studies concept.
	Ask probing questions to diagnose students' prior knowledge of the social studies concept.
	Focus students' attention on social studies experiences.
	Encourage students to work cooperatively in groups to relate prior knowledge to the concept.
	Make public students' prior knowledge of the concept.
Lesson Development	Provide concise, brief closure for the new social studies concept.
	Ask students to reflect on and explain exploratory experiences, concepts, and terminology in their own words to provide connections to the concept focused on in the lesson.
	Provide definitions, terminology, clear explanations, all characteristics, and elements of the new social studies concept as concretely as possible.
	Involve students in clear examples and nonexamples of the new social studies concept.
	Ask students to clarify the new idea and justify statements with evidence.
	Provide for student practice using the new social studies concept.
Expansion	Provide additional practice to help students use terms, definitions, and explanations of the concept experienced in the lesson.
	Provide application activities for the social studies concept in new, relevant contexts while at the same time helping students recall their original alternative explanations.
	Provide activities to help students transfer the new social studies concept to increasingly real world events.
	Provide a summary of the important events in the social studies lesson leading to the new social studies concept.

ities include sorting, student-only group discussion, small- and large-group discussions with the teacher, and informal discussions with the teacher during the activities. Students record their ideas in annotated drawings and diagrams, sequenced drawings, structured writing, and personal logs.

- Third, during the lesson development phase, students are guided to construct a new concept or reconstruct an existing one. An emphasis is placed on students presenting their ideas to others and learning to appreciate the ideas of other students and the teacher. Small-group discussion focuses on finding evidence for ideas. Large-group discussions bring a number of ideas together for consideration.
- Fourth, students experience many examples and nonexamples of the concept. Time is provided for students to explore all attributes and aspects of each attribute.
- Fifth, students use the new concepts to make sense of a new experience during the expansion. Students realize the usefulness of the new concept(s) in interpreting the world around them.

TEACHING CONCEPTS

COMPANION
WEBSITE

Concept learning requires students to relate new knowledge to prior knowledge, to apply the new knowledge, to become aware of all its important characteristics through many examples and nonexamples, and to have enough application practice so that it is used appropriately and automatically. The learning cycle shown in Table 4.3 motivates students and presents a concept and subconcepts in ways that help students construct a new understanding of the concept.

TIME FOR REFLECTION: WHAT DO YOU THINK?

Read the concept lesson in Table 4.3 and answer the following questions.

1. What concept and subconcepts are the primary focus of this lesson? _____
   _____
   _____

2. What makes the presentation of the concept and its subconcepts appropriate for elementary students? _____
   _____

3. What examples and nonexamples are provided in the lesson? _____
   _____
   _____

4. List at least two critical attributes, or characteristics, presented for the concept and each of its subconcepts in the lesson. _____
   _____
   _____

5. How is the concept applied in the expansion phase, and how is its use expanded to contexts beyond that in which it was learned during the development phase?
   _____
   _____

➤

TABLE 4.3

Learning Cycle	Productive Resources

Grade Level: Primary and Intermediate
NCSS Standards: Production, Distribution, and Consumption

NCSS

Exploratory Introduction

Objectives	Procedures	Assessments
Students review previous knowledge by identifying examples of natural, human, and capital resources.	The teacher asks: "Do you like brownies?" The teacher says: "Let's make some. What do we need to make brownies?" List items on the board. Affirm all items are necessary to make brownies.	Record, on a checklist, students who participate by offering appropriate suggestions.

Lesson Development

Materials: A set of three pictures of natural, human, and capital resources each, for each group

Objectives	Procedures	Assessments
Students define productive resources as the natural, human, and capital resources used to make a product or perform a service.	The teacher divides students into groups. Each group is given a set of pictures of natural resources. The teacher asks students to discuss the set in their groups.	
	The teacher writes *Productive Resources* on the board and identifies some of the pictures in the set as natural resources. Then the teacher writes *natural resources* on the board under the heading Productive Resources. Students are asked to identify other pictures in the set as natural resources and explain which characteristics in the picture they used to make the identification.	
	The process is repeated with the other two sets of pictures. The teacher has students consider the following questions: What (natural) resources do you see in this picture? Are these people examples of human resources? Why? Why not?	Correct classification of items on the list is recorded on a checklist.
	The teacher returns to the list for brownies. Students classify each item on the list. The teacher asks: "What can we say a productive resource is?"	
	Closure: Write the class definition of a productive resource on the board. Have students decide whether it needs revision. Have students write the final definition they develop in notebooks.	Class states an appropriate definition.

continued

T A B L E   4 . 3

Continued

Expansion

Materials: A set of five pictures of livestock production for each group

Objectives	Procedures	Assessments
Given a set of pictures of livestock production, student groups identify which of the items pictured are or are not productive resources in this business.	In groups, students develop a list of items from the pictures that are productive resources used in livestock production and a second list of items that are not used. Then students identify at least two examples of human, natural, and capital resources on their lists. The group recorder writes on the board. The class and the teacher compare checklists.	Teacher checks group lists for at least 80 percent accuracy.
	Assign Homework: Talk with a parent or neighbor about his or her job, and identify the productive resources required in it. Then put an *N* by those that are natural resources and a *C* by those that are capital resources. Be prepared to share this information the next day.	
	Students share findings from homework interviews and create a list of productive resources used by the people they interviewed. The teacher asks: "Why did some of the people you interviewed only use capital resources? How can we describe the jobs that used both natural resources and capital resources?"	
	Lesson Summary: Students briefly identify their lesson activities and conclude that those who produce goods are more likely to encounter natural resources as they work than are those people who perform services. Students conclude that natural resources were used to make the capital goods all workers use.	

➤   6. What purpose does the homework assignment serve in this lesson?

_____

_____

➤ **USING TECHNOLOGY**

Examples of Resources for Helping Students Build Concepts

Technology offers a wide range of resources that can be used to expand students' experiences as they construct new concepts and reconstruct existing concepts. Recordings represent an older but still very useful technology that engages students' sense of hearing, while a picture engages their sense of sight. When the two are combined, an opportunity to process many more observations is created. For example, students may understand a historical scene very differently when hearing it described by a bystander during an audiotaped interview than they might when looking at photographs of the same event. The teacher must preview each resource before using it with students. Some videos, audiotapes, and similar resources are outdated, are biased, have little useful information, or are of poor quality. Before using a technological resource, teachers decide on its purpose:

Will it stimulate students' exploration of a concept?
Will it help students construct the concept?
Will it expand a concept into new contexts?

Teachers introduce students to the focus of the resource before it is used. Students know whether they will be presented with information that cannot be personally experienced except by audiovisual means. Next, teachers outline key observations students should try to make and discuss how these observations are recorded. After examining the resource, students share and discuss their observations. Teachers then ask prepared questions to help students extend their observations. Subsequent activities build on these experiences.

Video has the advantage of being easily made. Video can be of a field trip, a guest speaker's visit, student presentations, local sites of interest to the social studies program, or of any number of other events and activities. Video can be edited and used on websites or in PowerPoint presentations. A script is prepared for a video by the students, teacher, or students and teacher working together. The script may lay out the exact words to be spoken, as in the case of a class play on a concept such as "human resources" or "voting." More often, a script indicates a sequence of activities and who is involved in each. Plans for activities and scripts are often general with specific details ad-libbed. Scripted videos allow for retakes if a major blunder occurs during videotaping. Students can feed video into a computer so that it can be watched when needed. The video title, credits, and other components can be added by using programs on the computer.

Concepts through Different Grade Levels

Concepts provide structure for social studies content in elementary and middle school lessons. The social studies program in kindergarten and primary grades classrooms begins with preoperational concepts and early inquiry skills. Creative repetition and transfer across all social studies content areas are necessary for the skills and knowledge to become automatic. During later elementary grades and middle school, social studies lessons emphasize concrete concepts along with the inquiry skills necessary to develop meaningful learning of the concepts. Lessons begin with concrete concepts and move toward the introduction of experiences relating to formal concepts.

TIME FOR REFLECTION: WHAT DO YOU THINK?

Return to the Time for Reflection activity on rivers at the beginning of the chapter. React, in light of your participation in reading and reflecting on this chapter, to the sample elementary textbook passage treatment of rivers. Reread the sample textbook passage and do the tasks below.

1. Identify which statements address concepts. _____
   _____
   _____

2. Identify statements that are procedures or other information about the social studies content. _____
   _____
   _____

3. Identify the statements you consider part of social studies content every student should understand and for which lessons need to be planned for meaningful learning of the content to occur. _____
   _____
   _____

Item 1: Statements 1–4, 6–16, 18–26, and 29–32 are concepts or descriptions of attributes of a concept. Twelve concepts are introduced in the passage: source (1), stream (4), riverbed (7), river (14), branches (15), tributaries (16), drains (17), river basin (18), silt (20), sandbar (22), and mouth (31).

Item 2: Statements 5, 17, 28, and 33 are procedures or other information about the social studies content.

Item 3: Students should understand the concept river and the attributes of the concept that distinguish it from others. All the statements except 5, 17, 28, and 33 present the concept, related concepts (subconcepts), and attributes of a river. This concept is important for students to understand. However, with twelve concepts presented in the passage, students may have difficulty constructing an appropriate understanding of the key concept: river.

SUMMARY

Concepts are a basic component of powerful social studies content. Although factual information is necessary for forming concepts, social studies content is not acquired by memorizing facts. Teachers planning lessons identify and distinguish among the concepts they teach. Different instructional methods are used to teach different concepts to students. Most concepts have more than one level of meaning and may be sensory, concrete, or formal, depending on the instructional methods used. Before being classified, a concept is clearly defined. All concepts are abstract because they are abstracted from many specific instances and examples.

Teachers use what they know about their students' ideas. They encourage students to talk about their ideas so they are better able to help students learn. When students have expressed their own ideas, learning activities help them test them out. Four conditions are needed to help students discard old beliefs and accept a new idea based on real-world facts:

1. A student must be dissatisfied with his or her existing idea.
2. Any new concept must be comprehensible to the student through the introduction of all important attributes essential to the understanding of the concept.
3. A new concept must appear as plausible as the student's own alternative conception.
4. A new concept or explanation has to be more useful for making sense of the environment than the previously held concept.

By design, the learning cycle helps teachers prepare lessons that provide the four conditions needed for conceptual change. The learning cycle fosters cooperative learning and a safe, positive learning environment; compares new alternatives to prior knowledge; connects new ideas to what students already know; and helps students construct their own "new" knowledge and apply it in ways that differ from the situation in which it was learned. When a teacher uses learning cycles in a classroom with a positive environment in which it is safe to take risks when learning and sharing ideas, students are more likely to have success in constructing powerful social studies concepts.

Expanding ON THIS CHAPTER

Activity

COMPANION
WEBSITE

Develop a concept analysis for one of the following concepts: *computer, scarcity, city, election,* or *friendship.* Include the following in the concept analysis:

a. Concept label
b. Definition
c. Attributes or characteristics
d. Examples
e. Superordinate concepts
f. Subconcepts
g. coordinate concepts (if any)

During which phase of a lesson should a concept be defined? Explain your rationale for identifying this phase of the lesson.

Recommended Websites to Visit

COMPANION
WEBSITE

Children's developmental stages
> **http://askeric.org/cgi-bin/printresponses.cgi/Virtual/Qa/archives/Family_Life/
> Child_Development/development.html**

"What's My Interest?" A lesson in economics education on the concept of interest
for grades 3–5
> **www.econedlink.org/lessons/index.cfm?lesson=EM377**

A lesson on the concepts of costs and benefits for grades 6–8
> **www.econedlink.org/lessons/index.cfm?lesson=EM376**

"Why Do We Need Authority?" An upper elementary/middle school lesson on the concept
of authority
> **www.civiced.org/fod_elem_auth02_sb.html**

"Look You're Wearing Geography." Teaching the concept of interdependence.
> **www.nationalgeographic.com/resources/ngo/education/ideas58/58wearing.html**

"Regions: A Hands-On Approach." Teaching the concept of region.
> **www.nationalgeographic.com/resources/ngo/education/ideas58/58regions.html**

CHAPTER 5

Helping Students Use Inquiry to Build Generalizations

INTRODUCTION

In addition to concepts, textbooks contain other important social studies statements called *generalizations*. Read the following passage on economic content from a sample fourth-grade social studies textbook. Each sentence has been numbered to simplify answering the questions following the passage. Be certain to record your answers because, later in this chapter, you are asked to do additional reflection and to refer to your initial thoughts about this passage.

(1) Have you ever thought about where the things we buy come from? (2) In the kitchen you have products such as baking soda and salt. (3) In the bathroom you might find products such as shampoo and shaving cream. (4) You might also find products such as aspirin. (5) When you go home today, look at the products in the kitchen and in the bathroom. (6) How many are brand-name items? (7) These are items you see advertised on television or in the newspaper. (8) How many are generic or store-brand items? (9) These are items you find only in a certain store. (10) Or they are items that are not advertised but are sold in several stores. (11) Make a list for each kind of item. (12) Which is more common among your items, generic or brand-name products?

(13) When you get back to school, find a partner and share your lists. (14) Which is more common among your partner's items, generic or brand-name products? (15) Which is more common when the items you both have are put together, generic or brand-name products? (16) Think about the products you both use and those that other people you know use. (17) Do you think generic or brand-name products are more widely used in your community? (18) Why do you think this type of product is more frequently used in your community?

➤

1. Which statement(s), if any, ask students to state generalizations about the products and families? _____

2. Which, if any, of the questions ask students to state a generalization? _____

3. What knowledge objectives for a social studies lesson can be developed from using this textbook passage? _____

4. Given what you know about fourth-graders, what do you think they may find interesting in the passage? _____

CHAPTER OVERVIEW

The most useful and powerful ideas in social studies are generalizations (Schwab, 1974). They enable us to explain processes and events we experience. Generalizations are often explanations of cause and effect that allow us to predict future events. Generalizations develop from inferences we make about many observations. They also arise from results gained from testing hypotheses. A generalization provides more information than does a concept. It describes two or more concepts and the relationships among them. Teachers can actively help students construct meaningful generalizations through questioning and thoughtful assignments.

This chapter involves the reader in activities that focus on enhancing the understanding of generalizations. To accomplish this goal, it is organized as a learning cycle. You will be working through the learning cycle as you read this chapter and perform the activities.

CHAPTER OBJECTIVES

1. Explain why generalizations are an important part of social studies content.
2. Suggest appropriate questions and activities for an inquiry lesson that helps students construct a generalization.
3. Describe the teacher's role in an inquiry lesson developing a generalization.
4. Describe how the process of developing and revising generalizations is continuous.
5. Describe thought processes used to construct generalizations to solve everyday personal and civic problems.

DEVELOPMENT OF GENERALIZATIONS

Before formal schooling starts, students construct alternative or inaccurate generalizations from their limited experiences (Driver, Leach, Millar, & Scott, 1996). For example, one generalization taught in social studies is that we depend on workers with specialized jobs and the ways in which they contribute to the production and exchange of goods and services. This generalization leads to statements such as "We use money to pay specialized workers and to exchange goods and services" and "An economic system determines what is produced by whom, how products are distributed, and who consumes them." Students might form an alternative generalization from a single experience, for example, people can do other people's jobs easily. This generalization can result when a child notes that a parent is able to take care of a garden, make and fire a clay pot, and put new spark plugs in a car.

Other alternative generalizations are formed from analogies made from seemingly related events, from statements of adults, or from information gathered from mass media (Thagard, 1992). Students may watch television programs or advertisements, for example, in which a gifted person is able to perform complex jobs such as computer programming, brain surgery, or plumbing without any training or experience, just because the person is very "smart." Students can use these media performances to construct the alternative conception "If you are smart, you can do any job." Social studies experiences provide students with a great number of opportunities to help them investigate relationships in the social world, construct generalizations through experiencing the interaction among concepts, and develop the knowledge and skills needed in reconstructing existing generalizations they brought into the classroom.

In a lesson constructing a generalization, a problem or question is posed. Questions are raised in the learner's mind by having students interact with information related to the topic during the exploratory introduction phase. Teachers help students identify questions using different strategies. Teachers can put students in a situation in which the information they acquire conflicts with what they expect or raises a question. They often find their prior knowledge isn't sufficient to resolve the conflict or to answer their questions.

In the textbook passage above, students were asked to find patterns in the types of products found in their home. The teacher could adapt the textbook passage by having students use it as a guideline for an activity they carry out at home. Then they can bring their data into class and compare it with that of a partner and with others. This exploratory activity can present students with a problem and involve them in collecting data that leads to the problem or question presented in statement 18 at the end of the passage: Why do you think this type of product is more frequently used in your community? This problem arises naturally from the activity with which students are involved.

Defining Generalizations

Generalizations are typically reconstructed as students gain more experience with the concepts included in the generalization. Instruction designed to help students construct meaning and learn generalizations is typically called *inquiry learning*. Distinguishing generalization statements from other statements is critical in deciding which instructional strategy to use. Social studies experiences with generalizations often begin with early childhood students and focus on personal decisions. As students grow cognitively, the curriculum content becomes more abstract and focuses on the civic or community impact of problems. Generalizations make up more of the content of social studies for older elementary and middle school students.

It is important to select and teach appropriate ideas that help students construct meaningful generalizations (Bianchini, 1998). Generalizations are "big ideas" formed and understood through both quantitative and qualitative encounters. Reading about a generalization, or having a teacher tell you what it is, leads to a weak understanding of it. Reading and telling might not be qualitatively rich enough in meaning for students to recognize the generalization as something relevant in life and worthwhile to learn.

Consider the following sample fifth-grade textbook generalization statements linking the economic concepts of specialization, productivity, and profit:

> The more specialized a worker is, the more profit can be made from the work. This is because each does the specialized work faster and with more accuracy.

On the basis of students' own experiences, the statements can only be accepted on authority and learned through memorization. These statements are not useful in students' everyday lives and only partly relevant to their prior experiences, so they may have difficulty understanding concepts such as specialization. Students do not encounter mass production as it is carried out in business and industry. They most likely see people individually completing an entire product, whether it involves building a model airplane or sewing a pair of drapes for the living room. Their own experiences with hobbies and class work are most often individually completed.

Even if students become highly specialized in particular tasks, such as assembling model airplanes or accessing information from books or the Internet, they are not likely to profit financially. Nor are they likely to understand the role of increased profits in the growth and success of business. Making or writing statements that try to simplify an idea so that a fifth-grader can understand it is largely futile. The student does not have the necessary prior experiences with which to understand the relationships in the statements, so memorization results rather than meaningful understanding. Memorized information has little chance of being applied in new settings because it is not linked to real experiences.

Generalizations differ from facts and concepts. They have the following characteristics:

- Identifying relationships between two or more concepts
- Constructing explanations of cause and effect
- Enabling predictions of a future occurrence of the relationship stated in the generalization (Driver et al., 1996; Eggen & Kauchak, 2001, p. 61)

Linking words and concepts together to form sentences is part of natural communication. In the discussion below, a third-grade student named Spencer uses both concepts and a generalization to describe an experience:

> The president makes speeches. The president meets important people. He signs laws. The president gives big dinners. He talks to television reporters and answers their questions. You have to be good at doing a lot of different things to be president.

Among the concepts Spencer uses are president, speeches, laws, dinners, and reporters. These concepts summarize Spencer's experiences with each of these events and items. Spencer also makes a generalization that goes further than the concepts alone. He relates being president to having many abilities.

Distinguishing Generalizations from Facts and Concepts

Because objectives for social studies lessons can be learning facts, concepts, or generalizations, teachers need to distinguish among them. The choice of an instructional strategy in a social studies lesson is matched to the type of statement selected for the learning objectives. Sometimes people mistake generalizations for facts. Consider the following statement: Riding in a limousine means you have a lot of money. This statement is a generalization, not a fact, for several reasons:

- The statement was not formed from one observation alone. We may have seen limousines and the passengers riding in them. We may have noted the quality of the clothes the passengers were wearing. But we have not seen their bank records or credit card bills. We are summarizing our experiences, not reporting a single event.
- The statement involves two concepts and a relationship. Predictions of future occurrences can be made from the statement. These characteristics distinguish it from a concept (Eggen & Kauchak, 2001).

Generalizations such as the limousine example occur when we make inferences from experiences we have had and generalize them to include all possible examples. If tested through predictions, or by using hypotheses to gather data, the resulting conclusion is a generalization.

Generalizations can be used to form a hypothesis or suggested explanation for which data can be collected. To test the limousine generalization, we may talk to various limousine riders and find out that they are not wealthy. For example, they may have hired the limousine to celebrate a personal event such as prom night or an anniversary. The results of our data collection may lead us to change our original hypothesis. Generalizations may be an inference from which a hypothesis is formed, or they may be a conclusion formed as a result of checking a hypothesis. Which of the following do you think is a generalization?

Margaret Thatcher was prime minister in the United Kingdom.

People in the United States are not sure that a woman can capably carry out the job of president.

The first statement is a fact; the second is a generalization because it is not formed from observation alone.

Because we have not seen all possible cases, we generalize from what we see to make the second statement. The statement tries to summarize what we are thinking. For that reason, it is a generalization from what was observed. We agree with the statement because no contradictory case has been observed. If a contradictory case eventually is observed, the generalization can be changed. For instance, if U.S. voters elect a woman to the presidency, we would have to reconstruct our generalization to become more confident in making predictions about who might be elected to carry out the job of president.

What generalization might this student form about the role of technology in her classroom activities?

MAKING A LITERATURE CONNECTION ➤

The Message Is a Generalization

Some literature for children and youth involves messages that are generalizations. One example is from *Not One Damsel in Distress: World Folktales for Strong Girls,* a book of stories compiled and retold by Jane Yolen. The message is "Anyone can be a hero if he or she has to be—even girls—especially girls. This generalization connects the concept of hero with that of girls and with that of a cause "if he or she has to be." It establishes a positive relationship between girls and heroism. Another book, *Cuban Kids* by George Ancona, uses many photographs to foster the generalization that Cuban children come in all shapes and sizes. A third book, *On the Same Day in March: A Tour of the World's Weather* by Marilyn Singer, emphasizes another generalization, the relationship between geography and various weather patterns: Weather patterns are affected by the geography of a region. A fourth book, *How I Became an American* by Karin Gundisch, explores the generalization: For immigrants to the United States, the hardships of language, finding work, and keeping a family united are balanced by the opportunities available.

Using Generalizations to Make Predictions

Generalizations are used to organize facts and concepts by summarizing them and describing the relationships among them. Once a generalization is formed, it can be used to make predictions of actions and events. Using the generalization that riding in a limousine means you have money, we can predict that a person who rides only in limousines would be considered wealthy by others in the community. Using the generalization that people in the United States are not sure that a woman can capably carry out the job of president, what prediction might you make about the chance a woman has of being elected president of the United States during the next presidential election? Using this generalization, you would predict that the chance a woman has of being elected president during the next election is poor.

Generalizations can be a starting point leading to the creation of a hypothesis and a test. If we use the hypothesis about the likelihood of a woman being elected president in the United States, we could test it by involving students in doing a survey of teachers and family members of students in our school. We could ask whether they think a woman could capably carry out the job of president, what the reasons are for their opinion, and whether they would vote for any of five potential female presidential candidates that students have identified. The results of our data collection, although limited, may lead us to change our original hypothesis and create a new generalization.

The predictive ability of generalizations is important because being able to predict events and actions gives us some control over our lives. Social studies helps students learn to predict, understand, and control events in their lives and as citizens of their society. Teachers help students form generalizations about their everyday life and use them to make predictions that affect their daily lives. They also help students discover inaccuracies in the generalizations they have formed and reconstruct the generalizations so that they have better predictive value.

Types of Generalizations

Generalizations have different levels of acceptance by people. They can describe a simple relationship among a few concepts with only limited explanatory and/or predictive power. Consider the following statement: Riding in a limousine means you have a lot of money. This is a generalization for which we can find exceptions. Other generalizations are highly complex and relate many concepts, show complex relationships, and/or make predictions with a higher degree of certainty or accuracy and a greater degree of confidence. These are laws, principles, and theories. Consider the following example: All people must eat to survive. This statement is a generalization that can be accepted as accurate and with confidence for all people.

CW

COMPANION
WEBSITE

T I M E   F O R   R E F L E C T I O N :   W H A T   D O   Y O U   T H I N K ?

Below is a list of social studies concepts. Write three or four statements linking together some of the concepts to form generalizations.

consumer	producer	election	law
advertisement	candidate	political party	leadership
voter	family	workers	investor

1. _____

_____ ➤

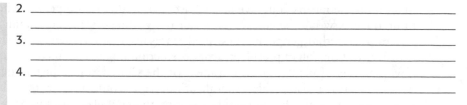

2. _____
_____
3. _____
_____
4. _____
_____

Consider the following generalization: The features of the earth's surface vary as a result of geologic events, weather, and human decisions.

1. Illustrate, by writing or drawing, your understanding of the generalization.

2. Suggest several topics or problems that upper elementary or middle school students might study to learn aspects of this generalization. _____
_____
_____

3. What inquiry skills might students need to study these topics or problems?
_____
_____

If students are to apply a generalization at appropriate times, teachers must help them understand the concepts and relationships found in the generalization. Memorization of a generalization with little understanding of the concepts it includes results in students being unable to use it or even judge when to apply it.

Teaching Powerful Generalizations

Generalizations are the most powerful form of social studies content for understanding and having some control over our lives. However, generalizations are also the most difficult form of social studies content to learn. To understand a generalization, a student must not only have first developed an understanding of the concepts used in the generalization, but have repeatedly experienced the relationship among these concepts. Students need to see that changing one concept creates a change in the other concept.

Reflect on the following generalization: The features of the earth's surface vary as a result of geologic events, weather, and human decisions. The effects of a heavy rain on the playground dirt need to be observed several times to ascertain the validity of this generalization. Students need to note that a heavy rain causes channels to form in the dirt and creates a delta where the dirt being carried off in the channel hits the sidewalk. They need to notice that lighter rain produces smaller erosion and deposits less dirt. They can measure approximately how long a rainstorm lasts and how much rainwater is collected in a rain gauge. They can predict the effects of storms of varying length and strength on the erosion of playground dirt, then go out to sketch and measure the depth and length of channels in the dirt after a storm.

At other times, students can build small dams out of heavy cardboard to see how they affect runoff and erosion on the playground during rainstorms. This is a time for checking predictions developed from prior knowledge against reality and modifying the generalization as needed. Eventually, students have enough experiences that they are able to apply them to the earth as a whole. They can begin meaningfully to understand the generalization that the earth's surface features vary as a function of geologic events, weather, and human culture.

A lesson focusing on a generalization has the following phases:

1. *Exploratory Introduction:* Identification of a problem or question
2. *Lesson Development:* Formation of a working hypothesis responding to the problem/question; gathering of data (information) related to the hypothesis; evaluation of the data to decide whether it supports the hypothesis
3. *Expansion:* Application of the generalization constructed if the hypothesis is supported, or reconstruction and testing of the generalization if the hypothesis is not supported

The complete cycle used in teaching a generalization is described in Table 5.1.

> **BUILDING ON DIVERSITY**

Using Resources to Support Learning a Generalization

Generalizations place a high demand on our thinking because they require us to understand the concepts they contain and the relationship that links those concepts. Students' cultural background will influence the concepts they have constructed and their ability to identify a relationship between them. Cultural differences will make a specific generalization easier for some students to construct and more difficult for others. Teachers must be aware of the influences of culture. Having specific information about the experiences students have within their culture can give teachers some insight into which generalizations students will be better able to construct.

All students benefit when teachers try to provide a large amount of context for a generalization (Cummins, 1996). High context supports students' learning through maps, visuals, gestures, clues, and similar resources. The higher the degree of cognitive demand or difficulty of a task or topic, the greater is the level of contextual support needed. This is especially true when students are English language learners (ELL). Cognitively, these students may be able to construct a generalization, but their proficiency in English might require high contextual assistance. With low context, ELL students have few prompts and might not recognize the concepts in the generalization as those they know. Or they might not understand that they need to

➤

T A B L E   5 . 1

Teaching Generalizations

Phase	Planning Required
Exploratory Introduction	Help students try out and confront their prior knowledge of the social studies generalization.
	Provide an opportunity for students to identify a problem or question that the lesson is focused on. Start students thinking with a key question that involves them in an activity.
	Encourage students to work in cooperative groups and relate prior knowledge to the problem or question.
	Bring out and make public students' prior knowledge of the problem or question.
Lesson Development	Ask students to investigate a social studies generalization as a response to the problem/question in the exploratory introduction activities.
	Allow students to gather data to provide evidence for a solution to their problem while exploring the generalization.
	Ask students to analyze the data and formulate a conclusion to their problem, comparing it to the generalization previously introduced.
	Provide closure to important aspects of the new generalization.
Expansion	Provide application activities for the social studies generalization in new, relevant contexts while at the same time helping students recall their original alternative explanations.
	Provide activities to help students transfer the new social studies generalization to more and more real-world events.
	Guide students in summarizing the important events in the social studies lesson that lead to the new social studies generalization.

➤ find out how these concepts are related. Students who are receiving special needs services but are not ELL also typically are better able to construct generalizations when a high level of context is provided to support their learning.

CHARACTERISTICS OF THE EXPLORATORY INTRODUCTION PHASE

The question or problem developed in the exploratory introduction phase is the starting point of a lesson helping students construct a generalization. A question can be posed by the teacher or, more meaningfully, by the student or a student group. Good questions are stimulating, making students take a closer look at something in their social and physical worlds (Schug and Beery, 1987; Spargo & Enderstein, 1997). Good questions lead to actions with people, objects, events, or ideas. The question or problem focuses the student on a cause and its result, or on an explanation. Good questions often start out as general "what" questions followed by more specific ones. Examples of general questions follow: What happens? What do I see, hear, or feel? What does it do? What do you think? What happens if . . . ? How many? What group . . . ? Can you make . . . ?

Poor first questions ask students about their knowledge of words or what the text or teacher previously said. They limit social studies to the recall of information by encouraging students to answer with what the teacher thinks is the "correct" reply instead of with what the students understand. If students ask poor questions, teachers need to help them rethink them. Good first questions ask students to focus their observation of an event, pose problems, initiate data collection, and make comparisons.

Students will probably not understand the generalization if they cannot (1) clearly identify the concepts, (2) identify the relationships in the generalization, and (3) actively engage in experiences and use data involving the relationships (Driver et al., 1996; Eggen, Kauchak, & Harder, 1979). The teacher must be aware of the limitations hindering students' abilities to work through an inquiry and construct a generalization:

1. Poorly developed prior knowledge containing alternative conceptions and misconceptions of concepts
2. The limited number of ideas students can hold in their short-term memory at one time
3. The need for help in addressing a question systematically
4. The need to examine concrete materials and experiences *while* they are engaged in the process of thinking and developing relationships

In planning the lesson, teachers think about these limitations in terms of the concepts involved in the problem or question, possible generalizations that could resolve the problem, and what kind of information students need to collect to determine whether their generalizations are supported by evidence.

CHARACTERISTICS OF THE LESSON DEVELOPMENT PHASE

The inquiry lesson continues as students gather information about their problem/question. Teachers provide guidance by asking questions such as the following:

What are some possible sources of information to be gathered?
What methods would help us gather the most useful information: direct observation, carrying out investigations, library and Internet research, surveys, or a combination of a few methods?
What materials and equipment do we need to carry out our investigation?
Can this method provide us with enough information to investigate our problem or do we need to combine it with another method to gather some different kinds of information?

How can we record and store the information obtained?

How can we communicate the information obtained to others?

How can we analyze the information we gathered?

Once students decide how they want to gather information, they are given enough time to do this. Some data gathering may be done out of school. Some in-school time is necessary, however, because students often need to discuss a next step in data gathering with their cooperative learning groups or they need advice on how to find and use an information source not previously considered.

➤ **USING TECHNOLOGY**

Supporting Students' Inquiry

As an example of data gathering, consider a problem that was investigated in an inquiry. Students studied drawings of Fort Duquesne (now Pittsburgh) in Pennsylvania and wondered why it was built in that location. After examining maps during the data collection phase of the lesson, they decided that it was built there because three rivers come together at this point: The Monongahela and the Allegheny join to form the Ohio. They decided that they needed to do further data gathering, so they checked this hypothesis by examining reference books that described why the fort was built at this location. They also used reference books and maps to examine the locations of other river cities to determine whether they were built at places where two or more rivers join. This led them to revise their hypothesis into a more comprehensive one: Cities are often built where two or more rivers join because the goods and people going up and down the rivers all come together here.

Several Internet resources were used in the project. Students found a useful map at www.Expedia.com with a close-up view of the three rivers. An overview of the site of Fort Duquesne was described on the History Channel site at http://historychannel.com/perl/print_book.pl?ID=87334. Pictures and historical models as well as blueprints of Fort Duquesne were found at http://historychannel.com/perl/print_book.pl?ID=87334. A search on Google at www.google.com found sites that deal with cities on rivers in the United States and in other countries. Technology resources were integrated into, and supported, students' data gathering and inquiry.

COMPANION
WEBSITE

As students gather data, they decide how to organize, classify, and categorize it. Data should be presented in a way that allows it to be easily and clearly shared with others. Students might use tables, charts, graphs, bulletin boards, drawings, oral reports, written reports, dramatic skits, panel discussions, models, or demonstrations. Well-organized data enables students to use it more successfully to decide the level of confidence they have in a generalization. Poorly organized data collection or presentation is of little use. It may not display identifiable patterns, encouraging false conclusions about the generalization.

CHARACTERISTICS OF THE EXPANSION PHASE

Teachers help students construct a usable generalization. They also help students understand that, once they have a usable generalization, they need to apply it and transfer it to a variety of settings. When students begin to apply a generalization, it is always necessary to encourage them to think about its limitations. This can be accomplished by asking students questions such as the following pair: When is this generalization useful? Does the generalization always make good predictions? Students decide how widely the generalization can be applied. For example, do all places where rivers join have a city? As questions are raised, students are encouraged to investigate them through further surveys, interviews, or the use of a website that sends queries to students at schools all over the world. Generalizations can be reconstructed when students find they no longer address the data they obtained.

TIME FOR REFLECTION: WHAT DO YOU THINK?

Return to the exploratory introduction activity about brand-name and generic products in our homes, presented at the beginning of this chapter. Answer the following questions.

1. The textbook passage contains no statements of generalizations. However, it contains questions that ask students to state generalizations. List these questions by their corresponding numerals. _____

_____

2. Complete this objective for the lesson: At the end of the investigation, students will conclude that families choose generic brands because _____

_____

3. Given what you know about fourth-graders, explain why students may be or may not be familiar with generic products? _____

_____

4. How would you suggest the passage be modified to make it more appealing, or better related, to the experiences of students? _____

_____

5. From what you have learned about teaching generalizations, explain why it is essential for students to go home and do the investigation of products the passage suggests. _____

_____

6. Design an assignment sheet with directions and questions you would use to ensure that students in your class, with the help of their family members, investigate their families' use of generic and brand-name products. Take into

➤

➤   consideration concerns for the safety of children and possible "house rules" concerning children's free access to all household items.

7. After students organize the data from the class assignment, what key questions will you ask to help state a generalization concerning the use of generic and/or brand-name products? _____
_____
_____

8. Write two hypotheses to test whether this generalization is applicable to students in other schools and to households in general.

a. _____
_____

b. _____
_____

9. Explain how a fourth-grade teacher might reasonably test your hypotheses with his students. _____
_____
_____

10. Compare your responses now with those at the beginning of this chapter. Explain whether they indicate that you have a more meaningful understanding of using inquiry strategies to teach students to formulate generalizations. _____
_____
_____

FORMATIVE EVALUATION AND THE INQUIRY PROCESS

Students are assisted in reviewing their investigative activities to determine which activities are productive and which could be done differently. For example, some data sources may be very helpful, whereas others are limited. Some ways of organizing data may be more effective than others. Evaluating their activities enables students to make better decisions, better direct their own learning, become more aware of their own thinking and planning, and become more dependent on internal rather than external reinforcement. This is important to teaching meaningful and powerful social studies that develops citizens who are independent judges and decision makers.

TIME FOR REFLECTION: WHAT DO YOU THINK?

Briefly describe an inquiry lesson that focuses on a generalization resulting from students' investigation of a physical or cultural problem in their school community.

Lesson objective: _____

Alternative student conception: _____   ➤

➤ **Exploratory Introduction Activity**

_____

_____

Problem or question generated by the exploratory activity: _____

_____

_____

Lesson Development Activity

_____

_____

Two sources or activities from which to gather data:_____

_____

_____

Closure: _____

_____

_____

Expansion Activity

_____

_____

1. How can the generalization be applied so that students can work further with it?

_____

2. How might you transfer the generalization to another situation? _____

_____

_____

3. Briefly summarize the lesson as you would with your students. _____

_____

_____

INQUIRY TEACHING AND THE NATIONAL STANDARDS IN SOCIAL STUDIES

The "Principles of Teaching and Learning" in the _Curriculum Standards for Social Studies_ describes five major components of a powerful social studies program (National Council for the Social Studies, 1994b, pp. 11–12). These components enable students to carry out inquiry-based social studies: meaningful, integrative, value based, challenging, and active. These principles note that in social studies, students learn _connected networks_ of knowledge, skills, beliefs, and attitudes that they find useful both in and outside school. Furthermore, the principles indicate that meaningful learning activities and assessment strategies focus students' attention on the most important ideas embedded in what they are learning. Teachers model seriousness of purpose and a thoughtful approach to inquiry. Teachers also show interest in and respect for students' thinking but demand well-reasoned arguments rather than opinions voiced without adequate thought or commitment. These principles, adopted by this national organization devoted to teaching social studies, support teacher and student involvement in inquiry-based and investigative learning aimed at helping students construct generalizations.

SUMMARY

The development of generalizations is a primary goal in elementary and middle school social studies teaching. It is the most powerful type of social studies content students learn. Knowledge of generalizations provides meaningful predictions to help control events in our daily lives and our civic associations. To create meaningful learning, students must be able to interact in relevant ways with the concepts and relationships involved in a generalization. Generalizations are meaningfully understood only through active involvement. For children and youth, such involvement is both physical and mental. It enables students to work with data used to construct the generalization and to predict the outcome of a generalization. Therefore, the generalization is verified each time it is used.

In teaching generalizations, the three phases of the learning cycle help students identify a problem/question related to the generalization (exploratory introduction), collect data with which to verify the validity of the generalization and to predict the results of the generalization (development), and apply or transfer the use of the generalization to different contexts (expansion). One significant step in planning a generalization learning cycle is checking the application of the generalization in a new situation during the expansion phase. Students need to use their generalizations in a variety of situations if they are to become usable pieces of knowledge. They also need to discover that the generalizations they construct (1) may not satisfactorily explain a different situation or their investigation, (2) may not use appropriate procedures or resources, or (3) may need additional or more diverse information. Because the modern world involves students in complex and changing situations, it is important that they use generalizations in a variety of situations to learn when they are appropriate and when they need to be reconstructed. If students are not able to do this, they will be less able to participate fully as citizens.

Expanding ON THIS CHAPTER

Activity

COMPANION
WEBSITE

Develop a list of generalizations appropriate for elementary or middle school students to learn about one of the following topics: maps and map reading, elections and the electoral process, jobs and careers, advertisements and advertising, television, or Saturday morning cartoons. Identify the national social studies curriculum standard(s) addressed by the list of generalizations.

COMPANION
WEBSITE

Recommended Websites to Visit

ESL Lounge: This excellent teachers' site is loaded with lesson plans, worksheets, teaching tips, printable board games, and reviews of notable ESL books.
www.esl-lounge.com

Pathways to School Improvement: An easy-to-navigate point of entry to gain access to some of the best resources on the Internet for teaching at-risk students.
www.ncrel.org/sdrs/areas/at0cont.htm

Urban Education Web: This site offers exceptional information about working with at-risk students but also includes resources on many other issues affecting the success of urban youth.
http://eric-web.tc.columbia.edu

"Made in the U.S.A." A lesson plan teaching the generalization: In today's interconnected world, customs and other aspects of culture are exchanged faster than ever, through trade, travel, and the media.
www.nationalgeographic.com/resources/ngo/education/ideas58/index.html

"Fighting Cholera With Maps." A lesson plan teaching the generalization: Mapping techniques can be used to understand social issues and to solve problems.
www.nationalgeographic.com/resources/ngo/education/ideas58/58cholera.html

"The Middle Ages." A lesson plan teaching the generalization: We learn about people from long ago by reading records, such as diaries, that they left behind.
http://school.discovery.com/lessonplans/programs/timesmedieval/index.html

Using Instructional Strategies That Help Students Learn

E X P L O R A T O R Y

INTRODUCTION

Compare the following two instructional strategies and respond to the questions:

Strategy 1: A 30-minute teacher lecture supplemented by photographs describing the characteristics of river formation. The focus of the lecture is on the cutting action of water running downhill.

Strategy 2: A 20-minute field trip in the school yard where student groups are asked to build a hill in a sandbox, then to pour a large glass of water down one side of it, and to make observations of the effects of the water. This is followed with sharing observations and a whole-group discussion.

What differences in student control are found in each method? _____
_____
_____

What difference would you expect in student learning from the two strategies for a first-grade student? _____
_____
_____

For a sixth-grade student? _____
_____
_____

CHAPTER OVERVIEW

Meaningful and powerful social studies knowledge, supportively taught using effective instructional resources, requires thoughtful planning and ongoing assessment of short- and long-term objectives. It also requires teachers who understand and use strategies that facilitate students' construction of social studies knowledge. What students learn is influenced by how they are taught, the quality of individual and social processes occurring in the classroom, and the perceptions and understanding of social studies as a subject to be taught and learned (National Council for the Social Studies, 1994b). The social studies program is supported by a mixture of appropriate and adequate technology, classroom facilities, and resources.

Social studies teachers are like orchestra conductors as they select and combine teaching strategies and instructional resources to help students learn. They emphasize different strategies at various times during the lesson. Because every strategy has strengths and weaknesses, effective teachers select strategies matching the objectives toward which their students work. They also select activities their students enjoy or need to practice and learn. This does not mean teachers should only use the strategies their students like best, but it does mean that teachers can be personally creative in their selections as long as they can professionally justify their selections and combinations of selections.

Throughout this book, the many classroom scenarios, teaching interviews, and learning cycles illustrate how individual teachers combine instructional resources and strategies to provide meaningful learning of powerful social studies skills, content, attitudes, and values. You will want to examine these carefully and to try them with students. They provide examples that we hope can inspire you to expand your own talents in lesson development.

CHAPTER OBJECTIVES

1. Describe instructional strategies that help students construct meaningful social studies learning of content, skills, values, and participation as an active citizen in a democratic nation.
2. Describe and evaluate cooperative group learning in a social studies lesson.
3. Describe and evaluate the teacher's role in social studies lessons focusing on fact acquisition, concept attainment, understanding generalizations, and developing cognitive and affective skills for active citizenship in a democratic society.
4. Describe the potential effects on social studies learning outcomes of varying the amount of student control in lesson activities.
5. Describe and evaluate appropriate instructional methods for each phase of the social studies learning cycle.
6. Describe important concerns to be addressed in an effective classroom management plan for teaching social studies lessons.
7. Explain how a teacher may benefit by doing action research related to particular instructional strategies or resources.

BECOMING AN EFFECTIVE PLANNER
OF A SOCIAL STUDIES PROGRAM

Effective classrooms require teachers who foster learning to the extent that most of their students learn most of what they are supposed to learn (Berliner, 1987a). A number of teaching dimensions and strategies are associated with effective teaching.

Teaching Dimensions That Support Meaningful Learning

Several dimensions of effective teaching support meaningful learning: *clarity, variety, task orientation,* and *student engagement.*

Clarity. *Clarity,* or clear instruction, includes:

- Knowledge of the social studies objectives for the activities
- Directions students can understand and follow
- Experiences related to, and relevant to, students' lives
- Multiple modes for presenting social studies content
- Opportunities for interaction, feedback, and self-evaluation throughout lessons (Jacobowitz, 1997)

Variety. Reading about a topic alone or using only a materials-rich activity is not sufficient. Combining instructional approaches such as materials-rich activities, student discussion, reading, and teacher questioning is needed to bring together the whole so that meaningful learning occurs.

Task Orientation. Classrooms vary greatly in the amount of time and emphasis devoted to specific educational goals (Perie, 1997). Powerful social studies learning for *all* students requires student involvement in social studies for a significant amount of time at every grade level. Effective teachers manage and reduce interruptions, plan for transitions between topics, organize materials distribution and return, and are aware of efficient techniques for managing student traffic flow. Social studies lessons are cycles of active learning and feedback. Lessons build on one another, leading to accomplishing unit objectives.

Student Engagement. Effective classrooms create and sustain a nonthreatening and supportive learning environment in which students focus on lesson activities with few interruptions or disruptions. If 40 minutes has been allocated for social studies but the students are engaged in learning only half that time, a powerful social studies program cannot result. The more consistently and completely students are engaged in lesson activities, the higher the student achievement will be. While students engage in learning activities, effective teachers continuously monitor their engagement.

Teaching Strategies That Support Meaningful Learning

Some teaching strategies are frequently used to support meaningful learning. Two such strategies are *questioning* and *cooperative learning.* You will see much use of these strategies throughout the learning cycles in this book.

Questioning. All learning begins by asking questions. The type of questions teachers use guide students' engagement in the lesson (King & Rosenshine, 1993). The amount of time a teacher waits between asking questions and calling on students for responses, or responding to answers, affects student responses (Rowe, 1996). Classroom research has found that teachers, on average, wait less than a second before calling on a student or responding to a student's comment. Waiting 3 or more seconds before calling on a student or acknowledging a response can increase the length of student responses, the number of appropriate responses, and the cognitive level of the responses.

Questions are planned in advance, relate to the lesson activities, and are written into lesson plans. Learning cycle lessons begin with questions that all students have a chance to answer, such as "What do you have to do to be elected president?" and "Why didn't many people settle in Florida until the middle of the twentieth century?" These are *open,* or *broad, questions,* which have many answers. Teachers accept all answers even though some answers may explain more than others. Such questions engage all students in the class. A central *key question* is planned for the exploratory phase of every learning cycle. In a lesson focusing on the concept of presidential election, for example, the teacher may ask the key question "What do you have to do to be elected president?" It is an open question that involves each student in thinking about the main idea of the lesson.

During the lesson development phase, questions focus student inquiry on the main concepts, skills, and attitudes of the lesson. After watching a film about the election campaigns of two recent candidates for president, the teacher might ask the questions "From whom did each candidate get the money to fund the campaign?" and "How much money was spent on television spots by each candidate?" These are *closed,* or *narrow, questions.* Their focus is narrow because they have one or a few appropriate or correct answers. Most questions during the lesson development are narrow or closed.

During the expansion phase of the lesson, questions are used to help students apply the concept in a new context. Again, the emphasis on open questions is greater although some closed questions may be used. For example, in the case of the presidential election campaign lesson just discussed, the teacher starts with an open question, such as "If you are going to design a winning presidential election campaign, what would it include?" Later, the teacher might ask the closed question "What is missing from our design for a winning presidential election campaign?"

Cooperative Learning. Cooperation is needed in all classroom learning as students share the time and talents of a teacher and learning resources. *Cooperative learning* is an approach and a set of strategies specifically designed to encourage student cooperation while learning. In a review of research on the use of cooperative learning in virtually all academic disciplines and in a variety of settings in the United States and in other nations, Slavin (1989) reported that students learn as well or better when using cooperative learning as when using competitive and individual learning strategies. Johnson and Johnson (1986) pointed out that students develop a positive self-image and an improved attitude toward, and acceptance of, classmates.

Because social studies is committed to fostering human and civil behaviors and active, responsible participation in the communities in which people live and work,

cooperative learning should be integrated into the learning and participation of social studies lessons (Stahl, 1994). Cooperative learning is uniquely suited for social
studies because the social skills it teaches are essential to democratic attitudes and
beliefs (Johnson & Johnson, 1991). When diverse students are brought together for
repeated face-to-face interactions in which they must use cooperative learning procedures, they become more supportive of each other (Johnson & Johnson, 1991).
Researchers Johnson, Johnson, and Holubec (1990a) reported that students in cooperative groups show higher academic achievement and increased motivation. Small
cooperative groups increase opportunities for positive reinforcement and reduce the
risks of negative reactions and ridicule for giving a wrong answer.

Traditional group strategies create barriers in learning (Johnson, Johnson, & Holubec, 1990a). Two major barriers include leadership dominated by one person and
work performed by a few in the group. Students do not develop group process skills
unless they are taught them directly and required to practice them (Roy, 1994). Only
through reflection on their cooperative efforts do students become committed to the
value of cooperative learning. To be successful, group interpersonal skills are carefully
planned for, taught, and reinforced by the teacher. Table 6.1 compares behaviors of students and teachers in cooperative groups with their behaviors in traditional classrooms.

Cooperative learning fosters four important goals (Johnson & Johnson, 1986).
First, positive interdependence among students is created through the division of work-
load, responsibility, and joint rewards. Groups establish positive interdependence when
they learn to work together to earn recognition, grades, rewards, and other indicators

TABLE 6.1

Behaviors of Students and Teachers in Classrooms

Traditional Classroom	Cooperative Classroom
Do your own work	Work with others to learn
Eyes to front and be quiet	Eye to eye, knee to knee
Listen only to the teacher	Listen to group members
Learn only from teacher/materials	Learn from one's peers within a group
Work alone	Work within a small group as a group
"Silence is golden"	Productive talk is desired
Teacher only makes decisions	Students make decisions
Learners are passive	Learners are active

Source: "Cultivating Cooperative Group Process Skills within the Social Studies Classroom," by P. Roy, 1994,
in R. J. Stahl (Ed.), *Cooperative Learning in Social Studies: A Handbook for Teachers,* Menlo Park, CA:
Addison-Wesley. Used with permission.

of group success (Slavin, 1989). They learn to work together for the common good. Discussions, explanations, questioning, and other verbal exchanges are important in sharing, exploring, discovering, applying, reviewing, and rehearsing the content.

Second, positive student interaction and accountability holds students individually accountable for their own learning and for the learning of others in the group. Assignments are frequently divided, with each student mastering a part and then instructing the other students in the area of mastery. Each student knows the others are depending on him or her. If one student chooses to do poor work or make trouble within the group, the other members of the group are sure to be affected and use peer pressure to change the student's behavior. Grades are often partially assigned by combining individual scores and group mean scores. Teachers and students evaluate and grade the working process of the group as well as the final product or presentation. They discuss the group process and how well the group accomplished its goals, and evaluate the individual roles of group members. Additional discussion topics include the sequence of tasks, procedures used in carrying out the tasks, and student responsibility for the tasks.

Third, students work to develop adequate interpersonal and small-group skills. Students are taught effective communication, willingness to accept and support each other, skills to resolve conflicts, and appreciation for learning about each other. Students evaluate their group skills and performance in planning and working together. Instruction in cooperative learning begins with short lessons or with carefully structured activities presented by the teacher. As students become more familiar with the group processes, activities may be longer and involve the students in selecting topics and assigning membership responsibilities.

Fourth, students develop awareness of the need for group processing. In face-to-face encounters students discuss the group process, determine how well the group accomplished its goals, and evaluate individual roles in the group. Some discussion topics include sequence of tasks, procedures to carry out the tasks, and student responsibility for the tasks. Group functioning is monitored by students and the teacher. The teacher instructs students in effective group processes, creates and facilitates a nonthreatening work environment, and intervenes when members encounter difficulty with group processes. Group processes include group formation skills, group achievement skills, and group interaction skills.

The method used in grouping students is important to the success of cooperative groups. Teachers plan heterogeneous, small cooperative groups. A typical group includes four students: one high achiever, two average achievers, and one low achiever. Leadership responsibilities for both the content of the lesson and the success of the group belong to all group members. One student might be the group *recorder,* writing down what decisions are made and keeping notes. Another student might be *materials manager,* collecting the materials needed and organizing them. Another student might be the group *spokesperson* in charge of communicating learning outcomes to others. One more student might be the group *organizer,* making sure that everyone has a chance to contribute to discussion and that each person has a clear task to do. Roles usually alternate over time among members of the group.

When large amounts of material are obtained for a topic, tasks are divided into about equal parts. For example, on the topic of the Great Depression in the United States in the 1930s, each group member focuses on one possible question:

- What were the major causes of the Depression?
- What were the effects of the Depression in our community?
- What major solutions were experimented with to try to ease the Depression?
- What was the role of the president, Franklin D. Roosevelt?

Each member may work with students in other groups who have the same question to answer. This division into specialist groups is called a *jigsaw*. An alternative sharing method requires each group member to develop a response individually, then to share it with his or her cooperative group.

In social studies activities using cooperative learning, teachers tend to have less difficulty with classroom management. Students assume greater responsibility for materials and help each other by answering questions and assisting in the completion of assignments. Because students realize they have valid contributions to make, they become even more willing to participate in small-group work (Hannigan, 1990). Students use their creativity to solve more difficult and complex problems than they would be willing to try individually. Social studies teachers are helping students learn to live in their social world: cooperative grouping facilitates this effort.

➤ **USING TECHNOLOGY**

Creating a Collaborative Classroom

Technology is used by teachers in developing a collaborative classroom. Available CD-ROMs, software, or the Internet offer many possibilities for enhancing student collaboration. Some software involves students in working in groups and in sharing thoughts as they solve everyday problems. Many software items record the choices students make and keeps information separately for each participant or role. Teachers can get copies of students' responses by consulting special pages in the software program. Students get clear directions and descriptions and readings for each role. Such programs can be used on multiple days. An example is the Choices, Choices series by Tom Snyder Productions on topics such as Kids and the Environment, On the Playground, Savings Pack!, and Taking Responsibility. These include a CD-ROM or disk accompanied by a picture card set and lesson plans. These problems involve students in simulation situations in which they balance their values with the expectations of friends, parents, and teachers. Another series from Tom Snyder Publications is Decisions, Decisions for grades 5–10 with a wide range of titles, including Lying, Cheating, Stealing; Prejudice; The Constitution; Violence in the Media; and Ancient Empires. This series comes with a CD-ROM or disk, student reference books, and a teacher's guide with lesson plans. Other software may not be targeted at use in group work but contains so many interesting kernels of information on a topic that group work, which is reported and shared with classmates, is the best way to harvest it.

An Interview with Mike Yell on Cooperative Learning

Interviewer: Mike, I understand that you have taught both high school and middle school social studies for twenty-eight years. Most social studies teachers I know begin in the middle school and progress to the high school. This makes me wonder—what brought you back to a middle school position this late in your career?

Mike Yell: I have taught history and all of the social science disciplines in every secondary grade and have enjoyed them all, but I really like the seventh-graders and find them most rewarding to teach. Middle school students have so much enthusiasm. When you engage this age group in learning and keep them active, they just keep going. So when a middle school position became available in our system, I jumped at the opportunity to have it.

Interviewer: You have described cooperative learning as being at the heart of your teaching. What would you advise teachers interested in using cooperative learning to do in order to use it effectively?

Mike Yell: Oh, yes, cooperative learning is one the instructional strategies to which the students respond with great enthusiasm. My advice to teachers just beginning to use cooperative learning is to be open to new strategies and be persistent with them. As with any strategy, you must be willing to try it, work with it, massage it, adapt it, make it your own.

Interviewer: Do you remember how you first encountered cooperative learning?

Mike Yell: One of my colleagues, who taught English, attended a workshop on cooperative learning conducted by David and Robert Johnson at the University of Minnesota. He was enthusiastic about it and shared some of his printed workshop materials and ideas with me. I became interested and started to try things. Later I attended a workshop by the Johnsons, too. Over the years I have attended workshops and read materials by all of the major advocates of and researchers on cooperative learning. It takes time to master any strategy and you have to modify others' ideas to fit your situation.

Interviewer: How have you made cooperative learning in your classes your own?

Mike Yell: Although I often have students interacting and processing class content in pairs or small groups, I generally use four specific cooperative learning strategies with which I have found the most success. I concentrate on designing or finding interesting and engaging activities through which the students apply their cooperative efforts.

Interviewer: What particular strategies do you use?

Mike Yell: It depends on the general learning objective for the activity. The four cooperative strategies I use most often include *Response Groups,* for working with primary and authentic resources; *Teams-Games-Tournaments,* for reviewing information; *Problem Solving Groupwork,* for research and synthesis of ideas in projects; and *Rotating Learning Centers* when I want my students to learn about many different aspects of a past culture.

Interviewer: How do you group students for a cooperative learning activity?

Mike Yell: I have different methods of forming groups, and although I usually assign them, often I do give the students an element of choice. At times, I will allow students to choose their groups, but I set certain rules for selecting those groups. For example, all groups must be mixed between guys and girls, and no one can be left out of a group. I disagree with total student selection because then some students will invariably be left out of that process and not chosen. I will not do that to any of my students.

Interviewer: With the great emphasis on assessment and student achievement, I must ask how you solve the problem of grading students and being certain that all students contribute to the work and learn about the topic.

Mike Yell: For cooperative learning projects that are graded, I do not give a group grade. For those in the school systems, group grading is the major criticism you hear from students and parents concerning cooperative learning. I agree with their concern. They tend to see it as an issue of fairness. Those familiar with the principles of cooperative learning understand that individual accountability is essential to good group work; if the teacher is to ensure that all students participate in the work, there must be individual accountability. I do not believe that you can ensure individual accountability by using group grades. Group grades not only ignore the accountability principle, in my opinion they are not fair to students. I let my student know right away that although we will learn together, we will perform alone. I find that most students are very relieved to hear this, as are their parents.

Interviewer: This sounds good, but how do you carry it out?

Mike Yell: If I'm giving a grade for a particular cooperative learning assignment, that grade for each student is based on their individual work in the group. For instance, students in a group have a separate and designated role that is graded, and a written/spoken assessment following the assignment such as a quiz, paper, or presentation. I also use rubrics in my evaluation; however, the specific categories of information and criteria for performance must not be universal but specific to, and reflective of, the content of the topic under study.

Interviewer: From what you are saying, I suspect that you tend to use cooperative learning as a means to help students perform the tasks of acquiring, processing, and evaluating social studies information and ideas.

Mike Yell: Yes, I have a variety of instructional strategies in my repertoire—some that are cooperative and some that are individual and some that are whole class. For example, I use writing strategies daily, and also reading strategies, discussion and lecturing strategies, project strategies, and concept attainment strategies. I believe that in addition to deep content knowledge, having a repertoire of engaging and active teaching strategies is an important component of good instruction.

Interviewer: If I recall correctly, I read an article describing your teaching of a lesson on Pompeii in *Social Education* a few years ago. Others could read that article and learn more about how you use and mix multiple strategies.

Mike Yell: Yes, as with all my lessons, *Uncovering Pompeii* uses a variety of instructional strategies to help my students learn. I should tell you that I don't teach that lesson today in exactly the same way as I did when I wrote the article; I've changed it quite a bit. I believe that lessons and units must be dynamic, incorporating new materials and improving as a result of their last use with students.

Interviewer: Mike, this discussion has been very interesting, and I can see why you were selected the Outstanding Middle School Social Studies Teacher in 1998 by NCSS. Thank you for sharing your time and ideas. Is there something that I have not asked that you would like to share with other teachers or teacher candidates?

Mike Yell: Thank you, I have enjoyed it. The last point that I would like to make is the importance of the teacher's own professional growth in terms of their content and pedagogical knowledge. I have found that one of the most important methods for increasing our own growth as teachers is to join and become involved in our professional organizations at both the state and national levels. My primary professional organizations are the Wisconsin Council for the Social Studies and the National Council for the Social Studies. The contacts, resources, ideas, and opportunities available to teachers through their organizations are fantastic! Great teaching is a continual process of growth, inquiry, and learning.

TIME FOR REFLECTION: WHAT DO YOU THINK?

1. Mike Yell indicates that teachers must continue to learn in different ways. What evidence do you see in the interview indicating that he learns through his teaching of students? _____

2. Mike Yell indicates he uses cooperative learning in four different instructional strategies. Which of these do you recall experiencing or observing? _____

3. How would you describe the student's participation in Mike Yell's classroom? _____

A CONTINUUM OF KNOWLEDGE AND INSTRUCTION

Teachers have different conceptions of the way social studies teaching and learning take place. One conception focuses on *fact acquisition.* The content to be learned is a list of facts and definitions of terms. Students receive and remember the information presented. Repetition is the key learning process. Students are evaluated by repeating facts and definitions provided by the teacher and textbook. The teacher exposes students to facts, provides drill and recitation sessions, and encourages motivation in students through a variety of media and external rewards.

A second conception of social studies teaching and learning focuses on *concept* or *idea attainment.* Attainment requires students to figure out the attributes and attribute values of a concept by comparing and contrasting examples and nonexamples of the concept. In this view, students are learning concepts created by others. Learning occurs when students search for these same patterns and relationships in examples and nonexamples to develop an understanding of the concept. The teacher presents and explains concepts in a coherent and interesting way by involving students in using examples, anecdotes, and activities to illustrate the concepts.

A third conception of social studies teaching and learning actively engages students in developing important social studies ideas on their own, identifying and using them in the real world. The emphasis in *idea formation* is on activities involving students with interpreting and constructing representations of what they read, observe, and try out. Students decide what to investigate and the methods to use. Students are encouraged, in a safe setting, to challenge their previously learned ideas. Students integrate this information with their prior knowledge, making changes or replacing old ideas as needed and appropriate. Teachers guide student learning and monitor student behaviors, ideas, and interpretations. New alternative ideas are attempted by applying them and by providing new evidence and situations, allowing the student to choose the appropriate new idea (National Council for the Social Studies, 1994b).

Effective social studies teaching through idea attainment or idea formation changes traditional student and teacher roles. No longer is the teacher just an information giver, motivating students to memorize concepts as understood by the teacher or text. Students actively participate in the learning process using exploration, testing their prior knowledge, and applying ideas in a variety of situations. Teachers help students learn, reducing their role as the knowledge authority. The activities of learning and the processes for helping others learn fall along a *continuum of instruction*. One end is the giving and acceptance of information to be learned; the other end is the search for learning and the puzzle of putting together data to create new meaning. People engage in all types of learning.

In planning for maximum learning, teachers identify the important social studies content to be learned and the amount of time and energy that can be devoted to its learning tasks. The more effective the teacher's planning is, the more likely the greatest number of students will learn. In the remainder of this chapter, you learn about some teaching strategies that can be used in social studies to help students attain specific objectives. Each is grouped and presented according to the amount of teacher and student control over the lesson and is linked to the phases of the learning cycle in which it is most appropriately used. You may recall that some phases of the learning cycle emphasize students having greater control over their learning than do other phases. Keep in mind that the teacher, in planning and selecting materials for use in the lesson, controls the range of possible student actions and discoveries. These teacher decisions are crucial to successfully teaching powerful and meaningful social studies. Figures 6.1 and 6.2 illustrate the relationships between types of activities and the behaviors of teachers and students.

MATCHING INSTRUCTIONAL STRATEGIES TO STUDENT NEEDS

One aim of education is to help students be self-directing (National Council for Social Studies, 1994a, pp. 11–12). A key factor varying with different instructional activities is the amount of student control during the learning process. The amount of control students have over their social studies learning activities is an important factor to consider when selecting an instructional strategy. Instructional activities for teaching social studies can be grouped into three categories of instructional methods based on the amount of student control. In order from least to greatest student control, the categories are expository, guided discovery, and inquiry and problem

Lesson Strategies or Models

Expository - - - - - - - - - - - - -Guided Discovery - - - - - - - - - - - - -Inquiry/problem solving and
decision making

Control over Lesson

Teacher control - - - - - - - - - - -Mixture of both - - - - - - - - - - - - -Student control

Student Behaviors

Receiving - - - - - - - - - - - - - -Mixed -Open inquiry

Intellectual Tasks

Memorize - - - - - - - - - - - - -Test and confirm or reject - - - - - - -Find meaning and act

F I G U R E   6 . 1   Parallels in Learning and Instructional Continuums

	Instructional Method		
	Expository	*Guided Discovery*	*Inquiry/Problem Solving and Decision Making*
Learning Outcome			
Content Goals	Facts ⟶	Concepts ⟶	Generalizations
Inquiry Skills	Low level ⟶ (use a ruler to measure)	Mid level ⟶ (predicting)	High level (investigating)
Affective Goals	Attending ⟶	Responding ⟶	Valuing

F I G U R E   6 . 2   Matching Learning Outcomes to Instructional Methods

solving/decision making (see Figure 6.1). These categories are described in detail in the next sections to demonstrate the range of social studies instructional methods. Teachers choose an appropriate instructional strategy that matches the student's level of social studies content, skill, attitudinal objectives, and developmental needs. Each instructional method is particularly effective and appropriate in helping students attain a particular level of learning objective.

Expository, or Direct, Instructional Methods

Expository instructional methods, or direct instruction, provide students with little control over the direction or extent of the learning process. Lesson activities using expository methods include the following characteristics:

- The teacher controls the situation, providing adequate directions and motivation.
- The teacher provides ample opportunities to practice the skill in a wide variety of situations.

- The teacher supplies immediate and continuous feedback focusing on correct answers.
- The teacher uses lecture and closed, narrow questions to control the learning situation but must provide extensive and adequate directions for the student.

Expository methods require external motivation and careful classroom management. These methods produce only lower levels of learning: recall and memorization. The usual result of lecturing or viewing a video or a computer-based tutorial is factual knowledge by rote memory. Expository methods facilitate development of the affective areas of attending and willingness to receive information. These methods are occasionally useful in the lesson development phase of the learning cycle in which the teacher explains the key idea of the lesson and the lesson focus involves the need for recall. The companion website contains guidelines for giving an effective lecture or presentation.

**COMPANION
WEBSITE**

Guided Discovery Instructional Methods

When using guided discovery instructional methods, students are involved in activities related to a concept and form an understanding of them before they are offered or explained by the teacher (Stefanich, 1992). The teacher creates a problem to investigate and determines procedures and materials needed, but students collect and analyze data and evaluate the results as they relate to the problem. The companion website gives more description of guided discovery. Guided discovery has five characteristics.

**COMPANION
WEBSITE**

1. Students are provided with the time and opportunity to study relationships in data and form a new idea.
2. Students use an activity focusing on one concept, generalization, value, or skill.
3. Students are involved in multiple activities illustrating the concept, generalization, value, or skill.
4. Students' main role is to investigate and discover answers to the questions posed, discussing and displaying data to do so.
5. The teacher provides directions and asks questions that help students begin activities with the learning resources selected.

An example of a guided discovery method is an activity helping students develop the concept of law by examining two different city laws: no spitting on the sidewalk and no playing checkers in public, as they appear in the city code in 1902, 1932, and 1962. The students look for patterns, then discuss what they find. For example, students may find that the law forbids spitting in 1902 is revised to allow spitting "on downtown concrete sidewalks" in 1932 and disappears from the city code by 1962. A number of discovery activities involving the concept occur: interviews with city officials, a health department official, and members of the historical society and research using city records to determine where sidewalks were found during each year that was studied. Students can learn inquiry skills such as inferring, predicting, organizing, interpreting, and drawing conclusions from data.

Inquiry and Problem-Solving/Decision-Making Instructional Methods

COMPANION
WEBSITE

The third social studies instructional method, inquiry, involves significant student control over the direction the lesson takes. Students create a problem to investigate, determine procedures and materials needed, collect and analyze data, and evaluate results. More description of inquiry is found on the companion website. These lessons have five characteristics:

1. Students are competent in basic social studies inquiry skills.
2. Students select problem areas to investigate.
3. Students work in groups, orally reporting the results of investigations.
4. The teacher guides students in defining the problem to investigate and in helping to identify resources.
5. A safe and supportive classroom environment is maintained.

Inquiry method activities are intrinsically motivating because students direct their own learning. Even a first-grader is likely to use higher thought processes during an inquiry than with other methods. A young student's social studies project, for example, could involve making a drawing showing where items in her personal materials basket (scissors, glue stick, crayons, etc.) should be placed. The drawing is made after the student lists three or more problems with the basket, such as the glue stick always falling over. The student asks questions, communicates information, makes inferences, and builds predictions. In writing stories about the experience, facts may form the basic content of the narrative, but students also often make inferences and construct generalizations.

Students involved in inquiry and problem-solving/decision-making method activities practice the full range of inquiry skills. Careful selection of key social studies ideas and skills is needed because inquiry methods reduce the amount of material covered to a greater extent than other instructional methods. However, meaningful learning of generalizations and higher-order inquiry skills, as well as improved long-term memory and transfer of learning, occur. Inquiry focuses on problem solving and decision making. It is important to bring students into contact with other people's various views and conflicting values. Therefore, inquiry problems are most often those found in the school and local community. Students plan how they can participate and work together (Dunfee, 1977; Dunfee & Sagl, 1967; Heacock, 1990).

COMPANION
WEBSITE

Teachers also use instructional methods that fall between expository and guided discovery methods to verify students' knowledge and communication abilities. At other times, teachers use methods lying between guided discovery and inquiry to discover relationships. Further description of the verification and discovery methods is provided at the companion website.

MATCHING TYPES OF INSTRUCTIONAL ACTIVITIES TO EACH PHASE OF THE LESSON

Teachers of powerful social studies instruction select teaching strategies that match the desired learning outcome and the needs of each phase of the lesson. The learning cycle provides a framework for lessons using multiple teaching strategies. As you read the classroom scene below, identify each phase of the learning cycle and note the various teaching strategies employed.

A Classroom Scene: One Teacher's Planning Decisions

Mrs. Cooper noticed that *scarcity,* the most fundamental economic concept, is identified for first-graders in the social studies standards of her school district. Because scarcity is a situation that affects everyone, including the very young, Mrs. Cooper wanted her lesson to help the students understand the concept and find solutions to a situation of scarcity.

Mrs. Cooper's first-graders do not have strong reading skills, but she wanted to incorporate the learning of problem-solving skills, so Mrs. Cooper selected the guided discovery model. In a structured exploration activity, she engaged students in making a thank-you card for school cafeteria workers. She suggested that a thank-you card should look happy. The students had previously said that yellow was a "happy color." She reminded them of their idea that yellow is a happy color, suggesting that every group might use some yellow on their card. However, Mrs. Cooper only had one piece of bright yellow paper. She introduced the concept of scarcity by asking, "How can each group have some yellow paper to decorate the card?" Students made a number of suggestions during a discussion in which they agreed on an idea that best solved their problem. After making their choice, the children started making their cards with their yellow paper and with a set of materials that included lots of other colored paper but not enough scissors and bottles of glue for all groups to use.

When the cards were completed, each group displayed their card, and the class noted how they had used the words *thank you* and the yellow paper. Then Mrs. Cooper asked whether any problems were encountered in completing the task, particularly with the use of scissors and glue. During the discussion, students identified the lack of enough scissors and bottles of glue. Mrs. Cooper asked students to tell her how they solved this scarcity problem, recording their solutions on a chart. Then she asked whether students noticed other times in the classroom or at home when there was not enough of something.

The children gave many examples, and Mrs. Cooper noted that everyone faces the problems of scarcity from time to time. She said, "When not enough of an item is available for you to use at a particular time and place, then there is a scarcity of the item." The children repeated the word *scarcity* and reviewed what was scarce when they made their cards. Mrs. Cooper read aloud the suggestions for solving problems of scarcity on the chart and asked, "What title should we give the chart?" and "Where should we post the chart so everyone can see it?" She encouraged the children to use the word *scarcity* in the title. The chart was posted so it could be used again when another situation of scarcity was encountered.

Later, when the students were using manipulatives in math, they discovered another situation of scarcity. They recalled, with Mrs. Cooper, how they had previously solved such a problem. Mrs. Cooper read the list and asked the students whether they could use one of these ideas to solve their problem or whether some new ideas could be added to the list. The students selected and used one of the ideas to solve the problem. The reuse of the chart during the mathematics lesson and throughout the week served as an expansion activity. As the week went on, the children became better at identifying situations of scarcity. They suggested additional ways to solve problems of scarcity, adding them to the chart. Mrs. Cooper found that her need to intervene in social problems involving scarcity decreased and that, if she reminded the students that a situation was one of scarcity, the children wanted to solve the problem for themselves rather than have her give them a solution. ■

TIME FOR REFLECTION: WHAT DO YOU THINK?

1. From the evidence offered in the description of Mrs. Cooper's teaching of scarcity, why would you say that she was or was not successful in teaching the concept to her students in a meaningful way? _____

_____

_____

2. In addition to learning the concept of scarcity, what other cognitive and affective objectives did Mrs. Cooper have for the lesson? _____

_____

_____

3. In what ways did Mrs. Cooper control the lesson? _____

_____

_____

4. In what ways did the students control what happened during the lesson? _____

_____

_____

5. What are some possible negative actions from students that might have controlled the lesson development? _____

_____

_____

6. How do you think Mrs. Cooper would have responded to the possible student actions? _____

_____

_____

The learning cycles throughout this book illustrate a wide range of instructional strategies, providing examples of how to combine various strategies discussed in this chapter.

Useful Instructional Activities for the Exploratory Introduction Phase

A sample of successful teaching methods for the exploratory introduction phase of a lesson is described next. These are sequenced from low to high student control.

Review. During review students recall related concepts and generalizations studied previously and relate them to the new idea that is developed in the current lesson. This strategy is often used in the exploratory introduction phase of a lesson, although it may be used in other parts of the lesson as preparation for the next activity.

Structured Exploration. Structured exploration of a concept, attitude, or generalization to be developed can occur at the beginning of the lesson. An open key question introduces the lesson and helps organize students' experiences. In the classroom scene above Mrs. Cooper might have asked, "What might happen when not enough materials are available for each person in a group to do a project?" She may then have had students predict what they thought would happen and try it. Next, students could predict what would happen when a third person was added and try that. Students should describe what is happening in each activity.

Cooperative Group Challenge. In a cooperative group challenge, a teacher describes what he is going to do and asks students to predict what happens next. For example, two students act out the beginning of a historical event but stop before it is finished. The class considers what happens next. Divide students into cooperative groups based on their answers and ask each group to provide evidence for its answer. Then provide each group with information about the event and ask students to test their predictions.

Confrontational Challenges or Discrepant Events. Confrontational challenges, or discrepant events, confront students' conceptions of the way the world works. Characteristics of these challenges include the following:

1. Students encounter a familiar experience in which they have an expectation of the next likely events but find the experience turns out differently than expected.
2. An inconsistency is introduced in one of several ways: through a silent presentation in which two people act out an event without speaking, having the event operating as students enter the room (for example, students enter to find two close friends arguing), cueing the students verbally, or using films or pictures that present an unexpected situation.
3. Students engage in discussion or manipulation of materials related to the inconsistent experience in an attempt to clarify their ideas.
4. Students inquire into all the discrepancies, even those they had not expected.
5. The teacher provides information only when requested, and only information that cannot be obtained through the students' own inquiry process.

For example, students are shown pictures of a man and a woman. They hear a description of one person's accomplishments, including that the person is a boxer and volunteer firefighter. Most likely, they select the large man's picture, after which they learn that the boxer and volunteer firefighter is the woman.

Problem Exploration. In a problem exploration, a teacher presents students with an open-ended problem and has them attempt to find a solution. Students might receive a map of a zoo showing drawings of animals, trees, restrooms, benches, picnic tables, waste cans, and snack machines. They are told that the city has received a gift of land next to the park that doubles its size. There is money to add pairs of moose, kangaroo, elephants, seals, and penguins. The number of tables in the picnic area will double. The zoo needs a new map, and the students have been asked to make the map. But the city wants the size of the map to remain the same 8½ by 11 inches as the present map. Groups of students work to make a new map for the zoo.

Open Exploration. Students explore an unstructured environment in response to an open key question. On a field trip to a tall building, for example, students observe the movement of people and goods in the community, then describe what they see and why this happens.

Useful Instructional Activities for the Lesson Development Phase

The second phase in the learning cycle, lesson development, explains a new concept or skill, leading students to perform and practice new skills and content. Instructional strategies ranging across a continuum from expository through inquiry-based problem solving and decision making can be used.

Field Trips. Field trips of short or long duration should be a common event. These activities include everything from a trip to the school playground to make observations of how people safely use playground equipment to a trip to a historic farm. Field trips require more advance planning than do classroom activities. Teachers visit the site to determine the potential for learning and possible problem situations. Complete planning for a field trip, particularly when it requires transportation elsewhere, is thoroughly described on this book's companion website.

CW
COMPANION
WEBSITE

Field trips have objectives similar to classroom-based activities. Depending on lesson objectives, the degree of student control of activities at the site varies. Practice or skill attainment is involved when the objective is fact acquisition or lower-level skills. Guided discovery is involved when the objective is construction of a concept or skill through an activity. Inquiry is involved when the objective is student discovery of a concept, generalization, or skill through an investigation the student structures.

Guest Speakers. A guest speaker is usually welcomed with great interest. Whatever the speaker's focus, the teacher carefully prepares both speaker and students for the visit. Students often spend some time studying the speaker's topic prior to the visit. Guidelines for using a guest speaker in the classroom are found on this book's companion website.

CW
COMPANION
WEBSITE

The objectives of the speaker's visit, how the students are prepared for the visit, what occurs during the visit, how the visit is expanded upon, and how it is evaluated must be identified in the lesson plan. Without a lesson plan, the visit is likely to be interesting, but it might not relate well to the specific social studies content.

Demonstration. A demonstration involves the use of real objects, physical analogies, or models to illustrate a concept, generalization, skill, attitude, or behavior. Students look for a particular event or one student performs the activity for others. A

A field trip offers this student a unique opportunity to operate bellows once used by a nineteenth-century blacksmith.

teacher may use a demonstration to teach students how to find directions with a compass or how to introduce oneself to a person about to be interviewed. A short film clip may be appropriate for demonstrating skills. Some demonstrations provide students with information they use in a follow-up activity. Younger students need concrete demonstrations. Any or all of the following criteria can be the deciding factor for using a demonstration:

- Limited availability of equipment
- Long-term phenomena
- Difficult or complex task
- Mixed developmental level of the students

Teachers can provide students with varying degrees of involvement by using different methods of presentation for demonstrations. When the teacher performs the demonstration, students have the least control over learning. A teacher might have students direct her by telling her what actions to take or students might perform the tasks as the teacher directs them. Allowing students to perform the demonstration for themselves provides the most student control.

Lecture or Teacher Presentation. Some lecture or teacher presentation is possible in the elementary and middle school. First-grade students should be exposed to a presentation of no more than 10 minutes if it is relevant to something they are studying and generates enthusiasm. Middle school students can attend to longer presentations. *PowerPoint* presentations are often illustrated lectures or presentations that may hold students' attention.

Games. Games are used during the lesson development phase or the expansion phase of a lesson. They provide an opportunity for students to practice both academic and social skills. Small-group games offer opportunities for players to interact directly, focusing on the educational content. Teachers in upper elementary and middle school classes may prefer to use whole-class games and model them on television game shows. Students help to prepare the game by writing questions and performing leadership tasks in such games. Competition among students and teams may undo the benefits such games offer, so teachers should be alert to such potential results.

Participation in answering questions can be increased by forming teams and requiring all team members to agree to an answer, or by having each team member write the answer on a piece of paper. One or two response sheets are randomly drawn, and a point is awarded for each correct answer.

Games must have a winner so that they come to an end. Teachers can reduce the amount of emphasis placed on winning, but for many students, the possibility of being a winner is part of the motivation for playing a game. However, keep in mind that a student's cultural background and experiences may focus not on individual wins but on contributing to the group's success. Games require following rules. Details and

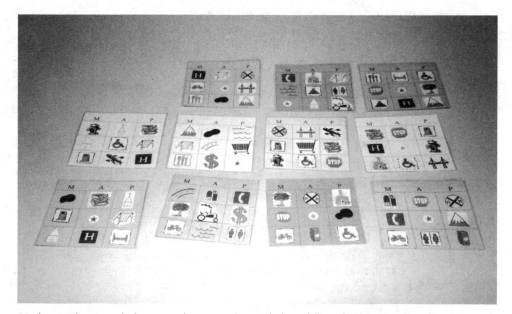

Teacher-made games help nonreaders recognize symbols, a skill used in map reading.

COMPANION
WEBSITE

guidelines for making small-group games to use with your own students can be found at this book's companion website.

Role Playing and Simulations. Both role playing and simulations provide opportunities to learn content, use critical thinking, make decisions, and practice social and communication skills. They also give students opportunities to hypothesize, test, revise, and retest their ideas. In role playing and simulations, students prepare for future experiences in a nonthreatening environment and receive help in developing sensitivity and tolerance for others. Done individually, role plays tend more to examine value and social issues, whereas simulations tend to stress content and cognitive skills. Simulations also incorporate role playing, adding to their interest and complexity.

Role Playing. Role playing examines interpersonal relationships and social behavior. Students become conscious of their values when they have to express and criticize the views and behavior of the characters in the role play. Young students role play situations with which they are familiar, such as selecting team members or telling the truth. Older students may confront familiar problems or explore real problems faced by historical figures to learn how the problem can be solved. Role playing is carefully taught. The teacher maintains a supportive class environment and is sensitive to the various personalities of the students. All students, including listeners, are actively involved in role playing. The teacher draws out all students. Role playing carries the risk of displaying emotions that might cause embarrassment or lead to criticism or ridicule. If the teacher takes time to develop a class atmosphere in which students respect individual differences and feelings, such problems are avoided.

A well-designed role playing lesson typically has eight parts. A *warm-up* makes students aware of the general type of problem and introduces the specific role play to be considered. Student understanding is checked with specific questions about the various characters and their views. Predictions of possible actions help to identify alternatives.

Selection of participants considers students' personalities, their cultural experiences, and the content goal of the role play. Different groups may replay the scene or subsequent scenes. More mature students should not be first to act out a scene because their choices might eliminate the consideration of alternatives and their consequences (Shaftel & Shaftel, 1982).

Setting of the stage occurs when the players come to a general agreement on the content to be portrayed in a scene but not its outcome—for example, "The scene is a conversation between a student and parent just after the parent has been called by the principal. The principal has said that the student cheated on a test."

The *listeners* in the audience are prepared for their role, receiving suggestions about what to listen for. The goal is to keep them intellectually involved in the role play, preparing them to take part in the discussion that follows. Different members of the audience may be assigned specific tasks, for example, observing a character's responses.

The actual *role play is introduced* by establishing who are the participants and when and where the action takes place. An introduction may state: "Mary is the mother who has just heard from the principal about her son cheating on a test. Tom is the son who enters the house through a door over there and sees his mother."

Following the enactment, the teacher leads a *discussion* investigating the realism portrayed by the roles. The characters' words and actions are evaluated. A discussion of alternative responses that could have been made by the characters and the consequences of those responses dominates this section.

A *reenactment* of the role play follows. Students portray different interpretations by the characters, so a new set of alternatives and consequences are examined. Additional scenes in the drama may also need to be portrayed. Different groups of students may act out these scenes to increase participation.

To bring *closure,* the teacher and students examine how representative is the problem they enacted. They may draw some generalizations about the ways people respond when facing a problem. During this time students may share similar problems with which they are familiar. A teacher never prods students into revealing personal problems that might cause embarrassment. Teachers remember that they are not trained counselors. Therefore, teachers ask appropriate questions:

Have you ever heard of someone having a similar problem?
Was the outcome realistic?
What were important comments or actions that led to this outcome?
What might have been said or done to change the outcome?
Can you imagine a situation in which a similar problem might take place?

The question "Have you ever personally experienced this type of problem?" is not appropriate (Shaftel & Shaftel, 1982).

Simulations. Simulations are activities similar to a real-world situation or problem, simplified for use in a short time period. Students perform tasks or assume roles and act out a problem situation. Participants are provided with descriptions of their tasks, roles, and the problem situation. Very young students might take part in assembling paper masks on a simulated assembly line or in a simulated early American school day. Older students might take part in a simulated Nigerian marketplace, court of law, or stock market investment.

Teachers can construct simulations, locate them in resources such as ERIC, or purchase them from special publishers. Many computer programs and Internet websites are examples of simulations. Computer software and Internet simulations usually provide interesting graphics and keep track of student progress. Students apply their knowledge and skills as they solve the simulation problem. Sophisticated simulations may last for several days or weeks and present additional problems for the players to solve as the simulation progresses. The teacher prepares the materials, introduces the simulation, and conducts the final debriefing discussion.

When they begin the simulation, students have all materials ready to use and clearly understand the problem and issues. Roles are assigned with care. Ideally, roles are equal in the amount of time and work needed for preparation. Simulation materials provide each student with a detailed written description of his or her role, including talents, concerns, and viewpoints about the topic.

When the teacher is certain that the problem and roles are clearly understood, the simulation begins. When the problem is solved, the simulation is completed. Debriefing of the simulation requires students not only to recall events, but also to reflect on their consequences and importance to the solution. Debriefing questions follow:

> How realistic was the simulation?
>
> Did the participants perform their roles realistically?
>
> Are the participants happy with the outcome? What could have been done differently to increase their satisfaction?
>
> What additional knowledge might help them better perform the simulation?
>
> What are other possible outcomes for the simulation had different views prevailed?
>
> What did we learn that might help us understand other similar problems?

A simulation has some element of competition. The teacher, however, stresses the goal of solving the problem in a realistic manner. The objective of a simulation is that the students learn through the process, including the debriefing, not that they get the "right" or "best" solution to the simulation problem. If grades are given in connection with a simulation, they should be assessed after the completion of the simulation and the debriefing discussion.

Teachers might choose to repeat the same simulation after students have studied the topic with the expectation that students create a more sophisticated and complex solution in the expansion phase. However, a short simulation experience cannot provide students with an adequate understanding or emphatic experiences for complex historical events such as the Holocaust or the slave trade (Totten, 2000). If a simulation is used for a complex cognitive and affective event, it may be best to reserve it for the exploration phase so research and study on the issues and values of the real event can be undertaken during the lesson development phase.

Discussion Strategies. Discussion entails verbally sharing ideas with the goal of improving one's thinking on a topic (Parker, 2001a). Students share ideas, reasons, facts, and questions. Powerful discussions involve higher-order thinking. Students who take part in successful discussions come to the situation with a set of skills they have learned and are willing to use, and some knowledge about the topic to be discussed. The knowledge may come from real-life experiences or be acquired indirectly through printed media. The teacher has four roles in discussions (Eggen & Kauchak, 2001; Parker, 2001b). First, teachers create a focal point for the discussion that attracts and maintains students' thinking by framing a question or problem of interest to students.

Second, teachers orient students to their role by giving clear directions for the specific tasks facing them. For example, a teacher might inform students that a homeless student living in a nearby shelter will become part of the class tomorrow and ask them, in pairs, to identify ways in which they can help the student maintain his school materials and be a successful partner in projects while respecting the difficulties of his situation. Next, the teacher uses small-group discussions in which each group focuses on a specific strategy that can be used to help the new student become a partner in the classroom. Finally, the whole group meets to share specific strategies discussed in small groups and plan how these will be implemented over the next week. The teacher might provide students with a discussion guide that presents a topic and asks them to perform certain tasks in keeping with the skills required for discussion of the topic (see Table 6.2).

TABLE 6.2

Discussion Guide: What Is This Artifact?

Before you examine the artifact, recall the rules for group discussions and decide on procedures you can use to help the group reach a conclusion.

- Listen to others and ask questions so you know what every other person in your group thinks.
- Give everyone a fair chance to express their ideas.
- Discuss what the group can do if you don't have the same idea at first.
- Discuss what the group should do if you can't all agree on an idea after talking about everybody's ideas for a while.

Each member of your group should examine your group's artifact carefully. When everyone has had a chance to examine the artifact, discuss and complete the following instructions.

1. Give the artifact a name.
2. Describe what you think the artifact is used for.
3. Describe what you think the artifact is made of.
4. Describe how you would make the artifact.

Third, teachers facilitate interaction during the discussion by the kinds of tasks they provide (for example, starting with discussion among pairs, moving to small groups, and then to a whole group). Teachers also facilitate interaction through using open-ended questions such as Why? How? and In what ways? Teachers foster willingness to participate by personally modeling skills and by recognizing students' efforts in the discussion. To do this, teachers clarify students' comments: "We don't have the facts to make a conclusion or know whether this idea is accurate or realistic" or "Carol is right, you must make an inference to make this conclusion." Arranging seats so that students have eye contact with one another and easily hear each other promotes the interchange of ideas.

Teachers teach skills for discussion and have students practice them, including the following:

- Listening to others
- Asking questions to draw out or clarify the ideas of others
- Paraphrasing the views of others
- Identifying areas of agreement or disagreement

Fourth, teachers keep the discussion focused and on track. They use focusing questions such as "How does that relate to our question?" Teachers also summarize and review at critical points. Throughout, teachers work hard to keep from dominating the discussion.

The biggest problem with discussions arises when a teacher cannot allow students to develop ownership of them (Eggen & Kauchak, 2001, p. 98). To give students ownership, teachers must sit back, take a less active role, and let student leadership develop. Teachers cannot, however, let discussion flounder but must provide sensitive direction that maintains students' central, active role. When some students dominate the discussion, teachers steer it by calling on a wide sample of students with comments such as "Let's hear another point of view from ___" and "We haven't heard from ____ yet. What do you think?"

Another alternative is to use small-group discussion in which everyone participates followed by whole-group discussion so that all students feel as though they have something to contribute. When the whole class is involved in a discussion, they are usually working toward the construction of a concept, generalization, value, or other portion of social studies content. This occurs during the lesson development phase. Small-group discussions are often used during the exploration but may follow during the expansion when students take the knowledge or skill they have constructed and consider its application elsewhere. They may try it out in a new situation and discuss how well it worked.

A discussion needs closure so that students feel their efforts have produced something. Teachers can ask students to create a summary of major points made in the discussion or to indicate their agreement to a consensus by a show of hands. Because discussions do not always lead to similar conclusions, teachers address this point at the end of the discussion noting that "Different people have different ideas about our question. That's okay. What is important is to know what you think and why." The teacher emphasizes that the purpose of discussion is not necessarily agreement but the honest exchange of ideas and opinions.

Writing in Social Studies. Writing can be utilized in many ways to create powerful social studies learning (Sunal, Powell, McClelland, et al., 2000). Writing helps to process information to examine what point of view exists and to determine how much the information explains about an event, idea, or value. The steps of the writing process are often incorporated: prewriting, drafting, revising, editing, and sharing/publishing to organize facts and express conclusions and beliefs.

An "I used to be . . . , but now" poem or paragraph is one example of using writing to create meaningful social studies (Sunal, Powell, McClelland, et al., 2000). Students take a look backward at their own lives and the way they used to be. Initially, as a prewriting activity, the teacher asks students to bring in and share photographs of themselves at different ages and also favorite toys from different ages. The teacher follows up with questions: How have you changed since you were little? and How have you stayed the same?

Another prewriting activity has each student complete a then/now chart on any number of topics. For example, the following chart considers the topic of emotions:

	Then	Now
Emotions	looked up to older brother	my older brother is a pain
	afraid of the dark—needed a light in the hallway	don't need a light any more

Next, students begin drafting a poem or paragraph using their then/now chart. The teacher may read the beginning of a piece she has partially drafted from her own then/now chart. Students put aside their drafts for a couple of days, then revise them focusing on their ideas rather than on mechanics. When satisfied with their ideas, they move to the editing stage in which they consider issues of form and correct grammar, spelling, and punctuation. Finally, students share their writing in a read-aloud from the classroom author's chair.

Students are helped to structure their writing in social studies using four sections: aim or purpose of the investigation, method or how it was carried out, results, conclusions, and action plan. Students can be told what type of information to write in each section and how it can be written. Table 6.3 shows how all these parts are related. The writing process can be used in creating the report of an investigation. Other social studies activities include creating a comparison and contrast chart, composing a photo essay, and developing a survey. As teachers reflect on social studies and writing, they should become aware of the many opportunities to use writing to organize and reflect on social studies content and citizenship values and actions.

MAKING A LITERATURE CONNECTION

Reading Literature

Only high-quality trade books that are appropriate for social studies should be selected for use in a unit. To maximize their use, trade books are carefully selected for small-group, whole-group, and teacher read-alouds. Trade books are used to support or introduce attitudes

TABLE 6.3

Guide for Writing Up a Social Studies Investigation

Heading	What to Write	How to Write It
State Problem, Aim, or Purpose	What do you think you were trying to find out in this investigation?	Write a short, single-sentence statement that begins "To find out...."
Method	Describe, in your own words, exactly what we did.	1. Write numbered statements. 2. Use the word *we* instead of *I*. 3. Use past tense: *was* and *were,* and so on.
Findings	What did you discover?	Write a few sentences about what you discovered. Illustrate with two or three examples of supporting evidence. Include a table, chart, or timeline showing the results.
Conclusions	What did you discover in this investigation?	Write a few sentences explaining what you found out.
Action Plan	What can or should people do to tell others about the situation and start to improve it?	Write one or two sentences about how people can use this information.

and values. It is important for teachers to read the books they select and to consider both their content and the attitudes and values that can be affected by reading the book. The selection of trade books must accurately represent differing perspectives. A trade book does not replace other sources used in social studies but is a support. Student self-selection of books to read from those identified by the teacher is a way to expand an individual's learning. Reading provides the student with information and viewpoints on issues, people, and events.

Carefully guiding students in reading textbooks and factual books is important because the styles of writing are different from a fictional story. Students need to identify the facts that illustrate ideas and recognize the conclusions made by the author. Help needs to be given to students in reading the words on maps and charts because writing on such items does not follow the same sentence construction as in the books they are familiar with reading. Indeed, some of the writing may be headings, which are not constructed in complete sentences. When reading documents, students also may encounter these same unusual ways of stating information.

➤ BUILDING ON DIVERSITY

Prereading Activities

Prereading activities can involve students in making their own responses to literature that bring their cultural experiences into the social studies classroom.

Going Home by Eve Bunting, illustrated by David Diaz, is a picture book about a farm-worker family who takes a car trip to visit relatives in La Perla, Mexico. This book can be used with many unit topics, for example, a study of continuity and change. A teacher may have students create a contrast chart before reading the book. After reading, students revisit their charts, commenting on what they now think to add.

Contrast Chart for *Going Home*

Good Things about Moving	Bad Things about Moving

An anticipation guide is another form of prereading activity useful in social studies for getting students to explore their attitudes, opinions, and beliefs (Wiesendanger, 1985). After reading *Going Home,* students tell why they responded as they did during the initial discussion. Does their response come from direct experience, what they have read or seen, or what they have heard others say? A partial anticipation guide for *Going Home* follows (Sunal, Powell, & McClelland, 2000, p. 255):

Anticipation Guide for *Going Home*

Agree	Disagree	
_____	_____	Most people who leave Mexico to live in the United States do this to make more money.
_____	_____	Farm workers have a hard life.

➤

➤ Journaling is used to find out what students think about a book. The double-entry journal encourages students to select meaningful quotes (Barone, 1990). The quote is written in a column on the left side of the page. The reader writes on the right side, across from the quote, his or her reaction to what the author wrote. An example of a double-entry journal for *Going Home* follows (Sunal et al., 2000, p. 255):

Double-Entry Journal for *Going Home*

Quote	**Response**
"Mama looks so young and beautiful and Papa . . . so handsome. She has forgotten about her sore shoulders," I say. "And he's forgotten about his *bad knees,*" Dolores adds.	Mama and Papa seem like they were young. Like when they met before they were married. It's like they are going back in time.

Venn diagrams and book charts help students compare two different texts. Students might read and compare *Going Home* with Allen Say's book *Grandfather's Journey* about the Japanese American narrator's grandfather and his move to the United States from Japan. An example of a book chart follows (Sunal et al., 2000, p. 256):

Book Chart

Title	**Author**	**Narrator**	**Lessons Learned**
Going Home	Eve Bunting	Carlos	Moving can be both good and bad. People miss where they were born.
Grandfather's Journey	Allen Say	grandson	War creates big changes. Moving can be both good and bad.

Many nonfiction reading materials, as well as informational books, can be used to create powerful social studies. These include student magazines, such as *Cobblestone,* and magazines written for a general audience, such as *National Geographic.* As with the examples provided for fiction, many prereading, reading, and postreading strategies can be used. Some of the strategies that work well with nonfiction follow (Sunal et al., 2000, p. 257):

Prereading	**Reading**	**Postreading**
anticipation guide	double-entry journal	Venn diagram
contrast chart	directed reading/thinking activity	book chart
K-W-L	note taking	summarizing
questionnaire	webbing of information	response journal

Difficulties in Reading Textbooks. Textbooks often define the social studies curriculum and the units within it. Many social studies textbooks contain lots of pictures, illustrations, maps, and graphs. Teacher guides suggest activities to help introduce and expand on the text presentation. Still, many students have difficulty reading social studies textbooks. Their difficulties often stem from a lack of experiential background and the complex social studies content in the textbook. Students who have little experience outside their neighborhood or local community may find it hard to be interested in learning about faraway places. Students who have little sense of personal or family history may find it difficult to relate to historical settings (Hoge, 1986).

Social studies textbooks tend to have a heavy load of technical concepts and generalizations. Technical concepts are specialized ideas in social studies, such as interdependence and political party. Technical concepts are related to each other to form generalizations, for example, the economies of countries in today's world are interdependent on each other. Most students have an incomplete and inaccurate understanding of these concepts. Many social studies textbooks pile too many concepts and generalizations into a few paragraphs without enough supporting examples and with little discussion.

Textbooks are made more complex because they include hard-to-pronounce names of cities, faraway countries, and foreign words. References to long periods of time and huge distances are frequent. What does a 10-year-old student think when a textbook says, "Our country was founded over two hundred years ago" or "long, long ago"? What do expressions such as "far to the north" or "over a thousand miles to the east" mean to students who are not sure which direction is which and have never traveled further than across the state (Hoge, 1986, p. 1)?

Doing a Content Analysis of a Textbook. Teachers carry out a content analysis of their school curriculum guide and think about what they intend to teach. When they have identified a unit they plan to teach, they examine a copy of the textbook to see whether it contains relevant material. Next, teachers analyze the unit in a student edition of the text before reading the teacher's guide. Many teachers use textbooks as resources for students. Often, textbooks from different publishers are used. When textbooks are used as a resource, they support a unit but do not directly determine its content.

TIME FOR REFLECTION: WHAT DO YOU THINK?

Try a textbook unit content analysis now. Using a student copy of a social studies textbook, choose one unit and ask yourself the following questions.

- What should be learned from reading this unit?
- What is most important here?
- What are the most important facts presented?
- What are the most important concepts presented?
- For which of these concepts can students currently give an example?
- Which concepts are likely to be completely new to students?
- What inquiry skills are presented or required?
- What attitudes are evident?
- What values are incorporated?
- Which words will students have difficulty pronouncing?
- Do the objectives match those in the state or local curriculum guide?
- Which national social studies standards are addressed?

The content analysis procedure in this Time for Reflection activity is also useful in carrying out a content analysis of a curriculum guide, a prepared unit, and other teaching material. A content analysis helps teachers identify the most important skills, facts, concepts, generalizations, attitudes, and values in the textbook unit. If these match what the teacher intends to teach, the textbook provides good support.

Developing a Teaching Plan Using a Textbook. Once the content of a textbook unit has been analyzed and the most important inquiry skills, facts, concepts, generalizations, attitudes, and values identified, the teacher develops a teaching plan. The teaching plan sets up learning cycles for the important material identified. If students can learn important material, the teacher relegates other material to the more cursory treatment of reading about it in the textbook. It is critical to identify what is most important and implement learning cycles to teach it. The textbook, or a portion of it, can be used in the learning cycle but is best used during the lesson development phase.

A new teacher may have difficulty accomplishing effective teaching because of the demands of many subject areas. New teachers usually cannot develop more than one or two complete, well-elaborated units in each subject area during the first year of teaching. Therefore, a new teacher identifies the one or two most important social studies units in the textbook and develops a teaching plan using learning cycles for those units. During the following year, the teacher can add one or two more units to his or her repertoire.

Usually, the teacher's guide has suggestions for activities to support the textbook. However, these often do not match the social studies content. They may also try to integrate other content areas and, consequently, include literature and math problems that align with literature and math skills for that grade level. Often, this approach is not appropriate for the social studies content under consideration. As a result, the social studies skills students need to learn are neglected (Alleman & Brophy, 1996).

When reading the textbook, students use a variety of strategies to help them with text material. Study guides help students identify important facts, concepts, and generalizations. In cooperative groups, students can each read passages and share their study-guide responses. Struggling readers can be grouped with more proficient readers so difficulties that arise in a particular passage, such as pronouncing a word or understanding a sentence, can be quickly overcome by seeking help from another group member. Passages can be tape recorded by the teacher, an adult volunteer, or an older student for students having difficulty reading certain passages.

Social Studies Kits. Social studies teaching materials can be purchased as individual items or as kits designed for a specific topic of study, such as ancient civilizations or mapping. Kits contain materials used to conduct activities that fit the yearlong social studies plan. Most kits are supplemented with a teacher's guide and multimedia support materials. Some kits contain several other materials, such as large pictures, posters, models, artifacts, or both informational and fiction books.

Professional educational publishing houses, museums, government agencies, industries, and special interest groups all produce materials for classroom use. Often, they hire education specialists to work with them to produce professional-looking learning materials. Such materials may be free or inexpensive, but are always considered "sponsored" (Haas, 1985). Many sponsored materials are appropriate for classroom use, but they may express the viewpoint of the producer or sponsor. Sponsored materials are not subjected to the reviews and pressures that commercial educational publishers face. They are rarely reviewed by state or local adoption committees. When teachers decide to use materials that have not been screened for overall appropriateness by official adoption committees, they have the additional responsibilities of examining the methods used to present the sponsor's message and of evaluating the potential impact that message may have on students.

Teachers must judge whether commercially prepared kits and units match the curriculum and abilities of the students. Without such a match, even a high-quality kit makes only a limited contribution to meaningful learning. Additional criteria for judging social studies kits and units are important:

- How accurate is the information presented?
- Is the material in the kit illustrative of the diverse nature of the society?
- Do the materials present multiple viewpoints in an unbiased manner?

Visual Information and Literacy. Television, computer screens, signs, symbols, books, magazines, movies, photographs, and even body language provide visual messages, so, when these are combined with the words we read (which are also visual messages), about 85 percent of all messages we receive are visual (Doblin, 1980). Few people are visually literate enough to get full value from social studies pictures and illustrations (Benjamin, 2001). Although we live in a visual age, we do not always teach students to successfully read both a complex diagram and a photograph, although each of these requires different skills. Educational materials today compete for student attention in a highly visual environment.

Social studies visuals include realistic drawings, photographs, abstract diagrams, graphs, charts, tables, flowcharts, maps, line drawings, pictures, and symbols. In textbooks, there are three typical problems with illustrations. First, the written text conflicts with the illustration. Second, the illustrations are too simple, so they do not adequately support the level of the text. Third, the illustrations are too complex, so students do not take the time needed to examine and learn from them.

Teachers need to ask this question when using any visual: "What is its purpose?" The visual could be to gain attention, trying to keep the viewer interested. It could be explanatory, trying to assist comprehension by clarifying the text. Or it could be to assist in recall. *Maps* as visual images are discussed in Chapter 11.

Charts, graphs, and *tables* are used frequently in social studies. An example in history is data describing the amounts of something (bridges, voters, soldiers, warships, deaths from smallpox) at a specific time in the past. Usually, these amounts are being compared (for example, the number of soldiers compared to the number of warships needed for troop transport). Or changes are traced in the amounts over time (for example, the number of warships in 1840, 1940, and 2004).

In Figure 6.3, reading across the chart allows you to trace changes in the number of soldiers in a region following changes in 100-year intervals. You can note the change by region and also the rate of change. For example, there was slow change in North America until the 100 years following 1850. Reading down the

Number of Soldiers by Region

Region	Year			
	1650	1750	1850	1950
Europe	10,000	14,000	25,000	30,000
North America	20	500	2,500	57,000
Latin America	1,200	1,400	2,800	25,000
Africa	10,000	8,000	12,000	15,000
Asia	33,000	48,000	35,000	35,000

F I G U R E   6 . 3   Chart of Soldiers by World Region

chart, you can examine the number of soldiers in each region during the same time period. In North and Latin America in 1650, there were few soldiers compared to the numbers in 1950.

More complex comparisons can be made by reading down and combining the information with that gained by reading across (Benjamin, 2001). Thus, you will find that the number of soldiers in Africa did not vary greatly over the time periods, while those in North America showed great change. Information in a table can be presented differently to highlight various aspects of the data. For example, the data in Figure 6.3 could be presented as percentages of the total world's soldiers in each region, which would make it easier to compare regions.

Another way of representing data is by using graphs. Bar and line graphs make differences more obvious and comparisons easier but are less precise and require more space to convey the same information as a table (Benjamin, 2001).

Drawings, artwork, video, and *photographs* can be more difficult sources for gathering information than they may at first seem to be. You need to do more than look at them (Benjamin, 2001). First, you need to recognize the actual information they present, such as what Columbus's ships looked like or how Hiroshima appeared after the atomic bomb explosion. Then you need to interpret them by trying to understand what the artist or photographer is saying in the work. Artists do not just record a visual image, they make choices about which part of an event they focus on and how much emphasis they give that portion. Artists are sending a message to anyone who looks at their work. Interpreting visual material requires knowledge about the subject matter, the artist, the style, and the context in which it appeared. Like written descriptions, art does not simply speak for itself. There are different and controversial interpretations of some images such as those of a public demonstration against the Vietnam War in 1970. But not all images are controversial. A photograph of the main street in your great-grandparents' small home town decades ago might tell you that while horse-drawn vehicles were common, there were a few motorcars in town. You might also find that the sidewalks were filled with people, while today few people are seen on the sidewalks because they now shop at a mall on the outskirts of town. There is a wealth of information about life at the time in such a town that requires interpretation and is not controversial.

Resources for visual literacy on the Internet are found at the end of this chapter.

Learning Centers. Learning centers provide students practice in making choices. Students choose which activities they do at the center and evaluate their own progress. Giving students the opportunity to choose their own activities allows them to select how they most want to learn. This selection process contributes to students discovering their best way to learn while building their self-esteem.

The availability of space plays an important role in the physical appearance of a learning center. In a cramped area, the learning center might be confined to a single box while students return to their desks to work on each activity. In other settings, learning centers might be large bulletin boards or sections of the room divided into cubicles for different types of activities.

The objectives of social studies learning centers vary widely. They may involve either gaining knowledge, developing skills, or examining attitudes and values, or incorporate two or more objectives. Learning center objectives have common characteristics:

- Clearly established learning objectives
- Self-checking and self-evaluating procedures for individual activities
- Progress charts or records for each student

This learning center could address knowledge, skill, or attitudinal objectives.

- Multiple activities to accommodate various learning styles
- Student choice among the methods of accomplishing specific objectives
- Enrichment materials for both remedial and advanced study needs

Inquiry Invitation. An inquiry invitation helps focus students' attention on higher-level inquiry skills such as selecting variables, data interpretation, and data analysis. Students are presented with data for a given problem or situation; the students do not gather or collect the data because it is a time-consuming process. An inquiry invitation is a good task for cooperative learning groups. This strategy provides students with experience in later stages of the inquiry process where they tend to be weakest. Three examples of inquiry invitations follow:

1. Bringing in a copy of a newspaper article about a particular event—a major earthquake in the United States
2. Providing a table of data—the number of rainy days per month in a specific location
3. Showing a picture or diagram of an event—the movement of troops in the Battle of Lexington during the American Revolutionary War

Weekly inquiry invitations providing details from current event news reports, pictures, or video clips motivate students' interest in the news and in places and people throughout the world. Open questions accompany the data: "What does this mean to you?" or "What happened here?" Students do not have to provide, or even attempt, a "correct" answer, but they are expected to apply logical and critical thinking as they work. Periodic use of the inquiry invitation not only helps students practice their skills, but also provides teachers with an authentic assessment exercise they can use to document student progress in developing higher-order skills. Additional discussion of general considerations teachers should be aware of as they select instructional activities for use during lesson development are found on this book's companion website.

COMPANION
WEBSITE

Closure Statement. A closure statement summarizes and defines the main idea, value, or skill taught during the lesson development in a learning cycle. It enables students to hear how others have developed their ideas during instruction. The teacher assesses students' construction of the idea, skill, or value being developed. Closure is required and usually an oral activity, but this may be done through writing or illustrations that are shared with classmates.

Useful Instructional Activities for the Expansion Phase

In the expansion phase, students apply the new concept, generalization, attitude, and/or skill to additional examples. Without many widely varied applications, the meaning of the idea remains restricted to the examples used during its development in the lesson. Teachers should select two or more different types of expansion activities for each learning cycle. Some suggestions follow, but others are possible.

- Using the lesson idea in new situations or with technology
- An inquiry invitation involving an application of the idea
- Applying ideas on a field trip

- Games and role playing involving an application of the idea
- Art, music, science, or mathematics activities using the new idea
- Confrontational challenge either returning students to the event they attempted early in the lesson, or one that is new, using a different context
- Investigating a problem involving an application of an idea

A final lesson summary completes expansion activities, ending the lesson. It is accomplished in one or more ways. Students discuss a sample problem that relates to, and reviews, the objectives of the lesson. The students or teacher provide a review of the lesson events. The teacher provides a short question-and-answer review. The teacher leads students into a discussion of the lesson events with a question, such as, What have we found out about . . . ?

Powerful Instructional Procedures: An Overview

A summary of powerful instructional procedures promoting meaningful learning not usually found in traditional classrooms follows.

1. Group students heterogeneously and encourage peer interactions throughout.
2. Call attention to discrepancies or create confrontational challenges where students consider multiple perspectives or interpretations of the same event or idea, if necessary.
3. Ask students to explain or justify their conclusions, predictions, and inferences, and whether they are accurate, rather than accepting a simple answer.
4. Propose discrepant observations, unsatisfactory hypotheses, or incorrect conclusions, and challenge students to evaluate them.
5. Introduce new terms during the lesson development phase by using concrete examples, a demonstration, or an activity; without experience from the exploratory introduction and without appropriate activities in the development of the concept, the new term will be forgotten.

CLASSROOM MANAGEMENT STRATEGIES FOR POWERFUL SOCIAL STUDIES

Students use materials and are involved in a great number of student-to-student interactions in meaningful social studies activities. Students have more movement about the room, more questions, and more control of their own learning. General classroom management guidelines designed for a social studies program facilitate students constructing meaningful knowledge. These guidelines include advanced planning, giving directions, distributing materials, creating an organized beginning, grouping students, using classroom rules, creating lesson smoothness, and being a facilitator (see Table 6.4).

Advanced Planning

Lesson planning is critical to effective classroom management and high student achievement. An effective teacher tries activities that students must perform in the

TABLE 6.4

Classroom Management Techniques for Powerful Social Studies Teaching

- Locate materials where they are to be used.
- Prepare the lesson plan and materials ahead of time.
- Provide an overview to students before beginning.
- Give directions first before having students get materials.
- Plan materials distribution.
- Assign students to work in small groups.
- Direct students' energy toward the lesson objectives.
- Conduct smooth lessons.
- Post schedules.
- Reduce confusion.
- Serve as a guide.
- Ask broad, open questions.

classroom *before* they are used. Problem points are evaluated, and modifications are made if difficulties occur. Preparation eliminates delays that cause frustration.

Giving Directions

Before students receive materials, they are given directions on how the materials are to be used. The directions do not have to be specific or step by step. They can include a statement such as "You will be receiving a box of materials. When you get your box, make observations of each object in the box and group them. Write your observations on the sheet provided." This approach introduces a focus for the activity. Providing instructions while students are already involved in activities with materials is usually not effective because they are too busy to listen. Call students' attention to the directions before they start activities and refer students to the written directions when they ask, "What should I do?"

Distributing Materials

Distribution of materials to students can be the single most difficult part of a materials-rich social studies lesson. It is important to set up stations and place materials in easily accessible locations. This eliminates confusion and reduces the time students need to obtain materials. Appointing social studies helpers to distribute social studies resources is an effective technique. One role for cooperative groups is the resource manager, who collects, organizes, and returns instructional resources.

Distribution methods based on restaurant and home distribution of food at mealtime are a good analogy for planning materials distribution in classrooms. Social studies materials can be distributed *family style*. Designate a table or row of students as a group. A student distributes a set of materials to each group. Students in the group redistribute the materials among themselves. *Waiter/waitress style* involves identifying a student from each group to come up and collect a set of materials to be used by the whole group. The student delivers items to each individual member of the group or the whole tray to the group as a single set. In a *cafeteria-style* approach, one student from each team proceeds through a line in which items to be used by the team are picked up. *Food court style* involves students going to different locations in the room to pick up needed materials. *Home style when dinner guests are late* involves distributing materials to student group locations before the lesson begins.

When making a decision about materials distribution, consider the following factors: time, amount of student involvement, amount of teacher time, and efficiency/smoothness. Reducing the amount of time is the most important factor. A distribution method that increases student involvement is preferable because it provides additional time for students to become aware of the materials and to understand how to use them, increasing their learning. The method that most reduces the involvement of the teacher provides more time to work with individual groups or monitor the classroom. The distribution method that gets the materials to the students quickly reduces class disruption. The importance of an individual factor depends greatly on classroom context. Factors to take into account include students' ages, number of materials to be distributed, type of materials, and amount of potential mess that could be caused during the distribution process.

Organized Beginning

When all materials are ready to be distributed and students are ready for the social studies lesson to begin, it is important to provide an introduction or overview to the lesson. This introduction provides students with an expectation of what is to come next and a focus for relating the events of the activity. Most introductions do not tell students the expected outcomes of the activities or the specific lesson objectives if doing so takes the excitement out of learning.

Grouping Students

Before beginning the lesson activities, students are grouped for cooperative learning. Not only do cooperative learning groups provide effective learning, but also they are useful in organizing the classroom for the distribution and return of materials. Groups should be given names or numbers and assigned work spaces.

Using Classroom Rules

Effective classroom management in powerful social studies requires that all classroom rules are taught and modeled. Posting daily and weekly classroom schedules and a student helper list is important. During the beginning of the lesson, teachers monitor and redirect the behavior of students who are not on task. Getting students involved in the learning task quickly enables teachers to identify topics that motivate students to remain engaged. Nonverbal communication is best when possible. If necessary, ask misdirected students to describe their task and to demonstrate responsibility. Refer to written directions if needed. When further redirection is required, discuss quietly the effects of the present behavior if continued, as well as the positive effects on fellow classmates of the requested behavior if observed.

Lesson Smoothness

Students stay on task when teachers provide smooth, evenly paced, relevant lessons. Teachers are aware of the various ways the flow of learning can be disrupted or enhanced. Lesson confusion is handled by appropriate lesson planning. Clearly knowing the sequence of activities, having all materials ready, and anticipating management problems creates a smoother lesson. Specific classroom management practices used during the teacher-guided part of the lesson can increase the smoothness and pacing of a social studies lesson:

- Completing instruction on the original idea before switching to a new idea
- Staying with an instructional activity
- Announcing only ideas or information relevant to the activity
- Avoiding disruption by overattention to minor student misbehavior (Kounin, 1970)

Being a Facilitator

Teachers help students having difficulty and monitor the progress of individuals and groups during student activities. The teacher moves from group to group around the class, asking mostly open-ended questions to help focus or redirect student learning: What evidence do you have for making that statement? Why did you say that? Why have you been doing that? In small groups, students usually feel freer to ask questions or provide explanations that may not be well thought out. It is important to create an atmosphere in which students are willing to try out new ideas and explanations without fear of embarrassment. The teacher's role during the student activity part of the lesson is one of facilitator and helper.

SUMMARY

Powerful social studies teaching involves knowing general procedures for effective teaching and learning, using a repertoire of social studies content-related teaching and learning methods, having adequate social studies content knowledge organized in a meaningful way, and knowing where and how social studies information can be obtained when it is needed. Although state and national organizations provide guidelines, the teacher has the responsibility of creating the social studies program. Having a basic set of criteria facilitates decision making. Teachers need to consider the amount of control given to students in various instructional strategies and where in the lesson a strategy can be used.

Expanding ON THIS CHAPTER

Activity

COMPANION WEBSITE

1. Identify two teacher actions from Table 6.4 that you have used, or seen used, in teaching a lesson. Explain how these helped or hindered the quality of the lesson.
2. Select one strategy you would like to use in the next social studies lesson you plan. Explain when you will use the strategy in the lesson and why.

Recommended Websites to Visit

COMPANION WEBSITE

21st Century Literacies Visual Literacy
www.kn.pacbell.com/wired/21stcent/visual.html
This website provides a general definition of visual literacy as well as lessons, worksheets, and further references. Links are also available for the study of media, information, and multicultural literacies.

Multimedia and Visual Literacy
www.mcps.k12.md.us/departments/isa/secondary_team/agendas/vis_lit_2_01/visual_literacy.htm
This website is a link to a workshop from the Montgomery County, Maryland, Division of Technology Training. It contains links for visual literacy definitions, activities, web resources, materials, clip art, virtual field trips, copyright, and several other resources related to visual literacy.

Media Literacy Webography
www.oneidany.org/media/literacy.htm
This site is dedicated to evaluating the information we receive. It includes the following helpful links: *What is media literacy?, How can we evaluate media?, What are some tips and things to watch for to help us be critical analyzers?, Special Link for Elementary Students, Links for Secondary Teachers, Sites for Library Media Specialists.*

ERIC Digests
www.ericfacility.net/ericdigests/index/
Presents thousands of articles, essays, and teaching ideas on a multitude of education topics, including diversity issues.

NOVA Online Teachers Site
http://pbs.org/wgbh/nova/teachers

Virtual Jamestown
http://jefferson.village.virginia.edu/vcdh/jamestown/

Geography Action! website
www.nationalgeographic.com/geographyaction

CHAPTER 7

Helping Students Relate to Individuals and Communities

INTRODUCTION

People's words and actions reveal the thought processes, beliefs, and values motivating their behaviors. Behaviors seen daily by teachers include impulsive or aggressive actions, acceptance of others, sharing responsibilities, thoughtful planning, shyness, confusion, conforming, and prejudicial or stereotypical responses. Read the classroom scenarios below and identify the belief or value expressed by the behaviors.

1. The teacher said, "I like how Betty is sitting straight and tall with her hands in her lap." Immediately, Charles and Elana folded their hands and sat as tall as they could. _____

   _____

2. Students view a civil rights video depicting a scene of Bloody Sunday at the Selma, Alabama, bridge. Mike says, "How could people turn fire hoses and dogs on people?" "Don't you know?" Jesse replies, "Police always beat you up."

   _____

3. After an art activity, the teacher notices that not all the supplies have been returned to the materials table and asks, "Where is the other pair of scissors and bottle of glue?" Sushila responds, "Our materials manager is absent, and we forgot we needed to put the supplies back." _____

   _____

➤

➤ 4. Write your own scenario in which a child expresses confusion, aggression, or impulsivity. _____

_____

_____

_____

5. Think about the behaviors you want children to exhibit in your classroom and in the community. Describe one way that teaching social studies can encourage and help children increase their performance of prosocial behaviors and reduce or eliminate those behaviors that hinder or destroy individuals, families, and communities. _____

_____

_____

_____

CHAPTER OVERVIEW

Within social studies, psychology focuses on understanding and accepting our individuality whereas sociology helps us understand our social nature and the groups formed within our communities, nation, and world. Research in psychology helps teachers assist students in developing positive self-image and self-confidence, better accepting and understanding themselves, and learning to accept and relate to others. This understanding enables us to live with others as social beings (Pagano, 1978). Developing the attitudes and values integral to each person's personality supports goals for individual and social development. The National Council for the Social Studies Standard IV, *Individual Development and Identity,* Standard V, *Individuals, Groups, and Institutions,* and Standard X, *Civic Ideals and Practice,* emphasize the importance of developing each person individually and socially as members of groups that contribute to communities, nations, and the world (1994b).

Social studies programs work to develop civic-minded citizens. In doing so, both teachers and the curriculum confront individual selfish behavior, lack of experiences, and misinformation that contributes wrongly to classifying and stereotyping others. Developing attitudes and values that support responsible citizenship entails education that promotes the development of both character and ethical behavior. Character education refers to helping students build a set of values and attitudes enabling them to be responsible, active citizens. Ethical behavior refers to helping students make decisions to behave in ways reflecting a system of ethics focused on what is best for all people.

Various aspects of psychology, sociology, and values education are controversial. The disagreements revolve around what to teach and how to teach it. Controversy can be expected in a democratic society because such a society encourages a variety of opinions. This chapter describes research and teaching practice related to psychology, sociology, and values education. Where controversy exists, a variety of viewpoints are presented. Consider them all and remain open to new information and viewpoints in the future as well.

CHAPTER OBJECTIVES

1. Explain how the classroom environment, curriculum, and instructional activities indicate the level of respect teachers and students have for each other.
2. Analyze classroom events in terms of the presence or development of values.
3. Describe social factors that affect the development of self-concept and teachers' ability to work positively with students from various social environments.
4. Identify three aspects of morality.
5. Describe theories of moral development.
6. Identify two means by which teachers can facilitate students' moral behavior.
7. Compare the goals and procedures of values clarification, value analysis, and teaching a specific value.
8. Explain the purpose of character education and its relationship to the social studies curriculum.
9. Explain why values and character education strategies are sometimes controversial.
10. Explain how values are present in the school and its curriculum.

RESPECT FOR STUDENTS AND FOR ONESELF AS A TEACHER

When exploring students' conceptions and understandings of the idea of hero, Steven White and Joseph O'Brien (1999) found that students identify with those people who demonstrate moral excellence, not with those who achieve prominence through displays of glitz and glamour that appeal, however superficially and temporarily, to society. As students mature, they move from exercising moral excellence in single events to actions sustained over a period of time. Teachers who create an environment of respect and encouragement help to promote such moral behaviors.

The Classroom Environment

Students sense, with their first step into a classroom, how much a teacher respects them. Room arrangements and instructional procedures suggest whether the teacher will encourage informal, frequent communication among students and between students and the teacher. The expectation for student discussion and cooperation is created by arranging the classroom into areas where small groups work together. Such an arrangement encourages students to demonstrate the ability and desire to exercise control over both their behavior and their learning. Within this environment, teachers view themselves as learners enthusiastically exploring new ideas and information along with students.

A teacher's respect for students does not mean that they should always be expected to know what has been taught nor that they should be penalized for making mistakes. When reading through the learning cycle in Table 7.1, note teacher behaviors that encourage students to grow in confidence and respect for each other as they work with the concepts of sharing and negotiation. The teacher uses an activity related to a holiday as a vehicle for setting up a dilemma students have to work through. Also note how discussion is used to encourage reflection and to draw out implications for how to better work together while appreciating individual differences and wants.

TIME FOR REFLECTION: WHAT DO YOU THINK?

1. How could student independence be fostered during the lesson development phase in the lesson in Table 7.1? _____

2. What teacher actions in Table 7.1 indicate that the teacher respects students? _____

3. What is a sample statement third-graders might make to define sharing? _____

4. What important characteristic do students need to add to their definition of negotiation to differentiate it from sharing? _____

5. How would you change the lesson plan if, during the making of the mailboxes, several students began arguing or became upset over the behaviors of others and complained to you or quit making their mailboxes? _____

Curriculum

Acceptance of, and respect for, students is communicated through the curriculum and the strategies used to teach it. The communication is evidenced through positive actions:

- Students have some responsibility for actively contributing.
- Discussions demonstrate a respect for students and diverse opinions.
- Students have a responsibility to make decisions relating to the lessons.

TABLE 7.1

Learning Cycle	Sharing and Negotiation

Grade Level: Primary
NCSS Standards: Individual Development and Identity, Production, Distribution, and Consumption

NCSS

Exploratory Introduction

Materials: For each pair of students, two shoe boxes; one pair of scissors; one glue bottle and glue stick; 10 sheets each of red, pink, and white construction paper; one large, red, lacy paper heart; a set of marking pens; five small valentine stickers; one vial of glitter—all per each pair of students; one response sheet per student; one checklist per student; one observation sheet per observer

Objectives	Procedures	Assessments
Students construct a Valentine's Day mailbox using only materials supplied by the teacher.	The teacher divides students into pairs and tells them they will be making a project. One pair of students acts as observers/reporters while the others work. The teacher asks for volunteers for this job. The teacher provides pairs of students with only the materials listed for use, and has all other supplies put away. The teacher tells students they are to make mailboxes to be used on Valentine's Day for collecting valentines. They must use only the supplies they are given to decorate their box. The teacher points out that there are not enough supplies for each student to use at one time. The teacher asks students: "What are some ways you can share some of your materials?" The teacher hears suggestions from several students and asks students to begin working on their boxes. The teacher shows the observers how to use the checklist sheets.	Students complete mailbox using only materials given them

Lesson Development

Objectives	Procedures	Assessments
Students identify problems they encountered in making the mailboxes.	When all have completed their mailboxes, the teacher asks: "Were you able to complete the mailbox in the way you wanted? Is anyone unhappy with the way their mailbox looks?" The teacher asks the observers: "Did you observe anyone who looked unhappy while making the box? Describe what you observed." The teacher asks the class: "Did you and your partner have any additional problems in completing your mailboxes with the materials	Students share their feelings and problems. Observers share their observations and others give evidences of listening to those observations.

continued

T A B L E   7 . 1

Continued

	you were given? What does sharing mean to you? Were you able to get equal amounts per person of all the supplies? Why? How? What are some behaviors, or ways you need to act, when you are sharing?"	Students identify behaviors indicative of sharing and identify behaviors that are nonexamples.
Students list ways to solve a problem of scarcity.	The teacher talks with students about scarcity, focusing on when there is not enough of something that is needed. The teacher asks: "What were some examples of scarcity when you made your Valentine mailboxes? In what other school events or home events have you experienced scarcity?" The teacher asks: "How do people solve problems of scarcity? Raise your hand if you thought sharing in the mailbox project was easy." The teacher discusses their responses, asking: "Why? Why not?"	Students provide appropriate examples of scarcity in the mailbox-making activity and in other events.
Students identify behaviors needed in sharing.	The teacher asks: "What are some suggestions for behaviors to use when sharing?" The teacher records student responses on board or chart.	Students identify appropriate behaviors.
Students define sharing as dividing things equally or, if not exactly the same, dividing them in a way those sharing think is equal.	The teacher asks: "From the ideas we put on our list, how can we define sharing so that we can write a definition of it? Does everything have to be equally divided? What happens if two people have three things to divide? Is it sharing if one person takes two of the items and the other gets only one? How can that be fair?"	Students decide that "fair" is not always an equal division of everything in sharing.
Students describe examples of negotiation.	The teacher explains how sometimes people decide that one person might get more of something and the other person gets more of something else that they want. I have heard students say: "I'll give you the purple marker if you will let me have the orange and yellow markers." They agree to do this. The teacher asks: "Who has heard something like I described? Do you know what this is called?" It is called negotiation, or making a deal. The decision is made and agreed to before the people get what they want.	Students share examples of negotiation.

TABLE 7.1

Continued

Students describe how negotiation and sharing can solve a problem of scarcity of materials and satisfy everyone.	Negotiating is a different way to solve the problem of scarcity, but it doesn't work unless people agree to the way things will be distributed. The teacher asks: "Why are sharing and negotiating worth taking the time to do?" Record answers in a list.	Students include in their description the characteristics of jointly talking over what their problem is and deciding that each person has equal access to materials or they decide beforehand what is a fair way to share.
	Closure: The teacher asks: "What title should we give this list of reasons?" Title it appropriately.	

Expansion

Materials: Materials to decorate covers of work folders, with some scarcity present in certain colors of paper; glue and scissors, for each pair of students.

Objectives	Procedures	Assessments
Students apply sharing and negotiation in solving a new problem involving scarcity.	The teacher gives pairs of students materials to decorate the covers of folders for their work, making sure that some materials are scarce.	Students offer appropriate explanations of how they solved problems of scarcity in the assignment.
	The teacher explains that some of the supplies are scarce and suggests that they recall the discussion of sharing and negotiation. The teacher encourages them to use the strategies previously discussed in the new task.	
	When the assignment is completed, the teacher asks: "Who used sharing in the task? Who used negotiation for supplies? Are you satisfied with the way your folders look? Where in the room can we post our ideas of sharing and negotiation behaviors so that we will remember to use them in the future?" The teacher posts a chart where students suggest and calls attention to it at other times throughout the year.	
Students appropriately illustrate and write about their individually created examples of sharing and negotiating.	The teacher has students draw a picture of two people sharing or negotiating and has them write a sentence or two describing the situation and solution they are describing.	Students present accurate descriptions and drawings demonstrating examples of sharing and negotiating.
	Lesson Summary: The teacher asks the students to briefly review the lesson activities and to identify the two important ideas with which they worked.	

continued

T A B L E 7 . 1

Continued

Checklist

Pair number: _____   Observer: _____

Observe the pair of workers once every 5 minutes, and record in a sentence or two the way they are behaving and working.

Observation 1   Time: _____

_____

_____

_____

Observation 2   Time: _____

_____

_____

_____

Observation 3   Time: _____

_____

_____

_____

Observation 4   Time: _____

_____

_____

_____

Observation 5   Time: _____

_____

_____

_____

TABLE 7.1

Continued

Response Sheet

Name: _____

What was the main problem you had in using the materials you were given? _____

_____

_____

_____

What was one way you used to solve this problem? _____

_____

_____

_____

What does sharing mean? _____

_____

_____

_____

How can sharing and negotiation help to solve the problem you had with the mailbox materials?

_____

_____

_____

- Family members are regularly involved in the curriculum and in lessons providing information or artifacts, in discussing ideas as part of homework assignments, and in visiting the classroom to examine students' presentations or to make guest presentations.
- Community members and public employees are requested to provide information and to help make connections between classroom studies and community experiences.
- Family members and volunteers, including older students, tutor or provide help for special activities, for field days or trips, and to photograph or record class activities (Alleman & Brophy, 1998; Sunal, 1986).

Consider the following example. Courtney's father came to class with digital photos of his childhood home in Tennessee. He showed a photo of a panel in the kitchen that could be opened to reveal log walls of what was originally a cabin. Later, these walls had been covered over with wood planks, and the cabin was expanded into a large farmhouse. He also told them some traditional Appalachian Mountain ghost stories.

Involving family members in the curriculum incorporates the student's culture and lays a foundation for a powerful social studies program for all students. As students experience a wider range of cultures, they are likely to overcome some of their prejudices. A curriculum that provides students with opportunities to examine interpersonal problems arising in the classroom and community (as demonstrated in the lesson in Table 7.1) promotes individual and civic development.

AREAS AFFECTING THE DEVELOPMENT OF SELF-CONCEPT

An individual's self-concept is the complex product of all life's experiences (Christensen & Dahle, 1998). It is affected by the cultures of the home and school. During the elementary and middle school years, students develop a sense of independence; they learn to cope with feelings of jealousy, fear, and aggression; and they form friendships (Kostelnik, Stein, Whiren, & Soderman, 1998). Each of these social areas seems to be universal across cultures, although they may be expressed differently in various societies (Ekman & Davidson, 1994).

Independence and Responsibility

Elementary and middle school students act independently but at times depend on adults (Sears, 1963). As they develop cognitively and socially, students become better able to plan solutions to problems and to understand the social environment. As a result, they are more and more able to act independently. Becoming ever more independent and responsible is part of maturation and an expectation in human societies. Students usually try to be independent when they find an opportunity to do so. Teachers usually reward positive attempts to be independent. When time is short, many teachers do not value student independence enough to provide the extra time needed for independent planning and decision making. Sometimes students' attempts result in unsafe or disruptive behavior. When students' independent attempts do not work, teachers are usually expected to assist them and guide them in learning from their mistakes (Macoby & Masters, 1970). But when help is given too quickly, it reinforces dependency, frustration, and sometimes aggression or withdrawal.

Students become independent when they are expected to be responsible (Quilty, 1975). For example, putting away materials when one is finished using them and keeping things in one's own locker both demonstrate responsibility. Expectations of responsibility are best met when accompanied with reasons. A teacher might demonstrate the benefit of being responsible by saying, "The scissors and stapler you need are on that shelf. It's nice that the last person who used them returned them to where they belong because now everyone can easily find them when they need them." Students may work responsibly on a task, but they often start, then stop and attend to

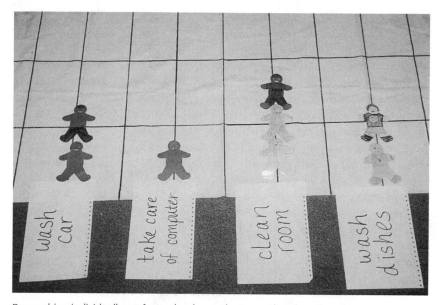

By graphing individually performed tasks, students see that they share some experiences with their classmates but not others.

something else, then return to what they were working on, and so on. Teachers should recognize and reward efforts at responsibility.

Independence and responsibility depend on one another. A student who is not expected to be responsible is not likely to be thought of as capable of independent behaviors. Students from various cultural backgrounds can be expected to display independence and responsibility differently. For example, students from Asian backgrounds often assume responsibility for tasks and carry them out well but might not be as likely to organize others to do a task unless the teacher indicates permission to do so (Scarcella, 1980). These students are demonstrating respect for the teacher in a manner they have learned through their personal cultural experiences. Teachers help students develop independence and responsibility by (1) planning carefully, (2) anticipating difficulties, (3) giving clear directions, and (4) providing outlines of suggested procedures. Expecting and encouraging responsibility and independent behavior show respect for students as individuals who are in the process of growing up.

Jealousy

Jealousy is a natural feeling that results partly from egocentrism, especially in younger students, who sometimes find it hard to accept another student being the center of attention even for a short while (Seifert & Hofnung, 2000). Reflecting on the learning cycle in Table 7.1, how much potential for jealousy is there in using this lesson's development with first-graders? With fourth-graders? As students mature, their egocentrism and the resulting occasional jealousy weaken. Even though jealousy in students is normal, it threatens their self-respect because it often means that a person is uncertain of the affection of another person in the presence of a third party.

Students express jealousy in several ways, including aggression, immature behavior, and boasting. When a student displays any of these behaviors much more frequently than is common among his or her peers, teachers may have cause for concern. Teachers who use peer behavior as their basis for comparing students' behavior recognize that some behaviors are more common among certain groups of people than among others. Teaching that encourages students to discuss concerns and analyze their behavior, as suggested in the sample learning cycle (Table 7.1), assists students in learning to cope with feelings of jealousy.

Contests resulting in winners and losers foster jealousy and reduce self-respect (French, Brownell, Graziano, & Hartup, 1977). Instead, an emphasis should be placed on each student performing as well as possible. Cooperative group efforts at completing a project are effective replacements for contests. Each student contributes personal strengths, gains in self-respect, and is less likely to be jealous of others. A closely related problem occurs when a teacher identifies one student as a model and tells others they should emulate this model. Although a teacher cannot avoid all situations that produce jealous feelings, a teacher can recognize potentially negative situations so efforts can be made to reduce their effects on students.

Students should have opportunities to examine situations whose development and outcome may have been influenced by jealousy. Both historical situations and current events provide ample opportunities for students to examine jealousy and to evaluate how people respond to jealous feelings. Teachers may ask questions to help students do so: How much did jealousy influence racist attitudes toward Jackie Robinson? Was European American control of major league baseball being jealously guarded? Do jealous feelings prevent us from logically viewing someone's success in a course we find difficult? Teachers find many opportunities to discuss portrayals of jealousy in children's literature. Were Cinderella's sisters jealous of her beauty? Was this why they were mean to her? Considering emotions such as jealousy should be a part of the social studies program at all grade levels. Students' own feelings, development of the situations in the classroom, literature, and historical and current events can all serve as a starting point for a discussion about emotions.

Fears

Fear is part of life. Fear can produce wariness, anxiety, suspicion, dread, dismay, anguish, and panic (Kostelnik et al., 1998). Students often have fears that are not reasonable. Very young children develop fears frequently between ages 2 and 5. As they mature, their ability to interpret observations and events develops; fears weaken and students become more realistic. Teachers should remember that because students' thinking processes are immature and their personal experiences are limited, students think their fears are reasonable. Students usually grow out of their fears as they mature. Adults who use threats to enforce discipline, such as telling a child to eat her food or the police officer will make her eat it, may cause children to develop fears.

Fear is often expressed so strongly that the adult cannot help but be aware of it. The best approach is to listen to the student, discuss the fear, and show sympathy for the student's feelings (Kostelnik, Whiren, Soderman, Stein, & Gregory,

2002). Although the fear cannot be talked away, the student will know that the fear has been recognized as real and upsetting. Activities in which students describe situations in which they feel fear and how they try to cope with it can be helpful. Focus on inventing strategies with the students that are successful in helping them recognize and cope with their fears.

Middle school students often develop fears related to their social situations. Students entering adolescence often fear ridicule. They worry when placed in a situation they feel has the potential for ridicule, such as making an oral presentation. Young teens may be nervous, or freeze entirely, unable to remember a word of what they want to say. The growing pressure young teens feel in social situations and the fear of ridicule cause inhibitions and anxiety.

Teachers need to help students develop confidence. Because young teens often compare themselves with the polished presentations actors create for videos and commercials, it is important to discuss the bloopers that professional actors make and to encourage students to watch a program that features such bloopers. Once they realize that professional presentations are the result of many retakes and much editing, as well as years of professional training, they may be able to set more realistic expectations for themselves and their peers. Allowing students to videotape their presentations beforehand or to use PowerPoint to revise and perfect them before presenting them helps overcome fears.

Teachers have limited ability to help reduce fears generated by personal situations. Therefore, it is important to work to reduce fears when possible but to be aware of whom to contact for assistance when a student is involved in a situation in which the teacher can provide only limited assistance or none at all. Fears that may be shared by several students should be examined. Reflect on how fearful students were during a recent weather event—a tornado warning, a severe rainstorm with lots of thunder and lightning, a blizzard. How did other students react? Are students afraid of getting caught in the middle of older adolescents shooting at each other because of an insult? How frightened are they of getting AIDS?

Aggressive Feelings and Conflict Resolution

Do you view yourself as more or less than, or about as aggressive as the average person? What situation(s) cause you to feel aggressive? Terms such as *desk rage* and *road rage* have surfaced in the news in recent years. Complaints about increased aggression in sports, even among young athletes and spectators, are of increasing concern. Other nations think that U.S. culture is so aggressive and violent that no one is safe on our streets.

Some students are consistently more or less aggressive than the average student. Their aggression is part of their personality since they are temperamentally noisy, active, and distractable with more difficulty in adjusting to changes in routine (Berk, 2000). Situations, however, also create many aggressive feelings. Some are poor social observers, finding it hard to accurately interpret others' facial expressions and words. So they do not understand that no hostility was intended and develop a history of not getting along with peers (Dodge & Crick, 1990). Some students become aggressive when frustrated. Often, positive reactions to frustration, such as sharing, cooperating, talking, and other prosocial behavior, have not been strongly reinforced in these students (Herrenkohl, Egolf, & Herrenkohl, 1997). Such students often associate with other aggressive students (Seifert & Hoffnung, 2000). Families who use erratic physical punishment often have aggressive children. These students believe the only reason not to be aggressive is to avoid getting caught and punished. Punishment often pushes them into further aggression. Aggressive models in real life and in the media teach aggressive behaviors. Some students come from cultural backgrounds that encourage higher or lower levels of aggression than are typical among most students. Most students also learn to feel guilt when they act aggressively in situations for which their society does not sanction aggression. As a result, they are more likely to avoid aggression as they get older (Seifert & Hoffnung, 2000).

One way to reduce aggression is to eliminate conditions that promote it. These include frustrating situations and aggressive media programs. Another way to reduce aggression is to teach students that aggression does not reward them, for example, by using time-out procedures. Teaching students how to resolve conflicts and interact positively with others helps. Using cooperative learning exemplifies the type of learning students need to practice if aggression is to be reduced. Finally, helping students monitor and control their own behavior is important. These strategies help students realize that less aggressive behavior results in more positive attention, affection, and approval (Seifert & Hoffnung, 2000).

Students should examine the aggression that occurs in current events. One country fights with another: Who is the aggressor? A traveler is attacked on a subway train: Who is the aggressor? Historical events can be examined in light of aggression. How did the Choctaw first react to the aggression that settlers exhibited as they appropriated the native lands and began to farm them? One major source of aggression is being unable to identify alternative solutions to conflict situations.

When children can think of just a few ways to get their point across, they tend to use some kind of attack as the fastest, surest choice (Smith, 1982). Children who come up with several choices less often use violence (Spivack, Platt, & Shure, 1976). So teachers have group discussions about possible solutions, teach assertiveness and negotiation skills, and teach conflict resolution.

Conflict resolution abilities are important for managing students' personal and interpersonal aggressive feelings. Conflict resolution refers to programs encouraging students to resolve disputes peacefully outside traditional school disciplinary procedures (Conflict Resolution Education Network, 2000, p. 27). Schools with conflict resolution programs teach, model, and incorporate the processes and problem-solving skills of mediation, negotiation, and collaboration. Fundamental to such programs is the idea that the disputing parties solve the problem themselves. Peer mediation is the most common type of conflict resolution process, having students act as neutral third parties to resolve disputes. This is most effective in middle school and to some extent in upper elementary grades. Components of conflict resolution can be used effectively with younger children. The Conflict Resolution Education Facts section of the Conflict Resolution Education Network website is a useful source of information on conflict resolution.

CW
COMPANION
WEBSITE

Conflict resolution requires specific skills: knowing how to listen, empathizing, reasoning analytically, thinking creatively, and understanding another person's viewpoint. Generally, six steps are followed:

1. Agree to meet and set ground rules.
2. Gather information about the conflict.
3. Identify what the dispute is really about.
4. Suggest possible options for resolution of the dispute.
5. Select one or more workable options.
6. Reach agreement (Conflict Resolution Education Network, 2000, p. 27).

Conflict resolution programs support school polices to prevent violence by teaching skills and processes for solving problems before they escalate into violence. Such programs help students develop personal behavior management skills, act responsibly in the school community, and accept the consequences of their own behavior. Students develop fundamental competencies, such as self-control, self-respect, empathy, and teamwork, that are necessary throughout life. Cognitive and other skills needed for academic achievement are taught. Students learn to respect others as individuals and as members of a group. Finally, students learn how to build and maintain responsible and productive intergroup relations (Conflict Resolution Education Network, 2000, p. 27).

A Special Note: Bullying. Bullies are unhappy children who likely will make poor social academic progress. Proactive strategies must be used with bullies and their victims. Teachers support victims by supporting verbal assertiveness so that they establish their desires and protect their rights. Assertiveness training reduces bullying. It helps to teach children how to appear more confident and how to interpret social cues. Finally, helping children form friendships reduces their victimization. Bullies must be told that their behavior will not be tolerated and must be taught ways to control angry impulses (e.g., talking oneself out of a quick reaction, deciphering behavioral cues that tell how someone else is feeling, and experiencing logical consequences from bullying.)

Friendship

Throughout childhood, students add to the number of acquaintances they have and develop close friendships. At different ages, students have different expectations for friends, so the character of friendship changes over the years. Students usually are closest to others who are similar in age, race, sex, interests, degree of sociability, and values (Hartup & Stevens, 1997). Through the early elementary school years, students prefer a friend who is easily accessible, has nice toys, and plays easily. Students, also prefer someone who quickly rewards attempts at friendliness (Seifert & Hoffnung, 2000). During the middle of the elementary school years, shared values become important. Beginning in middle school, students really start to care about what happens to a friend. They stress mutual understanding and closeness but still expect friends to be useful to them (Reisman & Shorr, 1978).

Students who make and keep friends are skillful at initiating interactions with their peers, maintaining ongoing interactions, and resolving interpersonal conflicts.

These skills are developed through four primary strategies that teachers can help students develop:

1. Greeting another student directly ("Hi! What's your name?")
2. Asking appropriate questions ("What's your favorite TV show?")
3. Giving information ("I like to play checkers.")
4. Trying to include the new friend in their activities ("Do you want to play tag at recess?")

Students need to know that it is important to keep trying even when rejected. Teachers should recognize that the willingness to keep trying depends on self-confidence.

Media, particularly interactive computer programs, can be aids in helping students develop skills in making and keeping friends. One example of a primary grades computer program is On the Playground, produced by Tom Snyder Productions. Designed to be used on one computer with the whole class, the program sets up a situation in which a new student has arrived and the other students must decide whether to spend their recess time getting to know the new student and involving him in their games. The program branches so that, as various choices are made, different events occur, based on students' choices. Discussion between class members is encouraged as consequences are projected, and analyses of the results of various strategies for handling the situation are encountered. Students can see how various decisions lead to different results.

Through daily classroom activities, teachers can effectively coach students in social skills that help them begin and continue satisfying friendships. Coaching involves telling or showing students how to use a specific social skill. This includes giving students opportunities to practice the skill and giving feedback with suggestions for improving the use of the skill. Among the skills that are effectively taught are asking questions, learning to give positive reinforcement to others (such as smiles), making good eye contact, and taking turns (Kostelnik et al., 2002). Once a friendship has begun, many skills can contribute to its continuation:

- Rewarding a friend by smiling at him or her
- Imitating the friend's actions
- Paying attention to the friend
- Approving of what the friend does
- Complying with the friend's wishes
- Sharing things with the friend
- Communicating well
- Being a good listener
- Giving information needed by the listener
- Judging whether your own actions have shown or not shown respect for others' rights and welfare (Hartup, Glazer, & Charlesworth, 1987)

Friendships can be examined by discussing current events and historical situations. Consider the following questions as ideas for content that can be discussed within social studies units:

At one time the United States has been both a friend and an enemy of Germany. What might be the characteristics of friendships between the leaders of these nations?

What is meant by a media report that someone got a city building contract because he was the friend of the mayor?

Does a real friendship mean you do illegal things for your friends?

Henry Ford and Thomas Edison were close friends. What was the basis for their friendship?

Self-Esteem

Self-esteem and self-concept are closely connected. If a person is pleased with his self-concept, he will have high self-esteem. Longitudinal research indicates that most students have formed a stable sense of self-esteem by the middle school years. Self-esteem appears to be related to social behavior. Students with high self-esteem participate frequently in discussions and other activities rather than simply listen passively (Coopersmith, 1967). Expressing opinions, approaching new tasks with self-confidence, resisting peer pressure, and making friends easily are thought to be the result of high self-esteem based on positive self-concept. However, high self-esteem could be the result of these positive characteristics rather than the cause of them. Teachers need to work to foster a positive self-concept in each student and to indicate respect and appreciation for each student's abilities and cultural background. Because self-esteem affects motivation and the desire to study and learn, teachers use instructional strategies and management procedures to support its formation.

MAKING A LITERATURE CONNECTION ➤

Supporting Development of Self-Respect

Literature can be used to focus discussion on social development with one student, among small groups of students, or with the whole class.

Students should have opportunities to discuss stories and historical events in which an individual deals with fear. For example, *Island of the Blue Dolphins* (O'Dell, 1960) offers opportunities to discuss the fears of a young Native American girl surviving on her own for years on a Pacific island. For very young students, a book such as *Will I Have a Friend* (Cohen, 1967) engages them in considering how others cope with fears. Reading biographies, trade books, and historical fiction provides students with safe opportunities to encounter and critically discuss the diverse fears and feelings of people throughout history.

Children's literature can also be used to explore aggression. *The Runner* (Voight, 1985) offers an opportunity to talk about aggression and conflict in a family. *A December Tale* (Sachs, 1976) focuses on child abuse. *Cider Days* (Stolz, 1978) describes conflict and aggression in school caused by racial bias.

Literature also serves as a possible starting point for discussions of the meaning of friendship. Many books discuss friendship between children and young adolescents. *Jennifer, Hecate, Macbeth, William McKinley, and Me, Elizabeth* by E. L. Konigsburg (1976) describes, for younger children, how a shy child makes friends. The actions of friends in such stories can be examined and compared to those of the students.

VALUES AND MORAL EDUCATION

Our values are an important part of our self-concept. Values are decisions about the worth of something based on a standard we set (Sunal, 1990). When an individual decides something has value, he or she decides that it is worthwhile and compares that worth to the importance and worth of other things. Something that is judged "right" is valued. Not all things of value are "moral" because their value may not be measured against the standard of "right" behavior.

Three Aspects of Morality

Morality has three aspects: (1) moral reasoning, (2) self-evaluation, and (3) conscious resistance to unacceptable thinking and behavior. Growth in moral reasoning is aided by finding that others have different moral perspectives, which may conflict with one's own perspectives (Seifert & Hoffnung, 2000). Some evidence indicates that moral judgments are multidimensional social decisions (Bandura, 1977). Moral judgments depend on synthesizing several varieties of social information to arrive at conceptions of appropriate and inappropriate behavior (Bandura, 1977).

Self-evaluation views guilt as empathic distress accompanied by the belief that you are responsible for someone else's distress (Hoffman, 1977). When children are tempted to do something they are not supposed to do, the likelihood of succumbing to temptation depends on child rearing and school experiences, understanding of the misconduct, and situational factors. When children have families and teachers who firmly and consistently insist that they learn and practice habits of self-regulation, who justify their disciplinary action with inductive reasoning, who are warm and communicative, who avoid the use of unnecessarily harsh discipline, and who are models of self-controlled behavior, they are most likely to display desirable conduct away from adults. Parents' and teachers' use of explanations and inductive reasoning helps children learn to accept responsibility for their misbehavior. In inductive reasoning, an individual becomes familiar with examples and nonexamples of something and then uses them to develop a concept or generalization. Bandura (1977) suggests that children develop personal standards of appropriate conduct and that they learn to guide their behavior by rewarding and punishing themselves for attaining or falling short of goals they have set for themselves.

Children who think of themselves as internally motivated to behave morally, who pride themselves on good behavior, who anticipate blaming themselves for misbehaving and know how to talk themselves out of misbehaving, and who know how to avoid thinking about forbidden activities are better able to resist temptations than are children lacking these qualities. At a time when nobody else is nearby, a student might, for example, notice, on the desk of another student, a brightly colored, fancy new pencil that is considered the latest thing in pencils. This student is tempted because her mother won't buy her something just because it is a fad; she buys her only the customary yellow pencils. This student could take the pencil, hide it, and use it out of class so that nobody would know she took it. However, this student knows she would feel guilt and would not want to look the owner in the face. She understands that the guilt she would feel from this misconduct isn't worth it, so she quickly moves away from the area and puts the temptation well away from her.

Situational factors that can influence the likelihood for resisting temptation include specific aspects of the situation as well as of the individual (Kostelnik et al., 1998). A specific situation often affects a person's reaction to each aspect of morality. For example, a student might feel guilt in one setting but not in another. In addition, depending on an individual's mood, concerns, or even health, the feeling of guilt might be present in one instance but not in another even when circumstances remain the same. These individual aspects also influence how a person faces temptations.

Moral Development Theories

Jean Piaget and Lawrence Kohlberg have described moral development. Some disagreement exists about how accurately their theories predict moral development, but some implications of their theories should be considered in social studies education. Piaget found that children's conception of rules seem to occur in three stages (Ginsburg & Opper, 1979):

1. **The *Egocentric* Stage.** Children (about 4 to 7 years old) do not knowingly follow rules; they decide what is right and wrong on the basis of what adults permit or forbid them to do.
2. **The *Incipient Cooperation* Stage.** Children (about 7 to 10 or 11 years old) are more social and cooperative as they demonstrate an understanding that rules are made to help solve interpersonal conflicts.
3. **The *Real Cooperation* Stage.** Children (about 11 or 12 years old) begin to develop appropriate rules and understand why rules are needed.

Kohlberg (1969) tested individuals from a variety of cultures and economic levels, finding similarities in development. Building on Piaget's work, he outlined his ideas as follows.

1. Cognitive development is the major factor in social behavior. As cognitive development occurs, understanding of morally appropriate behavior and the reasons for that behavior also occur.
2. Cognitive and social development occur in stages. Each new stage is qualitatively different from the one that preceded it.
3. Maturational factors and the continuing restructuring of behavior through experience and maturation result in the requirement that no new stage may be achieved unless all preceding ones have been achieved.

Kohlberg developed a moral judgment scale to determine which of six stages a person is in (Table 7.2). A Stage 1 person obeys because she does not want to be punished for not obeying. A Stage 1 person might suggest, for example, that you should not steal something because you might get caught and go to jail. A Stage 4 person believes in maintaining authority and conforming to accepted law and order. He might say that no matter how good the result and no matter what the reason, stealing violates laws protecting someone else's property. A Stage 6 person has individual principles of

TABLE 7.2

Kohlberg's Stages of Moral Development

Level 1: Preconventional

Moral reasoning is related to the immediate consequences of actions and to the power of those in authority over an individual.

Stage 1   Obedience to power: "Daddy says I have to do this."
Seeking rewards and avoiding punishment: "Will Mommy send me to my room for doing this?"

Stage 2   Satisfying your own needs: "What will I get out of this?"

Level 2: Conventional

Moral reasoning begins to involve a consideration of others, especially family and peers, and a desire to maintain the existing social order.

Stage 3   Approval of others: "What would my friends think if I did this?"

Stage 4   Law and order: "Is this the best thing for my society?" "Does my society say I can do this?"

Level 3: Postconventional

Moral reasoning involves making decisions based on universal principles, not on the needs of any one person or society.

Stage 5   Good of society: "If this law isn't really good for society, it can be changed." "You should do what you feel is right even if the majority of people have democratically agreed on something else."

Stage 6   Good of all people: "Is this really the best for people in general, even though it will mean a sacrifice for me?" "My society isn't going to benefit from this, but it is the right thing to do because it will mean greater equality among all people on Earth in the long run."

Overall Characteristics

In these stages, two characteristics are evident:

1. The decisions people make through their moral reasoning move from selfish to unselfish decisions.
2. The decisions people make require them to decide what is right in a given situation. In making this decision, people may decide on the basis of selfish or unselfish reasoning, depending on the stage they are in.

conscience on which she always acts regardless of the popular norm of behavior. This person believes that stealing is usually wrong. If life depends on something that is obtainable only by stealing, however, then stealing is right, and the person who does not value life highly enough to steal what is needed to maintain it is wrong.

Kohlberg combined these stages to form three levels of moral development, each of which contains two stages. Level 1 is preconventional behavior, containing Stages 1 and 2. Level 1 reasoning is selfish, and the individual considers his own desires, not what is good for society. Level 2 is conventional behavior and contains Stages 3 and 4. Level 2 reasoning focuses on what is accepted by society and conforms to social expectations. Level 3 is postconventional behavior and contains social expectations. It contains Stages 5 and 6. Level 3 reasoning goes beyond what is considered conventional by society and focuses on what is best in principle for all people, not just your own friends and citizens of your community or nation.

Kohlberg's theory has implications for teaching. Students cannot be expected to understand adult explanations of right and wrong because they do not have the cognitive ability to do so. Students are likely to be motivated by the reward or punishment an action brings rather than by whether it is right or wrong. Students can mature and begin to understand why if explanations are given. Eventually, they develop their own set of moral standards and values. They need to know and judge others' values and actions. Students need experience requiring reflection and logical reasoning to make moral decisions. Five guidelines have been used to develop teaching materials that stimulate students' considerations of moral dilemmas.

1. Students consider genuine moral issues they encounter in life, or about which they are personally concerned, and for which there are no quick and easy choices of right behavior.
2. Students focus on moral and social conflicts experienced during the discussion of the dilemma.
3. Students practice applying their moral reasoning to new problems.
4. Students are exposed to peers who reason at the next higher stage of development.
5. Students are confronted with their own inconsistencies in reasoning and action over time by being asked to explain why they make a particular moral decision (Beyer, 1974).

Teachers supply the basic data needed in a dilemma, remain neutral, and facilitate discussion of varying viewpoints in an open, nonthreatening atmosphere. Dilemmas, often present in events occurring in the classroom, in current news stories, or in historical studies, provide many opportunities for moral discussions. Teaching moral dilemmas uses a learning cycle format similar to that used for developing generalizations. Students are confronted with the dilemma during the exploratory introduction. In the lesson development, they identify the moral problem presented by the dilemma and state tentative solutions. In discussions, they explore rationales for their positions and make judgments concerning the effectiveness of the various positions. Finally, each student selects what he or she believes to be the best solution by prescribing what the person in the dilemma should do. During the expansion, students can develop a scenario describing what happens as a result of the decisions they made, or they can consider a similar problem.

Judgment has been found to become increasingly abstract up to about age 16, indicating that Kohlberg's insistence that cognition cannot be separated from moral development is well founded (1969). Kurtines and Greif (1974) found, in their research, using Kohlberg's moral judgment scale that their subjects tended to function at two or more stages, not at one stage as Kohlberg proposed in his theory. Because moral development requires practice in making and examining moral questions, teachers should concern themselves with providing students with lesson experiences in which they actively confront moral issues.

Carol Gilligan (1982) challenged Kohlberg's view that equal justice for all is the highest moral criterion. She stated that females have a concern for care and responsibility as the highest moral criterion that is missing from Kohlberg's work. She claims that men and women have a different sense of self and identity that leads to two different views of highest moral values. Women strive to be connected and relate to others, while men strive to be separate individuals. Snarey (1985) suggests that people integrate both justice and care and that the focus might be more a result of social class than of gender—where middle-class people might strive more for individuality and justice—while lower-class people might strive more for care.

The justice orientation results in ideals of equality, reciprocity, and fairness between individuals. The care orientation results in ideals of attachment to others, loving and being loved, listening and being listened to, and responding and being responded to. Brown, Tappan, and Gilligan (1995), indicate that children experience both perspectives and learn lessons about justice and care in early childhood relationships that generate expectations that are confirmed or modified in later childhood and adolescence. These lessons result in two moral injunctions—not to treat others unfairly and not to turn away from others in need—defining two lines of moral development; providing different standards for assessing moral thoughts, feelings, and actions; and pointing to changes in the understanding of what fairness means and what constitutes care (Brown et al., 1995, p. 315). Both high moral criteria should be fostered at home and in school.

Three ways are suggested for developing care (Brown et al., 1995). First, students should be helped to consider the peculiarities of a situation and to understand others in order to develop care. Activities fostering the development of care include: writing; reading fictional and historical accounts of human lives, societies, and cultures; demonstrating through art how meaning depends on context; frequent classroom discussion; constructing and discussing meaning as we interact with text (Brown et al., 1995, p. 316). Second, students need opportunities to tell their own stories about their real-life moral experiences (Brown et al., 1995, p. 217). Interviews with the teacher or other students enable students to tell their stories to an interested listener. Journals and essay assignments focus students on the moral decisions they have made in their own lives. Teachers must be sensitive and sympathetic, providing students with the kind of response to their stories that indicates they have heard and understood them. Teachers acknowledge the author's own moral perspective and encourage the continued authorization of that perspective (Brown et al., 1995, p. 327). Third, students dramatize their own moral stories through skits, plays, or video productions. This requires sharing a story with a peer audience, which can be uncomfortable for some but provides an opportunity for students to learn important lesson from their peers' stories (Brown et al., 1995, p. 328).

Teaching Approaches in Values Education

Three approaches have played important and often controversial roles in values education in recent years: values clarification, values analysis, and character education.

COMPANION
WEBSITE

Each requires preparation and thought to be used appropriately and effectively. This book's companion website contains links to Internet sites related to each of the approaches discussed next.

Values Clarification. Values clarification is a teaching approach focusing on moral reasoning. This approach emphasizes the process of thinking about what is valued more than the specific values themselves. The values clarification approach is used to help students decide what value they personally attach to something. Teachers help students explore a value such as being trustworthy by asking thought-provoking questions: Would they keep a friend's secret when another friend is curious? Would they keep silent when the teacher is threatening to punish someone else for damaging a computer disk that they know their friend damaged but have promised not to tell?

Teachers often take advantage of events to involve students in values clarification. For example, suppose a student says, "Anybody who burns the flag or does something like that should get out of this country. Love it or leave it." The teacher responds with a series of questions that encourage the student to explore the feelings that led to this statement. The teacher tries to remain neutral and to serve as a facilitator of the student's own exploration of his feelings. In so doing, teachers help students recognize that they live in a complex society in which many different values are present and often conflict. The teacher tries to help students decide what they think is worth valuing and how great a value they place on it (Raths, Harmin, & Simon, 1978).

When values clarification questioning strategies are employed in a learning cycle lesson, the exploratory introduction presents a decision-making situation or scenario in which the students make a decision. In the lesson development phase the first six steps of the seven-step process for values clarification developed by Raths et al. (1978) are followed. Table 7.3 presents the seven steps with sample teacher questions appropriate for each step. During the expansion phase, the teacher engages students in step 7 by considering situations in which the same value as that examined in the original problem is appropriately applied or not applied. Values clarification questioning is used as a whole-class, small-group, or single-student strategy.

Values clarification exercises using paper-and-pencil responses include rank ordering alternatives, forced-choice sets of statements, and checklists. To rank order, students are given a list of statements, or items, to rank from most to least important, useful, desirable, or any of a variety of other categories. Table 7.4 is a sample exercise for ranking the qualities students think are important in a good friend. Following the individual decisions, the students discuss their rankings and reasons for the rank ordering.

Forced-choice activities have students choose between two or more choices in responding to a statement. Table 7.5 illustrates a forced-choice exercise. Nonreaders may be asked to choose between drawings of situations, or they can raise their hands to register their choice as the teacher reads the items aloud. As student choices are discussed, the teacher uses clarifying questions such as those in Table 7.3 to help the students probe the reasoning for their responses.

Table 7.6 demonstrates a checklist approach. Students are first presented with a statement, situation, or story that involves valuing. Then they check off those adjectives from a list of positive and negative adjectives that describe how they feel about

TABLE 7.3
The Values Clarification Process

1. **Choosing freely**
   "Where do you suppose you first got that idea?" or "Are you the only one among your friends who feels this way?"

2. **Choosing from alternatives**
   "What reasons do you have for your choice?" or "How long did you think about this problem before you decided?"

3. **Choosing after thoughtful consideration**
   "What would happen if this choice were implemented? If another choice was implemented?" or "What is good about this choice? What could be good about the other choices?"

4. **Prizing and being happy with the choice**
   "Are you happy about feeling this way?" or "Why is this important to you?"

5. **Prizing and willing to affirm the choice publicly**
   "Would you be willing to tell the class how you feel?" or "Should someone who feels like you stand up in public and tell people how he or she feels?"

6. **Acting on the choice**
   "What will you do about your choice? What will you do next?" or "Are you interested in joining this group of people who think the same as you do about this?"

7. **Acting repeatedly in some pattern of life**
   "Have you done anything about it? Will you do it again?" or "Should you try to get other people interested in this?"

Source: Adapted from *Values and Teaching* (2nd ed.), by L. Raths, M. Harmin, and S. Shore, 1978, pp. 63–65, Columbus, OH: Merrill.

TABLE 7.4
Sample Rank-Ordering Form

What Is Important in a Friend?

In class, everyone listed those qualities they thought were important in a friend:

_____ Has ideas for games	_____ Likes things I like
_____ Is happy	_____ Listens to me
_____ Does the same things as me	_____ Agrees with me
_____ Shares	_____ Does what I say
_____ Dresses like me	_____ Tells me what he or she finds out

Which of these qualities do you think are the most important in a friend? Number the qualities from 1 to 10 from the most important to the least important quality.

Most Important Quality in a Friend: _____

Least Important Quality in a Friend: _____

TABLE 7.5

Example of a Forced-Choice Questionnaire

People have ideas about what makes a good friend. Some people's ideas about which qualities a good friend has are given below. Read each idea. If you agree with the idea, circle *Agree*. If you disagree with the idea, circle *Disagree*.

What Makes a Good Friend?

Agree Disagree	1. A good friend smiles at you a lot.
Agree Disagree	2. A good friend likes the same clothes you like.
Agree Disagree	3. A good friend has ideas for things to do together.
Agree Disagree	4. A good friend likes to do the same things you do.
Agree Disagree	5. A good friend shares things with you.
Agree Disagree	6. A good friend likes the things you like.
Agree Disagree	7. A good friend listens to you.
Agree Disagree	8. A good friend does what you say.
Agree Disagree	9. A good friend agrees with you.
Agree Disagree	10. A good friend takes the blame when something goes wrong.

TABLE 7.6

Sample Checklist

What Is a Friend?

A class surveyed all the students in their school. Their survey was about what a friend is. After they put together all their information, they decided on the following description:

A friend is someone who is just like you. A friend dresses like you, likes the same jokes, talks like you, and likes to play the same games. A friend never disagrees with you. A friend always lets you have first choice and shares everything. A friend never gossips about you and stands up for you to everybody else. A friend will lie about something if the truth will get you in trouble. A friend never gets mad at you.

What do you think about this description? Put a checkmark beside each word that tells what you think about this description.

_____ Helpful	_____ Silly	_____ Thoughtful
_____ Bad	_____ Impossible	_____ Important
_____ Wise	_____ Unimportant	_____ Good
_____ Strong	_____ Useful	_____ Weak
_____ Honest	_____ Tough	_____ Fair
_____ Mean	_____ Unfair	_____ Accurate

the statement, situation, or story. Student responses on the checklist are used as the focus of a discussion that follows.

The values clarification approach has been criticized for three reasons: (1) its focus, (2) broad interpretation of what a value is, and (3) lack of attention to what cognitive structures are needed for this type of questioning to help students successfully clarify their values (Fraenkel, 1977). The values clarification approach today is recommended as one component of a moral education program but not as the only part.

Value Analysis.   Value analysis strategies help students think in an organized, logical manner about the following issues:

- Their values
- Their reasons for making specific choices
- The consequences of having a particular value
- The conflicts between their values and other people's values (Banks & Clegg, 1979)

Because value analysis involves asking questions, it is appropriate to use in all three phases of the learning cycle. Sometimes an incident from a person's life or a story might lead to using value analysis. In *Goldilocks and the Three Bears*, Goldilocks goes into someone else's house, eats their food, breaks their furniture, and sleeps in their beds. What values was Goldilocks displaying? Why did she do what she did? What were the results? Did her values conflict with the bear family's values? Students' skills in value analysis can be built using a sequence suggested by Banks and Clegg (1979). See Table 7.7 for an example.

The values-analysis approach has been criticized as too logical to attempt to analyze what is affective. Certain values, particularly religious values, must be taken on faith and cannot be logically analyzed. Situations in which value analysis is helpful occur in pop culture (Joseph, 2000), legal cases (Naylor & Diem, 1987), classroom incidents, personal incidents, current events, and historical events. Some computer software, such as Taking Responsibility (Tom Snyder Productions), offers opportunities to analyze values in a situation that is hypothetical, in this instance a situation in which two students have sneaked back into their classroom during recess and accidentally broken an item belonging to their teacher. Value analysis may not always be appropriate, but it gives students a means by which they can analyze social issues and problems.

Character Education.   Character education is a movement that has become prominent in recent years (Benniga, 1991). This approach is focused on teaching and modeling specific character traits, for example, honesty, courage, perseverance, loyalty, caring, civic virtue, justice, respect and responsibility, and trustworthiness. Both values clarification and moral reasoning focus on the processes of reasoning and selecting values. Character education focuses on behavior that demonstrates the value (Lopach & Luckowski, 1989).

People with good character habitually display good behavior, and such habits are embedded in a person (California Department of Education, 2000). A list of desirable character traits might not produce any consensus, but the desirable moral values that

T A B L E   7 . 7

Value Analysis Sequence Using the Story of *Goldilocks and the Three Bears*

1. **What is the value problem?**
   Is it right for Goldilocks to be in the bears' house?

2. **What is occurring that might involve values?**
   Goldilocks is eating others' food and sleeping in their beds without their permission and breaking their furniture.

3. **What does Goldilocks' behavior tell us about what she values? What does the bears' behavior tell us about what they value?**
   Students might decide Goldilocks values her own needs above all else and/or the bears value their right to privacy more than Goldilocks' right to satisfy her needs.

4. **How do these values differ or conflict?**
   Students may decide that Goldilocks' and the bears' values conflict. The bears cannot have their privacy if Goldilocks feels the only way she can satisfy her needs is not to wait until they get home.

5. **What are the sources of the values expressed?**
   Students may decide Goldilocks learned at home that she doesn't have to wait to satisfy her needs. The bears may live in a community that regards the right to privacy as important.

6. **What other values could be expressed? What alternatives are there?**
   Students might decide Goldilocks should respect the bears' right to privacy and wait until the bears get home to ask them to share their food and for a place to sleep. Or they might decide that the bears would expect Goldilocks to come into their home and would be upset if she didn't make herself comfortable in their home.

7. **What are the consequences if various choices are made?**
   Students might decide that the consequences of Goldilocks' present choice is that the bears find their food eaten and their furniture broken. Making another choice, Goldilocks might have waited until the bears came home and asked them for help. Or maybe Goldilocks would have looked like a tasty morsel to the bears and they might have eaten her!

8. **What choice do you make?**
   Students might decide that Goldilocks should wait until the bears get home and ask for their help.

9. **Why did you make this choice and what will its consequences be?**
   Students might decide that Goldilocks should wait until the bears get home and ask for their help because she wasn't dying of hunger and should have had some respect for the bears' privacy.

underlie these traits yield much agreement. Meaningful learning is important: Children should learn to behave and display good conduct with an understanding of the importance for such behavior.

The Task Force on Character Education in the Social Studies, formed by the National Council for the Social Studies (1996), recognized the role of character education in citizenship. The task force report, *Fostering Civic Virtue: Character Education in the Social Studies,* states that citizens must be committed to core, or fundamental, values such as life, liberty, equality, truth, pursuit of happiness, and promotion of the common good. To accomplish such a commitment, social studies teachers foster

This learning center is part of a study of advertising and the values it promotes.

students' meaningful understanding of core values. Teachers involve students in discussions and projects tied to issues about which the students have concerns. Involving students in studying, researching, discussing, and debating issues can be controversial. But according to the report, timid teaching does not support students' meaningful understanding of core values. Nor does timid teaching spark students' willingness to behave in ways that are consistent with these core values.

A number of curricula address various aspects of character education, including different perspectives, content, and instructional approaches. Teachers and school systems critically examine these to decide which are appropriate for their students' needs and can best foster meaningful learning and understanding of behavior consistent with core values that underlie human societies. Examples of character education curricula follow:

American Promise (Farmers Group, Inc.) provides a teacher's guide with a 3-hour documentary aimed at grades 5 and up.

Discover Skills for Life (American Guidance Service) addresses character traits as skills for students in grades K and up.

Lessons in Character (Young People's Press) is intended for grades K and up.

Life Skills (Globe Fearon Press) works with interpersonal relationships and related character education topics with students in grades 4 and up.

Peace and Nonviolence Curriculum (Violence Prevention Education, Minneapolis, MN) provides a curriculum for grades 1 and up.

Second Step: A Violence Prevention Curriculum (Committee for Children, Seattle, WA) uses kits with a Spanish language supplement available for preschool through grade 8.

Wise Skills (WiseSkills Resources) provides a curriculum, skill cards, awards, and a poster for grades K–8.

We the People (Center for Civic Education) provides workbooks and participatory exercises for students in grades 4 and up.

These curricula and others typically have Internet websites or are identified in the content of websites focusing on character education.

Many websites provide access to lesson plans, links to a variety of other character education websites, bibliographies, and/or online discussion groups. As with any other topic, teachers need to identify who is supporting the website and evaluate the perspectives represented. Teachers need to decide whether the perspectives support character education or indoctrination. The perspective should focus on students' meaningful understanding of the core value represented by a character trait and how that value helps us decide what behavior is consistent with the value. Among such websites are the Character Education Partnership and Character Education Resources.

In character education lessons, the exploratory introduction typically involves preparing a situation in which the trait value is demonstrated. For example, students can role play a situation, such as returning money they have found to its owner. During the lesson development, the trait or value is modeled, described, and discussed. Students read and analyze stories in which honesty is demonstrated. Honesty is then demonstrated by students during the expansion. The students devise their own role plays to demonstrate honesty as a way of expanding the trait into new contexts. Concerns raised by this approach include the selection of traits and values for the content of character education and who selects them.

Advocates believe that it is impossible to have a value-neutral education but that it is possible to agree on a common set of core traits or values to be taught. They emphasize promoting cohesion across all groups in our society by promoting a common set of core values. Concerns exist about whether teachers are expected to indoctrinate students with a set of values selected by an elite group. Concerns also exist about whether young children can meaningfully understand character traits. The research literature on moral development indicates that cognitive development is important in understanding the abstract ideas represented by character traits and in knowing when and how to behave consistently with the values incorporated in those traits. Some traits, such as respect for others and taking responsibility for oneself, appear to have consensus. However, it is important to consider whether some traits represent the perspectives of one or more cultural groups but are not core values for peoples the world over.

We have discussed multiple approaches illustrating the range of purposes for values education. Values are basic to social studies curriculum and to all education. Yet this area has no clear specifications. Researchers and curriculum developers have put great effort into developing and testing the approaches described. Each has something to offer, but each must be considered with attention to how it is carried out and why it is being used.

COMPANION
WEBSITE

The companion website contains examples of children's literature dealing with character, values, and morals. It also contains books for teachers on character education.

➤ USING TECHNOLOGY

Stimulating Discussion

Television can be an excellent resource for stimulating discussion about how each of us relates to others as individuals and to our communities. Useful programs explore social situations in our society and in other societies. Nationally produced programs are sometimes of interest in a particular community. Locally produced programs often introduce students of members of interest groups such as the League of Women Voters, citizens who are concerned about an issue, and local and state government officials.

Teachers generally do not have an opportunity to preview a television program. They must depend on descriptions found in the teaching guide accompanying it or, more likely, on a description in a newspaper or commercial television guide. For this reason, many teachers prefer to tape a program and then show it in class. This is considered fair use and is permitted if the tape is shown within 10 days and erased within 45 days after it is used. Viewing videotaped programs in class allows the teacher to guide students' viewing and to help them view a program critically.

In many states, the Public Broadcasting System (PBS) provides educational services directly to schools. Some programs are broadcast for immediate use and often are accompanied by viewing guides and other materials for use by teachers and students. Other programs can be copied and kept by schools. Teachers need to check every year with their local PBS station to find out what new resources are available.

It is always important to talk with students both before and after the program is viewed. Misconceptions, bias, incomplete reporting, and other problems can be analyzed. Areas in which the quality of the program is high should be discussed, including the presentation of multiple viewpoints about an issue, attention to details, in-depth coverage of a topic, citation of sources, the use of language that is clear and free from bias, and the use of leading or prejudicial terms. Students are most likely to recognize areas of quality in other programs they watch if their attention has been drawn to such factors in class.

When a program is selected for viewing at school or at home, a viewing guide should be prepared. If the program is watched at home, the viewing guide is sent home with a note requesting that family members watch the program with their children, discuss questions and concerns raised, and be involved in expansion activities.

ATTITUDES

Attitudes form a mindset toward taking action based on how desirable we think the anticipated consequences will be. Desirable consequences create a positive attitude toward the action, whereas undesirable consequences result in a negative attitude toward the action. Social studies is concerned with social attitudes and also with attitudes toward social studies and the social sciences. Attitudes are manifested when a behavior is displayed as a regular pattern in a range of similar situations. They limit or facilitate the application of skills and ideas. For example, the ability to understand an argument or an explanation does not matter if students are not willing to try. Even though the students are capable of understanding, their attitude may prevent them from doing so.

Attitudes are learned from experience, developing gradually as a result of encouragement and example. Prosocial attitudes are encouraged by taking the perspective of others, through empathy and role taking. Learning to take the perspective of others increases students' ability to set moral standards and use them to make mature value decisions (Honig & Wittmer, 1996). Taking the perspective of others involves knowing what others want, feel, and believe. Teachers also call attention to, and explain, others' perspectives so students become sensitive to them.

Empathy involves reacting to another person's situation or display of emotion with the same emotion the other is experiencing. A student who feels happy when another student feels happy is responding empathically. Role taking involves accurately understanding what another is feeling, thinking, or perceiving, but it does not necessarily involve feeling the same way as another person. A student who realizes another student feels happy but who does not himself feel happy is involved in role taking. Both empathy and role taking are "other-oriented" capacities that contribute to prosocial behavior. In elementary and middle school students, empathy is associated with a willingness to help others who are having problems, including people who seem to be lonely and people who have accidents and may be hurt (Williams & Bybee, 1994).

Empathy develops when students are involved repeatedly in experiences in which they both have the same emotion, such as happiness. Teachers using small-group activities increase the likelihood that students experience the same emotion as a result of the activity they are jointly involved in. A student's empathic responding can be strengthened if, when disciplining the student for causing another's distress, teachers draw the student's attention to the other's distress while at the same time scolding the student (Macoby, 1980). Teachers can also do this by encouraging the class to acknowledge the happiness or pride of fellow students in various accomplishments. Role taking can be strengthened by providing students with opportunities to practice the behaviors desired. Students who are involved in skits in which they act out how each of several story characters was feeling are later more likely to share with a needy other (Iannotti, 1978).

Attitudes are not taught in the way that specific facts and skills are. Teachers need to be aware of the potential influence of the attitudes they model. Teachers need to address students' attitudes, discussing them in an open manner while avoiding

An artist's sculpture interests this young man and illustrates national attitudes toward soldiers killed in action.

indoctrinating students with the teacher's attitudes. Evidence shows that an attitude has been learned when teachers see in their students a new willingness to take (or refrain from) an action based on the learner's (1) concept of what the action is and (2) predictions as to the desirable or undesirable effects of taking (or not taking) the action (Seiger-Ehrenberg, 2002, p. 278). The development of attitudes that promote meaningful learning is a fundamental role of the social studies curriculum (see Table 7.8).

Curiosity

Curiosity is wanting to know, trying a new experience, exploring, and finding out about things. It is an attitude that promotes all kinds of learning. Curiosity often appears in the form of questioning. Inviting students to ask questions is one way of showing that curiosity is valued. Asking students to verbalize their questions too early can create problems, however. Students need time to process data and relate it in their minds to what is already known. Then they will be ready to ask questions to help make sense of it. After having some time to examine and think about a bullfight picture, for example, a student might ask, "Why do these people think it is fun to kill a bull?" Young children and those with a limited attention span might get no further than asking the superficial question that expresses interest before they turn to another topic.

TABLE 7.8

Values for Learning Social Studies

1. **Curiosity**
   a. Questioning
   b. Wanting to know
2. **Respect for evidence**
   a. Open-mindedness
   b. Perseverance
   c. Desire to know the evidence behind statements
   d. Willingness to consider conflicting evidence
3. **Flexibility**
   a. Willingness to reconsider ideas
   b. Recognition that ideas are tentative
4. **Critical thinking**
   a. Willingness to consider methods
   b. Wanting to improve on past ideas and performance
5. **Responsibility to people and the environment**

Questioning brings satisfaction if it helps students share their pleasure and excitement with others. Wanting to know stimulates efforts to find out, perhaps by investigating, using a library, or making a special visit. Satisfaction resulting from expressing curiosity helps students gradually sustain interest for longer periods of time and ask more thoughtful questions relating what the student knows to the new experience.

Open-Mindedness

To examine the social world and to make decisions about it, evidence must be gathered and used to develop and test ideas. Students and teachers must be open to seeking various views and to examining problems before they make meaningful generalizations. Adults often expect students to accept statements because of the authority of their position. This can reduce the students' desire to ask for evidence. If a teacher appears to accept statements without evidence or offers no evidence for a statement, the attitude that evidence is not necessary is transmitted.

Perseverance

To obtain really convincing evidence often takes perseverance. Perseverance does not mean keeping on trying if something is not working. It does mean being willing to try again, learning from earlier difficulties, and changing your ideas as a result of what has been learned. Teachers provide students with social studies assignments that require seeking out information rather than just accepting the most easily available information.

Willingness to Consider Conflicting Evidence

Extending a respect for evidence to situations in which other evidence or other ideas might conflict with what you think you already know is not easy. A respect for evidence involves willingness to do this. Students are more likely to be willing to consider conflicting evidence, even if it leads to mistakes, if their teacher accepts the mistakes and rewards their efforts.

Reserving Judgment

A respect for evidence requires reserving judgment. An individual does not make a judgment until an effort has been made to find out whether information is conflicting and then willingly considers the conflicts. The diverse perspectives represented by conflicting information enter into the final decision that is made. Students find this a difficult process that involves a period of uncertainty and of mental challenge before judgment occurs.

Flexibility

Mental flexibility relates to the products of social studies activities in a manner similar to the way respect for evidence relates to the processes occurring in social studies activities. The concepts and generalizations that we form when trying to understand the social world change as experience adds evidence that develops or contradicts them. Unless students have mental flexibility, each experience that conflicts with existing ideas causes confusion and creates a rival idea instead of modifying and developing an existing one. Flexibility and a recognition that conclusions are always tentative are important in social studies. We can never have all the evidence needed to be certain that our ideas are absolutely correct. Elementary and middle school students might not be able to understand the tentativeness of ideas, but teachers need to promote attitudes that enable them eventually to develop this understanding. One way of doing this is to preface conclusions with a statement such as "As far as we can see. . . ." It also helps to talk with students from time to time about how their ideas have changed and about how they used to think.

Critical Thinking

Both before and after arriving at a conclusion, students need to be willing to consider the process they followed in reaching the conclusion. Are their methods logical? Are they making unwarranted assumptions? Are they skipping a necessary step? A willingness to consider methods used helps students evaluate the methods, discover problem areas, and reflect on how they might do things differently. Wanting to improve on the ideas they have and on the processes they use to come to conclusions is an important attitude in students. Such a desire to improve leads to a willingness to consider the processes followed in reaching conclusions. It makes students more willing to identify problems and to seek alternatives.

Robert Ennis (1991, p. 68) provides a working definition: "Critical thinking is reasonable, reflective thinking that is focused on deciding what to believe or do." It requires us to be disposed toward seeking a clear statement of a question, seeking reasons, trying to be well informed, using credible sources, taking into account the whole situation, trying to keep with the main point and the original question, being open-minded, reserving judgment, persevering, being willing to consider conflicting evidence, being flexible, and being curious. These dispositions are accompanied by abilities constructed over time. Teachers have an important role in helping their students construct these abilities. Ennis (1991, pp. 68–71) summarizes these critical thinking abilities in five categories:

1. Clarification (focusing on a question, analyzing arguments, asking/answering clarification questions)
2. Support (judging credibility of sources, making observations)
3. Inference
4. Advanced clarification (defining terms and judging definitions, then identifying assumptions)
5. Strategy and tactics (deciding on an action and carrying it out)

Responsibility to Others and Their Cultures

In social studies, students investigate and explore their social environment to understand it and develop skills for future understanding, which may promote active civic participation. Such investigation and exploration involve an attitude of respect for others and the environment and a willingness to care appropriately for people and the environment. Growth in inquiry skills should be accompanied by a development of sensitivity and responsibility toward the social and physical environment. A sense of responsibility toward someone or something is more likely to occur when a person has had experience with that person or thing or knows something about him, her, or it. For example, a person who has painted walls in a house and understands the effort that goes into this task is likely to take more care of the walls than is someone who has not been so involved.

Many of the concepts relating to responsibility for and sensitivity to people and the environment are complex (interdependence, for example) and sometimes controversial (the use of coal for generating power), but it is still possible to begin to develop attitudes toward people by example and rules of conduct. Rules that teachers and students agree on help establish a pattern of response, but only when students begin to act responsibly (e.g., not taking others' supplies). The way to accomplish this is gradually to hand over to students the responsibility for making decisions about how they should behave. The development of attitudes is important not only in learning social studies but also in becoming a responsible citizen in a democracy. In developing attitudes, students can begin to perceive social studies as a search for knowledge and understanding.

➤ **BUILDING ON DIVERSITY**

Learning from the Voices of Our Family and Community

Teachers must offer family and community members opportunities to speak about their life experiences and give this knowledge an important place in the classroom (McCaleb, 1994). One way to accomplish these goals is to build student and community books on themes such as Our Family History, Teachings from My Childhood Community, the Wise Person I Remember, My Family's Dictionary: Words That Are Special to People in My Family, My Mother (or Father, Grandma, Big Sister, etc.) Is Special, Words of Advice from My Family, Friendship across Generations, the Most Frightening Time in My Life, or a Book for Peace (McCaleb, 1994).

To begin, a teacher might share a literature selection on the topic or have a brainstorming session. Next, a decision should be made about whether family or community members will be interviewed to obtain information. If interviews are to be used, questions are identified for the interview. Information from interviews can be discussed and put on thematic maps and charts. Many books should be joint student and family/community projects. Students will find that they have to weave together several stories and sometimes multiple perspectives. They might need assistance from their teacher and/or family members. A first draft can be edited with help from the teacher or other students. Some books, however, may be a coproduction of the student and family and may be brought to school as a completed project.

Even the youngest students can create a book. Their books may be mostly artwork of people or events. A description of the artwork may be short and written by the student or can be dictated to an adult who writes it down for the student. A special book day should celebrate the completion of books on a topic. Students from other classes can come in to listen to books as they are read, or the book can be shared with family members on a family night.

SUMMARY

Personal and social development occur through maturation and experience. Teachers provide experiences encouraging students' development, help them cope with difficulties they encounter, develop morals and values, and develop prosocial attitudes conducive to citizenship. Both adults and students' peers have some effect on students' development. The teacher is a powerful person in a student's life and works to ensure that his or her effect is a positive one for the student as an individual and as a participating citizen in a democracy. The area of psychology and values education is one that is generally acknowledged to be part of the school curriculum. However, it is an area requiring sensitivity to the needs and cultural background of each student.

Each student has different needs, and each of these needs has a strong impact on the student. Because of the needs each student has, and because of the differences between students, controversy erupts over how psychology and values education should be taught. Moral reasoning and values clarification are two areas that have generated a lot of controversy. Much of the controversy is due, first, to the recognition that psychology and values education are both important and sensitive issues, and, second, to conflicting ideas on how to teach them well. The controversy often involves people's basic beliefs about morality and students' relationships with each other. Because this is an area in which issues have not been resolved, we most likely will continue to see debate.

Expanding ON THIS CHAPTER

Activity

COMPANION
WEBSITE

Create a graphic describing how values and morals differ. You might use a concept web, a chart with columns, or, perhaps you think a Venn diagram will best fit your description because you think they overlap in some ways.

Recommended Websites to Visit

CW
COMPANION
WEBSITE

CIVNET
   www.civnet.org
   This is an international gateway to information on civic education providing a vast library of civics teaching resources, discourse on civil society, information on organizations and programs, book-length documents, lesson plans K–12, an online global discussion group on civic education, and research findings on democracy.

Giraffe Project
   www.giraffe.org/projectinfo.html
   This is a literature project devoted to informing others about people who "stick out their necks for the common good." It has a curriculum called *Standing Tall* whose goal is to teach children how to stick out their necks through a three-part instructional plan: "Hear the Story" in which children read and are told stories about over 800 real people; "Tell the Story" in which children find out about and speak or write about the real-life heroes in their local communities; and "Be the Story" in which children put into practice their own plans for being helpful.

Utah Department of Education: Character Education Partnership
   www.usoe.k12.ut.us/curr/char_ed
   This website provides lesson plans, a discussion of the theory and history of character education, and links to other related sites.

Conflict Resolution Sources and Websites
   www.crenet.org/cren/facts.html
   The Conflict Resolution Education Facts section of the Conflict Resolution Education Network website is a useful source of information on conflict resolution.

The U.S. Department of Education's Safe and Drug-Free Schools Program
   www.ed.gov/offices/OESE/SDFS

The U.S. Department of Justice's Office of Juvenile Justice and Delinquency Prevention
   http://ojjdp.ncjrs.org/

Helping Students Become Citizens in a Democratic Society in an Ever More Interdependent World

INTRODUCTION

"Beyond Basics, Civics Eludes U.S. Students," David J. Hoff, *Education Week*, 11/24/99.

"Election 2000: Young Americans Turned Off by Politics, Polls Show," Lori Lessner, Knight-Ridder Tribune, printed in *Fourth Estate*, *31*(16), 1/27/00, University of Wisconsin–Green Bay.

May 9, 2000—Some of the nation's most prominent organizations and leaders today acknowledge that the challenge is too big for any one group. . . . The National Alliance for Civic Education (NACE) was launched with more than 80 groups . . . committed to advancing civic knowledge and engagement. Formation of the coalition was ➤

➤ spurred by the disturbing rise in civic indifference, mistrust, and disengagement among young adults (retrieved from www. cived.net/about_prel.html, October 26, 2003).

February 13, 2003—THE CIVIC MISSION OF SCHOOLS, a report issued by the Carnegie Corporation of New York and CIRCLE: The Center for Information and Research on Civic Learning and Engagement, provides a framework for creating more effective civic education in our schools and represents, for the first time, consensus about this issue among the nation's leading scholars and practitioners.

February 16, 2003—But schools do remain the last, best hope to train those of the next generation in civics skills, to imbue them with civics knowledge and to awaken them to the importance and satisfaction of taking an active, informed role in civic life (Jane Eisner, The Philadelphia Inquirer, retrieved from www.philly.com/mldinquirer/5190396.htm).

1. How do these headlines and excerpts from newspaper articles make you feel?
   _____
   _____

The Civic Mission of the Schools identifies six promising approaches to civic education from a review of the research: (1) Provide instruction in government, history, law, and democracy; (2) incorporate discussion of current local, national, and international issues and events into the classroom; (3) design and implement programs that provide students with the opportunity to apply what they learn through performing community service that is linked to the formal curriculum and classroom instruction; (4) offer extracurricular activities that provide opportunities for young people to get involved in their school and communities; (5) encourage student participation in school governance; (6) encourage students' participation in simulations of democratic processes and procedures.

2. In which of these six promising approaches to improving civic education did you take part as a K–12 student? _____
3. Which of these do you think you would particularly like to do with the students you anticipate teaching? _____

CHAPTER OVERVIEW

Since the end of the Cold War, many U.S. social studies educators have been asked by leaders and educators in nations who have not had democratic traditions for many years to help them plan new civic curricula and train teachers to teach for democracy. These requests and domestic problems have stimulated dialog concerning the practices of civics education in the United States. As a result of his experiences, John Patrick (2003) has concluded that the twenty-first century civic mission of schools requires that at all levels of preadult education and in teacher education students should learn a minimal universal definition of democracy so that they will be able to compare and evaluate nations and regimes throughout the world according to a common basic understanding of democracy and democratic behaviors.

Being born in the United States or having an American parent makes a child a U.S. citizen. Citizenship, however, must be learned and practiced as the child grows and comes into contact with people and groups both in and out of the home. Patriotism, or love of country, is an attitude established early in life. Children and adolescents tend to be positive about national symbols, to like and trust their political leaders, and to be highly supportive of their political systems. Researchers have found such positive attitudes even when students have little understanding of their country or its government (Torney-Purta, 1990). But are love of country and positive attitudes toward symbols and leaders enough in a democracy?

The school, especially a public school, is an important societal institution that greatly affects young people. It teaches, through formal and informal processes, attitudes and behaviors toward society. This chapter examines political knowledge, values, and law in light of concepts students need to learn to become responsible, participating citizens. It examines the ways in which children learn to become active citizens and the roles schools and teachers play in this process. As you read and reflect on the chapter, keep in mind that (1) the United States is more ethnically diverse than ever before, (2) citizens of a democracy must share common values, and (3) governmental actions must reflect those values while protecting the rights of minorities.

CHAPTER OBJECTIVES

1. Explain the importance of knowledge, values, and participation to citizenship.
2. Explain the importance of the individual to a democracy.
3. Explain the role of the hidden curriculum in forming students' ideas about power, authority, and governing.
4. Identify political science concepts and values that are essential to understanding democratic government.
5. Identify lesson characteristics that are helpful in accommodating learning in a multicultural democracy.
6. State a rationale for community participation or service learning.
7. Give examples of student participation activities that are appropriate for elementary and middle school students.
8. Explain how democracy can be modeled and practiced in the school and classroom.
9. Assess recommendations on ways in which elementary and middle school students can study law.
10. Explain the media's role in educating citizens.
11. Identify ways to help children make wise use of the media in school and their lives.
12. Reflect on the ethics teachers need to practice and model that support the learning of democratic ideals and practices in the school, community, nation, and world.

DEFINING CITIZENSHIP IN A DEMOCRATIC SOCIETY

Because citizenship is a given to those born in a nation, how the population learns appropriate behaviors necessary to be a member of this group, called *citizens,* is determined by that group. Schools are one of the societal institutions that have an active role in helping children and youths learn to live and work in their nation. In the United States the centrality of citizenship education in the social studies curriculum has enjoyed widespread acceptance. Political scientists, with their emphasis on rational thought and decision making, often criticize what is taught in the schools as being a naive, unrealistic, and romanticized image of political life. They say that the ideals of democracy are confused with the realities of politics (Jennes, 1990). The elementary curriculum is singled out for criticism because it tends to fail to recognize the presence of conflict and failure within a democracy. Ideals for the appropriate focus span a continuum from stressing patriotism and loyalty through examining and solving social problems to centering on social and governmental criticism.

During the 1970s, social studies educators involved with Project SPAN defined the role of the citizen as focusing on relationships between individuals and political entities and organized efforts to influence public policy (Superka & Hawke, 1982). Because such relationships are found at neighborhood, community, state, national, and international levels of government, citizenship activities fit into all levels (K–12) of the expanding horizons curriculum model that dominated the field for many years. Social studies is the subject that is primarily responsible for teaching the knowledge, skills, and values needed to understand and participate effectively in the political system and to deal responsibly with public issues.

Rapid changes in the 1980s and 1990s increased not only the amount of knowledge in the world, but the speed with which individuals encounter this knowledge and the need to process information critically and react appropriately. During this same time period, the old political balances and forces of the world changed greatly. As a result more nations tried, and are continuing to try, to implement democratic forms of government while at the same time becoming increasingly ethnically diverse and economically interdependent. New problems for people emerged or became more difficult to solve as the number and complexity of their variables increased. Unfortunately, given our time and resources, the ability of many adults and children to understand and intellectually grow as rapidly as the social world changes is limited.

During this same time, the National Council for the Social Studies (NCSS) developed standards for social studies programs that identified power, authority, and governance and civic ideals and practices as separate, equally important strands of the social studies K–12 curriculum. Also included were science, technology, and society and global connections, two often-neglected themes in past curricula.

In the 1990s, the International Association for the Evaluation of Education Achievement (IEA) began preparations for its second study of civic education. This study would assess not only knowledge about government and power, but also student attitudes and beliefs about government and the future in the United States and 23 other nations. Preparing instruments for such a large undertaking required careful planning and the establishment of common goals. Judith Torney-Purta, a distinguished educator and researcher on political socialization, who is currently chair of the International Steering Committee for the IEA Civic Education Study, summarized five views of citizenship education (May, 2000):

1. Knowledge of facts about government and constitutions, as "real citizenship"
2. Willingness to vote (and to look for information about candidates, their positions on issues, etc.)
3. A basic level of trust in institutions, sense of political efficacy, an ability to be thoughtfully critical about government policies, and other political attitudes (sometimes related to participation)
4. Respect for political opinions different from one's own and respect for the rights of ethnic, racial, or language groups
5. Participation in service learning or community projects (or politically relevant youth organizations)

Dr. Torney-Purta points out that her research and that of others clearly indicate that different people and different nations emphasize one or more of the five definitions.

DEVELOPING POLITICAL AWARENESS

The model of civic education the IEA committee used to guide their planning and research for development of assessment instruments is given in Figure 8.1. It is complex and illustrates the many contributing factors or forces in a person's political socialization (Torney-Purta, Schwille, & Amadeo, 1999). Its complexity suggests that even a carefully planned civic curriculum with explicit objectives might not be equally successful for each child or group of children to whom it is taught. The model applies to children in more than 20 nations.

In the center of the model is the individual child surrounded by socializing agents with various degrees of contact with the individual. In the United States, where various forms of media, including television, radio, movies, and the Internet, greatly affect the lives of children, perhaps media should be included in the circle surrounding the individual labeled *carriers of goals into actions*. The outer ring represents the more distant community of national and international institutions whose laws, policies, and theories impact nations and communities (Torney-Purta, Schwille, & Amadeo, 1999).

Political science is the discipline that studies governments. Political scientists focus their studies on three very different types of questions concerning governing:

Who has the right and power to govern?
How do governments organize themselves to make and enforce political decisions?
How do groups of people influence the political process?

The first question examines historical and philosophical ideas; the second question deals more with the formation of governmental and public policies. The third question addresses politics as it is formally and informally practiced.

All citizens have the need for, and the right to, services from their governments. Citizens in a democracy have special powers and obligations:

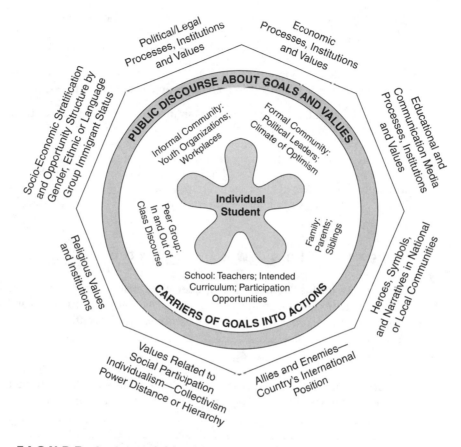

FIGURE 8.1 **Model for IEA Civic Education**

Source: Civic Education Across Countries: Twenty-four National Case Studies from the IEA Civic Education Project. (1999) Edited by Judith Torney-Purta, John Schwille, and JoAnn Amado. Amsterdam, Netherlands: IEA. Used by permission.

- Bestowing both the power and right to rule on a government of their choice
- Selecting those who perform day-to-day governance
- Debating and compromising to instruct the government on the needs of the people and the types of policies desired
- Monitoring the actions of governments and keeping informed on issues related to the collective good
- Balancing their own self-interest with the collective good

Political scientists believe that the capacity to participate effectively in the politics of a free society requires knowledge of the political system and a real understanding of what one is trying to accomplish. Citizens must have the following qualities:

1. An interest in public affairs and a sense of "public regardedness"
2. Tolerance and respect for conflicts arising from divergent values and beliefs

3. The ability to examine consequences and to assess the likelihood of alternatives achieving desired goals
4. The ability to assess both long- and short-term consequences (Brody, 1989)

In summarizing the first phase of the IEA assessment in civics, the editors of the report identified a number of agreements in goals and some accomplishments, concluding that

> there is a universal or near-universal commitment to certain goals or themes. Civics education should be cross-disciplinary, participative, interactive, related to life, conducted in a nonauthoritarian environment, cognizant of the challenges of societal diversity, and coconstructed with parents and the community (and nongovernmental organizations) as well as the school. Despite extensive efforts, however, there has not been universal success in any country in formulating programs that optimize the possibility of achieving these goals for all students. (Torney-Purta, Schwille, & Amadeo, 1999, p. 30)

TIME FOR REFLECTION: WHAT DO YOU THINK?

1. As you examine the IEA model of civic education, at about what age do you think children are likely to begin functioning politically: that is, encountering and solving interpersonal problems with people whose viewpoints differ from their own? Explain your reasoning. _____

   _____

2. What are some possible ways in which teachers and educators can work with other community groups to help attain the goals of civic education? _____

   _____
   _____
   _____

CITIZENSHIP AND STANDARDS

In elaborating on the meaning of power, authority, and governance and civic ideals and practices, NCSS (1994b) identifies understanding the historical development of the structures of power, authority, and governance and their evolving functions in contemporary society as essential for civic competence along with examining the dynamics between individual rights and responsibilities. The study and practice of civic ideals with the goal of full participation in society through multiple interactions with individuals, groups, institutions, and organizations is the means to attaining a democratic government.

Goals 2000: Educate America Act of 1994 called for every U.S. adult to possess the knowledge and skills necessary to exercise the rights and responsibilities of citizenship. The Center for Civic Education directed the development of the *National*

Standards for Civics and Government (1994). These K–12 standards focus on answering five questions:

1. What is government and what should it do?
2. What are the basic values and principles of U.S. democracy?
3. How does the government established by the Constitution embody the purposes, values, and principles of U.S. democracy?
4. What is the relationship of the United States to other nations and to world affairs?
5. What are the roles of the citizens in U.S. democracy?

These standards focus on both the content and students' actions that demonstrate that they understand and value the content. The skills are embedded in the standards through the use of verbs such as *identify, describe, explain, evaluate a position, take a position,* and *defend a position.* The development of participatory skills for democracy is present in recommended community and classroom activities. The goals of these activities are devoted both to monitoring politics and government and influencing politics and government. The standards provide specifics for two of the NCSS themes: VI (Power, Authority, and Governance) and X (Civic Ideals and Practice). As with other statements of standards, many state and local school systems used the *National Standards for Civics and Government* and incorporated its ideas into their own standards. So also did the National Assessment of Educational Progress and private testing organizations developing tests for states and school systems.

KEY CONCEPTS AND VALUES

In some states, courses focusing only on civics have been designed for eighth grade. However, government and civics have also been assigned by the curriculum to all social studies classes. Emphasis in civics and government has been placed on preparing the individual to deal with the structure of U.S. government and its agencies and to be a future voter. The focus tends to be on the mechanics of government rather than on concepts and values underlying the procedures of governing and making and enforcing laws.

The task of identifying concepts to teach young students has been left largely to textbook authors. In K–4 textbooks, publishers have included political science concepts, but to a much lesser degree than geographic and economic concepts. The most frequently appearing concepts include *law, president, government, citizen, nation, rules, taxes,* and *Congress* (Haas, 1991). Table 8.1 suggests concepts that have been derived from the professional literature and through joint deliberation among civic educators worldwide. Despite the fact that political science concepts are often highly abstract, several of the organizing concepts listed in Table 8.1 have examples that are present in any situation where a number of people interact, including at home and in the classroom.

School is often the first experience in which children interact with a variety of people who judge them on their actions. Schooling requires students to behave in new and different social situations. Lessons on political concepts such as rules, leadership, viewpoints, conflict resolution, and compromise, and the relationships

TABLE 8.1

Essential Concepts and Values in U.S. Democracy

authority	diversity	justice/fairness	power
Bill of Rights	due process	law making	privacy
changing laws	equality	law/rule	representative democracy
civil society	freedom	leadership	respect for the individual
compromise	government	loyalty	rule of law
conflict	honesty	majority	security
conflict resolution	human dignity	minority	self-discipline
consensus	human rights	nation	social responsibility
Constitution	influence	open-mindedness	tolerance
decision making	interdependence	order	viewpoint
democracy	international	pluralism	citizenship

among those concepts help students understand how to act in their school social situation in which they are one among equals. These lessons also provide rationales for desired classroom behaviors for the collective good of students and learning opportunities.

Socialization is the name given to processes whereby young people learn proper behaviors. Elementary and middle school teachers devote much time to socializing students. When elementary students attend school they are likely to learn to function in a larger, more diverse, and pluralistic group than they have previously encountered. Middle schools bring together students from several elementary schools and often create environments with a greater and more diverse pluralism than do elementary schools. Middle school students are engaged in another developmental task with political overtones: identifying appropriate roles in the larger community where, because of greater personal and cognitive powers, they are beginning to function more independently. Youthful maturing often brings countersocializing experiences. Students challenge the authority they previously assigned, without question, to certain people including parents, teachers, and government officials.

To function democratically, democracies have faith in their citizens to do what is right. Agreement on what is right comes from having common convictions and beliefs about what is important or of value. At a minimum, these include the provision for the basic needs of individuals and the respect for the human dignity of individuals. Such ideas are learned through socialization. However, socialization can become conformity for the wrong reasons and to the detriment of the human dignity of some or all of the population. For that reason, citizens are encouraged to question what is happening and decide whether the consequences of actions are those they consider important and of most worth or value. Democratic values and beliefs (civic ideals) associated with democracy and identified in formal position statements from the NCSS (1989, 1994b) are listed in Table 8.1.

Schools reflect the values of the society. Such values as self-discipline, consensus, equality, tolerance, fairness, loyalty, honesty, and freedom are of great concern in the functioning of all classrooms. Citizens must agree on the values and their importance if society is to function smoothly and have its laws observed. Elementary and middle school students need to examine the meanings of the values and predict what life would be like if people did not practice these values. In so doing, students decide on the type of society they want and need and come to understand the reasons for acting in ways that bring about such a society. Citizenship education in a democracy is going beyond conceptual understandings to include the development of *participatory skills:*

- *Interacting* through communication and cooperation in political and civic life
- *Monitoring* the work and actions of political leaders and institutions
- *Influencing* others and institutions to deal with issues consistent with democratic values and principles (Patrick, 1999)

The contribution of political science to social studies includes helping students find out how people use their own *personal power* to make a difference in their lives and others' lives. It also examines how individuals join together to make decisions *collectively* for their common good.

Research on democratic attitudes reports that the classroom climate and the hidden curriculum of the school directly affect students' attitudes. Even if they are not recognized formally in the social studies curriculum, concepts and values related to politics, law, and political science are presented indirectly throughout the K–8 curriculum. Students or groups of students may witness and experience discrimination, favoritism, and tyranny rather than tolerance, equality, and justice. This can result from classroom or school climates in which teachers accept stereotypes as facts about individuals or seek to keep particularly vocal or influential parents happy at the expense of equal opportunity for all individuals in the school to grow and learn.

Conflicting individual or small-group interests concerning school curriculum have resulted in various pressure groups seeking changes in school board policies or state and national laws. Formal instruction in democratic citizenship through the social studies curriculum is needed to help students overcome misconceptions and misunderstandings about democratic philosophy and U.S. government. A commitment to democratic principles, a willingness to engage in the democratic process, and the affirmation of core values are key elements of the bond that joins us as "We the People" (NCSS, 1997).

The primary-grade learning cycle in Table 8.2 defines voting, one of the most fundamental concepts related to decision making and the individual use of power. A clear understanding of the concept of voting and its consequences is essential if students are to be involved in the process of making some decisions concerning their activities.

T A B L E 8 . 2

Learning Cycle	Voting Is a Way to Make Decisions

Grade Level: Primary
NCSS: Power, Authority, and Governance; Civic Ideals and Practice

NCSS

Exploratory Introduction

Materials: A picture for each child to color that includes a boy wearing a shirt; crayons for each child

Objectives	Procedures	Assessments
Students recall decisions they have made in the task given and during the day.	Provide each student with crayons and a picture to color. When pictures are completed, have a class discussion asking small groups to stand and show their pictures. Ask: "What are some of the decisions you made when you colored your picture?" Note that lots of individual decisions were made to color the pictures.	Students identify decisions made when coloring their pictures.
Students explain that people can make their own choices for many things.	Ask: "Besides the colors on the pictures, what are some other decisions you made today? Let's think about why we made these decisions today." Ask students to raise a hand if they colored the boy's shirt red. Ask: "How did you go about deciding to color the boy's shirt red? Who colored his shirt blue? Why did you pick blue instead of red?" Repeat with other colors. Ask: "Just because I like yellow (or another color) the best, does that mean everyone should wear yellow shirts? Why not?" Restate and affirm students' conclusion: When each person makes their own choice and does their own action, it is called *individual choice.* Practice saying the term *individual choice.* Ask: "What is an example of an individual choice you made today? What might be an individual choice you will make later today when you are home?"	Students give personal and logical reasons for their choices in the task, such as for their choices of color(s) to use. Students affirm and accept the right of others to make individual choices. Students offer appropriate examples of individual choices.

Lesson Development

Materials: Large poster for each group to color and crayons or markers

Objectives	Procedures	Assessments
Given a whole group problem, students	Tell students: "Suppose that the principal came to our room and gave us a great big picture	Students identify at least two appropriate

TABLE 8.2

discuss the problem and decide important ways in which individual decisions differ from group decisions.	like the one you colored earlier. Suppose she said that she wanted the class to color this picture to be displayed on the classroom door. Suppose she wanted the class to decide, as a group, how to color the picture so that everyone is happy with the way the picture looks. Ask: "How could we make the decisions on what colors to use for the various parts of the picture?"	and important ways individual decisions differ from group decisions.

Taking a vote is suggested. |
| Students decide that everyone should have a fair way to take part in the whole-group decision making and offer ways for this to happen. | Explain to students that a popular way groups of people in the United States make decisions is to vote on possible choices. Ask: "Has anyone heard of voting? Can anyone tell us about voting?"

Provide examples of possible voting choices if needed. Sometimes members of a family might vote on where to go for lunch or what to buy for someone's birthday present. | Students respond and give some information about voting taking place. |
| Students list steps used in the voting process, placing them in logical order. | Ask: "Can anyone tell us what happens when a vote is taken?" List students' responses and continue discussion or fill in missing parts to get at least the following events. Number the statements in chronological order. Ask: "Of the things we have listed, which would be done first? Then what would happen?"

Be certain that the minimum steps include the following:

1. A problem with two or more possible choices for answers is identified.
2. Members of the group discuss the good and bad points of selecting each choice.
3. Members think about what they have heard and decide what they believe to be the best choice.
4. A vote is taken with everyone voting for only one choice.
5. The winner is the choice with the largest number of votes. | Students listen and offer suggestions for the steps in voting, placing events in logical order. |

continued

T A B L E   8 . 2

Continued

	Practice the voting process, using the steps. Perhaps vote on the colors to use on a large poster of the picture colored earlier or some other poster. Follow the steps identified, referring to each as it is done.	Students suggest colors, give reasons, vote, and count votes in an orderly manner.
Students decide that voting with the largest number as the winner is a fair way to make a choice.	Ask: "Are you pleased with the choice we made as a group?"	Students list steps and say the most votes wins.
	Have students take turns coloring the poster using the colors they voted to use. Then display the finished poster and discuss students' reactions to its appearance. Ask: "What steps did we follow in making our decisions?"	
	Ask: "Do you think you would like the poster as well if only one of the students in the class colored it and made all the choices? Would a poster completed by one person reflect what the class wanted?"	
	Ask: "What are some other times when we need to make choices in our class." List responses and post the list in classroom.	Students offer logical times for voting decisions in the classroom.
	Closure: Ask: "How do you suggest that we make such choices? Will you remind me when we have choices to have a class vote?" Throughout the year, have students vote on these and add them to the list when appropriate.	

Expansion		
Objectives	**Procedures**	**Assessments**
Students explain that the winning choice is not everyone's first choice when voting is used. (Some people might not be as happy with the result of the vote as those who voted for the winning choice.)	Ask: "When we voted on the colors to make the large poster, did any of you get all of of your first choices?" Raise your hand if that happened to you. (Some might not raise their hands.)	Students respond that not everyone got their first choice and that some people were not as happy as others with the choices made.

TABLE 8.2
Continued

	Ask: "Were you happy with the way the poster looked? Were you disappointed that your first choices were not all what the class selected?" Ask: "Think back, did anyone complain?" Ask a specific student why he/she did not complain. Ask others also. Discuss the responses.	Students respond that not everyone got their first choice and that some were not as happy as were others with the choices made.
Students state their acceptance of the principle of supporting the choice of the group to maintain harmony and fairness within the group.	Explain: When we vote on something, we are making an agreement with the others in the group. We are willing to go along with the group's choice.	
	Ask: "Why would someone be willing to do this? When have you done this before? Is there ever a time not to do what a group votes to do?" (Expect students to say when someone gets hurt, sick, etc.). Respond appropriately. Give hypothetical examples of group decisions and have students say whether they are acceptable decisions and explain their reasons. (1) We vote on what songs to sing for Grandparent's Day. (2) We vote that Betty should have a chocolate birthday cake.	Students identify times to accept and not to accept the group's decision. They indicate they want "fair votes" and appropriate group choice. Students say yes to #1 and no to #2. (Betty should select her own cake because it is her birthday.)
Students state that citizens should accept the winner of a fair election and give appropriate reasons.	Give examples of some adult group votes with which children might be familiar. For example: "Teachers in the school decided...."	Students say that citizens should accept the winner of a fair election and give at least two appropriate reasons.
	Explain the election of the president is a vote by the citizens for someone who will represent the American people and work for all of the people. Ask: "Why do we need someone to make these decisions?" When a president is elected, those who voted for the winner celebrate.	
	When we elect a president, someone else doesn't get elected. Ask: "How do the people feel who voted for the person who did not win? How do they act? Why don't they move to another country?"	

continued

T A B L E   8 . 2

Continued

Explain that every four years, we have a presidential election and can select a new president. Citizens can replace a president with a new vote. Some people will like the new president better than the old one. We also use the courts to be certain that the president makes fair decisions. The president also shares some of the law making with other elected people. The president can't just make any decision he or she wants to make. We will talk some more about how that is done on another day.

Lesson Summary: Ask: "What is the name of the way in which groups make decisions? Why is voting a good way to make decisions? Will people support the choice of a vote even if it is not their choice?"

Students respond with correct answers and logical related explanations.

Note: This lesson may be followed with
1. Other lessons on decision making and alternative forms of decision making
2. Practice voting on decisions made in class
3. A lesson on the election of the president, especially in a presidential election year

T I M E   F O R   R E F L E C T I O N :   W H A T   D O   Y O U   T H I N K ?

1. In what potential daily activities might teachers systematically help children learn to use their power for the good of the entire class? _____ _____ _____ _____

2. Why do you think it is important to teach children in grades K–2 about voting? _____ _____ _____

3. List four typical classroom decisions you believe primary students could make during the school year to practice democratic procedures and values associated with voting. _____ _____ _____

4. For an exploratory introduction for primary-grade students, a teacher selected a coloring activity followed by reflecting on the decisions made in coloring the picture. It is possible to teach, with different activities, a very similar lesson to older

➤ students. How would you modify the beginning of the exploratory introduction for grade 4 or 5? _____

_____

5. If children are allowed to vote on specific issues throughout the school year, what possible conflicts might arise among students? _____

_____

6. What additional values, concepts, and skills might you have to be ready to examine and teach as students begin to practice voting and accepting the results of a vote? _____

_____

_____

7. Older students may be familiar with formal voting carried out in elections. What concepts related to formal practices used in voting in the United States might you add to the learning cycle for older students? _____

_____

_____

8. What other concepts associated with government do you think young students and teens would profit by studying? _____

_____

_____

If possible, discuss your responses with a peer.

In the United States, citizens make their wishes known by voting for representatives, voting directly on issues in referendums, signing petitions, writing letters, displaying signs, taking part in support rallies, and giving speeches. The rights of freedom of speech, freedom of the press, peaceful assembly, and petitioning the government are guaranteed by the First Amendment of the U.S. Constitution. Participation in such activities is expected to reflect evidence of truthfulness and thoughtful consideration of the issues. Provisions are stipulated for legal redress of grievance for untruthful information and malicious intent. Information and the ability to use it gives a person the power to influence others, make better decisions, and exert control in his or her life. To make decisions on political issues, people must be informed. The information and skills learned in school contribute to the goals of informed citizens.

ASSESSING CIVIC EDUCATION IN U.S. SCHOOLS

The most recent assessment of what U.S. students have learned about government is the 1998 National Assessment of Educational Progress (NAEP) test in civics. It measured three interrelated components: knowledge, intellectual and participatory skills, and civic dispositions. Questions for measuring the knowledge of students in grades 4, 8, and 12 were written using the five questions concerning government that the *National Standards for Civics and Government* (1994) posed as the basis for the curriculum. Results from this assessment can be used to provide a base for evaluating the impact of the standards in future years.

The overall average scores for students in grades 4, 8, and 12 were similar to those for other major school subjects. The number of students at all grade levels scoring at the proficient level, which the National Assessment Governing Board says all students should reach, was less than 25 percent of the sample tested. In grades 4 and 8, 31 percent and 30 percent of the students, respectively, scored below the basic level. Hence, the reason concern was expressed with students' achievement in the headlines at the beginning of this chapter and why an examination of civic education and the curriculum by civic organizations and NCSS has ensued. Analysis of individual questions revealed areas of successful accomplishment by nearly all students but also areas that very few students had mastered. At each grade level, higher percentages of white students were at or above the proficient level than African American, Hispanic, or Native American students (Lutkus, et al., 1999).

The intellectual and participatory skills were measured with questions asking students to identify, describe, explain, analyze, evaluate, and take and defend positions. Students were asked questions measuring knowledge and understanding of important civic dispositions. At all three grade levels, students were asked multiple choice, short constructed response, and extended constructed response questions.

Students and teachers were also surveyed about the topics studied and the approaches taken in classrooms. They were questioned about student interactions with parents and the media, two additional powerful sources of political knowledge and socialization for youth. Students in grades 4 and 8 whose teachers devoted between 30 and 44 minutes per day to teaching social studies had the highest scores; students in classes in which less than 30 minutes per day was devoted to social studies had the lowest scores. Students who reported involvement in at least some use of such instructional activities as using computers, participating in mock trials, writing letters related to civic topics and reports of three or more pages, and using small-group activities had higher average scores.

At grade 4, students whose teachers had taught for 3 or more years had higher scores, but analysis of their teaching activities indicated that the differences were less likely to be a result of the type of activity selected or the frequency of instruction but instead with what the teacher does with the activities. Every grade revealed a positive association between the frequency of discussion of schoolwork at home and the average score on the civics test. At least two-thirds of the students across the three grades reported discussing schoolwork at home at least once a week.

Both fourth- and eighth-grade students who took the 1998 NAEP civics test were asked to indicate the ideas about government that they had studied in the last year. Over 70 percent in both grades 4 and 8 indicated they had studied the U.S. Constitution and Congress. Other concepts receiving the most emphasis included the president, rights and responsibilities, laws and rules, how people solve disagreements, the court system, and state and local government. Most of the emphasis was on U.S. government procedures, with fewer than half of the students in grades 4 and 8 indicating they had studied other countries' governments or international organizations such as the United Nations.

RESOURCES FOR CITIZENSHIP EDUCATION

An Interview with a Teacher: Emily Wood

In 1999, Emily Wood won the Outstanding Elementary Teacher award from the National Council for the Social Studies. She is a veteran elementary teacher in the Tulsa, Oklahoma, schools. Since her retirement, she has taught social studies in a private elementary school in Tulsa and history at Tulsa Community College. Over the years, Ms. Wood has taught all grade levels, including gifted and special education students. She currently teaches in a multigrade classroom. Ms. Wood's interview reveals the benefits students and teachers receive from using the resources of the local community.

Interviewer: Emily, I am particularly interested in your reaction to the conclusion that today's elementary teachers tend not to place much emphasis on teaching civics ideals and values and government (Haas & Laughlin, 2001). You said that you didn't understand this because it is so easy to teach civics in the elementary school. Would you elaborate on this statement?

Emily Wood: I have found that in every class there is usually at least one student whose family is in some way connected to government as a police officer, lawyer, or government employee. I also find that locally elected officials are willing to come to the school to visit classes and for special events. These people provide a wealth of information. Students' interest in these people further motivates the students' interest in civics as students interview and write letters to the mayor, council members, judges, and so on.

Interviewer: What are some of your favorite teaching strategies and approaches for teaching civics?

Emily Wood: I think it is important to involve the students in the learning process. Relying on pen-and-pencil tasks doesn't work very well. Mock trials are very good. There are a number of already prepared mock trials available from the American Bar Association. My students like to construct their own trial cases from local events reported in the newspaper. One class wrote a mock trial about eagles being found dead. I find that students love to debate, act out things, and write plays on events in their own community. In a mock city council meeting, my students have acted out deliberation on an animal ordinance stating the number of dogs you can have and whether people can keep wild animals. Simulations and role playing require lots of classroom management and time for kids to think and form solutions. Field trips are also helpful. I have always found that judges welcome having students come to court. This year we went to the municipal court. Once you get started, ideas and opportunities just seem to flow naturally. There really are unlimited things to do.

Interviewer: Could you give me an example of the natural flow you mentioned?

Emily Wood: This year we examined the Preamble to the Constitution word by word and illustrated each phrase in a student-written book. Students were very clever with their illustrations. *Posterity* was a word that really interested them. We studied our own family lines to help understand this term. Many of the children's families came from Russia, and only a couple were Native Americans. In Oklahoma, that is a bit unusual, as there are many Native Americans living here. One of the mothers came and explained how she took the test for citizenship and became a citizen. The children realized that they would someday have children and grandchildren and illustrated *posterity* with things that they wanted to leave to their future grandchildren as well as things that have been left to them. Because many of their families had not been wealthy, this group of children thought general welfare was important. One of the boys illustrated this term using public transportation. Our book on the Preamble was quite large because the students wanted to include things about immigration, including pictures of their families and Ellis Island. They all got a copy of the book to take home and want to make another book about the Constitution that will illustrate the three branches of the government.

Interviewer: You described having your students write a book. Do you use trade books with your students?

Emily Wood: Yes, trade books are good at bringing out the issues in the lower grades. For example, some Dr. Seuss books focus on law and the environment. I will use the books written by Peter Barnes and illustrated by his wife to help teach about the branches of the government. You know the books I mean. They are the ones in which the mice hold elected positions modeled after our national government. At first, the children are drawn to, and like, the illustrations of the mice, but I use the details in the drawings to help them focus on the governing process and structure of the government. The books by Peter and Cheryl Barnes are much more than cute pictures and rhyming lines. Again, teachers must prepare well to get the most possible from a trade book.

Interviewer: What are some words of advice or encouragement that you would give to beginning teachers concerning the teaching of civics and social studies?

Emily Wood: Civics can be lots of fun. I majored in government as an undergraduate and so had the interest from the beginning. But it really can be developed. Get interested in government yourself. Develop your own interest. Social studies is all around; use current events to spark interest. You will see lots of things to do. Then join educational organizations: really take part in them. Read their publications, go to the conferences, and serve on committees. This will help you learn and grow and open more opportunities to you.

Interviewer: Emily, it has been a pleasure to talk with you. You are always enthusiastic about teaching. Thank you for sharing your time and experiences.

Emily Wood: I hope that this will help. I have learned so much about my city as I have explored its government with my students. It has been a joy!

TIME FOR REFLECTION: WHAT DO YOU THINK?

1. Reflect on the interview, then describe what makes Emily Wood an award-winning teacher. _____

   _____

   _____

➤ 2. Those who performed the analysis on the 1998 NAEP civics test classified the following as "traditional" instructional activities: social studies textbook; using quantitative data, charts, or graphs; completing worksheets; hearing a teacher's lecture; and using books, newspapers, or magazines. How do you think Emily Wood sees these instructional strategies? _____

_____

_____

3. What reaction do you have to the following finding? "Traditional" instructional activities were among the strategies children said they were the most likely to do every day in the classroom (NAEP 1998 Civics Report Card for the Nation, 1999).

_____

_____

_____

4. Why do you think that teachers choose to use group work, mock trials, debates, primary documents, computers, writing three-page reports, doing projects, and writing letters only on a weekly or monthly basis with their students rather than more frequently? _____

_____

_____

Because many groups view citizenship education as one of their roles, the resources for citizenship education are literally countless and, as Emily Wood said, "all around us." Even before the Internet made materials readily available, many interest groups and businesses were working to promote their views about citizenship and their values by making free materials and guest speakers available to clubs and schools. These resources promote their perspectives on public or civic issues. Determining the quality of such materials for use in the classroom is important. Commercially prepared materials such as textbooks, video, film, and software often go through official state procedures to receive adoption approvals. But materials sponsored by interest groups and businesses generally do not go through such a screening process.

Parents and teachers find it increasingly difficult to assume that the resource materials students can obtain are appropriate and within the abilities of students to understand and evaluate. To assist parents and teachers, various education agencies and organizations have joined forces to assess materials and to provide rating systems. The education department for the state of California provides a large database of resources matched to the state objectives. A link to their website can be accessed at the companion website.

COMPANION
WEBSITE

The National Council for the Social Studies joins in coalitions with educators, business, government, and civic organizations to promote the teaching of powerful social studies. Professional education organizations make teachers aware of opportunities, issues, and resources through meetings and publications. They also investigate, debate, take positions, and speak out to promote their goals related to improving the teaching of their subject matter. Among the groups with which NCSS works are The American Promise and Children's Book Council.

MAKING A LITERATURE CONNECTION

Selecting a Trade Book That Stresses Social Studies

In her interview, Emily Wood indicates that teachers have an important role when using trade books for social studies instruction. Perhaps the most important is selecting a book to use as a read-aloud with all students. Such a book needs to focus on social studies content and objectives. Young learners need help in recognizing fact from fiction and identifying what is important for solving social problems from what is irrelevant, imaginative, or distracting. When taking class time to read a particular book, the teacher indicates to the students that this particular book is important. While reading a book to a class, the teacher has the opportunity to model critical reading behaviors with social studies content. This is not possible if the social studies content in not present or if the facts and issues addressed are not related to the learning objectives. Two important advantages of using a good social studies book over other instructional resources are the ease of selecting to read only a part at one time period and reviewing portions by simply turning a few pages. Books that deal with the complexities of the American political system and its abstract ideals present a challenge to young learners. But do cartoon illustrations represent the topic in a way that is appropriate to the importance of the content or the office and its impact on people? Cartoons, as they are and have been used in newspapers, use symbols and exaggeration to comment on issues and send a message. In learning social studies information, many topics are very serious, and a teacher must examine the illustrations that send lasting and powerful messages. The words that are used to explain pictures should guide the thinking of the reader to the important social studies information and attitudes. Gaining the attention of young learners is never more important than teaching accurate and important content and democratic, civic ideals and practices. Teachers must be careful when they hear or read that a book has won an award because awards are given to books for different reasons. A book might excel in the criteria for the award and fall far short on other important aspects, especially the criteria of meeting the objectives for a lesson on the presidency. *Woodrow for President* (1999), *Woodrow, the White House Mouse* (1998), *Marshall, the Court House Mouse* (1998), and *House Mouse, Senate Mouse* (1996) by Peter W. Barnes are worth examining for the balance in treatment between interest for young readers and selection of important content. While the mice are visually appealing for young learners, older students and adults can find many cleverly illustrated details and recognize many historical accuracies in American political life. The words, while rhyming, incorporate actual historical quotes and popular phrases. Future teachers who have used these books in field placements say that the students are quick to recognize some of the historical facts, such as the use of names of former presidents and office holders. They report that their younger students enjoy making detailed comparisons between the appearance of the real rooms in the government buildings and the illustrations in the books. Older students enjoy the challenge of using their textbooks or the Internet to search for references to historical events and quotations. Another idea would be to research the events of real presidential campaigns and compare them with what Woodrow G. Washingtail did to get elected. Woodrow G. Washingtail and his families and supporters also have values and character traits that can be identified and discussed. A good trade book can be used to motivate students to study as well as providing information and raising important questions about how and why people behave in particular ways or make particular decisions.

MEDIA RESOURCES

Freedom to discuss and comment on the actions of government and its representatives is essential in a democracy. Freedom of the press is among the specific rights guaranteed by the first amendment to the U.S. Constitution. Throughout history, newspapers, magazines, and books have provided citizens timely information. The critical use of such resources is among the skills promoted in social studies education. Media plays a major role in forming public opinion because it controls the knowledge of citizens. Failure to be media literate is a major obstacle to successful adult civic participation (Nelson, 1990).

Special newspapers and magazines for students at various ages, such as *Scholastic Magazine* and *Time for Kids,* attempt to encourage them to develop skills and habits necessary to keep current with events and acquire civic knowledge. Local newspapers have allied to create a program called Newspapers in Education whereby lessons on how to use the newspaper are provided to teachers, and the local paper is provided for every student in participating classes for a week. News magazines such as *Time* and *Newsweek* have created special educational programs in which students subscribe to the magazine at a reduced rate. Teachers receive weekly teaching guides and have the opportunity to select specially prepared packets on issues and enduring concerns prepared from the news agency archives. Most of these organizations also have websites that support teachers with lesson ideas and special sections for students that explain concepts related to stories receiving current media coverage.

Teachers often help students learn about events and the obligations and procedures for reporting news through activities such as producing a newspaper on events in their own classroom or in a time period under study. Often students or teachers ask questions about events in the local community or about international issues they encounter through studying current events. Such questions make excellent topics for units of study or local problem-solving activities. Students in grades 4 and 8 who took the 1998 NAEP in civics and who reported using newspapers, magazines, and books weekly or once or twice a month scored higher than students who said they rarely or seldom ever used them.

Elementary and middle school teachers who regularly use current events report doing so because they illustrate social studies content with current examples, helping students see the authenticity and need for studying the social studies curriculum. Current events is a vehicle through which students can learn about other nations. Students need important skills to become active citizens: gathering information, analyzing statements, identifying bias, defining problems, summarizing viewpoints, and drawing conclusions. These skills are taught and reviewed by studying current events. The outcomes of studying current events are values and attitudes such as developing empathy, reducing ethnocentric thought, building global awareness, recognizing interdependence, appreciating others and their views, encouraging tolerance, and realizing the need and importance of being an informed, active citizen. Teachers use a variety of resources when studying current events, with local newspaper and large urban papers being the most frequently mentioned, followed by television. News magazines including special youth editions and programs rank third in frequency of use (Haas & Laughlin, 2000).

Mary Hepburn, director of the Citizen Education Division at the Carl Vinson Institute of Government at the University of Georgia (1998), elaborates on the impact of electronic media as a socializing agent that needs serious reconsideration in the social studies curriculum. Hepburn relates that as early as 1979, Neil Postman predicted that television was fast becoming "the first curriculum," meaning that it would surpass the influence of schools as a civics education agent. Today, the vast majority of people in the United States receive their news through electronic media; nearly two-thirds of U.S. homes have more than one television; and more than half the children have their own televisions. The increase in individualized media use, especially by young children, means that both teachers and parents need to help students learn to use electronic media, including television, video, and computers, in meaningful and appropriate ways that help them gain knowledge and still have prosocial, democratic interactions with the great diversity of people who are their fellow citizens. More attention needs to be given to the power of the media to influence directly and indirectly people's knowledge and perceptions. Everyone needs to be aware of the media's potential to distort and mislead through repetition, bias, and stereotype.

Television relies on pictures to present its stories. Television journalists criticize their medium for having scripts so short that they distort the news. Time restrictions prohibit providing a perspective to frame stories and impede providing complete statements of the various viewpoints (Trotta, 1991). The Children's Television Act of 1990 limited the number of minutes of ads per hour in children's programs and required stations to air educational shows for children as a condition of license renewal.

Because all youth and especially those from lower socioeconomic backgrounds spend much time watching television, television is a socializing and educating force in their lives. Allen Smith (1985), a teacher in New York City, developed lessons critically examining popular television shows as a way of asking his students to examine the character traits of good citizens and ways in which people can influence the quality of programming.

COMPANION
WEBSITE

A website devoted to creating critical viewers of the media is associated with the Yale University Family Television Research and Consultation Center (see the companion website). The site contains activities to help learn and teach about television viewing habits, careers in television, determining reality from illusion, avoiding the reinforcement of stereotypes, dealing with controversial issues, reasoning with ethics and morality, and researching the impact of acts of aggression and societal violence. Each of these topics reveals the great impact television has on U.S. culture. Another comprehensive site on media issues, containing teacher lesson

COMPANION
WEBSITE

plans for the elementary grades teachers, is the Media Awareness Network (see the companion website).

COMPANION
WEBSITE

Computer usage is increasing in schools and holds great potential for social studies education and for bringing together people from all over the world to address shared issues and problems that are often global in scope and characteristic. C-Span provides teachers with daily lesson plans on breaking news that can be downloaded (see the companion website). It presents news broadcasts for use with students along with special newscasts that support school subjects. Computer use has created many new words, one of which is *teledemocracy,* which has three dimensions:

- Using the Internet for sources of public information
- Engaging people in electronic discussions
- Facilitating political participation, including signing petitions and communicating through letters and articles (Larson & Keiper, 1999)

COMPANION
WEBSITE

Websites such as Speakout.com and UNICEF's Voices of Youth are examples of teledemocracy (see the companion website).

Computer usage places an increased demand on social studies educators to teach the full range of media literacy skills. This is particularly evident when computers are connected to the Internet with its wide use of video, pictures, and cartoons. With the glut of information, students more than ever need to be active in critically evaluating what they see, hear, and create. Teachers can accomplish these objectives through lessons in which students study and use each form of media and compare the various forms of media. Lesson ideas that accomplish these ends are included in the following list:

1. Examine the presentation of a story as it appears in a television news broadcast, a newspaper, and a news magazine. Compare how each medium covers the story. Use a chart with categories such as facts, background explanation, emotional words, opinions or viewpoints, and graphics or pictures.
2. Analyze news stories in the newspaper and television for their length and content. Discuss these findings and students' feelings about what they have found.
3. Compare different types of television programs and written articles. Have students identify what they like and dislike about various programs and articles and which are most appropriate in answering various types of questions.
4. Follow a big news story through its development over time. Make lists of the knowledge learned on each day. Ask new questions and form tentative conclusions as the study progresses. When the story is over, review the experience. Identify which of the tentative conclusions were accurate. Identify the most helpful questions asked. Make final conclusions and judgments on how objectively and completely the story was presented.
5. Examine the trade-offs involved in the quality of information and the speed of transmitting a story. Decide at what times speed or details are more important.
6. Ask students to generate questions that they still have after reading or hearing a news story. Research these questions.
7. Interview adults about some very significant event (past or present) and ask how they got their information.

8. Interview local journalists about their profession and the problems they encounter in their work.

9. Have students assume the role of a journalist. Have them write various types of articles and produce their own newspaper, video, or website. As they encounter the problems of the journalist, discuss these problems, having students describe their feelings about the problems and the solutions used by the class or by the editor.

LAW-RELATED EDUCATION

The law-related education movement began because of the concern of lawyers and educators over the failure of the traditional textbook approach of civic education to provide a living content and vibrant activities for students (Starr, 1989). Advocates of law-related education (LRE) often criticize school civics curricula because students are taught the unrealistic perspective of a society that is in harmony and free from conflict. Law-related education provides many opportunities to examine the conflict between self-interest and the common good. Legal issues require careful examination of disagreements and conflicts. Mediation as a procedure for settling disagreements is usually taught as a way to avoid costly and negative actions that might lead to involving formal justice procedures. Examining the resolution of issues illustrates how society deals with conflicts for the common good and protects dissent through the concepts of individual, minority, and human rights.

COMPANION WEBSITE

Law-related education (LRE) is supported and promoted by the American Bar Association, which can be contacted through its website (see the companion website). Often, local and state bar associations work with school systems by training teachers and by providing guest speakers. Judges, police officers, and lawyers are frequently asked to speak to classes. Field trips to courts to observe the daily meaning of the loss of personal freedom and to legislative bodies to observe the process of making laws supply students with information on LRE topics.

Lessons in law-related education stress active student participation in learning concepts and performing value analysis. Role playing, simulations, mock trials, structured discussion, and analysis of stories containing moral dilemmas or expressing viewpoints are frequently used. Lesson content centers on the need for laws, human and legal rights, individual and civic responsibilities, processes of the legal system, and the important legal principles and values found in the Constitution and the Bill of Rights. Special projects on criminal justice and the judiciary system have been developed for intermediate and middle school students.

Law-related education seeks to foster the growth and development in students of knowledge and behaviors needed by citizens living in a pluralistic and democratic society. Law-related education is appropriate to use with primary-grade students, and its topics are authentic problems children have as they relate to children, adults, and institutions (McBee, 1996). It is recommended that LRE programs be designed to promote growth in several of the LRE learning outcomes listed in Table 8.3 (Anderson, 1980). Table 8.3 suggests how teachers can evaluate their success in teaching about the law. The desired outcomes of LRE are listed in the right column. The left column lists behaviors and perceptions that not only are opposite, but also reflect a person

TABLE 8.3

Critical Learning Outcome Continuums in Law-Related Education

Outcomes Children Move Away From	Outcomes Children Move Toward
Perceiving law as restrictive, punitive, immutable, and beyond the control and understanding of people affected	Perceiving law as promotive, facilitative, comprehensive, and alterable
Perceiving people as powerless before the law and other sociocivic institutions	Perceiving people as having potential to control and contribute to the social order
Perceiving issues of right and wrong as incomprehensible to ordinary people	Perceiving right and wrong as issues all citizens can and should address
Perceiving social issues as unproblematic	Perceiving the dilemmas inherent in social issues
Being impulsive decision makers and problem solvers who make unreflective commitments	Being reflective decision makers and problem solvers who make grounded commitments
Being inarticulate about commitments made or positions taken	Being able to find reasoned explanations about commitments made and positions taken
Being unable to manage conflict in other than a coercive or destructive manner	Being socially responsible conflict managers
Being uncritically defiant of authority	Being critically responsive to legitimate authority
Being illiterate about legal issues in the legal system	Being knowledgeable about law, the legal system, and related issues
Being egocentric, self-centered, and indifferent to others	Being empathetic, socially responsible, and considerate of others
Being morally immature in responding to ethical problems	Being able to make mature judgments in dealing with ethical and moral problems

Source: "Promoting Responsible Citizenship through Elementary Law-Related Education," by C. C. Anderson, 1980, *Social Education 44*(5). © National Council for the Social Studies. Reprinted by permission.

who is uninformed and lacks both a sense and desire for community. Table 8.3 can be turned into an assessment record by adding a rating scale and comment space under each statement so teachers can track the classes' or individual student's responses over a period of time. By rewording the statements into sentences and adding a numbered rating scale between the statements, Table 8.3 can be changed into a self-rating attitudinal measure for older students.

At the basis of our nation is the importance of the U.S. Constitution and the principles of government set forth in the document and its amendments. The flag and the president are the symbols of the United States with which most people, especially children, are most familiar. Knowledge about the Constitution, its content, and importance is an essential objective for social studies lessons. The learning cycle in Table 8.4 addresses the importance of the Constitution.

T A B L E   8 . 4

Learning Cycle	Presidential Oath

Grade Levels: Middle and Intermediate
NCSS Standards: Power, Authority, and Governance; Civic Ideals and Practices

Exploratory Introduction

Materials: Several pictures of current and/or former U.S. presidents

Generalizations

The United States is a nation ruled by a body of laws, not by any one person. The U.S. Constitution is the guide for all laws and acts of our government.

Objectives	Procedures	Assessments
Students recall and identify different actions that the U.S. president can and cannot do.	Assign students to small groups. Show several pictures of the president or past presidents of the United States Ask: "What are some of the things the president does?" Then ask, "What do you think the president can't do?" Assign small groups and ask students to create a list of responses for each question. Share lists, creating a class list on the board. Discuss questions: "Would you want to be president? Why or why not?"	Record students' responses on a class list noting the accuracy of their responses.

Lesson Development

Materials: Picture of a U.S. president taking the oath of office; poster on which is written the presidential oath; Internet materials, or appropriate websites, through which students can explore process of becoming a president

Objectives	Procedures	Assessments
Students identify the steps a person follows to become president of the United States.	Ask: " What is the process by which a person gets to be president of the United States today?" Discuss and help students, in small groups, compile steps of the process using reference materials from Internet sites or the websites themselves. Share group ideas about the process and create a list. Add any ideas students have not identified. 1. Declare yourself a candidate. 2. Win pledges of votes in primary elections. 3. Be nominated by a political party as their presidential candidate. 4. Campaign for office.	Students use materials and discussion to identify the steps a person follows to become president of the United States.

TABLE 8.4

Continued

5. Win the election.
6. Prepare to take over and appoint major helpers and advisors.
7. Be inaugurated (officially and formally sworn in by taking the presidential oath).

Students use the presidential oath in determining the relationships of the Constitution to the duties of the president	Display a picture of the president taking oath. Tell students that all U.S. presidents have taken the same oath. During the campaign, candidates for president promise they will do lots of things. Ask: "What are some of the things they promise? What do you want the president to swear to do?" List students' ideas. Ask: "Does anyone know what the actual oath is?" It is written in the Constitution, Article II, section 1:	Appropriate summary statements describe the relationship of the role of laws and the president.

I do solemnly swear (or affirm) that I will faithfully execute the office of president of the United States, and will to the best of my ability preserve, protect, and defend the Constitution of the United States.

This is the promise that tells us what a president must do, no matter what has been promised.

Discuss the meaning of the presidential oath Ask: "Are there any words in the oath that you don't understand?" (*Execute* means to carry out, not to kill.) "Does this oath include some or all of our ideals? Do you think it says all it should say? Why or why not? What appears to be the most important part of this oath?" How important is the Constitution to the United States? Is it more important than the president, Congress, the Supreme Court and the military forces? Why? What does the Constitution do for us? What does having the president swear to preserve, protect, and defend the Constitution tell us about how our founders, and Americans in general, view the law? What does it say about the importance of particular people or particular offices or positions?"

continued

TABLE 8.4

Continued

Closure: Ask students, in their small groups, to develop a summary statement describing how the United States is ruled. They should point out the role of laws as indicated in the lesson's key idea. Share statements. Develop a class statement.

Expansion

Objectives	Procedures	Assessments
Students predict which other occupations might take an oath to protect and defend the U.S. Constitution.	Review what was learned about the oath of the president. Present the following list of occupations and ask students to identify those for which the person swears an oath: lawyer, town council member, judge, teacher, doctor, soldier, governor, mayor, police officer, accountant, senator, member of Congress, citizen, member of the clergy. Ask: "For which of these occupations would a person be asked, as the president, to take an oath to preserve, protect, and defend the Constitution?" Mark the list according to the students' predictions.	Students' create a logical list of predictions.
Students collect data to determine the accuracy of their predictions about who takes an oath to preserve, protect, and defend the U.S. Constitution.	Check the predictions. In pairs, have students write letters, do library or Internet research, or interview people in these occupations. Assign each pair one occupation. Ask about their oaths and how the oath influences what they do when working. Ask students to prepare a summary statement on the occupation for which they collected data. Conclude by discussing the summary statements and the importance of the Constitution to people in the United States. Lesson Summary: Ask students to review activities of the lesson. Then ask: "Who has responsibilities to preserve, protect, and defend the Constitution? Should all Americans, or just some, take an oath to the Constitution? How and when should they do this?"	Students prepare an accurate summary statement identifying who takes an oath to preserve, protect, and defend the U.S. Constitution.

Note: Appropriate topics for learning cycles relate to various aspects of the Constitution, political and legal occupations, and the process of naturalization.

TIME FOR REFLECTION: WHAT DO YOU THINK?

1. What types of things do you anticipate the students saying they want the president to do? _____

   _____

2. What answer would you accept from students to the question "What does the Constitution do for us?" _____

   _____

3. At the beginning of the Expansion, the plan says to review what was learned about the oath of the president. List several things that you would want the students to say. _____

   _____

   _____

4. Examine your answers to question 3. Which responses recall facts? Which require statements of conclusions? _____

   _____

   _____

5. Students might not finish their reports for the expansion in a short time during class, especially if they interview someone. How do you suggest handling this problem to complete the lesson including all responses? _____

   _____

   _____

PARTICIPATING IN DEMOCRACY

Citizens are expected to participate in their communities. At the beginning of this chapter, you were asked to consider whether certain behaviors were those that would be performed by a good citizen.

In the nineteenth century, when fewer people were educated, most students were being prepared to become political, economic, or military leaders. Schools specifically taught students to be leaders and stressed the obligations of leadership as an important value. At the beginning of the twentieth century, when the rural nature of the United States was quickly giving way to the rise of industrial cities accompanied by a great influx of immigrants, Arthur Dunn of Indianapolis became one of the first public school educators to focus the social studies curriculum on identifying community problems and developing solutions. In 1915, Dunn became a member of the Social Studies Committee and convinced other members to incorporate service learning into two of their recommended course offerings: Community Civics for ninth grade and Problems of Democracy for twelfth grade (Wade & Saxe, 1996).

Even though service learning was promoted as an appropriate pedagogical model for citizenship education, it was largely replaced by other elements of the social studies curriculum, and only individual schools and teachers remained devoted to its use. Today, participation and service learning are being examined again because of changes in society. Some potential claims and benefits for community participation have been identified:

- Gaining a sense or a stake in the community
- Gaining a sense of self-worth and responsibility
- Practicing such important skills as cooperation, decision making, problem solving, and planning or organizing projects
- Gaining exposure to positive role models and career possibilities
- Increasing a sense of control over their environment
- Increasing personal interaction with a wider variety of people of other ages and cultural backgrounds (Procter & Haas, 1990)

Wade and Saxe (1996), in their review of empirical evidence for the impact of community service learning, reported that research was far from conclusive on the positive impact of service learning on social studies–related goals. Still, educators, politicians, business, and service communities consider service learning viable, and the number of people and schools taking part in it is increasing. A survey by the National Center for Education Statistics (Skinner & Chapman, 1999) found that 38 percent of middle schools in the United States had students participating in community service activities.

TIME FOR REFLECTION: WHAT DO YOU THINK?

Before reading further, record your answers to the following questions:

1. In what type of situation(s) might the average citizen assume a leadership role?

_____

_____

_____

2. What are three ways in which citizens of differing interests and abilities might serve their community? _____

_____

_____

3. What variables can you think of that might help or hinder a citizen's ability to serve his or her community? _____

_____

_____

4. In what kinds of service activities can the elementary and middle schools involve their students? _____

_____

_____

5. What opportunities are present in the school for students to perform services?

_____

_____

_____

Traditionally, citizen participation has been categorized as one of four types of behavior:

1. Participation in aspects of the electoral process
2. Participation in grass-roots citizen actions
3. Involvement in providing advice to form governmental policies and practices
4. Participation in obligatory activities

Recently, participation has been viewed with a broader sociopolitical definition: volunteer service through the donation of time and money and mutual self-help group projects addressing common problems (Langston, 1990). *Service learning* is a particular form of community service that incorporates service in the community with curriculum objectives and classroom activities and discussions (Hepburn, 2000). In social studies, Rutter and Newmann (1989) advocate the connection be to issues such as social responsibility, improvement of the common good, and opportunities for meaningful political participation.

All people have personal power. Only a few people exert political power daily. The informal use of power most likely occurs within less formal social institutions, such as family, friends, neighbors, and community-based organizations or clubs. The organized and formal use of power and influence is associated with political institutions beginning at the community level. In today's world, many issues and concerns are not limited by geographical boundaries. The larger the distribution of the issue, the more likely it is that legal and political organizations play a role in the solutions. Whereas political activism receives the greatest amount of publicity, social activism has responded more quickly to the needs of people throughout history, improved the lives of vast numbers of people, and prompted many of the social organizations and much of the social legislation taken for granted today. Social action is of particular importance to a large and diverse democracy.

School-Based Community Service Projects

Today, citizens are greatly concerned with the apparent alienation of youth and various population groups. Many see volunteer and mutual self-help types of community service as having an important role in correcting societal problems. They seek to involve young people in community and service activities. Several states have joined Minnesota and Pennsylvania in including statewide service programs in their schools (Clark, 1990). These community participation programs include a "passionate commitment to promote reasonableness, tolerance, fairness, and respect" (Langston, 1990, p. 304).

In 1996, NCSS and Farmers Insurance Group joined forces to start the American Promise Network to conduct educational outreach activities promoting the use of *The American Promise,* a video series and program that encourages service learning and community participation. A link to its website is found at the companion website. This program encourages teachers and students to practice service learning and promote the values of preserving freedom, encouraging and acknowledging responsibility, fostering participation, making hard choices, using information, providing opportunity for all, using leverage for change, deliberating with others, and seeing common ground.

In addition to individual character-building attributes, community service is seen as having the potential to vitalize the curriculum though authentic life experiences that require students to use social and intellectual skills. Following an extensive survey of community service projects, Procter and Haas (1990) identified six specific types of school-based activities that are often labeled as community service:

1. Using the community as a laboratory in which to practice skills learned in the classroom as a part of the regular curriculum. For example, students might record an oral history of the community and prepare it for use in the school or local library.
2. Special events or co-curricular activities sponsored by the school or a club. An example would be students taking part in a disaster relief drive.
3. Service programs that require a minimum number of hours of service for graduation.
4. Specially designed courses with class work and participation components. An example is helping organize a recycling center.
5. Programs designed for specific groups of students, such as students at risk or those with disabilities. An example is having these students use their skills to tutor or read to younger students or to help with a Special Olympics contest.
6. Career-oriented programs with emphasis on specific work skills or a professional orientation in which the students work part of the school day.

Participation activities are undertaken by students after careful study and preparation. Students must know why they are involved and how to carry their projects to completion. Teachers and other adults assist students in preparing for such projects. According to Wade (2000), quality service-learning projects require willing and honest reflection throughout the project in a classroom climate based on caring, mutual respect, and openness to divergent ideas. Table 8.5 illustrates social participation. Three types of service found in schools today are school, community, and individual. Social participation is shown on a continuum of possible activities ranging from a one-time activity requiring only a small commitment of time to long-term projects requiring a regular commitment of time and using multiple intellectual and social skills. Sustained periods of service in the field are needed for gains in political knowledge, participatory skills, and a feeling of understanding politics (Hepburn, 2000).

School service projects are centered on activities in the school. Tutoring younger students, performing skits to teach safety or health information to other students, making tray decorations for hospital or nursing home patients, and collecting food or blankets for the needy are examples. Community projects involve students in working with or through governmental and community organizations. Helping on a cleanup drive, planting trees in a park, and helping to build a children's playground are examples of community service projects. School and community projects are more predominant in grades K–8.

The individual service project is one in which the individual assumes the major responsibility in carrying out the service for an extended period of time. Tutoring in an adult literacy program, being a scout leader, and volunteering in a nursing home are examples of individual service projects. Table 8.5 also lists the skills, values, and citizenship concepts that are learned or practiced in each type of project. The projects

T A B L E   8 . 5

Hierarchy of School-Based Community Service Projects and Learning Outcomes

Project Type	Skills	Values	Citizenship Concepts	Grade Levels	
School Service Project	Identifying needs, organizing, group dynamics	Cooperation, self-esteem, pride in accomplishment	Participation, activism	K–12	**Basic**
Community Service Project	Communication, critical thinking, decision making	Respect, brotherhood, empathy	Community and democratic values	3–12	
Individual Service Project	Time management, problem solving, adaptability, self-direction	Human dignity, justice, responsibility	Appreciation of cultural diversity, social justice	7–12	**Complex**

are arranged in a hierarchical order to demonstrate that individual projects use the skills, values, and knowledge of the other two projects as well as those listed for individual projects. Individual service projects are more predominant in the upper grades (Procter & Haas, 1990).

Participation in Student Government

Student participation in the government of their own school through student councils has long been a tradition in middle and high schools. Such participation allows at least some students to practice democracy when the school administration gives students the freedom to initiate issues and solve problems. Today, many middle schools are attempting to encourage student government. In schools in which such programs are successful, the entire school and the principal have a strong commitment to the process. Student government is considered an important learning experience for all students.

Students elect representatives, who meet regularly, then return to share concerns and progress with classmates. Students identify the problems and needs of the school and are assisted in making the appropriate contacts in the school system and community to carry out their plans successfully. Students carefully research their ideas and develop workable plans. Students then present the plans to classmates, explaining the concerns of the adults and administrators and calling on fellow students to exhibit the behaviors needed to make the program a success.

For example, when the students at one school wanted soap in the restrooms, the janitor told them that uncaring students would break the soap dispensers, which would only create problems. The students mounted a campaign to educate their fellow students, pointing out the need for soap and the necessity for all students to use the dispensers properly. Students also set up a monitoring system to check on student behavior in the restrooms (Sadowsky, 1991). In some schools, student government representatives welcome and orient new students by explaining the school community and its government. Through such a process, students learn how to present their needs in petitions and address the concerns of public officials in their presentations. They also learn about the responsibilities of citizens to help care for government property and to share its use for the common good.

The democratic classroom is another way of involving students in learning about democracy. The work in such classrooms is designed to have students practice behaviors that reflect the democratic ideals of rights, responsibilities, and respect for self and others. Democratic classes make use of techniques such as cooperative learning, free expression and discussion of ideas, and the involvement of students in making decisions and setting goals (Holmes, 1991). Involving students in the assessment of projects is also an important aspect of the democratic school. The teacher models respect for all students and their ideas by inviting students to take part in making age-appropriate decisions. Through questions and involvement, students are guided to consider their needs and the common good. They are asked questions during the decision-making process and are involved in evaluating their choices and revising procedures or instituting new choices as needed. Teachers in democratic classrooms trust their students and allow them to make errors and face the consequences. However, they monitor the classroom activities carefully and encourage the realization and correction of errors before they become big problems.

➤ USING TECHNOLOGY

Discussions That Promote Greater Understanding through Combining and Evaluating Ideas against Criteria

Bouncing ideas off others is a technique many people like to use to help them to examine an issue or problem. Threaded discussions on a computer can provide such a forum for students and teachers. On an electronic mailing list, people respond if they want and as often as they like. As part of an assignment, teachers usually require a minimum number of responses or questions. Individuals are asked to respond and then to wait a day or so before responding again. This allows time for others to enter into the discussion and for people to reflect and word their responses carefully and to locate citations or references that are also helpful. Threaded discussions, which are asynchronous rather than a face-to-face opportunity, provide time for the responders to reflect on the discussion. These are important skills to teach young students so that they gain the learning benefits of discussions and understand the important role and benefits of discussions to the democratic process.

Threaded discussions begin with the asking of a question that cannot be answered with a simple yes-or-no response. The person who asks the question might provide a little bit of information related to the question and the type of responses that would be helpful. Those who are assigned to take part in a discussion are usu-

➤

➤ ally told to ask a question related to an assignment. Opening questions need to stimulate multiple responses and additional questions. Good questions to ask include those for clarifying or understanding points and relationships, for suggestions that might lead to creative applications of an idea, or for examples of experiences and concepts that support or challenge an idea.

A threaded discussion among middle school educators about an activity related to social studies illustrates the helpfulness of threaded discussion in teacher planning. A teacher indicated that he liked gardening and thought he could use the growing of plants as a connection to people in other areas of the world as a content focus of the seventh-grade course he teaches. His students would contact students in nations they were studying and ask that the students send them the seeds of native plants. These would be planted in an international garden. He added that he thought there were many ecological reasons why he should not do this, but he would like responses from list members.

Several responders replied with more than one comment that indicated that they had read what others said. The first responder explained about the U.S. Customs Service procedure of holding scientific plant, soil, and animals for a period of time before letting them proceed to their final destinations. This writer explained that many plants and animals have gotten into the United States that have not had natural enemies. In some cases, this resulted in massive populations that took the food sources of other species, resulting in extinction or endangerment. In new climates, some species grow much faster than in their natural habitats and become pests. The author indicated that this is an international problems and that rabbits, a feral species in Australia, are a major cause of the loss of habitat for many of Australia's native species. Hawaii was also mentioned as having similar problems dating back several hundred years. Rats from ships were mentioned as a danger to the egg-laying species on the Galapagos Islands, a location of unusual reptiles and birds. The gypsy moth was named as a major killer of trees that has cost the United States millions of dollars. This writer also indicated that the early settlers brought their domestic animals and turned them loose in the forests, where they ate and trampled plants, which allowed weeds mixed in with the European seeds to spread rapidly. Today there is a problem with the dogwood trees dying off in the mountains, which has a negative impact on the bird population that needs their seeds for food to migrate. The writer suggested that importing seeds was not a good idea but that the study of some of these problems throughout the world and the role of the Customs Service in protecting and controlling unhealthy trade might be appropriate. She indicated that the Customs Service does more that look for drugs and that students, as future decision makers, should be aware of the problems and attempts at solutions.

Several Southern teachers responded by naming kudzu, hydrilla, and water hyacinths as costly and troublesome imported species affecting their states.

A science teacher said that she was planning to work with a social studies teacher by coordinating the plants and animals that she studied with the nations studied in social studies. She recommended searching the Web for information about invasive species and said that she had found one website (www.invasivespecies.gov) that is loaded with information on the topic. She suggested that instead of planting ➤

➤ potentially dangerous seeds, students discuss gardens and how they are cared for, examine the role of gardens in various cultures, and exchange pictures or drawings of gardens with students in other nations via the Internet.

A second-time responder indicated that there were many good suggestions and wanted to add something that came to her mind as she read the responses of others. She suggested investigating successful importations, if not of species to grow, then of the crops themselves. She asked, "Where were the last shrimp you ate caught?" Indicating that in her state, fresh strawberries are available almost all year because of interstate and international trade, she suggested focusing a study on interdependence, a major concept in social studies that is discussed in the content disciplines of geography, economics, politics, anthropology, history, and global connections.

The threaded discussion provided the original teacher and several others with many good ideas and possible resources from a question that he originally thought might be a bad idea. Rather than discarding his idea, he now has several different approaches that he might develop into powerful social studies units that can make use of the resources on the Internet in several helpful ways.

Political Participation

Some elementary teachers work directly with their students to influence the formation of public policies at the local, state, and national levels. The political activities of third-grade students at Weber Elementary School in Fairbanks, Alaska, are a case in point. The students' activities included the selection of a current issue, in-depth study of facts and claims, and the use of communication skills and mathematics skills to gather data and inform citizens and politicians of their findings. Newspaper articles, guest editorials, and letters regularly flow from their classroom throughout Alaska and the continental United States as students study issues and share their knowledge and views. Not only do the students learn to gather and process information cooperatively, but they learn to respond appropriately and usefully in the democratic tradition. Their teacher, Grace Ann Heacock explains, "they are being empowered to keep a government of, for, and by the people" (Heacock, 1990, p. 11).

Over several years' time the efforts of the Extended Learning Program at Jackson Elementary School in the Salt Lake School District in Utah have resulted in the cleanup of a hazardous waste site, the passage of two laws, the planting of hundreds of trees, and $10,000 in neighborhood sidewalk improvements. Teacher Barbara Lewis writes: "Solving social problems will bring excitement and suspense into your life" (Lewis, 1991, p. 2). To assist other students, teachers, and interested adults, Lewis has written *The Kid's Guide to Social Action*. The following 10 tips are among her advice for taking action:

1. Choose a problem.
2. Do your research.
3. Brainstorm possible solutions.
4. Build coalitions of support.
5. Identify your opposition.
6. Advertise.

7. Raise money.

8. Carry out your solution.

9. Evaluate.

10. Don't give up.

Through actively taking part in examining political issues and trying to influence political decisions, students learn much about the functioning of the government. They also learn important principles concerning the use of power in society and test their reasoning skills and values. Such projects are filled with hard work and emotional ups and downs. Not every elementary or middle school teacher wants to use direct political participation with students. However, because many options for social action exist, all teachers can find a form of participation in which to engage their students.

Young people observe adults and model their behaviors on those of adults. Educators, especially social studies educators in a democracy, play a major role in helping youths to focus on civic choices and to encourage youths to evaluate possible choices, gather facts and opinions on issues, and make their decisions on the basis of the values that support democratic principles. Young people need to develop the full range of instructional goals that will lead to an ethical stance if they are to become good citizens who take civic action for the common good of their community, state, and nation. As part of examining the role of the social studies professional, members of the NCSS wrote and agreed to a code of ethics for the social studies profession. The code of ethics (see Table 8.6) identifies the six principles that describe how a social studies professional should approach teaching the knowledge, skills, and values associated with enlightened political engagement to young people. The entire statement that further explains each principle can be easily accessed through the companion website for this book.

TIME FOR REFLECTION: WHAT DO YOU THINK?

Read the six principles of the Code of Ethics for the Social Studies Profession in Table 8.6 and answer the following questions:

1. What are the characteristics of classroom management that are most compatible with the free contest of ideas? _____

_____

2. Who besides teachers are members of the social studies profession? _____

_____

3. In teaching which of the NCSS Standards does the teacher have the opportunity to model good citizenship for students? _____

_____

4. In teaching which of the NCSS Standards might the teacher have the opportunity to have students judge the civic virtues in the behaviors of a person or group?

_____

_____

➤

TABLE 8.6

Revised Code of Ethics for the Social Studies Profession

Principle One

It is the ethical responsibility of social studies professionals to set forth, maintain, model, and safeguard standards of instructional competence suited to the achievement of the broad goals of the social studies.

Principle Two

It is the ethical responsibility of social studies professionals to provide to every student the knowledge, skills, experiences, and attitudes necessary to function as an effective participant in a democratic system.

Principle Three

It is the ethical responsibility of social studies professionals to foster the understanding and exercise the rights guaranteed under the Constitution of the United States and of the responsibilities implicit in those rights in an increasingly interdependent world.

Principle Four

It is the ethical responsibility of social studies professionals to cultivate and maintain an instructional environment in which the free contest of ideas is prized.

Principle Five

It is the ethical responsibility of social studies professionals to adhere to the highest standards of scholarship in the development, production, distribution, or use of social studies materials.

Principle Six

It is the ethical responsibility of social studies professionals to concern themselves with the conditions of the school and community with which they are associated.

Retrieved on September, 16, 2003, from http://databank.ncss.org/article.php?story=20020402120622151.

➤ 5. When you think about your experiences with social studies professionals what specific principles of the code of ethics do you recall their exhibiting? _____

_____

_____

_____

■ SUMMARY

Citizens in a democracy must know the structure and procedures by which their government works and the ideals and values that support its beliefs and actions. They must also develop and practice civic skills and attitudes to carry out their responsibilities and duties as citizens. This includes examining the concerns of others and rec-

Memorials and monuments honor those who serve their nation.

ognizing that differences and similarities exist within each society. Students need to learn to respect and appreciate the multicultural nature of U.S. society and view diversity as providing greater possibilities rather than as a threat.

Schools have long been viewed as a place where students learn to get along with others and acquire and practice the skills of active participation in society. Many are calling for youth to play a more active part in their communities. Schools are changing their curricula to increase the participation of their students in various aspects and efforts in their communities. Active participation by citizens is a requirement for democracy to flourish. Today, technology has increased the speed of communication between people and opened new sources of information to all. This dramatic change presents new opportunities and challenges for educating students to be civil individuals in their personal and civic lives.

Expanding ON THIS CHAPTER

Activity

CW
COMPANION
WEBSITE

Contact the juvenile justice department of your state and learn how the legal system for youth is different from that for adults. Write a learning cycle lesson that teaches several fundamental concepts of law and examines how and why they are different for young children than for adults.

Recommended Websites to Visit

**COMPANION
WEBSITE**

Projects for students to participate in helping children in selected nations throughout the world have a better life.
   www.freethechildren.org/

A middle school project and lessons on civics.
   www.civiced.org/project_citizen.html

Ideas for how children can serve communities and people, especially other children.
   www.50ways.org/kidshelp/index.html

Persuasive reading and writing graphic organizers (click on Persuasive writing tools on chart).
   www.greece.k12.ny.us/instruction/ELA/6-12/Tools/Index.htm

CHAPTER 9

Helping All Students Experience Meaningful Social Studies

EXPLORATORY

INTRODUCTION

Professional development should help teachers understand the complex characteristics of ethnic groups in U.S. society and the ways in which race, ethnicity, language, and social class interact to influence students' behavior (Center for Multicultural Education, 2000).

1. Give two examples in which race, ethnicity, language, and social class impact your behaviors. _____ _____ _____

2. How did cultural experiences make you different from one or more of your elementary or middle school classmates? _____ _____ _____

3. List the characteristics you would use to describe a teacher. _____ _____ _____ ➤

➤ 4. Consider a sixth-grader whose grades usually range from C– to D and whose parents have a long history of complaining about the school. List the characteristics you think this student would use to describe a teacher. _____

_____

_____

_____

CHAPTER OVERVIEW

Powerful social studies means that every student has an equal opportunity to learn social studies, regardless of culture, gender, or disability. In recent years, the inclusion of students with special needs in regular classrooms has greatly increased. The majority of all students in the United States now attend regular classes. More than one-third of our students are from diverse cultural backgrounds. We must step away from the traditional whole-class approach to teaching social studies and encourage students to use, interact with, and respect not only their own heritage but also those of their peers.

Curriculum Standards for Social Studies (NCSS, 1994b) endorses the belief that students should be helped to construct a pluralist perspective based on diversity. This perspective respects differences of opinion and preference, race, religion, gender, class, ethnicity, and culture in general. Students need to learn that cultural and philosophical differences are not "problems" to be solved, but healthy and desirable qualities of democratic community life. Likewise, disabilities may limit individuals in some respects but enrich the group as students respond to and include each other in their work toward the common good of all.

This chapter describes the process for planning, developing, and carrying out lessons involving diverse students in a powerful social studies program. The types of accommodations that can be made to involve all students in a lesson are not unmanageable or difficult when included in a meaningful approach to social studies.

CHAPTER OBJECTIVES

1. Describe the purpose and rationale of social studies for all students.
2. Distinguish traditional social studies teaching from teaching that involves all students.
3. Describe general instructional strategies for social studies teaching in inclusive classrooms.
4. Describe the factors to be considered when adapting social studies instruction for students with special needs.
5. Identify and describe accommodations to be made in adapting a social studies concept for several specific special needs.
6. Define multicultural social studies teaching.

7. Describe modifications that are helpful in attaining meaningful social studies that accounts for differences in gender and cultural heritage.
8. Describe strategies for assessing social studies learning in diverse student populations.

MEANINGFUL SOCIAL STUDIES FOR ALL STUDENTS

Americans from all cultures need social studies to solve everyday problems. Multicultural education can be defined in many ways. A comprehensive definition describes multicultural education as at least three things: an idea or concept, an educational reform movement, and a process. Social studies is a critical component of multicultural education. Citizens need to observe events perceptively, reflect on them thoughtfully, and understand explanations offered to them (NCSS, 1994b). Social studies, in the past, has been depicted as an expendable class subject, particularly for special learners and diverse students. Social studies instruction is valuable to "special" students for many of the same reasons that it is valuable to all other students (Mastropieri & Scruggs, 2000).

All students should be as competent in civic matters as possible. They should have knowledge, skills, and attitudes that enable them to "assume 'the office of citizen' (as Thomas Jefferson called it) in our democratic republic" (National Council for the Social Studies, 1994b, p. 3). Four other reasons for teaching social studies to all students follow:

1. Social studies activities broaden and enrich personal experiences.
2. Special needs learners benefit from guided or selected activities that are based on reality and have predictable outcomes.
3. Social studies activities involve learning about cause-and-effect relationships.
4. Social studies develops and refines thinking and problem-solving skills.

An Interview

The following is an example of the results of an interview with a woman who works at a commercial business that helps people fill out their income tax forms. Ms. N explains how she uses social studies in a practical manner at work.

Ms. N: My company provided me with training on income tax law, what information is needed to fill out a wide range of income tax forms, and how to work with stressed-out people. I have always enjoyed working with mathematics problems and consider myself pretty good at mathematics. I have experience in sales and in a business office where I worked with lots of people and had to keep accurate accounts.

At first, my job seems like one that requires only mathematics knowledge. But when you really think about it, a great deal of social studies background is required. First, it is necessary to understand that paying taxes is part of a citizen's role in a country. Without taxes, many government functions could not occur. There would be no road paving, no garbage collection, and no monitoring of public health needs such as safe water. Next, it is necessary to understand the role of laws in the country. Laws help us to live together well. I need a detailed understanding of income tax laws. My company provides quite a bit of training on income tax law and updates the training every year. Finally, I need to understand how people think, what they worry about, and how they can be helped to make decisions about solving problems they have. All this is social studies knowledge that is important to doing my job successfully.

I have a community college degree. I learned a lot of what I know about my job in school. My high school and community college economics, psychology, and political science classes were important in helping prepare me for my job. I also learned a lot of what I know from my previous job experiences and from the training my company has given me. I think that nobody in my job ever knows all there is to know. So I am always learning.

A friend of mine works for my company doing the same work, and I got her interested in working here. My friend has helped me by answering questions and being supportive when it has been a busy day. Both of us have taken two accounting classes at the local community college.

SOCIAL STUDIES EDUCATION FOR STUDENTS WITH DISABILITIES

The U.S. Department of Education has interpreted the Individuals with Disabilities Education Act (IDEA) to mean that the regular classroom in the neighborhood school should be the first placement option considered for students with disabilities (Riley, 2000). IDEA requires that, to the maximum extent appropriate, children with disabilities "are educated with children who are not disabled, and that special classes, separate schooling, or other removal of children with disabilities from the regular environment occurs only when the nature and severity of the disability is such that education in regular classes with the use of supplementary aids and services cannot be attained satisfactorily" (IDEA, Sec. 612(5)(B)).

Students with disabilities who are placed in the regular classroom must have appropriate supports and services to succeed, including instructional strategies adapted to their needs. Some supplementary aids and services that educators have successfully used include modifications to the regular curriculum, the assistance of a teacher with special education training, special education training for the regular teacher, the use of computer-assisted devices, the provision of note takers, and the use of a resource room. In these classrooms students are viewed not as separate groups, disabled and nondisabled, but as students with shared characteristics who also vary.

Teaching resources continue to play a crucial role. Five areas that are examined to help students comprehend social studies resources are vocabulary level; content in terms of conceptual complexity (concrete versus formal ideas); writing style; organization of materials; and special features such as illustrations and graphics. A list of appropriate classroom strategies in social studies for special needs students follows:

- Activity-oriented instruction
- Instruction related to students' everyday experiences
- Interesting social studies activities
- Appropriate linguistic and conceptual social studies content demands
- Efficient classroom management, establishing ground rules and procedures for social studies activities
- Focus on skills development throughout social studies activities
- Examination of textbooks for the impact they may have on students

A primary reason for including students with special needs in the regular classroom is to increase their contact with a broader range of students. Excellent opportunities exist during social studies activities to promote such contact. Most social studies curricula hold the potential for a wealth of activity-centered small-group experiences appropriate for a wide range of students. When students work together to achieve a social studies objective, the potential for positive interactions within the group increases. Constructive interactions in the context of a group experience reinforce the interaction skills of all students and develop an appreciation of differences among peers. Other positive results of having students with a varying range of attributes work together cooperatively include tolerance, better appreciation for what a person can do, and opportunities to perform services that help others.

Meeting the personal needs of students with special needs requires thoughtful consideration of many factors. The identification of conditions needing accommodation may require modification of the learning experience to most fully benefit the student. Student abilities and characteristics, combined with the specifications of the Individualized Education Plan (IEP), determine the degree of modification of instructional strategies, curriculum, and evaluation procedures necessary to best serve the student.

General Instructional Strategies for Inclusive Classrooms

Many teachers have successfully adapted social studies curriculum materials to meet individual needs (Klumb, 1992). Adapting social studies materials for students with disabilities is accomplished through six general steps:

1. Identifying the learning needs and characteristics of the students
2. Identifying the goals for instruction
3. Comparing the learning needs and goals to the teaching materials to determine whether the content, instructional techniques, or setting require modification
4. Determining specific modifications of the teaching materials
5. Modifying the materials
6. Conducting ongoing evaluation as the materials are used

The following activities have proven useful in working with many special needs students. However, the teacher must have a clear understanding of the student's special needs and appropriate instructional strategies for the student. When peers work with the special needs student, the teacher must monitor the situation. Appropriate preparation includes selection of peers for working with the student and giving thorough guidelines for the activity.

Multisensory Activities. Multisensory activities throughout a lesson provide positive experiences for all students because motivation is enhanced through working with materials. Activities incorporating more than one sense or a different sense from that commonly used increase access to learning for all. For example, asking students to create a picture of an event by building it with clay on a piece of paper lets a visually impaired student "feel" the reported event. Other students are engaged in considering their activity from a new perspective: Rather than writing a report of an event, they must communicate it through the clay model. Such a challenge can result in some students utilizing or adapting little-used skills. All students may better understand that those who lack the physical ability to perform some skills are able to use other skills to accomplish a task. When more modes of presentation are used, everyone is likely to benefit both cognitively and affectively. Meaningful social studies activities occur throughout the learning cycle in an integrated manner, enabling students to construct their understanding of social studies content. Open-ended, multisensory, exploratory learning approaches are effective with students who have learning disabilities and related mild disabilities and for many students with visual, auditory, and physical disabilities.

Cooperative Group Activities. Cooperative group activities provide needed help for students and assist in social integration. Each student within the group has a role with a specific assignment. For example, a student might record responses, encourage contributions, or manage materials. Research on cooperative learning involving special needs and regular students indicates that cooperative learning experiences, compared to competitive and individualistic ones, promote more positive attitudes toward peers who have disabilities (Johnson & Johnson, 1978). Chapter 6 discussed cooperative learning in greater depth.

Classwide Peer Tutoring. Classwide peer tutoring involves assigning social studies tutoring activities to all students in a classroom. Students can work with an idea, a demonstration, or a procedure. Then they teach it to other students, perhaps through a group activity such as a jigsaw. When they have mastered the idea, demonstration, or procedure, they return to their home cooperative group and teach it to the members of that group. Having opportunities to teach peers can reinforce students' own learning and motivation (Vandercook, York, & Forest, 1989). Special needs students may have abilities that enable them to be effective at carrying out a demonstration, creating a map, putting information to music, or some other activity. Such abilities are used in classwide peer-tutoring sessions. When the idea is by other students through various modes of presentation, each student has multiple access to the idea, since each way of tutoring uses different senses or different perspectives.

Peer Buddy System. In the peer buddy system, students serve as friends, guides, or counselors to fellow students who are experiencing problems. For example, a student with an arm in a cast works with a peer buddy to complete a project such as a map that sometimes requires both arms and hands to be used in making it. A variation is to pair a student with special needs, such as one with a severe visual impairment, occasionally with another student whose vision is normal. Another variation is occasionally to pair two students who are experiencing similar problems so that they can give each other moral support. The opportunity to talk with someone else about how they have approached problem situations can lead to sharing advice, greater motivation, and better learning.

Reciprocal Teaching. Reciprocal teaching engages students in learning strategies aimed at improving their comprehension of social studies textual material by questioning, summarizing, clarifying, and predicting what is in a document, table, book, or other text. Textual material found in social studies textbooks, trade books, children's magazines, Internet sites, software programs, and in instructions for carrying out an activity can be used. Students take turns leading discussions in a cooperative group that focuses on each of the strategies. A student may lead a discussion about one of the following:

1. Questions the text raises
2. Ways of best summarizing the ideas in the text
3. Ways of explaining or clarifying the ideas in the text
4. Predictions based on the ideas in the text

Reading Alone. Reading alone can present difficulties, yet it is an integral part of most social studies activities and curricula. Although materials can be chosen to reflect the reading levels of most students, variations in individual reading levels within the classroom are still likely to be wide. Reading should be done *following* students' experiences with the events discussed in the reading materials. Reading is most effective when it is part of the lesson development phase of a learning cycle. It should occur after students have explored the lesson idea and formed the idea in their minds through active experiences. Students should be taught how, and encouraged to examine, the pictures and graphics in a book before they read explanations. This helps them comprehend what they read.

Lecture-Based Presentation. A lecture-based presentation is used primarily to give instructions, describe procedures, and provide short explanations. Lectures need to be supplemented to be successful in classes that include learners with disabilities and special needs (Bulgren, Deshler, & Schumaker, 1993). Lectures can create problems when students in the class have very short attention spans. They can result both in inappropriate behavior and in students simply "tuning out." When lectures are used, they must be brief. Important concepts and vocabulary are learned best through a variety of activities involving a range of modalities. If repetition is necessary, short lectures may be tape recorded so the student can hear them again.

The concept mastery routine has been described by Bulgren and colleagues (1993) as a way to assist students who have difficulty processing new information when trying to construct concepts. Teachers create a concept diagram. This visual device has several aspects:

- The concept name
- The concept class or category
- Important information associated with the concept
- Examples and nonexamples of the concept

- A blank space for additions to the diagram
- A definition of the concept

Media Presentations. Media presentations and the use of all types of *technology* can be a positive aspect of the curriculum for all students. Students with low reading abilities benefit from a multisensory approach. Media content may require reinforcement before and after its presentation. Repeated opportunities to work with the media presentation may be of value to any student in the class.

General Curriculum Adaptation for Inclusive Classrooms

Strategies for Using Social Studies Textbooks. Students need to be familiarized with the organization of the textbook over a period of days. Teachers first point out the overall parts of the textbook: table of contents, glossary, index, references, and appendices. Then the organizational system of the textbook is introduced: units, chapters within units, and sections within chapters. Next, specific features within chapters or units are examined: chapter objectives; chapter openers, such as motivating stories; chapter outlines; types and levels of headings and subheadings; use of boldface type, underlining, or colors; vocabulary; illustrations, maps, charts, diagrams, and graphs; chapter, section, or lesson summaries; follow-up activities or extensions; end-of-section, chapter, and unit questions; checks for understanding; different question-and-answer formats; skill builders; application activities; and critical or creative thinking extensions.

Finally, teachers help students examine features associated with supplemental materials, such as workbooks, activity sheets, student directions, textbook-related websites, textbook-related CD-ROMs, the amount and types of practice activities, and the formats of materials (Mastropieri & Scruggs, 2000).

Social studies textbooks and materials differ in structure from other types of text materials used in classrooms (Cook & Mayer, 1988). Text structures include the following examples:

Time, order. Information is provided in a chronological sequence; clue words include *next, later,* and *after this.*

Cause–effect. Events or actions are related as causes with consequences; clue words include *because, caused,* and *resulted in.*

Compare–contrast. Similarities or differences are highlighted among concepts, events, or other phenomena; clue words include *in contrast, similar, differ,* and *difference between.*

Enumeration. Items are listed by number; clue words include *one, another, the next,* and *finally.*

Sequence. Items are placed in a specific order; clue words include *first, second,* and *third.*

Classification. Types of items are placed into groups; clue words include *type of, labeled, classified, member of,* and *group.*

Main idea. An overriding thought or concept is presented (often in the first sentence) followed by supporting or elaborating statements (Cook & Mayer, 1988; Mastropiere & Scruggs, 2000).

Teachers help students decide which is the essential information by verbally describing why they are selecting certain sections, and not others, to highlight. For example, a teacher might say, "This looks like a new social studies concept, so I will highlight it. This next section just provides more information on the new concept, so I won't highlight it." Teachers can provide students with a self-monitoring sheet for highlighting that contains questions such as the following.

Did I examine my book for boldfaced print, types of subheadings, and charts, maps, or figures that seem important?

Did I find what information in my book is important to highlight, by asking and answering the following questions:

Is it new information?

Does it describe an important event in history?

Does it list or order causes of events or things?

Does it tell a main idea?

Does it compare and contrast things?

Did my teacher emphasize it?

Did I select information to be highlighted?

Did I test myself on the highlighted information by asking and answering questions about the highlighted information? (Mastropieri & Scruggs, 2000, p. 521)

This young student shows his ability to sequence by matching and aligning these traditional Russian figures.

Study Guides. Teachers often make study guides to reinforce their lesson objectives. Students use information in the textbook or other text materials to complete short-answer questions on the study guide form to reinforce major ideas and practice skills.

Semantic Feature Analysis. A semantic feature analysis is an activity to help students learn concepts from a social studies unit and/or textbook chapter (Bos & Anders, 1990). In using semantic analysis, the teacher analyzes the content within a chapter and develops a hierarchical web (see Chapter 15 for a discussion and examples). The web contains ideas introduced in a hierarchy of main ideas to lesser ideas. Students discuss the web with the teacher and fill in sections the teacher has left blank, or add examples for the ideas on the web.

Another strategy for using social studies textbooks with special needs learners is POSSE (Englert & Mariage, 1991; Englert, Tarrant, Mariage, & Oxer, 1994). POSSE is an acronym:

Predicting ideas from prior knowledge
Organizing predictions based on the forthcoming text structure
Searching/Summarizing for main ideas within the text structure
Evaluating comprehension

During instruction, POSSE begins with prediction activities. Students predict the content to be covered, activating their prior knowledge. As they discuss in small groups, or in the whole group, they record their predictions on sheets structured in the following way.

Students *predict* what ideas are in the textbook section: The Underground Railroad

Ideas	Questions
It's about a railroad.	Was there really a train?
Slaves try to run away.	Where could they go?
It is a long trip.	How did they get food to eat?

During the *organizing* component, students organize their ideas into semantically related groups. Figure 9.1 is an example of organizing ideas in a web format. After recording and organizing their ideas, students are asked to *search* for the structure in the ideas presented in the textbook (see Figure 9.2). Then they are asked to *summarize* the idea in their own words. Students use Figures 9.1 and 9.2 to help them make their summary explaining what they now see as the idea. Finally, students *evaluate* their work by comparing their summaries, using their search for the structure webs, clarifying their ideas, and perhaps predicting about a next related reading on the topic.

General Suggestions for Adapting Textbook Materials for a Diverse Classroom.
There are four major components of adapting textbook materials for a diverse classroom. First, the teacher might need to provide alternative text formats. Audiotapes of texts or those developed by the teacher and a volunteer reader can be used. Computerized text with audio components can be helpful. Enlarged-type versions of materials or Braille versions of text materials can be acquired. Finally, peers can read the text to the student.

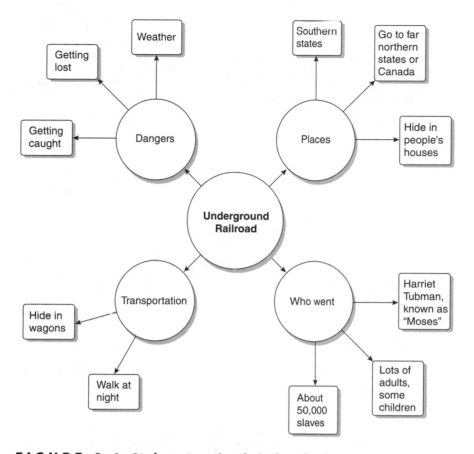

F I G U R E   9 . 1   Students Organize Their Thoughts in a Concept Web as Part of the POSSE Procedure for Reading Text

Second, the teacher develops or plans for the use of alternative curriculum materials. Study guides, outlines, or other types of guided notes can be prepared. Text materials can be supplemented with pictures, software, material from Internet sites, and activities.

Third, the teacher frequently talks with special needs students to find out what they are thinking and what meaning the material being investigated has for them. Students maintain journals that describe the meaning they are giving to new concepts.

Fourth, teachers use peers and parent volunteers as assistants (Mastropieri & Scruggs, 2000).

Factors to Be Considered in Adapting Social Studies Curricula and Instruction

Time is the variable that, more than any other, distinguishes the learning behavior of students with disabilities. Students with physical disabilities may need various

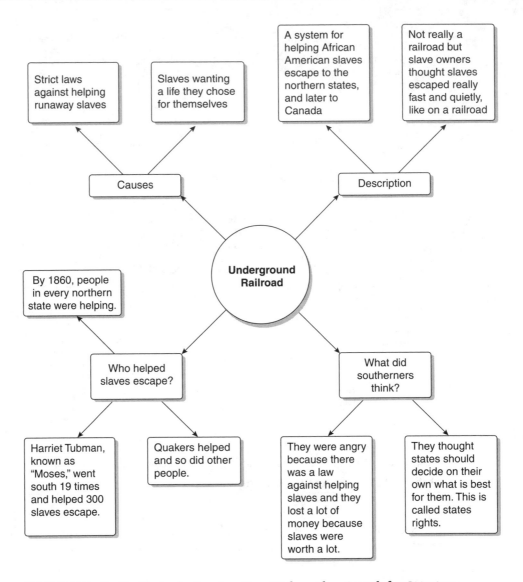

FIGURE 9.2 Students Create a New Web as They Search for Structure in the Text

sensory experiences to supplement learning. Students with visual impairments need tactile and auditory materials to explore while visual materials are being set out for other students eventually to pick up. Students with hearing impairments usually get less experience at abstracting information because they may have fewer opportunities to discuss their experiences with others. Their response time might be longer than that of other students in a specific situation because they have less experience and need more time to work through ideas.

Students with nonphysical disabilities might need more time and different learning strategies to supplement learning. Emotionally conflicted students often cannot suppress competing responses or cannot ignore one stimulus to pay attention to another. As a result, they spend less time anticipating the course of some event and adjust accordingly. Students with mental retardation often cannot integrate events, assign meaning to them, or pick out an appropriate response. For all these students, making predictions over a short interval of time may be difficult, but the reasons for this difficulty differ and depend on the type of disability. Teachers need to provide and support appropriate opportunities to increase the amount of time these students are engaged in data-processing activities.

Different modalities take in information at distinctive rates. An individual's eyes, for example, can display a whole spatial array at one time. The eyes keep track of information as a whole set. By contrast, information that comes in over auditory tracts is strung out in time and must be sequenced and patterned by the listener before it becomes intelligible. The wide range and depth of distance over which the eyes pick up information permit people to "see ahead in time." Before an event reaches its conclusion, or even before it takes place, people who can see may anticipate and adjust their responses accordingly. Because vision permits interaction at a distance, it provides a little lead time in which to adjust a response before an event happens.

When experiencing events, students with visual impairments usually must arrive in the midst of them. They may use sound and other perceptive cues, but because these are received over a much shorter distance and range than vision, the lead time is shorter. The visual cues, telling an inquirer what to look for and when to collect data, must be supplanted with other devices for visually impaired students. Because students with visual impairments have so little information before arriving on the scene compared to sighted children, they require more time to collect comparable cues.

Students with hearing impairments often don't get sufficient early clues. The task of abstracting information from the social world and then processing it into language to be logically manipulated depends on the availability of language models or appropriate communication substitutes for sound. Schools frequently spend a huge amount of time teaching language in a stand-alone format rather than in the context of some concrete event. As a result, students with hearing impairments are often denied the chance normal students get of trying to map experience with language in social studies activities.

Students with hearing impairments need to engage in social studies activities in which they can observe the history of events or systems. Students with visual impairments usually come to use verbal information very efficiently. They usually can hold longer chains of directions and verbal information in their memory than can sighted students.

Involving Students with Visual or Hearing Impairments in Social Studies.

Much of what is done in powerful social studies programs can be adapted for use by students with visual and hearing impairments for whom early social studies instruction is even more important than for other students. Teachers have successfully used the following steps to adapt materials for students with visual and hearing impairments (Sunal & Sunal, 1983):

1. Identify the factors in an event.
2. Identify the kinds of evidence associated with the factors.
3. Identify all the modalities or combinations of modalities that could be used to supply evidence that is equivalent to what would be collected by students without visual or hearing impairments.
4. Adapt the materials where necessary.
5. Devise a technique for recording data that the student with hearing or visual impairments can use.

Doing Social Studies with Mentally Retarded or Emotionally Conflicted Students.
Emotionally conflicted students and students with mental retardation often share the problem of a short attention span. Almost without exception, however, teachers who involve these students in social studies activities find that attention to activities is much longer than attention to passive tasks. These students often repeat or practice the same interactions many times.

TIME FOR REFLECTION: WHAT DO YOU THINK?

Evaluate a classroom lesson you have taught or recently observed that included one or more special needs students. On a separate sheet of paper, answer the following questions:

1. Describe the social studies lesson that was taught in the classroom. What types and number of interactions occurred between the students and the teacher and between the students? What role in the learning process did the teacher play? What role did the students play?
2. What strategies did you observe that involved all students in the lesson?
3. What learning outcomes do you infer for all students from the observed lesson? What difficulties did the students have in accomplishing the lesson objective(s)? Provide evidence supporting your evaluation.
4. During which tasks in the lesson did students with special needs have difficulties? During which tasks did thy perform well? Why do you think this might be the case?

SOCIAL STUDIES EDUCATION IN A CULTURALLY DIVERSE SOCIETY

The United States is more culturally diverse than most societies are. This diversity has led to an important question: "How can all students participate in and meaningfully learn social studies?" (Hursh, 1997). Classrooms are becoming more diverse. Some students are recent arrivals from other countries and are learning English as a second or third language. Many children are raised in urban settings that differ greatly from the national mainstream experience. Some students have moved from an urban area to a small town. In all such instances, these students increase the diversity of a classroom.

Important systems of beliefs are transmitted from one generation to the next. Children learn belief systems through direct teaching and through the behavior of those around them (Kostelnik et al., 2002). As a result, children learn different character traits. For example, in some societies, children learn to value cooperation more highly than in others; in some societies, children learn that competition is good. In some societies, time is treated as a commodity not to be wasted; in others, time is fluid and not so pressing. One cultural group might interpret a child's loud behavior as healthy exuberance, while another group might interpret it as disrespectful. Belief systems broadly define how people believe children should be treated, what they should be taught, and what behaviors and attitudes are socially acceptable (Shaffer, 2000).

> ➤ **BUILDING ON DIVERSITY**

Variations in Belief Systems

Children learn their culture's rules for how emotions are shown and for which emotions are acceptable in certain situations and which are not. Students carry these cultural rules with them into the classroom. For example, when most European American children are reprimanded, they are expected to maintain eye contact to show respect and to adopt a solemn expression to communicate remorse. Many Mexican American and Nigerian children are taught to cast their eyes downward to indicate respect. Chinese children might learn to smile as an expression of apology when being scolded. Navajo children often learn to lower their voices to express anger, whereas European American children learn to raise theirs in order to get the message across. In Japanese and Korean cultures, children typically learn to keep their emotional expressions in check and to avoid crying. In the United States, many people approve of young children expressing their emotions, but older children are expected to hide certain emotions out of consideration for the feelings of others; for example, they should smile when they receive a gift even if they are disappointed because it is not what they hoped for. In all cultures, children who learn the rules of conduct are perceived as more likeable and socially competent by peers and adults (Kostelnik et al., 2002).

People in most societies support social responsibility, behaving in ways that contribute to the common good. However, cultures place different emphases on prosocial behaviors such as sharing, helping, or cooperating. The emphasis that is placed on prosocial behaviors is expressed in laws, economic policies, through the media, and in the institutions people create. The ways in which people think about children, how children spend their time, what they see and hear, how they are treated at home and in the community, and the expectations people have for their behavior are all culturally based. Across all cultures, adults at home and in school most strongly affect whether children become more or less prosocial. Teachers must understand the variations between cultures and even within a single culture because not all subgroups teach their children exactly the same rules or promote the same behaviors. Activities such as making the student-family-community books presented in Chapter 7 on themes such as "Words of Advice from My Family," "What Kind of Work Did My Grandfather Do?" or "Teachings from My Childhood Community" enable a teacher to gain some insight into the cultural rules a student has been taught at home.

In the United States, three significant minority student groups—African Americans, Hispanics from numerous Latin American countries, and Native Americans—are often underachievers in social studies. The National Assessment of Educational Progress (NAEP) documents very low performance for Native Americans on its tests. Asian American immigrants generally have limited English proficiency, yet many groups of Asian Americans are more successful in the United States than are members of some other minority groups who are native English speakers (Tobin & McRobbie, 1996). However, each group exhibits a wide range of performance. Subgroups within each group also vary widely. Yet the members of each group tend to share cultural similarities. Teachers must consider these similarities because the needs of various groups within our culture differ.

Teachers need to think and learn about what makes a multicultural social studies program. In what ways is it different from a traditional program? The classroom has both a content and a context. To be responsive, teachers must present meaningful social studies that incorporates strands of specific content that are relevant to the experience of the students. Just providing a social studies program with a variety of experiences and an environment in which students are free to explore is not adequate. The social studies program must consistently invite all students to participate in experiences fostering different forms of communication: spoken, written, graphic, and mathematical.

All students—regardless of their gender and social class, their ethnic or cultural characteristics, and their special needs, if any—should have an equal opportunity to learn in school. Three basic premises of multicultural social studies education are as follows:

1. All students can learn social studies.
2. Every student can participate effectively in the social studies program.
3. Cultural diversity is appreciated in the social studies program because it enhances rather than detracts from the richness and effectiveness of learning.

Five goals have been identified for meeting the needs of culturally diverse student populations. These can be fulfilled through a multicultural approach to social studies education:

1. Acquire the knowledge and skills needed to study children's heritage
2. Present appropriate lessons for particular students, including powerful teaching strategies such as role playing and cooperation to increase instructional effectiveness with diverse students in the classroom.
3. Eliminate school and teacher stereotypes and expectations that narrow student opportunities for learning and displaying competence.
4. Create and sustain a communal setting that is respectful of individual differences and group membership where learning is valued, engagement is nurtured, and interests are encouraged (Holmes Group, 1986).
5. Assess students in the context of social studies activities.

Sample Strategies for Multicultural Social Studies

In classrooms where all students learn powerful social studies, three major strategies have been successfully used. The first strategy is to use *history* and the lives of *historical figures* as illustrations of the concepts being taught. The second strategy is to provide examples from *present-day social issues*. The third strategy involves using examples and applications of social studies concepts that fit a student's *culture* and *ethnic background*.

Historical Approach. Well-chosen examples of history incorporate a range of time periods, cultures, and genders to demonstrate a variety of perspectives. Long ago, Socrates taught through the use of questions and discussions in small groups; Elizabeth Peabody was an American who opened the first training school for early childhood teachers in the United States; Sarah Winnamucca encouraged Native Americans to build schools for their children in the late 1800s; and Freidrich Froebel established the first kindergartens in Germany in the early 1800s. Examples from history can be used to illustrate how various people's perspectives on a concept have changed education and are a part of important, larger cultural changes. In so doing, students can learn that the average citizen's role is not universal, inevitable, or unchangeable. This kind of understanding is needed to encourage critical thinking about social studies concepts.

Current Social Issues. Providing examples and references from current social issues can have a bearing on students' lives and arouse their interest in social studies. Also effective is discussing the people involved with these issues and how they are affected by addressing them. Some examples of issues are water quality, health care for all, urban sprawl, low voter turnouts, discrepancy in wages between men and women, how to provide adequate housing for all, and gun control. Such national issues have local import, and specific examples often affect the lives of a school's students.

Using Student Culture. Experiences that students have at home, in school, and in the community are rich opportunities for the development of relevant social studies concepts. It is important that the activities, problems, investigations, and variables in social studies lesson plans use student culture and relate to students' daily lives. They must encourage acceptance and appreciation of different views and behaviors by valuing all cultural and ethnic backgrounds.

Role Models and Relevancy

Limited experiences of students, especially those from some minority groups mean that they do not always have models who understand the role of social studies in their lives and occupations. Therefore, they might not see how social studies is relevant to their lives. Social studies may be viewed as boring and unnecessary. Some have considered this problem to be particularly acute in the African American community (South Central Bell, 1994). Similar situations often apply to large numbers of Hispanic Americans and Native Americans. The factors that have produced this problem are complex.

The curriculum is enriched when students are encouraged to bring in objects associated with their ethnic heritage.

Role Models. Professionals from all cultures make outstanding contributions in their fields. African Americans follow occupations that heavily rely on social studies knowledge, such as being government employees or managers of local businesses. Still, African American youths are often not aware of, or do not recognize, these historical and contemporary individuals as role models. Also, many African American youths do not realize the need for a strong early education in social studies or understand how to prepare for a professional career.

The investigation of the lives of people pursuing a wide range of occupations, both historical and contemporary, is important if all students are to have opportunities to succeed economically. Such an investigation must move beyond the individuals who are typically studied, such as George Washington Carver (a botanist and agricultural researcher) and Benjamin Banneker (a self-taught mathematician and astronomer). By restricting study to "great men and women" from a cultural group, recognition is removed from the important roles and services of average citizens. It is with average citizens that young people can interact and through whom they identify the important role of their own cultural group within the community. Most important of all is the chance to talk with local community members. These people are real and meaningful to students. When they come from the local area, they demonstrate to students what can reasonably be achieved with some effort and guidance.

COMPANION
WEBSITE

Internet resources that may be helpful for learning about potential role models in historical periods or from cultural groups at a distance from your community can be found on this book's companion website. These include Biographical Dictionary, which provides biographical information on more than 18,000 people from a wide range of time periods in a searchable database; African American History, which has links to people in African American history; Historic Audio Archives, with sound clips of a variety of people from the past; and Women in World History Curriculum.

MAKING A LITERATURE CONNECTION

Role Models

Role models from the community and local cultural group are an important component of social studies. These can be extended through biographies and autobiographies to include diverse role models from different locations and times. Examples include the following:

Bad Boy: A Memoir (2001) by Walter Dean Myers tells about growing up in Harlem in the 1950s and becoming aware of racism and his own identify as a black man (for middle school).

Hokusai: The Man Who Painted a Mountain (2001) by Deborah Kogan Ray and illustrated by the author is a picture book biography of Hokusai, one of Japan's most famous artists and gives an intimate look at the life of peasants in late eighteenth century Japan (for grades 3–5).

John Blair and the Great Hinckley Fire (2000) by Josephine Nobisson introduces readers to a not-well-known firestorm that devastated Hinckley, Minnesota, in 1894, burning a huge area and killing many. John Blair, an African American railroad porter, led 300 passengers out of burning rail cars to safety at a nearby lake (for grades 3–5).

America's Champion Swimmer: Gertrude Ederle (2000) by David A. Adler discusses the first woman to swim the English Channel and her never-give-up attitude (for primary grades).

Pick-and-Shovel Poet: The Journeys of Pascal d'Angelo (2000) by Jim Murphy focuses on an Italian immigrant's determination to write poetry as he teaches himself to read and write in English while earning his living with a pick and shovel (for middle school).

Cal Ripkin, Jr.: Play Ball! (1999) by Cal Ripkin, Jr., and Mike Bryan uses many photographs to tell the story of the Baltimore athlete who, in 1995, broke the record for the most games played in a row (for K–6).

Tallchief: America's Prima Ballerina by Maria Tallchief uses extensive pictures to tell Tallchief's story through her own words (for grades 3–5).

The Journal of Sean Sullivan: A Transcontinental Railroad Worker (1999) by William Durbin and illustrated with photographs and prints tells about a boy working on the transcontinental railroad and how he witnesses the legacy of the Civil War, the growth of the West, the courage and also the racism of some workers, and the appalling conditions that were part of working on the Union Pacific Railroad (for middle school).

COMPANION
WEBSITE

Boss of the Plains: The Hat That Won the West (1998) by Laurie Carlson tells how John Batterson Stetson created the most popular hat west of the Mississippi (for K–5).

Story Painter: The Life of Jacob Lawrence (1998) by John Duggleby and illustrated with Lawrence's paintings describes how he powerfully presented twentieth century African American experiences from the Harlem Renaissance to civil rights rallies (for grades 4 and up).

Seven Brave Women (1997) by Betsy Hearne highlights the brave exploits of seven of Hearne's female ancestors, celebrating the determination of "ordinary" women who have found many ways to be brave (for grades K–6).

Additional biographies and autobiographies are found on the companion website.

Relevant Social Studies. One way of addressing the needs of all students is to use everyday objects and experiences for social studies activities to make concepts more relevant (Rea, 1999). Although few students may become historians or politicians, they "will all become citizens with civic responsibilities and rights" (Rea, 1999, p. 4). Historical ideas in social studies can be made more relevant by tying them into students' prior knowledge, encouraging students to consider alternatives and reactions. Teachers could ask, "Has anything ever gotten you fighting mad?" and then help students tie their experiences to those of the American colonists who were "fighting mad" about the British Tea Acts (Rea, 1999, p. 4). Likewise, slaves and laborers reacted violently on some occasions. They also rebelled by slowing down tasks or only minimally performing them.

Not everything can be experienced firsthand, yet teachers can strive to make vicarious social studies experiences relevant. Teachers may use audiobooks, the Internet, trade books, guest speakers, storytellers, biographies, and video as ways of bringing experiences alive and increasing their relevance. An audiobook, with accompanying trade book, that would enable students to have vicarious experiences of a very different ecosystem is *Whalesong* (Siegal, 1998). This audiobook has strong emotional impact, enabling students to explore the Pacific Ocean world into which humpback whales are born and mature and the dangers they face from pollution as well as calls for renewed commercial whaling, both caused by humans.

Using such an example helps students contextualize social studies concepts (Sunal, Pritchard, & Sunal, 2000). The example makes use of an experience that many students have not had but ties it to experiences with which they are familiar. Teaching that works at making social studies relevant and that provides role models for students is good teaching for everyone. Other chapters discuss and give examples of teaching appropriate for diverse students.

CULTURE AND GENDER DIFFERENCES IN STUDENT–TEACHER INTERACTIONS

Many teachers interact differently with different students (Bernard-Powers, 1997). Male students are often given extended teacher help when answering questions. Females who give wrong answers are usually not asked to elaborate on their answers. Females are often rewarded for the neatness, but not the correctness, of their work. African American males might be ignored until they misbehave. Few African American females are praised for their learning. Native Americans are often introduced to social studies concepts in a manner that is not meaningful to them (Bellamy, 1994). The research indicates that teachers need to focus their attention on how they interact with students. They need to reflect on their observations of themselves to decide whether their interactions are based more on their expectations of students and preconceived ideas than on what each student needs and how each student participates in class.

Although it can be a time-consuming and complex process, teachers must read about the cultures represented by their students and interact closely with students and their families to learn about their cultural experiences. Gradually, teachers will develop an understanding of the cultural backgrounds of the students with whom they work. Teachers can address gender concerns by paying attention to how they interact with boys and girls, how they respond to both passive and active behaviors from boys and girls, whether and how their expectations for the behaviors of boys and girls differ, and how they include both males and females as role models in the curriculum.

Specific teaching strategies are needed to provide a powerful social studies program for students of both genders and of all cultural heritages. Many strategies have been shown to be effective in the research literature (Hampton & Gallegos, 1994; Pugh & Garcia, 1996):

1. Having high expectations for all students
2. Varying social studies learning activities
3. Addressing the affective dimension, considering feelings and motivations
4. Overcoming language barriers
5. Respecting different cultural mores and traditions by learning about them
6. Discussing gender and cultural inequities
7. Analyzing classroom management for equity
8. Providing role models of both genders, who represent a range of cultural heritages
9. Acknowledging and using the culture and home environment as a vehicle for learning

HELPING THE ENGLISH LANGUAGE LEARNER PARTICIPATE IN SOCIAL STUDIES

English language learners (ELL) bring diversity to the classroom that can be enlightening and educational. Encouraging ELL students to contribute to the classroom is a key to fostering their desire to learn a new language and to be academically proficient in the classroom (Cruz et al., 2003). A 2001 report from the National Clearinghouse for English Language Acquisition identifies the eleven most common primary languages of ELL students in the United States as 77 percent Spanish, 2 percent Vietnamese, 2 percent Hmong, 1 percent Haitian Creole, 1 percent Korean, 1 percent Cantonese, and just under 1 percent Arabic, Russian, Navajo, Tagalog, and Cambodian. Teachers are not likely to have a basic knowledge of all of these languages but can be expected to use strategies that help ELL students no matter what their primary language. The nature of social studies requires more language use, both verbal and written, than many other school subjects, such as mathematics, do (Cruz et al., 2003). Learning some basic words in your students' primary languages will help you to provide a comfortable, safe, and secure classroom environment.

There are two types of language use: basic interpersonal communications skills (BICS) and cognitive academic language proficiency (CALP) (Cummins, 1984). Language that is used to interact with others for social purposes, BICS, is developed through social interaction when students talk with others about a new pair of shoes or a school day off last week because of a severe storm. Specialized language used for academic purposes, CALP, is acquired at school and used for academic purposes. For example, classifying city, county, state, and nation in a hierarchy in which one includes another as a subcategory requires a high degree of CALP. Some English language learners developed CALP in their native country if they had adequate schooling; others did not develop it because of inadequate or no schooling. Those with CALP in their primary language more easily develop it in English when some support is provided. Those without CALP will need greater support for a longer time. Social language proficiency, BICS, takes about two years to develop to an age-appropriate level while CALP will take five to seven years. Teachers may assume that because social language is well developed, academic language is equally developed, but this should not be expected (Cummins, 1984).

Four proficiency stages in communication are found with ELL students (Bell, 1988; Cruz et al., 2003). At the preproduction stage, students point to items and can follow commands but mostly listen. Teachers use gestures and act out directions, use repetition, use pictures and props, and ask simple yes or no questions. In the next stage, early production, students give one or two word responses, label and match items, and list items. Teachers model tasks and language, use simple role plays, ask either/or questions, and ask who and where questions. In the third stage, speech emergence, students use phrases and simple sentences, compare and contrast items, and describe items. Teachers focus content on key concepts, use frequent comprehension checks, use expanded vocabulary, and ask how and why questions. In the fourth stage, immediate fluency, students demonstrate beginning CALP, participate in dialog and discourse, demonstrate reading and writing abilities, and comprehend academic text. Teachers provide alternative assessments, check for language bias and cultural bias, and provide contextual support. Teachers identify their ELL students' stages and focus on using the instructional strategies that are appropriate for each student.

Effective communication with ELL students includes modified input and modified interaction (Cruz et al., 2003). Modified input occurs every time the teacher directs something specifically at an ELL student, such as providing pictures, speaking slowly and clearly, and focusing on the here and now (Cruz et al., 2003, p. 21). Also important is the interaction between teacher and student and the ELL student and native speakers in cooperative groups. Interactions are modified to scaffold the ELL student's comprehension and production of the language and content. The teacher uses more comprehension checks and supports negotiation of meaning by teaching ELL students to use phrases such as, "please repeat that," "what does ___ mean?" and "how do you say ___?" (Cruz et al., 2003, p. 21). Peer students in cooperative groups are taught how to rephrase, expand, and check for indications of miscommunications. As ELL students advance through the communication stages, teachers match their development with appropriate instructional strategies.

Some of the strategies and techniques that help to provide a comfortable, safe, and secure classroom environment in which academic competency in social studies is the goal include the following (Cruz et al., 2003, p. 31):

- Learn to correctly pronounce the names of your ELL students.
- Use a community resource person to help you send a letter home to family members in their native language on class expectations and policies, major topics, projects, and the like.
- Provide a visual for class routines with a picture to depict each routine.
- Invite ELL students to make a presentation about their culture to the class. If their English proficiency is low, or if they decline, assign more proficient students to investigate the cultures of your beginning ELL students and to present the information to the class.
- Provide clear directions verbally, following up with written directions on the board and modeling of directions.
- Label items in the classrooms in the languages of your ELL students and in English.
- Set high expectations for all students with an understanding that it is often a language barrier, not an academic one, that impedes instruction.
- Check continuously for comprehension by asking for simple one-word responses, asking yes-or-no questions, and making true-or-false statements.
- Assign ELL students to an English-speaking classmate.
- Monitor your classroom, placing ELL students in the middle or at the front of the room, where they have your attention and you have many opportunities for frequent eye contact and interaction.
- Send home updates, weekly assignments, or class news in the ELL students' languages if possible through help from a community resource person.

ASSESSMENT OF SOCIAL STUDIES LEARNING FOR ALL STUDENTS

Tests fail to consider interpersonal skills, language abilities, and talents that students need in the real world. Culturally relevant alternative assessment is needed to improve educational options for students from diverse backgrounds. Alternative formats for assessments are discussed below.

Group Assessment through Cooperative Learning. Through discussion, students construct and negotiate a shared meaning of their social studies experiences, beginning to understand and appreciate cultural differences. Research indicates that cooperative learning experiences, more than competitive and individualistic ones, promote positive attitudes toward members of a different ethnic group or gender (Johnson & Johnson, 1978).

Graphic Organizers. Culturally diverse students share ideas, discuss, and agree on meanings through the use of graphic organizers.

Oral Interviews. Students are given an opportunity to share experiences through personal narratives. This enables them to demonstrate their individual questions, perspectives, and understandings.

Portfolios. Use of the portfolio provides multiple sources for profiling student growth and helps ensure equitable treatment of culturally diverse students.

Journal Writing. This activity encourages students to connect social studies to their personal experiences. It is more culturally relevant when it becomes a personal process in which grammar and punctuation are unimportant. These continuous entries throughout the unit provide evidence of learning in the context of the student's life experiences. When students share their journal comments in pairs or in their cooperative group, they communicate with each other about their learning. A continuous sharing back and forth of ideas helps students accept each other's ideas and the evaluation of their own ideas by others.

➤ **USING TECHNOLOGY**

Alternative Assessment

Authentic evaluation involves students in carrying out a variety of performances that show their understanding of an idea (Perkins & Blyth, 1994). Students express what they are learning by using word processing, desktop publishing, graphics, and multimedia display programs. With the help of software programs, students make graphs, timelines, and maps showing the results of a project. Examples of software useful for alternative assessment in social studies include TimeLiner and Neighborhood Map by Tom Snyder Productions.

TIME FOR REFLECTION: WHAT DO YOU THINK?

Evaluate one of your previously written social studies lesson plans or one that you find on the Internet or in a collection of lesson plans. Consider how appropriately the planned lesson involves culturally diverse students in the classroom. Answer the following questions:

1. What strategies would involve all students in the social studies lesson? _____
_____
_____
_____
_____ ➤

➤ 2. What additional strategy could be added to increase the effectiveness of the lesson for students from all cultural backgrounds? _____

_____

_____

_____

_____

SUMMARY

A powerful social studies program is a planned and deliberate effort to help students, regardless of special needs, cultural heritage, or gender. It is an effort to maximize their potential for success in social studies and as active citizens. Teachers focus on making social studies relevant and meaningful to each student. They expect that all students can learn social studies and that doing so is a worthwhile endeavor.

Expanding ON THIS CHAPTER

Activity

CW
COMPANION
WEBSITE

Your middle school students have decided to volunteer to help out at a local hospital as a community service project. One student in your class has developmental disabilities and cannot read, another is wheelchair bound, and three others are recent immigrants who speak just a little English. Yet all want to be involved in the project. How can you structure the project so that each student will be involved in it?

Recommended Websites to Visit

CW
COMPANION
WEBSITE

U.S. History Out Loud
   www.hpol.org
Student's Friend—World History and Geography
   www.studentsfriend.com/sf/sf/html
Ben's Guide to U.S. Government for Kids
   bensguide.gpo.gov
Kids' Money
   www.kidsmoney.org/
Selected Links for ESL & EFL Students: Easy to navigate with a lack of advertising
   iteslj.org/ESL.html
ESL Standards for Pre-K–12 Students
   www.tesol.org/assoc/k12standards/it/01.html

CHAPTER 10

Helping Students Interpret History

INTRODUCTION

Think for a moment about your experiences studying history, then answer the questions in the space or by putting an X on the scale beneath the statement. Identify at least six things that define, for you, the study of history.

_____
_____
_____

1. What appears to dominate your list? _____
_____

2. To what extent do you emphasize people, events, and dates?

none   a little   moderately   very much

3. To what degree does your definition indicate that history is an ongoing process of providing meaning?

none   a little   moderately   very much

4. To what degree does your view of history indicate that history provides you with a set of true relationships that connect the past, present, and future?
_____

none   a little   moderately   very much ➤

➤ 5. To what extent do you mention the process or methods of obtaining information?

_____

    none   a little   moderately   very much

6. Discuss your answers with friends. Do they see history as you do? Explain your findings. _____

_____

_____

CHAPTER OVERVIEW

People need to know about their pasts and their places in world history. This chapter is concerned with how we learn about our past and how that past can be made meaningful to us as individuals and as citizens of an increasingly interdependent nation and world. The study of history is personal and exciting but is often viewed by students as remote and uninteresting. Students have difficulty giving reasons for studying history because it does not seem to serve a utilitarian need. Perhaps this is more a factor of what and whose history has been taught than of the nature of history and its importance to people.

Elementary teachers play an important role as they provide students with formal learning experiences in history. Recent investigations into how elementary and middle school students understand history have described the naïve concepts or imaginative and inaccurate assumptions students hold. These investigations challenge the validity of past ways of introducing the study of history to young people. Therefore, the curriculum and instructional strategies that adults often experienced in their elementary and middle school years are being seriously questioned and reevaluated. This chapter investigates several reasons for studying history, the skills required to study history, the role of interpretation and evidence in the study of history, and research on how young students begin to examine and interpret history to identify the contributions it makes to their lives.

CHAPTER OBJECTIVES

1. Differentiate between the definition of history given by scholars and that used in schools.
2. Identify four goals or purposes for the study of history.
3. State a rationale for the study of history in all grades K–8.
4. Distinguish between the roles of primary and secondary resources in studying history.
5. Explain why the teaching of history must include the examination of conflicts.
6. Explain why studying particular historical topics is suggested for elementary and middle school students.
7. Suggest instructional procedures needed to teach young students to think critically about historical events and people.

8. Describe how timelines are used to assist in developing an understanding of time.
9. Reflect on how the learning cycle approach to lessons is appropriate to the needs of students studying history.
10. Identify various resources that can be used to teach history to students.
11. Explain why the role of narrative in teaching and learning history needs additional study.

DEFINITION OF HISTORY

History means different things to different individuals. Even historians do not agree on a single definition of history or on what constitutes an appropriate historical problem for investigation. Historians actually refer to themselves by different names: social historian, military historian, oral historian, archivist, public historian, interpreter, reenactor, genealogist, and archaeologist. However, historians generally agree on three important aspects: History is a chronological study that interprets and gives meaning to events and applies systematic methods to discover the truth.

Unlike social scientists, historians cannot rely on direct observations and experiments to gain facts. The historian has only what has been left behind and preserved to provide hints as to what may have taken place. Some people leave much; others leave practically nothing. Like the detective, the historian conducts exhaustive research to find many clues. Discoveries are mostly just clues, not complete records. They reflect the perspectives and memories of their preservers. Therefore, the historian *interprets the evidence,* deciding on the degree of its importance and accuracy. This is done by applying logic and "best guesses" to knowledge about the people and their times.

Often a discovery leads to more questions than it can answer. The ability to place times and events in chronological order is important in establishing cause-and-effect relationships. Historians not only examine the motives and actions of people, but also often apply principles from science and scientific discoveries to help them interpret the evidence. Working in history requires logic and persistence. The task is not complete when the answer is found; the results must be communicated to others, or the knowledge could be lost forever.

Actually, this explanation is not quite what a professional historian might indicate. Elliott West, a specialist in the social and environmental history of the American West, explains that history has no beginning and no end. There is always more to learn. Of necessity, historians bound their studies with a beginning point and an end point. But in reality, events took place that predate the topic of your study, and more history transpires afterward. Knowing about these events can contribute to a deeper and greater understanding and a more meaningful interpretation of what you have learned. West describes history as an infinite study "that celebrates a diversity of viewpoints and emphasizes our continuity with, and responsibility to, the past and future" (West, 2000, p. 1). West goes on to say that in this infinite quality, the study of history has much in common with the nature of education for teachers.

Students have various experiences before coming to school and return to different situations each afternoon. Teachers try to bound their teaching by knowing developmental characteristics of students at particular ages, but this is only a small help. Teachers who know the details of the lives of individual students have a better understanding of the students' interests, fears, and behaviors. Like the historian, the more teachers know about their students, the better they understand them.

When studying history, the more students know, the better they can learn. Young students with limited knowledge and experiences can learn history but not with the same understanding that the teacher, parent, or scholar has. Just what students know and are capable of doing at different times throughout their school careers is largely unknown. Only in recent years has research tried to discover how students learn history.

Additionally, if constructivists are correct, the problems of teaching history today differ from those perceived as problems of teaching history in the past. What you knew and could understand as a child might not be, because of changes in society and the world, what today's child can understand. Recent research points out that students understand time and lots of other concepts needed to learn history in more sophisticated ways than educators realized in the past. Other research, particularly large sample test results, illustrates that students might not know things that we think they know or what we think we knew when we were their age. Teachers must decide how to use the research findings to improve the teaching of history while resisting the temptation to do what has always been done or what others who have little experience with teaching tell you to do.

Brophy and Van Sledright (1997), in reviewing the new research concerning elementary students' understanding and learning of history, recommend that teachers ask themselves the following questions to reflect seriously on their approach to teaching history:

What are the big ideas I need to teach?
How can the study of history pique students' interests?
How can I encourage students to ask important questions about what happened in the past?
What inaccurate conceptions do my students hold that keep them from completely understanding the objectives?
How can I help students understand the past and get inside others' experiences?
How can I help students understand that history is an interpretive construction based on evidence?

They also remind us that some students introduce imagination into their interpretation of events. They recommend that teachers create assignments and opportunities to recognize the improper use of imagination and replace it with analysis of facts to help students make more accurate and logical interpretations.

HISTORY IN SCHOOLS

Historians have played a major role in all the national commissions and committees since 1892 that have addressed both history and social studies (Hertzberger, 1989). History is one of the specifically identified subjects in goal 3 of the U.S. Department of Education (1990), which states that history helps to prepare students for "responsible citizenship, further learning, and productive employment in our modern economy." The statement goes on to say that "all students will be knowledgeable about the diverse cultural heritage of this nation and about the world community" (U.S. Department of Education, 1990, pp. 5–6).

Two important dimensions of citizenship education in a democracy are identified by Engle and Ochoa (1988). One dimension is *socialization,* the process whereby a child comes to accept and support his or her culture. This provides for the continuity of the society. Engle and Ochoa suggest that for a democracy to continue to reflect the will of its people, its citizens must also experience a second dimension, the *forces of countersocialization.* Such forces require people to examine their personal and social beliefs and analyze the problems of their nation and world. Countersocialization activities require views to be supported with *reason* and *evidence.* Such behaviors are needed if citizens in a democracy are to be able to decide which ideas, institutions, programs, and behaviors should continue, change, or be abolished.

The study of history provides the opportunity for both socialization and countersocialization experiences. Engle and Ochoa suggest that very young children receive instruction that is largely socialization but that some countersocialization instruction is appropriate in the later elementary grades. The learning cycle on the first Thanksgiving in the United States is an example of how history helps socialize students (see Table 10.1).

TIME FOR REFLECTION: WHAT DO YOU THINK?

1. Why is the lesson in Table 10.1 classified as a lesson that socializes students into U.S. society? _____
_____

2. What prior knowledge did the teacher assume students would bring to the lesson?
_____

3. What role does the lesson expansion play in socializing students? _____
_____
_____

4. What do you recall learning about Native Americans in your school years?
Elementary _____
_____
_____

TABLE 10.1

| Learning Cycle | The First Thanksgiving in the United States |

Grade Levels: Primary and Intermediate
NCSS Standards: Time, Continuity, and Change

National Standards for History:

Standard 4: How democratic values came to be and how they have been exemplified by people, events, and symbols; Standard 6: Regional folklore and cultural contributions that helped to form our national heritage

Exploratory Introduction

Objectives	Procedures	Assessments
Students identify the tasks people must do when they move.	Ask students: "How many of you have ever moved?" Divide class into groups of four. Have groups select four roles: recorder, chairperson, materials manager, and facilitator. Each group is to pretend it is a family and make a list of things they must do because they are moving in a month or two. They are to consider how to get to their destination, where to stay when they arrive, and what to take with them. Have groups share their lists and record on the board. Discuss tasks with which the children in the family might help. As a homework assignment ask students to do the following: "From your own things select those that you would take if you were moving, but everything you take must fit into one large, brown grocery sack. Bring only a list of these items to class tomorrow."	Students working together in groups make logical choices. Record using a tally sheet.

Lesson Development

Materials: Overhead transparency of Sheet 3—*Coming to America* kit, for each student; copies of Sheets 4 and 5, *Coming to America* kit; world map or globe; trade books and materials downloaded from Internet (see the link at the companion website).

COMPANION
WEBSITE

Objectives	Procedures	Assessments
Students express their awareness of the difficulties of moving and make decisions based on personal priorities.	Students share their lists and discuss the reasons for their selections. Ask: "What was the first thing selected? What did you want to take that you had to leave behind? Would you have made the same selection if you knew there were no stores in the place you were going to?" Discuss any changes they would make and their reasons.	Students identify appropriate difficulties in moving and select items to take with them if moving today and in 1620. Use a checklist for participation in making a list of differences, attending to discussion, and giving or agreeing with ideas.

continued

TABLE 10.1

Continued

Objectives	Procedures	Assessments
Students identify at least five physical differences between moving today and in 1620.	Trace the route of the Pilgrims on a map or globe. The trip took 66 days. Show Sheet 3 from the *Coming to America* kit, about how the Mayflower was loaded with people and supplies. Discuss how the Pilgrims' trip was different from traveling today. Record differences on a list. Have a show-of-hand vote on suggestions before listing. Ask: "Do you think the Pilgrims had as much difficulty deciding what to take as you did? Why?"	At least five physical differences are identified by class in list on the board.
Students identify eight items Pilgrims brought with them based on what students recognize as their needs and space and classify these as tools, household items, arms, clothing, or food.	Ask students to make a list of what they think the Pilgrims brought with them. Classify the items. Did the students mention tools, household items, weapons, clothing, and food? Examine Sheets 4 and 5 in *Coming to America* kit for additional ideas and to confirm suggestions. Tell students that no one knows for certain what the Pilgrims brought with them.	Students classify appropriately using indicated categories.
Students work in small groups, gathering appropriate data from books about Pilgrims and Thanksgiving.	Students work in small groups, using books about Pilgrims and Thanksgiving to find answers to assigned questions. Give each group different questions from categories such as reasons for leaving England, problems on ship, surviving/living in Massachusetts, and celebrating first Thanksgiving. Groups report their research to the class and discuss why Pilgrims felt they should celebrate.	Students work together to find information to answer questions given.
Students draw conclusions regarding how contemporary and Pilgrim Thanksgiving celebrations are similar and different.	Compare the modern-day celebration of Thanksgiving with the first Thanksgiving by listing similarities and differences on the board. Students describe their sources of evidence.	Students share ideas for both categories and their sources of evidence.

T A B L E   1 0 . 1

Continued

Objectives	Procedures	Assessments
	Closure: Write two summary statements as a class: one for similarities and one for differences. The class repeats/reads statements together.	

Expansion

Materials: Short readings on Chusongnal in Korea and Pista Ng Aniham in the Philippines

Objectives	Procedures	Assessments
Students give reasons and identify supporting evidence for why other nations may or may not celebrate a thanksgiving.	Ask the students to recall reasons for Thanksgiving and when it is celebrated in the United States. Ask: "Do you think Thanksgiving is only celebrated in the U.S.? Why? Why not?"	Students identify reasons and give their evidence for those reasons in terms of whether a thanksgiving is celebrated in nations other than the United States.
Students compare celebrations of the harvest in Korea, the Philippines, and the United States by identifying similarities and differences.	Provide a short reading on Chusongnal in Korea and Pista NG Aniham in the Philippines. Ask the students to listen and identify at least three similarities with the way the Pilgrims celebrated. Ask the students to identify at least one idea from each celebration they find interesting and different from the U.S. Thanksgiving celebration. Ask them to tell why they selected it.	Students give accurate comparisons and show interest. Record on a checklist.
Students identify tradition, remembering history, and the efforts of the Pilgrims and Native Americans to live and work together as important reasons to celebrate Thanksgiving.	Discuss: "Why do farmers throughout the world celebrate at the end of the harvest?" Today, few people in the United States are farmers, but we still celebrate Thanksgiving. Ask: "Why do you think we continue to celebrate Thanksgiving?" *Lesson Summary:* Ask students to briefly summarize the main ideas of the lesson and the activities that supported them.	Students say people have same needs and wants. Students give, as a reason, recognition of hard work and a need for reward. Students recall evidence from history and celebrations accurately.

➤   Middle school _____
_____
_____

High school _____
_____
_____

College _____
_____
_____

5. Educators Frances V. Rains and Karen Gayton Swisher (1999) are Native Americans who have an interest in social studies. They recommend *against* special units on Native Americans. Why do they make such a recommendation? _____
_____
_____
_____

6. Explain why it would or would not surprise you to learn that African, Hispanic, and Asian American educators make similar statements about their ethnic groups. _____
_____
_____
_____

7. Identify three units in social studies in which a teacher can naturally and easily include instruction about Native Americans or indigenous peoples. _____
_____
_____
_____

The role of the study of history in the schools has been mostly to socialize students in the U.S. democratic tradition and to prepare them to be citizens. Much study has been devoted to learning about the origins of the nation and its struggles to grow physically, politically, and economically. Famous people and events have tended to dominate the study of history. Perhaps your definition of history greatly reflects this traditional approach to history. In recent years, social and ethnic groups have argued for the inclusion of important events and groups of people not previously studied in an attempt to present a more accurate interpretation of the nation and world. When asked to reflect on changes in social studies during their careers, more veteran social studies educators identified the inclusion of multicultural/global/gender-related education within the scope of social studies programs as the most important single change in the field of social studies. Catherine Cornbleth described this broadening of social studies to include more people as an important force because it "enables greater numbers of people to believe that they are a part of the U.S. and have a stake in it" (Haas & Laughlin, 1999b, p. 10).

STANDARDS FOR HISTORY

NCSS Standard II, "Time, Continuity, and Change," names three key concepts for the study of history: "Social studies programs should include experiences that provide for the study of the ways human beings view themselves in and over time" (NCSS, 1994b, p. 22). In seeking to understand their historical roots and locate themselves in the expanse of time, students are linked to people and ideas that remain the same over generations. They also come to see the struggle to institute change as a way of exerting control over their lives. Developing a historical perspective helps individuals and groups answer the following questions:

Who am I?
What happened in the past?
How am I connected to those in the past?
How has the world changed and how might it change in the future?
How do our personal stories reflect varying points of view and inform contemporary ideas and actions? (NCSS, 1994b, p. 22)

Young children are studying history when they sequence and order events in their daily lives, hear stories about today and long ago, recognize that other individuals hold different views, and understand links between their actions and decisions and their consequences. The curriculum, beginning in kindergarten, has plenty of opportunity to examine these basic historical concepts. Students enjoy solving puzzling questions about an unusual site they see on a walk through their community or about their school in years gone by, as pictured in old photographs brought in by a visitor. They might also learn about the people for whom local buildings and streets have been named. Through the study of people and events in world and U.S. history, middle school students experience expanded historical inquiry. They have in-depth instructional opportunities to learn about people's lives in various time periods by comparing, contrasting, and judging the lives, actions, decisions, values, and cultural traditions of individuals and groups.

After dialog and a major revision, the National Standards for History were published in 1996. The standards address U.S. history, world history, and historical thinking skills. Table 10.2 explains the five common historical thinking standards (skills) for grades K–12: (1) chronological thinking, (2) historical comprehension, (3) historical analysis and interpretation, (4) historical research capabilities, and (5) historical issues analysis and decision making. As you read descriptions of behaviors needed to perform historical thinking, you might wonder whether you were asked to do these tasks when you studied history. Note that some skills the historian uses are not common to the thinking skills elaborated for the various social sciences. This is a result of the differences in the available data and ways data is obtained.

In Table 10.2, skills in italics are for introduction and mastery in grades 5–12 when students are more likely to be formal operational thinkers. Although these skills are similar to those for K–4, they differ qualitatively in the complexity and number of tasks the student must perform before making a final conclusion. Note the

TABLE 10.2

Standards in Historical Thinking

Note: Skills listed in italics are additions from the grades 5–12 standards for historical thinking.

Standard 1: Chronological Thinking

A. Distinguish between past, present, and future time.
B. Identify the temporal structure of a historical narrative or story.
C. Establish temporal order in constructing students' own historical narratives.
D. Measure and calculate calendar time.
E. Interpret data presented in timelines.
F. Create timelines.
G. Explain change and continuity over time.
H. *Reconstruct patterns of historical succession and duration.*
I. *Compare alternative models for periodization.*

Standard 2: Historical Comprehension

A. Identify the author or sources of the historical document or narrative.
B. Reconstruct the literal meaning of a historical passage.
C. Identify the central questions(s) the historical narrative addresses.
D. Read historical narratives imaginatively.
E. Appreciate historical perspectives.
F. Draw on data in historical maps.
G. Draw on visual and mathematical data presented in graphs.
H. Draw on the visual data presented in photographs, paintings, cartoons, and architectural drawings.
I. *Evidence historical perspectives.*
J. *Utilize visual and mathematical data presented in charts, tables, pie and bar graphs, flow charts, Venn diagrams, and other graphic organizers.*
K. Draw on visual, literary, and musical sources.

Standard 3: Historical Analysis and Interpretation

A. Formulate questions to focus their inquiry or analysis.
B. Compare and contrast differing sets of ideas, values, personalities, behaviors, and institutions.
C. Analyze historical fiction.
D. Distinguish between fact and fiction.
E. Compare different stories about a historical figure, era, or event.
F. Analyze illustrations in historical stories.
G. Consider multiple perspectives.
H. Explain causes in analyzing historical actions.
I. Challenge arguments of historical inevitability.
J. Hypothesize influences of the past.

TABLE 10.2

Continued

K. *Identify the author or sources of the historical document or narrative.*
L. *Differentiate between historical facts and historical interpretations.*
M. *Analyze cause-and-effect relationships and multiple causation, including the importance of the individual, the influence of ideas, and the role of chance.*
N. *Compare competing historical narratives.*
O. *Hold interpretations of history as tentative.*
P. *Evaluate major debates among historians.*

Standard 4: Historical Research Capabilities

A. Formulate historical questions.
B. Obtain historical data.
C. Interrogate historical data.
D. Marshal needed knowledge of the time and place, and construct a story, explanation, or historical narrative.
E. *Identify the gaps in the available records, marshal contextual knowledge and perspectives of the time and place, and construct a sound historical interpretation.*

Standard 5: Historical Issues Analysis and Decision Making

A. Identify problems and dilemmas in the past.
B. Analyze the interests and values of the various people involved.
C. Identify causes of the problem or dilemma.
D. Propose alternative choices for addressing the problem.
E. Formulate a position or course of action on an issue.
F. Identify the solution chosen.
G. Evaluate the consequences of a decision.
H. *Marshal evidence of antecedent circumstances and contemporary factors contributing to problems and alternative courses of action.*
I. *Identify relevant historical antecedents.*
J. *Evaluate alternative courses of action.*

Source: National Standards for History Basic Edition, by the National Center for History in the Schools, 1996, Los Angeles: National Center for History in the Schools.

emphasis in Standard 5 on multiple perspectives and alternative viewpoints that encourage the historian to view history as an infinite story. Historians recommend that all five standards be approached in grades K–4 at a beginning, but not superficial, level that goes beyond retelling a story and beyond accepting only one possible outcome. They want teachers to emphasize the need for evidence to support ideas.

Because of differences in the cognitive and affective development of students and in the curricula found in various states, two sets of standards for historical knowledge are presented: one with a K–4 or primary grades focus (Table 10.3), and one for grades 5–12 (Table 10.4). Table 10.4 provides details on the recommended content standards identified by eras of time. Each standard may be addressed in multiple ways. Teachers, states, and school systems make many decisions concerning the specifics to be addressed. However, addressing history with elementary students

T A B L E 1 0 . 3

Standards in History for Grades K–4

Topic 1: Living and working together in families and communities, now and long ago

Standard 1
Family life now and in the recent past; family life in various places long ago

Standard 2
History of students' local community and how communities in North America varied long ago

Topic 2: The history of the students' own state or region

Standard 3
The people, events, problems, and ideas that created the history of their state

Topic 3: The history of U.S. democratic principles and values and the peoples from many cultures who contributed to its cultural, economic, and political heritage

Standard 4
How democratic values came to be and how they have been exemplified by people, events, and symbols

Standard 5
The causes and nature of various movements of large groups of people into and within the United States, now and long ago

Standard 6
Regional folklore and cultural contributions that helped to form our national heritage

Topic 4: The history of peoples of many cultures around the world

Standard 7
Selected attributes and historical developments of various societies in Africa, the Americas, Asia, and Europe

Standard 8
Major discoveries in science and technology, their social and economic effects, and the scientists and inventors responsible for them

Source: National Standards for History Basic Edition, by the National Center for History in the Schools, 1996, Los Angeles: National Center for History in the Schools.

TABLE 10.4

Sample U.S. History Standards for Grades 5–12

Era 3: Revolution and the New Nation (1754–1820s)

Standard 1
The causes of the American Revolution; the ideas and interest involved in forging the revolutionary movement; and the reasons for the American victory

Standard 2
The impact of the American Revolution on politics, economy, and society

Standard 3
The institutions and practices of government created during the Revolution and how they were revised between 1787 and 1815 to create the foundation of the U.S. political system based on the U.S. Constitution and the Bill of Rights

Era 8: The Great Depression and World War II (1929–1945)

Standard 1
The causes of the Great Depression and how it affected U.S. society

Standard 2
How the New Deal addressed the Great Depression, transformed U.S. federalism, and initiated the welfare state

Standard 3
The causes and course of World War II; the character of the war at home and abroad; and its reshaping of the U.S. role in world politics

Source: National Standards for History Basic Edition, by the National Center for History in the Schools, 1996, Los Angeles: National Center for History in the Schools.

through topics and events with which they are likely to have some personal knowledge or experiences clearly must be emphasized.

The National Center for History in the Schools describes activities keyed to the National History Standards for grades 5–12 in two sourcebooks, titled *Bring History Alive.* One sourcebook is devoted to U.S. history and one focuses on world history. These illustrate the Center's recommendations for using multiple resources to teach history. Table 10.5 provides sample activities for grades 5–8 from these books and indicates the several content standards for each lesson. Students use both primary and secondary resources and a range of intellectual skills to interpret the data and assess the interpretations that others have made of historical events and trends. The entire set of K–12 National History Standards are on the Internet (see the companion website for this book) and also listed as a recommended website at the end of this chapter.

COMPANION
WEBSITE

TABLE 10.5

Sample Student Activities for Teaching the National Standards for History

Activities Recommended for Grades 5–6

- **Transformations in Europe following the economic and demographic crises of the fourteenth century**
  Drawing on an assortment of picture books, discuss and compare examples of Italian Renaissance art. What is appealing about Renaissance painting or sculpture? What differences of composition can be seen in comparing a Renaissance painting with one from an earlier period in European history?

- **How increasing economic interdependence has transformed human society**
  Construct an illustrated chart depicting major scientific, technological, or medical breakthroughs of the postwar decades. What would your life be like without these advances?

- **How liberal democracy, market economies, and human rights movements have reshaped political and social life.**
  Interview a family member or friend who was a teenager or adult before World War II. How do they think women's lives are different today in regard to social equality and economic opportunity?

- **The social experience of the war on the battlefield and homefront**
  Explain how the war affected the lives of women by drawing evidence from diaries, letters, and stories about the lives of Clara Barton, Harriet Tubman, and Rose Greenhow. What responsibilities did women take on at home during the war? What role did women play on the battlefield?

Activities Recommended for Grades 7–8

- **Transformations in Europe following the economic and demographic crises of the fourteenth century**
  Write short biographical sketches of prominent figures of the late medieval and early Renaissance periods, such as Dante, Petrarch, Boccaccio, Giotto, Botticelli, Donatello, Dürer, Brunelleschi, and Isabella d'Este. Did these individuals share similar values and attitudes? How did writers and artists portray life in the early Renaissance? What is meant by Renaissance humanism? Why did wealthy or powerful persons become patrons of the arts?

- **How liberal democracy, market economies, and human rights movements have reshaped political and social life**
  Research the U.N. Declaration on Human Rights of 1948. Why was this document written? Write an expository essay on the progress or lack of progress of human and civil rights around the world or in one country.

- **The course and character of the Civil War and its effects on the people of the United States**
  Locate and label major areas of combat on a historical map. Explore firsthand accounts of a major battle using letters, diaries, photographs, and art reproductions. Plan a hypothetical class trip and map a selected battle or campaign. Explain how the physical geography of the area played a part in the battle.

- **The social experience of the war on the battlefield and homefront**
  Appraise the contributions of African American soldiers during the Civil War by drawing on excerpts from the movie *Glory* and books such as *Between Two Fires: Black Soldiers in the Civil War* and *Which Way Freedom* by Joyce Hansen.

Source: National Standards for History Basic Edition, by the National Center for History in the Schools, 1996, Los Angeles: National Center for History in the Schools.

BENEFITS OF STUDYING HISTORY

In response to concerns over what they saw as an inadequate quantity and quality of history teaching in U.S. elementary and secondary schools, historians formed the Bradley Commission on History in the Schools in 1987. Their final report is the most recent examination by historians of K–12 history teaching. The Bradley Commission says that the study of history is "vital for all citizens in a democracy, because it provides the only avenue we have to reach an understanding of ourselves and of our society, in relation to the human condition over time, and how some things change and others continue" (Bradley Commission, 1989, p. 5). The benefits can be grouped into three categories:

1. Personal benefits derive from helping individuals attain their identity by finding their own place in the history of the world.
2. The study of history helps individuals better understand and study other subjects in the humanities.
3. Studying history helps unify citizens into communities by creating a national identity.

The intellectual skills used and promoted by the systematic study of history help people develop cognitively. The Bradley Commission refers to these intellectual skills as the "habits of the mind" (1989, p. 25). The Commission goes on to say that the principal aim of the study of history is the development of perspectives and modes of thoughtful judgment associated with its study. Table 10.6 lists the perspectives and particular modes of thought historians use in making their critical judgments and interpretations

TABLE 10.6
Habits of the Mind Associated with History

Perspectives	Modes of Thoughtful Judgment
Understanding the past is significant to individuals and society	Distinguish between significant and inconsequential
Comprehend the diversity of cultures and shared humanity	Develop historical empathy
	Identify causal factors
Comprehend the interplay of change and continuity	Determine consequences
	Identify multiple causation
Accept uncertainties of life	Evaluate ethics and character
Consider conclusions and generalizations as tentative	Explain role of geography and time
Read widely and critically	Identify assertions, inferences, facts, and evidence

Source: *Historical Literacy: The Case for History in American Education,* by the Bradley Commission on History in the Schools, 1989, New York: Macmillan Publishing Company.

of people, institutions, and events. The modes of thoughtful judgment are similar to the tasks of critical thinking required in making decisions whereas the perspectives are more similar to conclusions about the world from the study of history. Thus, historians view the benefits of studying history primarily from a personal perspective whereas the creators of the school curriculum tend to see the benefits of studying history deriving from its contribution to a sense of community and national unity.

TIME FOR REFLECTION: WHAT DO YOU THINK?

In creating a curriculum, teachers establish goals and rank them according to the knowledge, skills, and attitudes to be learned. They consult the standards of their state and ideas put forth by history scholars and educators.

1. Look at Tables 10.3, 10.4, 10.5, and 10.6. What evidence do you see of the historians' views concerning the skills and content conclusions in the National Standards for History? _____

   _____

2. What evidence in the National Standards for History suggests special interest groups or cultural groups may have influenced the topics to be taught or the perspectives to be presented by those using the National Standards for History?

   _____

   _____

   _____

Once goals are established by the state or local district, they are placed in an appropriate sequence for teaching. Teachers and researchers have important ongoing roles in this process based on their experiences and research activities.

STUDENTS AND THE LEARNING OF HISTORY

Although students might not be able to understand history as completely as do historians, they are able to address some aspects. In recent years, researchers have shifted their focus from understanding time to broader concerns about how children learn history. As a result, they are more able to make research-based recommendations for activities that help children construct more meaningful understanding of history. Students know more about some historical topics than others. Children often know a great deal about the content and interpersonal relations of social history but very little about the nature and purpose of government, politics, and economics (Barton, 1997a). This has great implications for the type of history to select, the topics to be addressed, and the need to provide motivation and links to the reality and importance of specific events and people when teaching history at various grade levels and various locations.

The National Standards for History are used by most states in establishing state social studies standards. They have incorporated many research findings into their recommendations. In the remainder of this chapter you will encounter specific references to research related to instructional strategies and resources for teaching history to elementary and middle school students. You also are provided learning cycle lessons and ideas that model the proper use of research findings. Much of the research has been done in single classrooms using in-depth interviews and analysis of students' discussion and activities. These intense studies provide a type of data that has not previously been gathered systematically or in large amounts. Most of the studies indicate that students in a class do not view historical events or individuals in the same way, although their explanations and responses might show some possible trends.

Also available are the analyses of extensive tests such as the National Assessment of Educational Progress (NAEP). These test data indicate a great need for improved practices. The NAEP has redirected the focus of their testing to attempt to gain information on both the learning of historical content and historical skills. Some state tests are also using these types of questions, so large-scale state tests may be helpful to individual states and school districts. At present, the NAEP is the best single test educators have to measure both present successes and failures and any large-scale impact of reforms in the teaching of history. Past NAEP testing, conducted in 2001, is the best source of knowledge about U.S. students' understanding of history. Great similarities can be found in the NAEP findings reported on the teaching of civics and of geography in Chapters 11 and 14. The following statistics are of particular concern to social studies educators:

- Black and Hispanic students had significantly lower scores when compared with white, Asian, and Native American students.
- Students attending nonpublic schools performed at a higher level than did those students attending public schools.
- The percentage of students in grade 4 and of students in grade 8 who had teachers who reported that they never, or hardly ever, used primary documents was 62 percent and 23 percent, respectively.
- Almost half the students had teachers who reported using textbooks daily.

Overall, no statistically significant differences were found between the scores of male and female students in grades 4 and 8. At grades 4 and 8, 47 and 48 percent of the students, respectively, performed at the basic level, indicating only partial mastery of the material tested. Relatively few students, 18 percent at grade 4 and 17 percent at grade 8, earned scores at the proficient level, indicating solid academic performance and competence of challenging subject matter. Much room for improvement exists, and great concern has been shown about reasons why children in particular subgroups have not performed as well as other groups of children.

U.S. Secretary of Education, Rod Paige said at a press conference on May 9, 2002, that the high percentage of students who did not score at the basic level was "unacceptable. History is a critical part of our nation's school curriculum. It is through history that we understand our past and contemplate our future. Our shared history is what unites us as Americans" (Paige, 2002a).

Various states are introducing testing in social studies and presenting samples of the test questions at their respective state departments of education websites so that teachers, students, and parents can view sample test questions. These test questions are linked to the state standards for the curriculum and the various benchmarks for various grades. The state of Louisiana is one such state, and the following illustrate typical questions for fourth graders found at the website (www.doe.state.la.us/conn/assessments.php?dispPage=6):

Settlement of the west was most helped by the fact that the pioneers:

A. were granted many of the important government jobs
B. were not afraid of the Indians
C. used new inventions and tools to help meet their needs *
D. participated in searching for and mining gold

Which of the following shows the forms of communication in chronological order as they occurred in history?

A. telegraph, pony express, newspaper
B. newspaper, telegraph, telephone *
C. telephone, telegraph, newspaper
D. pony express, newspaper, telegraph

What is the purpose of the Bill of Rights?

A. To say how much Americans should pay in taxes
B. To protect freedoms like freedom of speech *
C. To describe the jobs of the President and the Congress
D. To make Washington, D.C., the capital of the United States

Correct answers marked with an asterisk.

USING TIMELINES TO DEVELOP CHRONOLOGY

The concept of time is very abstract. Timelines are concrete devices used to assist students in understanding time-related concepts. Physically making a timeline is only part of the process. Questions and exercises using the timeline are essential if students are to discover the meaning and relationships embedded within the timeline.

Whereas the primary emphasis on the calendar in kindergarten might appear to be the recognition of numbers and counting, the calendar also helps to mark the passage of time and important changes that occur over time. Recording changes in the weather and seasons and recognizing holidays and birthdays are beginning points for the study of time in history. By acknowledging these events, the teacher helps students to recognize important ideas related to history. As time passes, certain things change and others remain the same, illustrating continuity. Students need to recognize these and mark regularities in the passage of time. Appropriate questions related to the calendar include the order in which things were done during the day and the recall of past activities. Marking the class calendar with a favorite event from their day is a way students record the history of their school year together.

The first timelines that students are assigned to make are concerned only with the correct ordering of events. Recording one event for each day of the week or one event for each year of their life is a helpful structure for young students to use when creating personal timelines (Hickey, 1999). Using a clothesline on which items are attached with clothespins is a good way to make a timeline in the classroom. In the classroom, timelines are placed where they are easily seen and easily reached to make additions.

Complete timelines not only identify dates or time periods for which the events occurred, but also order them over the uniform passage of time. Placing events along the timeline requires the ability to add and subtract. When long periods of time are considered, multiplication and division are needed. Neatly placing drawings or pictures on a timeline and labeling events with words are physically difficult tasks. Young students need large pieces of paper and small time spans with which to work. Equal time spans are marked along the timeline. This can be done with the help of colored paper or knots along a rope. As students progress through the grades, longer timespans are studied. A century is a very abstract concept. Large time spans are divided into more understandable divisions. A decade represents the entire lifetime of fourth- and fifth-graders. A generation, 20 years, is a time period that is understandable and helpful.

When considering events over a longer period of time, students can be asked questions linking the passage of time to generations to assist them in their understanding:

How many generations passed between the events (e.g., the Civil War and the Spanish-American War)?

Are there many people still alive who had firsthand experience with the Civil War and its aftermath or is their understanding based on secondary sources?

Have there been any important events that might change the probabilities of what events are likely to happen to people in a war or because of a war at the time we are working with?

Thinking about cause-and-effect relationships and hypothetical predictions can be stimulated by activities involving removing and/or moving events along the timeline. Question are also stimulating; for example, ask students what events might not have happened if the compass had been invented 200 years earlier. Teachers can also rearrange the events on the timeline, asking students whether the new arrangement is a possibility. Students can be asked to consider if a particular event were removed from or added to the timeline, what other events might also be removed or added (Sunal & Haas, 1993). Timelines are a part of most history chapters in textbooks, and they are often illustrated with words, colors, and pictures. Teachers need to encourage students to read and interpret the timelines in the texts as well as the words and pictures of a book.

RESOURCES FOR TEACHING HISTORY

When teaching children about history, educators use a variety of resources in addition to, or instead of, textbooks. Additional resources provide opportunities to learn history by using a greater variety of learning skills. Part of learning history is learning how the historian gets and processes information. See Table 10.2 for the list of skills used in historical thinking. Historians use many resources. Each learning resource is evaluated for its usefulness, accuracy, and limitations. Some resources are readily available; others can be obtained through inquiries and using the Internet. Access to most of the great libraries and museum collections in the United States and in much of the world is possible through the Internet. These resources greatly extend the resource base available to all teachers and students and hold the potential of changing the way history is taught to K–8 students.

Locating and Using Historical Resources

Resources for teaching history can be obtained by asking for help. People are very willing to help when they are asked politely for specific things. Students' family members often have much to offer. Students should write a letter of thanks, including some of the things they learned as ways of reviewing and illustrating their attention and learning. Students are prepared in advance for any special behavior needed in encountering or handling resources. Make students aware of their learning objectives in advance before the experience and excitement of encountering the resources distract their attention. Prepare data collection sheets that match the learning objectives for use during the resource experience.

People as Resources

History is a part of everyone's life. Through examining similarities and differences in lifestyles and using resources from various racial, ethnic, and social groups in the community, a multicultural dimension is added to the study of history (Hickey, 1999; Singer, 1992). Whereas some people can relate experiences firsthand, others can tell about them because they remember what others have told them. Begin by talking to students' family members or neighbors. Have students write letters to local history buffs, leaders of business and civic organizations, or the local newspaper asking for specific information or for answers to questions. Some teachers have had great success in dealing with senior citizen's groups or nursing home residents whereas others have worked well with collectors or craft makers. Not all people might want to visit a class, but many are happy to receive one or two students. Students in small groups or as a whole group prepare a written list of meaningful questions to ask. Tape recording presentations helps to get information correct, but permission must be obtained before recording. For longer units of study, it is often useful to have one or two individuals who work well with the age group visit several times as the study progresses.

Artifacts and Museums

Museums are an important source of artifacts, but so are attics and antique stores. Larger museums often make reproductions available at reasonable prices. One or two carefully selected artifacts can provide many opportunities for students to use their observation and thinking skills. Interesting questions and discussions that lead to forming hypotheses and investigations can be initiated by examining artifacts. Artifacts are successfully used as instructional resources in each phase of the learning cycle. Examining the materials, craftsmanship, and workings of artifacts reveals much about the values and lifestyle of both the maker and user. Artifacts provide the opportunity to examine concepts such as change, continuity, and creativity and offer clues to the local habitat and level of scientific knowledge and its application during the time period when they were used.

A trip to a museum or restoration is often reported as a positive memory in the study of history. Many small local museums have some very different or unusual things students have never seen. Sometimes observers are surprised to find items displayed that they see every day but never think to be of value or related to history. Because museums display collections, they are often appreciated by middle grades students who delight in collecting and learning all about their own collections. Many museums and restorations provide active programs especially for students: allowing them to handle things, to take part in live demonstrations, or to remain several days to live and work in another time period.

Students learn best if the opportunity for instruction both before and after the visit is provided. Teachers should contact the facility well in advance of the visit. Many museums have planned activities or reading lists to assist the teacher in preparing for the visit. They also provide special guides or programs for student groups. One of the largest collections of artifacts in the world is that of the Smithsonian Institution, sometimes referred to as "America's attic," in Washington, D.C. Through the educational services of the National Portrait Gallery of the Smithsonian Institution website (see the link at the companion website) for example, students can visit the 1999 special exhibit of the portraits of George and Martha Washington.

COMPANION
WEBSITE

The Community as a Resource

State and local history is often included in the elementary and middle school curriculum. These provide the opportunity to gather data firsthand as a historian might and to process it into meaningful conclusions and displays. Third-grade teacher Caroline Donnan (1988) explains that she was able to meet all the social studies skill objectives through a third-grade study of the local community.

Cemeteries are often the locations of commemorative monuments to events or people. A trip to the cemetery can help teach students about the life cycle and about how and why people are remembered. Older students can look more closely at tombstones and discover changes in lifespans and the reduction of infant and child mortality. Rubbings can be made or epitaphs copied to provide information about a person and the times in which he or she lived. Often, ethnic, religious, or racial groups are buried in separate cemeteries or sections. Examining this phenomenon can raise a number of interesting questions:

Why did a family bury their son with other soldiers rather than in the family plot?
Why are people of one religion all buried together?
How many generations of a family are buried in one plot? What might this tell
     you about the people?

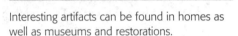

Visiting a restoration involves learners in the lives of people who lived in other times.

Interesting artifacts can be found in homes as well as museums and restorations.

The architecture of your community illustrates the origins of ethnic groups, changes in preferences, and the wealth of each owner. It indicates the technology and materials available to the builder. The names of streets reflect their functions and the people and places admired by the citizens. Some buildings have been used for a variety of purposes, and some are no longer in use. Speculation and investigation of their future usage are worthy activities. Many communities have special memorials, statues, and buildings. These acknowledge important people, businesses, and events of local concern. They often link the community to national and world events students read about in textbooks. In small communities, walking field trips provide students with opportunities to gather data and identify questions for future study. Sketching, photographing, and interviewing are helpful on a walking field trip and serve as discussion and project inspirations when students return to the classroom. Dot Schuler (2002) took her class on such a walking tour, which eventually led to their writing and illustrating a book that is sold as a guide to their community for tourists.

Documents as Resources

Every U.S. citizen should be aware of the content of important documents such as the Declaration of Independence, the Constitution, and the Emancipation Proclamation. Many textbooks include reproductions of such major documents. Here, documents are defined as the official or public record of events in the lives of individuals, businesses, communities, and institutions. Historians examine many documents.

Locally, documents often can be obtained through government offices, individual businesses and organizations, and local museums. Families may have deeds, wills, and certificates to share. The National Archives and Records Administration has prepared teaching resources and regularly publishes lessons based on a historical document from their collection in *Social Education*. Original documents are often handwritten and difficult to read. Most educational packets of documents include more easily read printed copies. As part of the federal government's emphasis on putting information online for use by citizens and in education, it is possible to gain access to many collections of documents through the National Archives and historial data from the U.S. Census manuscripts are at their website after the information is 50 years old (see links at the companion website).

COMPANION
WEBSITE

Questions to be answered when examining documents include those that help in gathering information, interpreting it, and establishing its meaning. Data-gathering questions follow:

What does the document say?
What values are expressed in the document?
Does the document include any words indicating bias or prejudice?
Does the document order action? By whom? To whom?
Is the document sworn to or legally binding?

Questions that assist in establishing meaning and interpretation follow:

What things happened as a result of issuing the document?
Does the information in the document agree with other resources?
Is this document likely to be more accurate than data in another source?
Why might this document have been preserved?
At what specific truth or what conclusion does this document help me arrive?

Diaries, Letters, and Pictures as Resources

Diaries, letters, and pictures are also primary sources of data. Some books contain these resources pertaining to specific events and time periods. Local families and museums may have such items that can be copied to share. Estate and garage sales are good sources of old pictures. Table 10.7 is a learning cycle lesson that develops skill in gathering information and comparing pictures. Because those who produce primary sources are likely to state their opinions or interpretations, questions concerning the author's or photographer's credentials and views must be asked:

Who wrote the material or took the picture, and for what reasons?
How likely was the author to know the facts and to make accurate conclusions?
Does the author or photographer have a reason to support one view or another?
Are any facts present or does the writer present only conclusions?
What other sources agree with the facts or views presented?
What word(s) might indicate a bias or lack of objectivity?
What does this document help me understand?

Teachers can make documents into learning resources. Teachers Leah Moulton and Corrine Tevis (1991) found the local museum a great source of historical pictures of their community. On the back of each picture, they copied and then covered the museum's description. As their second-graders examined the pictures, they identified

TABLE 10.7

Learning Cycle	Skills in Picture Analysis

Grade Levels: Intermediate and Middle
NCSS Standard: Time, Continuity, and Change

National Standards for History

Family life now and in the recent past; distinguish between past, present, and future; draw on visual data presented in photographs; analyze interests and values of various people; formulate historical questions; marshal needed information of a time and place

Exploratory Introduction

Objectives	Procedures	Assessments
Students describe toys with which they are familiar.	Ask: "Of all your toys, which is your favorite?" Call on several students to share their selection. Ask: "Have you ever asked your parents or grandparents what their favorite toys were like? What were the toys? What do you think they would have selected?"	Students offer appropriate responses. Record participation on a checklist.

Lesson Development

Materials: Copies of pictures of children and their toys from two time periods (10.2a and 10.2b for each pair of students)

Objectives	Procedures	Assessments
Students gather data from pictures.	Explain: "Today we are going to work with a partner and compare two pictures of children and their toys. One picture was taken recently and the other about 1906." Ask: "How many years ago was 1906? Does anyone know an individual that old? How do you think the pictures will compare?" Receive a few predictions. Ask for a show of hands for those who agree with each prediction. Assign partners.	Students answer correctly or logically.
	Distribute the pictures and questions to consider when comparing the pictures. (Allow about 10 minutes for this activity.)	
	1. List at least three things about the people shown in each picture. 2. Identify at least 10 items shown in each picture. 3. Where do you think each picture was taken? 4. Who do you think took each picture? Why? 5. How are the pictures alike?	Note student participation on a checklist: task, sharing ideas, and so on. Note evidence used by students.

T A B L E   1 0 . 7

Continued

Students make conclusions concerning the role toys play in training children for their adult lives.	6. How are the pictures different? 7. Identify at least three changes that you see illustrated in the pictures. 8. How have the lives of children changed in the years between the time the pictures were taken? 9. What do you think children learned from playing with the toys in the pictures? 10. Which one of the children shown in the two pictures would you most like to be? Why? Ask students to discuss their findings to questions 5, 6, 7, 8, and 9. *Closure:* "Do you have any questions about the pictures? How many of you think that toys have some purpose other than entertaining children? What purposes?"	Students provide correct or logical answers.

Expansion

Materials: Photos from 10.2a and 10.2b from Lesson Development

Objectives	Procedures	Assessments
Students suggest toys that might have belonged to children in the early 1900s.	Discuss the following questions: "Do you think boys and girls should be kept from playing with any particular toy? Why?" In the 1906 picture, most of the toys probably belonged to the girl because very young children did not have as many toys. Ask: "Is that still true today? When the little boy was as old as his sister, what kind of toys do you think he had? Where could we find out what toys were available for boys around 1906?"	Students' answers reflect the content of the lesson in support of their ideas.
Students check their predictions with research.	Students look in books about old toys, old catalogs, consult an antique dealer, or do Internet search to see what toys were available to check their predictions. *Lesson Summary:* Have students briefly describe the activities of the lesson and the main ideas.	Students affirm predictions or explain their research discoveries.

First picture for the history learning cycle on data gathering (Table 10.7).

Second picture for the history learning cycle on data gathering (Table 10.7).

the first thing they noticed, and two things they might not see at the location today. Finally, they gave each picture a title. Following class discussion, the descriptive paragraphs were uncovered and read aloud. This allowed students to check the accuracy of their predictions and to learn more about what was in each picture.

VISUAL LITERACY AND HISTORY

Before photography was available, artists preserved the likenesses of people and landscapes in paintings, on the walls of caves and on pottery, in stone, or on canvas. Artwork decorates buildings, homes, and tombs. Artists and, more recently, photographers made a living preserving images of the rich and powerful or what governments or news agencies paid them to photograph.

Study of ancient civilizations often calls on the evidence recovered by archaeologists. Because the languages of many people are not written or cannot be translated, works of art provide us with our best sources of information about many people and how they lived. For nonreaders in the primary grades or for students whose first language is not English, works of art provide important sources of information and are instructional resources for learning social studies. Children often like to handle pictures, examining them closely. Smaller pictures cut from magazines, or travel folders and postcards, which can be laminated or placed in page protectors, make good instructional resources for small groups. Or they can be placed in learning centers with questions to prompt exploration and data-gathering tasks. Another technique is to project a large image in which people are shown. Students discuss what they see, focusing on the people and how they might feel in this situation and what they are doing. Finally, small groups of students role play the scene several times and discuss their various interpretations and the likelihood of the role play being an accurate depiction.

Pictures do not always tell the truth. Painters and photographers include and exclude things from pictures. A painting, drawing, or photograph is an interpretation of what was. Cartoon drawings are especially known for carrying messages, but messages in other visual images are often overlooked. Visual literacy requires skills in interpretation, the exercise of judgment, and the desire to question what is seen. It also requires taking time to look carefully at the whole and at its parts. Questions that promote visual literacy follow:

> Does the object contain a signature or clues about the creator?
> What is being shown?
> What does the artist want you to see first and foremost?
> Does the work contain secondary messages?
> Do regular patterns or shapes present a message or feeling?
> What use do you think the owner intends to make of this object?

Films and children's film-length cartoons are resources with which students are very familiar. When films and videos are used, students need to analyze differences between fact, fiction, artistic license, and the need to create a story that sustains the viewers' interest. Many children's versions of films use a grain of truth, lots of special effects, and creative imagination. Ethnic groups particularly charge that stereotyping is used and untrue facts are presented in many popular children's films. The use of dialog, music, emotion, and visual stimuli make film and video powerful presenters of information that may not be accurate or fair. As with all learning resources in the classroom, teachers carefully evaluate these. When using them, teachers address the errors and try to assist students to differentiate between facts, fiction, and entertainment. When teachers have students present their learning in video or Power-Point presentations, students' special effects need to support accurate facts and interpretations of events.

TIME FOR REFLECTION: WHAT DO YOU THINK?

1. An assistant superintendent attended a presentation of the Boston Tea Party by a fifth-grade class. Native Americans tossed the tea overboard and then set fire to the ships. If you had been the assistant superintendent who was called on to comment after the students' program, what would you have said? _____

_____

_____

_____

➤ 2. How might the teacher have facilitated the students' recognition of the differences between fact, fiction, and dramatic presentations so that the Boston Tea
Party presentation reflected these understandings? _____

_____

_____

3. Children's literature is often beautifully illustrated. As students learn the importance of reading and the written word, they often entirely neglect the illustrations
in a book. What questions can teachers ask to encourage students to identify the
facts, emotions, and interpretations present in the pictures of books? _____

_____

_____

4. Identify at least three appropriate categories of tasks for a rubric for a history project that requires the students to illustrate what they have learned in drawings or
through other artistic endeavors. _____

_____

_____

5. Establishing the evaluative criteria to differentiate the quality of the tasks often
requires several tries. Write what you think might be some fair evaluative criteria
for the tasks you identified in question 4. _____

_____

_____

_____

REENACTMENTS AND DRAMA

Visits to historic sites and weekend festivals often bring people into contact with reenactors who assume the role of people who lived and worked during the period being
reenacted. History is taught by reenactors through presentations and answering questions as if the spectator had stepped into the historic scene. These historians are quite
knowledgeable about the individuals they portray and how the individuals performed
their work and lived their daily lives. It is possible to arrange for these historians to
come to schools for special presentations or for special days of celebration. A day in
a one-room school, at a medieval or Renaissance festival, visiting a colonial village,
or at a frontier fort are activities used by many teachers. These are usually done during the lesson development or expansion phases of the learning cycle. Older students,
after researching a topic or skill, might take part in a schoolwide presentation. They
become instructors, presenters, or members of living displays to inform and teach
classmates, younger students, community visitors, and family members about a particular era. These types of presentations may be part of a learning assessment.

Some teachers use the acting out of history as a regular instructional strategy. Students use their background knowledge to role play people and events while teacher questions focus their thoughts and help them to reflect on and evaluate the likelihood of their interpretations. Teachers carefully plan these scenarios so that students focus on acquiring and using facts and interpersonal understandings to attain meaningful learning of social studies objectives. Students are confronted with making decisions as they believe people of the era would have made them. Then they reflect on, and perhaps revise, their dramas. This strategy gives students control over the direction of the lesson and their learning assessment. In the process of using drama and acting to learn history, students develop affective skills related to empathy and skills to interpret acts and events giving them greater meaning. Students often say that they learn and remember more having engaged in the acting out of history (Morris & Welch, 2000). Teachers help students successfully act out history in several ways:

1. Researching the historical topic or event thoroughly
2. Mentally summarizing all the research in a series of events and relationships
3. Making a large chart to post in the classroom of the objectives, in the form of questions, to consider about the event:

    What actually begins the situation?
    Who are the leaders of the action?
    How do the poor people in the community view the importance of this situation?

4. Focusing students' attention on learning and answering the questions in an accurate or realistic manner
5. Providing for large amounts of verbal student expression
6. Allowing students freedom in their learning and interpretations, but helping them examine their reasoning and interactions through discussion, reflections, and writing
7. Keeping a record of students' daily participation using rubrics with which the students are familiar and on which students know they will be assessed

BIOGRAPHIES AND HISTORICAL LITERATURE

Each May, *Social Education* publishes an annotated list of notable children's books in conjunction with the NCSS Book Review Committee and the Children's Book Council. All the books are related to social studies content and classified by grade level topic. These lists serve as excellent resources for teachers and resource learning center coordinators. The decision to use these books as part of the curriculum depends on their contribution to appropriate social studies objectives.

Many believe that trade books provide a better, or at least an important, source to use in learning history and social studies. Claims for their success include the illustrations and engaging language are an improvement over dull textbooks, and literature expresses feelings and emotions with which students can identify. Some students seem to prefer trade books because of these characteristics (Levstik, 1986). The storylike format is familiar and can help students to read and understand the material because the story links information with casual relationships. However, the author of the story provides an interpretation of the facts that may or may not be accurate. Students tend not to question these relationships if the story plot makes sense or if they personally identify with a character in the story.

Because historical events are open to multiple and conflicting interpretations, the study of history must deal with such conflicts. No one story can substitute for a study of an event or historical issue. Simply reading, discussing, or acting out a story is not a study of history. What is necessary is the examination of stories by different authors and documents that present new and conflicting information. Conflicting information prompts students to look for the truth of what really happened. Historical fiction books must be written in the context of the real historical events involving a particular place and time period.

A story may be used as part of an exploratory introduction to help raise interest in or questions about events. During the lesson development phase, narrative histories and biographies, both fictional and factual, can serve as the source of data to be analyzed and evaluated. Teachers may read to students, stopping and discussing difficult passages with them. This helps students relate other information they know to the passage to clarify understanding. This approach models good historical thinking and reading skills. Alternatively, a teacher may have students select from a group of books on one topic and share their findings and questions with others. Using multiple books provides an opportunity to accommodate students with different abilities. Various authors are likely to present different facts, come to different conclusions, and express different viewpoints and interpretations. The use of multiple books requires students to examine different opinions, just as the historian does.

Successful experiences with the use of narratives and biographies in the study of history in grades 3 through 6 have been examined (Drake & Drake, 1990; Levstik, 1986; Zarnowski, 1990). In each case, multiple books were used, and the study lasted for a month or more. These studies reported that students tended to react strongly to the characters and their situations and that history knowledge was learned. Researchers have found that the meaningful examination and learning of history from trade books is not automatic.

Teachers should not be surprised to discover that students often read stories differently from adults because they have different interests and experiences. Zarnowski (1990) reported that an examination of the biographies students wrote while studying biographies showed that students tend to include more details and reactions concerning the early life of the person but only a rather matter-of-fact statement concerning the person's adult accomplishments. Perhaps this happens because students bring a better understanding of youthful experiences to their reading and do not have a great enough understanding of adult work and the challenges and interactions required in adult society. Each student provides her own meaning to every educational encounter.

Many have advocated the use of literature in the study of history and social studies. Some states, such as California, require its use as part of the curriculum guide-

lines. Middle schools often require literature study to help provide additional practice in reading to improve reading test scores. Middle school teams often use a novel
or chapter book with their integrated units or as the inspiration for an integrated unit.
Teachers in a team relate their instruction about the book to their school subject. The
social studies teacher might help students to understand the story in relation to its historical context. Teacher behaviors can assist students in learning history through literature by doing the following:

- Selecting resources and helping students obtain additional resources
- Organizing formal assignments that require students to manipulate data gath-
  ered or obtain new data related to the study
- Providing a time for reading each day
- Monitoring and providing positive reinforcement for individual and group efforts
- Providing timely feedback on student efforts and work
- Providing students with the opportunity to share their knowledge with each
  other and those outside their own class, especially family members or a mentor
- Encouraging students to examine stories critically for fact, opinion, fiction,
  and causal relationship

Some have warned that simply adding literary works to textbooks often trivi-
alizes or demeans the content and fails to address meaningful social studies objectives (Alleman & Brophy, 1994). Extremely complex and emotional topics deserve
much more attention and adult assistance to understand than do the limited perspectives often found in a piece of children's literature. However, such a book can
provide an introduction to a topic with strong affective influences. But although it
might have merit for individual students, a book might not be appropriate for class
use.

Few research studies support claims of better content learning with the use of literature. Research is needed on the effects of a literature approach, especially its impact on skill development and values formation (Eddington, 1998; McGowan,
Erickson, & Neufeld, 1996). Naturalistic studies have revealed that some student responses can actually have a negative impact on learning social studies or history
thinking skills. Students might identify so strongly with the character of the story that
they are inhibited from critically examining the issues that the character encounters
(Levstik, 1986).

After considerable review of research and their own investigations, Van Sledright
and Brophy (1992) concluded that students need to be taught how historical narratives are created if they are to develop meaningful understandings of the differences
between evidence-based accounts and fanciful elaborations. Barton (1997b) says that
educators need to be extremely cautious in their use of historical narratives. History
must be based on evidence, and this necessity must be made clear to students. Books
selected for students to read and learn history must have, as an essential criterion, descriptions of the sources of their information and acknowledgment of the conflicts
among the sources (Levstik & Barton, 1997). At the companion website for this book
is an evaluation form helping teachers make a sound decision about the use of a trade
book for teaching history and social studies.

COMPANION
WEBSITE

MAKING A LITERATURE CONNECTION

Various Types of History Books

Biographies and historical fiction are two types of trade books that have long been popular among young readers. Biographical series abound and are written for all grade levels. Often authors stress the subject's childhood and gloss over or omit the later life with its struggles and accomplishments. Other authors stress the values learned at a young age and used or practiced that led to an important accomplishment. Teachers might use such books to stress the importance of civic values. Another popular use of biographies is to expand the coverage of women and minorities to fill in the gaps of what they consider limited coverage in the textbooks.

Books of historical fiction are also available for all grade levels. For the youngest students, these books tend to present a storyline about a historical event and make extensive use of pictures or drawings. These make good read-aloud selections. Good historical fiction presents a plausible story in the context of a particular time period in which the sequences of events, buildings, dress, customs, and various attitudes and dialects are historically accurate for the time and setting. Real people referred to within the book should have lived and performed the actions ascribed to them by the author. The popular American Girl Series of books that describe a year in the life of a girl at various time periods in America is an example of historical fiction that attempts to promote positive images in young girls. Books of historical fictions are often selected by middle school teams for integrated units. The social studies teacher's contribution to the unit is to help students examine the events and the historical context and values. *Storm Warrior* (2001) by Elisa Carbone is the story of Nathan and his fictional family, who moved to a small cabin near the Pea Island Life Saving Station on the Outer Banks of North Carolina in the 1890s. The descriptions of the storms and rescue efforts of the African American station keeper and crew are true. As a postscript, the author includes a description of her research procedures and a dedication that lists the names of the keeper and crew who inspired the book.

There are several new trends in history trade books that attempt to present individual and social history to youth. One style is called the catalog book because it includes lots of pictures and illustrations with brief explanations grouped by topics such as entertainment, transportation, children's lives, and life inside a particular building. These books require that a reader observe the illustrations, many of which are quite small, for details and to make connections between items on the page. The narration tends to set the items in the context of the times and to comment on some details to illustrate and explain trends. Such books appeal to young learners who are great seekers of new, clever, or different ideas. They contain so many facts that the book can be examined many times and still bring out new findings and questions. These books are not appropriate for read-aloud strategies. Mary E. Haas (2000) illustrates how teachers can use small-group and whole-class discussions that prompt students to explore and ask questions about such books. A sample of individual and series of catalog books include *A Street through Time* (1998) written by Anne Millard and illustrated by Steve Noon, *A Farm through Time* written by Eric Thomas and illustrated by Angela Wilkes, *Pompeii: The Day a City Was Buried* (1998) by Melanie and Christopher Rice, *A Medieval Castle* (1990) by Fiona MacDonald and Mark Bergin, and *Welcome to Addy's World 1864* (1999) by Susan Sinnott.

EXPANDING YOUR SKILLS IN HISTORY

COMPANION
WEBSITE

In-service programs for teachers are widely available to help expand their skills in teaching history. The Internet helps to meet teachers' needs to increase their knowledge when they need skills at a low cost. The website Dohistory (see the link found at the companion website) is an excellent site to help teachers and older students develop the skills historians use. This site concentrates on the lives of ordinary people using as its primary resource a diary written by Martha Ballard more than 200 years ago. From the age of 50 until she died in 1812, Martha Ballard served her community as a midwife, delivering 816 babies. The site helps you examine the entries in Martha Ballard's diary as would a historian. Also included is a historian's tool kit. Among its instructional programs are how to use primary resources and how to conduct oral history. Another website addressing how to use primary documents is the teacher's resources section of the National Archives and Records Administration website (see the link at the companion website).

COMPANION
WEBSITE

COMPANION
WEBSITE

Teachers often need assistance in finding information about the cultures and viewpoints of various ethnic groups present in the United States. The history network is a website linking the history of other nations and many ethnic groups (see the link at the companion website). This site is a useful place to begin looking for additional historical information so that you can help students examine multiple views on historical events and issues. Guest speakers can assist a teacher and students in learning skills, viewpoints, and information. Smaller communities often have a helpful local antique dealer or auctioneer. Museums, universities, state libraries, local and state historical societies, and the state humanities council usually provide outreach services, loan artifact kits, sponsor workshops, and research guest speakers.

➤ USING TECHNOLOGY

An Interview with Jim Shipp

Jim Shipp, a third-grade teacher in Loma Linda, California, has created a rich learning environment for the third-grade classes in his community. Through his research efforts at local archives, third-graders examine old documents, maps, and pictures even though these students are too young to visit the archives. He shares aspects of his experience with us in the interview next.

COMPANION
WEBSITE

Interviewer: Jim, I saw your website: How Big Were Their Footprints? for teaching about Loma Linda [see the companion website]. I thought it was a great example of using local resources with your students. It is hard to believe that it is your first website. Tell me about how you got inspired to make the website.

Jim Shipp: Two things came together. First the principal asked us to carefully look at the new state standards and find any gaps between what we were already teaching and the new standards. The last time I taught third grade, the community study focused mainly on the services within the community. I noticed a new standard, "Students draw upon historical and community resources to organize the sequence of

➤

local history events and describe how each period of settlement left its mark on the land." I knew what general content to include and started gathering a collection of old books and newspaper articles. But I didn't have a satisfactory way for students to use these local resources. Most were not written for use with third-grade students. Then a workshop was offered as part of our continuing education by the Schools of California On-Line Resources for Education (SCORE) representative for our county, and I signed up. Over a series of sessions throughout the year, I received help in how to approach the study of history and how to put the information on the website.

Interviewer: For years, social studies professionals have been telling teachers to use local resources. How did you get access to the resources and how long did it take you to complete the site?

Jim Shipp: Our schools run year-round with a month off at various times. We had our first workshop sessions in the fall, and I spent most of December visiting the museums, libraries, and archives. This was a new experience for me and also for the people in the archives. They had not experienced producing educational materials for young children, let alone something that would be placed on a website and burned into a CD-ROM. In some instances, I helped them learn how to use hardware that had been purchased which they did not know how to use. At other times, I learned how to locate new primary data sources from the library and museum professionals. The biggest problem was the existing policies at the various facilities for the cost of duplication of documents and pictures. Most had a flat fee per picture, which they charged authors and publishers.

Well, I didn't have any money to put into the project, and certainly no money was to be made from the project. I had to make the case at each archive for a new policy. Luckily, the school had a good digital camera and I could use it to copy pictures, documents, and artifacts in low light that would not damage old pictures and documents. Because digital pictures will often only reproduce well on a computer screen, and when printed out, they are often of rather low quality, my using digital pictures would not result in the archive having a loss of control over their collection. In the end, I was able to get all the materials for no dollar costs. I also made a lot of new friends and came to understand what historians really do. It is rather like being a detective, and I think that if I had I learned that as a student, I'd have liked history in school.

Interviewer: Well, you have worked into your lessons the important skills of collecting and interpreting data by the students. I especially liked the use of the footsteps to summarize each time period.

Jim Shipp: Yes, the students are quite good at seeing the impact of the decisions and actions of people on the landscape. We work all year with the universal theme of continuity and change, seeking to see the environmental impact people make. In our study we can see the immediate impacts of the different people who came to our area, and some of their impacts have lasted for over 200 years, and students can still see their "footprints" today. Toward the end of our study we began linking the environmental impacts to economics, examining both the cost of the changes and the economic benefits. Our community has recently changed one of the old water drainage systems flowing right through the center of the community into a concrete drainage system, whereas the neighboring community made a political decision not to change the old way because they preferred to keep the natural features for control of their storm waters. As a class, we will be watching to see whether we made a good choice and comparing the choice of our community to that of our neighbors.

Interviewer: You have mentioned your students several times. Tell me how you used the website materials with the students.

Jim Shipp: I can best tell you how I will use them. Last year I did have the students engaged with part of the website as I was preparing the various parts. Each of the 10 time periods will be part of a one- or two-week unit in which the students will read and do the activities associated with the site and be tested on them. They will visit museums and see the artifacts in person. They will try to make some of the artifacts as outlined in the teacher's lesson plans. We actually made a Cahuilla house (kish) only to have it flattened by the Santa Ana winds, just as happened to the Native Americans in the literature book we read in which an entire village was destroyed. The students really understood that the houses were fragile. In the book they rebuilt their village, but we made the decision not to rebuild our house.

I see the website, or the CD-ROM version, as being a helpful way to provide the information to third-graders, which they can return to multiple times as they learn about their community. Students see their community and its problems; they also see the names of the streets and the old buildings and can link their observations to what they have learned in their history lessons. Through SCORE, the website is available for all teachers in the community to use. Some teachers in neighboring communities have a similar sequence of inhabitants and may also find parts helpful in their teaching. In the fourth grade students will learn about the history of the state. But California is a big state, and not everything that applies to the history of our community is true for all areas of the state. Still, the underlying principles of studying history learned in the community study can be used and built upon in fourth grade.

Interviewer: I see your project as a wonderful model for other teachers to view because it illustrates how the textbook can be supplemented with local resources. In the future other teachers or archives may use your site as an inspiration for their own efforts. Thank you for sharing your time and experiences with my students.

Jim Shipp: I was very pleased to do so. What I did was on the shoulders of the work of others, and I hope that my experience has been helpful to others. I have come to believe that the textbook is never enough, and teachers must also become the writers of curriculum and developers of learning resources. Maybe you can't do it all the time, but you can do it when necessary, and also make wise use of other resources. I know that having mastered the technology, and having completed one major project, I will do more materials developing in the future and the projects won't take me as much time to complete as this one did.

TIME FOR REFLECTION: WHAT DO YOU THINK?

Even though it took Jim Shipp almost a year to complete the CD-ROM and the lesson plans posted at the website, he will not need to do all of the work in future years. He can, however, return to the website and make changes as new materialsbecome available or he finds better questions or activities to use to assist the students in their learning.

1. What do you remember learning about the history of your local community in elementary school? _____

_____

2. What site in your community could students visit and learn about some aspect of the history of the community or the United States? _____

_____

3. How might you use a computer exercise to better prepare students to visit the actual site? _____

_____

4. What might be another local issue or topic that could be studied by third-grade students with the help of a website? _____

_____

Membership in professional organizations and attendance at state, regional, and national meetings is helpful. Professional journals and newsletters provide the opportunity to learn and think about issues and to become aware of workshop opportunities, and conferences providing scholarships for teachers. Individual membership brings all the benefits to your own address and the opportunity to become involved in leadership positions within the organization. NCSS membership information and publications information is available on the Internet, along with a list of the state and local affiliates and links to other social studies related organizations (see the link at the companion website).

**COMPANION
WEBSITE**

SUMMARY

History is an important subject for students to study in grades K–8. Many ways of stimulating and maintaining students' interest in the meaningful learning of history are available. Most researchers agree on the need for in-depth study of historical topics, the use of multiple resources, and the consideration of multiple perspectives. Rossi (2000) concludes that the clear implication for curriculum development of the research on the teaching of history is the need for in-depth study providing a conceptual framework that allows students to find meaning in the details.

Some controversy exists over what content and type of history to stress, but there is no shortage of potential content. Our families, the things around us, the issues influencing our lives, and our common heritage of values and beliefs all provide ample content. The data, too, is present if we look for and examine it carefully. The study of history can stimulate us to examine our present behaviors with an eye toward making appropriate changes while maintaining continuity with our worthy past.

Expanding ON THIS CHAPTER

Activity

COMPANION
WEBSITE

Locate several artifacts from a particular time period and construct a memory box or memory trunk. Write a lesson plan with clearly stated behavioral objectives that introduces the memory box to the students and includes a list of questions prompting them to make predictions and ask about the artifacts. Include a list of questions you anticipate second-grade students might ask about the items in the box. Then write the directions you would give to the students to take home and, with the help of an adult, create a memory box that tells their personal life history. Limit the number of items to eight (one per year of their life) so that the students will have to make choices. Include guidelines in the lesson plan for students' presentations of their boxes to classmates and write a rubric that shows how you will grade students for the assignment.

Recommended Websites to Visit

COMPANION
WEBSITE

Library of Congress with its lessons and American Memory Collection
   www.loc.gov

The Smithsonian Institution, sometimes called the nation's attic, with its museums and teacher pages
   www.si.edu

The National Archives and Record Administration of the U.S. government with its educators' pages
   www.archives.gov/

The National Standards for History 5–12
   www.ssnet.ucla.edu/nchs/standards/

Test questions for the fourth-grade examination of Lousiana
   www.doe.state.la.us/conn/assessments.php?dispPage=6

Plimoth Plantation presents the site and life of early settlers
   www.plimoth.org/

Virginia Center for Digital History, which provides ideas and lessons for teaching history using digital materials
   www.vcdh.virginia.edu/

National History Day contest and lessons on Our Documents, the 100 most important documents in U.S. history
   www.NationalHistoryDay.org/

A fine lesson plan about primary documents and how to teach about them to young students
   http://sunsite.berkeley.edu/calheritage/k12/primary_lesson.htm

History/Social Studies for K–12 Teachers
   http://my.execpc.com/~dboals/boals.html

A portal for African American history and culture
   http://blackquest.com/link.htm

A site to help teachers and older students develop the skills historians use
   www.dohistory.org

The History Network, which provides links to the history of other nations and many ethnic groups
   www2.h-net.msu.edu/lists/

A graphic organizer for cause and effect (click on cause and effect in chart)
   www.greece.k12.ny.us/instruction/ELA/6-12/Tools/Index.htm

CHAPTER 11

Helping Students Interpret the Earth and Its People through Geography

INTRODUCTION

1. List six activities you did in the past couple of days. _____
_____
_____

2. Perhaps you drank juice, drove to a supermarket, talked with a person from another nation, or dressed appropriately for a storm. In which of the activities on your list did you use geography? _____
_____
_____

CHAPTER OVERVIEW

Geography is an integral part of daily life. When was the last time that you were conscious of using geography? When was the last time that you sought out specific geographic information to help you make a personal or family decision? What issue in your community or in the nation are politicians discussing that is better understood and answered with the help of geographic information? In this chapter, geography is viewed as an integrated subject fundamental to people's lives and to the social studies curriculum. This chapter discusses the many ways we use geography in our lives and how children can meaningfully learn it.

CHAPTER OBJECTIVES

1. Evaluate your own experiences learning geography and compare them to the practices in today's elementary and middle school classrooms.
2. Analyze geography standards to develop a comprehensive definition of geography that is more than a tool for locating places.
3. Explain how geography is an integral part of all subjects and is used in many careers and daily work.
4. Identify and locate resources for teaching geography.
5. Identify activities that help students describe the three-dimensional characteristics of the world and translate them into a two-dimensional map.
6. Describe the advantages of using the globe with students.
7. Identify key concepts and skills geographers use to describe and interpret their world.
8. Analyze geographic lesson plans.
9. Identify variables that positively and negatively impact meaningful geography learning.
10. Hypothesize actions educators can take to increase geographic achievement for all.

An Interview with Billy Fitzhugh, A Second-Grade Teacher

Billy Fitzhugh teaches second grade at Reisterstown Elementary School in Reisterstown, Maryland. He is the 1997 winner of the outstanding elementary teacher award of the National Council for the Social Studies. He shares some of his ideas and activities in this interview.

Interviewer: Have you always been interested in teaching geography?

Billy Fitzhugh: Yes, I had the interest in geography and history in college, and then I came to education. Geography is good for children to learn, and its visual qualities help the children learn geography.

Interviewer: Do you teach social studies or do you teach predominately geography?

Billy Fitzhugh: Well, I stress cultural geography, not just the physical geography, so all elements of culture and economics are included.

Interviewer: How do the students respond to studying geography?

Billy Fitzhugh: They like learning about other children and what their lives are like.

Interviewer: How do you select the nations to study?

Billy Fitzhugh: In Maryland, each county makes its own selection of nations. In our county, second-graders study South Korea, Japan, Canada, and Denmark. At other grade levels, they learn about different nations or groups. I have been to Israel and Australia and also teach units about these nations.

Interviewer: You have said that having prior knowledge is important to your teaching. How do you get it?

Billy Fitzhugh: I brainstorm with the children at the beginning of each unit on various topics to learn a lot about my own students and the things they know. We talk about our own country and what it is like so that we can make comparisons to the things that are done in other nations. Making comparisons helps children understand ideas so they don't just try to memorize a lot of separate facts.

Interviewer: When you do your units, how do you go about preparing them?

Billy Fitzhugh: I like to center my units on the five themes of geography [see Table 11.1]. This provides a content guide for the unit and activities. The unit then kind of evolves. There are particular activities that students respond very well to which I incorporate into each of the units. The discovery kit is one of these. I have been to most of the nations our system has second-graders study, so I have collected some artifacts they can handle and see for themselves. This encourages them to ask questions and speculate on the ways these artifacts are used.

I like to use lots of picture books, and I always try to find one book to read for each of the units that includes some similar practice that we have in the United States. The students can relate to such a book. But, I want a book that clearly shows the other culture's perspective on the topic. I think it is important for the children to see that people around the world are much more similar than they are different. They also learn more about the United States.

Interviewer: Do you have difficulty finding such books?

T A B L E   1 1 . 1

The Five Themes of Geography and Related Concepts

Location	Place	Relationships	Movement	Region
Absolute	Environment	Attitudes	Migration	Nation
Grid system	Landform	Adaptations	Diffusion	Physical
Map/globe	Climate	Inventions	Barriers	Cultural
Legend/key	Land use	Technology	Systems	Community
Relative	Vegetation	Pollution	Currents	States
Directions	Elevation	Changes	Winds	Middle East
Distance	Population	Industry	Transport	Europe
Scale	Rural/urban	Deforestation	Communicate	Historical
Equator	Buildings	Conservation	Causes	District

Billy Fitzhugh: Well, yes and no. I want the focus of the book to provide something unique for each unit. For the Israel study I use the book *The Never-Ending Greenness* by Neil Waldman, which tells of the holiday Tu b'Shvat. It is similar to our Arbor Day, a celebration that children may not be too familiar with, but one which we can use for comparison to show similarities and differences.

Interviewer: I notice that you make lots of charts and keep a list of vocabulary words posted. How do you use these?

Billy Fitzhugh: Yes, I am a visual learner, and I use lists, charts, and diagrams a lot with the children. We use them to record information and as references for our assignments. For example, when we write about our nations, I usually give the students a few minutes to think about the topic for their writing and then we go through the alphabet giving words associated with the topic. I record the first word they give, and we just hear the rest of the words. This helps to build vocabulary in the study as well as review what we studied. I think encouraging vocabulary is very important at this age. Without the proper vocabulary, the children can't understand what you are reading to them. When they begin writing, I remind them that the lists are a reference to use and that the words on the list must be spelled correctly. Our state testing requires students to write a concise essay, so I provide lots of practice with expressing ideas in writing. There must be a topic and concluding sentence and support with information in the paragraph. I tell my students to provide two ways places are like or similar to the United States and two ways they are different. I feel that when they see the words *similarity* and *difference* on the test, they know the types of things that are appropriate to write.

Interviewer: How do you approach map studies and map skills with your students?

Billy Fitzhugh: With maps, I do a lot of learning from the ground up. I have the students make their own maps. Sometimes they look like they should, and sometimes they don't. But that doesn't matter because they are learning the elements of the map. It also keeps them from learning a lot of misinformation, like thinking north is "up." The children really like constructing the maps, and it teaches them the everyday practical use of maps. Again, on the state test, they will have to make a map and so they need to know what constitutes a map. We map our own area first, and I always make them draw their own maps for everything. The computer will give everyone a very pretty map with the push of a button, but that doesn't assure that the children really understand what is on a map or where places are located. Today you will see them making a cylinder map of the world and they have to correctly locate each of the continents in relationship to the equator and each other.

Interviewer: I notice that you have a map on the playground. I have heard you use the phrase "stand on the map." Is this where you do it?

Billy Fitzhugh: Yes, this was a project that I promoted, and the parents painted it. It cost about $400 and has held up pretty well for 8 or 9 years now. The students stand on it and walk from place to place. They get a better understanding of directions, the idea of where places are in relationship to each other, and an idea of the distance between places.

Interviewer: I noticed quite a bit of artwork from the fifth-grade class in the school's entrance hallway. Do you use artwork with the children?

Billy Fitzhugh: Yes, we are encouraged to integrate our subjects, and you can help children see that there are many art forms. In our South Korea study, we make a fan and study how calligraphy is a form of art that is important to the Koreans, something that is taught be-ginning in elementary school. We draw and write the appropriate kinds of things on our fans that Koreans would have on their fans.

Interviewer: What advice do you have for teachers who want to prepare better geogra-phy units?

Billy Fitzhugh: The more that you read and learn about a nation, the greater will be your ability to understand it and teach it. You have skills for teaching and will see many ways to teach the children about a nation as you yourself learn more about the nation.

TIME FOR REFLECTION: WHAT DO YOU THINK?

1. What evidence do you see in Mr. Fitzhugh's comments that he bases his instruc-tion on accurate social studies content? _____
   _____
   _____
   _____

2. Mr. Fitzhugh insists on correct spelling of social studies terms but is not as con-cerned that students make professional-looking maps. Why do you think this is the case? _____
   _____
   _____

3. What in Mr. Fitzhugh's statement indicates that he thinks students construct their own understanding of the world? _____
   _____
   _____
   _____

4. From what Mr. Fitzhugh said, how would you describe the state of Maryland's so-cial studies curriculum for elementary students? _____
   _____
   _____
   _____

5. What evidence indicates Mr. Fitzhugh makes an effort to learn about students' prior knowledge? _____
   _____
   _____

DEFINING GEOGRAPHY

Everybody wants to know what is happening around them. Joe Stoltzman (1990), a longtime geography educator, explains that geographically literate citizens are aware of (1) what is happening in the world, (2) why it is happening, and (3) how it affects other people throughout the world as well as themselves. Therefore, geography is good citizenship education.

STANDARDS FOR GEOGRAPHIC EDUCATION

Geographers are unique because they apply their efforts to understanding both the physical and cultural characteristics of the world. They have the perspective that location is an important characteristic of everything on earth. Through the study of locations and their relationships to each other, geographers help to explain the dynamics of what is happening in the world or in various places in the world. Geographers begin their study by asking where, but spend the vast majority of their time investigating the questions, Why is this where it is? If people do something in this location to change the physical or cultural conditions, what will be its impact on other locations? In what ways will the impact be positive and in what ways will it be negative? Because everything that has happened, is happening, or will happen must take place at a location, geography is a part of all 10 social studies standards.

Geography and the National Social Studies Standards

Clearly, geography is strongly evident in the social studies standard for People, Places, and Environments. Geographers know that places do not exist in isolation; all parts of the world are interrelated and important. Global systems in the natural habitat, such as winds and currents, impact people's lives. There also are many connected cultural systems, such as communications, transportation, economic development, environmental quality, and human relations. Geography helps citizens understand our nation and interdependence with other people. This cross-national interdependence and the potential for regional and cultural conflicts is an important assumption underlying the problems encompassed in the social studies standard Global Connections.

The social studies standard, Culture, is addressed in geography when people make decisions about the use of the earth's resources that are influenced by their culture. Some cultures exploit as many resources as possible, often bringing about major changes in the habitat. Other cultural groups view nondisruption of the habitat to be the correct decision. The final decision often is related to which group has the greater political or economic power or the legal authority to enforce decisions. Or it is related to who will devote time and effort to get their way or to force another group to compromise. Active citizens need to understand how geography is related to the social studies standard Power, Authority, and Governance and the standard Civic Ideals and Practices.

The Five Themes of Geography

Before the standards movement, geography was defined by a joint committee from the American Association of Geographers and the National Council for Geographic Education, which developed five themes: (1) location, (2) place, (3) relationships within places, (4) movement, and (5) regions as a working definition for K–12. Today, many teachers and geographers still use the five themes as they confront the daily pressures and tensions of the classroom.

Theme 1: Location, Position on the Earth's Surface. The importance of location is the fundamental assumption of geography. Sometimes, we need to know an absolute or exact location, such as in which classroom we can find Mr. Lopez's fourth-grade class. At other times, we can be satisfied with a more general or relative location; for example, much of the world's oil is found near the Persian Gulf. Some learning activities, including the location theme, help students learn to locate places in the community, state, or nation; on the earth; or on a map or a globe.

Theme 2: Place, Natural and Cultural Characteristics. This theme is descriptive of both the natural and human features of the landscape. Concepts describing features on the earth include mountains, capital cities, and the developing world. All are part of the place theme. Students gather data and answer questions such as the following to help them describe place:

What does the land look like?
How much water is present at this place?
Does the water usually come from the atmosphere as rain or snow or from a
    stream or body of water?
Why don't wild animals live in the area?
Do plants dominate the landscape or is the land largely barren or filled with
    buildings?
Why do so many (or so few) people live in this place?
What have people done to change the appearance of the area?

Theme 3: Relationships within Places, Humans and Environments. The natural environment tends to limit what people can do in a place. However, throughout history, people have been quite clever in dealing with these limitations. In dry areas where water was not sufficient to grow needed food, people found ways to import water. Today, people in dry places use advanced transportation to import food. A lesson presented in Table 11.2 addresses the theme of relationships within places.

Theme 4: Movement, Humans Interacting on the Earth. People often do not remain in one place, nor do they use only resources from the place where they live. The movement of ideas and products affects not only places of origin and destination but also places along the way. Raw materials are extracted, new products are grown or produced in factories, and transportation centers are expanded or established. Ideas such as preservation, conservation, and democracy are being attempted in new places. People travel to other nations to visit and may spend part of their lives working or living in other nations. There are systematic movements among the natural forces on the earth. For example, currents carry warm and cold water to new locations; they also carry pollution created by people to new locations throughout the

TABLE 11.2

Learning Cycle	People Change Their Environments

Grade Levels: Primary and Intermediate
NCSS Standards: People, Place, and Environments

Exploratory Introduction

Materials: Tape of soft music, tape player, flower-scented room freshener, marking pens, response strips

Objectives	Procedures	Assessments
Students suggest what the word *environment* means to them.	While the students are out of the room, rearrange the desks, turn off the lights, start a tape of soft music, and spray the room with a flower-scented room freshener. If the students do not notice the changes when they return to the room, ask them how the room has changed. Ask: "What changes in the environment do you notice? Do you like them? What do you think when you hear the word *environment?*" Record each response on a strip of paper and place it on the bulletin board.	Students offer logical associations for the concept of environment.

Lesson Development

Materials: Three sets of 10 pictures illustrating natural and human changes, various natural and cultural scenes of rural and urban areas, and pictures showing scenes including some of pollution or natural diasters, homes, roads, schools, stores, and so on.

Objectives	Procedures	Assessments
Students identify changes in the environments shown in pictures and suggest whether the changes were caused by nature or people. Students classify elements of the environment into natural and cultural (human made) landscapes. Students identify pictures that appear similar to and different from their own community.	Over two or three days, students use different sets of teacher-selected pictures and work in small groups. Teachers carefully select pictures for each group because the content of the pictures guides the classification possibilities. Each group uses a different set of pictures each day. Group activities: Students classify the pictures as: 1. Examples of natural and human changes. 2. Scenes similar to or different from their community scenes. 3. Changes they consider good or bad. When doing this, students must give reasons for their choices.	Students work cooperatively. Groups classify pictures as assigned or create their own logical classifications. Students offer logical reasons for classifying a change as good or bad.

continued

TABLE 11.2

Continued

Objectives	Procedures	Assessments
Students judge changes in the environments in the pictures as positive or negative and give reasons for their judgments.	Each day, students share their group's conclusions with the class. Groups decide on one picture to show the class to illustrate their classification and judgment. A different spokesperson makes the group report each day. Students ask clarification questions as needed.	Groups share work, listen to each other, and ask appropriate questions. Students ask appropriate questions. Disagreements are clearly stated.
	Daily closure: After each class discussion, teachers asks: "Are there any pictures or words we should add to or take off our bulletin board because of what we have learned today?" Changes are made when class agrees. Ask: "How does our bulletin board summarize what we have been studying about the environment?"	Class makes appropriate and logical changes. Students summarize accurately, giving important ideas.

Expansion

Materials: Chart paper and markers

Objectives	Procedures	Assessments
Students tell what they have learned about changes in the environment.	Tell students: "Think about what you have been learning and doing with the pictures of the environment this week. Will someone give me a brief statement of something you learned about the environment and how the earth is changed?" Call on several students. After each comment teacher says: "If you have also learned what Johnny said, raise your hand."	Students state what they have learned clearly. Students raise hands in agreement.
Students identify occupations that bring changes to the environment.	Display a list of occupations including doctor, clerk, contractor, janitor, tree trimmer, architect, fire fighter, farmer, and gardener. Ask: "Which of these people have jobs that cause them to change the environment as they work?"	Students offer answers and explanations.
Students list ways they can change their classroom environment.	Ask students: "How might students change the environment of their classroom?" List responses. If appropriate, have students also	Students offer logical answers.

TABLE 11.2

Continued

Objectives	Procedures	Assessments
Students agree on a set of changes to make in their classroom.	address how they could change the room to reflect a topic to be studied or coming season or holiday. (This procedure can be repeated during the school year.) Through voting and discussion select several changes to make in the classroom. Have students make these changes then reflect on their quality.	Students discuss and reach a conclusion by voting. Students take part in carrying out the changes on the classroom and express their concerns and willingness to make additional appropriate changes.

Note: This lesson may be expanded by students taking part in a school or community cleanup campaign or students extending their knowledge by learning about laws concerning the environment.

globe. Global problems are concerns of geographers as they study movements between places and regions.

Theme 5: Regions, How They Form and Change. It is difficult to conceive of the scale of the entire world, so geographers frequently divide it into regions. Within a region, geographers study all the places and activities defined by the other four themes. After studying many regions, geographers begin to get a picture of how the entire world works as they investigate the interactions between regions. Because the criteria for establishing a region are determined by the person doing the study, a region can be as small as an individual classroom, school, neighborhood, or community with which very young students are familiar. In this region, they can observe and investigate. As students develop their understanding of the five themes of geography, and develop their skills, they begin to study larger and more formal regions defined by physical and topographic features or political control. Those regions, such as the Middle East and Southeast Asia, defined by the interaction of many complex features, are appropriate for study by students who have well-developed concrete reasoning schemata or are formal thinkers.

Geography Education Standards and the Six Elements of Geography Education

Geography for Life is a statement of geographic education standards prepared by a committee of geographers and geographic educators. It details the basic concepts and generalizations of physical and human geography and illustrates how geography systematically approaches the study of the earth and its people. It explains how locations and interactions between people and natural habitats help students understand events and places today, in the past, and possibly in the future. These standards are helpful in selecting appropriate geographic content, concepts, and skills for lessons, curricula, and assessments.

The eighteen standards are grouped into six major categories or *elements*. Table 11.3 identifies the six elements and the eighteen standards. The standards subsume the five themes.

> **Element 1: The World in Spatial Terms.** Element 1 incorporates the theme of location, reminding instructors that finding places is not the only skill one uses when dealing with maps. It also identifies the variety of maps that students need to study and use.
>
> **Element 2: Places and Regions.** Element 2 combines two of the five themes, clarifying their meanings by pointing out that places are culturally defined by people, that they can be small or large, and that they may vary in importance over time.
>
> **Element 3: Physical Systems.** Element 3 serves as a reminder that the earth has patterns that are related to its physical nature, that many changes are a result of the physical processes acting on the earth, and that natural forces change Earth by moving materials.
>
> **Element 4: Human Systems.** Element 4 stresses ongoing changes in human patterns related to settlements, the movement of resources, and the struggles and conflicts regarding control of the earth's surface. The inclusion of these two systems reminds teachers to include detailed considerations of both.
>
> **Element 5: Environment and Society.** Element 5 shows how people, at times, adapt their behaviors to fit the environment, whereas at other times, they try to change the environment to fit their own needs and desires. This element ensures that teachers consider environmental perspectives and ask students to think about how various people view the earth.
>
> **Element 6: The Uses of Geography.** Element 6 encourages teachers to ask students to apply geographic knowledge to other school subjects and consider how people use geographic knowledge and skills in their jobs when making decisions.

T I M E   F O R   R E F L E C T I O N :   W H A T   D O   Y O U   T H I N K ?

1. Why do students quickly notice changes in the classroom set up for the exploratory introduction of the learning cycle on *People Change Their Environments* in Table 11.2? _____

_____

2. What initial terms do you anticipate students associating with the word *environment*? _____

_____

3. What procedures would you use to prevent or solve the problem of students being curious about the pictures that other groups of students have? _____

_____

_____

_____

T A B L E   1 1 . 3

National Geography Standards

Element 1: The World in Spatial Terms

1. How to use maps and other geographic representations, tools, and technologies to acquire, process, and report information from a spatial perspective.
2. How to use mental maps to organize information about people, places, and environments in a spatial context.
3. How to analyze the spatial organization of people, places, and environments on the earth's surface.

Element 2: Places and Regions

4. Know and understand the physical and human characteristics of places.
5. Know and understand that people create regions to interpret the earth's complexity.
6. Know and understand how culture and experience influence people's perceptions of places and regions.

Element 3: Physical Systems

7. Know and understand the physical processes that shape the patterns of the earth's surface.
8. Know and understand the characteristics and spatial distribution of ecosystems on the earth's surface.

Element 4: Human Systems

9. Know and understand the characteristics, distribution, and migration of human populations on the earth's surface.
10. Know and understand the characteristics, distribution, and complexity of the earth's cultural mosaics.
11. Know and understand the patterns and networks of economic interdependence on the earth's surface.
12. Know and understand the processes, patterns, and functions of human settlement.
13. Know and understand how the forces of cooperation and conflict among people influence the division and control of the earth's surface.

Element 5: Environment and Society

11. Knows and understands how human actions modify the physical environment.
15. Knows and understands how physical systems affect human systems.
16. Knows and understands the changes that occur in the meaning, use, distribution, and importance of resources.

Element 6: The Uses of Geography

17. Know and understand how to apply geography to interpret the past.
18. Know and understand how to apply geography to interpret the present and plan for the future.

Source: Geography for Life: National Geography Standards, by the Geography Education Standards Project, 1994, Washington, DC: National Geographic Research and Exploration.

➤ 4. Modifying the bulletin board helps students reconstruct their ideas about the environment and changes in it. What other activity might you use to help illustrate students' thoughts as they study? _____

_____

_____

RESOURCES FOR TEACHING GEOGRAPHY

An inexpensive but important primary teaching resource is just outside your school. Field work is possible on every walk or trip outside. With a little planning and encouragement, students can study geography. Even the youngest students can talk about, draw, list, and photograph what they consider important observations. In doing so, they begin to learn the usefulness of major geographic tools, such as graphs, charts, maps, photographs, aerial photographs, and remotely obtained information from satellites circling the earth. Making accurate observations and recording observations require instruction and practice using instruments and skills. But the first geographers began with nothing more than paper and pencils, tools that are readily available to all students.

As students explore the local geographic outdoors laboratory, they come to appreciate and take pride in some of its aspects. Some might express negative feelings or concerns and want to seek ways to improve a place, such as cleaning an empty lot or making a playground for neighborhood children. Such efforts recognize that the study of geography involves values. Conflicts among the values of people and groups become obvious, as does the need to consider civic ideals and practices for the common good.

Geography is integral to abilities to locate, move, or control natural resources in ways that contribute to the quality of our lives. So governments and private businesses collect, organize, and publish much of the geographic information that citizens may need as they make both personal and group decisions. Maps are available from governments at various levels. The most detailed and up-to-date maps in the United States are produced by the U.S. Geological Service, the U.S. Census Bureau, and the U.S. Weather Service. Links to their websites are available at the companion website.

**COMPANION
WEBSITE**

State offices responsible for natural resources, highways, and tourism frequently produce maps. The U.S. Department of Commerce and the U.S. Department of State organize and distribute information about various parts of the country and world. These are valuable resources for teaching, as are the employees of such offices. As guest speakers, these employees help to teach the proper use of maps and photographs as well as explain how they use geographic knowledge and skills in their work. Workers in the private sector, such as builders, architects, travel agents, and real estate agents, also encounter geographic problems and use geographic knowledge.

> ### USING TECHNOLOGY

An Important Contributor to Learning Geography

Inexpensive cameras and the ease with which digital pictures and streaming video can be placed on class websites and sent through email enable teachers and students to share their homes, community, and field work with parents and students in other schools and nations. Students get to share what they consider important with other students and directly ask questions rather than receive a secondhand interpretation or outdated information from hard-to-obtain printed sources. Students can also conduct joint research studies with students in other locations and in other nations. GLOBE is a website that assists in locating current data, provides tools for processing the data, and has projects with options for sharing data between schools

➤ and with scientists. GLOBE works with agencies of the U.S. government to coordinate these projects.

The proliferation of websites makes information more readily available to youths and teachers. News agencies' websites provide coverage of events all over the world 24 hours a day. Agencies and departments of governments, especially the U.S. government, provide easy access to data in the form of graphs and maps about weather, landforms, agricultural products, population demographics, and population distributions. The Census Bureau, U.S. Geological Survey, and the National Parks Service are just a few of the many U.S. government agencies whose websites provide data to teachers and students and lessons that assist in the use of their data. Organizations such as the United Nations, CARE, Oxfam, the Red Cross/Red Crescent, the National Wildlife Federation, and the National Geographic Society provide data and often have teacher and student pages to teach about their work. Because computers and other technologies are not universally available or used across the United States, there is no hard data that indicates how effective using technology is in increasing geographic knowledge and understanding among American students. However, NAEP data indicates that students who report having such experiences in their classes do score higher on the NAEP Geography Test.

DEVELOPING GEOGRAPHIC CONCEPTS, GENERALIZATIONS, AND SKILLS

Geographic knowledge is found throughout the elementary curriculum in both social studies and science. When emphasis is placed on the people of a region, their culture is part of the study of geography. Geographic concepts, generalizations, and skills are all present in the classroom, on school grounds, and in larger regions such as local communities, states, nations, and throughout the entire world.

Even though geography is so much a part of our lives, it was often largely neglected in the school curriculum. Textbooks tended to reduce it to long lists of detailed facts and occasional map skills lessons. Geography often has been represented in textbooks by the place and location themes. Textbooks have emphasized the place theme by discussing concepts such as mountain, river, plain, continent, equator, suburb, community, transportation, and lake (Haas, 1991). The location theme has been emphasized through map exercises in which students locate places and symbols and identify directions on maps of classrooms and familiar locations such as shopping centers. A major problem of emphasizing only the location and place themes is that studying geography becomes a chore of trying to commit isolated lists of information to memory. The most important reason for learning geography is its usefulness, which is made clear through the relationship and movement themes (Pigozzi, 1990). It is only through learning all the themes that students combine a sufficient number of appropriate concepts to form generalizations in geography. The generalizations that students make are tested by examining how concepts that are developed with information from one region can be applied to another region.

All five themes of geography, or all six elements of the standards, are stressed in every grade level. Very young children begin learning geography through personal interactions with their own local environments and regions. They observe their surroundings in the school and on short walks or field trips, and they record their information in simple stories, drawings, and maps. As they increase their information and skills through direct experiences, they begin to use more indirect sources of information to learn about places they cannot visit in person. Gradually, they use pictures, maps, films, charts, and written descriptions to begin to compare places. By identifying similarities and differences, they refine and elaborate their concept definitions. They form conclusions and make generalizations about various relationships among geographic phenomena. In so doing, they develop an elaborate mental map of their world. The mental map helps them to understand events and problems they encounter.

Two chief characteristics of a powerful geography curriculum are (1) the organization of geographic information and (2) the involvement of students in minds-on learning through inquiry and the use of inquiry skills. Information is presented in connected ways so that students are assisted in organizing this information. Authentic activities show the usefulness of geography by involving students in hands-on geographic investigations that are not limited to watching television programs, looking at Internet sites, or reading a book. When information is presented in a connected way, students are better able to construct meaning from it. Research by Brophy and Alleman (2000) reveals that whereas primary grades students can identify details in pictures and give reasons why different people might construct houses from different materials, they need help from teachers. Such help includes involvement in lessons

This young man's interest in places is enhanced by studying the atlas and sharing information with family and friends.

with activities and prompting questions that enable them to construct geographic generalizations, such as that people build houses from the natural materials found in their physical environments.

It is no coincidence that the NCSS standards use important superordinate concepts, such as People, Places, and Environment, as labels for their themes. Among the important superordinate concepts suggested by geographers in the five themes and six elements of geography are location, place, movement, physical systems, human systems, environment, and society. Questions using these superordinate concepts and relationships among them make excellent focus questions for units and curriculum for the entire year. Following is an example of a classroom scene showing how geography is meaningfully learned. As you read it, consider and examine the following:

- How students' prior knowledge is activated
- How concepts are developed
- How students use and expand on their new knowledge

A Classroom Scene

Mr. Boyd noticed that his state's third-grade social studies guidelines included teaching landforms and bodies of water and emphasized reading maps of the United States and the world. He knew that, although their community was located on the coast of one of the Great Lakes, most of his students had not seen a river. He planned and implemented a short unit using river as the superordinate concept to organize it.

He began by asking the students to think about Lake Michigan. Then he asked, "What can you tell me about the lake?" After students responded, Mr. Boyd refocused the discussion by asking, "Using the information we have been talking about, tell me how a river is similar to or different from Lake Michigan?" After some discussion, the children agreed that rivers are long and skinny and that you can see across them and build bridges to cross over them. Valesca said, "I saw pictures on television where a river had flooded over fields and into a town." Some students agreed with Shenana, who said, "Rivers are dirty and not pretty and blue like our lake." Mr. Boyd told the students that they certainly knew a lot about Lake Michigan and how people in their city use the lake. He told them, "In the next few days, we will be learning more about rivers and thinking about how the people who live along them might use rivers and what they think about rivers."

The next day, Mr. Boyd began the lesson development by putting students into small groups and giving them each a black-and-white outline map of the United States. He told the students, "Take a close look at the lakes and rivers on your maps. Then, make lists of differences and similarities." After a few minutes, he provided them with an additional colored map of the United States and colored pictures of scenes of the Great Lakes and several different rivers. He told them, "Look carefully at these colored maps and the pictures your group has. Add to your lists of similarities and differences if you want to."

The students' lists lengthened. They noted that cities were located along both the rivers and the lakes and that both rivers and lakes were shown in blue on the colored map. They also noticed that the colored map had some small lakes on it that were not present on the black-and-white maps. The students were surprised to see white water in some of the rivers that appeared to be moving fast. Some rivers seemed to be way down among rocks, whereas others were even with the land as the lakes were. All the groups decided that rivers that were even with the land did not look like they were moving. They noticed lots of trees and shrubs along the edges of rivers. Fields and cities seemed to sit back away from the river a bit.

Students grouped their pictures of rivers into those they thought might cause flood damage and those they did not think would be likely to cause flood damage. The students responded by placing those that were in rocky areas in the "not likely to flood" category. Mr. Boyd showed the students pictures of rivers that had flooded. The students concluded that their classifications were correct.

Mr. Boyd explained, "Rivers that flood have flood plains. This is an area that is expected to be covered with water in an average flood." He asked, "Where would you find the flood plain of a river?" Then Mr. Boyd told the students that one frequently flooded river in the United States today is the Mississippi River and that another great river that floods is the Nile River. After locating the Nile River on a world map, he showed the students pictures taken along the banks of the Nile River and asked them, "Where is the Nile River's flood plain?" The students quickly identified the flood plain. They explained why it was planted in crops, whereas the villages were on higher ground just beyond the flood plain.

Next, the students examined a map of the Nile River as the teacher called their attention to the various colors on the map along the course of the river. Students consulted the legend and discovered that elevation was shown by various colors. Part of the Nile River was at very high elevations shown in brown, whereas green indicated the lowest areas. The teacher then asked, "Where along the Nile do you think the pictures of the flood plain were taken?" The students decided that these pictures had been taken in green areas in Egypt.

The teacher then asked, "Where does the Nile River begin and where does it end?" The students found one end of the Nile but had trouble with the other end. So Mr. Boyd suggested starting at the end they found and tracing the Nile with a finger until they could not trace it any further. A controversy developed when they reached the city of Khartoum, Sudan, over whether this was the source of the Nile. The students said that each of the two rivers beyond the city, the Blue Nile and the White Nile, had *Nile* in its name and each came from high areas. Mr. Boyd took the opportunity to define the *junction* as a place where rivers flow together, forming a bigger river. He then asked the students to decide whether there would be a Nile River if there were no Blue Nile or White Nile. After some discussion, the students decided the source of the Nile River was the source of both the Blue Nile and the White Nile. At this point, Mr. Boyd provided the names for the regions in which rivers begin and end, telling the students that the region where rivers begin is called a *source* and where it ends (by flowing into the ocean or a lake) is called the *mouth.*

The students had noted that the Nile River divided at its mouth into branches with a triangular shape. Mr. Boyd told them the region in which a river divides is a low swampy area called a *delta.* He explained that *delta* is a letter in the Greek alphabet that looks like a triangle, and he drew this letter on the board.

Then Mr. Boyd refocused the students' attention on the junction of the Blue Nile and White Nile at the city of Khartoum. He wrote the word *tributary* on the board and said that the Blue Nile and White Nile were tributaries of the Nile. He asked, "Knowing they are called tributaries, what do you think the word *tributary* means?" After some discussion and looking at maps, the students developed a class definition: "A tributary of a river is a smaller river that comes in and helps to make the big river."

Next, Mr. Boyd challenged the groups to look at the map of the United States and trace the course of the Mississippi River. They had to identify the states where its source and mouth are located and count and record the names of its tributaries. They also decided whether the Mississippi and its tributaries had deltas. After about 10 minutes, the groups shared their findings. Mr. Boyd ended the session by asking for a volunteer to trace the course of the Mississippi River on a map of the United States he put on the overhead projector. He called on several students to name one of the parts of a river that they had learned about that day. Then they briefly summarized the lesson activities and the major concepts they had investigated related to the superordinate concept of river. These were similarities and differences between rivers and lakes, what rivers look like, which rivers might flood, flood plain, river junction, river source and mouth, delta, and tributary.

On the next day, the small groups traced the courses of the Ohio, Colorado, St. Lawrence, Columbia, Snake, Missouri, Arkansas, and Rio Grande rivers. They predicted which rivers might have large flood plains and where flooding might frequently present problems. They presented their evidence for making their predictions. Then they described inconveniences flooding might cause people living along the rivers. They offered explanations about why some rivers have large tributaries and others do not. They also explained why they thought only some of the rivers have large cities located along their courses. Then they were asked to decide whether the locations of these cities were in places where flooding might cause lots of problems. To conclude, Mr. Boyd said, "Both lakes and rivers are bodies of water." He asked the students to review the lists they had made previously of ways in which rivers and lakes are similar and different. They were encouraged to revise their lists. As a summary, Mr. Boyd asked one group of students to list on the board the activities of this short unit and the concepts discussed. Another group added one activity that had been overlooked.

As an evaluation, Mr. Boyd asked students to write about the following in their journals:

Imagine that you and your family are moving to a new community. Which type of community would you want to live in: one located on a lake or one located along a river? Explain the reasons for your choice. ■

TIME FOR REFLECTION: WHAT DO YOU THINK?

1. How did Mr. Boyd help students construct the concepts of delta and tributary?

2. What examples were used to help the students construct the concept of delta?

3. What inquiry skills did the students use to gather information?

4. How did Mr. Boyd assess student learning of each concept?

5. Why do you think Mr. Boyd asked the students to make the decision about living by a lake or a river as the evaluation activity?

➤ 6. Having completed this study of rivers, what might be a good choice for the content of the next social studies lesson for these students? _____

_____

_____

_____

When planning, the teacher keeps in mind students' experiences, skills, interests, and developmental level, as well as the themes and standards of geography. Because a single theme or standard can be studied through the use of a variety of content, teachers decide what important content students should learn. A first-grade teacher in an area where flash flood watches are common might include a discussion of such watches and how to respond to them. A teacher in Iowa might talk about flooding resulting from snowmelt or rainstorms, whereas a teacher in Oklahoma would be more likely to disucss tornadoes than floods.

As students develop their skills, they study more complex regions and issues. The complexity of the region makes it more difficult to understand—not its distance from the student as the expanding environments curriculum assumes. There is a difference between actual geographical distance and psychological distance. What is understood is directly related to common experience and empathy. Therefore, it is possible for young students to be interested in, and learn, accurate and legitimate information about areas of the world that are far away from them in geographical distance. With young students, it is particularly important to carry out the following tasks:

- Provide enough accurate information
- Have students look for similarities
- Link similarities with familiar concepts
- Help students imagine how people in other places feel or respond to an issue

For example, young students who learn about children in northern Nigeria celebrating a holiday with special foods and dancing should be led to see that the children in other cultures get treats on special occasions just as they do.

Whether a teacher thinks of geography as elaborated in the NCSS standards, the five themes, or *Geography for Life*, geography education should stress content, concepts, skills, and generalizations across the range of the standards. Many people associate geography with map skills. Geographers may use map skills far more frequently than the average citizen or people in other careers, but they also use many other skills commonly practiced by all social scientists. Table 11.4 identifies these inquiry skill categories and illustrates them with specific examples of classroom activities. Because geographically literate citizens need to become familiar with these skills, they also must be an integral part of the curriculum.

TABLE 11.4

Student Behaviors Illustrating the Five Geographic Skills

Ask Geographic Questions	Acquire Geographic Information	Organize Geographic Information	Analyze Geographic Information	Answer Geographic Questions
Ask questions: Where is it? Why is it there? What is important about its location?	Locate, gather, and process information from a variety of maps and primary and secondary sources.	Prepare maps to display data; construct graphs and tables displaying geographic information.	Use maps to observe and interpret geographic relationships.	Prepare oral and written reports that use maps and graphics.
How is one location related to other locations of people, places, and environments?	Make and record observations of physical and human characteristics of places.	Construct graphs, tables, and diagrams displaying geographic information.	Use tables and graphs to observe and interpret trends and relationships.	Acquire geographic information; draw conclusions; and make generalizations.
Distinguish between geographic and nongeographic questions.	Make and record direct field observations.	Summarize data integrating various types of materials.	Use text, photos, documents to observe and interpret trends and relationships.	Apply generalizations to solve problems and make decisions.
Plan ways to gather information.	Locate information in computer databases.	Make models of physical and cultural landscapes.	Make inferences and draw conclusions.	Assess validity of generalizations and revise if needed.
Formulate geographic hypotheses and plan their testing.			Interpret geographic information.	Apply theories from geography to help explain events and places.

Source: Adapted from *Geography for Life: National Geography Standards,* by the Geography Education Standards Project, 1994, Washington, DC: National Geographic Research and Exploration.

TIME FOR REFLECTION: WHAT DO YOU THINK?

Thoughtful decision making by citizens is essential in a democracy and therefore is an important social studies goal.

1. Which of the five geographic skills helps to define a problem? _____

_____

_____

➤

➤ 2. Which of the five geographic skills helps to process information to be able to understand and interpret relationships and evaluate their importance? _____

   _____

   _____

   3. Which of the five geographic skills is used when students evaluate or revise their conclusions and generalizations? _____

   _____

   _____

   _____

MAKING A LITERATURE CONNECTION   ➤

Books Provide Different Cultural Perspectives

Most people experience a geographer's curiosity when encountering spectacular sites prompting thoughts about origins and creations. Today the appearance of the surface of the earth is explained as the result of erosions, depositions, and plate tectonics. Today's scientific culture makes explanations in relationships and theories from science. But people in other cultures have explanations concerning important events and places that have been passed on for hundreds and thousands of years. *Legends of Landforms: Native American Lore and the Geology of the Land* (1999) by Carole G. Vogel presents pictures and contrasting explanations about the creation of many striking landforms from across the United States. A teacher can use this book to stimulate discussions that encourage learning about and appreciation for the cultures and values of the people that formulated the explanations. Speculative questions prompt students to think and examine the nature of cultures, including their own. For example, why would Native Americans want to provide explanations for certain locations? How might nomadic or settled people use stories to help them teach their youths? Who are the actors in the stories and why do you think they were given their specific roles in the story? What do you think is the role stories play in the culture of the Native Americans? When reading various explanations, help students examine their personal reactions to the stories. Ask students, "Which explanations do you like the best? What did you learn from each explanation? Which explanation do you understand the best? Which do you think you will remember the longest? How has each explanation helped you to remember the characteristic of the site? Which explanation would you tell another person who looked at this site in wonder? What does the scientific explanation tell you about our society and its culture? Does the scientific explanation make sense to you or does it make you want to ask more questions? What do the Native American explanations tell you about their views of the world?"

Research Findings on Geographic Education

Reviews of research on geographic learning by the teams of Rice and Cobb (1978) and Buggey and Kracht (1985) concluded that elementary students have the ability to learn geographic skills. Carefully planned instruction in the elementary and middle grades is effective in increasing both geographic knowledge and skills. In 1985, the president of the National Geographic Society (NGS), Gilbert Grosvenor, noted that U.S. students taking part in an international test on geography had done poorly compared to students in other nations. With the support of geographers, the NGS launched Geographic Awareness Week in 1987 to promote the study of geography at all grade levels. The NGS also raises money to fund the teaching of geography and encourages states to help form and maintain geographic alliances. These alliances, whose members are largely classroom teachers, focus efforts on increasing the knowledge and skills of teachers and promoting geographic education.

The results of the 2001 National Assessment of Educational Progress (NAEP) test in geography showed improvements in achievement over the 1994 NAEP tests (National Center for Education Statistics, 1995, 1996, 2002). Most likely, the higher levels of performance were related to efforts to increase the study of geography in the United States. Examining results of the 2001 NAEP assessment in geography provides information on what students knew and could do. This can help in making decisions for teaching geography to elementary and middle school students.

- At grade 4, 71 percent and at grade 8 74 percent of the students were at or above the basic level, whereas 21 percent of the fourth-graders, and 30 percent of the eighth-graders performed at the highest (proficient and advanced) achievement levels.
- Students scoring at the higher percentiles were more able to work with a range of geographic tools, create maps based on tabular or narrative data, grasp processes and relationships, bring outside knowledge to bear on answering questions, and analyze data.

The results from the NAEP geography test make it clear that some groups of students perform better than others. Some individuals in lower-performing groups do well on geographic tasks. But group differences indicate that schools in certain regions or serving specific demographic groups need extra efforts and assistance. Personal activities, such as doing geography projects, and home activities, such as discussing geography topics with a parent, also resulted in differences in performance on the test. Differences associated with demographic variables include the following (the terms identifying groups of people based on race and ethnicity are those used by the U.S. Bureau of the Census):

- White and Asian students had higher scores than African American, Native American, and Hispanic students.
- The higher the level of parents' education, the better the performance of students.
- Overall, male students performed better than female students.
- Students attending nonpublic schools performed at higher levels than did those in public schools.
- Students who were not eligible for free or reduced-price school lunch scored higher than students who were eligible for the program.

Differences in scores related to home and school behaviors include the following:

- Eighth grade students who reported studying countries and cultures scored higher than those who said that they never or hardly ever studied countries or cultures.
- Fourth- and eighth-grade students whose teachers had them use the Internet scored higher than those whose teachers did not have students use the Internet.

In addressing the press on June 21, 2002, when the findings of the 2001 NAEP test in geography were released to the public, Rod Paige said,

> Geography not only helps students explore the world's people and civilizations across time, it also helps them understand the complexities of the world we live in today. . . . This is not the same planet our parents knew or their parents. . . . It's a world of 24-hour-news cycles, global markets, high-speed Internet and big challenges for all who inhabit it. And in order for our children to be prepared to take their place in that world and rise to those challenges, they must first understand it. . . . I am pleased to hear that this report shows improved achievement among the fourth and eighth graders. . . . But the results also show us that, clearly, there is much more work to do. (Paige, 2002b)

TIME FOR REFLECTION: WHAT DO YOU THINK?

1. How do you think the results of national tests are best used to improve student learning? _____
   _____
   _____
   _____

2. Using the above information, identify the out-of-school variables that seem to impact student learning of geography. _____
   _____
   _____
   _____
   _____

3. If a class or school does not provide opportunities for students to learn geography, what are some activities that parents or communities can do to provide geographic learning experiences to the students? _____
   _____
   _____
   _____
   _____

Research on Map and Globe Skills

Students in grades K–5 understand space differently from the geographer. Even older students may have difficulty understanding the world as it is spatially presented on maps. This means that the types of maps used in grades K–5 should differ from those used by older students. The types of information included on a young student's map or observed by a student on an adult's map will probably be interpreted differently by the student and the adult.

Spatial understanding begins developing in the first few months of life. Early development of spatial understanding is influenced greatly by the egocentric nature of the learner. At first, children view things from their own perspective. Later, they come to recognize multiple perspectives from various locations. Last, they are able to use an abstract reference system to locate items in relationship to one another. The three types of space children come to understand are topological, projective, and Euclidian. Teachers who recognize the characteristics of these types of space help children organize and gain information from maps in developmentally appropriate ways throughout the elementary and middle school years. These teachers also recognize opportunities to integrate the learning of geography and mathematics.

Topological Space. Topological space is the first type of space students come to understand. Preschool children master some of its elements. Topological perceptions include proximity (or "nearby-ness"), separation, order, enclosure, and continuity (Holloway, 1967). The concept that something stands for something else, or that of symbol, is understood by very young children. They can identify simple symbols on maps and locate them in order. Young children can differentiate shapes and are taught to place labels on them.

Elements of topological space continue to dominate mapping until the onset of concrete operations about age 7 (Downs, Liben, & Daggs, 1988). The child's concept of form is more accurate than that of distance. Several researchers report success in teaching students ages 4–7 the elements of topological space that appear on maps (Atkins, 1981; Downs, Liben, & Daggs, 1988; Savage & Bacon, 1969). However, all report variation in success within a class and greater success when concrete items and terms are used.

Projective Space. Beginning in the preoperational stage (approximately ages 4–7), students start to understand elements of projective space. This enables students to see that items appear differently from various distances and angles. These new understandings enable them to develop the idea that locations are related to other places. This leads to a better understanding of distance and direction. Their maps become roughly accurate (Catling, 1978). Students' understanding of space continues to develop through age 11.

Euclidian Space. As students become formal operational (between ages 12 and 16) and increase their knowledge of concepts, mathematics, and language, they relate locations correctly to one another simultaneously (Holloway, 1967). Direction and distance become accurate and are measured in relationship to such abstract coordinates as the prime meridian, the equator, and the poles.

HELPING STUDENTS LEARN AND USE MAP AND GLOBE SKILLS

Maps and globes are important tools for geographers because they provide a convenient way to organize information by location. By their very nature, maps and globes are quite different from the real world. They are not a picture of the world but an interpretation by the mapmaker, containing only information the mapmaker considers important to include for the purpose of the map. The title tells the reader the major idea shown on the map.

One of the best ways to learn the definition of a map is to make your own maps. When doing so, students encounter and solve the same kinds of problems professional mapmakers encounter. Mapping the classroom, schoolyard, or route taken on a neighborhood walk are excellent experiences for primary-grade students. Such mapping might begin with making three-dimensional models in a sandbox or on the floor with blocks or plastic models. Older students might map their individual routes to school or their rooms at home. Students of all ages should examine a variety of maps so that they can compare and judge their own ideas against those of professionals.

Globes and maps today are durable, less expensive than in the past, and made from a variety of materials. Schools can afford to have several globes so that small groups of students can explore and mark on a globe rather than gaze at it from afar. It is possible to buy inexpensive maps and atlases so that each student or pair of students has an atlas or placematlike map. Such instructional materials provide students with opportunities for more active involvement in learning. Publishers of atlases and globes produce research-based materials that are appropriate for students at the various elementary grade levels. Many schools are painting maps on their parking lots and playgrounds, providing children with the opportunity to stand and walk across maps representing large areas such as the United States or the entire world.

If you put a globe where young children can get to it easily, they explore it and ask questions. This model of the earth is studied before maps are studied for several reasons. First, a globe is more concrete and realistic than a map. Second, students are familiar with models because of their toys. Third, although maps may include more specific information, all the information that is required in reading a map is available on a globe, and the globe presents the information more accurately. Shapes, locations, relative locations, distances, and sizes are all more accurately represented on a globe than on a map. Because of their two-dimensional nature, maps represent distances and shapes inaccurately. Such inaccurate information can lead to misconceptions.

Misconceptions not only limit a student's ability to answer geographical questions correctly, but often remain even after instruction tries to correct them. For instance, many U.S. children believe that Alaska and Hawaii are islands located just a little west of California and Mexico or in the Gulf of Mexico. It is the visual impact of the items on a map that helps to create and maintain such misconceptions. By using a globe first, children are more likely to learn geography correctly. After becoming familiar with a globe, students are likely to question the inaccuracies on maps. Eventually, they can discover why the mapmaker must make choices about what to include on a map and how to show it as accurately as possible.

Making three-dimensional maps helps students see new ways to illustrate elevation.

Reading a map or globe requires knowledge of the five superordinate concepts of (1) shape or pattern, (2) symbols, (3) directions, (4) distance, and (5) grid systems, as well as the conventions of their presentations on globes and maps. Like most concepts, each of these can be understood at a variety of levels. It is possible to use these concepts correctly on a map without thoroughly understanding them, just as it is possible to drive a car without understanding how its various systems work. However, understanding accounts for greater success in using globes and maps and for knowing when maps are most effectively used. Each of these concepts is introduced, practiced, and refined by the student throughout the elementary and middle school grades.

The first maps students use should depict familiar locations with only few symbols. Map and globe publishers such as Nystrom, Cram, and Rand McNally produce instructional programs and sets of globes, atlases, and maps for children starting in kindergarten. By the sixth grade, most textbook series include various types of maps usually found in commercial atlases. Because students at this age are just beginning to develop their understanding of the abstract Euclidian space on which these maps are based and just starting to read locations, distances, and elevations with exact measurements, teachers need to encourage lots of discussion and involve students in a wide range of activities with these maps.

Geographers divide map and globe work into three sets of skills: mapmaking, map reading, and map interpretation. The interpretation of data on maps is related to the complexity of the question being asked and to the data students can read and understand from the map. Young students can make inferences and interpret data from a map based on their mastery of spatial concepts. Older students begin making inferences from data shown on two or more maps.

Shapes and Patterns

Continents, nations, states, and distributions covering areas such as the Corn Belt or a low pressure system have distinct shapes or form patterns with a shape. The ability to recognize these patterns and describe them is key to the study of geography. The first step is to be able to recognize the patterns, and the second step is to be able to identify the pattern when it is seen again. Because maps are made in different scales, patterns based on shape must be recognized when shown in various sizes. How people determine what they see as a shape of a portion of the earth is a matter of personal choice. Few patterns repeat, and few have simple shapes, such as a square. Teachers encourage students to describe places by the shape they have when a dark line is drawn around the edges. This is helpful in learning the locations of states and nations. Very young children are capable of doing this task. Many children enter kindergarten knowing various states because they played with a puzzle of the United States. Teachers encourage children to make associations to help them learn patterns. They allow children to make their own shape description rather than tell them what shape someone else has decided it is. Teachers might need to encourage children to do so with examples, by suggesting, for instance, that Indiana is shaped like a stocking or that Antartica is shaped like a toy rubber duck.

Symbols

The idea that something represents another thing is learned in the preoperational stage, around ages 5 to 7. Globes and maps are symbols and they make extensive use of other symbols. Two types of geographic symbols are point symbols and area symbols. *Point symbols* identify those locations that cover small areas appearing as a point on a globe or small-scale map. The simplest point symbols to identify are called pictorial symbols because they appear similar to a picture of the real item. Maps for the beginner use a few pictorial or semipictorial symbols. As mapmakers include more information on a map, they simplify the symbols by making them more abstract. *Area symbols* show features that cover acres or square miles of land. Shading and colors are used for area symbols, and they are very abstract. Few universal symbols appear on maps and globes, partly because so many features might appear on a map. Even the meaning of a color may change from map to map.

Maps have legends or keys to specify the meaning of symbols used on them. Students must learn the habit of using the legend to be able to read maps. Symbol is one of the first superordinate concepts a student must come to understand to be able to read a map. Complex maps layer area and point symbols on top of one another.

Direction

Directions are learned first in relationship to oneself and then to other objects. Pointing to things and describing where they are in relation to yourself, to other people, and to objects is the beginning of directional activities. Students in the early primary grades can do this. Knowing left from right is important for learning map directions because east is 90 degrees right of north and west is 90 degrees left of north. Take students outside to locate north. As they face north, have them locate east and west by raising their arms. Tell students that south is to their backs when they are facing

The grid on the classroom floor allows students to practice locating items and classmates in order to better understand the use of the grid on maps.

north. Then label the walls in the classroom with correct directions. Using the cardinal directions, have students locate items outside and inside in relation to people and objects. For example, a student might say, "Mary sits two desks north of Joan."

When maps and globes are introduced, they should be oriented toward the north. Because maps show what is on the earth's surface, they are best placed on a desk or on the floor parallel to the surface of the earth. Students are encouraged to trace directions with their fingers over the surface of the globe or map. In the early primary grades, many children quickly memorize directions on a map and give correct answers to questions, but this does not mean that they understand direction or can use directions, except on a map.

Distance

Correctly measuring distance on a map with the use of a scale is complex. It requires accurate use of mathematics knowledge, an understanding of proportionality, and the ability to divide quickly. Students must be able to conserve distance, recognizing paths of the same length. Distance is not only a straight-line measure; it is also important in determining the correct size and shape of an area. Therefore, exact measures of distances are best attempted in the intermediate grades. However, relative distances are used in the primary grades. Near, farther away, and farthest can be introduced to young children, as can measures such as small, big, and very big.

Because the globe provides a more accurate presentation of distances in all directions than does a world map, measurement of world distances and comparison of the sizes of regions is done first on the globe. Pieces of string are stretched over a globe between two points to get a relative measure of distances between places. The pieces of string are cut and compared to see whether they are the same length and, if not, which is longer. As the string is laid on the globe, the student observes the direction of the path one would travel to get between the points. When actual measurements in miles are needed, a string or thin strip of paper is placed between the two points and cut at the end point. The string or strip is moved to the scale where the distance is read by placing the paper or string next to the scale. Pieces of string or dental floss are used when measuring curved rivers or roads because their flexibility yields more accurate measures. Measuring with string the equator, meridians (longitude), and lines of latitude on a globe and comparing the lengths greatly assist students' meaningful learning of these concepts, along with the concepts of sphere and hemisphere. Without an accurate understanding of these concepts, students can't master the grid system of latitude and longitude.

Grid Systems

The grid system is the most complex of the concepts. It is a way of finding locations. A vertical line and a horizontal line intersect at only one place. To use a grid system, the student needs to understand this principle and practice locating intersections. Grid systems are taught first by using a system similar to that used in locating a seat in an auditorium with numbers for the rows and letters for the seats. When transferred to a map, letters are placed along the horizontal axis and numbers along the vertical axis. Road maps of individual states usually include this type of grid system as do city maps. Such a grid system gives an approximate location. The grid system can also be introduced with a dot-to-dot game.

For additional practice, letters can be placed in the boxes formed by a grid and secret messages can be decoded for practice. For example, Kathleen's mailbox address might be C5. Some teachers have labeled the tiles on the floor or ceiling of the classroom and encouraged students to practice locating people and things in the classroom. So the aquarium might be at E8. Exact locations are given by the system of latitude and longitude. Each line of latitude and longitude is identified by a number and a direction. Because every line of latitude or longitude is not on a map, locating places by latitude and longitude requires the ability to sequence numbers in relationship to the rectangular grid. It also requires the ability to estimate and understand directions on a map.

Numbers: The Amount or Quantity
on Maps, in Atlases, and in Textbooks

Geographers cannot escape encountering and interpreting the meaning of large numbers. Population, gross national product (GNP), dollar value of crops, acres, miles, and elevations are just some of the geographic facts that are given as numbers. Comprehending the amount in a large number is quite difficult. Therefore, many people ignore the numbers and end up with great misconceptions about important characteristics of places. Geographers use charts and graphics, particularly histograms, pie graphs, bar graphs, and population pyramids. These graphics provide a visual image of numbers and sometimes compare parts to a whole or make symbols in graduated size to allow for more meaningful comparisons. Sometimes graphs are placed directly on a map to focus on location as well as amount. One of the most common graphs combines a line graph of the average monthly temperature and vertical bars indicating the average monthly precipitation at a location. These graphs are often shown on or with the maps that illustrate the types of climates and illustrate the variations in the temperature and precipitation during the year. Population pyramids are often printed with population distribution maps to indicate the age and sex distribution of the people. Other maps use area symbols to illustrate the amount of rainfall, length of growing season, and values of products produced in a state, nation, or continent. Typically, the colors on such map use shades to indicate amounts, the lightest shades indicating small amounts and the darker shades the greater amounts.

Atlases prepared for grade 6 are filled with graphic representations of facts and concepts. Maps for primary grades may categorize cities by size, such as small city, medium size city, and big city. Atlases for primary grades also use aerial photographs of the region with the map to help students gain the vertical perspective from which the map is drawn and to illustrate how symbols represent real objects. Teachers use such maps to encourage students to make predictions and conclusions that can be tested. Students who examine the variety of maps in an atlas should be asked, "Why is the information important in explaining the characteristics of a place?"

Activities using maps and graphs to learn about places include the following:

1. Students explain why a map shows only some of the objects visible in the aerial photograph and tell why they think the mapmaker omitted several specific items. Students make their own map of a familiar location, explaining what they included and identifying several things they decided not to include.
2. Students explain why there are so many more young people or old people in some nations than in other nations. They predict the special needs that a region has because there are many old people or young people living there.
3. Using climate maps and graphs, students decide what clothing they would take if they were to travel today to a specified place. Then they decide what would be the best time for a tourist to visit that location.
4. Students pretend that they are starting a fudge factory that will need tons of various ingredients each month. Using the product maps, students decide from where in the United States they will purchase their products and where in the world they will find the chocolate and nuts needed for the fudge.
5. Using land use maps, students identify places that are home to cowboys and cowgirls, miners, and those who catch fish or raise fish.
6. Examine the climate and product maps and predict where people might have a harvest festival and the month in which they would be celebrating the harvest.
7. Students write reports on a nation explaining how the people earn their living and how they spend their recreational time using only resources available in an atlas. Students are challenged to provide at least six specific facts to support their ideas.

Reading and Maps

Reading words on a map is different from reading words in a story. Except for the title of the map, words on a map are labels for specific locations. Reading left to right is not always the standard convention on a map. Sometimes the words are written at odd angles and spread out to cover the areas being designated. Many words are spread out much wider than the normal reading eye span. This is particularly true on large wall maps and road maps. The style of print is also used as a symbol. More important features have fonts that make them more visible. The same font is used to designate all features or regions of the same type. The teacher needs to assist students in discovering the unique ways in which words appear on a map.

Creating a complex mental map of the world is a worthy goal for each student. Building this knowledge of locations is accomplished throughout the years. The following instructional activities help students to construct map and globe concepts and practice using the skills needed to read and interpret information from maps and globes:

1. Students arrange a box of crayons, a pencil, a book, and a pair of scissors on their desktop and draw a map illustrating the arrangement. They remove the items and give them and their map to a partner. The partner uses the map to place the items on a desktop. The mapmaker checks to see whether the arrangement is correct.
2. Young students make Me Maps. A tracing is made around the body. Then the children use previously agreed-on symbols to draw their eyes, nose, heart, knees, ears, mouth, waist, and elbows in the correct locations.
3. Students follow a map to go on treasure hunts within the school or on the school grounds. The map may be drawn by the teacher or other students.
4. Students map their classroom or school grounds, selecting information to include and symbols to use. Then they place each symbol in the appropriate location. Actual measurement of distance is used if the students have such skills.
5. Each student makes a map illustrating the route taken to school. Older students also write directions to their homes, which classmates follow to mark a route on a city or county map.
6. When taking a field trip, students use a city or state map to plan the routes to and from their destinations. Older students measure the distance involved and try to locate the shortest route. They also write out a set of directions for the trip.
7. Students plan trips to visit famous cities and landmarks. They measure or compute the distance traveled.
8. Students use a world atlas and an outline map of the world to locate a natural resource or crop and draw its transportation route to the factory or marketplace where it is used or sold.
9. Students use a gazetteer to find the latitude and longitude of cities they hear about or read about in the news so they can locate them on the map.
10. Using the equator, prime meridian, and other selected meridians and parallels as a guide to location, students make freehand drawings of regions of the world, placing them in the correct locations relative to each other.

Meaningful learning of map and globe skills is linked to real-life experiences and to the use of maps. Too often, textbooks and teachers have taught map and globe skills as something unrelated to gathering and interpreting information. Using latitude and longitude is one of those skills often taught without consideration of its use beyond answering a question correctly on a standardized test. The learning cycle lesson in Table 11.5 teaches how to perform the skill of locating things exactly. It helps students consider the practical use of latitude and longitude.

TIME FOR REFLECTION: WHAT DO YOU THINK?

Read the lesson in Table 11.5, then reflect on it as you answer the following questions:

1. Think about when you were taught how to use latitude and longitude. How well did you accomplish the task? What did you find most difficult? Did you find anything relatively easy about latitude and longitude? _____

_____

_____

_____

2. How would you describe your memory of the study of latitude and longitude?

_____

_____

_____

3. Have you used latitude and longitude or seen references to them outside a school setting? If so, how were they used? _____

_____

_____

_____

4. In a skill lesson, the teacher must provide practice in the use of the skill. Where in the lesson in Table 11.5 are practice opportunities suggested or provided?

_____

_____

_____

5. What are some of the strategies the teacher uses to help students succeed in using latitude and longitude? _____

_____

_____

_____

6. How does the teacher assess students' progress toward learning these skills?

_____

_____

_____

7. Skill lessons are best taught as part of larger units that focus on geography content. What would be an appropriate content focus for a unit that incorporates the teaching of latitude and longitude? _____

_____

_____

_____

8. During the remainder of the school year, when might a teacher provide some additional practice using latitude and longitude? _____

_____

_____

_____

TABLE 11.5

| Learning Cycle | Latitude and Longitude |

Grade Level: Middle school
NCSS Standards: People, Places, and Environments; The World in Spatial Terms

Exploratory Introduction

Materials: Two cards with information about specific cities or vacation sites for each small group of three students (each group should have different cities or sites on its cards); maps and atlases

Objectives	Procedures	Assessments
Given questions about places to eat lunch at a mall, students explain the difference between seeking a specific site or a general site.	Present the following puzzle to the students: "Imagine that you have been shopping at a large mall and that you are hungry and start to think about eating a hamburger. Your friend suggests going to the food court because she wants a slice of pizza. Will going to the food court meet your want for a hamburger? How would you respond to your friends' suggestion?" Ask: Why do you think the owners of malls include food courts in their plans? Would a restaurant owner want to locate in a mall with a food court? Is there any time when you would definitely not want to go to the food court for lunch?"	Students respond with logical suggestions and explain that, when a person has specific wants, he or she must go to a place that can fill those specific wants.
	Ask: "Can you think of other examples of times when specific locations rather than general locations are the place to go?"	
Given a city or vacation site to visit, students try to describe its location to classmates so they can locate the mystery place.	Divide the class into groups of three and provide them with information about a particular city or vacation site. Without naming the place, students try to develop clues that enable their classmates to determine the site.	Students make an effort to describe city locations and try to guess the cities described. Students say that they need a way to find the exact location of a place.
	Have the class establish a number of tries the class has for each clue. Then have groups present their clues and have students try to determine the locations.	Students try to locate the places in the clues.
	Ask: "Why was it hard to determine these locations?"	Students discuss the difficulties of finding the places from the clues

TABLE 11.5

Continued

		concluding that it is difficult to locate places in other cities or nations. They decide that there should be a way to do this.

Lesson Development

Materials: A globe for each small group with locations marked with three differently colored stickers; a diagram for each small group showing the world divided into northern and southern halves by the equator and into eastern and western halves by the prime meridian; a grid for each student labeled with the equator and prime meridian and with other lines of latitude and longitude unlabeled; a world map for each group; a task sheet for each group with a set of 10 cities in the world whose location the group identifies; an atlas for each group; plain paper and one pair of scissors per group

Objectives	Procedures	Assessments
Given a globe on which are placed three colored stickers, students attempt to describe all three locations in words.	Tell students we have learned about using a grid system to find an approximate location on a city or state map. Ask: "Can someone explain how we found the location of the city, vacation site, or store on the map?"	Students respond that, after finding the area, they searched the area for the specific symbol and name on the map.
	Ask each group's materials manager to get a globe. Tell them you have put three stickers, each a different color, on the globe. Tell them, as a group, to try to figure out a way of describing the locations of each of the colored dots. Tell them they will have five minutes to try to figure out how to describe in words the locations of the three dots. (Note: A blue dot is located on the equator, a green dot is at the intersection of the prime meridian and a line of south latitude on the globe, and a red dot is between a line of north latitude and a line of longitude either east or west and near but not on a city that is labeled on the globe.)	
	After five minutes, ask: "How are you doing? Can you describe the locations of the dots? Which was the easiest to describe? Why?"	Students use the lines and perhaps the names of the lines (numbers) to identify the locations.

continued

T A B L E   1 1 . 5

Continued

Objectives	Procedures	Assessments
	Tell students: "When we used the grid system, each square had an address or two names, what did we use to label the coordinates of the grid?"	Students reply that letters and numbers were used.
	Ask: "Did you find any labels on the line on the globe that we could use to name the lines?" Help the students find the numbers and the words *equator* and *prime meridian.* Students should already know that the equator divides the world into a northern and a southern half while the prime meridian divides the world into an eastern and western half. Review this and give each small group a diagram to reinforce the point. Ask review questions.	Students look carefully at the globe finding the words *prime meridian* and *equator* and numbers.
Given a latitude and longitude grid and several locations, students practice locating places with latitude and longitude, circling the correct locations on the grid.	Provide students with a grid with a labeled equator and prime meridian. Help students label the other lines of latitude, also called *parallels,* in intervals of 20 degrees. Label each line with the number and an appropriate direction. Repeat similarly for longitude lines (also called *meridians*). Stress that each line has an address. Make an analogy to each line having a first and last name just as each student does. (The first name is a number and the last, a direction—north, south, east, or west.)	Students follow directions, accurately labeling lines and circling locations on the grid.
	Have students note that any combination of a vertical line and a horizontal line can cross, or intersect, at only one place.	
	Provide practice locating several intersections and circling them (0 and 20E, 30N and 40W, 50S and 0). After a few additional practice numbers, have the groups give you the locations of the green dot on the globe.	
	Follow these steps to locate places by latitude and longitude:	
	1. Begin at the equator and locate the correct latitude N or S. 2. Mark that line.	

TABLE 11.5

Continued

3. Begin at the prime meridian and locate the correct longitude E or W.
4. Make the line.
5. Find the place where the two lines meet.

Present the question: "Is the line for 15N on the grid? 28E?" We must estimate the locations of these lines. Stress always starting by looking from the zero line (*equator* when locating the N or S parallel and the *prime meridian* when locating the E or W meridian).

Practice several of these as a class. Have the groups locate the red sticker on their globe. Ask: "Why aren't all the lines drawn on the globe?"

Students identify lines of latitude and longitude as a *parallel* and a *meridian*.	Review the terms *latitude* and *longitude* and *meridian* and *parallel*. Ask: "Which line is also called a parallel? What directions will be the last name for a line of latitude?"	Students identify meridians and parallels accurately.
	Provide each group with a world map and have them locate the parallels and meridians. Ask: "Are the lines labeled the same on the map and the globe?"	
Working in groups, students correctly locate cities on the globe and on the world map.	Provide the groups with a set of 10 world cities to locate on a globe and a world map. Each pair locates all cities on both the globe and on a world map. Include the coordinates of your own city or that of a nearby city that can be found in the gazetteer in the back of an atlas (5N, 0W; 41N, 72W; 48N, 2E; 34S, 139E; 37N, 122W; 33S, 70W; 14N, 90W; 52N, 40E; 1S, 36E; 35N, 139E).	Students work cooperatively in pairs correctly locating the cities on the globe and world map.
	Ask: "Was it easier to locate places using latitude and longitude on the globe or on a world map? Why? Why do you think a map of a city uses a number and letter grid and not latitude and longitude grid?" (Answer: The city is too small an area for different numbers to be read and estimated.) "What are the latitude and longitude coordinates of our own city?"	

continued

T A B L E   1 1 . 5

Continued

Ask: "If you hear or read the name of a place and want to know its latitude and longitude so you can locate it on a map, where can you find the latitude and longitude?" Show students how to use the gazetteer in the atlas.

Provide for additional practice by using volcanoes, mountain peaks, or other cities. Have students use the gazetteer to find locations and write them on slips of paper to use in additional practice. (Such practice activities can be in a learning center also for those who need additional practice or are curious and want to do more.) Students can draw slips of paper at random from a box and locate the sites on a globe or map.

Closure: Ask students to describe and demonstrate how to identify the location of a city using its latitude and longitude.

Expansion

Materials: Large world map, grids and list of hurricane plots downloaded from NOAA Internet site (given below) for each small group

Objectives	Procedures	Assessments
Students direct another student in how to locate a new place on a transparency or wall map of the world.	Teacher asks review questions on vocabulary associated with latitude and longitude. Teacher presents a new place. Students give verbal directions for locating the place to another student, who tries to find it. Teacher asks, "What is the first step John must do to locate the city? What next?" and so on.	Students give accurate answers and directions and check for correctness.
	Teacher explains, "There are some occupations in which people use latitude and longitude because exact locations are very important to the success of their jobs." Ask: "Can you think of one such job?"	
Given an activity of plotting the course of a hurricane, students	Teacher explains the assignment: "You will need to plot a number of locations using latitude and longitude. Because the places to	

T A B L E   1 1 . 5

Continued

identify the need for weather services to track and predict hurricanes and other dangerous storms to help many people.

plot are close together, I am giving you a large map of a small region of the world."

Provide student groups with a new grid for tracking hurricanes (obtain from the NOAA at the link on the companion website). Using a world map, locate this area and show students that this map has symbols for individual degrees of latitude and longitude. When you estimate locations on the larger grid, you should notice that the lines are 1 degree apart. Ask: "New Orleans is located 30N and how many degrees west?" and "What is the latitude and longitude for Key West?"

COMPANION WEBSITE

Provide small groups of students with lists of places to plot. When they complete the plots they should connect the locations.

Students complete assignment correctly.

Ask: "What do you think is plotted on the map? Who would want to know this information?" Consult Internet sites on weather (see the companion website) for information on hurricane paths to plot for the lesson).

COMPANION WEBSITE

Ask: "When does the average citizen need to use latitude and longitude to help them locate places? People in which occupations might need to use latitude and longitude?" Ask students to describe the regions in the United States where hurricanes often strike.

Students conclude that shippers, tourists, farmers, and people living in potential hurricane paths would be interested.

Lesson Summary: Ask students to describe the activities in this learning cycle.

S U M M A R Y

In recent years, more emphasis has been placed on teaching geography. Geographers recommend that map skills be taught beginning in the primary grades through the use of developmentally appropriate activities. They see drawing maps, reading maps, and making inferences and comparisons as techniques that help students develop thinking skills and knowledge of geography (Winston, 1984). The emphasis in the elementary grades on learning map skills has given the impression that location is geography. Approaches such as the introduction of a completely meaningful definition of geography, teacher training in geography, and preparation of standards and themes to be taught at all grade levels help students learn the importance of geography in everyday life. Students learn that through their own actions they decide how the physical and cultural resources of the earth can and should be used.

Expanding ON THIS CHAPTER

Activity

COMPANION
WEBSITE

View a video, film, or filmstrip that attempts to teach children about people who live in a region of the nation or world. Write a one- or two-page evaluation of the film. Identify which of the five themes of geography or standards in *Geography for Life* are presented to the students. Explain why you think the film would be successful (or unsuccessful) in presenting geographic knowledge and motivating students to want to learn about the region.

Recommended Websites to Visit

COMPANION
WEBSITE

The National Geographic Society
> **www.nationalgeographic.com/**

World Heritage sites are recognized internationally as places of great importance or beauty. A separate page is available for each of the 750-plus sites throughout the world
> **http://whc.unesco.org/nwhc/pages/sites/main.htm**

A list of the world's 100 most endangered historic, artistic, and architectural heritage sites identified by the Word Monuments Fund, a private, nonprofit organization dedicated to preserving cultural heritage
> **http://wmf.org/a/watchlist.htm**

The U.N. Environmental Programme World Conservation Monitoring Center monitors endangered species and environmental concerns and reports
> **www.unep-wcmc.org/**

World gazetteer with statistics on nations and cities
> **www.gazetteer.de/**

GLOBE is a worldwide hands-on, primary and secondary school-based education and science program with a free site for creating maps and graphs
> **www.globe.gov/globe_flash.html**

The Environmental Protection Agency's portal to environmental issues and U.S. laws that affect the environment
> **www.epa.gov/highschool/**

Hurricane Tracking Chart for the learning cycle
> **www.nhc.noaa.gov/gifs/track_chart.gif**

Data on classic hurricanes for the learning cycle
> **http://weather.unisys.com/hurricane/index.html**

National Atlas of the United States provides maps for downloading and information and a program to make your own maps
> **http://nationalatlas.gov/**

Helping Students Make Economic Decisions

INTRODUCTION

- When was the first time you were told, "You can't have everything you want?" _____
- How do you use a credit card? _____
- Are you paying for part of your education with a loan? _____
- Why do you have a job, or why will you get one? _____
_____
- When have you refused to buy something because you thought the price was too high? _____
- If you were going to purchase a new car, would you be tempted to examine those that you have seen in TV commercials? _____
- Do you anticipate telling children in the classes you teach that they cannot have everything they want? _____
- If so, what will be the next sentence you will probably say to them? _____
_____

CHAPTER OVERVIEW

Economics is encountered every day by everyone. Chances are you cannot remember the first time you were told that you could not have everything you wanted; you were most likely too young to remember this incident. But you have probably heard it over and over again since then. This frequent caution is the basis of economics. The solutions people use to get around the reality that they cannot have everything they want is the study of economics. Economics is not limited to money, although this is the way most people view it. As a student you are likely to have a shortage of money, but you probably feel the shortage of other things as well, and perhaps even more. This chapter examines ways to help students understand the role of economics in their lives, their families' lives, their community, their nation, and the world. It also focuses on the process of making rational personal and group decisions about the use of the world's scarce resources. This chapter will give you ideas on how to approach teaching the NCSS standards Consumption, Production, and Distribution, Global Connections, and Science, Technology, and Society.

CHAPTER OBJECTIVES

1. Clarify the differences between microeconomics and macroeconomics.
2. List the key concepts for the study of economics and of economic decision making.
3. Explain why scarcity and decision making (cost–benefit analysis) are considered the key to economic understanding.
4. Explain how to use the economic decision-making model with students.
5. Explain how economics influences the lives of all people, communities, and nations.
6. Explain how interdependence impacts all nations bringing them benefits from economic cooperation and how a lack of cooperation works against some nations and for others.
7. Identify ways in which economic education is integrated into the social studies curriculum through such topics as career education, geography, history, community studies, and consumer education.
8. Reflect on the ways in which economic education is authentically taught and assessed.
9. Locate potential resources for teaching economics to students.

ECONOMIC LITERACY

The National Assessment of Educational Progress (NAEP) does not have a test for economic literacy. However, in 1999, the National Association of Economic Educators (NAEE) tested adults and high school seniors on fundamental economic concepts. Half the adults and two-thirds of the high school students failed, showing a lack of understanding of fundamental concepts such as money, inflation, and scarcity. Of the high school students, 35 percent admitted that they did not know what effect an increase in interest rates would mean. Just over half (54 percent) of the adults and fewer than a quarter of the high school students knew that a budget deficit occurs when the federal government's expenditures exceed its revenues for the year.

Many people in the United States have high rates of personal bankruptcies, large credit card debts, and no savings or investments. At the same time, others are reaping financial rewards for investing. Such findings are spurring a national campaign for economic literacy and the promotion of more economically sound behaviors in which social studies education has a major role.

An Interview with Nancy Braden about Teaching Economics

Nancy Braden, long an Arkansas elementary teacher, relates how she became an economic educator and the approaches she recommends for teaching economics.

Interviewer: Nancy, you are one of the most successful teachers of economics to young people in the country, having won multiple awards for your teaching over the years. How did you get started teaching economics?

Nancy Braden: I went to a workshop given in my school district by the Arkansas State Council for Economic Education. I anticipated just getting my in-service points, not ever dreaming I'd get interested in it or care anything about it. I planned to be bored for that week. I can't tell you now what was said, but whatever it was, it turned me on, and before it was over, I was planning what I'd do the next year.

Interviewer: You tell me that you didn't remember a lot of what you were told.

Nancy Braden: Not in that one week. No.

Interviewer: Well, I hear your students talking about such complex concepts as aggregate demand, profits, supply and demand, and investing. How did you learn all this information that you now teach?

Nancy Braden: I got the materials they [the Arkansas State Council for Economic Education] had published—the state curriculum guide. I got down and studied it. I was used to preparing my own units because we didn't have any social studies textbooks. I've never been one to use a textbook anyway, except as a guide and resource. Over the years, I've read lots of other books and articles and gone to other workshops and meetings, too. Plus I learn new things and more economic understanding with each unit I teach.

Interviewer: You are now teaching social studies in a departmentalized situation. How do you work the economics into your district curriculum?

Nancy Braden: Well, it just fits in. You couldn't teach social studies without it. There is just no way. All the direct areas and people we study from fourth through the sixth grade—all of them can't be understood without economics. You've got to study how the people live, how they meet their basic needs—food, clothing, and shelter. You've got to study their economy, their government. You can't study any of this without economics. There is no way to study any social studies without including economics, and I highlight a lot of it.

This year we've studied a lot about recycling. We are finding out that it is quite expensive to buy recycled materials, but since our opportunity cost is to ruin our country, we've got to do something. It's going to cost us, so we might as well pay for it now. We saved 26 trees in the last 9 weeks of the school year by collecting paper for recycling. We learned that in some cities and states people are required to recycle and that some local governments are making money by selling the recyclable materials, which is helping to pay for local services. That helps to keep from increasing taxes.

Interviewer: You just named a lot of economic concepts, and I've noticed they are an integral part of your vocabulary. How important is this set of economic concepts to your teaching?

Nancy Braden: Very, very. I've heard other teachers say they've had a hard time getting the concepts across, but I don't find that at all. I call the students entrepreneurs, and they want to know what I called them. Their parents may not know what the word means, but the students learn it, and how to spell it, and they think they are hot stuff. They get excited, and I'm excited. So I think the kids catch my enthusiasm.

Interviewer: Do you teach all the concepts first and then do your study of the economic problem?

Nancy Braden: I kind of do it all together. When I was teaching in a self-contained room, I mentioned economic concepts in all the subjects. Whenever there is an example of one of the concepts, I make certain that the students call it by the proper economic term. One year a co-worker told me that I was leaving out spelling, English, and math. Well, when we got back the results of the state test, my students had made a much larger gain in those areas than her students. It wasn't because I had smarter students; it was because they all got turned onto learning by the economics. They saw the connection between learning and real-life activities. The classes pull together in the study, and it carries over to other work as well. One thing I like is that it works well with all kids, the fast and the slow, and it has meaning for them and their families. When you say something that is going to affect them, they want to know about it.

Interviewer: So you make an extra effort to point out how what you are studying directly or indirectly affects your students, and you tend to use an in-depth examination of a particular problem each year?

Nancy Braden: Yes, usually. This year we did the ecology emphasis. We organized the whole school to put things into the recycle box. Recycling places used to pay for the newspapers; they don't now. But we weren't doing it to make money. We were doing it to teach the kids something about the wise use of resources. Instead of counting money, we took the total weight of the paper and figured out how many trees would need to be cut down to equal that much paper. That is how we know we saved 26 trees.

Interviewer: It sounds like you study a different problem or question each year. What are some of the other topics you've investigated with your classes?

Nancy Braden: The Economic Impact of Pets was my favorite. I loved that one. The Economic Problems of the Local National Park illustrated many interesting economic decisions and gave us the opportunity to learn about some careers working with government other than being a politician. The Cost of Crime study started because someone would drop a pencil and another student would take it and use it. Then the students would get into arguments concerning to whom the pencil belonged. We talked about taking something that belonged to another and why private property and government properties are important and should be respected and cared for by everyone. We also studied the interdependence of Barling, the small community where the school is located, and Fort Smith, the neighboring big city.

Interviewer: What was your first award-winning study?

Nancy Braden: It was called "The Economic Growth of an Industrial-Centered Community." It was a study of Fort Smith, Arkansas, where most of the parents work and shop.

Interviewer: Sounds like a topic where you would use lots of resource people.

Nancy Braden: Oh yes, I used a lot of fathers in that one. Later, I heard that the fathers started calling one another to see whether they were being invited to come to the class. I usually have visits from a banker and stockbroker. We've even had the governor. The governor had another appointment, and his aides kept trying to get him to leave, but he kept saying, "Just one more question." He was impressed because the students asked him specific questions about his economic policies and programs. Sometimes visiting speakers tell me that they don't think they can get to the low level of the children's understanding, but when they leave, they often say that they were afraid they didn't have good enough answers for the students.

Interviewer: Well, the school year has just finished. Do you know what you'll be studying in depth next year?

Nancy Braden: I think we will continue with the ecology and recycling study. There were a number of things we didn't have time to investigate. But I'm always open to a new topic and watch the news for possibilities. I enjoy the challenge of learning new things each year and gaining a greater understanding of economics at work in our nation and world.

Interviewer: I want to thank you for your time and explaining how you present economics to students. Through your enthusiasm and efforts you are making an important investment in your future and in the lives and futures of the human resources lucky to have you for their teacher.

TIME FOR REFLECTION: WHAT DO YOU THINK?

1. Ms. Braden says that economics "just fits" into social studies. How can economics fit into a study of your state? _____

   _____

   _____

2. What are economic decisions a person and a community can make concerning ecology and recycling? _____

   _____

   _____

3. Who are some local guest speakers who could help explain the role of economics in the growth of communities in your state? _____

   _____

   _____

DEFINING ECONOMICS

Several different groups of professionals deal with the economy, and they do not always agree on the goals for economic education. One group is composed of academics, who look at economics as a rational study of concepts, their relationships, and the decision-making process. Another group is composed of members of the business and labor communities who see economics as related to the importance of work, jobs, and production. A third group is the consumer advocates, who seek to help individuals learn how to get accurate information to make personal decisions. A fourth group is the conservationists, who seek to save natural and human resources from exploitation by what they claim is ignorance at best and a conspiracy at worse. The emphasis found in the economics curriculum of a particular state or school district tends to reflect the views of the economic education leaders in the community or state. All the groups agree that teaching economics is important, but what to teach and emphasize and how to instruct students are sources of much controversy.

Economics is based on the realization that people want more than the resources available can provide. *Scarcity* is the term economists use to indicate the imbalance of wants and resources. For some, the goal and definition of economic education centers on the analysis of how goods and services get produced and distributed. Others stress examining ways to make the system of production and distribution work better through the formation of governmental and business policies. Perhaps the most inclusive definition is the one that defines economics as both a set of knowledge and a way of thinking (Banaszak, 1987).

Economics as a body of knowledge includes the concepts, generalizations, and theories developed by people to try to extend their scarce natural, human, and capital resources so that they can fulfill their basic needs and as many of their wants as possible. An important key to the accomplishment of this goal is a systematic way of thinking and making economic decisions. Economic educators today recommend an in-depth understanding of scarcity and the influence of incentives and strategic thinking about how scarcity applies to personal examples and to the more complex and morally difficult issues in the international realm. Scarce resources have at least two valuable uses, and people are willing to make a sacrifice to obtain them. Entirely giving up one use is the sacrifice because the other use is considered more important or satisfying.

The National Council on Economic Education (NCEE) promotes and evaluates economic education. In recent years, changes in curriculum and technology and the collapse of command economies such as that of the Soviet Union have resulted in new efforts by the NCEE. Five trends in economics education have been identified by Nelson (1997):

1. Economics and citizenship education
2. Economic education in Russia and Eastern Europe
3. Consideration of the importance of the global economy
4. Content standards
5. Use of computer technology in economic education

Economists have made a continuous and long-term commitment to increasing and improving the teaching of economics, producing guides, standards, and instructional materials. They also evaluate their successes and failures. The human resources of economists, businesses, and educators are organized through state councils and centers of economic education. These organizations raise funds for selected projects that produce many high-quality supplemental instructional materials for grades K–12, applying the results of research into how economics is learned. Today, NCEE and its state councils and economic education centers continue to work to fulfill new needs in economic education, providing training for both prospective and veteran teachers.

NATIONAL SOCIAL STUDIES STANDARDS RELATED TO ECONOMICS

National social studies Standard VII: Production, Distribution, and Consumption focuses on the study of economics. All the remaining standards include consideration of aspects of economics. Standard IX: Global Connections and Standard VIII: Science, Technology, and Society are closely related to the current changes in the economy of the world. Throughout history, and across the world, people have had wants that exceeded their limited resources. People have tried, through decisions by rulers, inventors, and workers, to answer four fundamental questions:

1. What should be produced?
2. How should the production be organized?
3. How will goods and services be distributed?
4. What are the most effective allocations for their land, labor, capital, and management?

Science and technology often help to extend and make more productive some scarce resources, but these efforts come with opportunity costs. Siegfried Ramler (1991) describes the degree to which countries are interconnected. He says that connections occur in virtually every aspect of life: through world markets for the consumer goods we purchase and in such important elements of productive resources as labor, technology, and energy. The realities of global interdependence mean the impact of decisions go far beyond the local area in which they are made. In making economic decisions today, other cultures and nations must be considered. Social studies helps citizens to construct and build the knowledge needed to consider global influences on economic decisions. Taylor (1997) urges U.S. elementary schools to teach the impact of global issues on individuals and societies by giving attention to the interdependence of nations and the role of the United States in a global economy.

VOLUNTARY NATIONAL STANDARDS IN ECONOMICS

In examining the various published social studies standards, economists were concerned that some errors were present in the use of economic content. They also were concerned that students were being asked to do abstract thinking or perform tasks for which they were unprepared. They assembled a team of economists, teachers, and economic educators who wrote a set of standards stating 20 economic generalizations that can be addressed by K–12 students. Sample assessments were provided to guide teachers in determining whether they were being successful in teaching students about economics and economic decision making. Table 12.1 presents these standards in the left column and the assessment suggestion in the right column. By downloading the National Voluntary Standards (1997) from the NCEE website (see the link at the companion website), you can receive a rationale and benchmarks for grades 4, 8, and 12, with suggestions for activities on how to measure students' progress in their understanding of each standard.

COMPANION
WEBSITE

Voluntary National Standards for Economics and Assessments

Standard	Assessment
1. Productive resources are limited. Therefore, people cannot have all the goods and services they want. They must choose some things and give up others.	Students identify what they gain and what they give up when they make a choice.
2. Effective decision making requires comparing the additional costs of alternatives with the additional benefits. Most choices involve doing a little more or a little less of something: few choices are all-or-nothing decisions.	Students make effective decisions as consumers, producers, savers, investors, and citizens.
3. Different methods can be used to allocate goods and services. People acting individually or collectively through government choose which methods to use to allocate different goods and services.	Students evaluate different methods of allocating goods and services by comparing the benefits and costs of each method.
4. People respond predictably to positive and negative incentives.	Students identify incentives that affect people's behavior and explain how incentives affect their own behavior.
5. Voluntary exchange occurs only when all participating parties expect to gain. This is true for trade among individuals or organizations within a nation, and usually among individuals or organizations in different nations.	Students negotiate exchanges and identify the gains to themselves and others. They compare the benefits and cost of policies that alter trade barriers between nations such as tariffs and quotas.
6. When individuals, regions, and nations specialize in what they can produce at the lowest cost and then trade with others, both production and consumption increase.	Students explain how they can benefit themselves and others by developing special skills and strengths.
7. Markets exist when buyers and sellers interact. This interaction determines market prices and allocates scarce goods and services.	Students identify markets in which they have participated as a buyer and seller and describe how the interaction of all buyers and sellers influences prices. Also, they predict how prices change when a shortage or surplus of the product is available.
8. Prices send signals and provide incentives to buyers and sellers. When supply or demand changes, market prices adjust, affecting incentives.	Students predict how prices change when the number of buyers or sellers in a market changes, and explain how the incentives facing individual buyers and sellers are affected.

TABLE 12.1

Continued

Standard	Assessment
9. Competitions among sellers lowers costs and prices, and encourages producers to produce more of what consumers are willing and able to buy. Competition among buyers increases prices and allocates goods and services to those people who are willing and able to pay the most for them.	Students explain how changes in the level of competition in different markets can affect them.
10. Institutions evolve in market economies to help individuals and groups accomplish their goals. Banks, labor unions, corporations, legal systems, and not-for-profit organizations are examples of important institutions. A different kind of institution, clearly defined and enforced property rights, is essential to a market economy.	Students describe the roles of various economic institutions.
11. Money makes it easier to trade, borrow, save, invest, and compare the values of goods and services.	Students explain how their lives would be more difficult in a world with no money, or in a world where money sharply lost its value.
12. Interest rates, adjusted for inflation, rise and fall to balance the amount saved with the amount borrowed. This affects the allocation of scarce resources between present and future uses.	Students explain situations in which they pay or receive interest, and explain how they would react to changes in interest rates if they were making or receiving interest payments.
13. Income for most people is determined by the market value of the productive resources they sell. What workers earn depends, primarily, on the market values of what they produce and how productive they are.	Students predict future earnings based on their current plans for education, training, and career options.
14. Entrepreneurs are people who take the risks of organizing productive resources to make goods and services. Profit is an important incentive that leads entrepreneurs to accept the risks of business failure.	Students identify the risks, returns, and other characteristics of entrepreneurship that bear on its attractiveness as a career.
15. Investment in factories, machinery, new technology, and in health, education, and training of people, can raise future standards of living.	Students predict the consequences of investment decisions made by individuals, business, and governments.

continued

T A B L E   1 2 . 1

Continued

Standard	Assessment
16. There is an economic role for government in a market economy whenever the benefits of a government policy outweigh costs. Governments often provide for national defense, address environmental concerns, define and protect property rights, and attempt to make markets more competitive. Most government policies also redistribute income.	Students identify and evaluate the benefits and costs of alternative public policies, and assess who enjoys the benefits and who bears the costs.
17. Costs of government policies sometimes exceed benefits. This may occur because of incentives facing voters, government officials, and government employees; because of actions by special interest groups that can impose costs on the general public; or because social goals other than economic efficiency are pursued.	Students identify some public policies that may cost more than the benefits they generate and assess who enjoys the benefits and who bears the costs. They explain why the policies exist.
18. A nation's overall income levels, employment, and prices are determined by the interaction of spending and production decisions made by all households, firms, government agencies, and others in the economy.	Students interpret media reports about current economic conditions and explain how these conditions can influence decisions made by consumers, producers, and government policy makers.
19. Unemployment imposes costs on individuals and nations. Unexpected inflation imposes costs on many people and benefits others because it arbitrarily redistributes purchasing power. Inflation can reduce the rate of growth of national living standards because individuals and organizations use resources to protect themselves against uncertain future prices.	Students make informed decisions by anticipating the consequences of inflation and unemployment.
20. Federal government budgetary policy and the Federal Reserve System's monetary policy influence the overall levels of employment, output, and prices.	Students anticipate the impact of federal government and the Federal Reserve System's macroeconomic policy decisions on themselves and others.

Source: National Council for Economic Education (1997). *The Voluntary National Content Standards in Economics.* New York: National Council on Economic Education.

TIME FOR REFLECTION: WHAT DO YOU THINK?

1. Look at Table 12.1. Read the 20 standards in the left column. On the left line below, indicate the numbers of those you clearly recognize. On the right line, write the numbers of those you need help to understand.

   Recognize: _____   Need help: _____

2. Read through the assessments in Table 12.1. On the left line below, indicate those that you think could be done by students who by the end of grade 4 have received appropriate content instruction. On the right line, indicate those that you think could be done by students in grade 8 who have received appropriate content instruction.

   Grade 4: _____   Grade 8: _____

3. Read the assessment tasks. Indicate the numbers of the standards where the assessment focuses mainly on individual and family tasks. _____

   What are two curriculum implications of this focus? _____

   _____

   _____

   _____

ECONOMIC CONCEPTS AND VALUES

The National Council for Economic Education (NCEE) identified concepts providing the basis for both understanding economics and making reasoned economic decisions. Table 12.2 identifies these concepts and groups them to illustrate important relationships. The concepts within each of the major divisions vary in their degree of difficulty. The concepts shown in Table 12.2 are not comprehensive but are the broader organizing, superordinate concepts. A comprehensive list of concepts labeled Content Keywords is found on the Voluntary National Standards Contents: Index of Standards, at the NCEE link at the companion website. These are classified under each of the 20 standards for which they would most logically be taught.

COMPANION
WEBSITE

The fundamental concepts are necessary to understand all the aspects and specializations within economics. As you are teaching units, you might want to include only a small part of economics or perhaps a portion of one of the longer standards. However, as Nancy Braden said, you will always include at least some of the fundamental concepts. You are probably familiar with their meanings even if you do not call them by the term economists use. The University of Omaha Center for Economic Education has a matrix of economic concepts recommending the grade levels (K–6) for appropriately teaching or reviewing each concept. It can be found at the companion website.

COMPANION
WEBSITE

TABLE 12.2

Basic Concepts and Social Goals

Fundamental Economic Concepts

1. Scarcity
2. Opportunity costs and tradeoffs
3. Productivity
4. Economic systems
5. Economic institutions and incentives
6. Exchange, money, and interdependence

Microeconomics Concepts

7. Markets and prices
8. Supply and demand
9. Competition and market structure
10. Income and distribution
11. Market failures
12. The role of government

Macroeconomics Concepts

13. Gross national products
14. Aggregate supply and aggregate demand
15. Unemployment
16. Inflation and deflation
17. Monetary policy
18. Fiscal policy

International Economic Concepts

19. Absolute and comparative advantages and barriers to trade
20. Exchange rates and the balance of payments
21. International aspects of growth and stability

Measurement Concepts and Methods

1. Tables, charts, and graphs
2. Rations and percentages
3. Percentage changes
4. Index numbers
5. Real vs. nominal values
6. Averages and distributions around the average

Broad Social Goals

1. Economic freedom
2. Economic efficiency
3. Economic equity
4. Economic security
5. Full employment
6. Price stability
7. Economic growth
8. Other goals

Source: A Framework for Teaching the Basic Concepts and Scope and Sequences K–12 by P. Saunders and J. V. Gillard, 1995, p. 10, New York: National Council on Economic Education.

Microeconomic Concepts

Microeconomics is the study of individual households, companies, and markets and of how resources and prices combine to distribute wealth and products. The price of a new car at a given time helps to determine the demand for such cars. High prices may stimulate employers to work overtime to produce more cars. When lots of products are unsold, businesses hold sales to stimulate purchases. The government regulates those businesses that have a monopoly to protect consumers and ensure an adequate supply of the products produced by these businesses. Local, state, and national governments often own and operate some special facilities, such as power production, sanitation, roads, and transportation. Governments regulate taxes to help distribute fairly the burden of paying for public services in the society. Interest rates, the number of sales, and wages also distribute money throughout the economy because of the circular flow of wealth through various markets.

MAKING A LITERATURE CONNECTION

Trade Books Illustrating Economic Concepts

Using the story in a trade book to examine the impact of economics on the lives and actions of people, families, groups, and nations is a recognized procedure for examining economic ideas and theories (VanFossen, 2003). In examining economic principles within another cultural setting, students are helped to internalize concepts and to test the explanatory power of their economic generalizations. *The Ox-cart Man* (1979) written by Donald Hall and illustrated by Barbara Cooney describes a year in the life of a subsistent farmer family living in Appalachia during the 1800s. In contrast to today's family, each member of the farm family contributes to the production of what is needed by using his or her special abilities to produce something that the father takes to sell in the city at the end of his 10-day walk leading the ox and the cart he built to hold the products of their labors. The father sells all of the products, including the ox and cart. Then he purchases capital resources at the store and two pounds of wintergreen peppermint candy. He walks home, and the family continues their daily and evening activities. But what will the family purchase with the money that father brought home? And from whom will they purchase goods and services? Why do you think the farmer made such a long trip to the city rather that trading the family's products with people in the nearby villages? What would your students want their parent to bring back to them from a trip to a place very different from where they live?

Beatrice's Goat (2001), written by Page McBrier and illustrated by Lori Lahstoeter, is a true story of a subsistent farm family today. Beatrice, age nine, lives with her mother and five younger siblings in the small village of Kisinga in western Uganda. Beatrice helps her mother tend their crops and chickens, wash the clothes, and take care of her brothers and sisters. The book describes the changes that the gift of a goat from the Heifer Project International brings to Beatrice and her family. Beatrice did not understand how being the recipient of the goat would help her to attend school. In fact, she thought the family would never be able to save the necessary money for books and a uniform. At first, having a goat meant more work. Fetching water and elephant grass and selling their extra milk became additional daily tasks for Beatrice. The book provides details that allow students to answer such questions as these: What are some differences in the lives of children in the developing world from the lives of American children? Why did mama consider school for Beatrice more important than other needs of the family? How are schools in Uganda different from our school? Looking at the pictures, what other things do you think the family really needs? How can we find out how many boys and girls get to attend school in Uganda or other developing nations? How does the labor of the young people contribute to the common good of their families and community?

The illustrations in both of these books show landscapes that illustrate productive resources and the typical possessions of the subsistent farmers in the stories. Students should examine these illustrations to help gain a more accurate understanding of the quality of life for the subsistent farmers in different times and places.

To learn more about the work of the Heifer Project International and how your students might send another family in the developing world the gift of an animal and instructions in how to care for it, visit the project's website, which is listed at the end of this chapter.

A Basket of Bangles: How A Business Begins (2002) written by Ginger Howard and illustrated by Cheryl Kirk Noll relates how poor women in Bangladesh learn to work and support each other as they start businesses. Follow their progress as they learn how to get loans from a bank for their investment capital and the role of hard work, cooperation, and persistence in improving their daily lives and being able to pay back their loans with interest. This book prompts many questions about the lives of women throughout the world and the role of private enterprise, such as the following: Why would a bank want to loan money to women with no formal education? How do the women help each other throughout the year? Why doesn't the bank lend their money to men? Why, after paying off their loans, would the women want to get new loans that they will have to pay back with interest this year? Who, other than their own family members, benefits from the businesses the women start? Do you think the women will successfully expand their businesses and be able to pay off their new loans? How is starting a business in the United States similar or different from the way these women started their businesses? Invite a local merchant to your class to explain how his or her business got started and how the business continues to use the services of a bank.

Macroeconomic Concepts

Macroeconomics is the study of the big picture, of the economy as a whole. Macroeconomics provides an overview of the conditions in an entire nation. The gross national product (GNP) is the value of all the goods and services produced in a nation for a year. This information enables us to compare production among nations. When the GNP is divided by the population of a nation, the outcome is the GNP per capita. This figure gives an idea of how much money is generated per person. If the GNP per capita is $50, the lives of the people are quite different from the lives of people living in a nation with a GNP per capita of $3,000.

At various times during the year, different levels of employment occur because of temporary changes in the business rate. For example, before the Christmas holiday, more people in the United States are working, and the unemployment rate is lower because consumers are doing extra purchasing. After Christmas, the unemployment rate is higher because fewer people are buying products and services.

Inflation occurs when the prices of all goods and services tend to go up in the nation during the same time period. Monetary policy is the regulation of the amount of money in the nation's economy. This is regulated in the United States by the actions of the Federal Reserve System in raising and lowering interest rates. Lower interest rates offer incentives to people to expand and borrow, whereas higher interest rates tend to encourage investment and savings. Fiscal policy is the combined actions of the national government in taxing, spending, and borrowing, which adds to, or subtracts from, the supply of money available to business and individuals. Fiscal and monetary policies are means by which the economy is managed. Some people and some economists do not think that the national government always manages the economy correctly. These conflicts have the potential of making economics a controversial subject to teach in some communities.

International Economic Concepts

Nations have always been interrelated economically, but they are more so today than in the past and will probably become even more so in the future. Nations trade because they have something that other nations want and need and because they want products and resources from other nations. Some nations have an absolute advantage because they can provide something that other nations or regions cannot. Yet other nations provide a good or service better, faster, or in larger amounts and have what is called a comparative advantage. Because foreign-produced goods compete in the market with domestic products, some people want tariffs to stop the importing of certain products. However, when nations erect trade barriers, international trade slows. This slowdown can affect nations that have not raised their tariffs. Leaders in the U.S. government stress the need for free trade or trade without tariffs to promote the largest amount of sales between nations. Some economists warn that a complete free-trade policy may not always be in the best interest of a nation. The study of U.S. and world history is filled with discussions of international trade issues and their domestic and international consequences. Human rights advocates suggest that the international economy encourages lower salaries and poor working conditions in some nations and exploitation of poor people including children. When studying these ideas, students are also studying the NCSS Standards X (Civic Ideals and Values), II (Time, Continuity, and Change), and VI (Power, Authority, and Governance).

NCSS

   Nations do not want to buy much more from other nations than they sell. They seek a balance of payments between nations. If a nation does not sell about the same amount that it buys, it must find the wealth internally to pay for its international purchases. Such actions take away wealth for purchases and investments from the domestic economy. As a result, fewer domestic workers may be employed because money for workers' salaries and benefits must go to pay off the trade deficit. Nations can always print more money, but that money must be of constant worth or no other nation will want to take it in payment. The exchange rate is the price of one nation's money compared with another nation's. Most nations cooperate to keep the values of their currencies consistent.

   The economic conditions within a nation can prompt the movement of both goods and people. Throughout U.S. history, many people have migrated to countries such as the United States for economic opportunity. Such movements are often the sources of domestic problems in the nations receiving the immigrants. Because the most educated are often those who migrate, nations whose populations migrate face different types of economic problems prompted by the loss of human resources. Therefore, international economics cannot be totally separated from the other economic concepts previously discussed. The learning cycle lesson in Table 12.3 illustrates how the fundamental concept of interdependence is present in microeconomics and international economics.

Measurement Concepts and Methods

To help understand and interpret data concerning the economy, economists organize information into tables, charts, and graphs. Young elementary students can begin to use tables, charts, and graphs to help them organize economic information. Middle

T A B L E   1 2 . 3

Learning Cycle	Economic Interdependence

Grade Level: Middle school
NCSS Standards: Production, Distribution, Consumption, and Global Connections   [NCSS]

National Economic Standards

When individuals, regions, and nations specialize in what they can produce at the lowest cost and then trade with others, both production and consumption increase.

Exploratory Introduction

Objectives	Procedures	Assessments
Students give examples of situations where they are dependent on and independent from others.	Discuss the meaning of the concepts dependent and independent as the students understand them. Do this by asking: "What is an example of being dependent and being independent?" Encourage students to role play. Then form students into small groups and have them assign roles: chairperson, recorder, reporter, and materials manager. Ask groups to try to describe a situation involving two people when both of them are dependent on each other.	Students offer appropriate examples of dependent and independent situations.

Lesson Development

Objectives	Procedures	Assessments
Students define interdependence as "two people needing goods or services and providing them to each other so that both benefit and have some needs or wants fulfilled."	Tell the following two stories to the students: **Story 1** Mrs. Patrick was having a special dinner. She wanted to serve cheesecake with fresh strawberry topping. She went to her favorite fruit and vegetable stand and found bright red berries. "This is just what I need," she told the owner. "Don't ever go out of business!" "I won't," replied Mr. Fry, "as long as I have faithful customers like you." **Story 2** The Carmels' baby woke up early in the morning crying. On investigation, his mother discovered the baby had a temperature. She took the baby to the	

TABLE 12.3

Continued

pediatrician, Dr. Walker, that morning and got medications. That evening, when Dr. Walker left the office, the battery in her car was dead. She called Carmels' Garage to get the car back in running order.

Ask the student groups to make a list of the things the two stories have in common. Then ask them to identify differences. As groups report, list commonalities and differences on the board. Ask: "In our stories, what did Mr. Fry do for Mrs. Patrick? Mrs. Patrick for Mr. Fry? The Carmel family for Dr. Walker?" and so on. Ask: "Are these examples of two or more people being dependent on each other?" Discuss.

Students respond with correct answers.

Ask: "Does anyone know the word that describes two or more people being dependent on each other?" Introduce the term *interdependent*.

Review the meaning of words with the prefix *inter* such as intercom, intercept, interface, international, interchangeable, Internet. Reach a consensus on what the prefix *inter* means.

Closure: Develop a class definition of interdependent. Ask students to look at the list of what the two stories have in common. Ask: What does it take to have an interdependent situation? Write their definition on board.

Students' definition contains the elements: two people, those people's needs for goods or services, those people's provision of goods or services, those people benefiting from the process, and those people having some wants and needs fulfilled.

Expansion

Materials: A card with a different occupation written on it for each student; one card with the occupation of child written on it; one safety pin for each student; and a ball of string

Objectives	Procedures	Assessments
Students give correct examples of how people in a community are interdependent.	Give each student a card with an occupation on it. Have students pin on their cards and get into a circle. Give the student with the term *child* a ball of string. As the child holds on to the end of the string, he or she passes or tosses the string ball to someone with whom a	Students identify correct interdependent relationships, focusing on the connection between people.

continued

TABLE 12.3

Continued

Objectives	Procedures	Assessments
	child would be interdependent and explains that choice. As students get the ball of string, they repeat the procedure until all students are holding on to the string.	
Students predict that international independence is, or is not, a possibility and provide their reasons.	When everyone has had a chance, the teacher asks: "What does this illustrate about interdependence?" Ask: "Do you think we are only interdependent with people in our own community? Why? How could our families be interdependent with people in other areas of the world?" Students respond and explain as needed. Give students the following homework assignment. At home, tonight, identify three examples each of clothing, food, and appliances that were made in another country. Record the item by name and the country where it was made. Suggest how to find this information and that they might get help from family members. Provide a survey form on which to record information.	Students conclude that people are connected to each other through such economic concepts as jobs, goods and services, and needs and wants. Students discuss in a respectful, orderly way their predictions, supporting them with reasons.
Students make conclusions about their interdependence with other nations based on data collected in homework surveys.	In small groups, have students combine their examples, report, and compare the results. All the nations are located on a world map with a line drawn attaching the nation of origin to your city. Different maps can be made for the different categories of information by small groups, and displayed. Decide on a title for the map and put it on the map. Display maps and note similarities and differences. Ask: "Do we trade with the same nations of the world for all types of products? Can we find alternative sources for each of these products in the United States?" Discuss what would happen if their families stopped buying clothing, food, and appliances from other nations? Ask: "What things and why?	Students explain their answers based on the data on the maps and may add other data. Use a checklist to record participation.

TABLE 12.3

Continued

Students predict economic consequences of accidents and behaviors.	What would happen if a bad storm destroyed a crop or a big fire destroyed the port and its warehouses in Brazil or Korea?" and so on. "Do you know of any products from our community or state that are sold in other nations? How can we find out about this?" Students write letters asking local or state producers where products are sold in the United States and the world.	Students make logical responses, citing examples from past events and news items.
Students help plan additional data-gathering experiences and carry them out.	Assign students, or have them volunteer singly or in pairs, to interview produce managers in grocery stores to find out where foods such as tomatoes, strawberries, and grapes come from at different times during the year. Assign other students, or have them volunteer, to talk to older people to learn about the types of foods and produce available when they were young. Ask students to write a three-paragraph report discussing the survey results. In paragraph 1, they discuss the home survey; in paragraph 2, they discuss the produce manager or older adult survey; and in paragraph 3, they draw conclusions regarding interdependence.	Students develop and carry out usable plan for additional data gathering. Record participation on a checklist.
	Read sample paragraphs and read letters from local companies as received. A class map can be made of the answers received, with lines from your community to other nations drawn according to responses received.	
Students conclude that people all over the world have more goods and services because they are interdependent.	Conclude the lesson by discussing the pros and cons of being economically interdependent with people in other areas of the world. Make a chart of the students' points. Post it with the maps the groups made from their home surveys and the map of local exports still under construction.	Students state the conclusion that people all over the world have more goods and services because they are interdependent.
	Ask students to state three to four sentences telling:	Students state and give appropriate reasoning for their view concerning whether their actions can impact people all over the world in both positive and negative ways.
Students state that their actions can affect people all over the world in both positive and negative ways.	1. How their actions can affect people elsewhere in the world 2. Whether the effects are positive, negative, or both 3. The reason for their answer to Part 2	

school students can use percentages and averages. In the study of economics more than any of the other social sciences, students are called on to apply the knowledge and skills they have gained in mathematics to help them understand economic relationships. Integrated unit topics on economic issues and problems can involve the social studies teacher and the mathematics teachers. However, because many important economic concepts do not involve the use of mathematics, teachers of other subjects work on economic problems and issues as well. Case studies similar to those described by Nancy Braden in the interview included in the beginning of this chapter also use skills taught in the elementary curriculum.

ECONOMIC DECISION-MAKING SKILLS

Because people encounter scarcity every day, they have to make choices (Standard 1 in Table 12.1). Rather than accepting the first solution that comes to mind, people are encouraged by economists to make rational decisions that consider the economic long- and short-term consequences. The decision maker must weigh alternatives and be aware of the opportunity cost of what is given up when one alternative is selected. The alternative that is selected must be considered to give more benefits than the opportunity cost. Helping students to identify alternatives, criteria, and consequences and to select what they see as the best alternative is the essence of teaching decision making. It is also the essence of cost–benefit analysis. James Laney (1993) identifies cost–benefit analysis as the concept that should receive primary emphasis during the elementary school years. He identifies this concept because it is a problem-solving or decision-making model that works with elementary and middle grades students. This is consistent with recognizing that in making a choice for the use of scarce resources, some other opportunity to use the resource is seen to be of less value and is lost or given up forever.

People of all ages make snap decisions and impulse purchases. The rationale for teaching decision making is that it reduces such decisions. When students face an important decision, these skills help them take time to identify and weigh alternatives carefully. Students should be helped to see when they need to seek additional information from printed sources or ask for professional advice to help them make decisions. They need to learn to ask for specific information and evaluate it. The abstractness in the decision-making process is made more concrete for students when they investigate real problems with which the students are familiar and use a decision-making chart on which alternatives and consequences are recorded and rated.

Table 12.4 shows the type of decision-making chart used in the successful elementary video series *Trade-Offs*. The chart title is the question to be answered by the decision. Alternatives are listed in the column on the left, and the criteria are listed across the top of the chart. Students are asked first to identify specific criteria for their problem and then to offer alternative choices. Sometimes, as alternatives are listed or rated, new criteria or alternatives are discovered and added to the chart. The discussion of the solution is guided by the information written on the chart.

The teacher directs the discussion by asking questions about the chart and how various parts of the chart compare. Each alternative and criterion is discussed and

TABLE 12.4
Decision-Making Chart

Question: Which three students should represent our class at the program planned for the entire school day on March 3?

	Alternatives			
	Completes Regular Classwork in Advance	*Has Good Speaking Voice*	*Clearly Understands Ideas to Be Presented*	*Will Represent Class Seriously*
Tom	+	+	?	–
Betty	+	+	+	+
Mohammed	–	+	+	+
Cassandra	+	–	?	+
Mei Lin	–	+	+	+
Jacques	+	+	+	+
Cynthia	+	+	+	+

given a rating in the box created by the intersection of the appropriate row and column. Symbols such as smiley faces, frowning faces, question marks, pluses, zeroes, or minuses are drawn on the chart to conclude the discussion on each alternative and criterion. Rarely do all the ratings for an alternative contain positive symbols. The rating process does, however, narrow the list to the better alternatives. Next, the students reconsider each of these and decide which they believe is the best choice and second-best choice. The second-best choice is the opportunity cost. Students must decide whether their best choice is more to their liking than is the opportunity cost.

A second, more abstract, type of decision-making chart is shown in Table 12.5. In this chart, the students are asked to predict long- and short-term consequences, classifying them as having either positive or negative outcomes. After such information is recorded on the chart, students discuss the importance and chance of each consequence happening, and make their decision using information from the chart and its discussion. Making the final decision is important, just as letting students live with the consequences of their choices is a realistic learning goal for economics education and social studies—and for life.

Citizens make many personal decisions that affect the economy through the sales of goods and services and the use of productive resources. Their votes influence the ways in which governments spend and acquire money. Even rationally made decisions may not work out as predicted, because some criteria involve chance, or perhaps not all criteria are identified. Nevertheless, the consequences of such decisions cannot be avoided. Teachers should not come to the rescue of a poor decision with

TABLE 12.5

Consequences Decision-Making Chart

Question: Should the tariff on foreign-made cars be increased?

Alternatives   **Consequences**

	Short Term	Long Term
Yes	(+) Auto workers pleased, higher employment rate	(+) More U.S. cars produced
	(−) Auto agencies for foreign cars angry because sales decline	(−) Price of foreign cars up; nations raise tariffs on U.S. goods
No	(+) Price of foreign cars remains same; special sales on U.S.–produced cars	(+) United States produces better cars at lower prices through increased productivity and design improvements
	(−) United States produces fewer cars, more unemployed autoworkers	(−) Some U.S. auto plants close or reduce workers' hours

an unrealistic save. Instead, they should help by asking problem questions designed to stimulate thinking from a particular view.

Sometimes, teachers may suggest possible alternatives or consequences if students fail to mention them. Students are encouraged to take the time to consider these new alternatives before making a final decision. Revisiting a decision after several days, if the choice does not appear to be working well, is acceptable. It can result in the generation of new criteria, alternatives, consequences, and even a new choice of action. Indeed, it is a very authentic approach to problem solving and decision making.

Teachers make many decisions each day, yet some of these can be made by students. Such practice helps students to recognize their personal control over their lives and the responsibilities they have for their personal and group behavior. Economic decisions involve the use of scarce resources. Time is a scarce commodity in the classroom, as are art supplies, library books, computers, and individual moments with the teacher or an adult helper. Teachers provide students with opportunities to make age-appropriate decisions and practice the decision-making process. Although it takes time to teach decision-making skills, students become equipped to perform the task in small groups or individually. The teacher can assess and evaluate students' thought processes with a quick glance at the chart.

Students who make decisions are more accepting of the decisions of others, provided they see the rationality of such decisions. Teachers who encourage students to make some class decisions might find their own decisions questioned from time to time and might be asked to support their choices or to change them. In this way, teachers serve as role models of rational decision makers and citizens.

TIME FOR REFLECTION: WHAT DO YOU THINK?

Place an X on the line before the number of a decision that you would encourage students to make in your classroom. Focus your thinking on a single grade level and specify your choice of grade level here _____.

_____ 1. What refreshments to have for a class party
_____ 2. What assignments to do
_____ 3. What activity to do during free time
_____ 4. What criteria to use in grading a project or assignment
_____ 5. What books to read
_____ 6. What project to make
_____ 7. What type of program to present for a Parent Teacher Association (PTA) meeting
_____ 8. What topic to study next

Reflect on your answers, considering the following comments and suggestions. Feel free to change your first choices. You might also discuss your choices with peers. In the end, the decision is yours, but additional perspectives might be enlightening.

- The experience and age of students are determining factors, but teachers can provide some or all of the alternatives and criteria from which students may choose.
- If students are given responsibilities and teachers fail to treat their responses with respect, teachers lose the respect of some or all of the students.
- Some students might allow personal feeling to cloud their decisions about grades. Individual students view grades as personal rewards and punishments or may see them as part of their personal identity. Among some age and cultural groups, children expect adults to make such decisions and would not want to grade themselves or others.
- Teachers might feel negatively about the questions on evaluations. Evaluation is seen as the teacher's responsibility.

ECONOMIC GOALS AND VALUES

The correct decision for an individual or group is based on their values and morals. A society or nation holds some agreed-on values, beliefs, and morals. However, not all of the values and beliefs are universally held or are given the same priority by all the people in the group. Economists do not always agree on the priority of economic values when making decisions and policies. Individuals may find the priorities of their values conflict when fulfilling their different roles. For example, for consumers, a lower price is important, but for union members, job security and the unity of action that give unions power are also important. Citizens might want to help protect local jobs, but they also want government services that require increased taxation of individuals and businesses. This can be a problem when citizens vote on raising property taxes to pay for school improvements.

The NCEE has identified eight important goals in the economy that reflect some of the values encountered in economic decision making and policy formation:

Economic freedom	Economic equity
Economic efficiency	Economic security
Full employment	Price stability
Economic growth	Other goals

Economic freedom is an important characteristic of the market economy. This is the opportunity to make your own choices concerning how to use resources and how to obtain additional resources.

Economic equity or fairness to all comes from the realization that some differences in the abilities of participants, such as physical disabilities, are beyond their control. Policy makers need to take these differences into account to make things equal for all. Various groups in society often point out that their needs go unrecognized by the policy makers and that they do not have economic equity.

Economic efficiency has two distinct definitions. One is technical efficiency and is measured by getting the most output from the least input or resources. It is a reflection of high productivity. The second definition takes a broader view (macroeconomics), looking at the markets affected by the single decision and encouraging the choice that is best for all the markets. The total benefits must exceed the total costs. It is possible for a single person or company to benefit greatly while those choices have sum total effects that hurt many and cause an overall loss in productivity. Thus, the desire for economic efficiency creates situations in which the individual person or group is forced to place the larger group or society before his or her own good.

Economic security is a value highly prized by both individuals and society. We make economic decisions on the basis of the probability that we continue to be healthy, that we have employment, and that our savings and future are safe as long as we are willing to work. Individuals and citizens are often called on to make decisions that might affect economic security. In the United States, private and public policies have been made to try to give economic security to people. These include the Federal Deposit Insurance Corporation, worker's compensation, seniority rights, social security, and unemployment compensation. History is filled with examples of personal and group conflicts that relate to the values of economic security, and such conflicts will continue.

Full employment exists when everyone who wants a job has one. Although full employment seems desirable, it is probably never possible to attain this goal. There is always some unemployment as people enter the labor market for the first time, or decide to move or to seek new positions. When unemployment becomes larger than just these workers, it causes undesirable hardship because of the lack of economic security.

Price stability is another desirable value and goal that is probably never attainable. Prices do not all remain the same at all times. Controversy arises when increases and decreases in prices constitute inflation or deflation, which are damaging to the economy. Controversy also arises over managing the economy for price stability.

Economic growth is seen as necessary to continue to provide more products and jobs for a growing population, for investment, and for research incentives. Like many of the other goals and values, economic growth is interrelated with factors in a nations' economy and in the international economy. An economy can actually produce more, but the growth may not keep up with increases in the population as a whole or in the work force. Controversy exists as to the best ways to promote economic growth.

Perhaps you do not see how elementary or middle school students are involved in or concerned about some of these goals and values. Many values, such as hard work, accuracy, high standards, honesty, reliability, promptness, cooperation, competition, and social responsibility, are facilitated by the schools and related to economics. Unfortunately, other negative values, such as extreme self-interest, immediate gratification, and cheating, are also present and sometimes reinforced by schools, society, and the media.

Young people receive mixed messages concerning which values are important. Economic educators claim that by learning economics, how to use cost–benefit analysis for decision making, and how to examine the rationale for economic values, students come to see the reasons why they should act in particular ways and adopt desirable values and behaviors. Knowledge alone, however, does not bring about prosocial behaviors. Teachers need to actively facilitate and support their use.

CHILDREN AND THE LEARNING OF ECONOMICS

By the mid-1970s, economists and educators had reached a consensus on what aspects of economics to teach and how most effectively to accomplish the task. Their consensus includes the following four points:

1. An understanding of basic economic concepts is more important than a heavy dose of factual knowledge.
2. Instructional efforts should concentrate on aiding students to achieve a fundamental understanding of a limited set of economic concepts and their relationships.
3. Students should be given a conceptual framework to help them organize their understanding of economics, and they should be exposed to a manner of thinking that emphasizes systematic, objective analysis.
4. The real personal and social advantages of economic understanding become apparent as individuals achieve competence in applying their knowledge to a wide range of economic issues they themselves confront (Saunders et al., 1984, p. 2).

Economic education researchers have studied economic concepts presenting students with problems and asking them to explain what happened. Without formal instruction, economic reasoning begins to emerge between the ages of 5 and 7. Concepts with which students have the greatest personal experiences, usually the fundamental or microeconomic concepts such as work, want, and scarcity, appear to be the first that are understood (Armento & Flores, 1986). Two important conclusions come from these studies:

1. Children's economic ideas tend to follow a developmental sequence. Their thinking becomes more abstract and flexible with age.
2. Although economic thinking shows a gradual improvement with age, mature reasoning appears more quickly for some concepts than for others (Schug & Walstad, 1991).

With systematic instruction, even kindergarten students can learn economic concepts and economic decision making—weighing alternatives and what to give up against the benefits received (Kourilsky, 1977). Teacher behavior in teaching the concepts of specialization in grades 3–5 was examined by Armento (1986). Student achievement was greater when teachers did the following:

1. Gave more concept definitions and more positive concept examples and reviewed the main ideas of the lesson
2. Used accurate economic conceptual and factual knowledge relevant to the objectives of the lesson
3. Included more of the relevant knowledge generalizations and more of the related concept labels
4. Expressed more enthusiasm and interest in the content of the lesson (Armento & Flores, 1986, p. 98)

Students' drawings of specialists they know in their community.

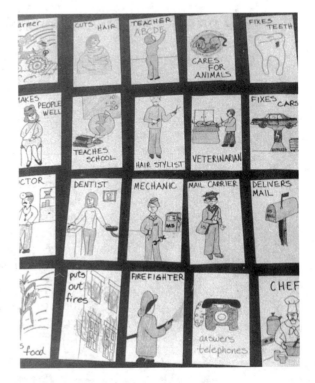

Research indicates elementary and middle school students can learn ideas about economics (Schug & Walstad, 1991). Even kindergarten students have been able to master concepts such as scarcity, decision making, production, specialization, distribution, consumption, saving, supply and demand, business organization, and money and barter (Kourilsky, 1977, p. 183).

APPROACHES TO TEACHING ECONOMICS

Students at all grades, at all ability levels, and from all socioeconomic levels can learn economics. "Although certain instructional approaches, techniques, and strategies have been shown to yield better results than others, comparative studies have concluded that elementary school studies can learn economics at some level of understanding through a variety of approaches" (Kourilsky, 1987, p. 200). Economics plays an integral part in all societies, including the one that exists when students interact within the classroom. Involving students in analyzing and solving classroom problems is the overall goal of two programs developed by Marilyn L. Kourilsky: the Mini-Society and Kinder-Economy. Both programs are for elementary-age students, although the Kinder-Economy is especially designed for students in kindergarten. Each concept is presented in a sequence of three types of lessons. First, students experience the concept in their own classroom society and decide how to solve the situation. Second, the teacher helps the students debrief the situation to learn the names, definitions, and relationships between the economic concepts. Third, the teacher provides reinforcing activities such as role plays, games, exercise sheets, stories, and art projects for the students to complete.

In beginning the study, the teacher performs two important tasks: arranging the initial scarcity situation in the classroom and leading the students toward reaching their own decision on how to solve their scarcity problem. Alternatives are generated, consequences are predicted, and the best choice is agreed to by the students. The students come to see that scarcity is frequently present in the classroom society and agree that the problem needs to be systematically reduced. Then students set about determining who in the classroom should get the scarce resources. Students usually decide that earning and free choice in spending are the best solutions. Once the decisions about the name of the society, the design of the money, the pay of officers, and pay procedures are established, the role of the teacher changes from leader to facilitator.

Instead of the teacher creating the experiences, the students, through their interactions, create the different problems to be solved. The teacher encourages them to examine the alternatives and consequences and to decide on the answer. If students make a poor decision, it becomes evident in new problems and can be corrected. The goal of these programs is to teach economic concepts and the relationships between concepts within society. The original opportunities to earn money must be activities that all students have an equal opportunity to engage in so that money gets into the classroom society. The key to the success of these classroom societies is the teacher's faith in the students' ability to discover problems and come to an acceptable decision supported by the class. For example, students might want to open businesses and sell items and services. Problems such as where to locate the business and when sales can take place must be solved. Can students sell services such as taking tests and doing homework for others?

The teacher, as a member of the class, has a role similar to that of the students in helping solve the problems. The teacher prods the students to use what they have learned about alternatives and consequences to help solve problems and, if necessary, suggests alternatives and consequences. Teachers have the additional responsibility of reinforcing learning through closure activities in the lessons and assignments. The teacher informs parents of the activities and their goals. Parents give written permission for students to bring items to school, specifying whether they are for use or may be sold or bartered.

The goals of classroom society programs go beyond the recognition of concepts requiring students to apply and analyze concepts and make decisions. The students must learn to live with both short-term and long-term consequences of their decisions. Because the Kinder-Economy and Mini-Society require a long-term, consistent time commitment during the week for students to accomplish their goals, the teacher needs to study the available books devoted to the program carefully. The Stock Market Game is a 10-week simulation sponsored by the Securities Industry Association. It runs three times each year for students in grades 4 through 12. Currently, there are two versions: a paper-and-pencil version and an Internet version. Student teams invest $100,000 and follow the progress of companies and markets as they interact with current events over 10 weeks. Students are allowed to buy and sell stocks and are guided and encouraged to learn the reasons for market changes. Teachers can enroll their classes through the NCEE website (see the link at the companion website).

COMPANION WEBSITE

Mark Schug, author of *Economics for Kids: Ideas for Teaching in the Elementary Grades* (1997), suggests the following criteria for elementary economics lessons:

1. Activities enhance citizenship understanding and skills.
2. Activities provide opportunities for manipulating data and using concrete examples.
3. Activities are formally planned, but informal opportunities are used to analyze and review concepts as they arise in the news and classroom.
4. Activities link to children's own experiences.
5. Activities link to the school district's curriculum.

Table 12.6 is a learning cycle lesson employing Schug's criteria in a lesson appropriate across grades K–8.

TIME FOR REFLECTION: WHAT DO YOU THINK?

1. How are the commercials for sporting events similar to and different from commercials focused on school-age students? _____
_____
_____
_____

2. How would you change the expansion of this lesson to focus on the study of elections? _____
_____
_____

TABLE 12.6

Learning Cycle	Advertisements and Making Good Choices

Grade Level: Modifications suggested for K–8
NCSS Standards: Production, Distribution, and Consumption

NCSS

National Economic Standard

Effective decision making requires comparing the additional costs of alternatives with the additional benefits. Most choices involve doing a little more or a little less of something: few choices are all-or-nothing decisions.

Materials

Three boxes of different sizes (one the size of a box that holds a birthday cake), each wrapped differently from plain to very fancy and colorful and containing one of the following: a stick of gum for each child, a box of cake mix, or a note providing an activity students would enjoy, such as a popcorn party at the end of the day, 15 minutes of free reading time, or choosing a book for a read-aloud; a video containing commercials students might see on prime-time television or in children's television shows; chart paper and markers for each small group; and a selection of advertisements from magazines, fliers, and newspapers.

Exploratory Introduction

Materials: Three boxes (described above)

Objectives	Procedures	Assessments
Students offer logical ideas on what might be in the three boxes the teacher presents.	Show the students the three boxes and ask: "Which box do you choose for your prize?" Tell the students you know that they will like each item but that they would especially like to have the cake. If they select the cake, you can call it an unbirthday party for all those whose birthdays are not on school days. Allow the students to discuss and decide which box to select. You might suggest thinking about the size of the cake or try to entice the students to take the most elaborately decorated box because it is wrapped like a birthday present.	Students make at least one suggestion that is appropriate for each box.
Students offer appropriate suggestions for arriving at a joint decision with which everyone will be satisfied.	After the discussion, ask: "How should we go about making the decision so that we know everyone will be satisfied?" Follow through with their choice and open the boxes. Begin with the boxes not selected and ask: "Would you have enjoyed getting these surprises? Why or why not?" If the box containing the cake mix is selected, open it and wait for the students to	Students make suggestions that consider everyone's viewpoints or decide that it is very difficult to satisfy everyone's wants.

continued

TABLE   12.6

Continued

respond. Ask: "Why did you respond this way? Isn't this a cake? What did I do or say that made you think there was a cake in here? What do we need to have before we have a cake to eat?" (With older students, the teacher might have them do things in class to earn the extra ingredients and frosting.) "Where do these extra items come from? How would you feel if we didn't have the eggs, oil, frosting, pans, and stove to complete the cake? What have we learned from this experience?" (If the box with the cake mix is not selected, provide the reward in their box and ask whether they enjoyed their present when finished. If the cake mix is selected, determine with the students a time when the cake is completed and served.)

Lesson Development

Materials: A video as described above, and chart paper and markers for each small group

Objectives	Procedures	Assessments
Students relate their past experiences with advertisements and the product advertised.	Ask: "Can someone tell me what we did with the three boxes? What did we say we learned from that experience? Were you satisfied with the present? Have you ever had another experience in which you thought, or were led to believe, that something was different from what it actually was? When?" After some discussion, explain that you are going to help them make better decisions by understanding advertisements and advertising.	Students identify instances of believing misleading advertisements.
Students characterize advertisements as attempts to try to get people to purchase something.	Form the students into small groups. Ask them to assign roles including recorder, chairperson, reporter, and materials manager. Show two advertisements from the videotape. Write questions on the board or overhead projector and ask each group to discuss the questions and record their answers on chart paper. "What do we call these two segments? Why are they on television? What do they have in common?"	Students state that, because television needs money to keep on air, time is sold for advertisements that get people to buy something.

T A B L E   1 2 . 6

Continued

	After groups share their responses to the questions, ask each group to discuss the following question, then share with the class: "What can we say is a definition for an *advertisement*?"	
	Show the two television ads from the videotape, one at a time. After each one, ask: "How did you feel when you watched this commercial? Why? Would you buy this item? Which of the two commercials did you like better? Why? What are some of your favorite commercials on television?" Get a quick list of four or five answers. Using a show of hands, ask "Who remembers and likes each commercial listed?" (Keep the list for future use.)	Students work cooperatively as a class or in small groups to identify types of ads.
Students identify examples of the use of advertising or propaganda techniques presented by the teachers, such as repetition, humor, endorsement, bandwagon, feeling good, glitz, or colorful language.	Depending on the time available and the age of the students, select several propaganda techniques and provide direct instruction on each as a separate concept. Use examples of each from the video and a short test for comprehension with a couple of commercials for which students are asked to identify the technique used and give their reasons. Affirm or explain answers. On the next day, review and perhaps teach an additional technique or two using advertisements from magazines. Have students draw their own ad and tell which technique they used as an assessment of comprehension.	Students correctly identify the various techniques in the commercials.
Students reword their definition to include using symbols and appeals that encourage buyers to make a choice that may not fit either their wants or their needs.	Discuss, with the students, their responses to the statement: Advertising is a bunch of lies. Ask the students whether they now want to add anything to their earlier definition of an advertisement. *Closure:* Ask: "What would be your advice to a consumer when seeing or hearing a commercial?"	Students' definition includes use of symbols and appeals by advertisements, and the reaction of consumers who buy what they did not originally want or need.

continued

TABLE 12.6

Continued

Expansion

Materials: Advertisements taken from magazines, fliers, and newspapers; chart paper and markers for each group

Objectives	Procedures	Assessments
Students conclude that newspaper advertisements and local ads use fewer special techniques than television and magazine ads.	Ask: "What have we concluded about advertisements and your making a choice as a consumer?" Give each small group several advertisements from magazines, fliers, and newspapers. Ask each group to identify, and record on chart paper, their response to the question, "What advertising technique is being used?" Have groups share findings. List techniques identified on the board. Ask class to draw conclusions from their observations with the question, "What are the differences you observe in these new ads and those on TV or in magazines?" List on the board.	Students identify less color, no famous people, and other logical observations from the ads, concluding that newspapers and local fliers use fewer special techniques than television and magazine ads because less money is available.
Students conduct an interview or use email to find out why business owners think advertisements are needed.	Ask: "Do you think you will remember the ads using fewer special techniques as long as the other ads? Why or why not? Why do these ads differ from the ones we looked at earlier? Can you think of any reason to advertise except to sell a specific item? Do you think there might be other reasons to advertise? How could we find out? Revise to include interview data. Interview local business owners, adverising people from the local newspaper, TV channel, or radio station, or people who sell or produce advertisements. Ask them why advertisements are needed. Alternatively, email such individuals for their replies, which students analyze for similarities, differences, and new ideas. Is our revised definition from yesterday still accurate?"	Students identify at least two reasons for the use of advertisements by business owners. Students consider changes in wording for their definition.
Students decide when they should consult ads for help and justify their answers.	As final closure, relate the following problem to the students for class discussion. Imagine that you moved to a new community and you need to get the following: a haircut, your bike repaired, a quick lunch, and a nice present for someone's birthday. For which of these items would you consult	Students identify logical instances when they can use advertisements to help them make a decision to satisfy a need.

TABLE 12.6

Continued

advertisements and for what reasons? Have students share their responses orally or in writing.

Lesson Summary: Ask students to describe briefly the major activities in this learning cycle and the important ideas each helped them to understand concerning decision making and advertising.

Note: Definitions of the various propaganda strategies can be found in books on propaganda and advertising, through the Internet, and on the website for this book, at the companion website.

COMPANION WEBSITE

RESOURCES FOR TEACHING ECONOMICS

COMPANION WEBSITE

The best single resource for help with understanding economics and teaching is the website of the National Council on Economic Education (NCEE) (see the companion website). This website is a portal for teaching economics at all grade levels, leading the user to lessons, assessment strategies, and the latest figures on the economy of the United States and for many other nations (Van Fossen, 1998).

➤ **USING TECHNOLOGY**

WebQuests: An Instructional Strategy Using the Internet

The WebQuest is an instructional strategy that focuses on inquiry, decision-making, and problem-solving activities. The resources of the Internet are used to obtain information and/or perspectives on the topic of study. WebQuests present students with a task or problem and provide scaffolding assistance for the students as they complete their projects. Students make extensive use of the computer and the Internet but are encouraged to use other available resources as well. Because individuals or groups of students perform research that differs from that of other students in the classroom, the computer is used to prepare WebQuest tasks and provide all or some website addresses (URLs) that assist the students in their research. Most teachers use a template to save time in putting a WebQuest together. Bernie Dodge, who developed the concept of WebQuest, has the information on WebQuests and includes a free template and examples of WebQuests for all grades K–8 (see the companion website).

WebQuests usually take from one to six weeks to complete. The instructional goal for a short-term WebQuest is the acquisition and integration of knowledge. When using a long-term WebQuest, students also analyze a body of knowledge and

➤

transform it in some way to demonstrate their understanding of the material. All WebQuests include a common set of similar types of activities:

1. Introduction overviews presenting the learning questions and task.
2. Presentation of the process and resources by the teacher, detailing the steps that the students follow in completing the tasks.
3. Provision of background knowledge to all students through common experiences or readings.
4. Provision of individual or small-group work for in-depth study of a portion of the topic so that various perspectives are examined. Scaffolding in the form of detailed instructions and guiding questions is provided, along with three or more Internet sites for each group or student to consult.
5. Provision of opportunities for students to debate and discuss what they have learned. A structure is provided for groups to help them examine individual contributions and to reflect and construct meaning from the information gathered.
6. Provision of an evaluation project or strategy that often is the creation of a product.
7. Presentation by the teacher of a narrative conclusion reviewing the goals of the WebQuest, making general content comments about what was learned and which skills and values were used by students, and informing students of other opportunities where they might use their knowledge or encounter it again. Students read this statement from the computer as a closure to their activities in the WebQuest.

COMPANION
WEBSITE

The website of the National Council for Economic Education (NCEE) (see the companion website) has many lessons that are presented as WebQuests to teach economic concepts and illustrate economic principles at work and that involve students in solving economic problems and make economic choices related to their personal lives and their public lives as citizens of the United States in an increasingly interdependent world.

Special resources for teaching economics are widely available. In addition to those resources generally available for educators, teachers often employ local citizens who are knowledgeable about specific economic issues impacting local government and businesses. Field trips to local businesses that include entrance into areas from which the general public is normally excluded are very enlightening to young people who know little about the specifics of many jobs and careers. Teachers also use locally conducted surveys and send out written questionnaires to gather information. All governmental agencies and institutions face economic issues. Printed government materials and government speakers prepared for the general public may be of help to students.

Federal institutions such as the Federal Reserve Banks, the U.S. Treasury, and the Internal Revenue Service have developed educational materials. Other economic institutions such as trade organizations, private corporations, insurance groups, and financial organizations have designed materials for use in schools. Many of these organizations are affiliated with NCEE and various state councils. One way to locate these materials is to contact your state's council on economic education. Your state department of education should be able to provide you with the appropriate address. Because economics is filled with controversy, some instructional resources have specific viewpoints. You want to apply the ideas discussed in Chapter 6 for evaluating the sponsored materials.

SUMMARY

Economics is integral to the lives of individuals and nations. Economists and economic educators place emphasis on research, teacher training, use of computers, and preparing instructional resources to improve economic knowledge. Although a variety of methods are successful in teaching economics, the best approaches emphasize economic concepts and rational economic decision making. Many economic concepts are present in elementary and middle school social studies curriculum. A study of economics for young teens is thought to be especially helpful because it has the potential to encourage students to make careful career choices and to develop good spending habits at a time in their lives when they begin to make their own decisions on many purchases and need to begin to select and prepare for working careers.

Expanding ON THIS CHAPTER

Activity

COMPANION WEBSITE

Ask five students to explain why they cannot have everything they want. Ask them how they learned this idea. Write a report describing their answers. Explain how formal lessons on economics will help the students to make better economic decisions in their lives and as citizens in a democracy in an increasingly interdependent world.

Recommended Websites to Visit

COMPANION WEBSITE

Learn more about Beatrice and the Heifer Project. Read a letter written by Beatrice when she visited the United States and helped to promote the book *Beatrice's Goat* in 2001.
   www.heifer.org/end_hunger/goats/12gen_main.htm

National Council for Economic Education website
   www.economicsamerica.org/standards/contents.html

The Econ Ed link of the National Council for Economic Education provides lessons for all grade levels linked to the standards, many of which are WebQuests.
   www.econedlink.org/

Website of the University of Omaha Center for Economic Education's matrix of economic concepts (K–6)
   http://ecedweb.unomaha.edu/elconpt.htm

The U.S. Mint has information on coins includes games for young people and lesson plans on coins
   www.usmint.gov/

Information and games for children at the money factory
   www.moneyfactory.com/

The website of the Center for Economic Education at James Madison University has many on-line lessons that are appropriate for elementary and middle schools.
http://cob.jmu.edu/econed/Default.htm

Definitions of the various propaganda strategies can be found in books on propaganda and advertising and through the Internet.
www.cyfc.umn.edu/Documents/C/C/CC1026.html

How Everyday Things are Made helps students learn about production of goods.
http://manufacturing.stanford.edu/

The Federal Reserve Bank of Richmond has an education site and teacher programs.
www.rich.frb.org/econed/

The best sources of information on WebQuests, including a template
http://webquest.sdsu.edu/webquest.html

Curriculum for personal economic fitness
www.fffl.ncee.net/

A list of many WebQuests with their URLs created by middle school teachers
http://sesd.sk.ca/teacherresource/webquest/midsocial.htm

CHAPTER 13

Helping Students Understand Local and Global Societies

INTRODUCTION

Read the following facts and then write your interpretation of those facts for teachers of social studies.

1. It took Thomas Jefferson 10 days to travel from his home in Virginia to Philadelphia in 1776.
2. In their homes around the world, people were able to watch the advance of U.S. troops on Baghdad during the 2003 war in Iraq on television.
3. *Through the Lens,* a book of the best pictures from the National Geographic Society, was published in 20 different languages in 2003.
4. Much of the athletic equipment and clothing sold by major U.S.-owned producers and purchased by large numbers of American youths, is made in the developing world by child labor in unhealthy working conditions.
5. Because people in Canada died as a result of the SARS virus in Spring 2003, tourists and businesspeople were discouraged from traveling to particular regions of Canada during that time.
6. Perishable fresh fruits such as strawberries and grapes are now available at most local grocery stores almost every week of the year.

My interpretation of the above facts is:

_____

_____

CHAPTER OVERVIEW

NCSS Standard IX, Global Connections, is interdisciplinary. Often it is addressed in part during units focusing on economic and geographic problems. The impact of this standard on the lives of people can also be part of units focusing on history. Civic ideals and practices essential to American democracy, such as free enterprise, equality, freedom of expression and religion, and separation of church and state, are being adopted in nations around the world and challenged by some who believe that these ideals are not appropriate. We live in a world where no place seems safe from physical attack. Global Connections and the impacts of Science and Technology, another interdisciplinary theme, on people and groups (society) have both positive and negative consequences as a result of decisions made by people and leaders who represent various nations and interest groups.

Citizens need a sound foundation of knowledge, skills, and attitudes that support and examine democracy and the character and ideals of their nation's people. Citizens also need to critically examine the themes of Global Connections and Science and Technology and Society that were not a typical part of the curriculum in the past. This is an important challenge for the curriculum in the United States because this country has such a large role in world affairs as a leading economic and military power. In this chapter, issues related to global connections and their impact on the lives and decisions of people are examined.

NCSS

CHAPTER OBJECTIVES

1. Explain how geography, economics, cultural institutions and practices, and human rights connect the people of the world.
2. Identify the characteristics of substantive cultural learning.
3. Explain how to confront misconceptions, stereotypes, and prejudice about people and groups through using instruction that focuses on substantive cultural learning.
4. Identify the multiple types of learning resources that provide accurate information and many perspectives on global and international issues.
5. Identify important issues that span national boundaries and potentially threaten the entire world.
6. Identify ways in which K–8 students can help take part in solving international and global problems.

GLOBAL EDUCATION: AN EVOLVING DEFINITION

Everyone's life is increasingly interdependent with the lives of people all over the world. American citizens directly and indirectly affect the lives of people throughout the world. Individual, group, state, and national decisions dealing with persistent global problems challenge our priorities and values. Governments, corporations, clubs, organizations, states, and individuals are all involved in transnational projects that contribute to global interdependence. Elements of global education can be found in all disciplines contributing to social studies content. Examples of lessons and resources related to global education issues are found in Chapters 7, 8, 10, 11, and 12.

Why, you might ask, is there a special chapter devoted to this topic? Educators need to make decisions on what is appropriate to examine in the school's curriculum, when topics should be examined, and what instructional resources to use. Each of these decisions stimulates debate, requires research to gain answers, and results in decisions that must be carefully documented and evaluated. People have ideas and are implementing lessons and programs in global education. Yet little hard data is available on the success of such programs, and the definition of global education is still tentative in the minds of many people.

Robert Hanvey's book *An Attainable Global Perspective* (1976) is often identified as a thoughtful statement concerning the knowledge and attitudinal bases for a global curriculum. Five dimensions of global education are identified:

1. **Perspective consciousness:** Understanding that others may view events and the world very differently from your own view.
2. **State of the planet awareness:** Knowing major trends in the world such as climate changes and population growth and the facts surrounding these trends.
3. **Cross-cultural awareness:** Knowing that there are differences in ideas and practices among nations and making an effort to view events from the vantage points of others.
4. **Knowledge of global dynamics:** Recognizing the interdependence of people and places because of dynamic world systems in the physical, cultural, and economic environments.
5. **Awareness of human choices:** Recognizing that events are shaped by the individual and collective decisions made by communities and nations. Decisions made in one area of the world may be prompted by decisions made by others or may affect the lives of people in far-off locations.

A set of guidelines for global and international education to assist teachers in establishing curricula was developed by H. Thomas Collins, Frederick R. Czarra, and Andrew F. Smith (1998). Their research led them to three broad K–12 themes for the curriculum:

1. Global challenges, issues, and problems
2. Global cultures and world areas
3. Global connections: the United States and the world

Their curriculum guidelines are built around these themes. Table 13.1 describes these guidelines. The knowledge, skills, and types of participation youths need to experience to gain a global or international perspective are identified in the guidelines.

In designing a global curriculum, it is necessary to try to define what such a curriculum is. Parker, Ninomiya, and Cogan (2002) approached defining a global curriculum through research with people from nine nations. People from several nations were involved because Parker and colleagues assumed that defining the nature of a world citizen requires multiple perspectives from people from many nations concerning the world and its issues. Their participants arrived at a consensus about the

T A B L E   1 3 . 1

Guidelines for Global and International Studies Education

I. Global challenges, issues, and problems
   A. Knowledge objectives
      1. Students will know and understand that global issues and challenges exist and affect their lives.
      2. Students will study at least one global issue in depth and over time.
      3. Students understand that global issues and challenges are interrelated, complex, and changing and that most issues have a global dimension.
      4. Students will be aware that their information and knowledge on most global issues are incomplete and that they need to continue seeking information about how global and international issues are formed and influenced.
   B. Skill objectives
      1. Students will learn the techniques of studying about global issues, problems, and challenges.
      2. Students will develop informational literacy about global issues and challenges.
      3. Students will develop the ability to suspend judgment when confronted with new data or opinions that do not coincide with their present understandings or feelings.
   C. Participation objectives
      1. Students will approach global issues, problems, and challenges with neither undue optimism nor unwarranted pessimism.
      2. Students will develop a sense of efficacy and civic responsibility by identifying specific ways in which they can make some contribution to the resolution of a global issue or challenge.

II. Global cultures and world areas
   A. Knowledge objectives
      1. Students will know and understand at least one other culture in addition to their own.
      2. Students will have a general knowledge about the major geographic and cultural areas of the world and the issues and challenges that unite and divide them.
      3. Students will know and understand that members of different cultures view the world in different ways.
      4. Students will know and understand that cultures change.
      5. Students will know and understand that there are universals connecting all cultures.
      6. Students will know and understand that humans can identify with more than one culture and thus have multiple loyalties.
      7. Students will know and understand that culture and communications are closely connected.
      8. Students will know and understand that cultures cross national boundaries.
      9. Students will know and understand that cultures are affected by geography and history.
   B. Skill objectives
      1. Students will analyze and evaluate major events and trends in a culture.

T A B L E   1 3 . 1

Continued

    2. Students will examine cultures in the world and recognize some interconnections with their life in the United States.

    3. Students will compare and contrast diverse cultural points of view and try to understand them.

    4. Students will examine the common and diverse traits of other cultures.

    5. Students will be able to state a concern position or a value from another culture without distorting it, in a way that would satisfy a member of that culture.

  C. Participation objectives

    1. Students will appreciate the study of other cultures.

    2. Students will appropriately tolerate cultural diversity.

    3. Students will seek to communicate with people from other cultures.

    4. Students will demonstrate an appreciation of universal human rights.

    5. Students will meet and learn from people from other cultures.

III. Global connections: The United States and the world

  A. Knowledge objectives

    1. Students will identify and describe how they are connected with the world historically, politically, economically, technologically, socially, linguistically, and ecologically.

    2. Students will know and understand that global interconnections are not necessarily benign; they have both positive and negative consequences in the United States and elsewhere.

    3. Students will know and understand the U.S. role in international policies and international relations, particularly since World War II.

  B. Skill objectives

    1. Students will recognize and analyze and evaluate major events and trends in U.S. and world history and examine how these events and trends connect to their local communities and the United States today.

    2. Students will recognize, analyze, and evaluate interconnections of local and regional issues with global challenges and issues.

    3. Students will recognize, analyze, and evaluate the interconnections between their lives and global issues.

    4. Students will generate alternative projections for the future and weight potential future scenarios.

  C. Participation objectives

    1. Students will value participation in the democratic process.

    2. Students will tolerate ambiguity.

    3. Students will read newspapers, magazines, and books; listen to radio television programs that relate to intercultural and international topics; and actively respond to news articles, books, and programs.

Source: Collins, H. T., Czrra, F. R., and Smith, R. F. (1998). Guidelines for global and international studies education: Challenges, cultures, and connections. *Social Education 62*(5), 311–317.

content of the curriculum. They based the curriculum on six ethical questions that focus on problems affecting people across the world. In using such a curriculum, students focus their efforts on inquiry and deliberation concerning the six questions:

1. What should be done to promote equity and fairness within and among societies?
2. What should be the balance between the right to privacy and free and open access to information and information-based societies?
3. What should be the balance between protecting the environment and meeting human needs?
4. What should be done to cope with population growth, genetic engineering, and children in poverty?
5. What should be done to develop shared (universal, global) values while respecting local values?
6. What should be done to secure an ethically based distribution of power for deciding policy and action on the above issues?

Studying people and culture is essential in global education because people form global perspectives, and students must be aware of them and must also think about being aware of the state of our planet, of other cultures, of global dynamics, and of the choices we make. The questions and themes above incorporate these dimensions identified by Hanvey (1976).

Global connections are complex issues. Some people believe that young learners do not have the ability to examine such complex issues and make decisions that will really help people. But young students are reported to have greater knowledge of political and social issues than was formerly assumed (Angell & Avery, 1992).

Many primary-grade teachers who teach students about people throughout the world are teaching global education. They are helping students become aware of the many commonalities we share. They are also helping students become aware of the differences that are found, especially those that are the result of human culture, such as religion, language, traditions, and the organization of communities. In addition, they are working to help young children better understand issues of which they are aware, including terrorism, environmental pollution, war, and health concerns.

APPROACHES TO GLOBAL EDUCATION

Two major ways of approaching global education are the cultural approach and the problems approach. They share some perspectives, but they also have different emphases in their approach to global education.

The Cultural Approach to Global Education

Elementary students should experience in-depth learning about several countries that provides an accurate treatment of the content and avoids blatant stereotyping or dull and superficial learning. In-depth country units can positively influence students' attitudes toward learning about other cultures and areas of the world (Hoge & Allen, 1991). When elementary teachers provide such high-quality instruction about other nations, they are helping students to build the understanding, attitudes, and skills needed to sustain our nation as a leader in the world community (Hoge & Allen, 1991).

Teaching about cultures around the world is a way of examining important social issues related to the lives of people everywhere (Merryfield, in press). The examination of cultures needs to be substantive and in depth. Table 13.2 illustrates substantive knowledge and skills that should be applied to the study of cultures (Merryfield, in press). The table contrasts the substantive global approach, which is a cultural approach, with the traditional approach that was often used in the past, which viewed other cultures through a narrow and nonglobal perspective.

The Problems Approach to Global Education

Global education is often conceived of as the study of economic, political, ecological, and technological systems and problems that extend across national boundaries. Four persistent problems encompass the entire globe and serve as the focus of global education:

1. Peace and security
2. National and international development
3. Environmental problems
4. Human rights

All these problems impact people and societies throughout the world. All are greatly impacted by changes in scientific knowledge and technology.

One way to study these four problems is to organize our instruction around five major concepts: interdependence, change, culture, scarcity, and conflict (Kniep, 1989). These major concepts can serve as five themes we study throughout the year. Through these themes, we can examine each of the four persistent problems found across the world. As an example, let's consider the problem of human rights and the major concept of interdependence. Because we are interdependent in our own society, we need each other's services, and this can lead us to deny the rights of some people to make sure that we get the services we need and want. So we might enact laws that make it hard to change jobs. Nations also might do this to other nations. Trade agreements might be set up to make sure that we get a resource we need from another country, such as oil or coffee. Because we need the resource, we might overlook human rights problems and the low wages, long hours, and unsafe conditions workers in those countries must endure for us to get the resource.

TIME FOR REFLECTION: WHAT DO YOU THINK?

Select one of the other three persistent problems identified by Kniep—(1) peace and security, (2) national and international development, or (3) environmental problems—and describe how the major concept of interdependence can be studied with this problem.

_____

_____

TABLE 13.2

Substantive Culture Learning

Content and Pedagogy	Some Practices of Nonglobal Educators	Some Practices of Global Educators
1. Developing skills in perspective consciousness	Teach one mainstream point of view. Teach that other viewpoints are wrong. Imply that other people are inferior, so there is no need to understand why they think the way they do. Assume that Americans know why people in Africa, Asia, or the Middle East behave the way they do (so there is no reason to ask them).	Teach students to recognize and understand underlying assumptions and values in their own perspectives and how they change over time. Teach students to analyze the perspectives of others as part of understanding how different people view events and issues. Have students develop the habit of examining the experiences, knowledge, beliefs, and values that shape people's world views.
2. Using skills in recognizing stereotypes, exotica, and cultural universals	Ignore stereotypes their students may have. May teach that all people in a culture or region are the same. May use exotica to motivate students. May ignore or play down commonalities. Do not teach cultural universals.	Identify stereotypes students bring to class. Address stereotypes directly. Teach students to recognize how exotica may interfere with cultural understanding. Aim for a balance between cultural differences and commonalities. Teach students to examine cultural universals.
3. Using primary sources from the cultures or regions under study	Use only American sources to teach about other cultures.	Use primary sources such as literature, documents, newspapers, and websites from the culture under study. Have students interact with people from the culture.
4. Understanding of the intersections of prejudice and power	Do not teach about intersections of prejudice and power.	Teach about prejudice and discrimination within and across diverse world regions.

TABLE 13.2

Continued

Content and Pedagogy	Some Practices of Non-Global Educators	Some Practices of Global Educators
		Teach about people's ongoing efforts to resist oppression or discrimination.
		Help students understand how minority cultures perceive the actions of those in power over them.
5. Understanding of dynamic change and increasing global interconnectedness	Do not teach how cultures change. Allow students to think a culture is static. May use images or content about a culture that are out of date. Do not teach global interconnectedness. Allow students to assume that the United States is not dependent on other nations or people in other countries.	Teach the dynamic nature of cultural change and diffusion. Help students understand how cultural norms change over time in real people's lives. Help students understand how cultural changes affect minorities and indigenous peoples. Teach economic, political, cultural, environmental, and other connections between their students and people in other cultures. Provide learning experiences to connect students with people in other countries.

Source: Merryfield, M. (in press). Engaging elementary children in substantive culture learning. *Social Education.*

INTERDISCIPLINARY CONNECTIONS

Many interdisciplinary topics that are frequently studied in middle school have global connections, especially those connected with preservation of species and changes in climate and atmosphere (Cruz, 1998). Political science, law, and civics are subjects that address global issues because many actions that are needed to solve global problems require the cooperation of nations, international organizations, and people living in several nations.

Closely related to global education is the peace education movement. The connection is evident when we consider peace and security as one of the persistent problems in the world. Peace is also important when we consider the problems of national and international development, of the environment, and of human rights. Originally prompted by concerns about nuclear war, peace educators soon recognized that

These youths, born in America, visited their grandparents and family in northern Nigeria. Such students and their parents are potential resources for teaching about other nations and cultures.

removal of nuclear weapons is not enough to stop war. Peace educators seek to preserve the world and to preserve the safety and security of our bodies and our consciences for all people.

TEACHING GLOBAL EDUCATION

There are many interest groups whose concerns fall under the umbrella of global education. Some of these groups sponsor special days or weeks throughout the year. These groups often supply free education materials and suggest activities that students might enjoy. Yet if such activities are done in isolation, they do not contribute to meaningful learning. Instead, students might develop only a vague awareness of the issues. Some students might experience despair because they see only huge problems with no solutions or they might be encouraged to embrace simplistic solutions. Sufficient time needs to be devoted if students are to gain the in-depth knowledge needed to understand global issues.

Teaching units that define the problems and investigate subtopics and alternative solutions are a more appropriate instructional approach than is the celebration of single-day events. Students need to investigate the consequences of actions designed to solve global problems along with the values that support the proposed solutions. As students examine global problems and their causes and consequences, they need to decide whether the solutions promote practices that are consistent with democratic civic ideals and whether the solutions will appear positive or negative to people in other nations. Some unit topics that can address global issues in these ways include the following:

- How can the needs of all people be fulfilled?
- How are changes in communication technology helping and hurting people?
- What makes a person a hero or heroine?
- Why have people or groups been nominated for or won the Nobel Peace Prize?
- How do we help people in places where a natural disaster has occurred?
- How are the lives of women and children changing in today's world?

Elementary and middle school students should examine global issues to help them deal positively with such issues. At school, students can examine many difficult issues with less emotion using a more rational thought process than will happen when they are involved in incidents that affect and challenge the lives of family members or a friend. The school curriculum can also address problems that have occurred in the past and examine and evaluate the various ways in which people and nations have tried to solve their problems. Although many possibilities exist, teachers must make careful decisions about which global issues to study and how to investigate those issues. Dorothy Skeel (1996) points out that one of the questions that each teacher must answer when selecting a topic for study is "Are the students sufficiently mature and experienced to thoroughly understand the study?"

Hoge and Allen (1991) believe that young students can and should learn about people in other nations. They recommend that teachers approach studies of other nations and people as a resource provider and co-learner with their students. In this role, teachers model effective ways of seeking answers for thoughtful questions. Such teachers help students to form conclusions and generalizations and test and revise their ideas as they encounter new facts and viewpoints. However, not all topics are appropriate for all students. Angell and Avery (1992) report that if a topic or problem is not clearly related to local situations, students tend not to see the issue as having local applications and cannot see ways to personally take action on such a problem.

Focusing on helping young students identify multiple perspectives on issues and problems is a major learning outcome related to global issues. So also is discussing what are good and positive actions, moral positions, and appropriate behaviors. For example, one of the most negative issues in the social studies curriculum is genocide. Examining such a difficult topic only superficially can result in students deciding to conform to what those in power want because they are afraid of them. By carefully examining the Holocaust, many educators hope to assist students in dealing with negative behavior and provide support for human needs and the value of justice. Some advocate teaching about the Holocaust in the primary grades. However, Samuel Totten (1999), an educator who has devoted years to the study of genocide and the Holocaust, recognizes the great complexity of the content of this topic and makes it clear that he does not view the Holocaust as an appropriate topic at the K–4 levels. However, he does identify a number of social skills and values that he believes should be taught in K–4 so that students will be more able to carefully consider the Holocaust in later grades. He recommends examining and teaching these values and attitudes with content that does not include the violence and extreme negative behaviors that are a part of the Holocaust. Global topics involving the environment and social conditions

Students' artwork reveals what they learned about the need to manage the world's renewable resources.

such as child labor also have many negative attributes and solutions that are very complex. Very young students should be helped to develop such skills as critical thinking and problem solving and values such as respect for justice and human dignity within the more traditional curriculum topics. Middle school students have greater cognitive skills and might address the more complex topics with accurate information. Middle school teachers must be sensitive to the needs of the students who are involved in developing their personal identities and need adult support in facing individual moral decisions and pressures from peers and a world that sends them confusing messages.

The learning cycle lesson in Table 13.3, "Teaching about War to Help Create a More Humane World," is presented as a large unit that takes place over at least 10 days of teaching. The early part of this unit serves as the Exploratory Introduction to the unit, with the middle section serving as the Development portion and the last part of the unit applying and expanding the key generalization taught forming the Expansion. This unit uses a number of instructional strategies suggested for use in addressing global issues. The unit requires several days to complete because it focuses on identifying multiple perspectives, using reflective discussion, and evaluating consequences of decisions. True stories from three trade books present the reality of war and its consequences in the lives of common people in different nations and at different times. The Expansion phase of the lesson looks at responses caring people and organizations have made to the negative impacts of warfare both between nations and within nations.

TABLE 13.3

Learning Cycle	Teaching about War to Help Create a More Humane World

Grade Levels: Intermediate and Middle School
NCSS Standards: Global Connections; Science Technology and Society; Culture; Time, Continuity and Change; Civic Ideals and Practices; and People, Places, and Environments

NCSS

Generalization: Because wars and civil wars kill some soldiers and civilians and severely change the lives of the surviving civilians and soldiers, warfare is an event that people and governments should work hard to prevent happening in the future.

Exploratory Introduction

Materials: Pictures from the U.S. Civil War from American history textbooks or the collection of the Library of Congress website (www.loc.gov)

Objectives	Procedures	Assessments
Given a set of pictures from the U.S. Civil War, students describe what they believe to be the characteristics of a war.	Arrange students in small groups and give each a set of pictures. Ask: "What do these pictures tell you about the characteristics of the Civil War?" Discuss this and be prepared to report your ideas to the class. Have groups share their ideas.	Students work together and share ideas.
	Teacher asks class: "Judging from your pictures, what did your group identify as characteristics of the people in the Civil War? From what you see in the pictures, who or what kinds of people were involved in the Civil War?" Have students point out or describe their sources of information in the pictures. Ask: "What messages did these pictures tell you about what things happened to the people in the pictures?"	
	Record students' answers on a chart titled "People and Events of War"	
Students indicate that only a few people's perspectives are present in the picture set.	Call attention to what is on the chart and ask: "Whose involvement in the war was not commemorated in the pictures? Why? Why do you think the photographers did not take pictures of old people, women, and children or why might the Library of Congress not have preserved such pictures? Do you think these other people had the same views toward the war as did the soldiers and	Students state that few views are present in the picture set.

continued

TABLE 13.3

Continued

politicians whose pictures we have seen? How can we find out what happened to slaves, wives, families, farmers, and factory workers during the war?"

Announce that the class will keep the chart and see whether it needs to be changed as the class continues to study. (Keep the chart and add, cross out, or put question marks beside ideas after reading and discussing each story. Use a different color marker for each day.)

Lesson Development

Materials: A copy of each of the following trade books: Polacco, Patricia. (1994). *Pink and Say.* New York: Philomel Books; Bereckler, Rosemary. (1996). *Sweet Dried Apples.* Boston: Houghton Mifflin; Cha, Dia. (1996). *Dia's Story Cloth.* New York: Lee and Low; chart paper and various colored marking pens; paper for drawing pictures for each student; world map.

Objectives	Procedures	Assessments
Given the reading of *Pink and Say* and discussion of its content, students examine the impact of the U.S. Civil War on two young men and their families, providing evidence from the book to support their ideas.	Tell students you are going to read them a book written about the U.S. Civil War. Showing its cover, ask: "What do you think the young men or boys pictured on the cover are doing? What does this picture lead you to believe about the young men?" Accept and record students' predictions. On a map of the United States, locate Michigan, which was Say's home, and Georgia, where the events in the book took place. Read the book, showing the pictures. Ask students to comment on the pictures, especially moods illustrated and facial expressions. After reading, say: "Think back on the pictures in this book and identify one that stands out in your memory. Tell me what is in the picture and what message the picture gives to you." After several students share, say: "Think about the picture you personally remember the most from the story or the picture that first comes to your mind and raise your hand if the picture could be described as happy." Count and record responses. Ask: "How many of you	Students attend to comments and questions of teacher and classmates.

TABLE 13.3

Continued

thought the first picture could be described as sad?" Count and record.	
Say: "Raise your hand if you think the story was sad. Next, raise your hand if you thought it was happy." Record the number of responses.	All students answer with a show of hands.
Begin a class discussion by noting that the book provides a few hints of what the lives of Pink, Mo Mo Bay, and Say were like before the war. Ask students to consider these questions and to support their responses with evidence from the story.	Students offer logical predictions and interpretations.

1. What do you think the lives of Pink and Mo Mo Bay were like before the war?
2. What do you think the life of Say was like before the war?
3. What happened to Pink, Say, and Mo Mo Bay during the war?
4. Describe how you think Mo Mo Bay felt about Pink and Say.
5. Pink and Say have feelings about the war. What do their feelings have in common? How are they different?
6. Why was touching Mr. Lincoln's hand "something important"?
7. What was the last request Pink made of Say? What do you think was the significance of this request and the actions of the two boys?
8. Why do you think Pinkus Aylee was killed within hours of entering Andersonville Prison and Say was not?
9. Who do you think was the hero of the story? What did Mo Mo Bay do that was heroic? What did Pink do that was heroic? What did Say do that was heroic?

Students offer logical predictions and interpretations, supporting them with evidence from the book.

Make a list of the words that describe Pinkus Aylee (Pink).

Make a list of the words that describe Sheldon Curtis (Say).

continued

TABLE 13.3

Objectives	Procedures	Assessments
	Make a list of words that describe the marauders.	
Students make changes on the chart that reflect their increased infor-mation from the evidence they identified in *Pink and Say.*	Closure: We have looked at a picture set and read a story of one soldier that was passed on through oral history in the family. Display the chart that was begun earlier. Ask: "Are there any statements on our list that you think we should remove from the list at this time?" If so, cross them out. If a question remains, put a question mark beside the statement. Ask: "Are there any new statements you think we should add to our list that tell us important things about the people and events of the war?"	Students evaluate their ideas and offer additions and sugges-tions for removal using evidence from *Pink and Say.*
Given the reading of the story *Sweet Dried Apples,* students identify the impact of the Vietnam War on the lives of Vietnamese people.	Display a world map, locating Vietnam, where the story takes place. Tell students that many people came to the United States from Vietnam after the war and most settled in California. Read the story and follow similar procedures with this book as with the previous book. Show pictures and ask students to predict what the face would look like on those pictures where the illustrator shows the backs of the people. Review the events of the story through a discussion based on the following questions, asking students to give supporting evidence from the book with their responses. 1. What was daily life like for the children before the war? 2. Little is said of what life was like for the adults, but judging from the pictures and the few words, how would you describe the lives of the adults prior to the war? 3. What were the first observable signs of the war that the children in the story encountered? 4. What things did the grandfather, Ong Noi, do for the children and the family?	Students make logical inferences about the impact of the Vietnam War on the lives of Vietnamese, using evidence from the story. Students answer questions with correct replies.

TABLE 13.3

Continued

5. How would you describe the relationship between the children and Ong Noi?

6. Why do you think Ong Noi did not smile when he told the children, "You must never wander from home!"

7. While the grandfather was gone, what did the children do as a surprise for him? Why do you think the children thought this would be a good idea? How was their village attacked during the war?

8. In the morning after the attack, what was the grandfather's concern and what did he do?

9. What happened to the grandfather?

10. What happened to the members of the village?

11. The book does not tell us what happened to Ba. What do you think most likely happened to him? Why do you think this is the case? Have the class vote with a show of hands on the predictions of the different responders and record their votes on the board. — All students vote, and logical reasons are offered.

12. What do you think happened to the people who reached the large boat?

13. Why do you think the girl promised herself that she would return and do several things for Ong Noi?

14. Who in this story do you think is a hero and why do you think that is the case?

Students identify war as one of the causes of immigration.	Tell students that many people have come to the United States as immigrants because of war. Ask the students whether they have heard the terms *migration* and *immigrant.* Define these terms if needed. Ask: "Can you name the nation from which one or more of your ancestors migrated when they came to the United States?" Record responses. Ask: "Do you know of anyone in the community who came to the United States from Vietnam?	Students identify war as one cause of immigration and provide logically acceptable answers to questions.

continued

TABLE 13.3

Continued		
Objectives	**Procedures**	**Assessments**
Students make changes on the chart that reflect their increased information from the evidence they identified in *Sweet Dried Apples*.	When people migrate, what do they leave behind? Why do you think more people would be willing to migrate during a war or just after a war?" Closure: Use same procedures as used for *Pink and Say*.	Students evaluate their ideas and offer additions and suggestions for removal, using evidence from *Sweet Dried Apples*.
Given the reading of the book *Dia's Story Cloth,* students trace the migration of the Hmong people and describe the lives of the Hmong during their migration.	Tell students that the people in the third book you are reading lived in Laos, a nation neighboring Vietnam, at the same time as the characters in *Sweet Dried Apples.* Locate both Vietnam and Laos on the world map. Note their shared border and the course of the Mekong River. Ask: "If I asked you to record the events of a trip, how would you do it? What media would you use to record the events?" The Hmong people of Laos have long recorded events that are important to them by sewing on a piece of cloth. Show the picture of the entire cloth in the center of the book. Ask: "What is your first impression of this cloth?" Share ideas. Have the students look at the picture and try to identify what happened in one or two events recorded on the cloth. Tell the students that the author of the book immigrated and now lives in the United States. The cloth shows the history of her ancestors' migration over many years. Read the names of the nations on the cloth. Use the map to locate these various nations where the Hmong people lived: China, Laos, Burma, and Thailand. Note the locations in relationship to the Mekong River. Say: "As we read this book, identify things that are similar and different from yesterday's story."	Students offer logical ideas based on scenes in cloth.

TABLE 13.3

Read the book and examine the pictures in ways similar to the other books. Then ask and discuss the following questions. Ask students to support their responses with evidence from the book.

Students answer correctly and predict logically.

1. Why have the Hmong people lived in so many different places?
2. What was the life of the Hmong people like before the war in Laos?
3. How were the lives of the Hmong people changed by the war?
4. Could the Hmong men have avoided fighting in the war?
5. How are the actions of a guerrilla soldier different from those of a regular soldier?
6. What happened to Dia's father? (The family does not know.)
7. What were the members of Dia's family forced to do to keep from being killed?
8. Hmong means "free people." In what ways do you think the Hmong people were "free" before the war?
9. Do you think the word *free* described the Hmong when they got to Thailand?
10. What did Dia's family get in the refugee camp in Thailand that helped them to eventually migrate to the United States?
11. What were some of the problems Dia and the Hmong people had to overcome in the United States?
12. Is there anyone in this book you think is a hero?

Students conclude that the cloth tells the history of the Hmong just as the picture set recorded U.S. history.

All of the events described in the narrative are shown on the cloth. Examine the cloth again, locating the different events. Ask: "What weapons are shown on the cloth? Which weapons do you think were most destructive to the Hmong? Why? What is the

Students agree that the cloth is a historical document that is important to all Hmong people and serves a function similar to that of photographs.

continued

TABLE 13.3

Continued		

Objectives	Procedures	Assessments
	importance of the story cloth to Dia and her family? To other Americans who are Hmong?"	
	Make a list of words that describe the cloth. Ask: "How has the explanation of the cloth and our detailed observation of it changed our thoughts about the cloth? What does the cloth tell us about the impact of war on people? In what ways are the presentation of the war on Dia's cloth different from what we saw in the picture set of the American Civil War? What does the cloth tell you happened to the people?"	
Students draw a picture that illustrates a way that war affects the lives of people.	Closure: Display the chart and read the statements. Ask: "Are there any statements on our list that you think we should remove at this time? Are there any new things to add about people, events, and war?" Read the final list aloud. Post the list on a bulletin board. Have students draw pictures to frame the poster that illustrate what they have concluded about war and its impact on people. Leave space at the top for a title to be added later.	Students offer appropriate changes to list. Students' pictures show the impact of war on people, including civilians.

Expansion Phase

Materials: Computers for research, a paper strip on which to write the title for the bulletin board, the list of past winners of the Nobel Peace Prize at http://almaz.com/nobel/peace/peace.html

Objectives	Procedures	Assessments
Given the request to reflect on their recent study, students describe what they have learned about how war affects the lives of people.	Call attention to the chart and pictures on the bulletin board. Refer to several pictures and ask: "Which statement on the chart do you think this picture illustrates? How are our pictures different from those we looked at from the Library of Congress?" Affirm the presence of civilian population and their losses as well as military. Tell students we need a title for our bulletin board that tells what we learned. Ask for suggestions, recording on the board, until there is a title on which students agree. Write the title on a strip of paper and attach it to the bulletin board.	Students indicate that more than soldiers are injured in war and mention immigration and refugees.

T A B L E   1 3 . 3

Continued

Students use the Internet to gather information about people and organizations who help civilians and refugees affected by wars, identifying their roles and the types of help provided.	Tell the students that World War I was called, "the war to end all wars," but there have been hundreds of wars since then. Many people have jobs in which they help the civilian people and those who become refugees. Display a list of winners of the Nobel Peace Prize. Note that some are people and others are groups or organizations. Ask: "What do you think they have done to bring about peace or prevent wars? How can we find out more about the winners and others who help to prevent wars or help people during wars?"	
	Assign students to small groups to research the organizations that help people who are affected by wars today. Find information on who works for the groups, how they get their money to work, where they are currently working, and what types of help they provide. (The teacher may make a short oral presentation explaining a poster the teacher makes that illustrates the main findings.) Display a list of organizations for reports; students may add others if they know of them. Students select groups and research the answers. Possible groups include the U.N. Commission for Refugees, Doctors without Borders, the International Red Cross/Red Crescent, Vietnam Veterans of America Foundation, winners of the Nobel Peace Prize, church-affiliated charities,* and nongovernmental organizations* such as World Vision and Children International.	Students identify role and types of help provided.
Students develop an action plan for sharing ideas about helping organizations and building an effort to support and participate in the work of those organizations.	Students present a short report with an illustration or PowerPoint presentation concerning the group researched. These illustrations may be added to the bulletin board under a heading that students select as appropriate. Students decide how they can inform others about what they have learned and why it is	Students offer plans and decide on an acceptable plan of action to share ideas about their research and to help an organization's work

* Teachers can search the Internet for names of such groups with local connections.

continued

T A B L E 1 3 . 3

Continued		
Objectives	**Procedures**	**Assessments**
	important. Then they develop an action plan in small groups and arrive at a whole-class consensus on a plan.	by supporting and participating in it.
	Alternative or additional options: Include a class visit from a person who works for such an organization or an interview with a person from the community who is a refugee.	
	Summary: Students briefly review the activities with which they have been involved and identify the generalization constructed as a result of those activities: Because wars and civil wars kill some soldiers and civilians and severely change the lives of the surviving civilians and soldiers, warfare is an event that people and governments should work hard to prevent happening in the future.	

T I M E F O R R E F L E C T I O N : W H A T D O Y O U T H I N K ?

1. What do you anticipate the students' response will be to the focus question for the exploratory introduction of this lesson? _____
_____

2. What immigrant groups are likely to be living in the school district where you hope to get a teaching position? Might any of them be refugees? _____
_____

3. When did you last read or hear in the media about refugees from war or famine?
_____

4. How can the NCSS Standard VIII (Science, Technology, and Society) be worked into this lesson? _____
_____

5. Write a values statement that you think sums up this lesson. _____
_____
_____

MAKING A LITERATURE CONNECTION

What Are the People of the World Like?

June 16, 1999, was called "Six Billion Day." One of the children born that day was the six billionth person living on the earth. Since that day, the world's population has continued to grow at the rate of 100 million people per year. Who are all these people and what do they have in common with you, an American? How do Americans rank among the various groups in the world? Trying to understand something that is expressed in large numbers is a challenge to most people, especially youths. In his book *If the World Were a Village: A Book about the World's People,* David Smith, a middle school teacher, has taken the large numbers from demographic reports and translated those numbers into smaller numbers that more people can understand. In his book, the world is a village of 100 people, so the numbers that describe the various characteristics are much easier to understand. The book is filled with many statements that can begin a thoughtful discussion. For example, in the world village, 22 people speak a Chinese dialect, 20 earn less than a dollar a day, 17 cannot read or write, 60 are always hungry, and 24 have a television in their homes.

RESOURCES FOR TEACHING GLOBAL EDUCATION

Computers and the Internet

Many sources of information and multiple perspectives about people and events throughout the world are available today. Whereas in the past, there were few opportunities for students to test or challenge perspectives or conclusions about how people live or feel in another area of the world, today students can communicate with students in classrooms throughout the world, read local reports in newspapers of many nations, and join in chats and discussions with individuals throughout the world. Technology has also changed the reporting of events, enabling reporters to provide live coverage as events are taking place that can include pictures and streaming video. All of these new sources of data provide more information but, in return, demand that students learn skills of critical thinking. Such skills are needed to evaluate information and decide which parts of the information are valid or biased, what conclusions can be made from the information, and how accurate those conclusions might be. In the past, students were likely to accept what was written in a book or presented in a single news presentation as true; today, that is less likely. When encountering the words of many people with varying wants and messages, students want to know the truth. Teachers need to help students by encouraging them to ask questions and by helping them to analyze and evaluate the many comments available.

Because young people are interested in the lives of youth in other nations and because so much of the athletic equipment and clothing worn by U.S. youths is made in foreign nations, U.S. students have become aware of the fact that the money they spend goes to workers and businesses around the world. The International Labor Organization website examines the plight of workers and the issue of child labor in today's world, while the U.N. website for teachers contains the texts and treaties on human rights (see the companion website) that can help students examine working conditions.

The impact of war includes the many people who are severely wounded every day by land mines, and more mines are being deployed each day. Through the project materials section of the United Nations website (see the companion website), students can learn about the serious problem of land mines and how to help families and children living in dangerous areas to have safer lives. Mark Hyman explains how students at Tenafly Middle School in New Jersey became interested in helping to eliminate land mines and raised $30,000 to finance the removal of mines in the small city of Podzvizd in Bosnia-Herzegovina (Hyman, 2001).

> **USING TECHNOLOGY**

Civics Impact of Technology Opportunities

A teacher of computer technology in a middle school wrote to the Middle-L mailing list requesting ideas for possible research topics for students. The teacher offered this beginning list of topics and hints for student development as examples of what he was seeking: fiber optics (from toys to communications), hydroponics (growing plants without soil), magnetic levitation (used in transportation), plastics (e.g., Bakelite, invented in 1909), robotics, solar energy for the home, solar-powered cars, and space travel and living.

Students might well be excited by each of these topics, and many would have personal experiences with some of them. Traditional research assignments, even when a computer is used to search for information and to produce the finished project, result in historic reports on scientists or inventors relating how discoveries or the first product were made. The focus tends to be on why individuals are important, and the easy conclusion of most young learners is that the person was extra smart or hard working and came in first, as in winning a race. Intelligence and hard work are desirable and important to teach youths, but the fact is that many hard-working, intelligent people never get recognized and continue to practice these and other virtues as part of their own self-respect and self-concept.

Recognition is bestowed on a person by others such as parents, teachers, friends, classmates, or communities of various types and sizes. Part of a person's identity is his or her place in the larger society. Preteens and teens are at the stage in personal development at which they are seeking to determine who they are in the larger community. Middle school students are beginning to look forward to becoming adults with jobs and legal rights. It is therefore an ideal time to ask students to examine why and how the civic society recognizes people by having students investigate or research the values and behaviors needed by a society and consider that type of society in which they wish to live and participate. Walter Parker (2001b) suggests that the Civic Ideals and Practices (NCSS Standard X) for a democratic society must be those of enlightened political engagement—not an engagement of blindly following a culture or leader, but behaviors that support the importance of all people and their rights to justice and equality associated with the ideals of the Enlightenment.

➤

NCSS

NCSS

> By focusing a research project such as that proposed by the writer to the mailing list on NCSS Standard VIII (Science, Technology, and Society), students must go beyond the traditional approach of investigating, researching, and communicating findings on a topic to include the reflection on and analysis of the impact or potential impact of a topic or invention on the lives and individuals in the larger community. Such an assignment forces students to pay attention to the civic role of all people and its potential impact on others, thus making a personal connection between the NCSS Standards VIII and X. Teachers prompt and encourage students to make such connections by the focus of the assignments they make and by discussing questions that require students to reflect and consider the impact of single events encountered throughout the curriculum. The discussion questions to ask (be they a reflection on history and cultures or a creative prediction) require responses to the phrase "So what?" A teacher focusing on communications and technology might ask the following series of questions: How did the invention of the telephone change the ways in which people communicated? How has the cell phone further changed communications? Which occupations benefit the most from this type of communication? Do you think the market for this particular invention will be large enough for manufacturing to occur? Will the people view this invention as a great advantage or an invader of their privacy? Accountability in schools includes student self-assessment as well as teacher grading. Research and investigation assignments need to be graded by rubric categories that require consideration of and reflection on the civic roles and impacts. When a teacher gives careful consideration to the NCSS standards and links them to assessments, students are helped to learn meaningful social studies and to view the importance of social studies learning to their lives and their future lives as citizens in a democracy in an increasingly interdependent world.

Book Series

Books with a variety of formats provide the information needed to study global issues. Picture books and reference books such as almanacs, atlases, yearbooks, and encyclopedias all provide some of the necessary data. There are a number of book series for young learners about families throughout the world. Especially helpful are those illustrated by photographs. Series of books such as those by Lerner Publications of Minneapolis address topics such as visual geography, the world in conflict, and globe trotters. Such book series provide similar information on nations and cultures that allow students to identify commonalities and differences among nations and people.

Resources for Current Events

Many teachers at all grade levels use current events to illustrate the importance of history and social sciences to the lives of people today. Current events are also used to internationalize the curriculum. Most teachers use current events for a few minutes each day or as a weekly or biweekly focus during a class period. Some teachers develop units based on a current event (Haas & Laughlim, 2000). There are numerous sources of information about current events, and today's technology makes it possible to gain access to international news broadcasts and articles. Local problems can be linked to similar problems in other areas of the world. Almost all of the news programs and publications have websites, and many provide lesson plans for teachers. Programs are available for purchase for all grade levels from *Scholastic, Time,* and *Newsweek.* C-Span in the Classroom broadcasts programs early in the morning so that teachers can tape them for use in their classes. C-Span also provides lesson plans for many of these programs. For URLs of major news organizations, go to the companion website for this book.

SUMMARY

Social studies educators see examining real-world problems currently challenging people and nations as part of the socialization duty of civic education that creates active rather than passive citizens. Social studies professionals view the global perspective as one important perspective for citizens of all nations to develop. Having both a national and a global perspective helps to counter the extreme nationalism that led to world wars and the abuse of basic human rights, freedom, and justice among many people promoted by nations in the twentieth century. A curriculum that includes powerful and meaningful instruction in all 10 of the NCSS standards promotes the development of citizens who are well aware of the importance of the long struggle of people to obtain democratic rights. Such citizens are also aware that solving international problems may involve some compromises but see the need to understand multiple perspectives in viewpoints among people and nations. Through examining global connections and their causes and consequences, students come to understand that the consequences and costs of proposed solutions must be examined and evaluated before action is taken and must be reevaluated as time passes. Students become aware of the importance of individual decisions and of the collective decisions of groups and nations.

Expanding ON THIS CHAPTER

Activity

From the local newspaper or newscast, identify an important local issue that is also an issue faced by people in other areas of the world. On a world map, identify other places where you expect that the problem is currently a serious concern for the people. Then go to a website such as www.worldpress.org and read about how the issue is being or not being confronted. Compare the problems in your community and the other regions using a Venn diagram. Then write a few sentences explaining what is revealed in the diagram. Offer an explanation for the reasons the decisions being made are similar or different.

Recommended Websites to Visit

**COMPANION
WEBSITE**

Translations of news articles appearing in the press in other nations
www.worldpress.org

Latest news from the United Nations on its efforts in all departments
www.un.org/News/

U.N. Voices of Youth with a link for teachers
www.unicef.org/voy/

Many other links from the United Nations related to youth
www.un.org/esa/socdev/unyin/links.htm

The International Education and Resource Network provides for joint studies between schools.
www.iearn.org/

Visit with children in other countries and learn about how they spend their days.
www.oxfam.org.uk/coolplanet/kidsweb/wakeup/index.htm

State of the World's Children for 2003
www.unicef.org/sowc03/

Document-based questions and rubrics
www.kn.pacbell.com/wired/fil/pages/listdocumentpa.html#cat2

Graphic organizer for DBQ by the Greece, New York, Central School District. Click on CEI
(Claim, Evidence, Interpretation) in the chart.
www.greece.k12.ny.us/instruction/ELA/6-12/Tools/Index.htm

The American Forum for Global Education—Free lesson plans to download and opportunities
for teachers
www.globaled.org/

UNICEF Voices of Youth—Information about youth and issues related to their lives, opportunities for students to communicate with peers throughout the world, ideas for service and
taking actions, teacher page.
www.unicef.org/voy/

World Movement for Democracy—Learn about efforts to promote democratic education
throughout the world. Links to many groups working on this task.
www.wmd.org

The website of the British Broadcasting Corporation, where clicking on NEWS WORLD EDITION
opens articles in English listed under African, Americas, Asia Pacific, Europe, Middle East,
South Asia, and the United Kingdom. Get the news and perspectives from other nations.
http://news.bbc.co.uk

Helping Students Learn through Multiple Assessments and Evaluation

INTRODUCTION

Think of a paper-and-pencil test you have taken. Now examine Figures 14.1 and 14.2, which present questions from the 1994 National Assessment of Educational Progress (NAEP) tests in geography and history for fourth-graders and eighth-graders, respectively. Answer the questions about geography written for fourth-graders in Figure 14.1 and about history written for eighth-graders in Figure 14.2. Review your test-taking experience by answering the questions below.

1. In what ways are they different from the tests you took in fourth and eighth grades? _____
_____
_____
_____ ➤

DRAW ISLAND MAP

In the box below, draw a map of an island.
On the island, draw in the following details by hand:

—Mountains along the west coast
—A lake in the north
—Houses along the east coast
—Forests in the south

Be sure to use the symbols shown in the key.
Use your colored pencils to help you draw the map.

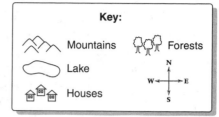

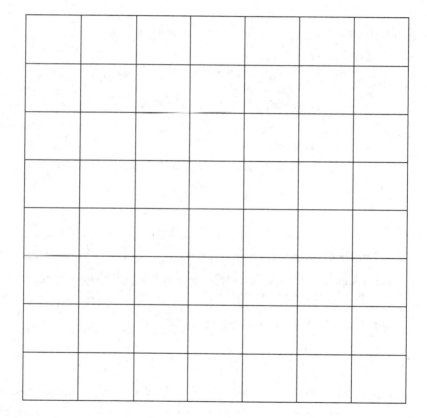

A **Complete** response includes an accurate map in which at least four elements are correctly placed. The response must be an isthmus and have directions of travel and river correctly indicated.

F I G U R E   1 4 . 1   Portion of 1994 NAEP Test in Geography for Fourth-Graders

Source: *Learning about Our World and Our Past: Using the Tools and Resources of Geography and U.S. History—A Report of the 1994 NAEP Assessment,* by E. Hawkins, F. Stancavage, J. Mitchell, M. Goodman, and S. Lazer, 1998, Washington, DC: National Center for Educational Statistics.

continued

USING A CHART TO CONSIDER TRADE BETWEEN COUNTRIES

The two questions below refer to the following chart.

Major Exports of Three Countries

Country A	Country B	Country C
Oil	Cars	Computers
Natural Gas	Televisions	Airplanes
Coconuts	Cameras	Wheat

1. The situation shown in the chart will probably lead to

   A. trade among all three countries
   B. trade only between countries A and B
   C. trade only between countries B and C
   D. a decision by each country to produce all nine goods listed

2. Is the United States most likely country A, B, or C?
   Give one reason why.

   _____

   _____

   _____

   _____

A **Complete** response correctly identifies country C and gives one appropriate reason why.

A **Partial** response correctly identifies country C but gives either no reason why, or an inappropriate reason for the choice.

FIGURE 14.1 Continued

2. How can subjectivity be removed from grading these questions? _____
   _____
   _____
   _____

3. Explain whether you think the questions are fair to all children living in various conditions and regions of the United States. _____
   _____
   _____
   _____
   _____

To answer the two questions refer to the newspaper report below.

A city of desolation, of vacant houses, of widowed women, rotting wharves, of deserted warehouses . . . acres of pitiful and voiceless bareness—that is Charleston.

1. The news report was most likely written in

    A. 1835
    B. 1845
    C. 1855
    D. 1865*

2. The new report best supports which statement?

    A. Cities on the coast saw the worst of the fighting in the Civil War.
    B. During the Civil War urban areas in the South suffered.*
    C. The destruction of cities had little effect on the progress of the Civil War.
    D. The Civil War had little effect on city life in the North.

FIGURE 14.2 Portion of 1994 NAEP Test in U.S. History for Eighth-Graders

Source: Learning about Our World and Our Past: Using the Tools and Resources of Geography and U.S. History: A Report of the 1994 NAEP Assessment, by E. Hawkins, F. Stancavage, J. Mitchell, M. Goodman, and S. Lazer, 1998, Washington, DC: National Center for Educational Statistics.

4. Explain whether you think most students would be able to answer these questions. _____

_____

_____

5. On the 1994 NAEP test in geography, 44 percent of fourth-grade students were able to draw an island and correctly place the mountains, lake, houses, and forest. Only a very small percentage omitted answering the questions or produced a map that had no appropriately drawn elements. However, when the scores were analyzed by race/ethnic group, 51 percent of white, 17 percent of black, and 33 percent of Hispanic students answered the question completely. On the 1994 NAEP test in history, 32 percent of the eighth-grade students answered correctly. The breakdown by race and ethnic difference was 34 percent whites, 31 percent blacks, and 30 percent Hispanic students answered correctly. What might account for these differences? _____

_____

_____

_____

CHAPTER OVERVIEW

How do you know whether the game has started as you approach the stadium? Does the crowd display certain behaviors that mark the beginning of a game? Suppose that, as you approach, a loud roar emanates from the opponents' side of the stadium. What would you suspect is happening? As you are considering such questions, you are assessing the situation. If teachers were asked what they do during the day, they might not mention assessment. However, teachers continually assess the behaviors of students to ensure that they are on task and accomplishing objectives. Administrators, state departments of education, politicians, and the public tend to pay attention to particular assessments they believe indicate students are learning. That selective coverage often calls forth negative feelings about a process that should be viewed for its positive role in education. This chapter examines the multiple ways in which teachers use assessment to determine the success of instruction and to adjust instructional procedures to improve individual learning and the curriculum. It also discusses ways to engage students in assessing their own progress toward learning.

CHAPTER OBJECTIVES

1. Explain the differences between assessment and evaluation.
2. Differentiate between informal and formal assessments and evaluations.
3. Describe how to modify assessments to determine more accurately the progress of students with various learning disabilities and culturally diverse students who lack English proficiency.
4. Discuss how the progress of nonreaders can be assessed.
5. Give examples of how students can be encouraged to assess their own progress and that of other students with whom they work.
6. Analyze and try writing rubrics appropriate for assessing projects and essays.
7. Examine test results and infer students' success and errors for the social studies curriculum.
8. Analyze how a middle school teacher uses assessment in teaching and planning.

ASSESSING AND EVALUATING SOCIAL STUDIES LEARNING

In the past decade, assessment has received greater attention than previously. This has required a complete reexamination of traditional assessment and evaluation. Educators are learning and developing new skills and inventing ways to assess more fairly and accurately student learning. Michael Yell, a seventh-grade teacher from Hudson, Wisconsin, and 1998 NCSS middle school National Social Studies Teacher of the Year, describes his efforts to overhaul his assessment practices as follows:

The journey toward using multiple types of assessment is compatible with the move toward constructivist and engaging teaching. I became dissatisfied with my methods of assessment. I realized that I was not teaching just for recall, and that assessing just for recall was defeating. As my journey continues, I want to expand my repertoire to include more student self-assessment, portfolios, and student-created rubrics. (Yell, 1999, pp. 328–329)

Aligning objectives and instructional procedures with assessment is the key to success in helping students attain standards and learning benchmarks. Learning is a journey. Unless you know where you are going (learning objectives), you don't know what roads and landmarks to look for (evidence), and you have no idea if and when you will get there (learning outcome). *Assessment* is collecting evidence of learning as you journey toward accomplishing your learning objectives. Similarly, unless you have accomplished your objectives, you won't know how well you like the results of your efforts. *Evaluation* comes after you complete the journey and ascertain how well that journey met your expectations. Evaluation in education comes when there is a collection of assessments that can be examined and compared with a set of expectations. Jane Pollock (1992), in reporting the outcomes of the Aurora, Colorado, schools' attempts to reform assessment, identified three results of the effort: (1) alignment with district goals, (2) improved instruction, and (3) greater student learning. Students are informed of the assessment criteria from the beginning, so they are more engaged in their learning tasks because they know what to accomplish during instruction.

Times When Evaluation and Assessment Are Needed

Evaluation is the process of using information to judge whether a program is meeting students' needs effectively. An evaluation should tell us (1) what students' needs are, (2) how well we have met those needs, and (3) what we might reform to better meet students' needs in both the affective and cognitive domains. Evaluation in social studies looks at students' understanding of their social world. The evaluation process is used to provide information with which the teacher can more effectively plan instruction for individuals and groups. It is also used to collect information so communication with parents is based on documentation of students' work and how they perform it.

Each evaluation serves one of two general purposes: formative or summative. *Formative evaluation* ascertains how well students engage in a lesson or unit and how well students are accomplishing the objectives toward which they are working. It begins with the exploratory introduction in which students' prior learning related to the lesson is diagnosed. Changes are made if it is evident students already know the content or skill to be taught or if reteaching of ideas and skills not mastered is needed. Throughout the unit, formative evaluation provides the teacher with information to determine whether and when students are ready to move on to new topics, objectives, or treatment of the information or whether additional time and effort are needed. Formative evaluation often is completed quickly as the teacher assesses students' comments, questions, and answers during discussions, in writing assignments, or while performing learning tasks.

In *summative evaluation,* students' progress is examined at the end of an activity, unit, or part of the curriculum. Teachers usually have available copies of students' work and charts from observations of participation and class discussion to examine for evidence of learning the necessary standard. If and when percent or letter grades are given, they are given for work on summative assessment materials.

The evaluation process depends on assessment. Assessment is the process of observing, collecting, recording, and otherwise documenting the work students do and how they do it. Evaluation is the process of interpreting the evidence collected through assessment and making judgments and decisions based on the assessment (Finkelstein, 1991).

Guiding Principles for Assessment and Evaluation

Social studies requires assessments reflecting all the content areas supporting the social studies—aspects of cognitive and social skills, values, and the predispositions for action required for competent citizenship and participation in our democratic society and in a global world (National Council for the Social Studies, 1991). One of the major complaints social studies educators have about standardized tests is that they assess only a limited range of what needs to be assessed for outcomes in social studies. Assessment is therefore a special challenge to social studies educators and one they need carefully to spell out for the public, for politicians, and especially for students.

Students often complain that social studies is not relevant and wonder why they study it. Yet the same students are very interested in their social world and in the lives of people. Social studies educators need to help students find connections between what they study and its importance to their lives and to the world in which they live. One way is to assess a wider range of what is expected to be learned and to recognize students' progress in an entire range of content, skills, attitudes, and dispositions. Students often have the misconception that only those things that are tested are worth learning. When testing and assessment focus on what is easy to test with a short reply, students are not given credit for their complete progress. In turn, they may react by focusing on the parts that are tested. Efforts to change the curriculum objectives and teachers' teaching methods must be accompanied by changing assessments and evaluations of the outcomes.

In 1991, NCSS adopted a position statement on testing and evaluation: "Only carefully designed evaluation strategies and tests will enable social studies educators to assess both the academic content and the thinking or performance skills stated in or implied by the objectives" (p. 4). To improve assessment and evaluation, the following guidelines were recommended:

1. Evaluation instruments should:
   —Focus on stated curriculum goals and objectives
   —Be used to improve curriculum and instruction
   —Measure both content and process
   —Be chosen for instructional, diagnostic, and prescriptive purposes
   —Reflect a high degree of fairness to all people and groups

2. Evaluations of students' achievement should:
   —Be used solely to improve teaching and learning
   —Involve a variety of instruments and approaches to measure students' knowledge, skills, and attitudes
   —Be congruent with both the objectives and the classroom experiences of the students examined
   —Be sequential and cumulative (NCSS, 1991, p. 4–5)

When making decisions about grades, class placement, promotion, or retention, the same NCSS document states, "Social studies educators can and should use all the information available about their students' social studies achievement—data gathered from a variety of assessment instruments and techniques . . ." (1991, p. 5).

If assessment and evaluation are to bring about improved learning, assessments and their evaluations must be made public and understood by those most involved in student learning: teachers, students, parents, administrators, and the public and its representatives, who make laws and spend state and school board monies. Finding ways to involve students in the assessment and evaluation of their own learning, or using assessment as a teaching strategy, is not an entirely new idea, but one that is and will continue to be increasingly practiced.

COMPANION
WEBSITE

Teachers plan assessments as a part of their lessons and the curriculum. The assessment questions in a textbook or standardized test should not be used unless the questions are determined to align with the objectives of the classroom. Groups of teachers cooperate to help each other improve their assessment skills and apply them to curriculum and classroom reform. The website Looking at Student Work (see the link at the companion website) is linked with many groups trying to learn how to evaluate various kinds of student work for use in educational reform. When evaluating students' thinking, Buchovecky (1996) suggests that teachers do the following:

- Focus on the evidence present in their work
- Look openly and broadly and not be led by expectations
- Look for patterns and clues as to how and what the student is thinking

Teachers reflect on the curriculum and their teaching in light of evidence provided by the students' work. In the process, questions for action research may be identified. Following are helpful procedures and questions for curriculum changes and action research:

- Compare what you see and what you think about the work with what you do in the classroom.
- Note what you saw in the students' work that surprised you or that you found particularly interesting.
- Consider what inferences you can make about students' thinking.
- Consider what questions about teaching and assessment the students' work raised.
- Consider how you might pursue these questions further.
- Ask whether there are things you would like to try in your classroom as a result of looking at the students' work. (Buchovecky, 1996)

National Testing of Social Studies

COMPANION
WEBSITE

A visit to the website of the National Assessment of Educational Progress at http://nces.ed.gov/nationsreportcard/ allows you to read sample test questions and the summaries of the most recent testing of geography, history, and civics. These tests provide the largest assessment of students throughout the United States. U.S. history and geography are to be retested in 2006, and economics will be tested for the first time in 2006. World history will be tested for the first time in 2010, and the next civics test is set for 2012. Testing of this type reveals trends in the learning of the various social studies contents and skills. When combined with demographic data and responses to survey questions, the data can be broken down to reveal average scores by groups. The information from such NAEP tests provides a snapshot of the accomplishments of the students at the time of the administration of the test. It does not tell us what causes differences in the accomplishments. However, there are consistencies in the findings over the years that, when combined with other types of research, indicate that the following five ideas are probably helpful in improving the scores and by implication the learning of students in social studies as summarized from *The Civic Mission of Schools* (Carnegie Corporation, 2003):

- Provide instruction in social studies on a regular basis beginning in the earliest grades.
- Discuss current local, national, and international events and allow students to examine a number of perspectives and to hold different perspectives on the issues.
- Use active learning strategies, including simulations.
- Apply what is learned in the school and community by taking part in service learning activities.
- Allow students to take part in governance in school and extracurricular activities.

TIME FOR REFLECTION: WHAT DO YOU THINK?

1. What do you think might account for variations in the scores of students in different parts of the United States? _____

2. What might account for differences in the ethnic and gender scores? _____

3. What can teachers, administrators, and the public learn from the NAEP tests that cannot be learned from state testing or from classroom assessments? _____

4. How do the recommendations from *The Civic Mission of Schools* support the vision of teaching social studies stressed in this textbook? _____

Assessment and Evaluation beyond Testing

Effective democratic citizenship requires gathering information, thinking, decision making, communications, social interaction, and civic participation. Assessment and evaluation limited only to testing fail to provide information about many of these requirements for citizenship. More authentic assessments of student work and behavior through projects, performances, essays, and portfolios are needed. Such forms of assessment require students to make decisions based on value judgments and to support their selections with facts and explanations. Continual assessment and evaluation of progress along the path to student learning help to facilitate thinking and actions that make students as productive learners as possible.

Students must enter into their own assessment and evaluation process and learn to assess and evaluate their own progress and that of their classmates in meaningful ways. When they do not like the way things are going, students need to recognize specifics that can be changed and approach these changes in ways that improve the quality of their efforts individually and collectively. When teachers facilitate students' development and integration of assessment and evaluation skills as part of the instructional process, they honor students' efforts by accepting and supporting their suggestions for changes. In this way, students assume some control in the assessment and evaluation process and are encouraged to use individual and group evaluation in ways that increase meaningful learning. When this is done, assessment and evaluation become instructional strategies. Such strategies are most often incorporated into the Development and Expansion phases of a learning cycle.

Learning takes time. Long-term assessment records are kept and charted so that teachers, parents, and students can see that adequate progress is being made and can identify areas of strength and weakness. One of the problems with relying only on teacher-made or standardized tests is that these tests are summative and do not provide the opportunity to refocus a student's efforts or to correct errors in a timely fashion. Summative-only assessment and evaluation reinforce poor habits and errors because students are unaware of the need to change. Teachers need to gather baseline data formally or informally through various forms of pretesting and then periodically evaluate progress. With the involvement of students and parents, a plan of action for each student is developed. An example of a progress report for incorporating the principles that guide assessment and evaluation appears in Table 14.1 (Finkelstein, 1991). Such a table might be completed during teacher–student conferences or teacher–parent–student conferences.

Many school systems have moved away from traditional report cards containing a letter grade per subject. These have been replaced with reporting forms containing greatly increased amounts and types of information related to class work or with conferences. Although states seem to be relying more and more on some form of test and/or standardized graduation requirements for entering and graduating from high school, what much of the public has not yet realized is that the assessment instruments are being modified from traditional, quickly scored, multiple-choice tests. Some states, such as Arizona, California, Connecticut, Kentucky, and New York, have mandated performance-based and portfolio-based testing formats (Wiggins, 1990). These decisions reverberate throughout the entire school system as teachers and students learn how to create, use, and interpret these new evaluations.

In many classrooms, self-assessment habits begin in the earliest grades with collaborative goal setting. Students help to decide what is to be learned through a task and what makes a complete assignment. Teachers post learning goals, stated as questions, and encourage students to refer to them when needed and at specified reflective times. Students may write a more formal final reflection or the teacher may conduct a reflective discussion focused on how well the students believe they attained their goals and asking for evidence to support their claims of success or failure (Hart, 1999).

T A B L E   1 4 . 1

Sample Progress Report

PROGRESS REPORT FORM: SOCIAL STUDIES

Name _____   Date _____

Task	Amount of Progress Low ◄——► High	Teacher Comments
1. Concept understanding as evidenced in		
a. Writing	◄——►	
b. Speaking	◄——►	
c. Graphic expression	◄——►	
2. Problem-solving ability as evidenced in		
a. Participation in discussions	◄——►	
b. Participation in activities	◄——►	
c. Willingness to take risks	◄——►	
d. Suggesting unique solutions	◄——►	
e. Focused thinking	◄——►	
f. Making appropriate responses	◄——►	
3. Thinking-skill development as evidenced in		
a. Exhibiting creativity	◄——►	
b. Exhibiting logical thought processes	◄——►	
c. Grasping main idea	◄——►	
d. Vocabulary	◄——►	

Group evaluation reports and rating of projects and working habits are used. Students also individually rate their group participation. These reports are combined with teacher observation and the final project to provide grades for cooperative group work. Young students begin rating only a few tasks, whereas older students have more tasks because of their increased skill and cognitive levels. Questions that students might address when rating the progress of their group and their own efforts within the group are shown in Table 14.2. The questions address skills and attitudes required for students to be successful in cooperating within the group. Questions ask students to identify specific tasks they do toward completing a project or assignment, for example, What ideas did you contribute to how the project should look?

Parent–Family Conferences.   Assessment and evaluation of individual students is often performed in collaboration with family members and the student. In student-led conferences, students present the information concerning their work and progress to

T A B L E   1 4 . 2

Guiding Questions for Self-Evaluation during Group or Independent Study

Suggested Questions for Self-Evaluation of Group Work

1. Did the group get to work promptly?
2. Did we understand our task?
3. Did everyone in the group have the opportunity to share their opinions and ideas?
4. Did everyone participate?
5. Did we wander off the topic at hand to other things?
6. Did we offer facts and experiences to help in solving problems?
7. Were disagreements settled through compromise and with agreement of all?
8. Did we seek help from each other when needed?
9. Did we listen to each other?
10. Did we seek clarification from the teacher only when we did not understand or could not solve the problem on our own?

Individual Self-Evaluation of Group Participation

1. Did you have enough chance to express your ideas and information about the topic?
2. Were you happy during the group work?
3. What would have made you happier during the group work?
4. Did anyone seem to do most of the group's work?
5. Who in the group listens to you?
6. Who in the group doesn't listen to you?
7. Did anything bother you during the discussions? If so, what was it?
8. What should the group do to improve its functioning?
9. Considering your abilities, assigned tasks, effort, and contributions, what grade do you think you should receive?
10. Using the criteria in question 9, suggest a grade for each member of your group.

the family members and teacher who ask questions. Then all help develop a focus plan for the student's efforts in the next grading period. Supporting activities can be agreed to, so that family members and the teacher work with the student to increase student knowledge and skills related to current events or to relate ideas learned through language and graphic means. Teachers offer students guidance in deciding what to present and how to approach the presentation as part of their classwork. With individual students, teachers may discuss particular selections and offer suggestions and encouragement. Students decide what to present and practice presentations in small groups to refine their presentation skills.

Involving parents and students in assessment is an important learning experience for all, including the teacher (Hackmann, 1997). In areas with large immigrant populations, teachers need to develop skills in relating to and talking with families who are not proficient in English and whose cultural views of parent and teacher roles differ from those of the teacher. Teachers need training in assessment and evaluation and in sensitivity, communications, and multicultural behavior. In some instances, students may serve as translators in conferences with family members. When teachers have large enrollments of students whose families do not speak English or do not speak it well, the teacher attempts to learn to greet family members and thank them for coming using short phrases from their language, even if these phrases have to be written out phonetically and read from cards. Such actions show respect for the efforts family members make in coming to the conference as well as respect for their culture.

➤ **USING TECHNOLOGY**

Improving the Use of Graphic Information

Many teachers have access to large-screen televisions. When these are connected to a computer, the two pieces of hardware provide new opportunities to expand and improve some old standby activities in new, more meaningful ways. One of the major benefits is the large size and the clear image. When students' posters and drawings are scanned onto a disk and displayed for oral presentations, not only is the image larger, so all students can see it, but parts of the image can be enlarged when the student speaks about elements of the poster or picture. This procedure not only helps to emphasize visual literacy, but also helps students to present information verbally because they can use the poster as an outline for the presentation. The poster or drawing becomes a part of the presentation instead of just being held up for a few seconds. The use of visuals is a standard presentation technique in many careers and makes such a presentation an example of an authentic assessment format. When graphs are presented as part of a report on a nation or state, it is easier for the listener to understand the meaning of numbers because graphs often present a number in comparison to other numbers. By putting graphic information into a PowerPoint presentation, the teacher has choices of bright colors and multiple fonts for displaying the information and the ability to copy and make a slight modification on the next graphic display in many ways to call visual attention to a part of the graph. Graphs can be made to illustrate many points and easily located and displayed as needed. In the PowerPoint presentation the teacher has the opportunity to move back and forth among the graphics rapidly as needed or to skip some graphs if they are not needed. Constructed response questions and some of the multiple-choice questions on standardized tests present data to students in graphics and ask students to use the data in answering the questions. Therefore, when a teacher encourages students to perform such tasks in an assignment and to present it to the class or when a teacher presents data and has the students discuss its meaning in class, the teacher is helping to prepare students to respond in accurate ways to the test. Authentic evaluation involves students in carrying out a variety of performances that show their understanding of an idea (Perkins & Blythe, 1994). The technology helps teachers and students to present data to students in multiple forms and to devote class time to its consideration in a more usable way than has been possible in the past. Some software programs such as Timeliner and

➤

➤ Neighborhood Map by Tom Snyder Publications help students to make clear and attractive graphs, timelines, and maps to illustrate their reports.

Performance Assessment. Performance assessments are testing methods in which students demonstrate both knowledge and skills. Formats vary, but in all instances, students construct or perform rather than simply select a response. For example, a performance test occurs when a student is asked to identify cardinal directions in the gym. More elaborate performance tests assess presentations on research projects, including reporting on research findings, proposing solutions to problems, supporting findings with reason and facts, working cooperatively with others, or planning a study. Lesson activities in the expansion phase of the learning cycle often provide opportunities for performance testing. Products of these activities are collected and graded or observed with the help of a checklist and rating scale.

Because many social studies activities cannot be completed without students applying learned skills and knowledge, the successful completion of social studies lessons and projects can serve as a form of evaluation. In addition to the project, students can write a description of the skills and steps used in completing the project or be interviewed about them. Performance assessment may also be a form of authentic assessment if the performance is the type of task that a citizen or an employee would be asked to perform as part of their work, and not just a contrived exercise for classroom use. In using performance assessments, students' performances can be positively influenced in several ways:

1. Selecting assessment tasks clearly aligned or connected to what has been taught
2. Sharing and scoring criteria for the assessment task with students prior to working on the task
3. Providing students with clear statements of standards and/or several models of acceptable performances before they attempt a task
4. Encouraging students to complete self-assessments of their performance
5. Interpreting students' performance by comparing them to developmentally appropriate standards, as well as to other students' performances (Elliot, 1995)

When performance assessment is used in standardized tests, it may be measured by open-ended questions. According to the Harcourt Educational Measurements, publishers of STAT 9, the social sciences and history are perhaps the ideal disciplines in which to use an open-ended assessment. Many questions concerning history and the social sciences have more than one cause, effect, or result. Open-ended questions require students to apply concepts and make inferences at a level beyond that required by the multiple-choice questions. They allow students to bring divergent thinking, relevant information, and different outlooks to their answers.

Rubrics. Assessing and evaluating authentic assignments and tasks requires obtaining information about the many parts of the task and the skills necessary to complete it. Terms such as *tasks, proficiency,* and *scoring criteria* are commonly used when discussing rubrics. Rubrics are used to identify both the content presented and the quality of the performance or presentation of information, skills, and values. Table 14.3

T A B L E   1 4 . 3
Rubrics for Assessing Students' Projects and Related Tasks

Student Assessment Rubric

Student Name

Category	Exemplary 4	Accomplished 3	Developing 2	Beginning 1	Score
Content	A. All unit objectives are mastered B. Topics are covered in depth C. Many pertinent details included D. Went beyond assignment requirements	A. Most unit objectives are mastered B. Topics are covered C. Includes pertinent details	A. Some unit objectives are mastered B. Covers topics in superficial manner C. Few details are included	A. Few unit objectives are mastered B. Topic is not fully covered C. Few or no details	
Inquiry Skills	A. Evidence that all content has been carefully analyzed and evaluated B. Substantial evidence that students sought out and found other relevant sources that have been carefully synthesized C. Students can carefully explain or defend their reasons for choosing sources in their presentation	A. Evidence that content has been evaluated and analyzed, but not effectively synthesized B. Clear evidence that students sought out additional source materials and made a good attempt to integrate them into a coherent statement C. Some attempt to explain why materials were chosen	A. Some evidence that content has been either evaluated or analyzed, but no evidence it has been synthesized B. Some evidence that additional materials have been sought out C. Little evidence that student can explain why materials were chosen	A. Little evidence that the content has been evaluated, analyzed, or synthesized B. No evidence that additional materials were sought C. No evidence that student can explain why materials were chosen	
Technology	A. Used a variety of multimedia effects (images, sounds, video, etc.) B. Used a variety of appropriate sources beyond the *CongressLink* site and employed at least one of the various technologies:	A. Used more than one multimedia effect (images, sounds, video, etc.) B. Used more than one appropriate source beyond the *CongressLink* site and employed at least one of the	A. Used one or no multimedia effects (images, sounds, video, etc.) B. Used one or no appropriate sources external to *CongressLink* and limited their use of technol-	A. Used one or no multimedia effects (images, sounds, video, etc.) B. Used no sources external to *CongressLink* and	

	scanner, other Web sources, digital recording, or digital camera to bring materials together	following technologies: scanner, other Web sources, digital recording, digital camera	ogy to the *CongressLink* website	no other technology
Presentation	A. Presentation is highly organized, thorough and cohesive B. Uses original approach effectively Terms and concepts are fully clarified for the audience C. Sources used greatly enhanced understanding of the topic D. Presentation of appropriate length E. Used multiple appropriate sources external to *CongressLink*	A. Presentation is organized, thorough and cohesive B. Used original approach C. Terms and concepts are clarified for the audience D. Sources used enhanced understanding of the topic E. Presentation is of appropriate length. Used some appropriate sources external to *CongressLink*	A. Presentation needs work with its organization thoroughness and cohesiveness B. All terms and concepts are not clarified for the audience C. Some sources enhanced understanding of the topic D. Presentation is almost of appropriate length	A. Presentation is not organized thorough or cohesive B. Terms and concepts are not clarified for the audience C. Few sources enhanced understanding of the topic D. Presentation is of an inappropriate length
Teamwork	A. Consistently demonstrated vital leadership B. Consistently on-task throughout the unit C. Maintained positive attitude throughout the unit D. Played a critical role in organizing and facilitating group learning E. Met all due dates	A. Frequently demonstrated leadership B. Regularly on-task throughout the unit C. Maintained positive attitude throughout the unit D. Played a role in organizing and facilitating group learning E. Met all due dates	A. Regularly contributed to group effort B. Usually on-task throughout the unit C. Generally had a positive attitude D. Played a limited role in facilitating group learning E. Met most due dates	A. Sometimes contributed to the group effort B. Rarely on-task C. Not always a positive attitude D. Played a very limited role in facilitating group learning E. Frequently missed due dates

Source: From CongressLink (www.congresslink.org), a service of the Dirksen Congressional Center, Perkins, IL.

contains rubrics for projects intended to assess the variety of tasks a student needs to perform in preparing for and presenting a project. Students usually vary in their knowledge of, and ability to do, the various tasks required to complete a performance assessment. Therefore, the use of rubrics identifies individual strengths and weaknesses so that students may set specific and individual goals for their learning efforts.

Students can be encouraged to participate in developing rubrics by asking several questions: What must be included in the answer for it to be complete? How important is it to make sure everyone has a chance to participate in their group's work? How will we know if the project is complete? Students can suggest a list of criteria that would be appropriate to include. The teacher adds to the list his or her expectations or asks a probing question, such as "We have learned how to write paragraphs, and our project includes writing, so do you think we should expect the answer to be written in complete paragraphs?" Alternatively, the teacher might suggest that because the class has learned that examples help to make ideas clear, the teacher expects students to include examples in their explanations. The teacher and students might discuss this idea and, together, agree on a minimum number of examples to include.

Students like to use rubrics because they help them see what is a complete report or project. However, complete projects are not all equal, and some work might not meet acceptable standards. Setting standards against which to evaluate work as acceptable, of high quality, or in need of improvement presents an additional set of problems. To be fair in evaluation, students need to know the rubrics or criteria before they begin their work. As they work, they use the rubrics to help them assess their progress and evaluate the quality of their work. Students help each other evaluate their work by applying the rubric and asking questions for clarification.

Often, teachers are not familiar with all that the students have learned and do not know what criteria to set until they have had experience reviewing the work of many and varied students. Rubrics and their scoring criteria are often developed over several years. At first, rubrics may resemble lists of criteria or tasks students perform. Many teachers start with general guidelines for evaluation, such as noting that grammar is acceptable, especially good, or needs improvement. After several years, the scoring criteria may be spelled out in detail, including the specific number of examples or types of examples to be provided and the types of reasoning strategies used for work of varying quality. Recommended scoring techniques call for using a checklist approach, narrative/anecdotal recording, or rating-scale approach (Brualdi, 1998).

For rubrics to be successful once the scoring criteria are established and distributed to them, students must be able to trust that fulfilling them as stated results in the grade indicated. Should a teacher find that one or more papers go well beyond the stated scoring criteria, the teacher cannot change the grading standard and award to these papers the best grades while lowering the grades of all who met the highest score (Nickell, 1999). Should this happen, Nickell recommends that students whose papers are exceptional also receive the top grade plus written comments from the teacher. These additional comments note the outstanding characteristics of the assignment and compliment the student's efforts. Other students who have accomplished the criteria for the top grade also receive that grade. Should many exceptional products be produced, scoring criteria might be modified in the future for this assignment. Table 14.4 is an adaptation of one of the sample social studies performance tasks and rubrics distributed to Wisconsin teachers as part of the Wisconsin Student Assessment System (WSAS) materials. It illustrates the alignment between the content standards, performance standards, task objective, and rubrics suggested as appropriate for use with students in grades 4 or 5.

The federal government is providing some leadership in the use of authentic assessments that incorporate rubrics for scoring. The most recent testing by the National Assessment of Educational Progress (NAEP) in history (1994), geography

---

TABLE 14.4

Social Studies Performance Task and Rubric for Comparing Advertisements Grade Level 4/5

Related Content Standard	Students will learn about production, distribution, and consumption in making informed economic choices
Performance Standard	Students will give examples that show how scarcity and choice govern our economic decisions.

Objectives	1. Given three examples of newspaper or magazine advertisements with the prices removed, students will write two paragraphs or complete sentences that
	   a. Identify similarities and differences between advertising claims
	   b. Conclude whether these claims are describing meaningful differences
	   c. Predict which products might be the most expensive, less expensive, least expensive, and give the reason for their decision

Rubrics	4. High Proficiency
	   Highly organized, shows creative thinking
	   Demonstrates a thorough understanding of basic content and concepts
	   Sentences are complete without flaw, and mechanics are without error
	3. Proficiency
	   Organization is logical—gets the point across
	   Demonstrates an adequate understanding of basic content and concepts—minor errors do not detract from overall response
	   Sentences are complete and mechanics are of quality
	2. Partially Proficient
	   Presentation is ordered in an acceptable manner
	   Demonstrates a marginal understanding of basic content and concepts—major errors of fact are present
	   Sentences are of inconsistent quality; errors in mechanics are visible
	1. Minimal Response
	   Poorly planned and disorganized
	   Demonstrates little understanding of basic content and concepts
	   Sentences are fragmented and mechanics are full of errors

(1994), and civics (1998) included some short-answer questions scored with rubrics. Many of these questions are published at the NAEP website and in copies that can be ordered free at the National Assessment of Educational Progress website (see the link at the companion website). These publications report the success students have with each question given, provide the scoring rubrics, and illustrate each level with student sample responses. Figures 14.3 and 14.4 provide samples from the NAEP tests and illustrate a range of types of questions they have begun to ask. As you study these figures, take note of those questions for which a partial score is awarded and notice the rubrics suggested.

U.S. Department of Education statistics concerning how many students correctly complete each NAEP question and analysis of the test using group comparisons stimulate questions about social studies curricula. Whereas politicians might focus on

---

After we anchored our ship in the ocean and went ashore to explore, we marched west. The forest was so thick we could only travel three miles in the first two days. Then we came to the mountains and climbed to the top. A rushing river flowed west out of the mountains. We continued to march two miles west and came down out of the mountains. Two miles further we came to the coast. It was obvious that the area we were exploring was an isthmus.

In the box below, draw a map of the region described above. Be sure to include all of the geographical elements mentioned in the description. Include a scale to indicate distance.

An **Essential** response includes a map in which three elements are correctly placed. The response may be a peninsula or an island.

A **Partial** response includes a map in which at least two elements are correctly placed.

F I G U R E   1 4 . 3   Portion of 1994 NAEP Test in Geography for Eighth-Graders

Source: Learning about Our World and Our Past: Using the Tools and Resources of Geography and U.S. History: A Report of the 1994 NAEP Assessment, by E. Hawkins, F. Stancavage, J. Mitchell, M. Goodman & S. Lazer, 1998, Washington, DC: National Center for Educational Statistics.

Scott wants to be a police officer when he grows up. He says the police get to wear uniforms with badges, use handcuffs, and drive cars as fast as they want.

What is wrong with Scott's ideas about why he wants to be a police officer?

<u>He thinks he gets to be big and powerful because he gets to brake [sic] the rules of others.</u>

Think about the things police officers do in their work. What are two good reasons to be a police officer?

1. <u>You discipline people so they can learn from their mistakes.</u>
2. <u>Make peace between people that are fighting and fix the problem.</u>

These constructed-response questions are designed to measure fourth-grade students' ability to make distinctions between power and authority. The response received a score of 3, or acceptable, on a 4-point scale in which a score of 4 was considered complete and a score of 1 was considered unacceptable. The first part of the responses did not receive credit because its meaning was unclear. However, both reasons for being a police officer were credited. Overall, 67 percent of fourth-graders wrote an acceptable answer.

F I G U R E   1 4 . 4   Completed Portion of 1998 NAEP Test in Civics for Fourth-Graders

Source: The NAEP 1998 Civics Report Card for the Nation (NCES 2000-457), A. D. Lutkus, A. R. Weiss, J. D. Campbell, J. Mazzeo, & S. Lazer (1999, p. 25), Washington, DC: U.S. Department of Education, National Center of Educational Statistics.

how well students in various groups (regional, racial, or ethnic) score, educators ask what results reveal concerning knowledge and skills being taught in the curriculum at various grade levels. Teachers make an effort to prepare students to do well on tests. When authentic tasks and thinking skills are included on tests, teachers provide practice with lessons and modify their own assessments to reflect the state or national test given. However, because of time constraints, many state and national tests still include a greater portion of questions that ask students to recognize the best answer suggested by the test writer, rather than to construct their own answer. NAEP has always provided much information free to the public, but the Internet makes it possible for more teachers and the public to examine the results of each test. In addition, people can submit requests and qualify to access additional information on tests given by the government for research purposes.

In recent years, states have placed great emphasis on revising the learning standards and establishing benchmarks of learning for the more broadly stated standards. States are administrating standardized tests to measure their success in meeting these benchmarks. The tests incorporate new types of questions to measure higher levels of learning and the multiple skills students must use to complete the questions at satisfactory and proficient levels.

Using documents in the teaching of social studies is a standard procedure, but students have not been formally tested on their abilities to use documents to form conclusions, make decisions, and solve problems. Document-based questions (DBQs) are appearing in larger numbers in social studies tests for elementary, middle, and high school students. Students are given several documents of various types (e.g., diary, cartoon, picture, legal papers, newspaper clippings, advertisements, or sections of government documents ranging from speeches to laws and the Declaration of Independence) that provide information on a social studies topic. The tests present a selected response question for each document and then present an essay question on the topic. Students are required to write an essay of several paragraphs in which they examine the documents' positions, explain relationships between the documents, and explain the importance of the topic to the social studies topic. Students are expected to relate the content of these documents to other information they know about the topic and to state a conclusion or position.

The value of standardized testing is in its ability to provide educators with information that helps to improve instruction for the students in the classrooms. Teachers in the Greece, New York, Central School District provide a model for use of data from standardized tests. They examined the scores of their students on DBQs across the grade levels, noting common accomplishments and where students failed to receive credit on their essays. They made inferences about student behaviors and knowledge when using the documents and writing the test essays. Next they interviewed students to learn whether their inferences were correct. The teachers noticed that the students did not write complete answers to the questions, writing well on one point and neglecting to provide the multiple examples and reasons asked for by the questions. Middle school students tended not to apply the rubrics given for the correct answers. Students told the teacher that they were confused about how to proceed with writing the essay because each year their teachers taught different approaches to writing essays. The teachers developed a common approach that focused on the claim, the evidence for the claim, and an interpretation of the meaning or importance of the claim. Teachers used this approach with a graphic organizer to writing essays using documents. They developed or located documents and used a DBQ essay writing assignment three times per year on topics selected by individual teachers in their own classrooms. They developed and used a generic rubric and had the students also apply the rubric by helping to evaluate their essays. As a result, student performance on the DBQ portion of the state tests inproved. For more information on DBQs and rubrics for grading them, consult one or more of the recommended websites for this chapter or the companion website for this book.

COMPANION
WEBSITE

NAEP tests a sample of students every four years in a particular content area. It also asks students and teachers to self-report selected behaviors that might help explain student scores. By law, NAEP is not allowed to ask questions that measure attitudes and predispositions for action. Therefore, neither the NAEP nor state tests can provide a complete measure of all social studies goals and objectives. Many questions remain for teachers and researchers to ask beyond those raised by standardized test results. Some argue that the best or most effective research is done by individual teachers in their own classrooms. Their rationale is that the individual teacher is most likely to use this information in a timely manner to bring about changes in classroom practices and curriculum for students.

An Interview with Mark High about How He Uses Assessments to Help Improve Instruction

Interviewer: Mark, when I read your comments on using mock trials on the NCSS mailing lists, I was delighted to read that you teach seventh grade and are willing to share your experiences. Please describe your school and community.

Mark High: Gunnison is a small town in the tourist area of Colorado. The population is largely homogenous and of European ancestry. A small number of students are of Hispanic origin. In Colorado, there is local curriculum selection, and we selected to model our social studies curriculum on the California curriculum. Sixth-graders study ancient civilizations, and seventh-graders focus on world history from the fall of Rome through the Renaissance and Age of Discovery. My curriculum revolves around four major research units. My librarian, Fran Carricato, and I team teach the Crusades unit, the Renaissance Unit, the Columbus Trial, and the Mongol Trial.

Interviewer: That accounts for your studying Columbus, but how did you become interested in putting him on trial?

Mark High: Back around 1991, I was reading a lot about the controversies concerning the 500th anniversary of the voyage of Columbus. In a National Geographic Awareness Week packet was the suggestion of trying Columbus for crimes against humanity. So I thought I'd do it but really didn't have a clue and fell flat on my face. A local lawyer whom I'd asked to serve as the judge told me that I had seen too many law programs on TV and to come in and let him help me. From that experience, I wrote trial procedure sheets that I give to the students when we start the unit to guide our study and their actions during the trial.

Interviewer: I noticed that you set out the procedures of the mock trial simulation in detail. Is the emphasis of the study on the legal procedures?

Mark High: No, I also stress the reading and thinking skills and the presentation of positions during the trial. I use the legal procedures and definitions to help construct the assignments and make them more authentic. For the mock trials, Fran and I cooperate in teaching the students, and we spend about three weeks with the students preparing for the trial. This has proven a wonderful experience, and students receive more individual help. After the trial, we carefully evaluate the trial with comments from all participants and experiment with new ideas for improvement each year. This year, we began to use Internet resources, which required students to learn to access information and evaluate the quality of sites before using the information to create the case.

Interviewer: How long is the actual trial?

Mark High: We travel to the district court to perform the Columbus trial, and we have only about 80 minutes to complete the travel and the trial. Being in the actual court helps the students to present their work in a serious manner. Going to the courtroom was a suggestion from one of the students. We were lucky to find that the judge traveled to another part of the district for several weeks at the right time of the year.

Interviewer: I'm amazed that you can complete the trial in only about 60 minutes.

Mark High: I emphasize preparing ahead of time and thinking on your feet to fix things or rehabilitate the testimony of a witness during the trial. One change from the legal process

I use is if the jury cannot reach an agreement within a reasonable time, I have them vote and accept the majority vote. The lawyers who act as judges don't particularly like this modification, but class time is limited.

Interviewer: Mock trials require lots of time and energy from the teacher. What do you particularly like about using the trials?

Mark High: Mock trials are inherently motivating for students. Students know the rubrics from the beginning and that I give 5 to 10 extra points to the winning side. Students' egos are on the line, and teams compete to win.

Interviewer: How do you assess the unit?

Mark High: When going to the court, I have never had a student behavior problem. Parents and other community members will stop me in the store and inquire as to how the mock trial went this year. One of the roles some students have is to be a reporter. Some of their written assignments have been published in the local paper. It is more difficult to make concrete rubrics for grading the mock trials than for some of the other assignments and units, and we are still working on clarifying the rubrics. About 80 percent of the grade comes from the different tasks in the research process and 20 percent on their presentation when they must remain in character. We videotape the trial, and it circulates throughout the rest of the year as students check it out and take it home to share with their parents. I also use the tapes as I help prepare next year's students for their trial. Another measure of success is the increase in the students' abilities to construct their arguments and responses for the second trial.

Interviewer: Speaking of the second trial, how did you come to the decision to try Genghis Khan?

Mark High: A number of reasons prompted the use of a second trial. Over the years, I discovered that whatever unit I used at the end of the year was not as successful as I wanted it to be. I attributed this to the time of the year. Additionally, the lawyers told me that criminal trials are a small portion of the cases brought to the courts and encouraged me to use a civil case because it is more representative of the legal system. We also wanted to make the historical content for the year focus on more than just traditional Western European history. The Mongols help to focus on elements of Russian and Asian history. In our trial, Genghis Khan, who represents all Mongols, is tried for outrageous conduct as defined by Colorado's law.

Interviewer: What words of advice do you have to offer others who want to start using mock trials with middle school students?

Mark High: Get help. Search the Internet under the term *law-related education.* This will narrow the search and provide you with state bar associations and national organizations for resources. Ask local attorneys to act as the judges. Use the facilities of the courthouse for the trial if at all possible.

Prepare the students for their roles. My partner and I select the attorneys based on class work and responses to activities during the first couple of days of the unit. Have students work cooperatively in preparing for the trial on specific assignments: writing the questions and answers they might need during the trial and deciding what to include in the opening and closing statements. Begin by learning important courtroom proceedings that attorneys, members of the jury, and court reporters need to know. For example, the prosecution must deliver the indictment and list of evidence to the defense. The rules of evidence require using relevant evidence, presenting the best evidence, and avoiding hearsay evidence. The types of questions that are legal to ask and the meaning of leading a witness need to be clear in the minds of the students.

During the mock trial, the teacher should concentrate on grading the student performance and allow the students to determine what they say and how to respond to the rulings of the judge.

Interviewer: All this is great advice. I can clearly see that you are teaching legal procedures and critical thinking, but how do you work in the history of the times which you said is the major focus for the curriculum?

Mark High: Well, the charges and evidence must be historically accurate, and the punishment and judgments must be within the possibilities of the times. Likewise, the witnesses' responses must be historically appropriate. I give students credit for staying in character and responding with historically accurate, or possible, replies.

Interviewer: Mark, this almost sounds too good to be true. You must encounter some problems. What are these likely to be?

Mark High: Remember that I have been doing this for a number of years, and we have identified problems over the years and rewritten procedures and assignments to help solve them. Actually, the students' interest and enthusiasm for the unit remove lots of the potential problems. Students being absent on the day of the trial is the biggest concern. If a witness is absent, I tell the attorney that sometimes a witness does not show for a trial and to deal with the problem as best they can. However, should one of the attorneys be absent, we would be in big trouble, so we have two attorneys for each side and have them work and plan together.

Interviewer: Mark, what you are doing is most impressive and shows you possess well-developed skills in planning and reflecting on your teaching. Your objectives, procedures, and assessments are carefully matched and reflect worthy and important knowledge, skill, and attitudes for students to learn. Thank you for being so willing to share your efforts with others.

Mark High: Thanks! The success of this unit is a direct result of my collaboration with Fran. I strongly encourage teachers, especially middle school teachers, to plan and to teach with other professionals. Fran has been instrumental in the success of our units. Through our joint planning and evaluations of the units, we have learned together and grown professionally.

TIME FOR REFLECTION: WHAT DO YOU THINK?

1. What resources does Mark use to ensure that his students learn about the various periods of history through the mock trials? _____

_____

_____

_____

➤

➤ 2. What student behaviors and outcomes could Mark use during the second mock trial (Mongols) to assess for student learning of important social studies skills and attitudes during the first trial and throughout the year? _____
_____
_____
_____

3. What do you think is the rationale for including the role of court reporter for some students? _____
_____
_____
_____

4. How do Mark and Fran assess the students during the precourtroom session?
_____
_____
_____
_____

5. What areas of social studies learning are addressed in this activity and therefore are in need of assessment? _____
_____
_____
_____

6. What evidence appears in the interview that assessment is included for more than learning content? _____
_____
_____
_____

7. *Teaming* is a characteristic advocated by many for middle school teaching and learning experiences. In what ways does Mark use teaming in the mock trial?
_____
_____
_____
_____

8. What evidence do you see that the data from the assessments have been evaluated and applied to make changes in the unit? _____
_____
_____
_____
_____

In your class work and field experiences, you have undoubtedly heard the term *action research.* Mark and Fran have done action research on the mock trials to improve their teaching and students' potential learning. They provide a model of its proper use. More is said about the role of action research as a form of teacher assessment and how it is linked to planning and instructional improvement later in this chapter.

➤ **BUILDING ON DIVERSITY**

Promoting Individual Needs

The law requires that some students with special needs have individual learning plans. Often these recommend specific ways to change learning activities and identify modifications needed in testing conditions. For those with special needs, the teacher aligns assessment strategies with changes in learning goals and changes in the duration or physical conditions of lessons in which students are taught.

When multiple types of assessments are used and teachers and students work together to assess and evaluate learning progress, one result is that many more students receive help in establishing their own individual short- and long-term learning goals. Students with attention disorders may find alternative assessments provide them with a more accurate assessment of what they can do than do traditional tests for several reasons: (1) Alternative assessments do not necessarily require students to sit quietly for extended periods of time. (2) Alternative assessments actively involve students in learning activities. (3) Alternative assessments tolerate constructive noise.

Teachers can make specific arrangements to address individual needs:

1. Provide additional time to complete assessments to address problems of anxiety, attention span, language, vision, and reading difficulties.
2. Provide recorded directions or readings of test questions students can listen to using headphones.
3. Provide the opportunity for students to dictate their answers into tape recorders.
4. Use pictures and graphics to illustrate directions and questions for those with reading difficulties or second-language learners; encourage students to express answers with combinations of graphic representation and words.
5. Post written directions and schedules for assignments so that students can refer to them for additional assistance as they work.
6. When students are asked to present materials orally for authentic assessments, allow them to make presentations on audiotapes or videotapes so that they can stop, start, and redo.
7. Establish a quiet work area in the room away from sound and visual distractions.
8. Cooperate with special education teachers who work with inclusion students or with aides for those with special physical needs.

Gifted students have special needs. They may be gifted in one or more ways. Often, they are very creative in their thoughts and presentations of what they know and learn. Not being forced into thinking and performing like everyone else is important in supporting these students. During assessments and evaluation, it is important to look at and listen carefully to the entire message a gifted person presents in his or her works, giving recognition to novel perspectives and encouragement for future independent efforts. When teachers conference with family members, they should support the use of special mentors who have talent in the same areas as the gifted student. Conversations with such a mentor are a way of learning how to better encourage a gifted student and to help that student work cooperatively with all classmates.

MODES OF ASSESSMENT

Assessment systems are evaluated to determine whether they provide teachers, students, and parents the kinds of information needed to foster meaningful social studies learning. Only then can results be used to make decisions about what is and is not working. Teachers work to ensure that both their informal and formal assessments consider each student at some point in a lesson. Procedures such as regular student–teacher conferences, teacher–parent conferences, student–teacher–parent conferences, and team meetings have been instituted in many schools to share information about students and plan for future learning. Such sharing is more productive when teachers increase their use of the following assessments.

Checklists.   Checklists identify desired student behaviors for lessons throughout the day. They provide a running record of the teacher's perceptions of students' participation and accomplishment. Table 14.5 illustrates such a checklist.

Individual Portfolios.   Individual portfolios are samples of student work illustrating what students are correctly able to do. Students select and organize best examples of work to illustrate clear progress over time. They present their portfolios to the teacher and family members. A portfolio contains a variety of products to demonstrate the range of knowledge and skills the student is developing. Periodically students remove and replace materials in their portfolio, or they begin a new section within it.

Teachers of younger students begin incorporating this form of assessment and evaluation by providing students with opportunities to select products from some of the

A student's drawing can
be part of a portfolio.

T A B L E   1 4 . 5

Sample Economics Education Checklist for the Student

Topic: Wants and Needs

	Activity	Glenn	Sue
Needs	1. Identifies food as a need	X	X
	2. Identifies shelter as a need	X	X
Wants	1. Identifies a television as a want	X	
	2. Identifies a computer as a want	X	X
	3. Identifies roller blades as a want	X	
	4. Prioritizes wants	X	X
	5. Develops a timeline for obtaining the item prioritized as #1 on the want list		X

assignments to be included in the portfolio. Or teachers provide young students with a list of required types of assignments to be included. Some schools save yearly portfolios throughout students' schooling and present it to them on their graduation.

Interviews. Interviews enable teachers to talk with students in some depth about their ideas and plans. Table 14.6 illustrates questions a teacher might ask students in an interview to help them organize their thoughts while informing the teacher of their progress on an individual research topic on the Hausa people of West Africa. A key

T A B L E   1 4 . 6

Interview Guide on Hausa Culture

The interviewer introduces the student to what will follow.

Interviewer: We have been exploring Hausa culture in West Africa. Because everybody has been following up different parts of Hausa culture, I wanted to talk to you about what you have found out.

1. What part of the culture did you decide to explore?
2. Can you tell me what you think is the most interesting thing you have found out?
3. Do you think this is really important for everyone to know, or is it something that is interesting but not something everyone should know? Why?
4. What are three things you have found out that you should share with everyone in this class because you think everyone should know them? Why?
5. If we think about these three important things, do you think we will decide that they are not very different from what we have here in our culture, or will we decide that they are really different? Why?

set of questions for each interview is preplanned. Additional questions probe students' ideas as the interview progresses. A record is kept of the types of responses students make and of any agreed-on goals identified as a result of the interview. All students in the class participate in interviews and are able to tell the teacher anything they want.

Classroom Websites. Assessment should involve not only the teacher and student but also the parents. Family members can be asked to share comments with their child on assignments and topics. By filling out short questionnaires or reports for the teacher on their child's learning and homework, parents help the teacher to gain a better understanding of their child's interests, abilities, and needs. Parents should be encouraged to share such reports with their children and to offer encouragement and praise for studying and learning in school. Students can contribute to positive benefits from assessment by assisting in making class newspapers or websites designed to inform parents or to provide information on class activities. Even the very young students can help select pictures that illustrate their school day and projects to put on a website and encourage their parents to visit a class website where the teacher may also post information and suggestions on ways parents might support student learning on current topics of study. In posting pictures from a field trip, the teacher provides parents and students with a prompt for questions and discussion. Posting of student artwork and writings concerning class activities shows parents a range of the class activities and skills in the class. Class websites usually provide an email address so that parents can easily communicate with the teacher. Formal parent conferences have replaced written report cards in many school systems, but these, while very helpful, are infrequent. The computer provides another opportunity for busy parents and teachers to communicate more often and for the continuous assessment of a student's learning. Websites may include daily assignments to aid family members in discussing or supervising homework. They also provide opportunities to download assignments for students who must miss class.

Journals. Journals are diaries or logs in which students reflect on their school experiences. They are especially helpful when students have individualized assignments. Journals encourage the use of writing as a learning process and as individual communication with the teacher.

Quality Circles. Quality circles are class or small-group evaluation sessions. They may be teacher led or guided with a questionnaire or rubric, or students might write and share a report similar to a journal entry. Table 14.2 suggests questions that might guide a group quality-circle discussion.

Self-Evaluation Reports. Self-evaluation reports are filled out by each student concerning his role in a group. They give the student the opportunity to reflect on personal contributions to the group and how he could better benefit from group efforts. The lower section of Table 14.2 suggests questions for a self-evaluation.

ACTION RESEARCH CLASSROOM ASSESSMENT FOR REFORM

Becoming an effective planner of a social studies program requires self-direction. Teachers need to know what really is happening in their classroom and not focus on what a few students' reactions tell them. Teachers assess what is going on and evaluate what they find. Then they make changes to improve a lesson or strategy. They try out the changes and record data on what happens. This data is analyzed, and a decision is made on whether the change has accomplished what was intended or whether further revision and trial is needed. Teachers do much of this intuitively as they work. However, they might miss important variables or incorrectly interpret some results. Action research is a way of taking what teachers often intuitively do and organizing it clearly so that the problem, the possible solution, and the results of trying the solution are clear.

Action research begins with a focus question or problem that narrows attention to one key factor for which information might be obtained. For example, one teacher set up several learning centers in her classroom, and it seemed to her that students did not use some centers as much as others. She decided to find out first which were most used. Then she would try to find out why some were used more than others. Her first action research project involved using a checklist of the centers. She counted the students using each center at five-minute intervals during center time on Monday, Wednesday, and Friday of one week. After totaling student usage, she found that it was similar on each day, with one center visited by no more than three students each day. This center had the lowest turnout. Now she had to undertake a follow-up action research project to find out whether she could make changes in the center that would attract students to it.

Action research provides the teacher researcher with a deeper understanding of the factors related to the problem being examined and leads to more powerful social studies learning outcomes in students. Of course, what works with one group of students and one teacher might not work equally well or at all in other settings. However, the focus of teacher action research is on increasing the quality of education within a specific classroom. Knowing more about the classroom situation, the teacher uses this information and experience to help make better decisions when planning for future learning experiences. Further information and help in carrying out practitioner research in daily classroom routine can be found by searching the Internet using terms such as *practitioner research* and *action research*. Some links to useful sites can be found at the companion website.

CW

COMPANION
WEBSITE

SUMMARY

Each student is special, and all students deserve complete assessments and fair evaluations. Each student must be treated first as a student, and evaluated in terms of similar needs to learn, grow, and develop into a productive citizen respectful of himself or herself and of others. Assessment and evaluation are positive processes involving the learner and helping teachers structure learning environments. Their goal is to meet the students' needs to reach the goals of the social studies program.

For proper evaluation, assessment begins with learning what the students know and do not know. It continues throughout the lesson, guiding the instructional process until students attain their unique degree of success in understanding the social world in which they live and act. Teachers take the time to learn about the students they teach and work with others to improve student success. They realize that students' physical, emotional, and cultural needs must be addressed to help them get the most they can from school and to be measured fairly and recognized for their accomplishments. Most often, teachers who use a range of assessment and evaluation strategies, coupled with rubrics that spell out required levels of expectations, find that they are able to evaluate their students appropriately.

Expanding ON THIS CHAPTER

Activity

COMPANION
WEBSITE

Everyone says to preassess your students' knowledge, but few teachers make an organized effort to do so. Try this method to help you plan a lesson. Show several pictures from a historical event or era that you plan to teach about individually to elementary or middle school students, and ask each student to tell you about the picture. Listen carefully to their comments. Ask a probing question only if it is needed to get a student to respond. Write a reflection on the experience, reviewing the characteristics of the students and their responses, both what they saw and told you and what they did not mention that you thought they would. Explain what the students' comments revealed to you about the place and time period, their sources of information, the accuracy of their knowledge, and their interest in the event and its people. Identify some of the implications this has for the classroom teacher. Tell how this preassessment of student knowledge helps you to prepare lessons that will be meaningful to the students and teach important social studies content.

Recommended Websites to Visit

COMPANION
WEBSITE

Website of the National Assessment of Educational Progress is the nation's report card
    http://nces.ed.gov/nationsreportcard/

View sample questions from the Louisiana test (PASS)
    www.louisianaschools.net/conn/assessments.php

Exemplary rubrics for assessing research skills
    www.fno.org/libskill.html

Help your students become good writers and publish on the Web
    www.education-world.com/a_tech/tech042.shtml

Rubric Generator allows you to use prepared or customized rubrics
    www.teach-nology.com/web_tools/rubrics/

Examine a sample document-based question for the primary grades
    http://comsewogue.k12.ny.us/~ssilverman/documents/example.htm

A draft test sampler of questions for New York social studies tests for elementary and intermediate grades
    www.emsc.nysed.gov/osa/samplerelint/elintsampsocst.html

Sources of primary documents and document-based questions prepared by Paula Goldstein
    www.kn.pacbell.com/wired/fil/pages/listdocumentpa.html#cat2

Planning Units
of Various Lengths
and Formats

INTRODUCTION

In examining the course of study from a local school system, you find that change and continuity is listed as a social studies unit topic in first grade and again in seventh grade.

1. On what three key ideas involving change and continuity might you focus the unit for first-graders? _____
   _____

2. On what three key ideas might you focus the unit for seventh-graders? _____
   _____

CHAPTER OVERVIEW

We receive many bits and pieces of information every day in isolation, ignore most of them, and choose to store just a few in our minds for future use. Lessons are organized to encourage students to link ideas and experiences. These linkages result in meaningful learning that deepens understanding. Effective teaching is organized around key concepts, generalizations, values, and inquiry skills. It seeks to help learners link their ideas and is best done in units of study. Social studies units can be focused on a social studies topic, several social studies standards, or can integrate several subjects. The *unit* is a set of interconnected, related lesson plans that introduce and explore, fully develop, and expand understanding of a topic. Related values and skills necessary for processing and communicating information about the topic are part of the unit. There are basic steps helpful in planning a unit. The unit-planning process is a critical professional skill because key ideas are interrelated with each other and with students' prior experiences.

Most social studies units are integrated. Social studies itself is an integrated subject. It organizes knowledge around themes that interconnect the social sciences, humanities, natural sciences, and technology. Some of the themes clearly indicate the integration of knowledge, such as Science, Technology, and Society and Global Connections (National Council for the Social Studies, 1994b). Indeed, some of the most meaningful social studies units involve several school subjects in an integrated unit approach (Sunal et al., 2000). This approach involves using a theme to interconnect significant and relevant knowledge from various disciplines in a coherent manner (Martin-Kniep & Soodak, 1995). Developing integrated units is complex because the topic of the unit is dealt with from a number of viewpoints. The range of viewpoints found in such a unit provides depth of study on a topic and makes it possible to address the needs of diverse students. Integrated unit teaching is known by a variety of names, including interdisciplinary teaching, thematic teaching, and multidisciplinary teaching.

National and state standards promote an interdisciplinary and integrated development of knowledge (National Council for the Social Studies, 1994b). The rationale for an approach that integrates knowledge from several disciplines is articulated by many professional organizations. For example, the American Association for the Advancement of Science stated: "To ensure the scientific literacy of all students, curricula must be changed to reduce the sheer amount of material covered; to weaken or eliminate rigid subject-matter boundaries; to pay more attention to the connections" (1993b, p. 104). Language arts specialists encourage elementary teachers to involve their students in writing and reading activities that are integrated with their subject matter studies. In the mathematics standards, mathematics is "process" involved with themes in all subject areas (National Council of Teachers of Mathematics, 1989). Integration is an increasingly important goal for education.

Units are the best means of involving students in powerful social studies and accomplishing the standards. The construction of a unit requires teachers to make many decisions: What steps are needed for planning a social studies unit that helps students develop meaningful learning about the social world? What does it mean for an elementary or middle school teacher to integrate social studies with other subject areas? Why is integration important in planning meaningful learning for students? What kinds of integrated teaching develop meaningful learning in students? What is the place of social studies in an integrated social studies unit? What conceptual organizers and organizational patterns are useful as evaluation criteria in the development of social studies units? This chapter discusses the process of unit planning and development and presents examples and guidelines for carrying out that process.

CHAPTER OBJECTIVES

1. Explain the importance of significance, relevance, and coherence as evaluation criteria for developing social studies units.
2. Differentiate between various types of units built on social studies topics.
3. Identify the strengths and weaknesses of each type of unit.

4. Describe unique problems in planning and teaching an integrated, interdisciplinary unit that are not found with units focusing only on social studies topics.
5. Identify systematic procedures for determining appropriate topics for social studies units.
6. Describe general steps in planning all types of social studies units.
7. Construct unit focus questions and link them to appropriate school subjects and content standards.
8. Analyze sample unit web diagrams.
9. Construct a web diagram illustrating relationships between focus questions, school subjects, and the information to be learned in a unit on a social studies topic.

PLANNING THE APPROPRIATE FOCUS FOR SOCIAL STUDIES UNITS

CW
COMPANION
WEBSITE

Planning units can involve a single teacher, a teacher pair, a group of teachers, various subject area teachers, a whole school, or several schools through use of email, discussion boards, and the Internet. When more than one person plans a unit, all participants respect the diversity of the planning staff, compromising and cooperating. This applies to both content issues and the use of a teacher's time for planning and instruction. Planning social studies units involves focusing on key ideas, addressing students' needs, selecting appropriate instructional strategies, and using relevant assessments. Many teachers do year-long planning for social studies. Extensive help on how to do year-long planning along with examples of such plans is found on the companion website.

Significance, coherence, and relevance are three evaluation criteria useful when constructing social studies units. *Significance* means that the content taught must be important to the discipline and to the student's need for powerful social studies. The unit and its activities focus on the nature of social studies knowledge, skills, and values. Interdisciplinary interactions connect unit ideas with prior knowledge and facilitate transfer to a wider set of experiences (American Association for the Advancement of Science, 1994). Less is more in the unit. Only the most critical concepts related to a topic are selected for the unit, and they are taught in depth (National Council for the Social Studies, 1994b).

NCSS

Coherence means that the investigative nature of social studies cuts across all parts of the unit and across the curriculum. Students receive direct experience with the inquiry skills and actions typical of work in the disciplines contributing to social studies. To ensure coherence, units stress acquiring and practicing inquiry skills, conceptual understanding, applications, and transfer of social studies knowledge to the student's own social world along with its attitudes, value agreements, and conflicts.

Relevance means that social studies content, activities, and breadth of experiences reflect students' current life, future goals, and aspirations. Social studies content and skills have an impact on students' decisions and their quality of life. Selecting a focus for a unit involves determining the guiding *goals* of the unit. The focus of the unit goals is determined by the social studies content, inquiry skills, amount of integration with other subjects, and the amount of time available for the study. The developmental level of the students and their experiences in life and with formal school social studies instruction are also variables teachers consider when determining the focus of a unit.

Some units focus on describing an event or idea from history or from the social sciences, such as community development, transportation, the voting process, or immigration. Other units focus on learning a skill used in organizing or processing social studies information, such as using a grid system to locate places on a map. Still other units focus on attitudes or values people in our nation believe to be important or in need of reconsideration, such as treating everyone equally and justly or recycling trash to conserve resources. Longer units that study themes, such as interdependence, or an issue, such as how to reduce drug use among young people, place more emphasis on learning content, attitudes, values, and skills. Each focus has its strengths and weaknesses. Each focus can be used in a thematic, integrated, and interdisciplinary unit or in a unit whose content is drawn only from the social studies. Table 15.1 provides an overview of the characteristic focus of each type of unit found in the social studies curriculum.

Descriptive-Focused Units

The traditional organization of social studies curriculum and that found in most textbooks has a *descriptive focus* emphasizing students' acquisition of knowledge. The content topics frequently spiral through the K–12 curriculum. Topics are introduced in the early grades and repeated at various points in higher grade levels. Each time they are repeated, more abstract and complex new information is introduced. When these topics are well taught, students gradually build an in-depth understanding of the topic. However, previous teachers might not have taught the topic, or they might have taught it with a factual emphasis neglecting conceptual development. As a result, students are unprepared for the more advanced investigation of the topic they find at a higher grade level.

With a content emphasis, descriptive units may provide a clear view of a topic such as colonization but do not make clear connections with other topics. Learning is isolated with little application of the content possible. Descriptive units should be taught sparingly during the year and supplemented with greater emphasis on thinking skills. They can be used for current events or commemoration of an event, for example, the anniversary of the nation or of the constitutional amendment giving U.S. women the right to vote. Units based on descriptive textbook materials need to be greatly modified by focusing on the key social studies concepts and thinking skills identified for the topic in local, state, and national standards.

Thinking Skills–Focused Units

In a unit with a *thinking skills focus,* the specific content learned is less important than the skills to be developed. A thinking, or inquiry, skill such as classification can be taught with almost any content. Students can classify agricultural products,

TABLE 15.1

Focus of Each Type of Social Studies Unit

Descriptive Unit

Focus	Mainly on content
	Stresses defining and describing concepts and examples of concepts
	Places a small emphasis on thinking skills
Examples	A unit on wants and needs
	A unit on the American Revolution

Thinking Skills Unit

Focus	Mainly on learning and using skills to organize information and make conclusions
	Uses content but content not expected to be remembered in detail
Examples	A unit on observing pictures and classifying their content as landscapes made by nature or by people
	A unit on investigating the evidence supporting a hypothesis, for example, the hypothesis that women living on the American frontier did hard physical labor so the family could survive

Conceptual and Thinking Skills Unit

Focus	Places equal emphasis on both content learning and development of skills
Examples	A unit on identifying and investigating factors relevant to an issue, such as a deciding how to involve more parents in helping at the school

types of government, or the climates of world regions. Students focus on a significant skill developed and practiced within a set of content. A strength of a thinking skills–focused unit is that it allows the teacher to provide help for students who have difficulty. Students are more focused on *how* they are learning. All students are helped to work with more abstract ideas as teachers select thinking skills, problem-solving skills, and other skills based on the students' needs.

The weakness of solely a thinking skills–focused unit is that social studies ideas may not be covered systematically, jumping instead from concept to concept without full development of any one concept. Higher-level concepts may not be learned because subconcepts providing a foundation for them are not adequately or systematically addressed. General connections between social studies and other subjects usually are not developed in thinking skills–focused units. Thinking skills–focused units are best taught from a systematic curriculum plan. They are interspersed with other types of social studies units throughout the year and from grade to grade. They ensure that students develop a thinking skill needed in upcoming units.

Conceptual and Thinking Skills–Focused Units

Units can combine social studies concepts and thinking skills with equal emphasis. A *conceptual and thinking skills–focused unit* works best with inquiry and investigative instructional strategies. Students work with a coherent set of content. At the same time, they develop skills necessary systematically to study and construct an understanding of the concepts and their relationships. They also examine the values related to processing the information and the attitudes of people toward the content.

As an example of such a unit, students can investigate why Native Americans and early European settlers in New England and the Middle Atlantic colonies used specific plants to dye clothing. The students collect the plants and boil them to make dyes. Their investigation involves making and testing predictions about which colors result from boiling a plant. They classify plants on the basis of observed properties, such as the dye color produced. Students use and further develop their skills in making observations and recording data. The concepts involved with this investigation include scarcity (of some plants), the opportunity cost or amount of time and effort required to achieve a specific dye color, and cultural preferences for colors and for sharing work among family members. A criterion for selecting appropriate topics for this type of unit is that key ideas must lend themselves to investigation by students. This type of teaching requires significantly more time than does a traditional approach. So it is important to select key ideas that are fundamental to powerful social studies.

T I M E   F O R   R E F L E C T I O N :   W H A T   D O   Y O U   T H I N K ?

Below are descriptions of several social studies units. Classify each of the units by its major focus: descriptive, thinking skills, or concept and thinking skills. Identify your choice by writing the letter D, T, or C, respectively, on the line provided.

_____ A. Ms. Brown teaches her students about the census that is taken by the government as ordered in the U.S. Constitution. Her students encourage their parents to fill out the form that comes to them in the mail on Census Day, April 1. She shows the students a sample form and has them take a census of their classroom using the form.

_____ B. Mr. Goldman stresses the personal benefits of saving money in the bank and how banks help business and government by investing the savings of customers in the local community. Students gather some of the information through surveying their parents and interviewing two local business owners who come to the classroom.

_____ C. Ms. Wang teaches her students about the importance of justice in U.S. democracy. She reads a book about the life of Martin Luther King, Jr. As she reads the story, the students identify the various actions Dr. King takes to gain justice for African Americans. Then the students divide up a list of people who have also worked to extend justice to larger numbers of people, researching and reporting on their actions. In a program, the students present their findings to their parents and tell why they believe that justice is something that needs to be preserved and promoted through the actions of all people.

➤

➤   _____ D. Ms. Herrera took a trip in the West and visited a number of historical sites. She uses her travels to help her students learn about the Westward Movement and settlement of the West. Students plot the Oregon and Santa Fe trails on a map and the paths of the transcontinental railroads. They locate today's major cities and rivers along the Oregon and Santa Fe trails. Pictures of places Ms. Herrera visited on her trip are examined and located on a map. Students seek to learn the appearance of the natural and cultural landscapes and to describe these places in words. They read passages from diaries of people who traveled west during the settlement period. They look at pictures that artists drew and photographers took of Western landscapes and of Native Americans who lived in the West during the 1800s. Students try to infer which locations the diary authors were describing. They also try to infer the places in which Native Americans were encountered, using the evidence in the drawings and photographs in which they appear. Last, students use websites to obtain and view pictures of the cities and national parks in the West today, pointing out major changes in the West since the mid-1800s. They decide whether the changes they have identified are positive or negative, explaining their reasoning for their decision.

1. If you were a K–8 student, in which one of the units above would you prefer to participate? Why? _____
_____

2. If you were a K–8 teacher, which of the units would you prefer to teach? Why?
_____
_____
_____

UNITS THAT INTEGRATE SCHOOL SUBJECTS

Two types of units can be used that integrate school subjects: theme units and issue and problem-solving units. *Theme units* cut across social studies topics and may include topics associated with other subject areas. An *issues and problem-solving unit* attempts to solve a problem that is relevant to somebody—an individual, a group of individuals, or society as a whole.

Theme Units

Powerful ideas are often used by people of all occupations. These ideas provide tools for thinking about the world and solving problems (American Association for the Advancement of Science, 1993a; National Council for the Social Studies, 1994b; National Research Council, 1996). Some examples include systems, classification, culture, interaction, production and distribution, models, time, decision making, interdependence, and scale. Other less broad but useful themes are concepts such as energy, neighbors, the dynamic earth, colonization, or space exploration (Mayer, 1995; National Council for the Social Studies, 1994b). A theme unit can have a descriptive focus, a thinking skills focus, or a conceptual and thinking skills focus. The focus is determined by the theme selected for the unit.

Planning and development of *theme units* begin when meaningful integration of the selected subjects around an important theme can occur. After comparing the plan for the yearly topics of each of the major subjects, a theme that fits the curriculum and appropriate topics in each of the subject areas is identified. For example, patterns of continuity and change could be investigated during the early childhood years in a theme unit that integrates the following:

> Examination of how people change their dress and activities in relation to weather events—carrying umbrellas on rainy spring mornings or wearing thick coats, hats, and gloves in cold weather (social studies)
>
> Observation and classification of common physical changes in the environment caused by a weather event—such as cracks in the ground following a hot and dry period (science)
>
> Investigation of number sets and problems related to daily and seasonal weather changes through activities—such as counting the hours of daylight in winter (mathematics)

A strength of this type of unit is its ability to make connections in several school subjects.

Many middle school teaching teams plan one or more integrated or thematic units each semester to help their students see the connections between what is being learned in different classes with different teachers. A weakness of this type of unit is the difficulty of focusing on significant aspects of the theme in each subject area. Some themes do not lend themselves to integration of all subjects. When planning a unit, teachers need to consider whether strong examples that students can understand exist in the subjects included.

Issue and Problem-Solving Units

An issue does not always have a clear or universally correct answer. Many issues are complex and not easily resolved or not resolved at all. However, students can explore such issues, identify possible solutions, examine the arguments for and against each solution, predict which solution(s) might be best implemented, and try out a possible solution. Such a unit is likely to have a conceptual and thinking skills focus. The issue involves one or more significant concepts and requires students to apply and further develop thinking skills to work with it.

Selecting developmentally appropriate issues or problems for investigation is essential. The strength of a unit focused on an issue or problem is that students can become highly motivated to investigate the issue because they perceive it as relevant. Such units combine content and skill development and stress the need to communicate and use social interaction skills. All students are involved in the investigation at some level even though each might not examine or perform the same learning tasks and activities. Another strength of these units is that they require examining the problem or issue from a variety of viewpoints. Most issues have social, political, economic, scientific, historical, and technological contexts. Such units allow students to see that life contains differences and controversies. Students learn how best to deal with differences within a democratic perspective.

The selection of appropriate key ideas for this type of unit begins with identifying an issue that is relevant to the students. The topic of endangered species, for example, cannot be meaningfully investigated by first-graders because of its abstractness. Instead, such young students might investigate the problems that result from acquiring a possible new classroom pet: a dog, a cat, a fish, a parakeet, a gerbil, or a lizard. They might have the pet permanently in the classroom or bring it in to visit for a day or two. They can note what, how often, and how much it eats and what must be done to keep it and its surroundings clean. They can consider whether they get tired of caring for the pet, whether they dislike and avoid cleaning it and its surroundings, and whether they pay it less attention over time. During their investigation, they can address the issue of responsibility for the pet and develop procedures that ensure that the pet is properly cared for. This unit investigates the general question "What are the responsibilities and problems of owning and caring for a pet?" A second related question students might investigate is "Why do pet owners need to teach their pets to be good members of the community?"

Choosing a yearly curriculum based on issues requires planning and reflection by teachers. Perhaps this type of unit is best when interspersed with other units in a well-sequenced curriculum based on local, state, and/or national standards. One effective way of using an issue-focused unit is as a follow-up to a previous unit. Students investigate in some depth an issue that was discovered in a previous unit. Such a unit might ask the question "How does the historian or anthropologist know that they are telling us accurate information about people who lived long ago when no written messages or books were left for us to read?"

An issue-focused unit is complex to manage and assess. Students are often pursuing different aspects of an investigation at the same time. Teachers must make sure that projects have an underlying organization, that all information is sequenced and communicated to all participants, and that information is analyzed and shared in relevant and clearly understood formats. Graphs, maps, charts, computer databases, and other means of organizing and communicating information are used. Teachers often hold class meetings in which students discuss common problems and suggest possible solutions to one another. Teachers meet with small groups of students about their individual progress to help coordinate and support student learning. Carefully planned rubrics for assignments are used to help students evaluate their own progress.

TIME FOR REFLECTION: WHAT DO YOU THINK?

A question can serve as the focus for a unit based on an issue, for example, "Why do pet owners need to teach their pets to be good members of the community?" This general question brings students into contact with (1) the needs of other people in the community, (2) personal responsibilities citizens have to others, and (3) laws and jobs related to caring for pets.

➤

➤ 1. Write two additional focus questions appropriate for lessons related to this issue.

  a. _____
     _____
  b. _____
     _____

2. Write a focus question that requires students to use either science or mathematical knowledge to answer it. _____
_____
_____

3. What are three social studies standards that are addressed in the focus questions you wrote in items 1 and 2 above? _____
_____
_____

4. What sources of information will students most likely use to get help to answer these questions? _____
_____
_____

5. How can the teacher help students understand the meaning and relationships among the pieces of information provided to them? _____
_____
_____
_____

6. What skills do students need to learn or practice to answer these focus questions? _____
_____
_____

7. What value(s) do you anticipate students embracing to explain why a pet needs to learn to be a good member of the community? _____
_____
_____
_____

How to Choose Appropriate Topics for Integrated Units

Perhaps the best way to start to think about the types of decisions required and the problems to be addressed in planning integrated social studies units is to consider an example of a theme-focused unit that is often taught in elementary schools: a unit designed around turkeys and the Thanksgiving Day holiday. In such a unit, students may make name tags in the shape of a turkey, read stories about turkeys, make turkey drawings from hand tracings, write stories about turkeys, make observations of a turkey egg and turkey feather, and visit a turkey farm. A major criterion for choosing these activities is how well they fit this particular theme.

It is difficult to identify an important concept or skill being taught in this unit. In selecting a topic, the teacher reflects on four questions:

1. What will be the important *key concepts* central to each of the subject areas integrated?
2. What will be the *guiding questions* that lead students into thinking?
3. What will be the *activities* that engage the students in reflective thinking?
4. What will be the natural and significant *connections* between key concepts?

An appropriate topic engages teachers and students in making choices that enhance the quality of student learning outcomes and the teacher's own feeling of the worthiness of the unit (Sunal et al., 2000). Although most topics interconnect subjects, *many* do not provide meaningful learning for the students, such as zoo animals or written communication. Integrated units are best used when they are appropriate for teaching important content and skills.

Planning Integrated Units

Two major planning techniques can be used for integrated teaching. The first is choosing a single key idea for a unit that interconnects the disciplines. The second major planning technique for integrated teaching is planning the yearly curriculum in several subjects. Teachers look at curriculum goals throughout the year, matching the goals for social studies to those for language arts, science, mathematics, art, music, physical education, and so on across several units. If the major goals in social studies, science, and mathematics all involve studying topics about the same time period, these could be taught at the same time. Then constructing a better understanding of the Constitutional Convention and the Revolutionary War period in social studies, electricity in science, and the metric system in mathematics can all be accomplished together.

Interconnections occur when students study Benjamin Franklin as a participant in the Constitutional Convention while considering other aspects of his life. Students could investigate his experiments with static electricity, for example. Within the next few decades following Franklin's experiments, liquid batteries were invented by Volta in 1800; electromagnetism was discovered by Oerstead in 1819; and laws of electrical interactions were devised by Ampere in 1822. Other inventions, such as electroplating, and the concept of basic circuits could be connected with events in history during and following this period. At the same time, a measurement unit in mathematics could be taught because the invention of the metric system occurred in this time period.

Curriculum Mapping. Curriculum mapping is one way to identify topics for integrated units for teachers who have already had at least one year in which to teach their curriculum. Michael Zulkoski, a principal in Grand Island, Nebraska, describes his teachers' use of curriculum mapping as follows (1999):

> We had all teachers write down what they taught and at what time during the semester. We put all of this on large posters and laminated them. . . . We grouped the teachers . . . with colored pens, they examined the posters looking for themes,

circling the topics supporting the themes in different colors. . . . Then they took one of the themes and built a thematic unit. (p. 17)

Teachers using curriculum mapping may find a lot of repetition in what has been taught as well as missing topics. Often teachers decide that they could do more with a topic or skill and reduce the time spent on something else. Teachers negotiate their curriculum with their peers.

Using a Wheel Design.   Some teachers have used a wheel design to identify topics. Edith Merritt and Martha Lockard, teachers from Tuscaloosa, Alabama, report their use of a wheel design (Sunal et al., 2000). They draw a circle, then draw another circle inside of it, and another circle inside of that circle, creating rings in the circle. They add in as many rings as there are subjects under consideration for topics.

For example, one year they started with six major social studies topics on the outermost ring, so the circle was divided into six sections by topic. Each of the six topics was written in a section of the outermost ring. Next, they examined the science curriculum and listed, where possible, a topic related to each social studies topic. One science topic, for example, was classification of organisms. This topic was written, along with the other science topics, in the second ring, next to the corresponding social studies topics written in the outermost ring. They continued this process, filling in a third ring with language arts/reading topics.

Teachers can use as many rings as they like. Filling in the rings makes visually obvious which topics from different subject areas go well together to form a theme.

Using a Column Design.   Another format for identifying possible themes for integrated units is a chart. The subject areas under consideration serve as the headings. Chart headings could be social studies, science, mathematics, physical education, art, or any other subjects. The teacher selects one subject with which to begin, such as social studies. Then all the topics to be taught in social studies that year are listed under the heading *social studies*. The second column may be reserved for science. Looking at the science topics, the teacher decides which ones correspond to the social studies topics and writes them in the column next, in the same row of the social studies topics they match. The process is repeated with mathematics and so on. An example of such a design follows (Sunal et al., 2000):

Social Studies	Science	Mathematics	Language Arts
Human communities	Animal communities	Numbers	Stories about communities
Graphing	Graphing	Graphing	Interpreting graphs

As the teacher fills in the chart, themes are built where many matches occur.

Using a Bubble Design.   Another alternative for planning integrated units is to use a bubble design (Sunal et al., 2000). In such a design, teachers select an issue, concept, skill, or attitude as a focus and place it in the center of a bubble or circle. Examples are interdependence, classification, culture, why U.S. citizens often choose not to vote in elections, and appreciation of family members' efforts to resolve personal conflicts occurring in the home. Once a central idea or skill is identified, teachers examine the curriculum for related ideas and skills, placing them in adjacent bubbles by discipline and connecting each with a line to the central bubble that contains the focus idea or skill.

For example, if interdependence is the central concept, the social studies curriculum may contribute concepts from economics and history. The science curriculum may contribute concepts of interdependence among plants, among animals, and among animals and plants. The mathematics curriculum may contribute concepts of calculating percentages of products exchanged between nations or regions. Physical education and dance may contribute concepts related to how people come to share others' games and dances. When deciding whether to integrate instruction, the teacher reflects on five key questions:

1. What important *key concepts* are central to each of the school subjects and can be successfully learned or practiced in the unit?
2. What *questions* can focus and direct students' thinking?
3. What *activities* can engage students in reflective thinking about the unit?
4. What natural and significant *connections* can be made to the students' world beyond the school?
5. How can students *connect the key concepts and generalizations* to be learned from studying the unit?

> **BUILDING ON DIVERSITY**

Units Incorporate Diversity

Units offer opportunities to incorporate and reflect on diverse experiences and viewpoints. Because units incorporate several lessons, they have built-in flexibility and can be used to have students investigate their own cultures, carry out compare/contrast activities that involve culturally diverse experiences, include show-and-tells that bring cultural experiences and artifacts into the classrooms, use videos that show aspects of people's lives and of the places in which they live in different societies, and use the Internet to investigate aspects of a topic in different cultures.

DEVELOPING INTEGRATED UNITS

Effective unit development requires thoughtful consideration of basic planning steps, purposeful organization, and reflective evaluation. Using any of the unit planning approaches and types of unit focuses already described requires a similar sequence of planning steps. The essential planning steps are summarized in Table 15.2. The model set of procedures presented next has worked well for many elementary and middle school teachers. The procedures are based on classroom use as well as on related research results. Although the procedures provide a useful set of steps with which to work, teachers generally adapt them and develop their own set of procedures as they gain experience in planning and teaching units.

T A B L E   1 5 . 2

Summary of Suggested Steps in Planning a Unit

1. Generate ideas for the topic.
2. Research the topic.
3. Develop focus questions.
4. Identify and accommodate special needs of students.
5. Name the unit.
6. Develop intended learning outcomes.
7. Categorize intended learning outcomes as knowledge, skills, and attitudes.
8. Create a web.
9. Develop a rationale and goals.
10. Begin the KWL chart.
11. Develop learning objectives.
12. Develop an assessment plan.
13. Develop lesson plans.
14. Develop accommodations for technology.
15. Implement the unit.
16. Evaluate student learning.
17. Reflect on the unit.

As you reflect on this discussion of teaching units, you might want to examine units already written. Sources for such units are many and include university education library collections, local school systems, and the ERIC system. The Internet also contains many websites that feature social studies units. Examples follow:

Crossroads: A K–16 American History Collection. Contains 36 units including several for the elementary and middle school levels.

Core Knowledge Lesson Plans and Units. Contains teacher-developed units for grades K–6 on world and U.S. civilization: ancient Egypt, Islam, the Renaissance, the thirteen colonies, and westward expansion.

Cities of Today, Cities of Tomorrow. Contains six interactive units designed for grades 5–12 that provide an overview of urbanization: its history, potential, and problems

COMPANION
WEBSITE

Addresses for all these websites are available at the companion website.

Step 1: Generating Ideas for the Topic of a Unit

Once a topic has been chosen, ideas about the content, skills, attitudes, and values related to the topic are generated. These ideas are a beginning point and are revised during the unit development process. Examples of initial ideas for an integrated unit on government at the fifth-grade level include laws, voting, structure of government, taxes, making inferences, school government, local and state government, comparing roles of government officials, problem solving, campaign literature and television advertisements, making changes in government, mapping electoral districts in our community and in our state, and decision making. Questions to stimulate ideas include "How do people decide for whom to vote?" and "What role does government play in our daily lives?"

Step 2: Researching the Topic

Researching the topic enables teachers to assess their prior knowledge, to add to this knowledge base, to identify alternative concepts and perspectives that students may hold, and to update their knowledge. Journals, encyclopedias, social studies texts, trade books, and an Internet concept search or sending queries via email are research sources.

Step 3: Developing Focus Questions

Teachers identify the main points or questions for a unit. This is especially important when the ideas have been planned for them, as in a textbook chapter. Textbook chapters and learning kits typically contain more information than students can meaningfully understand. Without focus or central questions, it is difficult to help students see the main point. *Focus questions* help students to link with their prior knowledge as well as to establish a rationale for studying the unit. For a single unit, several focus questions are appropriate. A focus question guides the development of a single lesson or of several lessons. For example, a middle school unit on local and state government could start with several focus questions:

What is government?
How are local and state government similar and different?
Who makes the rules by which local and state governments operate?
Who might provide these services if local and state government did not do so?

Once an initial list of focus questions is developed, teachers ask themselves: "Which of the focus questions really get at the heart of the unit? What kinds of questions are being asked? Are they mostly where or when questions? Are there any how or why questions? Do the questions represent a variety of thinking skills from recall and comprehension to application, analysis, and evaluation? To what extent do the questions relate to the students' interests and needs?" If needed, focus questions are modified to include a variety of social studies thinking skills and student interests and needs. For example, after evaluating the list of focus questions generated for a unit on local and state government, the teacher might decide to modify the following question: "How are local and state government similar and different?" The teacher might decide to change this question to read: "How can we create a Venn diagram showing similarities and differences of local and state governments?"

Step 4: Identifying Special Needs among Students and Making Accommodations

Special needs students might require adaptation of lesson plans. A list of specific adaptions may be compiled on the basis of students' needs identified through the special education program and others noted by the teacher. Some of these needs might include (1) students who are having difficulties academically, (2) students whose native language is not English and who are not yet fluent in English, (3) students who have physical and emotional difficulties, and (4) students who are experiencing severe family stress, such as divorce, death, a major illness, or relocation.

Step 5: Naming the Unit

Units need focus. Naming a unit is a way to arrive at a focus. The name can capture the importance or value of the unit, as well as its content. The name a unit is given is a way of making sure that the initial ideas are logically connected to each other. A way of naming a unit is to use a question that students strive to answer during the course of the unit:

How Do People and Things Move from Place to Place in Our Country?
How Can We Classify Types of Government?
Why Are There Rules in Human Society and in the Natural World?
Is Our Information an Inference or an Observation?

Step 6: Developing Intended Learning Outcomes

The initial list of ideas and the teacher's reflection on the focus questions help to create intended learning outcomes, which are usually written as learning objectives. Intended *learning outcomes* are statements of what the teacher wants the students to learn. These statements can address inquiry skills, concepts, attitudes, or values. The process of identifying learning outcomes begins with an examination of the initial list of topics generated in Step 1. Learning outcomes are not activities the students do during the unit. Instead, they describe what students construct in their minds. The following list contains initial ideas for a middle school unit on U.S. regional geography. Ideas marked with an X best represent potential intended learning outcomes. Those marked with an O are activities, not intended learning outcomes.

X 1. Explain the relationship of climate to features on the geographic landscape.
O 2. Write a letter or use the Internet to obtain information about local and state government.
X 3. Explain how the characteristics of a region relate to its economic strength.
X 4. Conclude that planning for movement of people around a region enhances economic opportunities.
O 5. View pictures of damage caused by natural disasters.

Step 7: Categorizing Intended Learning Outcomes

The next step is grouping the intended learning outcomes into categories. Each idea is defined as an inquiry skill, content knowledge, attitude, or value. Teachers ensure that outcomes are expected for each category. Inquiry skills, such as recalling, explaining, predicting, analyzing, creating, and evaluating, can be grouped into several levels. Content knowledge can be grouped into factual statements, concepts, or generalizations. Attitudes can be identified or explained in detail with possible consequences noted.

Step 8: Creating an Idea Web

As possible goals and intended learning outcomes are explored, the technique of webbing can be used to evaluate, complete, and relate the important ideas, skills, attitudes, and values in the unit. Teachers use the information and ideas from the previous steps to group and illustrate their presentation of the unit into a *web*. Webs are especially helpful when teachers jointly prepare units. As the web is constructed, additional ideas, skills, attitudes, and values may be identified to support the topic and create bridges among the components of the unit. Links represented by labeled arrows can be drawn to connect ideas and inquiry skills, showing relationships between facts, simple concepts, more abstract concepts, and generalizations. These links, or ladders, help students to understand relationships and integrate skills, concepts, and generalizations.

Two types of webs are generally used: a hierarchical web and a schematic components web (Novak, 1995). The teacher chooses one that best fits the topic. To construct a hierarchical web (Figure 15.1) the teacher performs the following tasks:

1. Selects the key idea(s), skill(s), attitudes, and values
2. Lists ideas, skills, attitudes, or values related to key ones
3. Ranks the ideas and/or skills from the most general to the most specific
4. Groups the ideas, skills, attitudes, and values into clusters, adding more if necessary
5. Arranges the ideas, skills, attitudes, and values in a two-dimensional array
6. Links the ideas, skills, attitudes, and values, and labels each link

Figure 15.1 shows part of a hierarchical web illustrating interdependence between different nations for a unit named "How Are People in Our Community Interdependent with People in Similar Communities and Other Countries?"

Many of the same procedures just listed for constructing hierarchical webs are followed in creating a schematic components web. In a schematic components web for the same unit in Figure 15.2, the unit topic is located at the web's center. Both web types connect main ideas, skills, attitudes, and values with interlinking inquiry terms, such as *has, depends on, as measured in,* or *as inferred in.* These terms define the thinking processes used to learn the content—inferring, measuring, and so on. Using a webbing technique is a way to analyze the nature of the unit at this stage. Does the web show meaningful ideas, skills, attitudes, and values? Are there too many abstract ideas? What concrete ideas, bridges, and ladders can be added to help students understand other concepts or more abstract ideas?

If a textbook serves as the source for a unit, the teacher lists important ideas, skills, attitudes, and values from it. This list is used to create a web. Using national, state, and local standards, the teacher modifies the web by changing or adding ideas, inquiry skills, attitudes, or values. Typically, social studies textbooks contain a large amount of content. The teacher deemphasizes and eliminates textbook ideas and facts that are not compatible with the standards used to implement a unit based on appropriate key

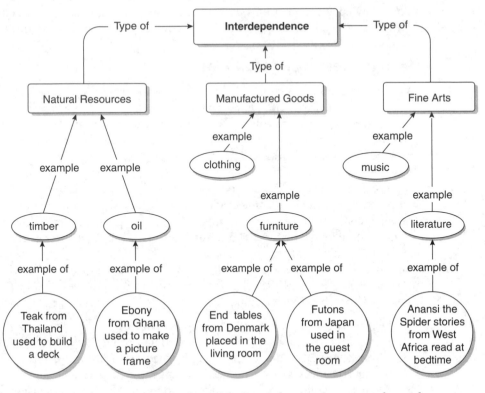

F I G U R E   1 5 . 1   A Partial Hierarchical Web for a Unit on Interdependence

ideas for powerful social studies. For example, modifications and deviations from the course of study in a second-grade textbook chapter on communities may be made:

Discussions and diagrams of community governmental structures may be deleted.
Field trips may be added so that students can investigate the characteristics of their community through real-life experiences.
Activities such as photographing the field trip can be incorporated.
Tasks such as charting similarities and differences between the neighborhoods observed in the photographs can be carried out.

Step 9: Developing a Rationale and Goals

It is important to think about the reasons for teaching the unit and how the *unit rationale* is communicated to students. A rationale statement is determined by the values influencing the teacher's perception of students, students' relationship to society, and students' interaction with social studies as a subject. Unit rationales are also influenced by current directions in social studies teaching and education in general. For example, since the 1970s, a shift has occurred toward a more student-centered approach. In the 1990s, more reflective thinking in effective and diverse classroom set-

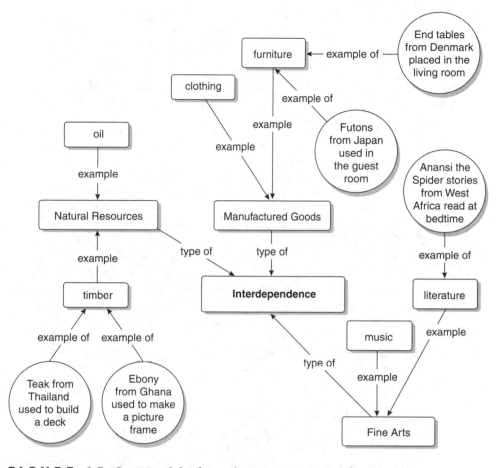

FIGURE 15.2 A Partial Schematic Components Web for a Unit on Interdependence

tings complemented the previous trend to create a hands-on, minds-on approach to teaching. A unit rationale statement answers the questions:

How is the unit relevant, affecting the future of the *students* as well as their current, individual needs and interests?

How does the unit examine *societal* issues and help students deal responsibly with them?

How is the unit *developmentally appropriate* for the students?

How is the unit a *self-learning enterprise*?

A rationale for a unit on U.S. life in the post–Vietnam War period might, for example, contain a goal statement such as "This unit is designed to give sixth-grade students insight into, and an appreciation of, U.S. life in the past 30 years; ideas concerning how life changed during these three decades; and the diversity of factors resulting from these changes." A complete rationale contains a goal statement and briefly describes how instruction is intended to proceed. Added to the goal statement above, for the unit on U.S. life in the post–Vietnam war period, is a rationale. An example of such a rationale follows:

> The unit begins with evidence from local newspapers and national magazines of the conditions of life found at the end of the Vietnam War. It continues with Internet searches and library resources to collect more examples. Students identify general patterns of change in the home, workplace, and schools. They examine changes brought about by social and environmental conditions. The unit concludes by investigating current local and global descriptions of life at home, in the workplace, and at school. The role of society is addressed to provide students with the appreciation that their actions have consequences and that their decisions affect the decisions others must make.

Step 10: Beginning the KWL Chart

The *KWL* chart is used over time in planning and evaluating the unit. It provides the teacher with some indication of students' knowledge prior to instruction, what knowledge needs to be obtained before instruction begins or as instruction progresses, and what knowledge the students learn through the unit. At the beginning of a new unit, a teacher asks students, "What do you *know* about _____?" Then the teacher asks students, "What *would* you like to learn about this topic?" After the unit has been taught, the teacher asks students, "What did you *learn* about this topic?" Students' comments are recorded on a chart under three columns headed K (*k*now), W (*w*ould like to learn), and L (what was *l*earned), respectively. Teachers may develop a personal KWL for a unit.

The KWL is extended by interviews with a sample of students. Questions can be used to ascertain the K and W parts of the chart, or teachers can use photographs, maps, artifacts, or other items related to the topic to probe students' prior knowledge and interests. For example, a teacher planning a sixth-grade unit on the Vietnam War might use a set of photographs including war scenes and a view of a protest march to probe students' prior knowledge during an interview. The KWL chart and interviews are used throughout the unit to help plan, modify, and assess to evaluate the extent to which the learning outcomes are being attained.

Step 11: Developing Learning Objectives

Initial learning outcomes are revised, written as objectives, and classified into practical categories for teaching. Several formats can be used to write learning objectives. All *objectives*, whatever their specific format, focus on what the student will learn and how success can be achieved. Examples of objectives indicating *knowledge* of a concept or generalization that students construct follow:

> Students compare the lives of colonial children with their own lives.
> Students give reasons why one brand of cereal costs more than another.
> Students state the meaning of a holiday in their own words.

Examples of objectives indicating *inquiry skills* that students develop and use follow:

Students gather data by interviewing.
Students organize data into bar charts comparing two variables.
Students write reports in the form of a newscast.
Students classify the items on their list into needs and wants.

Examples of objectives indicating *attitudes or values* that students learn to appreciate and accept follow:

Students demonstrate respect toward older people.
Students express a desire to seek out opportunities to learn more about the president's official activities.
Students conserve energy in their daily lives.

TIME FOR REFLECTION: WHAT DO YOU THINK?

During a lesson, students participate in a series of activities that result in one or more of the following: acquiring content knowledge, enhancing skills, analyzing values, taking a position, and making decisions on how to participate in society in ways that support democracy and its citizens. The teacher's role is very different from that of students: facilitating student learning and development and assessing student progress toward learning. To perform this role, the teacher must constantly be aware of what the students are to be doing and must observe and assess whether students' behaviors are those that indicate they are likely to be mastering the objectives of the lessons. Knowing what you expect of the student is important to successful teaching. In evaluating a teacher, the evaluator often asks, "Did the teacher teach to the objective?" For a social studies teacher, the evaluation question is "Did the teacher help students to learn valuable and important things that will help them become good citizens in a democratic nation in an increasingly interdependent world?"

Once the topic of a lesson has been selected, the teacher decides just what about the topic the students should learn. The emphasis of every objective must be on the accomplishment of the student. Some educators say that the objective should clearly state what students will be able to do after instruction that he or she could not do before being involved in the instructional process. This view of an objective sees the student's mind as an "empty vessel" that is "filled up" during instruction. Clearly, during social studies instruction, students do acquire new content knowledge. However, meaningful learning often requires learners to use skills they already have to reorganize their knowledge. This means that there are times when what the learners are doing during the instructional process is more important than new knowledge and the focus of the objective is on the use, or mastery, of a skill. At other times, students focus on what is important to do when making conclusions or decisions, placing the focus of the objective on attitudes/dispositions or values.

➤

➤   Perhaps you have learned to write behavioral objectives that include three parts:

1. Under what conditions (specific sources of information)
2. The action of the student (action verb)
3. The degree of acceptable accomplishment (minimum performance level) (Mager, 1962)

Some examples of such an objective are as follows:

- Given a map of the world and the latitude and longitude coordinates of 10 national capitals, the student will correctly locate the capitals with 90 percent accuracy.
- Given a list of the presidents and vice-presidents of the United States, students will correctly match the vice-presidents with their presidents with 90 percent accuracy.

The above form of an objective is helpful when the student is practicing a skill that has several rules to apply in performing the skill. However, many social studies lessons include tasks that do not follow a systematic series of steps. John Jarolimek (1991) says that there is a middle ground in the wording of objectives. Social studies specialists tend to view behavioral objectives as statements of what students will learn or do during the instructional process. The key to writing such objectives is to use a verb that describes what is done by the learner during the lesson. Among the verbs that accomplish this are *name, list, identify, explain, compare, locate, graph, analyze, tell why, choose, defend, evaluate, listen, order,* and *group.*

In the discussion of Step 11 above are examples of the three types of educational objectives written in the middle-ground approach suggested by Jarolimek. This is how you should word your objectives. Note how the descriptive verb hints at what will be done during the lesson and how the teacher might approach the evaluation of each objective.

1. What are the four different unit topics that the knowledge objectives indicate would be studied? _____

_____

_____

2. What are the four activities that students will be doing in the lessons guided by the skill objectives? _____

_____

_____

3. Look at each of the attitudinal objectives. What conclusion or generalization would the students have had to make and believe to motivate them to perform the actions described in each of the attitudinal objectives? _____

_____

_____

In the skill objectives listed above, you are not able to identify the topic being studied. Some teachers do like to write longer skill objectives and include the topic, for example, "Students will gather data about the daily lives of soldiers by interviewing   ➤

➤ members of the local VFW." However, including the topic is a matter of personal preferences and not a requirement for a skill objective.

4. Assume that you plan to teach fourth-grade students about Washington, D.C., in three to five days. Write three knowledge objectives for the study, three skill objectives, and three attitudinal or value objectives. Label the objectives by type.

_____

_____

5. How many learning cycles would you use in your unit on Washington, D.C.? Outline your unit identifying which objectives would be appropriate for the early, or Exploratory, part of the unit. Then describe which objectives would be appropriate for the middle, or Developmental, part of the unit. Then identify the objectives for the last, or Expansion, part of your unit. _____

_____

_____

Step 12: Developing an Assessment Plan

Two purposes of assessment are important at this stage in planning a unit: (1) feedback about student learning of a key idea and (2) data about the effectiveness of the lesson plans on student learning outcomes. Assessment also is used to provide feedback to students about their learning and to teachers about the effectiveness of the unit.

Types of assessment used by many teachers include a quiz or test, student writing projects, graphs and charts, cooperative group work, artwork, interviews, or group/individual projects. Informal and semiformal methods, as well as having students develop portfolios of their work, can be incorporated into an effective assessment plan. The assessment is designed to evaluate each type of learning outcome included in the unit. This requires several types of assessment methods. Measures are developed to evaluate ideas, thinking skills, and affects. Techniques for group and individual assessment are planned at the beginning of the unit. As part of a complete assessment plan, students are asked for feedback on their reaction to the unit (see Figure 15.3).

MAKING A LITERATURE CONNECTION ➤

Incorporating Social Studies Trade Books into Units

Social studies trade books are available for all themes found in the national standards. Once a unit theme and the major national standard(s) on which the unit will focus have been identified, teachers can consider which trade books might best accompany the unit. Trade books should be read by the teacher and then chosen to fit students' interests and developmental level, challenging students' thinking and moving it to a higher level of complexity and reflection. Each teacher will also consider whether bias or stereotyping appear in the book and whether the book can be used along with other books and materials to present multiple perspectives on an idea.

What Did You Think about Our Unit?

1. Place an X on the line before the choice that shows how satisfied you were as a learner during this unit.

   ____Very satisfied   ____Satisfied

   ____Unsatisfied   ____Very unsatisfied

2. What could you, your classmates, or your teacher have done to increase your satisfaction?

   _____

   _____

   _____

   _____

3. What were your favorite activities? Why? _____

   _____

   _____

   _____

4. What were your least favorite activities? Why? _____

   _____

   _____

   _____

F I G U R E   1 5 . 3   Sample Student Feedback Form

Trade books often address more than one national social studies standard and might be used more than once throughout the year for different purposes. Younger students often enjoy hearing a book read to them more than once. Some examples of recently published trade books are presented below to indicate the range of social studies trade books available for use by teachers in units. These books are organized according to the national standard they address.

Culture

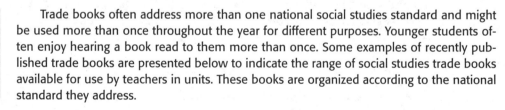

Amish Horses (2001) by Richard Ammon and illustrated by Pamela Patrick is a picture book describing the many tasks people and horses accomplish on an Amish farm (for primary grades).

Charley Waters Goes to Gettysburg (2000) by Susan Sinnott and illustrated with photographs by Dorothy Handleman uses Charley Waters and his father as Civil War reenactors to discuss what life was like for soldiers fighting in the Civil War (for grades 3–5).

Locomotive: Building an Eight-Wheeler (1999) by David Weitzman details step by step the process by which a wood-burning, steam-powered 4-4-0 eight-wheeler locomotive was made (for grades 3–8).

Time, Continuity, and Change

When Esther Morris Headed West: Women, Wyoming and the Right to Vote (2001) by Connie Nordhielm Wooldridge and illustrated by Jacqueline Rogers is the story of Esther Morris who not only voted but also ran for office and won before women were given suffrage throughout the United States (for primary grades).

The Sound That Jazz Makes (2000) by Carole Boston Weatherford and illustrated by Eric Velasquez tells the story of jazz from its beginnings in Africa to the Harlem nightclub (for grades 3–8).

The Way Things Never Were: The Truth about the "Good Old Days" (1999) by Norman Finkelstein contrasts the ways in which the "good old days" are often presented with some of the problems and realities of the 1950s and 1960s in areas such as health care, environmental concerns, family life, and eating habits (for middle school).

People, Places, and Environments

Africa Is Not a Country (2000) by Margy Burns Knight and Mark Melnicove and illustrated by Anne Sibley O'Brien passes a day with children in various African nations to introduce the distinctive customs of different regions of the continent (for grades 3–5).

Katie and the Sunflowers (2001) by James Mayhew depicts Katie's adventures in a museum and introduces us to the works of van Gogh, Gauguin, and Cezanne (for grades 3–5).

Pioneer Church (1999) by Carolyn Otto and illustrated by Megan Lloyd is based on the records of Old Zion Church in Brickerville, Pennsylvania, and depicts how communities change over time (for primary and middle grades).

Individual Development and Identity

Gershon's Monster: A Story for the Jewish New Year (2000) retold by Eric A. Kimmel and illustrated by Jon J. Muth is a Jewish folktale telling the story of Gershon, who regularly ignores his shortcomings and, on the new year, packs them up and tosses then into the sea (for primary through grade 5).

Just the Two of Us (2001) by Will Smith and illustrated by Kadir Nelson celebrates the dignity, maturity, and honor of being a father (for grades 3 and up).

Our Only May Amelia (1999) by Jennifer L. Holm describes May Amelia Jackson in 1899 as she struggles to grow up as the only girl among seven boys and the only girl ever born to settlers on the Nasel River in the state of Washington (for middle school).

Individuals, Groups, and Institutions

Racing the Past (2001) by Sis Deans is the story of 11-year-old Ricky Gordon, who lives in rural Maine and tries to deal with his father's death, rural poverty, bullies at school, and a needy younger sibling as he runs a long-term race with the school bus (for middle school).

Fighting for Honor: Japanese Americans and World War II (2000) by Michael L. Cooper recounts Japanese American life during World War II, highlighting the bravery of those who participated in fighting the war while also describing the daily life of those who were interned. The effects of the war and internment on the Japanese American community are given attention (for middle school).

O'Sullivan Stew (1999) by Hudson Talbott retells an Irish folktale in which Kate decides to recapture a horse the king has taken in order to save her village from destruction by a witch (for grades K–5).

Power, Authority, and Governance

Red, White, Blue, and Uncle Who? The Stories behind Some of America's Patriotic Symbols (2001) by Teresa Bateman and illustrated by John O'Brien is an easily read introduction to seventeen traditional American icons (for grades K–5).

Bound for the North Star: True Stories of Fugitive Slaves (2000) by Dennis Brindell Fradin uses primary source illustrations to tell the stories of fugitive slaves who took great risks to find freedom (for middle school).

Kids on Strike! (1999) by Susan Campbell Bartoletti illustrates the working conditions of the late 1800s and early 1900s with photographs of children working in coal mines, cotton mills, and the garment industry and talks about how strikes were used to change child labor laws in the United States (for grades 3–8).

Production, Distribution, and Consumption

Those Building Men (2001) by Angela Johnson and illustrated by Barry Moser is a picture book of the diverse men who build and the monuments they build including the Erie Canal, skyscrapers, and bridges (for grades K–5).

Made in Mexico (2000) by Peter Laufer and illustrated by Susan L. Roth describes a way of life in a remote Mexican village that touches music around the world (for grades 3–5).

A Big Cheese for the White House (1999) by Candace Fleming and illustrated by S. D. Schindler is a fact-based story of the efforts of Elder John Leland to organize his fellow townspeople to make a big cheese for President Jefferson (for grades 3–8).

Science, Technology, and Society

The Great Unknown (2001) by Taylor Morrison presents the efforts of artist and paleontologist Charles Wilson Peale to excavate and display the bones of the mastodon (grades 3–5).

Do Your Remember the Color Blue? And Other Questions Kids Ask about Blindness (2000) by Sally Hobart Alexander describes, by responding to 13 personal questions, the author's experience of losing her sight at 26 and going on to become a wife, mother, and award-winning author (for grades 3–8).

Fire in Their Eyes: Wildfires and the People Who Fight Them (1999) by Karen Magnuson Bell uses vivid photographs and text to show the training, equipment, and courage needed by wildfire fighters (for grades 3–8).

Global Connections

Who Really Discovered America? Unraveling the Mystery & Solving the Puzzle (2001) by Avery Hart and illustrated by Michael Kline outlines the tools of inquiry, rules of evidence, and some historical methodologies and activities for students to help answer the question "Who really discovered America?" (for middle school).

Uncommon Traveler: Mary Kingsley in Africa (2000) by Don Brown is a biography of the self-educated Englishwoman who, after a secluded childhood and youth, traveled through West Africa in 1893 and 1894 and related much about its inhabitants (for grades 3–8).

A Is for the Americas (1999) by Cynthia Chin-Lee and Terri de la Pena and illustrated by Enrique O. Sanchez is an alphabet book that takes you on a tour of the Americas (for grades K–5).

Civic Ideals and Practice

Food Watch (2001) by Martyn Bramwell presents issues affecting the planet's food supply and introduces professionals in the field, using the phrase "A day in the life of . . . ," then guides readers through experiments and actions they can take (for grades 5 and up).

Forging Freedom (2000) by Hudson Talbott is a tribute to the author's friend, Jaap Penraat, who saved over 400 Jews during the Nazi occupation of Holland (for grades 5–8).

Through My Eyes (1999) by Ruby Bridges is a personal account of the six-year-old African American girl who integrated the New Orleans public schools in 1960.

Step 13: Developing Lesson Plans

Potential activities emerge from the list of learning outcomes. One way to view the activities is to consider the resources available and related activities possible using these resources. Next, the appropriateness of the resources and activities for the special and developmental needs of the students is considered. Examples of resources are textbooks, field trips, games, guest speakers, the Internet, computer software, commercial videos, TV cameras and home-made videotapes, digital cameras, manipulatives from common materials, case studies, debates, and simulations. Each of these resources can provide an experience facilitating the accomplishment of an objective.

For instance, consider a unit on scarcity. One objective might be "Students will give examples of natural resources that do not exist in their local area." Possible resources and activities for accomplishing this objective could be as follows:

- Taking a field trip to a mine or a gravel pit
- Using the Internet to search for natural resources
- Reading newspaper articles on resources imported into the community
- Reading pages in a textbook

Each of these resources and resource activities can be used to achieve one or more different outcomes. The lesson plans drafted are based on the rationale and learning objectives that have been designed using the list of resources and activities.

Step 14: Developing Accommodations for Technology

Teachers ask themselves several questions:

How can technology enhance learning in this particular setting?

If concrete materials are not available for the concepts and skills involved, can technology provide the bridge to help students learn the concepts meaningfully?

Can technology provide additional practice or transfer experiences that are not possible in the real-life situation?

Is the use of technology economical in terms of the time it requires?

Is additional supervision necessary?

➤ **USING TECHNOLOGY**

Databases and Spreadsheets

Databases are files or sets of information students create about a topic made up of records, one for each event, each place, each monthly temperature, or each piece of data in any number of information categories. Databases and spreadsheets are useful in studying many unit topics. Each record in a database or spreadsheet has fields: subcategories containing information such as the name of a capital city and its height above sea level. Fields can be arranged or sorted in many ways. In using a database on U.S. cities, for example, students can ask for listings of those cities with a certain characteristic, such as population more than 100,000 or less than 500,000. Once a database has been set up, it is always available to answer questions related to the information it contains (Spooner & Barracato, 1998).

COMPANION WEBSITE

Ready-made databases are available on the Internet. Perhaps the largest is that of the U.S. Census Bureau (see the link on the companion website). This database is helpful in learning about the people of the United States and each state and territory. A number of databases can be purchased on CD-ROMs. Students can make their own databases quite easily. Most computers have programs such as Microsoft Office or Apple ClarisWorks installed that create databases.

Each student does research and then enters the products of the research efforts into the database. For example, students could set up a database focused on early settlers in their community. After deciding what sort of information to collect about each person (e.g., name, birthdate, date of death, whether married or single, occupation), each student searches and finds as much of the needed information as possible for a given settler and enters the information into the database. Once the database is complete, students ask questions and sort the data to help answer their questions. Figure 15.4 depicts screens from a fourth-grade class database.

When data is sorted to answer one question, the answer brings new questions to mind. As new questions arise, students carry out further research and add new information to the database. Sometimes the information is just not available. This clearly illustrates to students that not every question is readily answerable. Making databases as a class effort demonstrates the power of information and of cooperative efforts.

➤

(Screen One: list of information items given about each president)

OUR PRESIDENTS

Main Menu

President's Name
President's Term of Office
President's Political Party
State President Was Born In
President's Occupation
President's Age at Inauguration
President's Age at Death

(Screen Two: specific information about a president, Harry S. Truman)

Truman, Harry S.
1945–1953
Democratic
Missouri
Businessman
60
88

(Screen Three: answer to the question "Which former presidents were not lawyers?")

Washington, George
Harrison, William H.
Taylor, Zachary
Fillmore, Millard
Johnson, Andrew
Grant, Ulysses, S.
Roosevelt, Theodore
Wilson, Thomas W.
Harding, Warren G.
Coolidge, John Calvin
Hoover, Herbert C.
Truman, Harry S.
Eisenhower, Dwight D.
Kennedy, John F.
Johnson, Lyndon B.
Carter, James E.
Reagan, Ronald W.
Bush, George H. W.

FIGURE 15.4 **Three Sample Screens of a Database Developed by Fourth-Grade Students**

Spreadsheets can be used to extend data into the future. Data in a database can be put into a spreadsheet. Students can use the spreadsheet to add, subtract, multiply, and perform many other mathematical operations with numerical data. For

➤ example, a student might note that each year a state collects a certain amount of money from a gasoline tax. The average gasoline tax paid by a citizen can be obtained by dividing the total tax by the number of people in the state. Then it can be multiplied by an inflation error.

The learning cycle format offers many opportunities to build on the cultural diversity represented by students. Because the Exploration phase is open ended, it is expected that students' prior knowledge is diverse. As each student's prior knowledge is brought out, other students often discover varying perspectives among their classmates, setting up a challenge to what the student currently thinks. During the Development phase, the focus is on reconstructing prior knowledge into a new idea or skill level or attitude, so all students have equal opportunities to reconstruct their prior knowledge. The different perspectives and skill levels among the students are used to both broaden and deepen the reconstruction. During the Expansion phase, students use their newly reconstructed idea, skill level, or attitude in a new application that is different from the context in which they learned it. The more diverse the students, the wider is the possible set of applications.

Step 15: Implementing the Unit

After planning, the unit is taught. Adjustments and fine tuning are made to meet the needs of the students and the context of the learning experience while it is being taught.

Step 16: Evaluating Student Learning

Students provide their ideas concerning the unit activities and what they learned through the unit either as part of a lesson or in a separate class or group discussion (see Figure 15.3). Teachers add their observations to information obtained from examining assessments. Students' ideas are recorded on the KWL chart. Teachers may conduct some postunit student interviews. Teachers compare the learning outcomes with the information they have and decide to what degree the students have accomplished them.

Step 17: Reflecting on the Unit

Unit development and instructional planning are part of a large cycle. One of the most important parts of the cycle is devoted to gathering feedback on the unit and reflecting on its effectiveness. Some questions to consider are as follows:

What evidence of motivation to learn about the topic was found?
What evidence of learning about the topic did you see?
To what extent did students accomplish the learning objectives?
Did the ideas in the lessons flow together well?
What did the students remember and not remember from day to day?
Which lesson was the best? Why? Did you predict this?

Russian students gather with their teachers after a day at an outdoor camp to sing songs and discuss the unit they are just finishing on social issues and the evironment.

Would you use this unit again in its present form? If not, what specific modifications would you make?

Written responses provide a starting point for a teacher when considering whether the unit should be kept and revised for inclusion in the curriculum for the future.

TIME FOR REFLECTION: WHAT DO YOU THINK?

Figure 15.5 shows portions of a planning web for an interdisciplinary middle school unit addressing the question "What are the effects of war?" This web illustrates the use of focus questions for teachers in mathematics, social studies, and science. These are shown in rectangular boxes with question marks. Content for various answers that teachers incorporate into lessons is stated in the ovals. Because of space limitations, the arts portion—"How have people expressed their feelings and reactions to war?"—is not shown.

Planning webs such as this one help teachers focus the content and provides each team member with an overview of the content being presented in other courses. Webs help teachers better coordinate the timing of their other lessons in an integrated, interdisciplinary unit. As teachers write individual lesson plans

➤

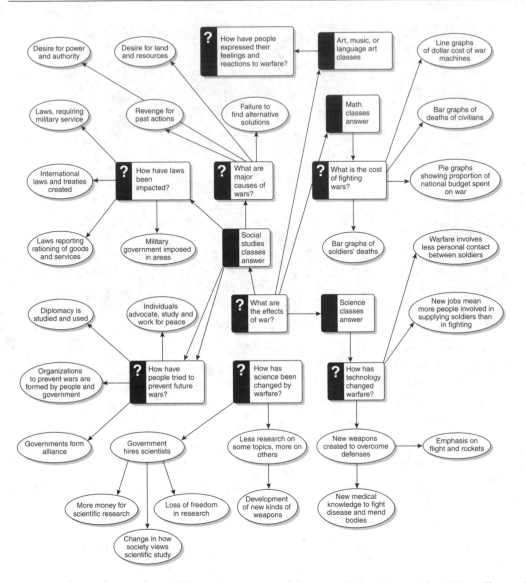

FIGURE 15.5 Planning Web for an Interdisciplinary Middle School Unit on the Effects of War

> and expand their research, they may add more questions and information, such as teaching dates, to the web.
>
> 1. After examining the content in the web, write two answers a teacher might expect students to give after they have completed the unit "What Are the Effects of War?"
>
> _____
>
> _____

➤ 2. Why is this unit more appropriate for middle school students than for primary grades students? _____

_____

3. What are two important concepts about warfare that students learn from this integrated unit that they might not have learned if the unit were addressed only in social studies class? _____

_____

4. Write another question that could be asked by the science or the social studies teacher. _____

_____

5. The question for the language arts/art/music teacher(s) is indicated on the web. Construct what you think might be an appropriate completion for this portion of the web. _____

_____

6. What skills are learned or practiced by the students as they study the unit illustrated in the web? _____

_____

7. What values do the various teachers ask their students to examine as they study this unit? _____

_____

_____

Teachers make many choices when planning a year-long curriculum. Because the year-long plan provides guidelines and encourages reflection on the purpose and success of the social studies program, some changes in the plan should be expected as the year progresses. Students may find one topic particularly interesting and want to pursue it further, or topics and ideas planned might not challenge students because they are too complex and abstract for their level of maturity or too simple to curry their favor. Unexpected issues of importance to the students and community may arise and stimulate students to investigate them.

SUMMARY

The unit-planning process is a critical professional skill because key ideas are interrelated with each other and with students' prior experiences to make them useful. Units can be developed with emphasis on key social studies ideas or on integrated ideas from several disciplines. Three evaluation criteria are useful during the construction of units: significance, coherence, and relevance. Selecting an appropriate focus for a unit involves determining the rationale and goals of the unit. Emphasis can vary in content, inquiry skills, attitudes, values, and the amount of integration with other subjects. Different foci for unit planning include a descriptive focus on content, a thinking skill focus, a conceptual and thinking skill focus, and an issues and problem-solving focus. Within a year's time, a teacher can probably teach some integrated units and some units devoted to a single subject or skill.

In planning an integrated unit, an appropriate topic involves teachers and students making choices that increase the quality of student learning outcomes and the teacher's own feeling about the worth of the unit. When the goals for social studies can be matched to those for science, mathematics, physical education, fine arts, or language arts across several units, individual teachers and teams of teachers often find that students learn the topic better through the connections made during integrated units. Effective social studies unit planning with an appropriate focus requires thoughtful consideration of basic planning steps, purposeful organization, and reflective evaluation.

Expanding ON THIS CHAPTER

Activity

COMPANION
WEBSITE

You are going to teach a unit about the job of the president of the United States. Write six focus questions for the unit. Reflect on the questions, deciding whether they address major aspects of this job.

Recommended Websites to Visit

COMPANION
WEBSITE

NESEA's curricular units are interdisciplinary on themes such as transportation, energy, and the environment.
www.nesea.org/education/

Erasing Native American Stereotypes at the Smithsonian Institution's Anthropology Outreach Office website offers teachers advice on how to accurately present and study American Indian cultures, an excellent and recommended starting point for teachers as they begin to create and prepare lessons and units.
www.nmnh.si.edu/anthro/outreach/sterotyp.html

Social Studies School Service provides many resources in support of social studies units.
www.socialstudies.com/holo.html

SPICE, the Stanford Program on International and Cross-Cultural Education has a large number of teaching and learning materials on the world.
http://spice.stanford.edu

Free Global Education curriculum materials
www.globaled.org

References

Alleman, J., & Brophy, J. (1994). Trade-offs embedded in the literary approach to early elementary social studies. *Social Studies and the Young Learner 6*(3), 6–8.

Alleman, J., & Brophy, J. (1996). Considering textbook limitations and strategies for compensation. *Social Studies and the Young Learner 9*, 4–7.

Alleman, J., & Brophy, J. (1998). Strategic learning opportunities during out-of-school hours. *Social Studies and the Young Learner 11*(4), 10–13.

Allen, R. (1996). The Engle-Ochoa decision making model for citizenship education. In R. Evans & D. Saxe, (Eds.), *Handbook on teaching social issues, NCSS Bulletin 93* (pp. 51–58). Washington, DC: National Council for the Social Studies.

American Association for the Advancement of Science. (1993a). *Benchmarks for science literacy* (pp. 3–4, 322). New York: Oxford University Press.

American Association for the Advancement of Science. (1993b). *Science for all Americans.* New York: Oxford University Press.

Anderson, C. C. (1980). Promoting responsible citizenship through elementary law-related education. *Social Education 44,* 383–386.

Anderson, O. R. (1997). A neurocognitive perspective on current learning theory and science instructional strategies. *Science Education 81*(1), 67–89.

Angell, A. V., & Avery, P. G. (1992). Examining global issues in the elementary classroom. *The Social Studies 83*(3), 113–117.

Armento, B. J. (1986). Promoting economic literacy. In S. P. Wronski & D. H. Bragaw (Eds.), *Social studies and social science: A fifty-year perspective, Bulletin 78.* Washington, DC: National Council for the Social Studies.

Armento, B. J., & Flores, S. (1986). Learning about the economic world. In V. A. Atwood (Ed.), *Elementary school social studies: Research as a guide to practice, Bulletin 79* (pp. 85–101). Washington, DC: National Council for the Social Studies.

Atkins, C. (1981). Introducing basic map and globe concepts to young children. *Journal of Geography 80,* 223–232.

Ayers, W. (1993). *To teach: The journey of a teacher.* New York: Teachers College Press.

Baker, D. R., & Piburn, M. D. (1997). *Constructing science in middle and secondary school classrooms.* Boston: Allyn & Bacon.

Banaszak, R. A. (1987). *The nature of economic literacy.* Bloomington, IN: Clearinghouse for Social Studies/Social Science Education. (ERIC Digest No. 41).

Bandura, A. (1977). *Social learning theory.* Englewood Cliffs, NJ: Prentice Hall.

Banks, J. A., & Clegg, A. (1979). *Teaching strategies for the social studies: Inquiry, valuing and decision making* (2nd ed). Reading, MA: Addison Wesley.

Barell, J. (1991). Reflective teaching for thoughtfulness. In A. Costa (Ed.), *Developing minds: A resource book for teaching* (Rev. ed., Vol. 1, pp. 207–210). Alexandria, VA: Association for Supervision and Curriculum Development.

Barone, D. (1990). The written responses of young children: Beyond comprehension to story understanding. *The New Advocate 3*, 49–56.

Barr, R., Barth, J., & Shermis, S. (1977). *Defining the social studies* (NCSS Bulletin 51). Arlington, VA: National Council of the Social Studies.

Barton, K. C. (1997a). History—It can be elementary: An overview of elementary students' understanding of history. *Social Education 67*(1), 13–16.

Barton, K. C. (1997b). "I just kinda know": Elementary students' ideas about historical evidence. *Theory and Research in Social Education 25*(4), 407–430.

Bell, B., & Barker, M. (1982). Toward a scientific concept of animal. *Journal of Biological Education 16*(13), 197–200.

Bell, J. (1988). *Teaching multilevel classes in ESL.* Carlsbad, CA: Dominie Press.

Bellamy, N. (1994). Bias in the classroom: Are we guilty? *Science Scope 17*(6), 60–63.

Benjamin, J. R. (2001). *A student's guide to history* (8th ed.). Boston, MA: Bedford/St. Martin's.

Benniga, J. M. (1991). *Character and civic education in the elementary school.* New York: Teachers College Press.

Berk, L. (2000). *Child development* (5th ed.). Needham Heights, MA: Allyn and Bacon.

Berliner, D. (1987). Knowledge is power: A talk to teachers about a revolution in the teaching profession. In D. Berliner & B. Rosenshine (Eds.), *Talks to teachers.* New York: Random House.

Berliner, D., & Casanova, M. (1987). How do we tackle kids' science misconceptions? *Instructor 97*, 14–15.

Bernard-Powers, J. (1997). Gender in social education. In E. W. Ross (Ed.), *The social studies curriculum: Purposes, problems, and possibilities* (pp. 71–90). Albany, NY: State University of New York Press.

Berns, R. M. (1996). *Child, family, community.* Ft. Worth, TX: Harcourt.

Beyer, B. (1974). *Ethnicity in America.* Pittsburgh, PA: Carnegie Mellon University, Social Studies Curriculum Center.

Beyer, B. (1985). Critical thinking: What is it? *Social Education 49*, 270–276.

Bianchini, J. A. (1998). What's the big idea? *Science and Children 36*(2), 40–43.

Bos, C. S., & Anders, P. L. (1987). Semantic feature analysis: An interactive teaching strategy for facilitating learning from text. *Learning Disabilities Focus 3*(1), 55–59.

Bos, C. S., & Anders, P. L. (1990). Interactive teaching and learning: Instructional practices for teaching content and strategic knowledge. In T. E. Scruggs & B. Y. L. Wong (Eds.), *Intervention research in learning disabilities* (pp. 166–185). New York: Springer-Verlag.

Bradley Commission on History in the Schools. (1989). Building a history curriculum: Guidelines for teaching history in schools. In P. Gagnon (Ed.), *Historical literacy* (pp. 16–50). New York: Macmillan.

Bredekamp, S., & Copple, C. (1997). *Developmentally appropriate practice in early childhood programs* (rev. ed.). Washington, DC: NAEYC.

Brody, R. A. (1989). Why study politics? In national commission on social studies in the school, *Charting a course: Social studies for the 21st century* (pp. 59–63). Washington, DC: National Council for the Social Studies.

Brophy, J., & Alleman, J. (2000). Primary grade students' knowledge and thinking about Native American and pioneer homes. *Theory and Research in Social Education 28*(1), 96–120.

Brophy, J., & Van Sledright, B. (1997). *Teaching and learning history in elementary schools.* New York: Teachers College Press.

Brown, L. M., Tappan, M. B., & Gilligan, C. (1995). Listening to different voices. In W. M. Kurtines & J. L. Gewirtz (eds.), *Moral development: An Introduction* (pp. 311–336). Needham Heights, MA: Allyn and Bacon.

Brualdi, A. (1998). Implementing performance assessment in the classroom. *ERIC/AE Digest.* (ERIC Document Reproduction Service No. ED 423 312.)

Bruner, J. (1961). The act of discovery. *Harvard Educational Review 31*(1), 21–32.

Bruner, J., Goodnow, J., & Austin, G. A. (1962). *A study of thinking.* New York: Science Editions.

Buchovecky, E. (1996). Learning from students' work. *Horace 30,* 2.

Buggey, J., & Kracht, J. (1985). Geographic learning. In V. A. Atwood (Ed.), *Elementary school social studies: Research as a guide to practice, Bulletin 79* (pp. 55–67). Washington, DC: National Council for the Social Studies.

Bulgren, J. A., Deshler, D. D., & Schumaker, J. B. (1993). *The content enhancement series: The concept mastery routine.* Lawrence, KS: Edge Enterprises.

California State Department of Education. (1988). *History–social science framework for California public schools: Kindergarten through grade 12.* Sacramento, CA: Author.

Calkins, S. (1994). Origins and outcomes of individual differences in emotion regulation. In N. A. Fox (Ed.), *The development of emotion regulation: Biological and behavioral considerations. Monographs of the Society for Research in Child Development, 240*(59, Nos. 2–3), 53–61.

Capron, B. (1972). University of Minnesota social studies project. *Social Education 36,* 758–759.

Carnegie Corporation. (2003). *The civic mission of schools: A report from the Carnegie Corporation of New York ad Circle: The center for information and research on civic learning and engagement.* New York: Carnegie Corporation.

Catling, S. (1978). The child's spatial conception and geographic education. *Journal of Geography 77,* 24–28.

Center for Civic Education. (1994). *National standards for civics and government.* Calabasas, CA: Author.

Center for Multicultural Education. (2000). *Essential principles for teaching and learning in a multicultural society.* Seattle: University of Washington Center for Multicultural Education.

Charren, P. (1990). What's missing in children's TV? *World Monitor 3*(12), 28–35.

Christensen, L. M., & Dahle, K. B. (1998). Is social studies different because I am included? *The Docket: Journal of the New Jersey Council for the Social Studies 8,* 19–23.

Christensen, L. M., Sunal, C. S., & Haas, M. E. (1995). Using the five themes of geography to teach about Mexico. *Southern Social Studies Journal 21*(1), 17–30.

Clark, T. (1990). Participation in democratic citizenship education. *The Social Studies 81,* 206–209.

Collins, H., Czarra, F. & Smith, A. (1998). Guideline for global and international studies education: Challenges, culture, and connections. *Social Education 62(5)*, 311–317.

Conflict Resolution Education Network. (2000). Conflict resolution in schools. *The ERIC Review 7(1)*, 27.

Cook, L. K., & Mayer, R. E. (1988). Teaching readers about the structure of scientific text. *Journal of Educational Psychology 80*, 448–456.

Cook, R., Tessier, A., & Armbruster, V. (1987). *Adapting early childhood curricula for children with special needs.* Columbus, OH: Merrill.

Coopersmith, S. (1967). *The antecedents of self-esteem.* San Francisco: W. H. Freeman.

Costa, A. (1991). The inquiry strategy. In A. Costa (Ed.), *Developing minds: A resource book for teaching* (Rev. ed., Vol. 1, pp. 302–303). Alexandria, VA: Association for Supervision and Curriculum Development.

Costa, A. (2002). Mediating the metacognitive. In A. Costa (Ed.), *Developing minds: A resource book for teaching* (3rd. ed., pp. 408–412). Alexandria, VA: Association for Supervision and Curriculum Development.

Cotton, E. G. (1999). The virtual tour. In J. A. Braun & C. F. Risinger (Eds.), *Surfing social studies: The Internet book* (pp. 33–40). Washington, DC: National Council for the Social Studies.

Council of Chief State School Officers. (1988). *Geography education and the state.* Washington, DC: Author.

Cox, A. C. (1997). Using the stock market game in the social studies classroom. *Social Education 61(6)*, 347–350.

Cruz, B. C. (1998). Global education in the middle school curriculum: An interdisciplinary perspective. *Middle School Journal 30(2)*, 26–31.

Cruz, B. C., Nutta, J. W., O'Brien, J. O., Feyten, C. M., & Govoni, J. M. (2003). *Passport to learning: Teaching social studies to ESL students.* Bulletin 101. Silver Spring, MD: National Council for the Social Studies.

Cummins, J. (1984). *Bilingualism and special education: Issues in assessment and pedagogy.* San Diego: College-Hill.

Cummins, J. (1996). *Negotiating identities: Education for empowerment in a diverse society.* Los Angeles: California Association for Bilingual Education.

De Costa, S. (1990). Using resources to teach the social studies. In C. Sunal (Ed.), *Early childhood social studies* (p. 223). Columbus, OH: Merrill.

Doblin, J. (1980). A structure for nontextual communications. In P. A. Kolers, M. E. Rolstad, & H. Bouma (Eds.), *Processing of variable language, vol. 2* (pp. 84–111). New York: Plenum.

Dodge, K. A., & Crick, N. R. (1990). Social information-processing bases of aggressive behavior in children. *Personality and Social Psychology Bulletin 16*, 8–22.

Donnan, C. S. (1988). Following our forebears' footsteps: From expedition to understanding. In V. Rogers, A. D. Roberts, & T. P. Weiland (Eds.), *Teaching social studies: Portraits from the classroom, Bulletin 82.* Washington, DC: National Council for the Social Studies.

Downs, R., Liben, L., & Daggs, D. (1988). On education and geographers: The role of cognitive development theory in geographic education. *The Annals of the Association of American Geographers 78*, 680–700.

Drake, J. J., & Drake, F. D. (1990). Using children's literature to teach about the American Revolution. *Social Studies and the Young Learner 3(2)*, 6–8.

Dreyfus, A., Jungwirth, E., & Eliovitch R. (1990). Applying the cognitive conflict strategy for conceptual change—Some implications, difficulties, and problems. *Science Education 74*(5), 555–569.

Driver, R., Leach, J., Millar, R., & Scott, P. (1996). *Young people's images of science.* Philadelphia: Open University Press.

Duit, R. (1987). Research on students' alternative frameworks in science—Topics, theoretical frameworks, consequences for science teaching. *Proceedings of the second international seminar: Misconceptions and educational strategies in science and mathematics,* 1, 151–162. Ithaca, NY: Cornell University.

Dunfee, M. (1977). *Social studies for the real world.* Columbus, OH: Merrill.

Dunfee, M., & Sagl, H. (1967). *Social studies through problem solving: A challenge to elementary school teachers.* New York: Holt, Rinehart, & Winston.

Dunn, R. E., & Vigilante, D. (1996). *Bring history alive!: A sourcebook for teaching world history.* Los Angeles: University of California, National Center for History in the Schools.

Eddington, W. D. (1998). The use of children's literature in middle school social studies: What research does and does not show. *The Clearing House 72*(2), 121–125.

Eggen, P., & Kauchak, D. (2001). *Strategies for teachers: Teaching content and thinking skills.* Englewood Cliffs, NJ: Prentice Hall.

Eggen, P., Kauchak, D., & Harder, R. (1979). *Strategies for teachers.* Englewood Cliffs, NJ: Prentice Hall.

Ekman, P., & Davidson, R. (Eds.). (1994). *Fundamental questions about emotions.* New York: Oxford University Press.

Elliot, S. N. (1995). Creating meaningful performance assessments *ERIC Digest E531.* (ERIC Document Reproduction Service No. ED 381 985.)

Engle, S. H., & Ochoa, A. S. (1988). *Education for democratic citizenship: Decision making in the social studies.* New York: Teachers College Press.

Englert, C. S., & Mariage, T. V. (1991). Making students partners in the comprehension process: Organizing the reading "POSSE." *Learning Disabilities Quarterly 14,* 123–138.

Englert, C. S., Tarrant, K. L., Mariage, T. V., & Oxer, T. (1994). Lesson talk as the work of reading groups: The effectiveness of two interventions. *Journal of Learning Disabilities 27,* 165–185.

Ennis, R. (1991). Goals for a critical thinking curriculum. In A. Costa (Ed.), *Developing minds: A resource book for teaching,* (Rev. ed., Vol. 1, pp. 68–71). Alexandria, VA: Association for Supervision and Curriculum Development.

Evans, R., Newmann, F., & Saxe, D. (1996). Defining issues-centered education. In R. Evans & D. Saxe (Eds.), *Handbook on teaching social issues, NCSS Bulletin 93* (pp. 1–5). Washington, DC: National Council for the Social Studies.

Farris, P. J., & Cooper, S. M. (1994). *Elementary social studies: A whole language approach.* Madison, WI: William Brown & Benchmark.

Finkelstein, J. (1991). *Appropriate assessment practices for early childhood/elementary social studies.* Paper presented at the annual meeting of the National Council for the Social Studies, Washington, DC.

Flaitz, J. (Ed.). *Understanding your international students: A cultural, educational, and linguistic guide.* Ann Arbor, MI: University of Michigan Press.

Fraenkel, J. (1977). *How to teach about values: An analytic approach.* Englewood Cliffs, NJ: Prentice Hall.

Francis, J. (1990). Hands-on legislation. *Social Studies and the Young Learner* 2(4), 6–8.

French, D., Brownell, C., Graziano, W., & Hartup, W. (1977). Effects of cooperative, competitive, and individualistic sets on performance in children's groups. *Journal of Experimental Child Psychology 24*, 1–10.

Gagne, R. (1965). *The conditions of learning.* New York: Holt, Rinehart and Winston.

Gilligan, C. (1982). *In a different voice: Psychological theory and women's development.* Cambridge, MA: Harvard University Press.

Gil-Perez, D., & Carrascosa, J. (1990). What to do about science "misconceptions." *Science Education 74*(5), 531–540.

Ginsburg, H., & Opper, S. (1979). *Piaget's theory of intellectual development* (2nd ed.). Englewood Cliffs, NJ: Prentice Hall.

Ginsburg, H., & Opper, S. (1988). *Piaget's theory of intellectual development* (3rd ed.). Englewood Cliffs, NJ: Prentice Hall.

Glatthorn, A., & Baron, J. (1991). The good thinker. In A. Costa (Ed.), *Developing minds: A resource book for teaching* (Rev. ed., Vol. 1, pp. 106–113). Alexandria, VA: Association of Supervision and Curriculum Development.

Goldman, S. R., Williams, S. M., Sherwood, R. D., & Hasselbring, T. S. (1999). *Technology for teaching and learning with understanding: A primer.* New York: Houghton Mifflin.

Goodman, J., & Adler, S. (1985). Becoming an elementary social studies teacher: A study of perspectives. *Theory and Research in Social Education 13*(2), 1–20.

Grosvenor, G. (1985). Geographic ignorance: Time for a turnaround. *National Geographic Magazine 167*, 6.

Grusec, J. E., Goodnow, J. J., & Cohen, L. (1996). Household work and the development of concern for others. *Developmental Psychology 32*, 999–1007.

Haas, M. E. (1985). Evaluating sponsored materials. *How To Do It Series 4 Number 3.* Washington, DC: National Council for the Social Studies.

Haas, M. (1989). *Teaching geography in the elementary school.* Bloomington, IN: Clearinghouse for Social Studies Social Science Education. (ERIC Digest No. ED-SO-89–6.)

Haas, M. E. (1991). An analysis of the social science and history concepts in elementary social studies textbooks grades 1–4. *Theory and Research in Social Education 19*, 211–220.

Haas, M. E. (2000). A street through time used with powerful instructional strategies. *Social Studies and the Young Learner 13*(2), 20–23.

Haas, M. E., & Laughlin, M. A. (1999a). *Meeting the standards: Social studies reading for K–6 educators.* Washington, DC: National Council for the Social Studies.

Haas, M. E., & Laughlin, M. A. (1999b). *Perspectives on social studies over a quarter of a century: Reflections from veteran social studies leaders.* (ERIC Document Reproduction Service No. ED 432 516.) Bloomington, IN: Social Studies Development Center and ERIC Clearinghouse for Social Studies/Social Science Education.

Haas, M. E., & Laughlin, M. A. (2000). *Teaching current events: Its status in social studies today.* (ERIC Document Reproduction Service No. ED 440 899.) Bloomington, IN: Social Studies Development Center and ERIC Clearinghouse for Social Studies/Social Science Education.

Haas, M. E., & Laughlin, M. A. (2001). A profile of elementary social studies teachers and their classrooms. *Social Education 65*(2), 122–126.

Hackmann, D. G. (1997). Student-led conferences at the middle level. *ERIC Digest.* (ERIC Document Reproduction Service No. ED 407 171.) Champaign, IL: ERIC Clearinghouse on Elementary and Early Childhood Education.

Hampton, E., & Gallegos, C. (1994). Science for all students. *Science Scope 17*(6), 5–8.

Hannigan, M. R. (1990). Cooperative learning in elementary school science. *Educational Leadership 47*(4), 25.

Hanvey, R. G. (1976). *An attainable global perspective.* New York: Center for Global Perspectives.

Hart, D. (1999). Opening assessment to our students. *Social Education 63*(6), 343–345.

Hartup, W. W., Glazer, J., & Charlesworth, R. (1987). Peer reinforcement and sociometric status. *Child Development 38,* 1017–1024.

Hartup, W. W., & Stevens, N. (1997). Friendships and adaptation in the life course. *Psychological Bulletin 121,* 355–370.

Harvey, T. L., & Pappas, C. C. (1987). Exploring the development of historical understanding. *Journal of Research and Development in Education 21,* 1–15.

Heacock, G. A. (1990). The we-search process: Using the whole language model of writing to learn social studies content and civic competence. *Social Studies and the Young Learner 2*(3), 9–11.

Hepburn, M. A. (1998). The power of the electronic media in the socialization of young Americans: Implications for social studies education. *The Social Studies 89*(2), 63–71.

Hepburn, M. A. (2000). Service learning and civic education in the schools: What does recent research tell us? In S. Mann

& J. J. Patrick (Eds.). *Education for civic engagement: Service learning and other promising practices* (pp. 45–59). Bloomington, IN: ERIC Clearinghouse for Social Studies/Social Science Education.

Herlihy, J., & Herlihy, M. (Eds.). (1980). *Mainstreaming in the social studies.* Washington, DC: National Council for the Social Studies.

Herrenkohl, R. C., Egolf, B. P., & Herrenkohl, E. C. (1997). Preschool antecedents of adolescent assaultive behavior: A longitudinal study. *American Journal of Orthopsychiatry 67,* 422–432.

Hertzberger, H. (1989). History and progressivism: A century of reform proposals. In P. Gagon (Ed.), *Historical literacy* (pp. 69–102). New York: Macmillan.

Hickey, M. G. (1999). *Bringing history home: Local and family history projects for grades K–6.* Boston: Allyn & Bacon.

Hoffman, M. (1977). Moral internalization: Current theory and research. In L. Berkowitz (Ed.), *Advances in experimental social psychology* (Vol. 10, pp. 86–127). New York: Academic Press.

Hoge, J. (1986). *Improving the use of elementary social studies textbooks.* (ERIC Digest No. 33.) Bloomington, IN: Clearinghouse for Social Studies/Social Science Education.

Hoge, J. D., & Allen, R. F. (1991). Teaching about our world community: Guidelines and resources. *Social Studies and the Young Learner 3*(4), 19, 28–32.

Hoge, J. D., & Crump, C. (1988). *Teaching history in the elementary school.* (ERIC Document Reproduction Service No. ED 292 749.) Bloomington, IN: Social Studies Development Center and ERIC Clearinghouse for Social Studies/Social Science Education.

Holloway, G. (1967). *An introduction to the child's conception of space.* New York: Humanities Press.

Holmes, E. E. (1991). Democracy in elementary school classes. *Social Education 55,* 176–178.

Holmes Group. (1986). *Tomorrow's teachers: A report of the Holmes groups.* East Lansing, MI: Author.

Honig, A. S., & Wittmer, D. S. (1996). Helping children become more prosocial: Ideas for classrooms, families, schools and communities. *Young Children 51*(2), 62–70.

Huntley, M. A. (1999). Theoretical and empirical investigations of integrated mathematics and science education in the middle grades with implications for teacher education. *Journal of Teacher Education 50*(1), 57–67.

Hursh, D. (1997). *Multicultural social studies: Schools as places for examining and challenging inequality* (pp. 107–120). Albany, NY: State University of New York Press.

Hyman, M. (2001). One step at a time: A land mine removal initiative. *Middle Level Learning 14,* 10–15.

Ianotti, R. (1978). Effect of role-taking experiences on role-taking, empathy, altruism, and aggression. *Developmental Psychology 14,* 119–124.

Jacobowitz, R. (1997). 30 tips for effective teaching. *Science Scope 21*(4), 22–25.

Jarolimek, J. (1991). *Social studies in the elementary school* (8th ed.). New York: Macmillan.

Jennes, D. (1990). *Making sense of social studies.* New York: Macmillan.

Johnson, D., Johnson, R., & Holubec, E. (1990a). *Circles of learning.* Edina, MN: Interaction Book Company.

Johnson, D., Johnson, R., & Holubec, E. (1990b). *Cooperation in the classroom.* Edina, MN: Interaction Book Company.

Johnson, D. W., & Johnson, R. T. (1978). Cooperative, competitive, and individualistic learning. *Journal of Research and Development in Education 12*(1), 3–15.

Johnson, D. W., & Johnson, R. T. (1991). Group assessment as an aid to science instruction. In G. Kulm & S. Malcolm (Eds.), *Science assessment in the service of reform* (pp. 281–289). Washington, DC: American Association for the Advancement of Science.

Johnson, R. T. & Johnson, D. W. (1986). Action research: Cooperative learning in the science classroom. *Science and Children 24*(2), 31–32.

Joseph, P. R. (2000). Law and pop culture: Teaching and learning about law using images from popular culture. *Social Education 64*(4), 206–211.

Joyce, B., & Weil, M. (1992). *Models of teaching* (pp. 159–179). Englewood Cliffs, NJ: Prentice Hall.

Joyce, W., & Alleman-Brooks, J. (1982). The child's world. *Social Education 46,* 538–541.

Katz, L. G., & McClellan, D. E. (1997). *Fostering children's social competence: The teacher's role.* Washington, DC: NAEYC.

King, A., & Rosenshine, B. (1993). Effects of guided cooperative questioning on children's knowledge construction. *Journal of Experimental Education 61*(2), 127–48.

Klausmeier, H., Ghatala, E., & Frayer, D. (1974). *Conceptual learning and development: A cognitive view.* Orlando, FL: Academic Press.

Klumb, K. (1992). *Generic consideration in adjusting curriculum and instruction for at-risk students.* Lucerne, CA: Lucerne Valley Unified School District. (ERIC Document Reproduction Service No. ED 342 141.)

Kniep, W. M. (1989). Social studies within a global education. *Social Education 53,* 399–403.

Kohlberg, L. (1969). Stage and sequence: The cognitive developmental approach to socialization. In D. Goslin (Ed.), *Handbook of socialization theory and research* (pp. 118–140). Chicago: Rand McNally.

Konner, M. (1991). *Childhood.* Boston: Little Brown.

Kostelnik, M. J., Stein, L. C., Whiren, A. P., & Soderman, A. K. (1998). *Guiding children's social development* (3rd ed.). Albany, NY: Delmar.

Kostelnik, M. J., Whiren, A. P., Soderman, A. K., Stein, L. C., & Gregory, K. (2002). *Guiding children's social development: Theory to practice.* Albany, NY: Thomson Delmar.

Kounin, J. (1970). *Discipline and group management in classrooms.* Huntington, NY: R. E. Kreiger.

Kourilsky, M. L. (1977). The kinder economy: A case study of kindergarten pupils' acquisition of economic concepts. *Elementary School Journal 77,* 182–191.

Kourilsky, M. L. (1987). *Mini-society experiencing real-world economics in the elementary school classroom.* Menlo Park, CA: Addison-Wesley.

Kurtines, W., & Greif, E. (1974). The development of moral thought: Review and evaluation of Kohlberg's approach. *Psychological Bulletin 81,* 453–470.

Kysilko, D. (Ed.). (1995). *Winners all: A call for inclusive schools.* Alexandria, VA: National Association of Boards of Education.

Laney, J. D. (1993). Economics for elementary school students' research-supported principles of teaching and learning that guide classroom practice. *The Social Studies 84*(3), 99–103.

Langston, S. (1990). Citizen participation and citizenship education in the 21st century. In W. T. Callahan, Jr., & R. A. Banaszak (Eds.), *Citizenship for the 21st century* (pp. 297–310). Bloomington, IN: Social Studies Development Center.

Larson, B., & Keiper, T. A. (1999). Creating teledemocracy. In Joseph A. Braun, Jr., & C. Frederick Risinger (Eds.), *Surfing social studies: The Internet book, Bulletin 96* (pp. 49–52). Washington, DC: National Council for the Social Studies.

Lawson, A., Abraham, M., & Renner, J. (1989). *A theory of instruction: Using the learning cycle to teach concepts and thinking skills.* Atlanta, GA: National Association for Research in Science Teaching, Monograph #1.

Levstik, L. (1986). The relationship between historical response and narrative in a sixth grade class. *Theory and Research in Social Education 15*(1), 1–17.

Levstik, L., & Barton, K. (1997). *Doing history: Investigating with children in elementary and middle schools.* Mahwah, NJ: Erlbaum.

Lewis, B. A. (1991). *The kid's guide to social action.* Minneapolis, MN: Free Spirit.

Lopach, J., & Luckowski, J. (1989, March). The rediscovery of memory in teaching democratic values. *Social Education 53,* 183–187.

Lutkus, A. D., Weiss, A. R., Campbell, J. R., Mazzeo, J., & Lazer, S. (1999). *The NAEP 1998 civics report card for the nation,* NCES 2000–457, Washington, DC: U.S. Department of Education, Office of Educational Research and Improvement, National Center for Education Statistics.

Lynch, E. W. (1998). Developing cross-cultural competence. In E. W. Lynch & M. J. Hanson (Eds.), *Developing cross-cultural competence: A guide to working with children and their families* (pp. 47–86). Baltimore: Paul H. Brookes.

Macoby, E. (1980). *Social development: Psychological growth and the parent–child relationship*. New York: Harcourt Brace Jovanovich.

Macoby, E., & Masters, J. (1970). Attachment and dependency. In P. Mussen (Ed.), *Carmichael's manual of child psychology* (3rd ed., Book 2). New York: Wiley.

Mager, R. (1962). *Preparing instructional objectives*. Belmont, CA: Fearon.

Magnusson, S. J., & Palinscar, A. S. (1995). The learning environment as a site of science education reform. *Theories into Practice 34*(1), 43–50.

Marshall, C., & Rossman, G. B. (1995). *Designing qualitative research* (2nd ed.). Thousand Oaks, CA: Sage.

Martin-Kniep, G., & Soodak, L. (1995). Curriculum integration: An expanded view of an abused idea. *Journal of Curriculum and Supervision 10*(3), 227–249.

Martorella, P. H. (1994). *Social studies for elementary school children: Developing young citizens* (2nd ed.). Columbus, OH: Merrill.

Massachusetts Institute of Technology. (1990). *Education that works: An action plan for the education of minorities*. (Quality of Education for Minorities Report.) Cambridge: Massachusetts Institute of Technology.

Mastropieri, M. A., & Scruggs, T. E. (2000). *The inclusive classroom: Strategies for effective instruction*. Columbus, OH: Merrill.

Mayer, V. (1995). Using Earth System for Integrating Science Curriculum. *Science Education 79*(4), 375–391.

McBee, R. H. (1996). Can controversial topics be taught in the early grades? The answer is yes! *Social Education 60*(1), 38–41.

McCaleb, S. P. (1994). *Building communities of learners: A collaboration among teachers, families, and community*. New York: St. Martin's Press.

McGowan, T. M., Erickson, L., & Neufeld, J. S. (1996). With reason and rhetoric: Building the case for the literature–social studies connection. *Social Education 60*(4), 51–60.

Merryfield, M. (in press). Engaging elementary children in substantive culture learning. *Social Education*.

Meyer, J. (1973). Map skills instruction and the child's developing cognitive abilities. *Journal of Geography 72*, 29–35.

Mitsakos, C. (1978). A global education program can make a difference. *Theory and Research in Social Education 6*(1), 1–15.

Morris, R. V., & Welch, M. (2000). *How to perform acting out history in the classroom to enrich social studies education*. Dubuque, IA: Kendall/Hunt Publishing Company.

Morrison, D., & Collins, J. (1995). Epistemic fluency and constructivist learning environments. *Educational Technology 35*(4), 60–63.

Morrissett, I. (1981). The needs of the future and the constraints of the past. In H. D. Mehlinger & O. L. Davis, Jr. (Eds.), *The social studies* (80th Yearbook of the National Society for the Study of Education). Chicago: University of Chicago Press.

Moulton, L., & Trevis, C. (1991). Making history come alive: Using historical photos in the classroom. *Social Studies and the Young Learner 3*(4), 12–14.

National Center for Educational Statistics. (1995). *NAEP 1994 geography: A first look: Findings from the National Assessment of Educational Progress*. Washington, DC: Office of Educational Research and Improvement, U.S. Department of Education.

National Center for Educational Statistics. (1996). *NAEP 1994 geography report card: Findings from the National Assessment of Educational Progress.* Washington, DC: Office of Educational Research and Improvement, U.S. Department of Education.

National Center for Educational Statistics. (2002). *Geography highlights: The Nation's report card 2001.* Washington, DC: Office of Educational Research and Improvement NCES 2002–485, U.S. Department of Education.

National Center for History in the Schools. (1994). *National standards for United States history: Exploring the American experience; National standards for world history: Exploring paths to the present; and National standards for history: Expanding children's world in time and space.* Los Angeles: University of California Press.

National Clearinghouse for English Language Acquisition. (2001). Survey of states' LEP students and available educational programs and services 1999–2000 summary report. http:// www.ncbe.gwn.edu/ncbepubs/seareports/99-00/sea9900.pdf. Retrieved August 16, 2003.

National Council for Economics Education. (1997). *Voluntary national content standards in economics.* New York: Economics America.

National Council for Geographic Education. (1994). *Geography for life: National geography standards 1994.* Washington, DC: National Geographic Society.

National Council for the Social Studies. (1976). *Curriculum guidelines for multiethnic education.* Washington, DC: Author.

National Council for the Social Studies. (1989). In search of a scope and sequence for social studies report of the task force on scope and sequence. *Social Education 53,* 376–387.

National Council for the Social Studies. (1991). *Testing and evaluation of social studies students.* Washington, DC: National Council for the Social Studies. Retrieved on February 3, 2001 from the World Wide Web: http://www.sociastudies.org/standard/positions/testingandeval/html.

National Council for the Social Studies. (1994a). *Charting the course: Social studies for the 21st century* (p. 59–63). Washington, DC: Author.

National Council for the Social Studies. (1994b). *Expectations of excellence: Curriculum standards for social studies.* Washington, DC: Author.

National Council for the Social Studies. (1996). *Fostering civic virtue: Character education in the social studies.* Washington, DC: Author.

National Council for Social Studies. (1997). *Position statement: Fostering civic virtue: Character education in the schools.* Washington, DC: Author.

National Council of Teachers of Mathematics. (1989). *Curriculum and evaluation standards for school mathematics.* Reston, VA: Author.

National Research Council. (1996). *National science education standards.* Washington, DC: National Academy Press.

Naylor, D., & Diem, R. (1987). *Elementary and middle school social studies.* New York: Random House.

Nelson, L. R. (1997). Recent trends in economic education. *ERIC Digest.* (ERIC Document Reproduction Service No. ED 412 171.)

Nelson, M. (1990). A future for civic education. In W. T. Callahan, Jr., & Banaszak, R. A. (Eds.), *Citizenship for the 21st century* (pp. 42–57). Bloomington, IN: Social Studies Development Center.

Nickell, P. (1999). The issue of subjectivity in authentic social studies assessment. *Social Education 63*(6), 353–355.

Novak, J. D. (1995). *Concept maps help teachers learn.* New York: Cornell University.

Novak, J. D., Gowin, D. B., & Johansen, G. T. (1983). The use of concept mapping and knowledge mapping with junior high school students. *Science Education 67,* 625–645.

Pagano, A. (1978). Children learning and using social studies content. In A. Pagano (Ed.), *Social studies in early childhood: An interactionist point of view* (pp. 82–94). Washington, DC: National Council for the Social Studies.

Paige, R. (2002a). Press Release, May 9. Retrieved from www.ed.gov/print/news/speeches/ 2002/05/5092002.html.

Paige, R. (2002b). Press Release, June 21. Retrieved from www.ed.gov/print/news/speeches/ 2002/06/062102a.html.

Parker, W. (2001a). Classroom discussion: Models for learning seminars and deliberations. *Social Education 65*(2), 111–115.

Parker, W. (2001b). Toward enlightened political engagement. In W. B. Stanley (Ed.), *Critical issues in social studies research for the 21st century* (pp. 97–118). Greenwich, CT: Information Age.

Parker, W., Ninomiya, A., & Cogan, J. J. (2002). Educating world citizens toward multinational curriculum development. In W. Parker (Ed.), *Education for democracy: Context, curricula, assessments* (vol. 2, pp. 151–182). Greenwich, CT: Information Age.

Patrick, J. (1991). Student achievement in core subjects of the school curriculum. *ERIC Digest.* (ERIC Document Reproduction Service No. ED 332 930.)

Patrick, J. P. (2003, May 7). Teaching democracy globally, internationally, and comparatively: The 21st century civic mission of schools. Paper presented at the third annual R. Freeman Butts Institute on Civic Learning in Teacher Education in Indianapolis, Indiana.

Patrick, J. J. (1999). *The concept of citizenship in education for democracy.* (ERIC Digest No. EDO-SO-1999-6.)

Patrick, J. J., & Hoge, J. D. (1991). Teaching government, civics and law. In J. P. Shaver (Ed.), *Handbook of research on social studies teaching and learning* (pp. 427–436). New York: Macmillan.

Perie, M. (1997). *Time spent teaching core academic subjects in elementary schools. Comparisons across community, school, teacher, and student characteristics. Statistical analysis report.* Washington, DC: American Institutes for Research in the Behavioral Sciences.

Perkins, D. (1992). Technology meets constructivism: Do they make a marriage? In T. M. Duffy & D. Jonassen (Eds.), *Constructivism and the technology of instruction* (pp. 45–55). Hillsdale, NJ: Erlbaum.

Perkins, D., & Blythe, T. (1994). Putting understanding up front. *Educational Leadership 51*(5), 4–7.

Perkins, D., & Salomon, G. (1991). Teaching for transfer. In D. Costa (Ed.), *Developing minds: A resource book for teaching thinking.* (pp. 215–223). Alexandria, VA: Association for Supervision and Curriculum Development.

Piaget, J. (1963). *Origins of intelligence in children.* New York: Norton.

Piaget, J. (1970). *The science of education and the psychology of the child.* New York: Orion Press.

Pigozzi, B. (1990). *A view of geography and elementary education* (Elementary Subjects Center Series No. 18). East Lansing: Michigan State University, Institute for

Research on Teaching, Center for the Learning and Teaching of Elementary Subjects.

Pintrich, P. R., Marx, R. W., & Boyle, R. A. (1993). Beyond conceptual change: The role of motivational beliefs and classroom contextual factors in the process of conceptual change. *Review of Educational Research 63*(2), 167–200.

Pollock, J. E. (1992). Blueprints for social studies. *Educational Leadership 49*(8), 52–53.

Potari, D., & Spiliotopoulou, V. (1996). Children's approaches to the concept of volume. *Social Studies Education 80*(3), 341–360.

Procter, D. R., & Haas, M. E. (1990). *A handbook of school-based community projects for student participation.* (ERIC Document Reproduction Service No. ED 326 467.) Bloomington, IN: Social Studies Development Center and Eric Clearinghouse for Social Studies/Social Science Education.

Pugh, S. L., & Garcia, J. (1996). Issues-centered education in multicultural environments. In R. W. Evans & D. W. Saxe (Eds.), *Handbook of teaching on social issues, National Council for the Social Studies Bulletin 93* (pp. 121–129). Washington, DC: National Council for the Social Studies.

Putnam, J. (1993). *Cooperative learning and strategies for inclusion: Celebrating diversity in the classroom.* Baltimore: Paul H. Brookes.

Quilty, R. (1975). Imitation as a dyadic interchange pattern. *Scandinavian Journal of Psychology 16,* 223–239.

Rains, F. V., & Swisher, K. G. (1999). Authentic voices: Advice for incorporating American Indians and Alaska Natives in the elementary school curriculum. *Social Education 63*(1), 46–50.

Ramler, S. (1991). Global education for the 21st century. *Educational Leadership 48*(7), 44–46.

Raths, L., Harmin, M., & Simon, S. (1978). *Values and teaching* (2nd ed.). Columbus, OH: Merrill.

Rea, D. (1999). Serious fun in social studies. *Middle Level Learning 6,* 2–5.

Reisman, J., & Shor, S. (1978). Friendship claims and expectations among children and adults. *Child Development 49,* 913–916.

Rice, M., & Cobb, R. (1978). *What can children learn in geography?: A review of the research.* Boulder, CO: Social Science Education Consortium. (ERIC Document Reproduction Service, ED 166 088).

Riley, R. (2000, May). U.S. *Secretary of Education Richard Riley announced the grantees for 2000 under the Partnerships in Character Education Pilot Projects Program.* Washington, DC: U.S. Department of Education.

Roach, V., Ascroft, J., & Stamp, A. (1995). *Winning ways: Creating inclusive schools, classrooms and communities.* Alexandria, VA: National Association of Boards of Education.

Rosenshine, B. (1983). Teaching functions in instructional programs. *The Elementary School Journal 4,* 335–351.

Rowe, M. B. (1987). Wait-time: Slowing down may be a way of speeding up. *American Educator 11*(1), 38–47.

Rowe, M. B. (1996). Science, silence, and sanctions. *Science and Children 34*(1), 35–37.

Roy, P. (1994). Cultivating cooperative group process skills within the social studies classroom. In R. J. Stahl (Ed.), *Cooperative learning in social studies: A handbook for teachers* (pp. 18–50). Menlo Park, CA: Addison-Wesley.

Rutter, R. A., & Newmann, F. M. (1989). The potential of community service to enhance civic responsibility. *Social Education 53,* 371–374.

Rye, J. A., & Rubba, P. A. (1998). An exploration of the concept map as an interview tool to facilitate the externalization of students' understandings about global atmospheric change. *Journal of Research in Science Teaching 35*(5), 521–546.

Sadowsky, E. (1991). Democracy in the elementary school: Learning by doing. In J. S. Bennina (Ed.), *Moral character, and the civic education in the elementary school* (pp. 84–106). New York: Teachers College Press.

Sanger, M. J., & Greenbowe, T. J. (1997). Common misconceptions in electrochemistry: Galvanic, electrolytic, and concentration cells. *Journal of Research in Science Teaching 34*(4), 377–398.

Saunders, P., Bach, G. L., Calderwood, J. D., & Hansen, W. L. (1984). *Master curriculum guide in economics: A framework for teaching the basic concepts* (2nd ed.). New York: Joint Council for Economic Education.

Saunders, P., & Gilliard, J. V. (Eds.). (1995). *A framework for teaching the basic concepts and scope and sequences K–12.* New York: National Council on Economic Education.

Saunders, W. (1992). The constructivist perspective: Implications for teaching strategies for social studies. *School Science and Mathematics 92*(3), 16–27.

Savage, T., & Bacon, P. (1969). Teaching symbolic map skills with primary grade children. *Journal of Geography 68,* 326–332.

Scarcella, R. (1980). *Teaching language minority students in the multicultural classroom.* Englewood Cliffs, NJ: Prentice Hall.

Scheurman, G., & Newman, F. (1998). Authentic intellectual work in social studies: Putting performance before pedagogy. *Social Education 62*(1), 23–25.

Schon, D. (1987). *The reflective practitioner.* New York: Basic Books.

Schrag, J., & Burnett, J. (1994). Inclusive schools. *Research Roundup 10*(2). Alexandria, VA: The National Association of Elementary School Principals. (ERIC Document Reproduction Service No. ED 367 077).

Schug, M. C. (1997). Economics for kids: Ideas for teaching in the elementary grades. In M. E. Haas & M. A. Laughlin (Eds.), *Meeting the standards: Social studies readings for K–6 educators* (pp. 166–168). Washington, DC: National Council for the Social Studies.

Schug, M. C., & Beery, R. (1987). *Teaching social studies in the elementary school: Issues and practices.* Glenview, IL: Scott Foresman.

Schug, M. C., Todd, R., & Beery, R. (1984). Why kids don't like social studies. *Social Education 48,* 382–387.

Schug, M. C., & Walstad, W. B. (1991). Teaching and learning economics. In J. P. Shaver (Ed.), *Handbook for research on social studies teaching and learning* (pp. 411–419). New York: Macmillan.

Schwab, J. (1974). The concept of the structure of a discipline. In E. Eisner & E. Vallance (Eds.), *Conflicting conceptions of curriculum* (pp. 162–175). Berkeley, CA: McCutchan.

Scott, T. J., & O'Sullivan, M. (2000). The Internet and information literacy: Taking the first step toward technology education. *The Social Studies 91*(3), 121–125.

Sears, R. (1963). Dependency motivation. In M. R. Jones (Ed.), *Nebraska symposium on motivation, 2* (pp. 25–64). Lincoln, NE: University of Nebraska Press.

Seifert, K. L., & Hofnung, R. J. (2000). *Child and adolescent development* (5th ed.). Boston: Houghton Mifflin.

Seiger-Ehrenberg, S. (2002). Concept development. In A. Costa (Ed.), *Developing minds: A resource book for teaching* (3rd. ed., Vol. 1, pp. 437–441). Alexandria, VA: Association for Supervision and Curriculum Development.

Shaffer, D. R. (2000). *Social and personality development*. Pacific Grove, CA: Brooks/Cole.

Shaftel, F. R., & Shaftel, G. (1982). *Role playing for social value* (2nd ed.). Englewood Cliffs, NJ: Prentice Hall.

Shaver, J., Davis, O. L., Jr., & Helburn, S. W. (1979). The status of social studies education: Impressions from three NSF studies. *Social Education 43,* 150–153.

Shaw, E., Jr., & Hatfield, M. (1996). *A survey of the use of science manipulatives in elementary schools.* Columbus, OH: Science, Mathematics and Environmental Education. (ERIC Document Reproduction Service No. ED 404160).

Siegal, R. (1998). *Whalesong.* (Cassette Recording YA 965) Read by Don West. New York: Listening Library.

Singer, A. (1992). Multiculturalism and democracy: The promise of multicultural education. *Social Education 56,* 83–85.

Singleton, L., & Asher, S. (1979). Racial integration and children's peer preferences: An investigation of developmental and cohort differences. *Child Development 50,* 936–941.

Skeel, D. J. (1996). An issue-centered element curriculum. In R. Evans & D. Saxe (Eds.), *Handbook on teaching social issues* (pp. 230–235). Washington, DC: National Council for the Social Studies.

Skinner, R., & Chapman, C. (1999). *Service learning and community service in K–12 public schools.* (NCES 1999-0443). Washington, DC: U.S. Department of Education, National Center for Education Statistics.

Slavin, R. E. (1988). Cooperative learning and student achievement. *Educational Leadership 46*(2), 31–38.

Slavin, R. E. (1989). Research on cooperative learning: Consensus and controversy. *Educational Leadership 47*(4), 52–54.

Smith, A. (1985). Channeling in on good citizenship. *The Social Studies 76*(91), 28–31.

Smith C. A. (1982). *Promoting the social development of young children.* Palo Alto, CA: Mayfield.

Snarey, J. (1985). The cross-cultural universality of social-moral development: A critical review of Kohlbergian research. *Psychological bulletin, 97,* 202–232.

Snarey, J. (1995). In a communitarian voice: The sociological expansion of Kohlbergian theory, research, and practice. In W. M. Kurtines & J. L. Gewirtz (Eds.), *Moral development: An introduction* (pp. 109–134). Needham Heights, MA: Allyn and Bacon.

South Central Bell. (1994). *Black achievers in science.* Birmingham, AL: Author.

Spargo, P. E., & Enderstein, L. G. (1997). What questions do they ask? Ausubel rephrased. *Science and Children 34*(6), 43–45.

Spivack, G., Platt, J., & Shure, M. (1976). *The problem-solving approach to adjustment.* San Francisco: Jossey Bass.

Stahl, R. J. (1994). Cooperative learning: A social studies context and an overview. In R. J. Stahl (Ed.), *Cooperative learning in social studies: A handbook for teachers* (pp. 1–17). Menlo Park, CA: Addison Wesley.

Stauffer, R. G. (1969). Directing reading maturity as a cognitive process. New York: Harper & Row.

Starr, I. (1989). The law studies movement: A brief commentary on its history and rationale. *ATSS/UFT Journal 44*(10), 5–7.

Stefanich, G. P. (1992). Reflections on elementary school science. *Journal of Elementary Science Education 4*(2), 13–22.

Sternberg, R. J. (1994). Diversifying instruction and assessment. *Educational Forum 59*, 47–52.

Stoltzman, J. (1990). *Geography education for citizenship*. (ERIC Document Reproduction Service No. ED 322 081). Bloomington, IN: ERIC Clearinghouse for Social Studies/Social Science Education.

Sunal, C. (1986). Parent involvement in social studies programs. In V. Atwood (Ed.), *Elementary school social studies: Research as a guide to practice* (pp. 146–164). Washington, DC: National Council for the Social Studies.

Sunal, C. (1990). *Early childhood social studies*. Columbus, OH: Merrill.

Sunal, C. S., & Haas, M. E. (1993). *Social studies and the elementary/middle school student*. Ft. Worth, TX: Harcourt, Brace, Jovanovich.

Sunal, C., Powell, D., McClelland, S., Rule, A., Rovegno, I., Smith, C., & Sunal, D. (2000). *Integrating academic units in the elementary school curriculum*. Ft. Worth, TX: Harcourt Brace.

Sunal, C., Pritchard, G., & Sunal, D. (2000, June–May). Whales in depth: An interdisciplinary study. *Middle Level Learning 8*, 11–15.

Sunal, C., & Sunal, D. (1983). Adapting science for the hearing impaired, *Resources in Education*. (ERIC Document Reproduction Service No. ED 273 177).

Sunal, C. S., & Sunal, D. W. (1999, April). *Reasoning and argumentation*. Paper presented at the annual meeting of the American Educational Research Association, Montreal, Canada.

Sunal, C., Sunal, D., & Haas, M. (1996). Meaningful learning in social studies through conceptual reconstruction: A strategy for secondary students. *Inquiry in Social Studies 32*(1), 1–17.

Superka, D., & Hawke, S. (1982, May). Social roles: A focus for the social studies in the 1980s. *Social Education 44*, 362–369.

Superka, D., Hawke, S., & Morrissett, I. (1980, May). The current and future status of the social studies. *Social Education 44*, 362–369.

Taba, H. (1967). *Teacher's handbook for elementary social studies*. Palo Alto, CA: Addison Wesley.

Taba, H., Durkin, M. D., Fraenkel, J. E., & McNaughton, A. H. (1971). *A teacher's handbook to elementary social studies*. Reading, MA: Addison-Wesley.

Taylor, H. E. (Ed.). (1997). *Getting started in global education*. Alexandria, VA: National Association of Elementary School Principals.

Tennyson, R., & Cocchiarella, M. (1986). An empirically based instructional design theory for teaching concepts. *Review of Educational Research 56*, 40–71.

Thagard, P. (1992). Analogy, explanation, and education. *Journal of Research in Science Teaching 29*(6), 537–544.

Tippins, D., & Dana, N. (1993). Culturally relevant alternative assessment. In S. J. Carey (Ed.), *Science for all cultures* (pp. 44–47). Arlington, VA: National Science Teachers Association.

Tobin, K., & McRobbie, C. (1996). *The significance of cultural fit to the performance of Asian Americans*. Paper presented at the annual meeting of the American Educational Research Association, New York.

Torney-Purta, J. (1990). Political socialization. In W. T. Callahan, Jr., & R. A. Banaszak (Eds.), *Citizenship for the 21st century* (pp. 171–198). Bloomington, IN: Social Studies Development Center.

Torney-Purta, J. (2000). comments in E-mail discussion. American Political Science Association. Posted March 28. Retrieved from APSA-CIVED@H-Net.MSU.EDU March 18, 2004.

Torney-Purta, J., Schwille, J., & Amadeo, J. A. (Eds.). (1999). *Civic education across countries: Twenty-four national case studies for the IEA civics education project.* Delft, Netherlands: Eburon Publishers.

Totten, S. (1999). Should there be Holocaust education for K–4 students? The answer is NO. *Social Studies and the Young Learner 12,* 36–39.

Totten, S. (2000). Diminishing the complexity and horror of the Holocaust: Using simulations in an attempt to convey historical experiences. *Social Education 64*(3), 165–171.

Trotta, L. (1991). *Fighting for air: In the trenches with television news.* New York: Simon & Schuster.

Turner, T. N. (1994). *Essentials of classroom teaching: Elementary social studies.* Boston: Allyn & Bacon.

U.S. Department of Education. (1990). National goals for education. Washington, DC: Author.

U.S. Department of Education. (2001). *No Child Left Behind Act of 2001.* Public Law No. 107-100. [On-line]. Available: www.loc.gov/.

Vandercook, T., York, J., & Forest, M. (1989). The McGill action planning system (MAPS): A strategy for building the vision. *Journal of the Association for Persons with Severe Handicaps 14*(3), 205–215.

Van Fossen, P. J. (1998). World wide web resources for teaching and learning economics. *ERIC digest.* (ERIC Document Reproduction Service No. ED 424 289).

Van Sledright, B. A., & Brophy, J. (1992). Storytelling, imagination and fanciful elaboration in children's historical reconstructions. *American Educational Research Journal 29,* 837–859.

Vockell, E., & Schwartz, E. (1992). *The computer in the classroom.* Watsonville, CA: Mitchell McGraw-Hill.

Wade, R. (1994a). Conceptual change in elementary social studies: A case study of fourth graders' understanding of human rights. *Theory and Research in Social Education 22*(1), 74–95.

Wade, R. C. (1994b). Community service-learning: Commitment through active citizenship. *Social Studies and the Young Learner 6*(3), 16–21.

Wade, R. C. (Ed.). (2000). *Building bridges: Connecting classroom and community through service-learning in social studies, Bulletin 97.* Washington, DC: National Council for the Social Studies.

Wade, R. C., & Saxe, D. W. (1996). Community service-learning in the social studies: Historical roots, empirical evidence, critical issues. *Theory and Research in Social Education 24*(4), 331–359.

West, E. (2000). At play with education and history. In S. W. Bednarz & R. S. Bednarz (Eds.), *Social science on the frontier: New horizons in history and geography* (pp. 1–17). Boulder, CO: Social Science Education Consortium.

White, S. H., & O'Brien, J. E. (1999). What is a hero? An exploratory study of students' conceptions of heroes. *Journal of Moral Education 28*(1), 81–95.

Wiggins, G. (1990). The case for authentic assessment. *ERIC Digest.* (ERIC Document Reproduction Service No. ED O-TM-90–10).

Williams, C., & Bybee, J. (1994). What do children feel guilty about? Developmental and gender differences. *Developmental Psychology 30*(5), 617–623.

Wilson, E. K., Bagley, W., & Rice, M. K. (2000). Virtual field trips and newsrooms: Integrating technology into the classroom. *Social Education 64*(3), 152–155.

Winston, B. (1984). *Map and globe skills: K–8 teaching guide.* Indiana, PA: National Council for Geographic Education.

Wisendanger, K. D. (1985). Comprehension: Using anticipation guides. *The Reading Teacher 39,* 241–242.

Yell, M. M. (1999). Multiple choice to multiple rubrics: One teacher's journey in assessment. *Social Education 63*(6), 326–329.

Yopp, H. Y., & Yopp, R. H. (1996). *Literature-based reading activities* (2nd ed.). Boston: Allyn & Bacon.

Zarnowski, M. (1990). *Learning about biographies.* Washington, DC: National Council for the Social Studies.

Zola, J., & Ioannidou, A. (2000). Learning and teaching with interactive simulations. *Social Education 64*(3), 142–145.

Children's and Youth Literature References

Adler, D. A. (2000). Illustrated by T. Widener. *America's Champion Swimmer: Gertrude Ederle.* New York: Gulliver.

Alexander, H. (2000). *Do You Remember the Color Blue? And Other Questions Kids Ask about Blindness.* New York: Viking.

American Girl Collection. (numerous years). Middleton, WI: Pleasant Company Publications.

Ammon, R. (2001). Illustrated by P. Patrick. *Amish Horses.* New York: Atheneum.

Ancona, G. (1999). *Cuban Kids.* New York: Cavendish.

Barnes, Peter W. (1996). *House Mouse, Senate Mouse.* Alexandria, VA: VSP Books.

Barnes, Peter W. (1998). *Marshall, the Courthouse Mouse: A Tail of the U.S. Supreme Court.* Alexandria, VA: VSP Books.

Barnes, Peter W. (1998). *Woodrow, the White House Mouse.* Alexandria, VA: VSP Books.

Barnes, Peter W. (1999). *Woodrow for President.* Alexandria, VA: VSP Books.

Bartoletti, S. C. (1999). *Kids on Strike!* New York: Houghton Mifflin.

Bateman, T. (2001). Illustrated by J. O'Brien. *Red, White, Blue, and Uncle Who? The Stories behind Some of America's Patriotic Symbols.* New York: Holiday House.

Bell, K. M. (1999). *Fire in Their Eyes: Wildfires and the People Who Fight Them.* Ft. Worth, TX: Harcourt Brace.

Bramwell, M. (2001). *Food Watch.* New York: DK Publishing.

Breckler, R. (1996). Illustrated by D. K. Ray. *Sweet Dried Apples: A Vietnam Wartime Childhood.* Boston: Houghton Mifflin.

Bridges, R. (1999). *Through My Eyes.* New York: Scholastic.

Brown, D. (2000). *Uncommon Traveler: Mary Kingsley in Africa.* Washington, DC: National Geographic.

Carbone E. (2001). *Storm Warriors.* New York: Knopf.

Carlson, L. (1998). Illustrated by H. Meade. *Boss of the Plains: The Hat That Won the West.* New York: DK Publishing.

Cha, D. (1996). *Dia's Story Cloth.* New York: Lee & Low.

Chin-Lee, C. & de la Pena, T. (1999). Illustrated by E. O. Sanchez. *A Is for the Americas.* New York: 1999.

Cohen, M. (1967). *Will I Have a Friend?* New York: Macmillan.

Cooper, M. L. (2000). *Fighting for Honor: Japanese Americans and World War II.* New York: Clarion.

Coy, J. (2002). Illustrated by L. Jean-Bart. *Straight to the Hoop.* New York: Lee & Low.

Deans, S. (2001). *Racing the Past.* New York: Henry Holt.

Duggleby, J. (1998). *Story Painter: The Life of Jacob Lawrence.* New York: Chronicle.

Durbin, W. (1999). *The Journal of Sean Sullivan: A Transcontinental Railroad Worker.* New York: Scholastic.

Finkelstein, N. (1999). *The Way Things Never Were: The Truth about the "Good Old Days."* New York: Atheneum/Simon & Schuster.

Fleming, C. (1999). Illustrated by S. D. Schindler. *Big Cheese for the White House.* New York: Ink/DK Publishing.

Fradin, D. B. (2000). *Bound for the North Star: True Stories of Fugitive Slaves.* New York: Clarion.

Goodall, J. (2002). *The Chimpanzees I Love: Saving Their World and Ours.* New York: Scholastic.

Gundisch, K. (2001). Translated by J. Skofield. *How I Became an American.* New York: Cricket Books.

Hall, D. (1979). *Ox-cart Man.* Illustrated by Barbara Cooney. New York: Puffin.

Hart, A. (2001). Illustrated by M. Kline. *Who Really Discovered America? Unraveling the Mystery & Solving the Puzzle.* New York: Williamson.

Hearne, B. (1997). Illustrated by B. Anderson. *Seven Brave Women.* New York: Greenwillow.

Holm, J. L. (1999). *Our Only May Amelia.* New York: Harper Trophy.

Howard G. (2002). Illustrated by C. K. Noll. *A Basket of Bangles: How a Business Begins.* Brookfield, CT: Millbrook Press.

Johnson, A. (2001). Illustrated by B. Moser. *Those Building Men.* New York: Blue Sky/Scholastic.

Kimmel, E. A. (2000). Illustrated by J. J. Muth. *Gershon's Monster: A Story for the Jewish New Year.* New York: Scholastic.

Knight, M. B., & Melnicove, M. (2000). Illustrated by A. Sibley O'Brien. *Africa Is Not a Country.* New York: Millbrook.

Konigsburg, E. L. (1968). *Jennifer, Hecate, Macbeth, William McKinley, and Me, Elizabeth.* New York: Atheneum.

Laufer, P. (2000). Illustrated by S. L. Roth. *Made in Mexico.* Washington, DC: National Geographic.

Lewis, B., and edited by Espeland, P. (1998). *What Do You Stand For?: A Kid's Guide to Building Character.* Minneapolis, MN: Free Spirit.

Littlesugar, A. (2002). Illustrated by F. Cooper. *Freedom School, Yes!* New York: Puffin Books.

MacDonald. F., & Bergin M. (1990). *A Medieval Castle.* Inside Story Series. New York: Peter Bedrick Books.

Mayhew, J. (2001). *Katie and the Sunflowers.* New York: Orchard.

McBrier, P. (2001). Illustrated by Lori Lohstoeter. *Beatrice's Goat.* New York: Atheneum Books for Young Readers.

Millard, A. (1998). Illustrated by S. Noon. *A Street through Time.* New York: DK Publishing.

Morrison, T. (2001). *The Great Unknown.* New York: Walter Lorraine Books/Houghton Mifflin.

Murphy, J. (2000). *Pick-and-Shovel Poet: The Journeys of Pascal d'Angelo.* New York: Clarion.

Myers, W. D. (2001). *Bad Boy: A Memoir.* New York: Harper Tempest/Amistad.

Nobisson, J. (2000). Illustrated by T. Rose. *John Blair and the Great Hinckley Fire.* New York: Houghton Mifflin.

O'Dell, S. (1960). *Island of the Blue Dolphins.* New York: Houghton Mifflin.

Otto, C. (1999). Illustrated by M. Lloyd. *Pioneer Church*. Ft. Worth, TX: Holt.

Polacco, P. (1994). *Pink and Say*. New York: Philomel.

Ray, D. K. (2001). *Hokusai: The Man Who Painted a Mountain*. New York: Frances Foster Books/Farrar, Straus and Giroux.

Rey, H. A. (1941). *Curious George*. New York: Houghton Mifflin.

Rice, M., & Rice C. (1998). Illustrated by R. Bonson. *Pompeii: The Day a City Was Buried*. New York: DK Publishing.

Ripkin, C., Jr., & Bryan, M. (1999). Adapted by G. Herman. Illustrated by S. Silver. *Play Ball!* New York: Dial/Penguin Putnam.

Robinson, S. (2001). *Jackie's Nine: Jackie Robinson's Values to Live By*. New York: Scholastic.

Sachs, M. (1976). *A December Tale*. Garden City, NY: Doubleday.

Sheindlin, J. (2001). Illustrated by B. Tore. *Judge Judy Sheindlin's You Can't Judge a Book by Its Cover: Cool Rules for School*. New York: Cliff Street Books.

Singer, M. (1999). Illustrated by F. Lessac. *On the Same Day in March: A Tour of the World's Weather*. New York: Harper Collins.

Sinnott, S. (1999). *Welcome to Addy's World 1865*. Middleton, WI: Pleasant Company Publications.

Sinnott, S. (2000). Illustrated by D. Handleman. *Charley Waters Goes to Gettysburg*. New York: Millbrook.

Smith, W. (2001). Illustrated by K. Nelson. *Just the Two of Us*. New York: Lee & Low.

Spies, Bornemann, K. (2000). *Franklin D. Roosevelt* (United States Presidents Series). New York: Enslow.

Stolz, M. (1978). *Cider Days*. New York: Harper & Row.

Talbott, H. (1999). *O'Sullivan Stew: A Tale Cooked Up in Ireland*. New York: Putnam/Penguin.

Talbott, H. (2000). *Forging Freedom: A True Story of Heroism during the Holocaust*. New York: Puffin.

Tallchief, Maria. (1999). *America's Prima Ballerina*. New York: Viking Press.

Thomas, E. (2001). Illustrated by Angela Wilkes. *A Farm through Time: The History of a Farm from Medieval Times to the Present Day*. New York: DK Publishing.

Vogel. C. G. (1999). *Legends of Landforms: Native American Lore and the Geology of the Land*. Brookfield, CT: The Millbrook Press.

Voight, C. (1985). *The Runner*. New York: Atheneum.

Weatherford, C. B. (2000). Illustrated by E. Velasquez. *The Sound That Jazz Makes*. New York: Walker.

Weitzman, D. (1999). *Locomotive: Building an Eight-Wheeler*. New York: Houghton Mifflin.

Wells, R. (1999). Illustrated by G. Kelley. *Tallchief: America's Prima Ballerina*. New York: Viking/Penguin Putnam.

Woolridge, C. N. (2001). Illustrated by J. Rogers. *When Esther Morris Headed West: Women, Wyoming and the Right to Vote*. New York: Holiday House.

Yolen, J. (1999). Illustrated by S. Guevara. *Not One Damsel in Distress: World Folktales for Strong Girls*. New York: Silver Whistle.

INDEX